At the Origins of Modern Atheism

Michael J. Buckley, S.J.

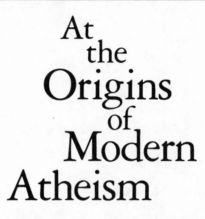

At
the
Origins
of
Modern
Atheism

Yale University Press   New Haven and London

For my mother and father
on the
sixtieth anniversary of
their marriage

"El amor, más fuerte es más unitivo"

Designed by Sally Harris
and set in Garamond type by Vera-Reyes, Inc., Philippines.
Printed in the United States of America by
Edwards Brothers, Inc., Ann Arbor, Michigan.

Library of Congress Cataloging-in-Publication Data

Buckley, Michael J.
  At the origins of modern atheism.

  Bibliography:
  Includes index.
  1. Atheism—History—Modern period, 1500–
I. Title.
BL2747.3.B83 1987   211′.8′0903   86–28248
ISBN 0–300–03719–8 (alk. paper)

The paper in this book meets the guidelines for
permanence and durability of the Committee on
Production Guidelines for Book Longevity
of the Council on Library Resources.

10 9 8 7 6 5 4 3 2 1

Contents

Acknowledgments

This book comes to publication trailing clouds of the kindness of others. From its earliest days in classes or seminars at the University of Chicago, Gonzaga University, the Pontifical Gregorian University, and the Graduate Theological Union, its initial investigations and subsequent research were made possible by the encouragement of such administrators as Charles Wegener, Clifford Kossel, René Latourelle, Claude Welch, Andrew J. Dufner, and T. Howland Sanks. I remember Santa Clara University for its great generosity over the two years in which I was its grateful guest, first as scholar-in-residence and then as Bannan Fellow, positions opened to me by the president, William Rewak, and the academic vice-president at that time, Paul Locatelli, and supported by the continual assistance of the chairperson of the Religious Studies Department, James Reites. My brother Jesuits gave me both room and community during those two happy and productive years when I was stashed securely on the second floor of Nobili Hall, and their religious fraternity, breadth of interests, lively conversation, and hospitality have left this book and its author deeply in their debt: "The thought of our past years in me doth breed / Perpetual benediction."

Students and colleagues whose names are too numerous to be mentioned have contributed so much over these years, but a particular place among my benefactors is taken by those who lent their expertise to individual chapters: James Collins, Frederick Copleston, Nicholas D. Smith, Helen Moritz, Anthony Ruhan, George Lucas, Joseph Chinnici, Theodore Foss, Frederick Tollini, Linus Thro, and John Heilbronn. Louis Dupré gave this entire project and every chapter of the manuscript his careful attention and insightful suggestions, and I count his openhanded scholarship as well as his friendship among the great gifts of these years. As I recognize the size of this volume, I cannot but ruefully recall from my student days the Greek reproach: A big book is a big evil! Without the generosity of so many colleagues, especially Professor Dupré, it would have been so much worse.

Secretaries and research assistants number among my heroes, doggedly deciphering scrambled handwriting or pouring hours of their days into the dark cavern of obscurities: Ethel Johnston, Amy England, Douglas Burton-Christie, and especially those who helped to pull the project out of danger, Michael Takamoto and Timothy Chambers. Kevin Fitzgerald and Paul Danove proofread much of the text; without their help I could not have met my deadline in a very crowded academic semester.

Above all, at this time, my thoughts turn gratefully to Paul Crowley, once my student in theology at the Graduate Theological Union, for a number of years my research assistant, and now a colleague and friend. He was with this book at its early stages of research, contributed continually to its growth, and has shepherded it through its final moments of redaction. I could not let this book go to press without registering my deep indebtedness and gratitude for his consistent generosity.

The final weeks of editing coincided with a period of difficulty unprecedented in my life. During this time, I was sustained and encouraged by the steadfast support of Archbishop John R. Quinn of San Francisco, Bishop John S. Cummins of Oakland, and Father John R. Clark, the Provincial Superior of the California Jesuits. They turned a dark period into a witness of integrity and fidelity. Great friends and a loving family gathered around me throughout this time. Of what they have been to me, as this book goes to press, I stand in a "grateful, never-dying remembrance."

Finally, the Jesuit School of Theology at Berkeley has continually surrounded this work and its author with encouragement. The former vice-chancellor of the school, Terrance Mahan, insisted upon its being given a prime focus in the threatening chaos of other academic demands; presidents and deans have made time available; and the faculty has given that heartening attention through the colloquia and conversations that constitute an academic community. The Jesuits with whom I live at "Virginia West" have supported me in every way possible, patiently enduring periodic torrents of explanation that might mark a breakthrough on Helvétius, Meslier, or Gadamer and sharing an enthusiasm as the inquiry lumbered to its conclusions. For their learning, their kindness, and their religious brotherhood, I am deeply grateful.

Introduction:
"This Damnable Paradoxe"

A *damnatio memoriae* followed the death of Akhenaten. His son-in-law reverted to the religious beliefs that had lain under ban and persecution. The Egyptian monarch's massive granite sarcophagi and alabaster Canopic chest stood unused. His body was either interred in a secondhand coffin or torn to pieces and thrown to the dogs. His capital stood abandoned to the desert, never again to serve as a royal residence and only to be recovered from the sands thousands of years later by German and English archaeologists in the decades surrounding the World Wars. The Ramessides of the succeeding dynasty worked out this obliteration, even excluding Akhenaten and his immediate progeny from the king-lists of Egypt. Whenever possible the symbols and figures of the hated Pharaoh were erased from monument and stele. His name was execration. If reference had to be made to his reign, he was characterized in a circumlocution as "that criminal of Akhet-Aten."[1] For his had been a regime, described by his successor, Tutankhamun, in which

> the temples of the gods and goddesses from Elephantine [down] to the marches of the Delta [had . . . and] gone to pieces. Their shrines had become desolate, had become *mounds* overgrown with [*weeds*]. Their sanctuaries were as if they had never been. Their halls were a footpath. The land was topsy-turvy, and the gods turned their backs upon this land. If [*the army* was] sent to Djahi to extend the frontiers of Egypt, no success of theirs came at all. If one prayed to a god to seek counsel from him, he would never come [at all]. If one made supplication to a goddess similarly, she would never come at all. Their hearts *were hurt* in their bodies, (so that) they did damage to that which had been made.[2]

The repudiated monarch is indicted not for heresy, as has been so often and so mistakenly alleged, but for an antitheism in which he opposed the other

1

gods of Egypt in favor of Aten, the Sun-God, an antitheism that led to a divine abandonment of the nation as all "the gods turned their backs on this land."

What this stele inscription decried as impiety and antitheism, however, successive generations read as religious advancement. For the scandal of Akhenaten, his true originality, lay with his uncompromising solar monotheism. Egypt had flourished for fifteen hundred years in religious peace through the assimilation of tribal cults into its hospitable pantheon. Hundreds of animalic heads perched on human bodies with a multiplicity that bespoke their origins, and a tendency to identify one with another indicated a strong drift toward monotheism or at least syncretism. Akhenaten brought that tendency to fulfillment not by assimilation, but by repudiation and proscription. The one God was the solar disk; the others were discarded and suppressed. Their temples were unsupported, their priests ignored, their names hammered away. Directives were issued for the plural form of the word *god* to be eradicated wherever it appeared.[3] The capital was moved from Thebes to El-'Amârna, and the site was rebuilt into the new city named Akhetaten to celebrate the Sun-God.

In a lyrically lovely hymn, Akhenaten worshiped Aten, the solar disk, as the "sole God, like whom there is no other! Thou didst create the world according to thy desire, whilst thou wert alone: all men, cattle, and wild beasts, whatever is on earth, going upon (its) feet, and what is on high, flying with its wings."[4] His successors and even more the next dynasty judged that such a worship and such a king had turned Egypt *seni-meni*, "passed-by-and-sick."[5] It had deprived the nation of its temples, the army of its victories, and the people of its recourse to the divine. In the middle of the fourteenth century B.C., as the eighteenth dynasty ran its course, Egypt made the collective judgment: monotheism was antitheism. The denial of the gods of the people destroyed the living presence of any god.

A thousand years later, in 399 B.C., Socrates drew from Meletus that same easy equation between the gods of popular belief and all divinity. Forensic theology had divided Athens since Anaxagoras of Clazomenae had introduced philosophy into this center of Hellenic culture. Anaxagoras had been indicted under the city's decrees against those "who do not believe in the divine or who teach *logoi* about matters transcendent" and had fled for his life to Lampsacus.[6] A bronze tablet displayed on the Acropolis publicly proscribed Diagoras of Melos, and a reward of one talent was posted for those who would kill him and two talents for those who would bring him captive into Athens. Diagoras was an "atheist." Indeed, his fame was to rank him among the great classic atheists in the ancient world, with his name heading the canonical catalogues of the godless. The tablet explains his atheism: he had ridiculed the Eleusinian Mysteries and spoken about what occurred within them.[7] Around the same time, 415 B.C., Protagoras of Abdera was reportedly banished from Athens and his book burnt in the *agora* for theological skepticism: "About the gods, I do not have [the capacity] to know, whether they are or are not, nor to know what they are like in form; for there are many things that prevent this knowledge: the obscurity [of the issue] and the shortness of human life."[8] Whatever solid ground of actual event and word lies beneath the mist and haze of story, allegation, and maxim surrounding Anaxagoras, Diagoras, and Protagoras, Athens was never the territory of untrammeled inquiry that the Enlightenment projected. It was protective of its gods, and Meletus accused Socrates of denying them.

Initially, Meletus denounces Socrates for corrupting the city's youth "by teaching them not to believe in the gods in which the City believes, but in other *daimonia* that are new." With breathtaking ease, Socrates induces Meletus to identify this indictment with a total denial of any divine reality: "This is what I say, that you do not believe in gods at all. . . ." "Do I believe there is no god?" "You certainly do not, by Zeus, not in any way at all." Socrates is τὸ παράπαν ἄθεος, completely godless.[9] Meletus associates him with Anaxagoras in the conviction that the sun is only a stone and the moon is only earth. Socrates finds the general charge of atheism so absurd that he treats Meletus like a jester, one who like Aristophanes features serious issues in the corruptingly inappropriate medium of flippancy. Socrates had taken the direction of his life from the revelation of Delphi and its negative governance from his *daimon*. His life was to be lived as "the god stationed me, as I supposed and assumed, ordering me to live philosophizing and examining myself and others."[10] If he had abandoned this station, then with some assurance one could have discerned disbelief in his conduct, since out of fear of unpopularity and death he would have disobeyed the divine directions given him by the oracle. The ambiguity of "atheism" in the *Apologia* stems essentially from the identification of the gods of the city with all gods, of an understanding of divinity accepted within one society with any understanding of the divine. Ironic as this identification might have seemed to Plato's Socrates, it resulted in the tragedy of his execution. One man's theism proved to be his indictor's atheism, the incarnation of impiety.

Socrates also introduced another factor into atheistic discernment: the differentiation of levels of confession between true and specious religious belief. Meletus insists upon an obvious profession that corresponds with the acknowledgment of the gods of the city; Socrates offers a quality of commitment in life that indicates actual conviction. Meletus does not attend to practice; Socrates collapses any ultimate distinction between theory and practice and makes practice an embodiment or instance of theory. This added consideration does not center on the kinds of gods who are worshipped, but on the difference between inauthentic and authentic confession, a distinction that the works of Plato broadened into the differentiation between the apparent and the real, between the phenomena and the truth of the phenomena. Plato did not distinguish, as he has been continually and facilely dismissed as distinguishing, between two different and independent worlds, the world of appearance and the world of ideas—as if these were two autonomous spheres. He does distinguish between the apparent and the form that is the truth of the apparent. There are not two worlds, but the imperfect phenomenon and its perfect truth now grasped in the modes of religious affirmation and denial. Socrates' discernment insisted both upon the differences among gods and upon the differences among the levels of knowledge.

The early opposition to Christianity would be unintelligible outside this ambiguity. Justin Martyr's *First Apology*, written at Rome in the middle of the second century, recognized the charge made against the Church, now a little over a hundred years old: "Thus we are even called atheists [ἄθεοι]. We do confess ourselves atheists before those whom you regard as gods, but not with respect to the Most True God."[11] Christians absented themselves from state temples and from common cults; they refused the recognized acts of reverence to imperial symbols and to the statues of the gods whom they called idols. Thus they stood apart from the cities and from the festivals which marked social religious life; at the same time, they were not assimilated into the Jewish nation. The scandal of such a refusal is hard to recapture, but it led the early Christians to the same indictment as that of Socrates. They were obviously atheists, despite the appeal that Justin, as so many of the apologists before and after him, lodged: "What sensible person will not admit that we are not atheists, since we worship the Creator of this world and assert, as we have been taught, that He has no need of bloody sacrifices, libations, and incense."[12] It is little wonder that the early Christians found in Socrates a common heritage and postulated Moses as his influence. The same charge that had led to his death introduced their centuries of persecution. Both philosophic convictions and religious commitments suffered the charge of atheism.

Akhenaten was never called an atheist, but he was described as such. Socrates was called an atheist but rebutted the charge. Justin Martyr was called an atheist and admitted the sense in which that indictment was true. These three figures expose the paradoxical history of a continually ambiguous term. Irenaeus accepts the term as applicable to Anaxagoras, but Augustine celebrates Anaxagoras' belief "that the author of all the visible world is a Divine Mind" and places him with the great natural theologians of antiquity.[13] Cicero, Sextus Empiricus, and Claudius Aelianus drew up lists of the atheists, but their indices covering so many centuries bear the same internal contradictions as the histories from which they draw.[14] Never do those named in the catalogues or in the remarks of others come to more than ten. Seldom would one of those so named admit the justice of the title; even more rarely would subsequent historians of philosophy insist upon it. Diogenes of Apollonia, Hippon of Rhegium, Protagoras, Prodicus, Critias, Diagoras of Melos, Theodore of Cyrene, Bion of Borysthenes, Euhemerus and Epicurus: almost always their "atheism" was an alien, unsympathetic reading of their theism or their natural philosophy. Too little is known about most of them, naturalists, sophists, and skeptics, to assert much with certitude. The naturalists won the name because they made air or water the primary substance, but Diogenes, like Anaxagoras, attributed Mind to his primary substance and identified it with Zeus, and Hippon was listed by Clement of Alexandria among those who were given the name of atheist without deserving it.[15]

A sophist, a politician, and a Cyrenaic won the name because they investigated the origin of the divine names: Prodicus of Ceos found that Hephaestus was a synonym for fire in Homer and that the Nile was worshiped as the source of life in Egypt. Linguistic analysis discovered that the term *divinity* was predicated in its original usage of that which is beneficial to humanity. Some in Athens found this atheistic, but others defended it as historically accurate and as profoundly insightful in identifying the divine with the universally beneficent.[16] Critias of Athens placed in the mouth of Sisyphus, in the satyric play by the same name, another explanation for the origin of religion. It arose not from the experience of beneficence, but from the primitive experience of limitless human exploitation. Laws by themselves do not eliminate crime; they only encourage secrecy in its commission. So a "wise and clever man invented fear for mortals. . . . He introduced the Divine, saying that there is a God flourishing with immortal life, hearing and seeing with his mind, and thinking of everything and caring about these things. . . . And even if you plan anything evil in secret, you will not escape the gods in this."[17] *Sisyphus* enunciated for the first time in Western civilization a political or social motivation for the origin of the gods. On the other hand, there is no reason to ascribe to Critias the opinion which he put into the mouth of his shifty protagonist; in fact, the location and the character of the speech should indicate the distance between its judgment and that of the author of the play.[18] Euhemerus, finally, never denied the gods. He asserted in his book of travels that the heavenly bodies were divine but that many of the popular gods were great men whose achievements earned their divinization after death.[19] Epicurus asserted the existence of the gods; indeed, he so asserted their happiness that he excluded from them any providential care for the human condition.[20] For Diagoras, Theodore, and Bion, and perhaps one or two more, the case was

different: their atheism consisted neither in whom they identified as divine
nor in what they characterized as divine activity, that is, in how they defined
the gods. Diagoras' Ἀποπυργίζοντες Λόγοι attacked any divine existence.[21]
Theodore's *On the Gods* submitted them to a searching criticism and final
denial, Bion initially denied their existence but underwent conversion before
his death.[22]

Greek philosophic history, then, exhibits the enormous paradox of
"atheism." The word could carry vastly divergent and even contradictory
meanings and could consequently be applied to figures whose ideas were
radically opposed. But its history does more than embody the ambiguity of
the term; it also exhibits something of the anatomy of the ambiguity. Men
were called *atheists* dependent upon a limited number of variables: whom
they identified as gods; the understanding they gave to the term; the
activities they defined as divine; the kind of denial attributed to them. Any
of these factors could tell critically in the attribution of atheism. A naturalist
could most easily be identified as an atheist by the first factor; the sophist
and the mythographer by the second; the atomist and the superstitious by
the third; the agnostic and the antitheists by the last. In other words, the
ambiguity of *atheist* is the classic indeterminacy that Plato held was true of
any linguistic unit, of any word: ambiguity about the appropriate instance,
the appropriate definition, and the appropriate word, with all of these
framed within varying degrees of knowledge, the kind of affirmation or
denial, the difference between appearance and reality, the definition and the
word. The term *atheist* is not hopelessly vacuous, but unless the instance to
which it is applied and the meaning in which it is used are determined, its
employment is profoundly misleading.

Plato maintained that ambiguity characterized any word or any instance
or any definitional articulation. The word does not define itself, and the
individual case does not explain itself. The need for the dialectical method
lies precisely in the discontinuity among these three, and the movement of
the dialectical conversation is toward their resolution, toward a coincidence
of word, thought, and thing. Thus the author of the *Seventh Epistle* could
summarize the elements and procedures of any method:

> For each of the things which are, there are three necessary means through
> which knowledge is acquired. Knowledge itself is a fourth factor. And the
> fifth, it is necessary to posit, is the thing itself, that which is knowable and
> true. Of these, the first is the name [ὄνομα], the second is the definition
> [λόγος], the third is the image [εἴδωλον], and the fourth is the knowledge
> [ἐπιστήμη]. If you wish to understand what I am now saying, take a single
> example and learn from it what applies to all. There is [5] that which is
> called a circle, which has for its [1] *name* the word we have just men-

tioned; secondly, it has a [2] *definition*, composed of names and verbs: "that which is everywhere equidistant from the extremities to the center" will be the definition of that which has for its *name* "round" and "spherical" and "circle." And in the third place, there is [3] *that which is being drawn or erased or being shaped on a lathe or destroyed*—but none of these processes affect [5] the *real circle*, to which all of these other [circles] are related, because it is distinct from them. In the fourth place, there is concerning these [4] *knowledge* [ἐπιστήμη] and *insight* [νοῦς] and true opinion [ἀληθής τε δό§α], and these must be assumed to constitute a single whole which does not exist in either vocal sounds or in bodily forms but in souls. Thus it is clear that it [4, knowledge] differs from [5] the nature of the circle itself and from [1, 2, 3] the three factors previously mentioned.[23]

No sensible person confuses the three physical or external means or factors that enter into the generation of knowledge.

The *Seventh Epistle* affords a very good instance of three expressive factors which must enter into any movement toward knowledge: [3] instance, [2] definition, and [1] word: To confuse [5] the circle that one [4] understands with [3] this *particular* circle that is being shaped on the lathe would deny all universal knowledge; to identify [5] the circle with the words of its [2] definition would fail to see that [1] words are always indeterminate apart from [3] instance, and that a [2] general definition never perfectly fits its [3] imperfect and phenomenal realizations; to seize upon the [1] word as if it were without divergent [2] definitions and contradicting [3] applications is to reduce language to sophistry and invective. The three must be coordinately present and grasped: word, articulated meaning, and imperfect realizations. Otherwise there is no knowledge. Knowledge itself may range from opinion to science to intuition.

What holds true in so simple an example of geometry becomes even more telling in the history of ideas. This Platonic enumeration identifies the elements which constitute the culture: the words we use, the understanding they are given within this use, and the stories, legends, persons, events, and theories in which they are appropriately used. Culture, the achievements of the past, is irreducibly linguistic. Whatever the kind of language, in culture the inner word has become the outer word, and this outer word remains to be read, assimilated, and interiorized in another generation's inner word.

The terms that run through intellectual history exhibit all the indeterminateness cited by this Platonic epistle against written or literary philosophy. These units do not keep a constant meaning. They function more like variables than constants in intellectual history. *Nature, substance, person,* and *principle* vary essentially in their meanings and in their applications in various philosophic or theological systems. To ask what is nature, outside such a context of relationships, is to ask a meaningless question. To assert that the notion of cause can no longer be admitted may evoke solid feelings of metaphysical rectitude, but this statement carries little but pathos when taken apart from a context of discourse in which it makes sense. The problem of language, though exhibited in language, is not simply linguistic, however.

It is equally, and perhaps more profoundly, a problem of thought, of the grasp of meaning and of the world. For thought exists only within language, whether this language be expressed vocally or remain in the inner *verbum*: "Thinking and discourse are the same thing, except that what we call thinking is, precisely, the inward dialogue carried on by the mind with itself without spoken sound."[24] The history of ideas can be formulated only if these ideas emerge as words; the history of terms can be illuminating only if this intrinsic unity between thinking and speaking is maintained. Expression is not artificially added to thought. Thought only takes place within inner expression, within an inner word, of which either written or oral discourse can properly be called an emanation.[25] External expression is not identical with thought. Our expression may be more than we understand or realize; it may also be inadequate to our thought. Both are possible. "That is not what I meant." "But it is what you said." And again: "In telling me that, he had no idea how much he was revealing about the matter." External word and concept are not identical, and a text can obtain a life of its own. But language is not external to concept; it is literally its ex-pression. There is no thinking without correlative expression. In terms of the Platonic triad, a definition is given in terms of names and verbs.

But the last member of the external triad is the single instance (εἴδωλον) to which it may refer, by which it may be exemplified, or in which it may be realized, however imperfectly. The instance embodies the meaning and carries the language in discourse, or it is the particular from which the universal can be induced or by which the word is judged in its appropriateness. The instance, "the case in question," is so critically important in the clarification of meaning that, above either word or meaning, it exhibits the intelligibility of that which is the object of discourse. It is not enough to have the word *justice* singled out as a unique term; the greater the instance of justice—as in the polis rather than the individual person—the more readily an exact meaning for it is discernible.[26]

Word, definition, and instance: knowledge must cover each of these, form them into a single whole. Knowledge in some lesser degree of perception or opinion can begin with any of them, for each is an expression—a limited expression—of the reality which one is attempting to reach in inquiry.

Any inquiry into an aspect of atheistic affirmation encounters all the twisted contradictions that the *Seventh Epistle* noted in the path toward knowledge. The word *atheist* presents unique problems. It occurs almost exclusively in a polemic context; it is the designation of another person; it is invective and accusation. It rides into the quarrels of human beings as the term *heretic* functioned in Europe's Middle Ages or as the word *fellow traveler* terrified the United States in the middle of the twentieth century. Those who were called heretics insisted almost universally that they represented genuine and purified belief; few of those branded as fellow travelers characterized themselves as such. So also ἄθεος. It is a brand imprinted by one's enemies. Its definition is parasitic; like any denial, it lives off the meaning denied. The amphibologies it gathers to its history are a product of the hostile interpretation of unsympathetic critics. As it occurs in Greek antiquity after names such as Anaxagoras or Epicurus, *atheism* denotes a denial not of all transcendent personal divinity but of popular gods, the figures of civic legend and preference. Thus, the use of the epithet is dictated by the definition of the gods denied or by the instances of those to whom worship is offered or refused.

"Atheism," then, exhibits in a double manner the indetermination embodied in each member of the Platonic triad. The name, the definition, and the instance both of the god or gods and of the "atheism" that constitutes their denial are undetermined. This sixfold ambiguity is increased almost beyond hope when one recognizes the forensic context in which all six occur, the passions that are engaged and the recriminations that are easily called into play. For, unlike the Platonic example of the circle, the affirmation or denial of god touches something so deep and so basic within human experience that it involves radical drives for meaning, for unity within experience, for final security, for autonomous freedom and self-determination—longings which have run through human history and choice.

If one begins with the term *atheist*," the promiscuity of its definition and application is evident from its first use in England. To Sir John Cheke, first Regius Professor of Greek at Cambridge, seems to belong the honor of its introduction.[27] In 1540 Cheke translated into Latin Plutarch's *On Superstition*, in which both superstition and atheism are condemned, but with different evaluations: the atheist thinks there are no gods, while the superstitious man, haunted by fear, "though by inclination Atheist, is yet far too weak-minded to think about the gods what he wishes to think. And again Atheism is in no way responsible for Superstition—Whereas Superstition has both supplied the cause for Atheism to come into being, and after it is come, furnished it with an excuse."[28] In Plutarch, atheism seems the mistake of the brave and superstition the conviction of the coward. In an essay appended to his translation, Cheke strove to redress the balance. His was an attack on the atheist, but atheism conceived as a denial not of the existence of

god but of the interventions of providence, an atheism that traces itself back
to Epicurus and Lucretius and that finds its practical, political embodiment
in Machiavellianism.

Books were coming out by the gross against atheism in England, which is
not so strange if one remembers the report made to Lord Burleigh in 1572 in
Carlton's *Discourse on the Present State of England*: "The realm is divided
into three parties, the Papists, the Atheists, and the Protestants. All three are
alike favoured: the first and second because, being many, we dare not
displease them; the third, because, having religion, we fear to displease God
in them."[29] Walter, Earl of Essex, died in 1576 seeing only religious ruin:
"There is nothing but infidelity, infidelity, infidelity, atheism, atheism,
atheism, no religion, no religion."[30] Twenty years later, Thomas Nashe's
"Christs Teares over Jerusalem" would find the atheists everywhere: "There
is no Sect now in England so scattered as Atheisme. In vayne doe you
preach, in vayne doe you teach, if the roote that nourisheth all the branches
of security be not thorowly digd up from the bottome. You are not halfe so
wel acquainted as them that lyue continually about the Court and City, how
many followers this damnable paradoxe hath; how many high wits it hath
bewitcht."[31] Cheke was not alone in his refutation of "this damnable
paradoxe." In 1530 John Rastell's *New Boke of Purgatory* took up the gage.
Roger Hutchinson's *Image of God or Layman's Book* (1550) identified the
group that had "already said in their hearts, 'There is no God'; or that they
may easily be brought thereunto," with the radical religious sects closely
akin to the Anabaptists. Perhaps no one surpassed the rhetorical zeal of John
Veron's title, *Frutefull Treatise of Predestination and Providence, against the
Swynishe Gruntings of the Epicures and Atheystes of Oure Time*, lumping
together "all the Vayne and Blasphemous Objections That the Epicures and
Anabaptistes of Oure Time Can Make."[32] John Veron was not original, but
he was straightforward. In general these sallies possessed all the accuracy of
the newly developed musket. For all the powder poured down the barrel,
the shot was wild. What sense could be found in a word that could cover
Machiavelli, Christopher Marlowe, the Anabaptists, and even Thomas
Nashe himself, a word of which the growing influence could be engaged by
men of the religious quality of the Earl of Essex and Lord Burleigh?

During the great controversies at the end of the nineteenth century,
George Jacob Holyoake coined a new term, *secularist*, to distinguish himself
from those who were called atheists. The distinction was imperative: *atheist*
was often taken to denote one who is not only without god, but without
morality.[33] At the same time, Thomas Huxley created the word *agnostic* to
distinguish his own skepticism, as well as that of John Tyndall before him
and Clarence Darrow in the next century, from the outright denial explicit in
atheist.[34] On the other hand, Charles Bradlaugh maintained the respectabil-

ity of those called atheists against Holyoake and vowed that he would fight until the designation *atheist* was generally accepted in civic life, allowing atheists to give evidence in court. Upon his own admission into the House of Commons in 1882, he pulled out a Bible and gave himself the oath of office.[35] Holyoake was the last man imprisoned on charges of atheism or blasphemy in England, in 1841; Bradlaugh had to defend himself and his *National Reformer* in 1868 and 1869 against the charge of blasphemy and sedition.[36] What Nashe called "this damnable paradoxe" runs through the history of Western civilization. It is difficult to discuss the issue at all. The ambiguity of name, definition, and instance makes it impossible to give some determination to the problematic situation, or to leave it to the open-field running of the sophists or the polemists.

If, taking another route, one begins with the term *god* instead of *atheism*, the same "damnable paradoxe" emerges. Perhaps its paradigmatic embodiment is best exhibited in the various evaluations which have followed the work of the gentle Jewish genius, Baruch de Spinoza. Spinoza's *Ethics* demonstrated the existence of god; the term pervades his treatise, building finally into an understanding of life in which human "blessedness is nothing but the peace of mind which springs from the intuitive knowledge of God, and to perfect the intellect is nothing but to understand God, together with the attributes and actions of God that flow from the necesity of His nature."[37] Yet this is the same Spinoza whom Pierre Bayle, usually detached and sophisticatedly distant from any dogmatic assertions, introduced in his *Historical and Critical Dictionary* as "a Jew by birth, and afterwards a deserter from Judaism, and lastly an atheist. . . . He was a systematic atheist."[38] The name of God was not in question—both Spinoza and his subsequent critics treated the name with reverence—but the definition. Spinoza's first public biographer, John Colerus (Köhler), put the issue squarely: Spinoza "takes the liberty to use the word *God*, and to take it in a sense unknown to all Christians."[39] For this reason, despite the piety with which his name is surrounded, Colerus and Diderot in the *Encyclopédie* and Hume in his *Treatise of Human Nature* could speak of the "true atheism . . . for which *Spinoza* is so universally infamous."[40] The abbé Claude Yvon, in the extended article on *athéisme* in the *Encyclopédie*, used Spinoza as the archetypal atheist, turning the issue of the existence of God into a contest between Bayle and Spinoza.[41] On the other hand, Novalis celebrated Spinoza as "ein Gottrunkener Mensch" while Lessing, Herder, and Goethe spoke of the religious sentiment which his work evoked in them.[42] The *Pantheismusstreit*, in which Moses Mendelssohn defended Spinoza against his critics, did not end the controversy; perhaps its most rhapsodic moment came when Ernest Renan hailed Spinoza's achievement, claiming, "The truest vision ever had of God came, perhaps, here."[43]

To heap enigma upon ambiguity, Friedrich Nietzsche wrote to Franz Overbeck in 1881 that he recognized in Spinoza his precursor. Three years before, however, at the age of sixteen, Vladimir Sergeyevich Solovyov had begun his acquaintance with Spinoza's writings, and he credited them with his return to the Christian faith he had abandoned. In "The Concept of God: In Defense of Spinoza" (1897), Solovyov, one of the greatest Russian philosophers, theologians, and ecumenists of the nineteenth century, wrote, "The concept of God, which the philosophy of Spinoza gives us, in spite of all its incompletion and imperfection, nonetheless responds to the primary and indispensable demand of a genuine idea and thought of God. Many religious people have found spiritual support in this philosophy."[44] The "atheism" of Spinoza obviously depends upon two distinct, but related, hermeneutical events: how one reads his text and how one interprets *god*.

This ambiguity of *god* and its definition inevitably involves ambiguity of instance, of what is either called "god" or should be characterized as theistic denial. The ironic comment of Harry Austryn Wolfson before a Harvard congregation touched heavily upon this point. Drawing upon his knowledge of the movements of philosophy, this great reflective scholar centered on the new instances of what is called "god" and hence the salvation of religion:

> Nowadays, lovers of wisdom are still busily engaged in the gentle art of devising deities. Some of them offer as God a thing called man's idealized consciousness, others offer a thing called man's aspiration for ideal values or a thing called the unity of the ideal ends which inspire man to action, still others offer a thing called the cosmic consciousness or a thing called the universal nisus or a thing called the *élan vital* or a thing called the principle of concretion or a thing called the ground of being. . . . I wonder, however, how many of the things offered as God by lovers of wisdom of today are not again only polite but empty phrases for the downright denial of God.[45]

Wolfson is not denying the existence of an idealized consciousness, a human aspiration for ideal values, or *élan vital*. He is questioning whether any or all of these instances can supply—even in an imperfect realization and existence—either an image or a subject of which the name *god* can be legitimately predicated. The reduction of the divine to any of these instances seems to be a covert form of denial. On the other hand, Whitehead and the process theologians who followed him characterized the principle of concretion as "god," and Paul Tillich founded his three volumes of *Systematic Theology* on god as the ground of being.

With god identified by Tillich as the furthest reaches of life, the atheist becomes correlatively understood as one who says that life has no depth, that it is shallow. The atheist affirms this in complete seriousness; otherwise he is not an atheist.[46] Friedrich Jodl's *Vom Lebenswege* takes up the human aspiration for ideal values as divine and contends: "Only the person without ideals is truly an atheist."[47] With so attenuated an understanding of what legitimizes a predication of "god," atheism is never in question. "God" has become so sentimentally amorphous that it admits any statement of meaning, even quite contradictory statements, and can be applied to any treasured phenomenon or friend behind the phenomenon.

Thus the first function of any inquiry into the origins of modern atheism is to determine whether one is talking about something at all, whether one has something definite enough to constitute a problem. The first problem is not to say something about modern atheism; the first problem is to determine the data and resources enough so that there is something, a subject, to talk about at all. "This damnable paradoxe" is constituted not simply by variant predicates attached to the same subject, by unresolved issues about a common topic. It consists, at least initially, in the name of the subject itself. For from the history of the terms and their correlative determinations in meanings and applications to doctrines and persons, a problematic situation emerges that is long on rhetoric and polemics, but short on the precision, the care, the seriousness, and the delimitation that allow an aspect of it to become the source of problem, inquiry, and assertions. The initial question, before any discussion of origins, dialectical or otherwise, is really quite simple: What are we talking about? Is it possible to think in some consistent way about the career of atheism at all? The value of even so cursory an attention to the history of atheism indicates that this question, simple as it is, carries complications which stretch back to writings, stelae, and battles at the beginning of the history of ideas.

The Parameters of the Inquiry

The problem with atheism is that it is not a problem. It is a situation, an atmosphere, a confused history whose assertions can be identical in expression and positively contradictory in sense. The ambiguity which marks such terms as *god* and *atheism* can be discovered in almost every critical proposition about this situation. Projection, for example, lies at the origin of religion for both Feuerbach and Freud, but in the *Essence of Christianity* what is projected are the lineaments of the perfectly human, while in the psychoanalytic treatment of Freud what is projected is the protecting and threatening father figure, "so patently infantile, so foreign to reality, that to anyone with a friendly attitude to humanity it is painful to think that the great majority of mortals will never be able to rise above this view of life."[48] In such an atmosphere, the first function of inquiry is not to frame its final and governing question, because the vocabulary in which it would be framed would be as ambiguous as the situation out of which it arose. The first function is to determine if there are any parameters in the historical career of atheism through which this vague, unsettled, indeterminate situation might be given consistency and consequence. These, in turn, might suggest the conditions necessary for understanding it and disclose some of the procedures by which these conditions could be met. Are there any constants in the history of atheism in Western civilization?

The characteristic of the indeterminate, of any problematic situation, is that its inner consistency is not apparent. Factors are concurrent or successive without their inner relations being established. Beliefs or implications become problematic when their emergence seems random or their conditions are hidden. Statements of meaning and truth become impossible when it is not evident that the phenomenon adequately represents reality or whether its present career exhibits anything about its future. Progression in knowledge is towards control, not in the sense of technical use, but in the sense that wonder or doubt or puzzlement advance toward an adequate grasp of a state of affairs, as the internal coherence of its material elements and their formal relationships is determined. Investigation is this development of a chaotic subject from indeterminacy to determination, and the initial step of this progress lies in discovering those parameters by which the chaos becomes intelligible.[49]

Atheism does not stand alone. The term and the persuasions which cluster around it take their meaning from the divine nature which has been asserted by the religions and the philosophies, by the superstitious practices and the mystical experiences of those who adhere to the divine existence. An essential unity in intelligibility lies between atheism and theism, and if only the negative moment of this dipolarity receives attention, the problematic situation remains undetermined. The reflective experience of millennia demonstrates this. Atheism does not simply displace theism. The conflict between them is mortal because of their more general unity in meaning. If the antagonism does not bear upon a single subject, there is no contradiction. Affirmation and denial are only possible if the subject remains the same.

This subject is determined not by the atheist but by the theist, by the going beliefs, by the popular gods of the city or what the political and social establishment has determined as its god, by the sense of the divine which is the issue of religious or philosophical sensibility and argument, or by the proclaimed personal god of the monotheistic religions. Any or all of these can be the object of skepticism, denial, or uncommitted opinions, but outside these affirmations the correlative negative loses any meaning whatsoever.

Perhaps the first instance of coherence in any attempt to understand atheism is this: the central meaning of atheism is not to be sought immediately in atheism; it is to be sought in those gods or that god affirmed, which atheism has either engaged or chosen to ignore as beneath serious challenge. The history of the term indicates this constant, and the analysis of its meaning suggests that it is inescapable: atheism is essentially parasitic.

This is the first parameter in any attempt to transform the vague, unsettled, and indeterminate situation of atheism into a serious question. This parameter allows the determination of the subject-matter to proceed one step further. The meaning of atheism is not only fixed by the content of theism: atheism depends upon theism for all three factors isolated by the *Seventh Epistle*. The name, the definition, and the instance for the atheistic negations are all set by the current theism.

Charles Bradlaugh had insisted upon this dependence:

> I am an Atheist, but I do not say that there is no God; and until you tell me what you mean by God I am not mad enough to say anything of the kind. So long as the word 'God' represents nothing to me, so long as it is a word that is not the correlative and expression of something clear and distinct, I am not going to tilt against what may be nothing-nowhere. Why should I? If you tell me that by God you mean 'something' which created the universe, which before the act of creation was not; 'something' which has the power of destroying that universe; 'something' which rules and governs it, and which nevertheless is entirely distinct and different in substance from the universe—then I am prepared to deny that any such existence can be.

Definition and instance must also come from the prior theological assertion. One of the many paradoxes inherent in this history is that the point made centuries before by Justin Martyr for Christianity is retrieved by Charles Bradlaugh in his battle against it: "The Atheist does not say there is no God, so long as the word simply represents an indefinite quantity or quality—of you don't know what, you don't know where: but I object to the God of Christianity, and absolutely deny it."[50] And again: "He did not deny that there was 'a God,' because to deny that which was unknown is as absurd as to affirm it. As an Atheist he denied the God of the Bible, of the Koran, of the Vedas, but he could not deny that of which he had no knowledge."[51] The assertions of the theist provide the state of the question for the atheist, whether that question bears upon the words, the meaning, or the religious subject. The initial parameter of an inquiry into atheism, then, has multiplied. Theism and atheism are not simply an accidental conjunction, a successive accumulation of contradictory opinions. A bond of necessity stretches between them: atheism depends upon theism for its vocabulary, for its meaning, and for the hypotheses it rejects.

Does atheism also depend upon theism for its very existence? This pushes the question of internal coherence one critical step further. Does theism not only shape, but generate, its corresponding atheism? This was the process in certain obvious historical movements. The polytheism of the Egyptians drifted slowly, almost imperceptibly, toward the amalgamation of gods into the single deity, until this development was frozen by the violent attempts in the eighteenth dynasty to force its growth. The cruelty and sexual promiscuity of the Hellenic gods evoked skepticism about their existence. Augustine recorded that the Roman pontiff Scaevola rejected the gods of the poetic tradition because "such deities cannot stand comparison with good human beings. One god is represented as a thief, another as an adulterer, and so on; all kinds of degradation and absurdity, in word and deed, are ascribed to them."[52] When Feuerbach attempted to eliminate any divine reality that is other than the human person, he argued that the intrinsic contradiction in Christian doctrine makes such an imagined subject impossible, that atheism is the secret truth of religion and that the incoherence of Christian dogma discloses that truth.[53] In all of these instances, atheism depends upon the content of the god proposed not only for its terms, its significance, and its adversary, but also for its existence. The internal contradictions within the nature of god generate its denial. In other words, the relationship with theism is not only definitional, it is dialectical.

Does that same relationship obtain in modern atheism? Does theism not only set the meaning, but also generate the existence of the atheism which emerges in the middle eighteenth century? Is the content of god, the idea of the divine, so internally incoherent that it moves dialectically into its denial? Dependence for meaning is one thing; dependence for existence is quite another.

Any attention to the origins of atheism in the West must attend as much—if not more—to the theism of the theologians and the philosophers as to the atheism of their adversaries. Atheism must be seen not as a collation of ideas which happened to arise in Western thought but as a transition whose meaning is spelled out by the process and whose existence is accounted for in terms of the ideas which preceded it. To be indifferent to atheism as a transition is to fix it as an abstraction, and never to understand it in either its starting point or its ideational context. Even more, it is to fail to deal with the deeper question which underlies much of the historical evolution of atheism. If the emergent atheism simply reveals dialectically the internal contradiction which was lodged within the content of theism itself, then the understanding of atheism is possible only through the understanding of its generating matrix, theism. One issues from the other; one cannot make sense unless the other does.

An inquiry into atheism as a serious idea, as a conviction not simply

reducible to external factors, sociological conditionings, or economic pressures, as a conviction that is taken precisely as a judgment that claims insight
into the nature of reality, must take the meaning of what it treats from those
whose claims are contradictory and must examine the evidence to see
whether it supports a dialectical reading of what is already a relationship of
dependence. In other words, an inquiry into the origins of atheism must
trace the intellectual process from god affirmed to god denied. The content
of one constitutes the content and explanation of the other. For atheism as a
problematic situation possesses a content which is determined by several
critical parameters. Atheism is necessarily dependent upon theism for its
vocabulary, its meanings, and its embodiments. Atheism has often been
dependent upon theism for its evocation and its existence. These parameters
advance the internal possibilities for inquiry significantly because they
indicate its methodological direction. Any study or investigation of the
origin of modern atheism must be equally a study of the theism of the
intellectual world which generated it. Atheism is essentially a transition.

This conviction governs the inquiry in this book. The history of atheism
suggests some of the conditions which are necessary for its understanding
and discloses the futility of the polemics which have been written to counter
its emergence. So strident have both sides become over the past century that
the debate itself has lost a good deal of its previous respectability. The voices
are too impassioned, the side-remarks too clever, the appeal to the audience
too blatant, and the whole quarrel finally sterile. There is no progress in
understanding when philosophic history or theology become tactics.

In order to understand atheistic consciousness, then, it is important to
investigate in some depth that which is proposed as divine. But there is
something further that needs examination besides the content of the divine.
It is the form of thought in which that content appears.

The distinction between content and form figures critically in the history
of human reflection, a theme running through one variation after another.
The *Seventh Epistle* numbered name, definition, and instance as various,
imperfect embodiments of reality, but also spoke of the forms of thought—
science, insight, and true opinion—by which these three could be grasped,
forged into a unity, and made productive of a highest form of knowledge
that would unite the knower with reality. In the medieval debates over the
existence of universals, the distinction was drawn between the *id quod* and
the *modus quo*, the content or essence and the mode of its existence either as
particularized in reality or as universalized in thought. The Hegelian
dialectic maintained that art, religion, and philosophy all have the same
content, the Absolute, but in art it exists in the immediacy of the sensuous
and as an individual object; in religion it exists in the mode of figurative
representation (*Vorstellung*) and in acts of worship; and in philosophy it

exists in its own proper form, that of thinking knowledge, as pure thought. The form is not identified with the content as such in the Platonic Epistle or in the medieval disputes or in the Hegelian dialectic, and its distinction from content allows various forms of thought and existence to exhibit similarity in content.

This does not tell the whole story, however. Content is not the same thing as form, but content and form are not indifferent to each other; the content will be significantly affected by the form in which it is cast. The Schoolmen of the Middle Ages put it in an axiom: "Quidquid recipitur per modum recipientis recipitur" (whatever is received [content] is received according to the mode [form] of the one receiving it). Aquinas attributed this insight to the Platonic tradition: "Plato saw that each thing is received in something else according to the measure of the recipient."[54] Human nature exists one way as a thought and another way as a particular man. Number is abstract as three and concrete as three cows. So profoundly does the form of thought or existence tell upon what is thought or upon what exists that for centuries philosophers have argued the reality of universals and the irretrievable singularity of each real thing. The content of what is known remains in some way through the various apperceptive forms of the processes by which it is known, but that way must be intellectually understood also if thought is not to be confused with extramental reality. The form in which the content exists must be concomitantly grasped—even if nonthematically—for it will tell upon the content. The modes of thought employed determine the truth or falsity of the statements which are made.

There is nothing all that mysterious in such a parameter. Everyone knows that the propositions made in a drama carry a different sense from those made in a physics or history textbook. One expects one kind of truth from myth, but not the truth of a chronicle. Even if it were possible to frame a single proposition identical in its formulation for drama, physics, history, myth, and chronicle, anyone would recognize that the literary form alters significantly the content of what is said, even if its grammatical structure and language remain the same. So also form will eventually change the meaning of an inappropriate content. What is said sarcastically will eventually become hostile, regardless of protestations that "I was only joking." What is repeated endlessly will eventually become meaningless, regardless of its intrinsic merit.

This gives our inquiry a third parameter: in considering the transition of theism into atheism, it is critically necessary to consider not only the content of the divine that is being negated, but also the form in which that content is advanced, the mode of thought in which it is given meaning, elaborated in a method, and grounded in principle. The dialectical movement of the content into its negation happens not only because of a contradiction lodged at the very heart of its own meaning, but also because of a contradiction or inappropriateness between the content itself and the form in which it is proposed. The dialectical movement progresses not only toward the internal coherence of the subject, but also toward the methodological coherence of the subject with an appropriate mode of thought or pattern of discourse. In this evolution of understanding, the form of discourse or the mode of thought will eventually work out its truth in the content. What one thinks about will eventually take upon itself the shape given by the way one is thinking.

This parameter is accepted in any philosophic tradition. For Hegel, its formulation is that "method is the absolute foundation and ultimate truth."[55] In Aristotle, it lies in the affirmation that internal privation is the unstable condition for movement and change. Method will eventually produce its idiomorphic, even unexpected, content. Thus it is misleading to abstract from the working context, whether religious, philosophical, scientific, or literary, in which the necessity of the affirmation or denial of god appears. Propositions ripped from their context can never be more than an accumulation of opinions, easily formulated and easily rejected. There is no thinker whose conclusions cannot be made to seem absurd by the reduction of his inquiries to a few pages in a "history of philosophy," where his conclusions are listed as if they were a series of idiosyncratic convictions, and his name placed under such hopelessly misleading titles as "empiricist" or "idealist." Stunted, parodied, and stamped, he takes his place in a series of futile predecessors and successors, each one refuting the one who came before and awaiting in the succeeding generations the turn of opinion against him.

One can only grasp the seriousness and the universal claim of a conclusion if the working inquiries have been carefully and methodically retrieved. This does not mean that the author is simply to be repeated; it does mean that his work is to be traced and analyzed as a whole. A work which is interpreted and sequenced by a succeeding generation of thinkers does not remain the same. The bringing of new questions to these texts, the indexing of them within their "effective history," that is, within the consequences of their thought and the history of their influence, the understanding of their latent power through the traditions which they have fathered—all of these inevitably alter the very works which are the objects of this study. But the alteration is not distortion any more than it is reproduction. It is interpretation, a new "fusion of horizons" in which the past is made present and the virtualities of a tradition may be newly discovered. The event of interpretation is an event of understanding, a dyadic relation, in which both the questioner and the questioned mutually influence one another. "To interpret means precisely to use one's own preconceptions so that the meaning of the text can really be made to speak for us."[56] But to be a serious part of that conversation, the text which gives permanence to the arguments and evidence and to the principles and conclusions by which an idea develops must be respected in its integrity.

This willingness to enter into the form, the labor of a work, allows it to achieve its rightful integrity that transcends the random citations of the pastiche, the accidental, and the final absurdity of oversimplification and easy dismissal. Atheism is essentially a transition, a movement from the affirmation of the divine into its negation, perhaps a negation awaiting in turn its own negation. Whatever its particular history and development, that transition will never be understood unless it is understood from within, and this interior knowledge will never be obtained unless the positive and the negative of the transition are interpreted both for their content and for the mode of thought in which this content is incarnate. Without this labor, the content is simplified, misrepresented, and misunderstood, and the dialectical movement into contradiction becomes only a surface cleverness. The portrait never comes quite into focus, leaving the impression that all has been polemics and arbitrary choice.

This insistence upon the importance of the mode of thought not only continues a determination of the problematic situation, rendering the indeterminate increasingly open to investigation, but implies still a fourth parameter for the investigation. Theism and atheism are not only mutually dependent in their content and form of argument and hypothetically dialectical in this dependence: they both exhibit modes of thought, which become in their expression modes of discourse. Amid the divergence of meanings and applications, and the dependencies and struggles among the proponents of contradictory positions, they have in common a literary community, a world of available discourse. The transition into atheism is not only a generation of negation; it is a literary event, whose progression spells out a world which remains available long after the agents and actors have passed on. The atheistic transition is available in this world of discourse, maintaining an independent life, in contrast to the thousand contingencies out of which it emerged. "Not only in the world 'world' only insofar as it comes into language, but language, too, has its real being only in the fact that the world is re-presented within it."[57] The modes of thought become concrete in discourse, however abstract the language, and take on a determined quality which opens up to even further investigation the problematic situation of modern atheism. Thus the fourth and final parameter: What theism and atheism have in common is discourse. For their study a neutral instrument is needed by which they may be interpreted in their working inquiries and compared without reducing their pluralism to one mode of thought or another. Discourse allows for this analysis.

For discourse itself contains four coordinates which Richard McKeon has isolated as inherent in any connected pattern of thought: selection, interpretation, method, and principle.[58] These coordinates allow a series of questions to be leveled at any tractate, speech, argument or discursive expression, and a subsequent relationship to be drawn between one text or inquiry and another, without either reducing every philosophy to a single true philosophy or regarding all positions as of equal worth because each represents a different perspective. To ask questions governed by these coordinates is to look for the values given to certain variables in every discourse. Like an operational matrix, these four coordinates of discourse will be progressively clarified as they are employed in the following inquiry, but some formal and initial discussion of them might be helpful.

Selection is operative because discourse must always be about something. Selection indicates the fundamental field or area which will provide the subject-matter and the terms with which the discourse deals. Selection indicates the radical focus of the discourse, whether that focus converges on the structure of things or upon the antecedent processes of thought whereby the structure of things can be known or upon expressions of these thoughts in language and in action. Philosophical periods differ as the major thinkers find their fundamental area of disclosure or of inquiry in the nature of things (a metaphysical selection) or in the structures of cognition (an epistemological selection) or in the nature of language and the implications of actions (a semantic or pragmatic selection). Selection responds to the question: What are you fundamentally talking about? What area is fundamental to all subsequent inquiry? It is usually indicated by the kind of categories which are operative in the discourse. A semantic selection would allow Gilbert Ryle to have categories of words, varieties of the types of proposition-factors that could complete certain "sentence-frames" without absurdity; an epistemological selection would indicate that the categories of Kant's *Critique of Pure Reason* would be deduced from the kinds of logical judgments deduced as the a priori conditions for all judgments because they make possible the syntheses inherent in experiential knowledge; a metaphysical selection would turn Francisco Suárez's *Disputationes metaphysicae* to a consideration of the categories of being, rather than of judgments or of words. Every discourse must have a focus or area of inquiry which is fundamental to all others. Selection characterizes what that focus or area is.

Interpretation addresses the second question about any discourse: What allows something to be said about the subject? How can statements or propositions be formed that are more than tautologies? This introduces the coordinate of interpretation since all judgments and all propositional knowledge involve an interpretation of a subject-matter. Propositions are made or terms predicated according to what is finally real within the discourse. Selection asks what are you talking about; interpretation asks how you can say anything about it, how you can form propositions. Statements are made or propositions are formed in accord with what passes as authentic evidence, what Plato called "the really real." There are four basic possibilities. Either the real can transcend the phenomenon, as it does for Plato (an ontological interpretation) or it can underlie the phenomenon, as it does for Freud (an entitative interpretation). In both cases, one distinguishes between the apparent and the real. For the ontological interpretation this distinction becomes that of the phenomenon and the real; for the entitative, this distinction becomes that of the surface or symbolic and the actual substratum. On the other hand, one can maintain that the real and the phenomenal are not to be so distinguished, that in some way it is the real that is phenomenal. This can be either because, as for Aristotle, the essential is the structure of the real (an essentialist interpretation) or, as for André Gide, human perspectives confer on the phenomena whatever meaning and value it possesses (an existentialist interpretation). In Aristotle, the intellect's activity does not give the structure to the real, does not confer its essential patterns, but it does make those patterns intelligible. In the existentialist interpretation of André Gide, on the contrary, it is perspective that constitutes the real, giving it intelligibility as well as structure. How one "interprets" the real, i.e. as transcending or underlying the given phenomenon or as merging either essentially or perspectively with the phenomenon, will provide the warrant for any statement. Interpretation indicates the final evidence on which judgments will be formed, and a difference in interpretation dictates a radical difference in judgments. Selection exhibits what the discourse has taken as subject; interpretation allows predicates to be joined to that subject.

Third, there is method. The word itself has an interesting history. The fundamental metaphor in μέθοδος is ὁδός, a way, road, or journey. Burnet maintains that it was taken originally from hunting, and Liddell and Scott give the "pursuit of a nymph" as one example of this sense. Richard Robinson, noting that only in the *Sophist* do hunting and μέθοδος come together, maintains that it is "more likely that the word came to have its technical meaning through Parmenides' 'way,' which was not a hunt or a pursuit of anything, but a pilgrimage to the presence of a goddess."[59] Etymologically, μέθοδος means the "way after" something, and Robinson argues that by the time of Plato and Aristotle the journey or search was purely intellectual, translating it with the English derivatives "method," "inquiry', "procedure," or "pursuit."

In any case, method indicates a pattern of discourse, a way of procedure, a manner of argumentation in which one is able to move from one proposition to another. Method is indicated by the way that one raises a question, establishes evidence, argues from evidence to conclusions, or verifies the conclusions tentatively accepted. Selection is a coordinate of discourse because discourse must have that which allows real predication; method is a coordinate of discourse because there must be a pattern to such movements as inquiry, proof, demonstration, and verification. Method allows the question: How is something done, established, composed, or contradicted? Method is the pattern within discourse.

The history of reflective discourse, whether philosophic, scientific, literary, historical, or theological, is rich in the possibilities and varieties of methods it exhibits. Some methods have been proposed as universal, as the single method or pattern appropriate to all serious discourse. The dialectical method of Plato and of the tradition which reaches from him to Hegel and Marx is the only method "that attempts systematically and in all cases to determine what each thing really is."[60] It moves through negation to resolve contradiction in a higher unity. The operational method of Galileo and Bacon lies in the elaboration of an initial matrix or series of distinctions or perspectives and in the bringing of this structure to bear upon any matter in question in order to achieve conclusions whose validity can subsequently be tested. Still other philosophers have proposed a series of differing or particular methods. The problematic method of Aristotle, Aquinas, and Dewey distinguishes a different method for each different kind of problem; much of the work of inquiry consists in discovering the method appropriate to the question to be treated. Finally, from Euclid to Newton to Santayana, the logistic method consists in breaking composites down to their simple elements and then synthetically recombining them, for the whole is nothing but the sum of its parts.

Each of these methods is modified and radically altered as it combines with the other coordinates of discourse, but the isolation of method as one of these coordinates allows an identification of the pattern which the discourse is taking, either initially, to establish questions and evidence, or subsequently, to formulate illation and verification. To ask the question about method is to inquire how it is that this text or this argument embodies coherence and pattern.

Finally, since human thought and speech must have its beginning, principle addresses the fourth question: What holds the whole together as the source of so much diversity? The principle is the source of the discourse, of its truth, its value, or its connection with reality. The question of principle probes for what is ultimate in the presuppositions that so many elements would be combined into what is one play, or that so many conclusions could follow in thirteen books of geometry.

Philosophic history contributes very different kinds of principles to the unity of discourse. For some philosophers, such as Plato or Newton, one single principle (a comprehensive principle) will be the source of all explanation, whether that comprehensive principle is the relationship of being to becoming as knowledge to opinion or whether it is the motive force to which all movement and natural phenomena can be resolved. For others, such as Aristotle and Descartes, the principle in each case is reflexively commensurate with a particular science or area of problem, a reflexive principle. In physics, Aristotle could have nature as a principle, as the source of movement in something which is intrinsically moved; in metaphysics, he could explain generation and corruption by thought thinking itself; he explains predication, finally, through categories which are predicates of predicates. For still others, the principle would be simple, that is, the parts of a whole, the "simple ideas" of Locke or the individual atoms of Democritus. Finally, the principle could be actional as Marx introduced revolutionary activity into the Hegelian dialectic as necessary for continual progress or as William of Ockham made the act of creation the arbitrary source of all finite reality.

The necessities of significant discourse are: a subject and terms of discourse, a reality which makes predication possible, a method by which these propositions can become an argument or an inquiry, and a source by which the discourse can be said to be fundamentally true or valuable or unified. Selection, interpretation, method, and principle, used as the coordinates of discourse, provide a way not of categorizing an author or his work arbitrarily, but of asking questions about a work which brings out its unique procedure. "With their aid, contrasts or corroborations can be asserted, and the real issues of disagreement can be separated from verbal contradictions or philosophical complementarities."[61]

Atheism, then, discloses four parameters by which its ambiguity can be clarified and its claims be made the subject of a consistent inquiry. These parameters dictate both the content and the method of the following inquiry into the origins of modern atheism.

Because atheism is parasitic on theism for its name, its meanings, and its adversary, it is imperative to investigate theism, its use of *god*, those who constitute the "theists," and so on. Because atheism suggests a dependence upon theism even for its generation and existence, it is imperative to investigate the transition in which theism gives way to atheism. This problem constitutes the question of this book. Since the form in which this content emerges is critical to its meaning, it is imperative to analyze the working inquiries in themselves and to notice the shifts from one mode of thinking to another, such as from theology to philosophy, and from one form of philosophy to another. Since both atheism and theism emerge as discourse, it is imperative that some attention be paid through the coordinates of discourse to those differences and interrelations of terms and meaning in which problems are raised and solutions offered. It is not that one of these imperatives should be followed, completed, and another then engaged. All these imperatives function together to form the structure of this inquiry. The parameters of atheism frame the question which will govern this book: How did the idea of atheism emerge in the modern world and take so firm a hold?

The Event and Its Inquiry

If "atheism" without parameters is not a problem, "modern" without qualifications is not a period. Cassiodorus' *Variarum libri* refers to the institutions or things of the present as the *moderna*, and one current usage has repeated this by identifying modern and contemporary. The word is postclassical in its Latin origins, derived from *modo*, "just now," as *hodiernus* was derived from *hodie*, "today." Cassiodorus employed it to segregate a later civilization from that of the *antiqui*, "ancient."[62] The word traveled from sixth-century Latin into French, Spanish, Portuguese, Italian, and German that flowed as tributaries from this original source. Its designation of a distinction from the past allowed periodic advancements or struggles in education to be characterized as battles between the ancients and the moderns. Vituperations between the "ancients" and "moderns" were exchanged by fourteenth-century logicians, the Thomists and the Scotists classified with those who followed the *via antiqua* and William of Ockham heading the *moderni*.[63] In 1585, Thomas Washington distinguished the "writings of the auncient and moderne Geographers and Historiographers," while Francis Bacon predicted to Tobie Matthew in Spain that "these modern languages will at one time or other play the bank-rowtes with books."[64] By the early eighteenth century, the battle had become one over humanistic learning in general, pitting against Richard Bentley the satire of Jonathan Swift's *Full and True Account of the Battle Fought Last Friday Between the Ancient and the Modern Books in St. James's Library* (1704).[65]

While "modern" has been contrasted with "ancient" since Cassiodorus, it has come increasingly to be distinguished from "contemporary." The *Oxford English Dictionary* notes as obsolete a once-accepted meaning,"being at this time; now existing," despite frequent sixteenth-century usage. "Modern" is more generous in its meanings now: "of or pertaining to the present and recent times," and in historical studies it denotes that period which begins after the medieval.[66] Some authors speak of the twentieth century as introducing the "post-modern world," and terminate the modern period with the end of colonialism, the emergence of atomic energy, the decline of Europe, the unifications of mass communication and transportation, or a particular turn in world consciousness or philosophic focus. James Collins opens his magisterial *God in Modern Philosophy* with the distinction between "the modern history of the problem of God and contemporary speculation about Him," and in two other works he confines the range of modern European philosophy to the three centuries between 1600 and 1900, while insisting that there is always something extrinsic and arbitrary about such boundaries in the history of thought or in the actions and persuasions of human beings.[67]

The overlapping of boundaries, the consequences of rereading ancient authors and former accomplishments and of their retrieval through new exegesis and commentaries, the parallel but independent streams of traditions which intersect at unexpected, unforeseen junctures, the interventions of genius and the misinterpretations by the faithful disciple,—all of these make any simple sequencing or sectioning of the history of philosophy or theology finally false. The series over time is true enough at first blush, but the interconnections of influences and inquiries render any dispersal over time or within a period only initial and tentative. It is true to say that Thomas Aquinas preceded David Hume by hundreds of years and held sway in a profoundly different philosophic and theological culture. It is also true, however, and perhaps even more accurate, to urge that Aquinas and Hume are intellectual contemporaries; part of the hermeneutical task is to overcome the historical and linguistic distance between them so that their concerns about god, freedom, causality, and understanding can be mutually related, differentiated, and criticized. In other words, it is banal to note that the procession of figures moves successively through the history of thought; the part of wisdom is to find a continual conversation taking place, a conversation to which each generation makes its contribution and from which it derives its tradition as it evokes from the older members latent insights and discoveries which emerge only during this continued encounter. Chronology is appropriate in intellectual history, but it is not the final word.

Nevertheless, it is a word that should be spoken. It is one thing to insist that wisdom is sempiternal; it is another to argue that it is static. Philosophy and theology contain events of inner development in which the initial principles of a system are allowed time for the maturation and emergence of their organic consequences. Often the master has not spelled out these conclusions of initial presuppositions; it is a task done within and over history. History seems in this sense to be the laboratory for ideas and assumptions. What lies hidden in the presuppositions only develops as the conversation continues; what is false or misleading is often recognized only when a hypothesis finally fathers a conclusion that is untenable. The history of philosophy or the history of theology in this sense is part of philosophy or theology in a distinctive manner. The verification principle for theoretic investigations often lies in the irreversible sequel of their presuppositions—not that these can be established as true by their conclusions, but they can be established as false by them. A true conclusion can come from a false or a true premise; a false conclusion can come only from a false premise. And when a philosophic or theological conclusion does not explain reality, but explains it away or contradicts something unquestionably established, the premises under which the inquiry was conducted become problematic. The conclusion translates what the assumptions mean; it spells out their implications. An assumption it is a statement about the world, and eventually the world will be formed which tells you what you have said. A plot must have an organic beginning, middle, and end, but the beginning will only deliver its latent sense when the end has been reached. The beginning is only a beginning because there is an end. In philosophy or theology, the plot is an inquiry or an argument, which also needs time to disclose the full power and significance of its principles, for these principles are only understood in their conclusions.

Within what is now called the modern period, a new conclusion appeared. It was not a judgment about atheism or books about atheistic doctrine, nor about adversaries who were judged atheists. The conclusion was that there were men who judged themselves to be atheists, who called themselves atheists. In the ancient world, and even more in the medieval world, this was unheard of. "Atheist" had been vituperative and polemic; now it became a signature and a boast. David Hume commented casually that he had never met an atheist, as John Duns Scotus or Aristotle might have said before him. But Baron Paul d'Holbach did what no one had done with Duns Scotus or Aristotle: he introduced Hume to a society he claimed to be filled with them![68] Paris boasted what medieval Oxford and ancient Athens did not command: a band of thinkers who celebrated their denial of anything which one could call "god."

Hegel recognized that something distinct had occurred in the Paris of the Enlightenment: "We should not make the charge of atheism lightly, for it is a very common occurrence that an individual whose ideas about God differ from those of other people is charged with lack of religion, or even with atheism. But here it really is the case that this philosophy has developed into atheism, and has defined matter, nature, etc., as that which is to be taken as the ultimate, the active, and the efficient."[69] Hegel was correct in recognizing that something new had occurred. What he could not know was that this persuasion of a very few would wax throughout the next century and increasingly become the mark of an elite. The opening of the twentieth century found that number swollen to a few hundred thousand, but it increased by 1985 to over two hundred million. (If one includes those devoid of any religious belief or interests, the total is over a billion, more than twenty percent of the world's population.) What began in Paris reached this extent in only two hundred years.[70] Some twenty years ago, Professor

Schubert M. Ogden registered his agreement with the German theologian Gerhard Ebeling that our culture is characteristically "the age of atheism," and explained his agreement in terms of context and alienation: "If the reality of God is still to be affirmed, this must now be done in a situation in which, on an unprecedented scale, that reality is expressly denied." Karl Rahner in his interview with Gwendoline Jarcyk spoke of world atheism as "un phénomène qui jusqu'à présent n'a jamais eu cette extension dans l'histoire de l'humanité. . . . Une telle réalité, voilà qui n'a jamais existé jusqu'à présent." What began in the Paris of the Enlightenment has become a religious phenomenon which Western civilization has never witnessed before. It is critical to notice the historical uniqueness of the contemporary experience: the rise of a radical godlessness which is as much a part of the consciousness of millions of ordinary human beings as it is the persuasion of the intellectual. Atheisms have existed before, but there is a novelty, a distinctiveness about the contemporary denial of god both in its extent and in its cultural establishment. The recent judgment of John Paul II coincides with these readings of the present situation: "L'athéisme est sans conteste l'un des phénomènes majeurs, et il faut même dire, le drame spirituel de notre temps."[71]

This massive shifting of religious consciousness was recognized as the nineteenth century drew to a close by men as diverse as John Henry Cardinal Newman and Friedrich Nietzsche. In 1887, after Nietzsche had published the initial edition of *The Gay Science* and followed it with *Thus Spoke Zarathustra* and *Beyond Good and Evil*, he returned to the prior work to complete it with the great fifth book. Earlier, the Madman in the marketplace had announced the death of God. Now Nietzsche spelled out the precise meaning which this striking parable carried: "The greatest recent event—that 'God is dead,' that the belief in the Christian god has become unbelievable—is already beginning to cast its first shadows over Europe. For the few at least, whose eyes—the *suspicion* in whose eyes is strong and subtle enough for this spectacle, some sun seems to have set and some ancient and profound trust has been turned into doubt."[72] In England, the aging Newman felt the same drawing on of night, the same shadow lengthening over what had once been Christian civilization. In the *Apologia Pro Vita Sua*, he wrote of the religious disintegration of Europe: "In these latter days, in like manner, outside of the Catholic Church, things are tending,—with far greater rapidity than in that old time from the circumstance of the age,—to atheism in one shape or another. What a scene, what a prospect, does the whole of Europe present at this day . . . and every civilization through the world, which is under the influence of the European mind!"[73] For both Newman and Nietzsche, this gradual but profound erosion of religious belief, an erosion not halted but promoted and embodied in the liberal attenuation of dogma, constituted a massive cultural phenomenon, the emergence of a certain cast of mind in greater and greater predominance, one whose sensibilities and educational background, whose ambit of intellectual interests and engagements, defined human beings constitutionally unable to believe, to know, or to be convinced in any way of the existence of the Judeo-Christian god. What Nietzsche and Newman foresaw was that religious impotence or uninterest would not remain a private or an isolated phenomenon, that it would increasingly characterize the "educated intellect of England, France, and Germany," and that its influence would eventually tell upon every routine aspect of civilization.[74] Both Nietzsche and Newman, albeit with vastly different evaluations, gauged the enormous importance of what was taking place, and in their assessments they stand as prophetic figures within the twilight of the nineteenth century.

In the oft-repeated scene from the third book of *The Gay Science*, when the Madman lights a lamp in the day and rushes screaming into the marketplace, it is the Madman alone who cries out: "I seek God! I seek God!" The marketplace convulses in ridicule: "Has he got lost? asked one. Did he lose his way like a child? asked another. Or is he hiding? Is he afraid of us? . . . Thus they yelled and laughed." The difference between the Madman and the market crowds was not that one believed in the reality of god and the other did not. Neither believed, and god died in the event of his own incredibility. But the Madman alone knows what they have done, what they have lost. "I will tell you. We have killed him—you and I. All of us are his murderers. But how did we do this? How could we drink up the sea? Who gave us the sponge to wipe away the entire horizon? . . . What was holiest and mightiest of all that the world has yet owned has bled to death under our knives." Here the Madman falls silent before the astonished listeners. He throws his lantern upon the ground, smashing it into pieces. "I have come too early, he said then; my time is not yet. This tremendous event is still on its way, still wandering; it has not yet reached the ears of human beings. . . . This deed is still more distant from them than the most distant stars—*and yet they have done it themselves.*"[75]

In his lectures with Paul Ricoeur, Alasdair MacIntyre maintains that the characteristic of the contemporary debate between the atheists and the theists is the decline in the cultural urgency of the question. It doesn't make any difference. The tension between religious belief and unbelief in the nineteenth century, which one can trace in the lives of Matthew Arnold and Henry Sidgwick, cannot be found in contemporary culture.[76] But this is to miss much of the point of Nietzsche's myth. It is precisely the absence of this tension within the latter-day nineteenth-century marketplace which convinced the Madman that human beings do not understand what they have done. Two things were poignantly obvious to Nietzsche: that the incredibility of god within the bourgeois world constitutes his death, and that this was the elimination of a god radically unimportant to those who clustered there. The god who had disappeared from conviction was finally irrelevant.

Nietzsche never draws out the implication of these two insights, but they are points of critical importance. For if the death of god is constituted by his massive incredibility and if this incredibility rests upon one who is fundamentally trivial, then the issues of the *Seventh Epistle* about meaning and instance can be legitimately leveled at the Madman of *The Gay Science* and the prophetic Zarathustra: What god has died beneath these knives? What is the content of theological meaning and the instance of its embodiment which has perished?

But Nietzsche's Madman does pose a central question, whose import bears more upon the modes of thought or the forms of discourse than upon the content: "We have killed him—you and I. All of us are his murderers. But how did we do this?"[77] *The Gay Science* sketched a very general answer by tracing out the history of science and morality, but the question still hangs on the air. How was it possible that such an event came about? The question of the Madman is not about cultural disappearance, as some have argued; much less is it a return to some lighter version of Hegelian projection into otherness through the incarnation. Nietzsche himself specified its meaning: God has become incredible. What was once the content and subject of unhesitant conviction and religious confession has become unwarranted. It is not that Europe has stopped defending or believing in the Christian god. The statement is not about Europe, but about god, about the transition from being credible to becoming incredible. This transition has been made, but it will take centuries for Europe or for the world to accept it. "In the main one may say: The event is far too great, too distant, too remote from the multitude's capacity for comprehension even for the tidings of it to be thought of as having *arrived* yet. Much less may one suppose that many people know as yet *what* this event really means."[78] Nietzsche's Madman and Zarathustra announce "this tremendous event" itself: the transition into incredibility, as belief in the Christian god became unbelievable, which demands inquiry. What is this transition, this event still so far distant from most human beings?

When a judgment so recent in its earliest proponents and so massive in the contradictions it offers to religious consciousness gathers force and adherents so swiftly that within two hundred years it commands the convictions of numerous major thinkers in the West and the attention of all, the event out of which it issued legitimately and urgently claims examination. Something crucial has happened in the realm of ideas.

Atheism cannot be dismissed simply as an epiphenomenon of the social order or as an understandable psychological maturation or, conversely, as another symptom of moral degeneracy. Whether it measures a remarkable advance in the revolutionary arrangements of social classes; or emerges in the conversion of common interests from the transcendent to the exploration and conquest of this world, a conversion for which enthusiasm is fed with heady advances in technology and science; or whether it appositely fits a world of comforts and alienation undreamed of by our ancestors, the disintegration of monogamous marriage, the widespread industry in death, the rise of totalitarian governments, and the recent nihilism of total war, atheism remains a judgment, a statement about the nature of things. What is more, it is primarily a religious judgment, whether that "religion" adopts the form of natural or revealed religion, of philosophy or humanism. As a religious judgment, atheism possesses its own plot, its own argument in the history of ideas, its own demands for coordinated inquiry. To postulate that religion arose and held its sway because of an ill-ordered society or an ill-ordered psyche was an option indulged in the nineteenth century, just as atheism had been reduced in earlier polemics to a collapsing social order or a guilty conscience. All of these hermeneutics have claimed their advocates and yielded diverse readings of the cultural histories they attempt to explain, yet all of them explained a conviction through its genetic occasion. But genesis and development exhibit the meaning and truth of ideas and of judgments only if the theoretical motives which justify these concepts and statements integrate that history and are submitted to an appropriate criticism. The empirical necessities of the irrigation of the Nile Delta may well have been the social and economic occasion for the formation of the early geometries, but this agricultural genesis says nothing about the truth of the theorems elaborated or the accuracy of the corollaries drawn. How an idea emerges from society or from interior and unconscious states is one question. Whether an idea is valid in both its content and its form of thought is quite another. The genesis of a conviction is philosophically or theologically critical to its understanding if the idea is not reduced to a social product or a psychic inevitability, that is, if it is not explained or explained away by contraction to something else, if the ideational integrity of idea, argument, facts, and principles is kept and submitted to a history and a critique on its own terms. Affirmation and negations have a right to be judged on their own evidence and traced out in their own presuppositions and sequels. Social histories and psychological analyses are rich in the illumination they provide, but they finally impoverish if they reduce the central judgments studied to symptoms of myriad hidden factors and refuse to take a conviction seriously enough to consider it in itself, with its own content and forms of appropriate discourse.[79] A doctrine so defrauded of its proper coordinates in history and in evidence becomes an ideology only symptomatically interesting: its metaphysical persuasions have only a subjective character and the influences which bring it about are seen as independent of all reasonable grounds and working with blind necessity. It is an idea alienated from its own grounds and argument.

This book proposes to investigate the origin of an argument, to explore the beginnings of a plot, not to follow its development through the great *dramatis personae* of the nineteenth and twentieth centuries or through the shifting patterns of the evidence then alleged and the methods employed. The question for this inquiry is prior to that development. What lies at the origins of modern atheism? How was it that over the period which Owen Chadwick has called "the seminal years of modern intellectual history" one of the seeds which germinated and flourished was that of atheistic consciousness?[80]

To this question the prior parameters of an inquiry into atheism must be brought. To understand the origins of atheism as an idea rather than as a cultural by-product, it is necessary to track the theisms out of which it came and to which it considered itself a counterposition. This job may not be prohibitively difficult if we begin with the great work of Baron Paul Henri d'Holbach, to which this comprehensive promoter of philosophic atheism brought the conversations of his friends, and by which he turned the long journey of Denis Diderot into system, the *Système de la nature*. The *Système* unquestionably deserves the assessment which succeeding generations have made of it: "the most important demonstration of materialism and atheism" until the middle of the twentieth century.[81] D'Holbach's book brought to culmination the philosophes' religious cynicism, and it made even such hardy patrons as Frederick the Great join the opposition with his *Réfutation du Système de la nature* and Voltaire enter the lists against it in his *Dictionnaire philosophique*. In the *Système*, the atheism of the Enlightenment had assembled its most careful argumentation and sounded its frankest insistence upon the atheistic conclusion. One can begin with this work and with the works of the philosophes out of which it came and to which it was sequel and crown. Then the theisms that are being attacked are immediately evident. Theology is considered in general confused and contradictory, yet two theologians are singled out as of principal importance: Dr. Samuel Clarke of England and Father Nicolas Malebranche of France. But both of these theologians are descended from figures that dominated the European philosophic and scientific world: Clarke sits at the feet of Newton and Malebranche on every page bears witness to his extraordinary conversion to Descartes. So d'Holbach and Diderot reached back to Newton and Descartes for their principal opponents.

Certainly there were other figures who stepped on the stage at diverse moments and who occupied it in more than a secondary role. Giordano

Bruno anticipated Diderot's dynamic matter by a century and a half, while the history of atheistic polemics could be written through the books composed to counter Spinoza. But Bruno and Spinoza were either too removed from the discussions in natural philosophy or too intrinsically ambiguous to form a concatenated series of disciples that advocated their heritage within the Enlightenment. Spinoza drew the fire of both Malebranche and Clarke, but it was not Spinoza's influence which told on Diderot and d'Holbach. Descartes and Malebranche, Newton and Clarke generated a tradition in a way that neither Bruno nor Spinoza did. These theistic traditions finally generated their own denials. One of the many ironies of this history of origins is that while the guns of the beleaguered were often trained on Spinoza, the fortress was being taken from within.

The remarkable thing is not that d'Holbach and Diderot found theologians and philosophers with whom to battle, but that the theologians themselves had become philosophers in order to enter the match. The extraordinary note about this emergence of the denial of the Christian god which Nietzsche celebrated is that Christianity as such, more specifically the person and teaching of Jesus or the experience and history of the Christian Church, did not enter the discussion. The absence of any consideration of Christology is so pervasive throughout serious discussion that it becomes taken for granted, yet it is so stunningly curious that it raises a fundamental issue of the modes of thought: How did the issue of Christianity vs. atheism become purely philosophical? To paraphrase Tertullian: How was it that the only arms to defend the temple were to be found in the Stoa?

This question pushed the inquiry back to the guardians of the temple, the theologians of the dawning seventeenth century. Two of them wrote elaborately and influentially against the atheists: Leonard Lessius of Louvain and Marin Mersenne of the Parisian Priory. One was a Jesuit, the other a Franciscan; both were scholars of immense erudition, and both took their posts in the great intellectual battles that brought the modern world into its initial configurations. Lessius and Mersenne shaped something of the intricate pattern which this new age was to assume; both of them told upon their culture. But perhaps more important, both were symptomatic of forces and persuasions more powerful than themselves and more pervasive than their teaching. It is with them, then, either as influences in the history of thought or as indications of its drift, that our story can begin. For these successive questions, cumulating one on top of another, suggest this history the way that history is always suggested, backwards. They arise from the religious storm that broke over Europe during the Enlightenment and probe for its origins, for beginnings which remained silent, unnoticed, a subtle drop in the temperature and a change in the humidity, clouds forming far on the horizon, stealing into the atmosphere and altering its climate, gathering moisture as almost imperceptibly they progress from albumen to slate gray to black, the first few drops of rain, then the torrents and the earth awash with water. From this, the governing question: How was it possible?

The emergence of modern atheism lies with Diderot and d'Holbach. This fact seems uncontestable. The inquiry of this book does not establish that fact; it presumes it. The problem for this book is how was such a fact possible? It is not remarkable that an atheist or two or three would appear in Paris. Almost anything will eventually appear in Paris! But how could such an idea appear with force sufficient to initiate the massive negation which has cast its shadow over Europe? Why could Nietzsche legitimately call this idea a "tremendous event?" "We have killed him—you and I. All of us are his murderers. But how did we do this?"[82] This question expresses as well as possible the problem of this book, an inquiry in agreement with Aristotle that the one "who considers things in their first growth and origin, whether a *polis* or anything else, will obtain the clearest view of them."[83]

Our effort, then, is to understand what has taken place as it emerged, rather than mount an effort of advocacy or of attack. The question which shapes this effort is twofold. In the generation of ideas, how did so powerful an idea as atheism arise? In the reflections of theology, what can be learned from such "a tremendous event"?

The first issue is one in the history of ideas rather than sociology, cultural anthropology, or psychology. Human beings wrote works which advanced ideas, urged convictions, appealed to evidence, and mounted arguments, and these works evoked agreements which combined into an intellectual tradition unique in the history of Western civilization. They established a community of meaning, even within clashing disagreement and violent repudiation, for one of the ways in which human beings can come together is to fight. Within the unity of this struggle may be hidden the possibilities of a further or more comprehensive truth for whose realization these contradictions are necessary, dialectical moments. But whatever the outcome, the first issue is that of the continuity, interaction, and genesis of ideas. The second issue is directly theological, constructive in its inquiry and inductive in its conclusions: Does this history of ideas exhibit anything that should bear upon the reflections of the theologian and upon the design of theology? Can the theologian learn from history, especially the history of the contention that the theologian has nothing to talk about? Granted that there is such a pattern in the origins of atheistic consciousness, granted even that this pattern is dialectical, that is, generated out of contradiction, what can theology gain from the knowledge that this structure lies at the procreation of atheism?

The task of hermeneutics is the restoration of communication, a fusion of horizons in which significant works are made present and fruitful in their effective history, in which what is alien is made familiar and restored to continuity, presence, and importance. Not only does the present ask of past assertions and texts questions about meaning and truth, but this restored tradition poses questions to contemporary reflection. Even the negativity of such an experience implies a question. The origins of atheistic consciousness place demands and challenges before contemporary theology, and perhaps the ensuing dialogue can discover new significance in both.

The first issue, then, bears upon the establishment of a tradition; the second, upon the discovery of its theological meaning. The inquiry is one of tradition and discovery. For there is only an apparent contradiction between discovery and tradition. The disclosure or the invention of what is new only superficially excludes the transmission or reception of what is old. Actually, discovery can only light upon what is hidden within the given, while a tradition can possess significance, can perdure, only if that which is past is continually made present, changed, reinterpreted, and transposed—if only to be understood by succeeding generations. Discovery is the grasp of new meaning; tradition is its mediation, posing the elements and the problematic situation which enables new disclosures. Discovery and tradition are not opposed; they are coordinated. They constitute the rhythm and the unity of inquiry. Tradition embodies an evolving history, symbolic continuities, resonances with varied human experiences. Discovery seizes upon a newness of meaning or a retrieval of significance, but the matter of discovery is tradition.

Discovery alone can have something hypothetical about its insights and something abstract about that which stands as revolutionary or as untried. Tradition adds time and development, consequences and implications, within conflicting conceptual schemata until the idea becomes a topic in the history of ideas and its propositions take on the flexibility of a theme. The new idea is an abstraction; tradition gives the idea an effective history, following its internal possibilities through the growth and testing of subsequent experience. In its initial invention, an art object or a literary work may possess a richness unseen by its author. History traces the consequent reflection of other minds and the cultural embodiment in different practices to bring out these hidden virtualities.

A tradition in the history of ideas, then, presents theological discovery with its own prior and repeated discoveries and verifications. Theology finds in this consequent history a field of experimentation, a laboratory in which its possibilities are elicited and tested. Tradition is this discovery in its continued richness, with some of its developmental promises or sequels realized. In this sense, tradition is the truth of discovery. Tradition confronts the present with a depth that nothing less settled can match.

This is deeply true of theological reflection. One does not reach back into the past to resurrect figures and arguments. Vital traditions are the situations of the present. Tradition is the contemporary presence of the past. It forms, as it surrounds, both the issues which are raised and the subject who questions. Theology and its research always stand within a tradition, not at a distance from it. And the richness of its reflection depends upon its awareness of this tradition.

This relationship between tradition and discovery is critically important to any understanding of atheism, perhaps especially so in an inquiry into the theological meaning of its origins. For the Western world, as indicated above, is presented now with a radically different state of the question. Unlike any civilization or intellectual culture that has preceded it in the past or accompanies it today, Western philosophical and theological reflection now confront the denial of god no longer as a random option or as an idiosyncratic philosophy, but as a heritage of two centuries. Atheism exists now in the West with a length of lineage and with a comprehensiveness of human commitments unlike anything which it has enjoyed before. Atheism has become a tradition, rather than a revolution. It possesses its own reading of the past as moments of crisis, insights, and a labored evolution towards its present moments of freedom and rationality. The twofold task of this book, then, is to trace out the origin of this atheistic tradition, or origin which is its transition from theism to atheism, and to understand its theological significance.

1 Religion as Bankrupt: Catholic Theologians and the Origins of Modern Atheism

Peter Gay traces the pluralistic coherence and the developing radicalism of the Enlightenment through three generations and finds its line of unity in an evolution from deism into atheism: "In the first half of the century, the leading philosophes had been deists and had used the vocabulary of natural law; in the second half, the leaders were atheists and used the vocabulary of utility."[1] The vectors which Gay charts are certainly there, but the distinction may be somewhat too neat, too overdrawn. Among his second-generation thinkers, only Diderot moved into unequivocal atheism, while d'Holbach attacked all forms of religious convictions as the Enlightenment ran its course. If Gay's matrix might be modified in a search for a pattern in this extraordinary rush of European intellectualism, it does evoke something of the character inherent in the Enlightenment. Who does or does not belong to the Enlightenment is arbitrary enough—with the exclusion of such figures as Samuel Johnson, Haydn, Mozart, Boscovich, Wolff, and Edmund Burke because of their sympathy with Christianity. It is one thing, however, to define the movement somewhat operationally as an anti-Christian army whose primary analogue is taken from the French philosophes, the "modern pagans" in Gay's felicitous phrase; it is quite another thing to find their generals increasingly godless. By and large, deists they were at the beginning, and deists they were when the great revolutions at the end of the eighteenth century incorporated them, as in the Americas, or engulfed them, as in France.

It would be false to tax the Enlightenment with indifference to religion. It would be more discerning to say that it was obsessed with it.[2] It would be even more accurate to assert that much of it was irrevocably hostile to supernatural revelation and confessional beliefs. "The strongest intellectual

37

forces of the Enlightenment do not lie in its rejection of belief, but rather in the new form of faith which it proclaims, and in the new form of religion which it embodies."³ That strangely gifted genius, Denis Diderot, summarized both the Aufklärung and its central persuasion in the title to his work, *De la suffisance de la religion naturelle*: individual, historical religions rise and fall. They have made the world ugly with their fratricidal wars and endless dogmatic controversies. Natural religion is beneath them all, foundational to all confessions, containing whatever truth they express, and possessing its own warrant directly within human experience. Natural religion is one which "I bear within myself, and I find it always the same."⁴ Diderot himself emigrated into a troubled atheism, but the Enlightenment in the main accepted and developed into a philosophic institution the deism whose forefathers were Edward, Lord Herbert of Cherbury and Charles Blount, and whose original naturalistic stamp was thoroughly imprinted in John Toland's *Christianity Not Mysterious* (1696) and Matthew Tindal's *Christianity as Old as Creation* (1730). The characteristic of this merger of the Enlightenment with deism was not the eclipse of religion as a focus of interest—and even of bitter controversy. Voltaire thought the existence of god a strictly demonstrable truth, and joined battle in what became the central theological issue of the period, a theodicy which would allow a provident god and a world of which he could remark, against Leibniz: "*Someday all will be well*, it is our hope; *all is well today*, is an illusion."⁵

Whatever the individual histories of Diderot and d'Holbach, by and large the Enlightenment did not countenance atheism; it rejected it. But in this repudiation, its major figures counted the Church and confessional religion not as allies, but as adversaries. If atheism was unacceptable, superstition and fanaticism were emphatically more so. Voltaire and the Enlightenment with him insisted that the evidence for the reality of god be obtained independently of any religious community. The natural religion of human beings sensitive to the world around and within them was discovered here, and it could provide criteria by which the truth and falsity of confessional doctrines could be sifted. Philosophic reflection was not the medieval *praeambula fidei* or *ancilla theologiae*; it was the truest religion or the "sister of religion" which "has disarmed the hands of superstition, which have so long been reddened with gore."⁶ To inhibit this therapy of confessional religion accomplished by a prior natural religion would return Europe to superstition and fanaticism. The existence and meaning of god must be established without appeal to the Church, and, even more critical for the historical European religious sensibility, without appeal to Jesus Christ.

That this should be done without appeal to the Church seemed obvious. The Church was part of the problem, part of the disease which was infecting any knowledge of god, not part of the solution. The Churches were the soil of atheism. As early as Francis Bacon, reflective thinkers had noted that "the causes of atheism are, divisions in religion, if there be many; for any one main division addeth zeal to both sides but many divisions introduce atheism."[7] Catholics and dissenters were hunted out of England; France revoked the Edict of Nantes and expelled thousands of Huguenots into the Dutch Republic; heretics were burned by the Spanish Inquisition and witches in the German principalities, the United Kingdom, and the early American religious colony of Massachusetts. Each major nation could tell of its slaughters in the wars of religions whose hatred had turned great portions of the earlier centuries into horror for Germany and France and whose animus energized the civil wars of England, Scotland, and the Netherlands. As the Enlightenment developed, first in England, then in France and Germany, and finally in the British colonies, the Western conscience found itself deeply scandalized and disgusted by confessional religions. The Churches and the sects had devastated Europe, engineered massacres, demanded religious resistance or revolution, attempted to excommunicate or to depose monarchs. Neither political compassion nor social tolerance, neither freedom for the Jews nor liberty of expression came from these fractious and ambitious communities, as the Enlightenment read them. Religious warfare had irrevocably discredited confessional primacy in the growing secularized sensitivity of much of European culture.

The abhorrence of this bloody practice reinforced a parallel aversion to relentless dogmatic conflicts and theological argument. Europe had become weary of the double predestination and the limited number of the saved, of an original sin which muted humanistic values, and of an Augustinianism which read human impotence and perversion everywhere. Jefferson wrote of the rejection that he represented: "I can never join Calvin in addressing *his* god. He was indeed an atheist, which I can never be; or rather his religion was daemonism. If ever man worshipped a false god, he did. The being described in his five points, is not the god whom you and I acknowledge and adore, the creator and benevolent governor of the world; but a daemon of malignant spirit. It would be more pardonable to believe in no god at all, than to blaspheme him by the atrocious attributes of Calvin."[8] The value of deism, in its last and American ambit, was that it prevented confessional religion from driving human beings into atheism as the only alternative! "As to the Christian system of faith," Thomas Paine wrote in *The Age of Reason*, the last popular manifesto of deism, "it appears to me as a species of Atheism—a sort of religious denial of god. It . . . is as near to Atheism as twilight is to darkness."[9] If one was to rescue allegiance to god, religious convictions, and theological seriousness, the history of confessional religions —either as social practice or as dogmatic teachers—was only hindrance. The existence and meaning of god would have to be established independently.

The position of Jesus in this attempt was strangely negligible. Not that the Enlightenment despised him. Quite the contrary. Both Diderot and Voltaire quoted the gospels to sustain the practice of tolerance.[10] For Lessing, he was the first reliable, practical teacher of the immortality of the soul: "To preach an inward purity of heart in reference to another life was reserved for him alone."[11] In 1778, Lessing published Reimarus' fragment, "Vom Zwecke Jesu und seine Jünger," delineating a Jesus fanatically persuaded that he is the anointed Messiah. After his death, his followers change this tragic picture in fictitious narratives to persuade the nations of his universal mission and divine importance. In the Enlightenment the distinction between Christianity and Christ became a contradiction between a moral teacher of some distinction and the corruption of tactically skilled communities.[12] Jefferson denied that he was in the profoundest sense anti-Christian: "To the corruptions of Christianity, I am, indeed, opposed; but not to the genuine precepts of Jesus himself."[13] No one denied the moral genius of Jesus. The only real question among the Enlightenment was how highly these "genuine precepts" should be regarded. For Jefferson, they present a fragmentary system of morals which "would be the most perfect and sublime that has ever been taught by man."[14] Thomas Paine would not travel quite that far down the road: Jesus "was a virtuous and an amiable man. The morality that he preached and practiced was one of the most benevolent kind; and though similar systems of morality had been preached by Confucius and by some of the Greek philosophers many years before; by the Quakers since; and by many good men in all ages, it has not been exceeded by any."[15] The Enlightenment agreed that Jesus was a Jewish ethical preacher, still illuminating a world in which tradition and Church had distorted his beliefs and maxims beyond recognition by any except . . . the philosophes.

But Jesus did not figure in their discussion of atheism. Aside from an occasional remark or rhetorical appearance in a subordinate position, the reality and message of Jesus did not support any assent to the existence of god. Nor should such an appeal be made, Jefferson contended. To insist upon the critical importance of Christ is to encourage atheism. Only one-sixth of the known world is Christian. To affirm revelation as necessary for the knowledge of god is to deny human beings that awareness which underlies the argument from universal consent. "Indeed, I think that every Christian sect gives a great handle to atheism by their general dogma, that, without a revelation, there would not be sufficient proof of the being of god." Jefferson, who numbers the disciples of Spinoza, Diderot, and d'Holbach among his atheists, shows here an inexplicable innocence of the history of Catholic theology, an innocence rendered more puzzling by his accurate citation of Cardinal Toledo's commentary on Aquinas in the same lengthy paragraph.[16] But he spoke for a revelation which insisted on the autonomy of reason. Revealed religion had so confused the native belief and trust in god with its battles of claims and counterclaims that the fundamental principle of natural religion must be established by means of the proper application of the mind to the evidence which is available to every person. If one is going to counter the atheists, it must be through appeal neither to Bible nor to teacher, but to nature.

Nature is the book that everyone can read, and its theological interpretation exercised the major thinkers of the period, whether philosophes or the scientific genius whom the Enlightenment reverenced above all, Isaac Newton. Newton called this a purpose of his writing the *Principia*: "When I wrote my treatise about our system, I had an eye upon such principles as might work with considering men for the belief of a Deity; and nothing can rejoin me more than to find it useful for that purpose."[17] Atheism for Newton, as for Voltaire, was senseless.[18]

Religion for the Enlightenment became a matter of action. When the question of religion focused upon god, his providence became the fundamental issue. When the question of religion focused upon the human person, the moral life became the fundamental issue. The shift in religious focus indicated a similar reassessment of Jesus; he became a teacher of ethics. Nature and, increasingly, issues of human history figured in discussions about the reality of god and his providence; Jesus figured—in the company of Cicero and Confucius—in discussions about the moral life of persons and cultures. Even when Lessing extended the importance of Jesus into the immortality of the human, he gave him unique status because Jesus had indicated that inward attitudes were ethically important before a final judgment of human worth.[19] The argument between the deists and the atheists lay in the interpretation of nature and the contradiction between what was found there and a human history of suffering and evil. The battle was an ancient one; only the nature of the terrain was revolutionary.

Or was it? Did the deist and the atheist actually shift the arena of religious debate and stake out new sources of evidence and new methodologies of interpretation—or was this the ground already? Did the Enlightenment insist upon a revised question or did the philosophes take over the state of the question from the discussion of the early seventeenth century? Did this "philosophic army" march into land that had been accepted as the place for the conflict and its resolution because Catholic theologians had long since abandoned the religious figure of Jesus as the principal evidence for the reality of god? To ask this crucial question another way: How emphatically did the theologians assert the witness and reality of Christ and the religious experience of the Judeo-Christian heritage in order to find warrant for the existence and nature of the Christian god? Were the discussions of the Enlightenment prepared by theologians?

Leonard Lessius and the Retrieval of the Stoic Topics

Like the first scene from *Hamlet*, this drama of the early seventeenth-century theologians might begin with the apparition of a ghost, but its land is England and the phantom is the wraith of Sir Walter Raleigh, come from the dead to petition a friend. Here, in the third decade of the century, Raleigh's ghost complains bitterly that the world "hath at sundry tymes cast a foule, and most unjust aspersion upon Me, for my presumed deniall of a Deity. From which abhominable and horrid crime, I was ever most free." No one knows this better than his friend, who must remember that Raleigh "was often accustomed highly to praise and esteeme the Booke of Lessius, written in proofe of the being of a Deity, and entitled, *De providentia numinis*."[20] The scene could hardly be more unlikely: the Flemish Jesuit, who crossed swords with James I over the powers of the papacy, now making his entrance into English letters through the man whom James beheaded.

Lessius' tractate "frustrateth with shame and confusion all the impugners of so illustrious and evident a Principle (Charactered in our Soules by Gods own seale;)" and Raleigh begs his friend—as a "Boone, or Favour"—to translate the Latin book into English and let it bear Raleigh's name. This would work a double grace: it would rescue Raleigh from the reputation of atheism and would pay some homage "to him who gave thee and me our Being."[21]

The ghost and its appeal were literary devices, a bit of preface to introduce the work of Lessius to the English audience and to smooth the passage between Louvain and London. In 1631, "permissu Superiorum," the translation was made and the book appeared at the market stalls: *Rawleigh: His Ghost. Or a Feigned Apparition of Syr Walter Rawleigh, to a friend of his, for the translating into English, the Booke of Leonard Lessius (that most learned man) entitled, De Providentia Numinis et Anime immortalitate written against the Atheists and the Polititians of these days.* The Latin original had appeared in 1613 and had met a general enough enthusiasm to be printed eventually in a Chinese edition.[22] What was this work which a theologian could offer to both Anglican divines and the Mandarins of the Central Kingdom as a defense of the existence of god and of his providence?

Leonard Leys, latinized into Lessius, was born in Brecht on October 1, 1554, and died on January 15, 1623, in Louvain. Louvain drew to itself most of his life. He was educated at its University, taking the doctorate as *primus* in philosophy in 1571. Leonard entered the newly founded Society of Jesus in 1572, even though the chancellor of the University attempted to dissuade him, the redoubtable Michael de Bay with whom Lessius was later to find himself in almost continuous conflict. From 1581 until 1584, he studied theology at the Roman College, sitting in the lecture halls of Francis Suarez and Robert Bellarmine. Upon his return to Louvain, Lessius assumed the chair of theology in the Jesuit College, and inaugurated there a change of critical importance.[23]

In 1526, at the University of Salamanca, the first theologian, Francisco de Vitoria, introduced an unprecedented procedure into the teaching of systematic theology in Spain. Following his former teacher, Peter Crockaert, he commented not on the *Book of the Sentences* of Peter Lombard, but on the *Summa theologiae* of Thomas Aquinas. Stealing into the great universities beyond the Pyrenees was the spring of the "Second Thomism." Lombard had held medieval theology together, presenting a common series of texts upon which vastly different theological structures could be built. The *Sentences* gave all the theologians of the Middle Ages, irrespective of the color of their convictions, a common language and a common tradition within which the conflicting theologies of Duns Scotus, William of Ockham, Durandus of St. Pourçain, and Thomas Aquinas could contact and speak intelligibly with one another. The *Sentences* provided for the Middle Ages what Catholic theology has never been able to regain: a focus or a unity precisely within dispersion, a common series of theological statements, a vocabulary and a common intellectual tradition which allowed substantial disagreements, and an irreducible pluralism within a shared culture. Vitoria's decision split from this common language and tradition, opting for the work of Aquinas over the Lombard's ordered assemblage of texts from the Fathers of the Church which were the common possession of all Christians. This factional schism within Catholic theology paralleled the sectarian divisions which were increasingly polarizing Christianity. The Jesuits of the Roman College followed Salamanca's suit, and Lessius in his turn brought the *Summa theologiae* of Aquinas into the Netherlands as the primary theological text. The University of Louvain first opposed and then adopted this innovation.[24]

The next thirty-eight years were rich in theological products as well as violent in their controversies. Lessius produced books on moral theology, mystical experience, economic theory, sacred scripture, and Catholic dogmatics. Almost from the beginning, the Baianists engaged him in the discussions cardinal among Catholic theologians of the relationship between efficacious grace and human liberty. Even three years after Paul V had prorogued the fractious *Congregatio de auxiliis* indefinitely and Molina's *Concordia* had passed through its fire unscathed, Lessius launched his own distinguished *De gratia efficaci decretis divinis libertate arbitrii et praescientia Dei condicionata*. Every noun and adjective in its title was a fighting word in those days, and the tract won both applause from his confrères for its defense of salvation *post praevisa merita* and a censure from the Jesuit General, Aquaviva, terrified that the newly buried controversy with the Dominicans would rise from its welcome grave.[25] Lessius' most celebrated work was undoubtedly the *De jure et justitia* of 1605, analyzing complex questions of economic justice, business interactions, law, and civil society within the heady atmosphere of Antwerp commerce and finance. The governing Duke of Brabant kept the work on his desk, next to his sword, "the one to dictate his rule and the other to sanction it!"[26] To the Protestant controversies, Lessius contributed his *Quae fides et quae religio sit capessenda Consultatio* (1609); to a rising Gallicanism and as a shot across the bow of England's James, there was the *Defensio potestatis Summi Pontificis* (1613); and at those religious who ate more heavily than was good for their health and died too early in the service of the gospel, he leveled the *Hygiasticon, seu vera ratio valetudinis*, a work on diet and living that went through thirty editions, translated into all the European languages and coming out in French under the inviting title, "The Art of Living a Century." Lessius, who was also as much a mystic as a Renaissance man, was continually in debate, taking up the major issues of his day and tilting with kings and Dominicans, irritating the Jesuit General and Michael de Bay in turn, and battling against expensive feasts at the conferral of the doctorate. It is not surprising that such a theologian wrote also "against the atheists and the polititians."

As the work is forensic in its intent, so the combination of topics—the divine providence and human immortality—indicate the methodological area within which its controversies are sustained. It is not finally a theoretical book, not metaphysical or physical in its interest; it is ethical. The existence of a provident god and the immortality of the soul constitute a knowledge which is "dignissima et inter omnia cognitu maxime necessaria." And why is it of such sovereign importance and pressing necessity? Because a negative decision on either of these issues would be the ruin of the moral enterprise. If one reduces the world in its ultimacies either to the impulses of nature (*naturae quodam impetu*) or to the chance intersection of causes (*fortuito causarum concursu*), one removes as governor of human life a providential god who punishes evil and rewards good. One removes an ultimate justice. To deny the reality of god is to deny that there is any final sanction in moral life, a judgment which ultimately allots to each according to his or her deeds. To eliminate the awareness of such a god is to eliminate the police force from human life, the terror that each life will be called before one by whom it will be eternally assessed.[27] Lessius follows a line of reasoning almost paradoxically contrary to Lucretius and Freud. Fear operates critically in religious choice for both positions. For Freud, however, it lies at the origin of religious affirmation because one feels fragility before the terrors of nature or horror before death. But for Lessius, fear lies at the origin of religious denial: atheism is an attempt to remove the threat of eternal judgment.

Perhaps another contrast will illumine the special character of Lessius' unity of scientific divisions. The subjects which Lessius is uniting in this work against the atheists are those which Kant also mutually implicates in his second *Kritik*. The existence of god and the immortality of the soul are for Kant, as well as for Lessius, convictions necessary to rationalize human ethical choice. For Kant however, they form necessary postulates, demanded by the principle of morality; for Lessius, they are demonstrable truths whose consequences sanction ethical life. Kant distinguishes sharply between the theoretical and the practical (moral) realms and insists both that it is pathological to attempt to demonstrate the existence of god from the experience of the world, and that it is heteronomous to use the existence of god to establish the moral life. This is precisely what Lessius *must* do. Lessius argues from multiple evidence to the reality of god, and the reality of god establishes a salutary fear out of which come proper moral choices. In Kant, pure practical reason possesses an independence and a primacy in its association with speculative reason. In Lessius, speculative reason supplies the principles by which practical reason is established and guaranteed: the ethical context is founded on what the world reveals. The whole business rests here, and the existence of god "wonderfully shineth both in the whole fabrick of the world, and in the creatures contained therein; as also in the most wise disposall and government of the same things."[28]

Lessius also wrote against the politicians, not just against the atheists. The obvious charge against his ethical interest is that his god is not so much true as socially expedient and that this line of argument makes religion useful (*conducibilis*), not intrinsically valid. According to Machiavelli's *Prince*, it is not necessary for the ruler to be religious; that could even be a hindrance; but it is very necessary to seem to be religious: "And it must be understood that a prince, and especially a new prince, cannot observe all those things which are considered good in men, being often obliged, in order to maintain the state, to act against faith, against charity, against humanity, and against religion."[29] The preservation of the control of the social order is nonnegotiable, and for this the reputation of being religious is helpful, but there will be times in which the appearance will be without substance. "These are those whom we call polititians," wrote Lessius, "because they reduce all religion to policy or to the *statum politicum*."[30] Lessius, in contrast, gives religion an absolute value, and bases its truth on the "fabrick of the world." He does not argue principally from its ethical consequences that it is true, but that it is necessary. The importance of religious conviction lies in its social and moral consequences; the warrant for this conviction of the existence of a provident god lies in arguments drawn from the reality of the world.

If Niccolo Machiavelli represented the politicians, who represented the atheists? Strangely enough, not contemporary figures, not Renaissance humanists, but classical names from antiquity. They can be designated either as those who simply rejected *omne numen a quo mundus dependeat*—and these were only five—or as those who denied a provident god, one who would care for and govern the universe. The five come in two groups. As in the ancient catalogues, Diagoras of Melos comes first, and Lessius adds the name of Protagoras with the note that both were disciples of Democritus, the atomist. The second group is composed of Theodore of Cyrene and Bion of Borysthenes, his disciple. Lessius calls Theodore, actually a Cynic, "sophista impurissimus pariter et impudentissimus." Two schools, then, are presented here as atheistic, the atomists and the sophists. To these two groups, Lessius adds a fifth name, that of Lucian, who aimed his second-century satire at the old Olympian gods and at Christianity. Those who denied only the providence of god were the leading atomists: Democritus, Epicurus, and Lucretius. While many would ascribe this denial also to Aristotle because of statements in Lambda in the *Metaphysics*, Lessius argues that the tenth book of the *Ethics* insinuates another position. Cicero's *De divinatione* denies both divination and providence because divine fore-knowledge would negate human freedom.[31] On both the divine existence and a divince providence, Lessius saw his adversaries as the atomists and the skeptical sophists.

Are there no atheists at the turn of the sixteenth century, only the classical figures returned to Europe through the Renaissance? Contemporary atheists could be legion, but a legion difficult to identify because the universal law in Europe made the profession of atheism a crime: "Although at this day," Lessius wrote, "there be many who deny in their secret judgments all divine power and Deity, yet are they not much knowne to the world; since the feare of the lawes doth impose silence to these kind of men, and only secretly among their familiars do they vomit out their Atheisme."[32] Why write against it, then? Because the vectors of religious division indicate that this is the terminus of heresy. All errors in religion have a natural path: once one begins to depart from the true religion, the human understanding finds nothing wherein it may firmly and securely rest, and it begins to doubt all religious mystery, "as if it were only a thing forged out of policy . . . that people be contained within the limites and boundes of their duties. And hence it proceedeth that among Heretickes, such as are of sharper wits doe inwardly doubt of all religion, and either deny, or at least rest uncertaine, whether there be any divine and supernatural power at al." It is critical to notice that the atheism against which Lessius wrote was not identified in 1613 with seminal thinkers or critically current philosophies. It was a revival; its names were standard names of antiquity. Atheism was seen not so much as a state of Europe nor as an atmosphere within it, but as a vector, whose initial stages were identified not with the new science but with the disintegration of a common religious confession sustained by a teaching Church. The denial of authority within religion was the initial moment of this development, Lessius wrote, and the skepticism embodied in the soph- ists and in the Third Academy, and, more important, the immanent mater- ialism of the Epicureans could provide fuel for its fires. Atheism was in an early renaissance.[33]

This makes somewhat intelligible the tack that *De providentia numinis* takes: the arguments which Lessius uses and the evidence to which he alludes are also from the classical philosophers. To deal with a putative atheism, Lessius steps back over almost fifteen hundred years of Christian theology as if these centuries had left no mark upon European conscious- ness, and revives the arguments of ancient, pagan masters.

The typical atheists are the ancient philosophers. So atheism in the sixteenth and seventeenth centuries is treated as if it were a philosophic issue, rather than a religious one; this shift characterizes Catholic apologetics for the succeeding four hundred years. The demonstration of the reality of god can proceed from "rationes philosophicae"—but the obvious ones, leaving out those which are more obscure and which "can be explored in the *Metaphysics*."[34] This locates the ultimate foundations or sanction of moral life, which in Europe had been traditionally the province of religion and the object of preachers, within philosophy. Atheism is taken as if it were simply a matter of retrieving the philosophical positions of the past, rather than a profound and current rejection of the meaning and reality of Jesus Christ. Christology has become irrelevant in establishing the reality of god. This shift of the question from religion to philosophy was dictated not merely by the adversaries enumerated and by whatever revived presence they com- manded through the European Renaissance. The wars of religion and the wrangling of theologians had discredited religion. The shift made possible a book acceptable to the Anglicans and to the Chinese, as well as to the Catholics—at the price of considering atheism principally, as in classical antiquity, as a philosophic position.

While Lessius collapses on principle the distinction between metaphysics and ethics, he insists methodologically upon that between faith and reason, the distinction between "credi ex revelatione," and "multis rationibus, ex iis quae nobis nota sunt, et sensibus percipiuntur, solide probari posse." They are separate areas of issues and methodology. Revelation is mentioned, connected with faith, and dismissed from consideration. Reasonings are mentioned, they are connected with proof or demonstration, and fifteen different "rationes" are elaborated by which the truth of providence can be established.[35]

And what an array of philosophical arguments there are: the universal consent of humankind, especially of the wise; the motion of the heavenly bodies, the existence of bodily things, the beauty of things and the structure of their parts—and entire squadron of arguments encompassing the parts of the world and the diversity of faces and voices; miracles, prophecies, spirits, the absurd consequences of the denial of god, and finally, historical examples in which sin has been punished and piety rewarded.[36] The list is a long one, but the discovery of its internal unity discloses not only Lessius' own philosophic coordinates but the direction which theistic argumentation takes through the Enlightenment. For all of the arguments are variations on the argument from design, from some particular evidence of structure which demands an intelligence to account for its complex interrelationship. Design is found everywhere.

One should have expected this line of argument. It is consequent upon the question which Lessius proposes. The title of the work is not the question of Aquinas: *Utrum Deus sit?*—an issue which the *Summa theologiae* would take up twelve questions before its discussion of the divine knowledge and twenty questions before treating divine providence explicitly. Lessius had often commented upon these very sections of the work of Aquinas. Here he is not asking a question, but sustaining a thesis, and in this tractate he merges the distinction between the divine nature and divine providence: "esse unum supremum numen, cujus providentia res humanae, et cetera omnia gubernentur, quod Deum vocamus."[37] The major influence here is not that of Aquinas; the vocabulary and the structure are much earlier.

The heritage is Cicero's. The debate is his *De natura deorum*. Lessius takes his place within the dialogue as the Stoic interlocutor, Quintus Lucilius Balbus. For both, the principal adversaries are the atomists: those who deny either the divine existence or divine providence are essentially equivalent. In Cicero's dialogue, the Stoic Lucilius Balbus is pitted against the atomist Gaius Velleius, a dialogue that is facilitated by the negative dialectic of the academic skeptic Gaius Cotta. In Lessius, the skeptics contribute the figures of the sophists Theodore and Bion, but the principal debate is with the materialists who attribute the origin of the universe to chance or to mindless nature. The attack mounted against the atheists is fought for mind over nature as the final explanation for all things. Lessius has taken over from Balbus, through a distance of sixteen hundred years. Like Balbus, Lessius is concerned to establish "esse aliquod numen praestatissimae mentis quo haec regantur."[38]

The "chiefe reasons" that Lessius assembles as causes of the convictions of atheism come out of an Epicurean tradition. The principal evidence is the lack of design. There is no relationship between virtue and historical success or between improbity, wickedness, or cruelty and punishment. "In the whole world there is such disturbance of order that we can hardly conceave a greater perturbation than it is." The good are oppressed and the wicked are affluent and powerful. Who would look upon a city or a kingdom and see such a disproportion, and believe that there is any governor? "For from this ἀταξία, and want of order, and from this confusion of things, the former men did conjecture, that there was no supreme governour." Chance rules the lives of human beings, not an orderly providence.

Second, in the conducting of business, human beings have found that "their success (for the most part) is answerable to the industry and endeavors employed in them," and not to any intervention of providence. Even the most unjust wars and the most pitiless business transactions have gained victory because of the industry employed in them. Where chance does not intervene in human affairs, the results are simply proportionate to human ingenuity and art.

Third, the routine order found in the things of nature indicates no outside governor. They and their movements are always the same: "things consisting of nature, doe ever proceed after one and the same manner, keeping one immoveable course and order." The lack of order in human affairs indicates the absence of a provident god; the eternal regularity of nature indicates "that there is no higher power, then Nature herselfe, by which all of these things are affected."

Fourth, the natural order of human life resembles that of the other more developed creatures; as they perish, so does every human being.

Finally, if there were any supreme spirit, it is inconceivable that it would concern itself with human beings or interfere in human affairs. Human beings would lie beneath its notice, as kings do not concern themselves with bond-slaves and men disregard the crawling of ants. Such a spirit would be too transcendent to involve itself in such triviality. What is more, any god would be "perfectly blessed, containing all sufficiency within itself, and seeking nothing, that is extrinsecall or externall." What reason is there to assert that there is a provident god, deeply and even poignantly associated with the sorrows and injustices of the human condition and history?[39]

These are the arguments of the Epicurean Velleius, representing this school's attack against the Stoa and reinforced by the skeptical Academy in the person of Cotta. All five arguments are drawn from the *De natura deorum*: "Intelligitur enim a beata inmortalique natura et iram et gratiam segregari."[40] For happiness or blessedness consists in tranquility of mind and in the freedom from any connection with sorrow: the divine and providence are self-contradictory.[41] As for the world, "natura effectum esse mundum, nihil opus fuisse fabrica," an opinion strengthened by observing the regularity of its movement.[42] And the shapes and forms which emerged so from the chance interaction of the infinite quality of atoms, not from some *sempiternus dominus*.[43] Finally, as one of the first counters against the Stoics, there is the evidence which the Epicureans advance and which their philosophy attempts to treat, evidence which the skeptics will develop at much greater length: "Ita multa sunt incommoda in vita."[44] If Lessius has assumed the position of the Stoic Balbus, in Cicero's dialogue he has drawn a very accurate picture of his Epicurean adversary.

There are critical differences, however, between the Stoic and the Jesuit, principally in the determination whether the *numen* is immanently identifiable with the universe or distinct from it. The Stoics merge god and the universe; Lessius makes them infinitely distinct. Yet in question, interest, evidence, and argument, Balbus and Lessius are virtually one. The question is about the provident god; the interest lies with social or moral importance; the evidence is the *notae* or *vestigia* which indicate the presence of a designing intelligence; and the arguments include the consent of the universal world, the nature of physical things, and the portentous events and life-stories which have occurred in human historical experience. Even when the ontological argument figures it is colored *a posteriori* in both the Stoic and in Lessius.

This is not the place to attempt to congregate and analyze the really remarkable assemblage of arguments which Leonard Lessius brings to support his central thesis, but to consider these arguments in general—the initial ones in greater detail to suggest the type of all of them. Such a survey will indicate the direction Catholic theology was taking in response to an early, rising atheism and how the stage was being set for the massive debates of the Enlightenment.

The initial argument is problematically distinguished from the remaining fourteen.[45] It is taken from the opinion of human beings; the rest, from the nature of things or the outcome of histories. The argument is from universal consent, an argument whose structure is Stoic but whose data had been extended by recent explorations. All people, of whatever clime or custom, confess belief in this *numen*, even the "Indians, the people of China, Japonians, Tartarians, and all others." Their ceremonies, priests, temples, vows, and prayers testify to a profound depth of conviction, universal both in history and in contemporary living, that this *numen* "tooke notice of their actions, that it was able to defend them, to free them from dangers, to imparte to them thinges which they desired, and to take revenge for injuries." Granted so pervasive and so enduring a conviction, what accounts for it? The devices of art and nature are translated into tradition and human nature in order to explore this question. Such a pervasive conviction cannot come out of story and tradition, because these religious persuasions differ among themselves on almost every point, coincident only on the reality of a provident power. If not from human ingenuity and tradition, the confession must emerge from deep within human nature itself—and Lessius actually quotes Cicero's Balbus here: "Hoc omnibus est innatum et insculptum."[46] If the conviction is innate, emerging from the nature of the human person no matter what his condition or time, then it has the same soundness as the conviction of the intellect that it must seek truth or of the will that it must love. What is of nature is not pathological, not radically disoriented. If the natural orientation of the mind, which is by nature geared to truth, includes a conviction—however diversified and hazy—about a provident god, then the conviction must be sound.[47]

Here Lessius adds his own unique twist to the classical ontological argument, which argues from the very concept of god that he must be. Lessius argues the parallel of Anselm. The very notion of the divine is that the potentiality and actuality are the same, for as Aristotle and all philosophers teach: "In divinis idem est esse actu, et posse esse; non esse actu, et esse impossibile." If this is the case, it is not adequate to show that as a matter of fact there is no god; one must prove that it is impossible that there be a god, that the notion is irreconcilably self-contradictory. Only if the potential is not real, is the act unreal. What is more, one would have to assert that there is a natural orientation, shown throughout every phase of human history, of the human mind towards that which is intrinsically impossible and absurd.[48]

Finally, this conviction, "which is so potent and hath such a secret agreement and sympathy with man's understanding, as it is even able to invade and possess (and this without any co-action or constraint) the myndes of all," is confirmed by the judgment of the wise, as Augustinus Steuco demonstrated in his work of 1540, *De perenni philosophia*. This tractate, to which Mersenne also refers, was a remarkable essay which traced as common themes those philosophical judgments which repeatedly appear in diverse forms and within conflicting systems throughout the history of human wisdom.[49] The existence of god counts as such an assertion, continually reaffirmed in the philosophic inquiries of the previous two thousand years.

Even this argument of Lessius is from design, not the placing together of mechanical parts, but the orientation found in natural structures. Universal and endless agreement indicate an origin placed by nature in the drive of the mind. This internal design of nature possesses its own warrant for the soundness of its conviction, confirmed by the passage of time and its perdurance in diversities.[50]

The argument from motion, the first of Lessius' "philosophical reasons," also assumes its basic outline from the Stoic Balbus, but takes increased factual data from the newly discovered telescope. The inference has been transposed into an astronomical argument, and the motion in question is that of the stars and planets. The geometric design of celestial movement cannot have originated simply from some sort of natural inclination or naturally impressed force. In either case, it would come to an end; but the heavenly bodies revolve continuously in orbits. There must be another cause operative irrespective of whether these motions "are performed by divers transient pushes (even as the rowling about of a potters wheele is occasioned by the Potter) or els by certaine stable, firme, and permanent forces, impressed in the celestiall Orbes (as some do affirme) for by whether meanes soever it is caused, it necessarily proceedeth from some incorporeall cause indued with mynd and understanding, and not from any peculiar propension and inclination of nature."[51] Later in the century, Isaac Newton argued in a somewhat similar fashion from the orbits of the planets that gravity could account for the tendency of the planet to move toward the sun, but a divine intelligence must have originated the transverse movement which combined with this gravitational pull to produce an orbit.[52]

What is more, the existence and the movement of the stars and planets do not benefit themselves, but they do benefit such an inferior body as the earth. The apparent revolution of the sun does not profit the sun, but it is indispensable for the earth. Vegetation, life, increase, growth, and conservation depend upon this movement of this body which is, of itself, certainly indifferent to the earth. But there is an orientation of the sun towards the earth, a structure or set of relationships by which it is beneficial to or at the service of life on this planet. Here the design is not so much geometrical as it is biological.

Finally, there is the extraordinary diversity and internal structure of the system of the universe. Certainly this is not from nature, "whose whole inclination is ever simple and uniform." There are the massive movements of the stars, the seeming random movement of the planets "to the demonstration of which poynts are invented the Eccentrick Circles, and the Epicycles," and the rich variety of the heavens, "lately discovered by the helpe of a Perspective glasse, invented by a certaine Batavian." With this glass, Lessius has seen the "spongious" nature of the moon, the four small moons around Jupiter, sun spots, and the phases of Venus from which "it may seem to be necessarily inferred that Venus is carried in a huge Epicycle about the Sunne." The *fistula dioptrica* was revolutionizing astronomy, radically changing it from Aristotelian and Ptolemaic description. Here, in 1613, about two years after Galileo's *Siderius nuncius* had announced the discovery of the uneven face of the moon, Jupiter's four Medicean planets, and the waxing and waning of Venus, this Flemish theologian had not only accepted these findings but confirmed them: "Saepe haec omnia ipse instrumento conspexi," he wrote, incorporating these new facts into his basic argument from the variety and design of the universe, "cum summa admiratione divinae sapientiae et potentiae." The infinite multitude of the stars newly discovered add to this wonder, as does the motion of the zodiac, whose final course is completed every 7000 years. Who could maintain that for such a multiplicity there could be other than a divine intelligence when everywhere "eadem cernitur varietas, idem motuum discrimen, eadem symphonia et proportio?"[53]

The argument from existence is similarly transmuted. How are we to account for the fact that bodily things exist and yet are dependent for their substance (*secundum suam substantiam*)? There are three possibilities: either they cause themselves, they are caused by chance (*casu fortuito*), or they are caused by an incorporeal cause endowed with mind. The possibilities lie with nature, chance, or divine art. The possibility of the world being produced by another world is dismissed; this answers nothing and leads to a *processum in infinitum*.

What exists by itself is neither composed nor has a beginning. But whatever is composed is caused by another. Furthermore, whatever has a beginning at one time was not, and therefore it was brought from nonbeing to being by another.

What about chance, as the atomists have classically taught? This fails to account for the structure and the form of the world, for the consistent order found within the movements of the universe, and for the orientation of anything material to a particular function. When the Stoic Balbus advanced this consideration, he appealed to the ordinary common sense of any human being who came upon a spacious, beautiful home. No one could be induced to believe, even in the absence of any master, that this structure "was built by mice and weasels!"[54] So Lessius argues in a manner that extends through the centuries to William Paley's watch. Chance cannot account for any of these determinations of matter, let alone those of great complexity and seeming ingenuity, "since to say thus were as much as to defend that some one most faire, sumptuous and stately pallace were not made at all by an artificer with art, but only by a suddain mingling and meeting together of certaine peeces of stones into this curious and artificiall forme." The design found throughout material things, in their relations or basic determinations to a particular function, does not permit chance to be an ultimate principle.[55]

All of the arguments receive such a transformation: miracles and prophecies show a knowledge of the designs of nature and the structures of the future. The argument from absurdity becomes a consideration of the disintegration of human order consequent upon a denial of god, and the final arguments show a design or order within the divine governance of human life. Design is everywhere in Lessius' argumentation, but it is not mechanical design, the composition and dissolution of wholes and parts. It is rather the orientation or relationship found within natural bodies and the entire universe. The axiom which underlies this design and the arguments which proceed from it are put in scholastic vocabulary, though its application is continually Stoic: whatever has a final cause to which it is oriented has also an efficient cause by which it has been oriented.[56] The finding of service is the finding of purpose is the finding of efficient cause which has the intelligence and power to set up such a web of connections.

The above analysis does not do justice to the depth of Lessius' arguments and to his assessment of the evidence, but the theologian is pressed to ask whether there is any Christology in these counters to a nascent atheism. The answer is somewhat disconcerting. Jesus, his life and the paschal mystery, become an expansion of two typical Stoic arguments: the argument from miracles and the argument from prophecy. Balbus had already outlined both of these, as portents which indicated divine presence or as prescience which was embodied in divination.[57] Now Lessius purifies and expands them with the miracles and prophecies of the Old and New Testaments, inferring finally that the fulfillment of the prophecies about Christ indicate that he is the savior of the world.[58] But this almost in passing. New facts are subsumed under classical arguments for divine providence. Just as European explorations and the newly discovered telescope expand the basic arguments from universal consent and from the movement of the heavens, so Jesus and the history of Christianity add more data to the evidence of miracles and prophecy—one more instance, albeit a capital one, among many.

De providentia numinis occupies a position from which the Church will seldom depart in its apologetic response to the gradual rise of atheism in the Western world. Lessius' problematic methodology separates the question of god from the cognitive claims of Christology in the classic distinction between revelation and reason. The centrality of Christ is relegated to revelation—Christ does not evoke faith in the Father; his intelligibility is consequent upon faith. What Lessius presents is not the person and message of Jesus, but those cosmological and historical experiences which are open to any human being. It is here that the *vestigia* and *notae* of god are found and carefully described and penetratingly analyzed against the renascent Epicureanism. The variations in the *notae* are simply variations in design. The search is always for the efficient cause which implanted these relationships with such skill or which imposed the harmonious movements. A metaphysics of being might look at such procedures and wonder what has happened to the more radical consideration of the act of being and to the issue of why is there something rather than nothing, a question which any real composition such as movement, causality, actualized possibility, participation, or finalized activity can raise—not as an inquiry to account for particular patterns of motion given by astronomy or for a widespread consensus given by the knowledge of world religions, but as an investigation of dependence in being. But the theologian can look at the same procedures and wonder what has happened to Christianity's Christ as the primordial manifestation of the reality of god and the victorious source of the possibility of religious conviction. The Enlightenment later takes Jesus as a teacher of morals, but nature and the cosmos teach it about god. One cannot but remark that this division was prepared by such theologians as Leonard Lessius of Louvain.

This choice of procedures is one which has been with Christianity at least from some of its great medieval theologies. Aquinas' problematic method and reflexive principles distinguish two ways to religious awareness and conviction. The initial questions of the *Summa theologiae*, which follow the discursive of *sacra doctrina*, are philosophical in their issues and methods, but philosophy integrated into theology as a moment within theology, as a *praeambula fidei*. They elaborate a doctrine of god whose warrant and argument are philosophic, buttressed by citations of supporting theological evidence. Only when the questions turn to the Trinity do the evidence and the argument become intrinsically theological as the evidence for argumentation becomes revelation. In the *Summa theologiae*, Christ make a central appearance only in the third part—after the doctrines of god, providence, the nature of the human person, creation, and human finality have already been defined.

From this, the shift exhibited in Lessius' *De providentia numinis* is an easy and understandable one. The question of atheism is raised. It is taken as a philosophical issue. The initial sections of the *Summa* are excised from the previous study of scripture and from their location within a total theological structure. The arguments are transposed from metaphysics, which is obscure, to the more evident data of the universe of Tycho Brahe, the consensus chronicled by Augustinus Steuco, and the biological measurements of the human body. An independent "natural theology" begins to emerge, one that does not look for the more difficult, fundamental questions but for philosophic arguments that are *perspicuas*. And it is here that the Stoics rather than Saint Thomas must fill in. Cicero has Balbus open his tractate with the exclamation about the existence of god from the evidence of astronomy: "Quid enim potest esse tam apertum, tamque perspicuum. . . ?"[59] Lessius agrees, even in his vocabulary, and incorporates the structure of inquiry from the Stoics with the additional evidence which the early seventeenth century provided, modifying the ancient masters in their identification of a provident god with the universe.

Natural theology, then, becomes no longer a part of metaphysics, but derivative by common sense or ordinary philosophic maxims from astronomy, comparative religion, mechanics, and biology. It is a world to which theology itself has very little contribution to make. So it remains in the centuries to come, an effort to provide a preamble to Christian convictions about god which does not include Christ.

Marin Mersenne and the Platonizing of Epicurus

If the first scene in this drama of the theologians opened with a spectral apparition, perhaps the second could begin with a poem. "Les Quatrains de Deists ou l'Antibigot" was widely circulated throughout France by 1622.[60] It is much more a manifesto than a poem, hammering away at Christianity, whether Huguenot or Catholic, as a superstition, arguing for an impersonal god, one as indifferent to human acts as unaffected by human prayers. It repudiates the god of the Christians as a god of vengeance, a hell disproportionate to any human evil, an omnipotence that makes either sin or freedom unintelligible. If god is all-powerful and all-knowing, human acts are determined and not free; if human acts are free, then god is limited both in his power and in his foreknowledge. Predestination, positive divine commandments, analogical attribution of perfections to god, asceticism—all instance the fatal weakness within Christianity. In place of this, "Les Quatrains" proposes the devotions of the deist: "Sa religion se borne à adorer la cause première, à ne faire de mal à personne, à aimer son prochain." Why worship an indifferent god? Virtue and truth have their own internal reward; there is no need for a response from god to warrant either adoration or human morality. Finally, in a contention which runs through the later history of deism, the deist is not an atheist; but it would be better to be an atheist than a Christian, predicating absurdities and horrors of god.[61] These 106 stanzas are hardly lyrical, but they effectively support the god of the Epicureans with the morality of the Stoics to challenge the Christian god. They also elicited from the Franciscan theologian Marin Mersenne his major riposte against the atheism and the deism of his time; the latter he thought a clever cover for the former.[62]

Framing an appreciation of the life and contributions of Père Marin Mersenne on the occasion of the tercentary of his death, the abbè Robert Lenoble noted that Mersenne figured pivotally throughout the first half of the seventeenth century. His voluminous compositions sustained friendships and arguments with the major intellectual figures of the period. Galileo and Hobbes, Gassendi and Descartes, Huygens and Torricelli, were his continual correspondents, and much of the philosophy and science which was rising to change the character of Europe was articulated, explored, and furthered in these letters.[63] It is impossible, for example, to study Descartes and not to read Mersenne. James Collins calls him "the clearing house for scientific and philosophical information in the decades just prior to the appearance of the first learned journals."[64]

The irony of his fame lies with two facts. First, he is read often in relation to others, but seldom for himself. As Richard H. Popkin put it, "Marin Mersenne, 1588–1648, was one of the most important figures in the history of modern thought, and has been until very recently most neglected and misunderstood."[65] His works are rarely analyzed for themselves, and the mention of his name in the history of thought is frequently as a counterpoise to his more remembered correspondents. Secondly, whatever place he has been ceded in intellectual histories is in philosophy, but he wrote essentially as a theologian, although one enormously involved in other fields.[66] Mersenne not only knew something of the contemporary scientific revolution, as did Lessius; he was expert in much of it and contributed to some. There have been few theologians of any time who were so seriously interdisciplinary in their competences, expert both in alien fields and in their reflections upon revelation. Yet in theology and the history of theology, Mersenne is unknown. Who was this remarkable, and remarkably forgotten, theologian?

Marin Mersenne was born in Oizé, near Maine, on the September 8, 1588, and died in Paris on September 1, 1648. At the age of sixteen, he enrolled in the Jesuit college of La Flèche, some years before the much younger René Descartes. From 1609 to 1611 he continued his theological studies at the Sorbonne while completing his classical education at the Collège de France. On July 16, 1611, he entered the Minims, a Franciscan order founded by Francis of Paola, and was ordained in 1613. Mersenne taught philosophy for three years after his ordination and later taught theology at Nevers. At the end of 1618, he was sent to Paris again, now as a member of the Minim Community of the Annunciation. Here he was to spend the rest of his life. In 1623 he published his first work, a commentary on Genesis.[67] But what a commentary! It fills nineteen hundred columns in the original folio and sets for itself a comprehensive refutation of the errors then plaguing France: "In this volume," the subtitle runs, "atheists and deists are battled and refuted and the Vulgate edition is vindicated against the calumnies of the heretics. The music of the Greeks and of the Hebrews is restored. The cabalistic dogmas of Francis George Veneti are fully refuted, which here and there occur in his book on problems. This is a work especially useful to theologians, philosophers, doctors, lawyers, mathematicians, musicians, and indeed to opticists." The work is not a simple exegesis of Genesis. It is an encyclopedia—a hundred years before the encyclopedists—of the science of the day: music, mathematics, physics, astronomy, agriculture, and linguistics all find their place within its pages. Mersenne is not exploring new sciences here: he is organizing the sciences of his time, and in the chair of a theologian commenting upon Genesis. The work is polemic in tone, taking aim at the errors of the naturalists such as Campanella, Paracelsus, and Pomponazzi, Cabalists such as Pico della Mirandola and Cornelius Agrippa of Nettesheim, atheists such as Vanini, deists like Charron, and the band of "novi theologi."[68]

In the following year, Mersenne published a book which caught up some of his former issues in a more organized fashion, *L'Impiété des Déistes, Athées, et Libertins de ce temps*. The subtitle of the work indicates which atheists he has especially in mind: "la refutation des Dialogues de Iordan Brun, dans lequel il a voulu establir une infinité de mondes, et l'ame universelle de l'Univers."[69] That Mersenne should write again against atheism is not surprising when it is recalled that *Quaestiones in genesim* had maintained that there were fifty thousand atheists in Paris alone in the second decade of the seventeenth century, the population of the entire city being four hundred thousand![70] The *Quaestiones* had used the term very loosely, to cover Bonaventure des Periers, Charron, Machiavelli, Campanella, Vanini, Fludd, Bruno—all the adversaries of Mersenne, men whose doctrine he thought dangerous or supporting dangerous tendencies.[71] The *Quaestiones* is an initial work, and when Mersenne turned to his "most orderly and economical treatment of the proofs of God's existence," *L'Impiété*, he did not cast his net with such indiscrimination.[72]

Who, then, were the atheists for Mersenne? If Lessius found it necessary to go back to antiquity, Mersenne could go next door. Three names figure before all others: Pierre Charron, Geronimo Cardano, and Giordano Bruno.[73] At first glance, such an assemblage seems impossible. Pierre Charron was a devout priest, who had wanted to enter the Carthusians but had remained in apostolic work in Paris, preaching with great success, a representative of the Catholic clergy at the meeting ot the Etats Généraux of 1595. He had written against atheism in *Les Trois veritez* (1593), establishing the distinctions between *religion naturelle, religion révélée*, and *religion catholique*. But Charron had reintroduced into France the skepticism of the Academy. While the Pyrrhonian skepticism of Montaigne would prescind from any statements based upon anything but faith, Charron's academic skepticism allowed nothing as certain; all the statements made by reasoned judgments were at best probable. Faith alone gave certitude for Charron; reason gave verisimilitude and the unbridled use of reason led to atheism. The skeptical therapy was the *via negativa*, the best possible road to walk in order to realize that all knowledge has its intrinsic hazards and that faith alone can found an unwavering conviction about god. In countering Charron, Mersenne was engaging the Third Academy of Carneades.[74]

Geronimo Cardano was the follower and popularizer in France of Pietro Pomponazzi, the great Neo-Averroist of Padua. His master was Aristotle, but Aristotle denying that reason can prove the immortality of the soul, the providence of god, and any doctrine of creation out of nothing. In his naturalism he also argued the profound inability of reason to deal coordinately with faith. The Padua school had its own version of the two truths: what philosophy could establish and what was received from revelation as truth. Cardano himself had made significant contributions to the study of algebra, but his first love was astrology, which he called "scientia iudiciorum astrorum," and which Mersenne found extravagantly and pretentiously deterministic: "Il veut quasi par tout faire àcroire . . . qu'il est si grand naturaliste, qu'il decredite la foy tant qu'il peut, comme vous pouvez voir en ce qu'il a escrit de l'Astrologie Iudiciaire: car il parle de la venué de nostre Sauveur, et de la loy Chrestienne, qu'il a instituée, comme si les Astres estoient causes de tout cela." In Cardano, Neo-Averroism became a version of physical determinism, leading to errors either "against the faith or against reason, or against sound morality."[75]

Finally, Giordano Bruno, the turbulent and tragic figure of early modern Europe, was read by Mersenne as almost the opposite of the others. While Charron was a skeptic and Cardano a determinist, Bruno was a thorough-going rationalist. His mathematics, Mersenne maintained, attempted to prove that at their depth the circular line and the straight line, the point and the line, the surface and the three-dimensional body are nothing but the same thing. He carried this movement into a comprehensive principle in theology also. There was no freedom in creation because "God is attached to this earth, and his infinity is bound up with the things which are finite in such a way that he is not able to be omnipotent and infinite without them." The god of Bruno was the immanent principle of the universe, out of which all things come and to which they return. Mersenne thought that Giordano Bruno had invented "une nouvelle façon de philosopher," in order to battle against Christianity. New such a philosopher might well be, but Bruno had returned to Europe the underlying god of the Stoics, identifying with the universe and being the energy from which things issue and to which they eventually all return.[76]

There are paradoxes in Mersenne's array of adversaries. They are all contemporaries, yet each brings into the century a tradition and a set of arguments whose antiquity was greater than Christianity's. Each of these principal representatives of atheism's hold on France spoke for a divine reality, a god. Charron proposed one so arbitrarily connected with the universe that his existence could not be inferred with certitude, but only revealed. Cardano's god contradicted by revelation the impersonal, disinterested nature which had been discovered by philosophy. Bruno's god so implicated the universe that there was no ultimate distinction: all differences or changes were only modifications of the single reality. Each of these, for Mersenne, was a species of atheism, and it was against this that he wrote his dialogue, *L'Impiété*.

As in Lessius some ten years before, Mersenne's adversaries can be found remarkably modeled in Cicero's *De natura deorum*. In that dialogue, the Academic skeptic Gaius Cotta maintains that the doctrines of the Stoics differ only linguistically from those of the Peripatetics. Lessius' *De providentis numinis* allows that coincidence to stand and resumes with significant modification the position of the Stoic Balbus, locating his argumentation within his statement of the problem, the kinds of evidence to which he appeals, and the problematic methodology which allows him to distinguish arguments built upon revelation from those built upon natural reason, and among the latter to distinguish those which appeal dialectically to the opinions of humanity from those which employ the nature of things as evidence. The adversaries for Lessius, as for Balbus, are the Epicurreans and the Skeptics.

In Mersenne, the same figures present themselves, again with significant modifications. But their roles are notably changed. The Peripatetic and the Stoic stand in counterposition. Charron retrieves the skepticism of the Academy. Cardano is the Peripatetic, now become the naturalist. Bruno represents the Stoic with a god both comprehensive and immanently identified with the universe. Mersenne seeks not to adapt these schools, but to refute them.

His dialogue is neither the careful and continual Platonic interchange between interlocutors nor the Ciceronian engagement of divergent views in order to test various positions in extended debate. It is neither dialectic nor controversy; it is instruction. There are two parties to the dialogue, the theologian and the deist. The theologian does not cross-question the deist in order to evoke a movement toward a unity of word, instance, and meaning; neither the theologian nor the deist gives the contradictory and extended orations which are found in the dialogues of Cicero and Tacitus. The theologian explains, cites, and encourages; the deist responds, follows the argument, and is eventually converted. The method or style of Mersenne's dialogue follows the method of his argumentation. He is not probing a question or proving a thesis as much as building a case.

And build he does: the entire movement of the twenty-six chapters is one of composition and division. One begins with an examination of the human body, its parts and its marvelous design. To this is added the world and all that is external to the human. The conjunction of both raises the question of moral life within the world; the moral law constitutes the moral life, and the influence of god constitutes the moral law. At this juncture, it is necessary to establish the existence of god.[77] In Lessius, the divine existence and action was a necessary sanction for the moral life; in Mersenne, the divine existence and action establish the moral life. Once the existence of god is demonstrated, Mersenne continues to build from god to the Catholic religion as that which is warranted by god. This done, Mersenne can take up the poem attacking Catholicism and analyze it stanza by stanza.

Mersenne's method is to build up his elements into a whole and to analyze the whole into its parts. It is the classic logistic method, used by Thucydides in his history to amass the reality of power and fear as the factors of conflict, and used by Newton in mechanics with such enormous success.[78] In the Boylean lectures of 1711–1712, William Derham spoke of Mersenne as belonging to the same tradition as Boyle and Newton.[79] This is true not only in the obvious way that all three connected a natural theology with scientific mechanics, but more profoundly in that all three used a method which could build complex wholes out of their component units and resolve the intelligibility of these molar realities by a reduction to their elements. In classic philosophy, it was the method of Democritus and Epicurus, and in the dialogues of Cicero it was represented by Gaius Velleius.[80]

It is in this gradual building of an argument which will eventually yield a religious system of the world that the deist asks the theologian for "de sortes raison pour preuver que Dieu est," in order to deal with the *libertins* who "ne croyent aucune divinité."[81] The theologian answers that he wants to deal with this subject so that in this way "l'Athéisme prenne fin" and "tout le monde recognoisse le grande moteur de l'univers pour créateur de toutes choses."[82] The choice of words is critical: "the mover of the universe" is an adaptation from Aristotle that runs through the Middle Ages and reaches its poetic expression in Dante's salute to the one who moves the sun and all the other stars. Dante has already connected this notion with the creator of the universe and the Father of Jesus Christ. One would expect Mersenne, the theologian, to bend his efforts to show the equation between the mover of the universe and the Christian creator-god. He does not. His efforts are to establish both at once, to collapse the distinction between them, and to argue to the creative mover of all. Just as Lessius blends the notion of god and the notion of providence, looking for evidence in the world of divine intelligence and power, so Mersenne merges the notion of the cause of movement and the cause of the creation of all things. It is an easy enough step, which Newton's scientific theism also takes, to identify *moteur* with the force which accounts for the setting up of created things, as gravity accounts for the movement of the heavenly bodies and as motive force accounts for any movement in mechanics.

The initial argument is a Platonic adaptation of the Epicurean discussion of an ultimate *plenum* or void as the context within which the world exists. In Mersenne, this issue becomes an ultimate decision for god or nonbeing as the situation for all finite realities. If there is a being supremely (*souverain*) good, one to whom nothing is lacking, anyone would acknowledge that this one deserves the name of god. If such a one does not exist, then his absence would be a privation, a supreme, sovereign evil—the privation of the supreme good being the supreme evil. Evil and nonbeing would be the sovereign context of all reality. But a privation cannot exist except in terms of a prior act. "Il n'y a nulle apparence que la privation soit plustost que son acte, lequel la doit necessairement preceder." Therefore, since the decision is between an ultimate good and an ultimate evil, and evil is nonbeing, and since nonbeing can only exist within a prior being, there must be a sovereign good. Not only are there no grounds to doubt that there is such a good, but god is so necessary that it is impossible for god not to be. Nothing would exist except eternal nonbeing—an eternal void—with which any kind of being would be incompatible.[83] In Epicurus, the gods could exist as a reflexive principle, indifferent to the human race and internally blessed, without providence and without miracles.[84] In Mersenne, the divine becomes a comprehensive principle, transcendent but comprehensive, the context for all reality. The ontological status of the good as *plenum* enables him to take Epicurean mechanics and totally rephrase the question of the existence and the reality of god.

The second argument shifts from the void to the infinite, but now—in contrast with Epicurus again—it is the *plenum* which is infinite as well as independent. "It is necessary that there be a being which is independent and which has no limits." Why independent? Because the world and the things within it are dependent—they exist and their intelligibility is derived from that upon which they depend. But this dependence cannot stretch out endlessly—for each of these things receives its being, is dependent for its being. There would be no reception if being were not received from someone. The real source of dependent being must be independent.

But why infinite? We know the things around us. With a little thought and imagination, we can imagine things which infinitely surpass the real around us. If there were no infinite being, human imagination and thought would surpass the real and move inexorably into the unreal. But only the infinite is greater than human imagination. How would it be possible to maintain that this infinite does not exist when either the understanding or the human will is borne towards it with such *ferveur*? It would mean that the object of the drive of the intellect and of the will were not true and, as the previous argument had indicated, not good.[85]

The third argument continues to advance the necessity of the infinite—now to account for the dimensions of the finite. Lessius introduces the experience of the place, the *Annales* of Ennius and the *Commentaries* of Livy. Each possessed a design or pattern before which a person would be made to talk about chance rather than intelligence as a cause. Mersenne uses the house or the town, a speech of Cicero or the *Aeneid* of Vergil—but as an example quite different. Each of these has its limits. Who or what set these limits? Now look at the sky: Why is it not larger? Why is it round rather than square or even six-sided? Everything that we see can be similarly queried. Each thing is limited, its dimensions or boundaries set. The finite is obviously made, obviously given its limitation. By what? Only the infinite can account for the particular limitations of the finite.[86]

The fourth argument brings the methodology of part-whole directly to bear upon the bodies introduced in the previous argument. One can resolve or analyze any body into its component parts, whether one takes those parts as chemical (salt, sulphur, and mercury), as substantial principles (body, spirit, and soul), or as physical elements (earth, fire, and water). Any body can be resolved or dissolved into its composing parts. But the same order (*la mesme ordre*) which one perceives in the dissolution is recovered or found again in the composition. If all bodies are composed, it is necessary that there be that one by which this composition is effected—and that this one be not a body, but *très simple*. One can argue the same point dynamically, that is, temporally: everything that we see, rocks, plants, animals, or minerals, or the stages of the development of the world, dissolves with time; it is equally certain that they all began at a time—as "le premier Historiographe du monde" so correctly said when he wrote that god created heaven and earth at the beginning of time. The one who began that which is in time must be outside of time, the eternal god.[87]

All of these four arguments build up to the fifth argument: the order found in the universe—*le bel ordre que est au monde*—in which one sees that each thing has its range and its place, although one sees within this vast order elements of disorder. The universe would never possess this order, either from the beginning or continously, if there were not "the divine Orpheus who touches the cordes of the great lute of the Universe." The order, for Mersenne, is the order of a great arch in which all of the parts contribute to the harmony of the whole, in their inner composition, their place, and their movement. Contemporary astronomy, here rendered in an extended poem, sustains the argument from the government of the universe, the system of the world.[88]

In the sixth argument which the theologian advances for the instruction of the deist, the proportions and composition of the various planets and the sun indicate more than a governor, they indicate a supreme architect (*un souverain Architecte*) who has given them these quantities, these measures, and these distances. Astronomers such as Tycho Brahe and Kepler have provided an enormous amount of material to support such an argument from the design of the universe. Almost any study of the sky or the earth will yield "the quantities, the measurements, and composition which indicate the presence of mathematical genius in its construction."[89]

The seventh picks up the eternal nature of truth, arguing with Augustine that to deny truth that is atemporal is self-contradicting. In the eighth, Mersenne moves from Augustine to Anselm's statement that "qu'on ne peut rien penser de plus grand" must necessarily exist. The ninth argues from a doctrine of "a true participation of all things in the divine perfection," using the maxim of all of the philosophers, "propter quod unumquodque tale et illud magis." There can be no finite justice or truth unless there is the supreme and infinite justice or truth.[90]

This turn in the development of Mersenne's series of arguments is startling: the first six build on the methodology and mechanics whose origins lie with Epicurus and whose application was the dynamic behind much of the new science. The last few come out of Platonic or Neoplatonic thought as it touched massive figures such as Augustine and Anselm. But it should be remembered that Mersenne was not Epicurus; he was not even Gassendi, who brought Epicurus into the emerging mechanics.[91] He uses the mechanical method in his writings, which allows him to understand Galileo perhaps better than any theologian of that century and to expound and defend him in a series of works.[92] It also enables him to work with Gassendi in the refutation of the Englishman Robert Fludd.[93] But there is also a very strong sense of transcendence in Mersenne, coupled with a comprehensive principle by which the world is finally made intelligible—and in this he looks much more like a Platonist. Only so comprehensive a principle could unite—what Lessius would have disjoined—such diverse subjects as Mersenne's *questions theologiques, physiques, morales et mathematiques.* The conundrum that his work poses for philosophers who find him either eclectic or accepting of a merely rhetorical persuasive line of theistic arguments might be somewhat resolved if one noted this strange series of philosophic coordinates.

But what happened to the theologian? Throughout the dialogue, the theologian speaks and alludes to Genesis and to the Latin Fathers. But neither Christology nor a pneumatology of religious experience figure in his apologetic. Despite his realization that atheism is a concrete rejection of Christianity and not simply a rearticulation of an ancient position, Mersenne deals with it as if it were a philosophy. He acts as if there were no presence of Christ within Western Europe, as if one did not have to confront this figure in a decision for or against the reality of god, and as if atheism were a profoundly religious decision and must be dealt with religiously. The integration which Mersenne's comprehensive principle brings about of diverse sciences and the subsequent demonstration he offers of the truth of the Catholic faith would have easily allowed him to follow another great Franciscan, Bonaventure, in making Christ Catholicism's immediate response to the denial of the reality of god, Christ as the supreme manifestation within the world of the divine actuality in its offer to human beings of the possibilities of faith and grace. It was not done. Bonaventure's path was not taken. The argument was cast differently, and this shape was to remain with Western Europe throughout the rise and increasing power of atheism.

The Issue Becomes Philosophic

If Leonard Lessius and Marin Mersenne, two of the most influential theologians of their time, among the first to write against the early awakenings of atheism as the Renaissance drew toward twilight, can be taken as typical, then the irony of the Church's position toward this new and fatally destructive force can be stated with some precision. The drama that was to become atheistic humanism was opening upon the European stage, and Catholic theologians stood ready to greet it as philosophers. The skeptical dialectic, the Epicurean mechanics, and the Stoic judicative logic were so well represented that one could find the topics of the arguments in Cicero's *De natura deorum* revived in the early seventeenth century. The wealth of new facts which the Renaissance had discovered were taken up into the natural philosophy which subsumed all the available sciences. Celestial mechanics, anatomy, comparative religion, botany, and architecture all contributed new facts whose intelligibility demanded the existence of god. What is more, each of the theologians not only incorporated these new sciences, but made significant contributions to them. Mersenne still figures in mathematics for the Mersenne numbers (his formula, $[2^p - 1]$, attempted to derive all the prime numbers) and for his investigation of cycloids. He is also remembered for his suggestion to Christian Huygens that the pendulum be used as a timing device, "thus inspiring the pendulum clock."[94] Lessius made substantial contributions to jurisprudence and economic theory and was one of the first to note the changed nature of money which capitalism was introducing.[95]

What is critically important about Lessius and Mersenne is not their individual genius or historical influence. They exemplify a broader movement within Catholic theology. Each presents a serious case against atheism, one arguing with a Stoic methodology to an intelligibility lodged in the nature of things, and the other with a Platonized Epicureanism that the appearances which we can know of the changeable world demand that the context of reality be the good. In both, the argument from design is preeminent, though the design in Lessius is spoken of as that between final and efficient cause and in Mersenne as that between quantities, boundaries, elements, and dimensions. Both can speak of god as the great architect, but in each it has a somewhat different ring. In each, the case is taken from a wide-ranging knowledge of natural philosophy.

Whatever the metaphysical judgment of such attempts, the theologian will look in vain for a critical position accorded to Christology or religious experience. Both Lessius and Mersenne treated the atheistic question as if it were a philosophic issue, not a religious one. Both acted as if the rising movement were not a rejection of Jesus Christ as the supreme presence of god in human history, whose spirit continued that presence and made it abidingly evocative, but a philosophic stance toward life brought about by either the scandal of the state of the world, the personal dissolution of the moral virtues, or the collapse of religious unity and the horror of the religious wars.[96] Whatever the causes, neither theologian indicated that the reflective understanding of god's self-revelation in the person of Jesus and in the depths of human religious experiences had anything to contribute to this most critical issue for the Church.

Two factors may have substantially contributed to this stance. Montaigne and the school that came after him seem to have already preempted this argument. Montaigne, systematically following Sextus Empiricus, attempts to destroy any natural philosophy which could attain certitude. Wisdom consisted in the Pyrrhonian: "Que sçay-je?" The only certitude could come not from philosophy ("Et certes la philosophie n'est qu'une poësie sophistiquée") but from revelation.[97] Pyrrhonian skepticism was matched with revelation to produce the devout Catholic. Charron follows this lead with a skepticism taken from the Academy: god's nature and existence are unknowable because of the weakness of the human mind and the greatness of god. One can only attain god through revelation. Charron employs what Popkin terms a "double-barrelled fideism" to attack atheism. His position is, very simply, that the atheists, because philosophers, are incapable of making any statement about the existence of god.[98] For Lessius and Mersenne to have appealed to the witness of Christ or to Judeo-Christian religious experience would have seemed to be lining up with the skeptics, those who pushed revelation at the cost of the soundness of reason, and neither man would content himself with this.

The second factor is the paradoxical influence of the *Summa theologiae*. In the *Summa* a doctrine of the one god is elaborated which is philosophical in its basic arguments, though its context is theological. But Aquinas was not writing against atheism. The *Summa* is not a polemical or apologetic work. These early questions inquire into the intelligibility and validity of those confessions which are made by faith. When the time for polemic came, the habit of mind was set: the existence of god would and could be demonstrated through philosophy from the evidence available to anyone. Through a shift in focus and interest, this proposition from Aquinas justified a purely philosophical approach to the apologetic problem posed by the new atheism.

Perhaps under both of these influences, neither Christology nor a mystagogy of experience was reformulated by the theologians to present *vestigia et notae* of the reality of god—as if Christianity did not possess in the person of Jesus a unique witness to confront the denial of god or as if one already had to believe in order to have this confrontation take place. In the rising attacks of atheism, Christology continued to discuss the nature of Christ, the unity of his freedom and his mission, the precisely constituting factor of his person, the consciousness of the human Jesus, the nature of his salvific acts; but the fundamental reality of Jesus as the embodied presence and witness of the reality of god within human history was never brought into the critical struggle of Christianity in the next three hundred years. The Enlightenment gradually took over the discussion of the meaning and existence of god. There was no need for the philosophes to draw up their own state of the question. It had been given to them by the theologians. Diderot resumed Charron's *religion naturelle* but in a form which had already been shaped by such theologians as Leonard Lessius and Marin Mersenne. In the absence of a rich and comprehensive Christology and a Pneumatology of religious experience Christianity entered into the defense of the existence of the Christian god without appeal to anything Christian.

The Existence of God and the New Philosophic Consciousness

SECTION 1. God as the Pledge of a Universal Mathematics: René Descartes

At the opening of the seventeenth century, there was a widespread conviction that the atheists were at the gates and the defense of the religious walls had passed from theologians, or at least from theology, to philosophy. Some theologians took the field against the argument drawn from the "Atheorum locis communibus," but they became philosophers in order to do so.[1] Cicero's dialogue had been flexible enough to incorporate new knowledge and new evidence, but the world had changed radically since the twilight of the Roman Republic sixteen hundred years before. New sciences were emerging, a new world had been discovered, assertive new intellectual interests were awakened. One could not put this heady new wine into old wineskins.

In fact, there were serious doubts whether any wineskins would be available again. Concomitant with the proud position of Cicero was the rising force of skepticism. Cicero represented the Third Academy, the skepticism which held nothing as certain and sponsored debates to distill from the various dogmatisms their most probable elements. Philosophic and scientific discourse was a laboratory of such probabilities. The elegance of the Latin style and the urbane open-mindedness of such an unpretentious goal commended itself to the modern world, so unsettled by the cataract of discoveries which had staggered the imagination and dislodged the old sense of security.

Skepticism, however, possessed a presence even stronger than Cicero's. Sextus Empiricus had been completely translated by 1569.[2] An equally polished French stylist read the *Pyrrhonian Hypotyposes* in his retirement at the family estate in Perigord and sharpened them into a question which would level even Ciceronian probabilities: "Que sçay-je?"[3] Doubt could not go further nor intellectual despair commend itself more charmingly than they did in the guise of this deeply sophisticated modesty. Michel de Montaigne asserted nothing as certain or probable. He did not even maintain what the contemporary Spanish physician François Sanchez offered in the title of his own book, *Quod nil scitur* (*That Nothing Can Be Known*). One was rather to prescind from affirmations that rang of any settlement. The responsible intellectual posture before the antinomies brought to bear upon every significant issue was to hazard no statement whatsoever. Montaigne's question allowed this strategy without the Spaniard's barefaced self-contradiction. Agrippa of Nettesheim, Omer Talon, François Sanchez, and finally Montaigne—the tradition which culminated in the *Essays* was in no sense an occult or esoteric persuasion. It was the atmosphere of profound epistemological renunciation, and it permeated the educated intellect of Europe, making doubtful from the start any mission to engage a putative atheism.[4]

Only within this situation can Descartes be understood. Etienne Gilson has made the point repeatedly that this horizon constitutes the context and challenge of everything he did: "The philosophy of Descartes was a desperate struggle to emerge from Montaigne's skepticism."[5] It is equally true, however, that Descartes incorporated into this desperate struggle the defense of religion against its most implacable foes, the atheists. One can judge his intent, he wrote, even from the full title of his *Meditations*: "I was altogether hostile to these [atheistic] beliefs, for it [my book] purports to give 'proofs of the existence of God.'"[6] What is never noted, yet is crucial for the interpretation of his project, is that he did not originate this conjunction between skepticism and the existence of god. It came to him already forged.

Montaigne's skepticism had achieved its highest articulation in handling the *Theologia naturalis sive liber creaturarum* of the fifteenth-century Raymond of Sebond.[7] Raymond had subtitled his treatise *The Book of Creatures*. Scripture, the other book, is limited in its scope, and only clerics know how to read it, but the book of the world or nature is common to all men and women and cannot be falsified, mutilated, or falsely interpreted. Raymond demonstrated not only the existence of god but "every truth that a human being needs to know whether concerning the human person or concerning God or all that a person needs to know for his salvation and perfection and progress in the way that leads to eternal life."[8] This was natural theology with a vengeance, in which "the whole Catholic faith is made known and proved to be true."[9]

At the request of his dying father, Montaigne translated this "Spanish scrambled with Latin endings" into flowing French, admiring with splendid condescension the high purpose which Raymond had set for himself: "His purpose is bold and courageous, for he undertakes by human and natural reasons to establish and prove against the atheists all the articles of the Christian religion."[10] It is hard to know at this point which will give out first, Montaigne's tongue or his cheek: In tracing Raymond's accomplishments, "I find him so firm and felicitous, that I do not think it is possible to do better in that argument and I think that no one has equaled him."[11] It was not possible to do better, but utter candor would have added that this is not very reassuring. How seriously should sixteenth-century France take this *Theologia naturalis*? Let this gallant work be revived as not only unparalleled in its forceful argumentation, but as representing in its full vitality the doctrine of Thomas Aquinas. Montaigne was told by the scholarly Adrian Turnebus, "who knew everything," that only the genius of the Angelic Doctor was capable of the erudition, the subtlety, and the invention of arguments which this work embodied.[12]

Montaigne had obeyed his father. He had translated Raymond. Then, in by far the longest of his essays, he went one better: he defended him. Montaigne's defense of the *Theologia naturalis* became the masterpiece among the presentations of Pyrrhonian skepticism. He demonstrated that reason is "so lame and so blind that there is nothing so clear and easy as to be clear enough to her; that the easy and the hard are one to her; that all subjects, alike, and nature in general, disavow her jurisdiction and meditation."[13] Montaigne supports Raymond, as Arthur Beattie remarks, somewhat as a gallows halter supports the hanging criminal.[14] It was not the first nor the last time that skepticism emerged from a disappointed rationalism. Perhaps it was the first time, however, that natural theology had been co-opted into the ranks of skepticism. Descartes was confronted with their united progress from a comprehensive natural theology to a comprehensive skepticism. He would have to go in reverse: from certitude to a new natural theology or metaphysics. Raymond of Sebond plus Michel de Montaigne had made the theological and the epistemological issues one.

The story of Descartes has often been told in the books and lecture halls of philosophy. The paradoxical fate of one who scorned the history of philosophy was to be condemned to initiate the history of modern philosophy, and the measure with which he scorned previous philosophers has been measured out to him, in abundance, pressed down and overflowing. Margaret Dauler Wilson prefaces her *Descartes* almost with a sigh: "There are already more books on Descartes' philosophy than anyone other than a near-maniacal specialist could assimilate in a single lifetime."[15] It could not be otherwise: Descartes represents the confluence of many great rivers, not the least of which are the unrelenting rationalism of Raymond and the equally absolute skepticism of Montaigne. Almost all modern thought has been fed in some part from his tributaries.

Perhaps the best scene to capture Descartes' entrance into Western philosophy would be the conference in Paris of November, 1628. The gentle Oratorian Pierre Cardinal de Bérulle, the Franciscan friar Marin Mersenne, René Descartes, and a "grande et sçavant compagnie" were summoned by the Papal Nuncio, Monsignor de Baigné, to hear the Sieur de Chandoux savage scholastic philosophy and propose "sa nouvelle philosophie."[16] La Rochelle had fallen in October to the troops of Richelieu, and Chandoux envisaged a similar fate for the methods of the schools. It would be an easy victory, one often won in the drawing rooms and among the clerics and literati of newly centralized France. When Chandoux had finished, the assembly applauded with a general enthusiasm. Only Descartes sat quietly. The Cardinal noted his silence and pressed him for a response. Descartes, after some halfhearted attempts to escape the charge, finally "praised the address, but did not praise the assembly because they had allowed themselves to be satisfied with what was only probable [quod *verisimili* tantum contenti fuissent]."[17]

Satisfaction with the probable (*vray-semblance*) is a fundamental error, the disorder that carries every other weakness in its wake.[18] It allows the false to pass itself off as the true; it is the halfway house to Montaigne. To put this to the test, Descartes gave the distinguished group a challenge: it might present any truth it held as obvious, as incontestable; with twelve equally probable arguments Descartes would demonstrate that it was false. Again, taking any admitted falsehood, with similar argumentation he could demonstrate its plausibility. The method was that of the Pyrrhonian antinomies. Contradiction is so elicited from any proposition that one finally abdicates any settlement between opposing claims. The point that Descartes drew from this brilliant display was similar to that which skepticism had been making in France for a hundred years: using probability as a criterion or as an unexamined reassurance, any sophist can prove anything. The inevitable end of the Third Academy is with Pyrrho.

Montaigne had ended here, but Descartes was just beginning. The assembly put to him the question that was being debated the length and breadth of France: whether there was any escape from skepticism. If probabilities led inevitably to skepticism, was there any possibility of transcending them to obtain certitude? The question was about method, how one goes about something, a pattern of thinking; it sought what Baillet termed an infallible method of avoiding sophisms.[19] It was the right question at the right time. "Ce fut là que je fis confesser à toute la troupe ce que *l'art de bien raisonner* peut sur l'esprit de ceux qui sont mediocrement sçavans, et combien mes principes sont mieux établis, plus veritables, et plus naturels qu'aucun des autres qui sont déjà reçus parmi les gens d'étude."[20] Descartes promised a new method that would deliver new principles, better established and more coordinate with what was natural to humanity.

Sebond himself had made a similar promise that his method would not depend upon a high degree of talent. In fact, he was breathtakingly in advance of Descartes. The *Theologia naturalis* was a science "accessible alike to laymen and to clerics and to every condition of men and can be had in less than a month and without trouble . . . nor can it be forgotten when once obtained."[21] Descartes advanced no such pretensions. On the contrary, he required steady labor over prolonged periods of time. But neither he nor Raymond demanded a genius as a student. Descartes offered a skeptical preface, however, which was fatally missing from Raymond. The land was to be cleared before one could begin to build. And how to build? "He replied that he knew of no [method] more infallible than the one he himself was wont to employ, adding that he had drawn it *from the treasury of the mathematical sciences*, and that there was, he believed, no truth which he could not, by its means, clearly demonstrate, in conformity with his own principles."[22] Much as this assertion might sound like Raymond's, Descartes was careful to distinguish from it all those things which were a matter of faith. Raymond's claim had been placed on the Index of forbidden books in 1595, some thirty-three years before.[23] Descartes did not wish to suffer a similar fate.

The Cardinal and the assembly were conquered. Bérulle asked for an interview, in which they discussed "those thoughts on philosophy that had first occured to him after he had come to recognize the usefulness of the methods commonly employed in treating it." He indicated further effects which this method of philosophizing might obtain in medicine and mechanics. This colloquy, however, subtly reversed their roles. Descartes told the Cardinal about the method to be followed if one wished to obtain certainty in knowledge; Bérulle, one of the greatest spiritual directors of his century, told Descartes about the obligations he had in conscience to pursue these studies if he wished to obtain salvation from the "Sovereign Judge."[24] Bérulle gave Descartes a mission that reinforced his own natural inclinations, a mission that was to last all of his life, "to publish his doctrine against the skeptics and atheists."[25] Never were two adversaries more fatefully merged into one mission.

The century-long battle between rationalism and skepticism, with the progressive temptation of the intellect to destroy itself first by overweening pretensions and then by their ineluctable disappointment, had been preoccupied with certitude, with an attempt to gain a reassurance free from haunting doubts, rather than with understanding. Among the theologians, the task given to a "natural theology" had been to establish the existence of god as an implication of either nature, thought, concept, or experience. Montaigne had merged these two preoccupations, and natural theology had disintegrated into "Que sçay-je?" Descartes merged them once more: to establish the certitude of cognition and of perception by establishing the existence of god who could not deceive. Indeed, this federation of purposes led to a conjunction of methods. The skeptical method, calling everything into doubt, became the initial *via negationis* to a foundation which was self-justifying and self-authenticating, principles intuitively so justified that they admitted no denial and were even sustained by the experience of doubt. From there one could build by a proper "art de bien raisonner" a metaphysics of the self which carefully deduced the existence of god and of the world, and thus lay the foundations for physics, mechanics, and morals. The prospect was universal, and the outlines of its execution basically simple—feasible enough to capture the admiration of Bérulle, and to evoke from him this serious charge to Descartes, whose spiritual director he remained until the Cardinal's death.[26]

God as a Problem for Philosophic Wisdom

E. M. Curley has been at some pains to maintain against L. J. Beck and Etienne Gilson that Descartes shows substantial development beyond the *Regulae ad directionem ingenii* in his subsequent *Discourse* and *Meditations*. These later works "pose a problem which is just not present in the *Regulae*, the problem of justifying our belief in the things that seem most evident to us." Curley suggests that until 1628, Descartes did not explore the problem of knowledge at a depth appropriate to its intrinsic challenge and that in this year Descartes "came to feel that Pyrrhonian skepticism was a more dangerous enemy than scholasticism."[27] In his attempt to nail down what occasioned this amplification of the problem with its consequent modulations of the Cartesian procedure, Curley neglects the critical intervention of Bérulle and the importance that Descartes himself ascribed to the November conference.

The problem of certitude had always been there. Perhaps Curley fails to consider sufficiently the demanding imperative of the second rule of the *Regulae* that one believes only "what is perfectly known and indubitable" (*perfecte cognitis, et de quibus dubitari non potest*) and the procedure recommended under the sixth rule that "before setting out to attack any definite problem, we ought first, without making any selection, to assemble those truths that are obvious as they present themselves to us."[28] The skeptical prolegomena is methodologically implicit in any regulation that made the *sponte obvias veritates* foundational and that demanded an evaluation of the extent of human knowledge.

The problem of the later works is significantly different from that of the *Regulae*. After 1628, Descartes joined to the problem of certitude the commission on atheism. He integrated the human search for intellectual reassurances with the contemporary attempts to establish the existence of god. The problem he set himself had become far more vast. But this development was an organic evolution of his initial concerns with true knowledge.

Montaigne had joined the issue of skepticism to natural theology not only by his use of Raymond of Sebond. Even more emphatically, he had made the Renaissance discussions *de potentia Dei absoluta* the grounds for doubting even the most apparent truths. Nothing could limit the power of god. Much less could a finite, fallible human intellect confine god's power within its own comprehension. In Montaigne, as Curley has pointed out, the power of god becomes a theological foundation for skepticism.[29] If the Eucharist looks like bread, and yet in Christian teaching is the body of Christ, who is to say that sense experience and even mathematical axioms cannot deceive? God cannot be reduced to the measure of the human. Consequently, whatever is asserted must be asserted hypothetically with the theological recognition that it may be totally otherwise. With such a challenge, there was no choice left for Descartes if he was to take the field against the Pyrrhonians. He had to deal with the existence and nature of god if he was to defend the existence and nature of certitude.

Even this universality, however, is already implicit in the initial pages of the *Regulae*. The sciences are not like the arts. The arts demand certain bodily dexterities, one of which might well exclude the others. The skills demanded of the harpist can be destroyed by the daily employments of the French peasant. The sciences were the opposite; there was an organic unity among them. The mastery of one helped in the mastery of the others, and all the sciences together formed human wisdom: "Nam cum scientiae omnes nihil aliud sint quam humana sapientia."[30] This is a radically different conception of wisdom from either the Aristotelian grasp of ultimate causes or the skeptical renunciation of all assertion. The sciences form a concatenated unity among themselves; a grasp of that complex whole, the mastery of all the sciences as well as of their interconnections, constitutes human wisdom. It is hard to exaggerate the importance of this notion of wisdom in Descartes. It makes understandable the first finality for the education of human *ingenium*: it should be able to make accurate judgments about "everything which is proposed to it."[31] This emphatically lays the foundation for the great work of French scholarship of the succeeding century, the *Encyclopedia*: "Quippe sunt concatenatae omnes scientiae, nec una perfecta haberi potest, quin aliae sponte sequantur, et tota simul *encyclopedia* apprehendatur."[32] Wisdom constitutes what Descartes elsewhere calls the "catenam scientiarum," and the command of this interlocking totality forms the end of all studies.[33] Human wisdom, then, is a universal wisdom ("de hac universali Sapientia") and it necessarily comprehends all the great objects of human inquiry: certitude about knowledge, the self, the being and attributes of god, the existence and nature of the external world. This wisdom is task enough for any human being!

One speaks not only of the internal unity of the sciences but of their certitude because science, like wisdom, has gone through a significant redefinition. It is knowledge, but that kind of knowledge which is both certain and evident: "Omnis scientia est cognitio certa et evidens."[34] Probabilities do not make one wiser. They simply extend the area in which one wanders less assured and more liable to essay false opinions. "Therefore," Descartes says, in a sentence that annihilates equally Aristotelian dialectic and the hypothetical methodology of contemporary physics, "we reject all knowledge [*cognitiones*] which is only probable."[35] Skepticism defines the parameters of the task, and it admits no room in its execution for that which gives entrée to doubt. The objects which this maxim excises will be discovered as one moves skeptically through opinions previously accepted. It will leave what he promised to the dazzled Bérulle: principles better established, more true and natural, than any that had been accepted by the scholastics. If these dismissed opinions are readmitted for scientific inquiry, as indeed they will be, it will be because metaphysics rather than sense perception has rendered them indubitable. The skeptical question must be leveled at everything because the problem that has been set touches everything and will be satisfied only by indubitable knowledge.

To anyone who wishes to treat everything, the problem of god is obviously inescapable. But there is a further consideration: the issue of god is a question intrinsically more appropriate to philosophic wisdom than to theology. Never was this appropriation so starkly signaled as in Descartes' letter of dedication to the dean and theological faculty of the University of Paris. To these "sapientissimis clarissimis viris," theologians all, he dedicated his greatest work, the *Meditations*, by indicating how theologians and philosophers should divide their turf. More elegantly, what was the task, the *opus*, of philosophy? "I have always been of the opinion that two questions—those dealing with God and with the soul—were among the principal ones which should be demonstrated by philosophy rather than by theology." Theology is limited by faith. The faithful can accept the divine existence and the immortality of the soul because of their belief, but faith is useless to persuade those who do not believe. Natural reason alone is effective. It alone provides appropriate means to bring one to accept either religion or a moral life. Descartes' evaluation of the urgency of this task sounds like the theologian Lessius: these convictions about religion and the moral life are the foundation of human civilization. "Few persons would prefer the just to the useful if they were not restrained either by the fear of God or by the expectation of another life." Here is a confluence of the Flemish theologian and the French master. Neither allows religion to have its own proper evidence in dealing with the atheistic question. Christology simply does not and should not figure. The existence and attributes of god become the primary preserve of the philosopher: "quae Philosophiae potius quam Theologiae ope sunt demonstrandae."[36]

What is more, theology itself has indicated that this is the way it should be. Philosophy did not come to this task simply on its own. Catholic theologians have assured the philosophers that the existence of god can be demonstrated from natural reason, and they found this assertion on the Wisdom of Solomon and the first chapter of Romans. The thirteenth chapter of the Wisdom of Solomon offers not only an encouragement, but a pattern which the arguments of Descartes follow: if one can know the world and its creatures, how much easier is it to know the existence of the creator-god! What Descartes takes from this is startling: that it is far easier, far more immediately evident that god exists than that the world does. In the Epistle to the Romans he discovers confirmation of this conviction, and the arresting exegesis Descartes performs for the theologians of the Sorbonne discovers an outline of his own philosophical program: "We seem to be instructed that all of those things which can be known about God, can be shown by reasons which we do not need to look for from any other source than our own mind." Faith gives no knowledge about god's existence that cannot be philosophically established; indeed, it provides the task for philosophy. Theology says the *ea omniaquae de Deo sciri possunt* can be established by natural reason and its evidence can be found within the human mind itself.

All that remains for Descartes is to take this commission as his philosophic task and demonstrate "how it can be done and by what method [*qua via*] God can be known more easily and more certainly [*facilius et certius*] than the things of this world." Theology indicates only that the undertaking can be done; Cartesian philosophy indicates how. The Fifth Lateran Council in its eighth session mandated to Christian philosophers (*Christianis philosophis*) the responsibility of defending the immortality of the soul. Descartes extends this mandate to cover his first philosophy, assumes the mantle of a Christian philosopher, and takes up the defense of the existence of god against "the atheists who are ordinarily more arrogant than learned and judicious."[37] By the time he had executed most of this commission, he could write to the Jesuit Provincial of France, once his instructor at La Flèche and subsequently confessor to the King: "I profess completely that there is nothing which pertains to religion which could not equally or even with greater ease be explained through my principles rather than through those commonly received."[38] Even more affirmatively to Père Vatier: "I make so bold as to say that never has faith been so strongly supported by human reasons, as it can be if my principles are followed."[39]

Christian philosophers have seldom been so comprehensive in their claims or so confident in their assessment of results, but Christian philosophers have seldom so minimized theology and conjoined at such depth the problem of god and the problem of human certainty, and then, within this problematic complexity, brought together all the sciences into an interdependent whole whose mastery was universal human wisdom. Massive as this task was, its outlines were registered in the very first rules of the *Regulae*. The unity which had been forged in the historical succession of Raymond of Sebond and Michel de Montaigne constituted the historical context in which Descartes worked, but it was the furthest reaches of skepticism, his own concept of wisdom, and the office of a Christian philosopher that raised this cultural horizon into the problematic situation of all that he thought and wrote.

Certitude and the Method of Universal Mathematics

Since wisdom is the constellation of the sciences, and the sciences are marked by clarity and certitude, the question before Descartes was inevitably what constituted certitude and by what method it could be obtained.

Oddly enough, the nature of certitude did not trouble Descartes at great length. It had been his experience that philosophers confused rather than clarified when they attempted explications of those things which were "perfectly simple in themselves." This phrase is critical in Descartes; it is not a sloppy passing over of primitive terms. The Cartesian method reduces complex wholes to simples—as would legions of philosophers before and after—but these simples are not to be asserted arbitrarily, as if method could go no further. The simples must be self-justifying, "simple in themselves." Descartes' principles are not like those of Democritus or Newton, however much his mathematical methodology resembles theirs. His principles are reflexively self-justifying or self-evident. Whether it is a question of the meaning of words or of the truth of propositions, these simples, which are the principles of more complex meanings and dependent propositions, must be self-instantiating. Like the principles of Aristotle and Spinoza, Cartesian principles are reflexive. Among those "which are of the simplest possible kind" are terms such as knowledge, existence, and certainty. Everyone knows what these notions comprise, and a prolonged examination of their meaning is neither necessary nor helpful.[40] One does not define in terms of something else what is obvious by itself.

For all that, "certitude" was worth more than a paragraph, and the second series of objections to the *Meditations* elicited more descriptive analyses, expounding "what seems to me the only basis on which any human certitude can rest (*omnis humana certitudo niti posse*)."[41] Certitude can best be seen in stages. As soon as we think that we have correctly perceived something, we spontaneously persuade ourselves that what we have grasped is true. The condition for this assertion of truth lies in the clear perception of something. We cannot conceive of it without at the same time recognizing its truth. If this connection between conception and truth is so strong that we "can never have a cause for doubting that of which we are persuaded," there is nothing further to search for. We have obtained everything which could be reasonably desired (*habemus omne quod cum ratione licet optare*). Regardless of what fictions are erected to shake this *persuasio*, if we have obtained a conviction that nothing can destroy, we have obtained absolutely perfect certitude (*perfectissima certitudo*). Certitude, then, is not a condition of the thing known, the *akribeia* of Aristotle—what today one might call a "sure thing." It is not a combination of things and knowledge, as was the *certitudo objectiva* of the Middle Ages; certitude is a condition of human consciousness, a *persuasio* that is *tam firma ut nullo modo tolli possit*.[42]

If Descartes' principles are reflexive, his semantic interpretation is existentialist, that is, it locates in human perspective the warrant for the assertion of the "really real." The clear and the distinct are predicates about reality, but reality assessed by the condition of human consciousness. The *persuasio* that indicates the clear and distinct, the certain, is in its own order of consciousness not unlike the divine immutability upon which it was founded. The Middle Ages also had a term for this condition of awareness; it was called subjective certitude. For Descartes, and for the entire tradition of philosophy after him, this constitutes the only kind of certitude. Its possibilities depend both upon the knower and upon the character of the object known. If there is any obscurity in the act of perception, no certitude is possible, for confusion of any kind is sufficient cause to raise doubts about the judgment to be made. Further, if the perception is sensible perception alone, irrespective of how clear this sensible perception seems, certitude is impossible. There are too many instances in which the senses deceive us. Whatever certitude is humanly possible can only be found "in those things which are *clearly perceived by the intellect*." These are the propositions which carry their own intuitive justification; they are both evident and simple. For example, "That I, while I am thinking, exist; that what has once been done, cannot be undone." What makes these propositions an experience of certitude? "We cannot doubt them, unless we first think about them; but *we are not able to think about them, without at that same moment believing them to be true*." The experience of certitude is the coincidence between the awareness of meaning and the awareness of truth; it is the conscious experience of indubitability.[43]

This is *perfectissima certitudo*. Rare indeed. In mechanics and medicine, the best that can be obtained is an explanation that fits all the phenomena. But even a total explanation does not possess the warrant for its own truth. Two clocks may function externally in precisely the same manner, but their internal constitution may be utterly different. As clocks, so the universe! Doubtless there is an infinity of different ways in which all the things we see could have been formed by "the great Artificer."[44] One can obtain from an exhaustive explanation only moral certitude, sufficient for the conduct of life and for all of those "arts which the knowledge of physics subserves." But moral certitude by itself, unless grounded in something more secure, can be the halfway house to skepticism. Coherence of explanation is no final judgment, no *firma et immutabilis persuasio*.[45] Perfect certitude, unchangeable persuasion, the only state that can constitute a destructive counterinstance to skepticism, must offer more. It must underwrite an existentialist confidence that the thing known cannot possibly be other than as we think of it. The conduct of life, the practice of medicine, the skills and theories of mechanics offer no possibilities for such reassurance.

But mathematics does. If one maintains that science, to be science, must be certain, or that only those questions should be objects of inquiry which yield certain and indubitable resolution, then "of the sciences already discovered, Arithmetic and Geometry alone are left, to which the observance of this rule reduces us."[46] What mechanics and medicine cannot offer, arithmetic and geometry are commonly acknowledged to possess. Consider, like Father Clavius, "the Modern Euclid" and major authority in the Jesuit colleges of the early seventeenth century—consider the effect of mathematical demonstrations upon the mind: they leave no room for doubt. Contrast this effect with the chaos in philosophical schools, the Aristotelians with their internecine battles waged through the Greek and Arab commentaries, the continuous, nagging, unresolved struggles between the Nominalists and the Realists. Contrast this sectarianism and irresolution with the history of mathematics: "I suppose that everyone sees how far all of that is from mathematical demonstrations. The theorems of Euclid, as well as those of the other mathematicians, are just as purely true today, safe in their results, as firm and solid in their demonstrations, as they already were in schools many centuries ago."[47] It does not take a genius to read this text, which Descartes may well have read. It did take a genius to take the next step: make perfect certitude the criterion for any scientific knowledge, maintain the *Regulae*, and mathematics is left.

Let us examine arithmetic and geometry to determine what singles them out. What allows this quality of scientific reassurance to emerge? We find two characteristics: one touches upon the objects of mathematics and the other upon the structure of their demonstrations. Mathematics deals with line, with figure, with number—objects that are so simple, so unmixed with alien attributes, that mathematics does not have to make any assumptions that are open to subsequent invalidating experiences. Once these elements are grasped in their purity, mathematics moves through the strict deduction of consequences (*totae consistunt in consequentiis rationabiliter deducendis*). These two methodological characteristics impart a solidity to mathematical propositions unmatched by any other science, a security so intrinsically warranted that "in them it is scarcely humanly possible for anyone to err except by inadvertence." The impossibility of error—this is what the demonstrations of mathematics possess. The lesson they teach is not that they alone constitute serious inquiry nor that their presence destroys the counterclaims of the skeptics. The lesson they offer is that of object and procedure, a subject and a pattern of discourse through which one can obtain wisdom. In its search for a correct method (*rectum veritatis iter*), all human inquiry should take as the object of its study those things whose purity allows a similar certitude and as the pattern of its study those procedures that guarantee its attainment. Arithmetic and geometry offer the scientific suggestion that the objects and the processes involved in their construction be universalized. If one is to obtain an equal certitude, it must be through a generalized mathematical method.[48] The universal wisdom, with its double task of defending human knowledge and the divine existence, demands a generalized mathematical science, a Universal Mathematics. Since all science must be certain and since the only science which measures up to this stringent requirement is mathematical, it is critically necessary to abstract and universalize the mathematical method; to be concerned with objects that are simple and can be grasped by intuition; and to move from these simplicities into their implications by a carefully linked series of deductions.[49]

A Universal Mathematics! This was not the first time that such a phrase had been coined. In 1597, A. van Roomen in his *Apologia pro Archimede* had urged a *mathesis universalis* as a science which would be analogous to first philosophy or metaphysics. Just as metaphysics, the science of being as being, comprised the consideration of the subjects of all the sciences and dealt with the demonstration of their first principles, so the *mathesis universalis* "would deal with the subject-matters of all the mathematical sciences, both pure and mixed."[50] The universal mathematics of van Roomen considered quantity as precisely measurable, together with the properties commensurate with all quantities. It treated the foundations both of pure mathematics, in the abstractions of number and size, and of applied mathematics, in the measurements of time, sounds, places, motions, forces, and so on.[51] Van Roomen was not repeating the common sixteenth-century expression, *mathesis universa*, which denoted all the mathematical disciplines in their unitary relationship to one another. His was a *mathesis universalis*, a first mathematics that would study the nature of those things fundamental to all mathematics.[52]

Descartes moved far beyond that. Initially, he reported to Isaac Beeckman his proposal to give the public "not an *Ars brevis*, such as Lully's, but an entirely new science which will allow of a general solution of all problems which can be proposed in any and every kind of quantity, continuous or discontinuous, each in accordance with its nature . . . so that almost nothing will remain to be discovered in geometry."[53] The discovery of analytic geometry was the achievement of the young Descartes that transformed the world of mathematics and gave to geometry a universality that deserved all his enthusiam. But this was only the beginning, only a hint of what might be done if the mathematical method subsumed all the chaotic philosophic questions and gave them a new order and procedure.

The *mathesis universalis* of Descartes extends far beyond the confined area allotted it by van Roomen. *Mathesis*, after all, is the Greek word for something as general as the Latin *disciplina*. Why should it not develop to deal with those things that would make science scientific, that is, certain? And what would that entail? The order and the measurement in which subjects are investigated—an order for those things that cannot be literally measured. "I saw, consequently, that there must be some general science which investigates [*explicit*] everything which can be explored [*quaeri*] about *order and measurement*, restricted as these are to no special subject matter."[54] It is not that the Universal Mathematics will have order and measurement as devices in its methodology. Order and measurement have been abstracted from mathematical methodology and form its specific subject.

Universal Mathematics, then, is the heart of all mathematics. It can deal with all the objects which customarily fall to the various parts of mathematics, and many more besides (*et insuper alia multa*). Taking order and measure wherever they may appear releases the mathematical focus from figure or number, sound or stars. It allows a "general science" to emerge which deals with anything in which order and measure are to be found. This general science of order and measure is entitled to the name of Universal Mathematics.[55]

Is there still some single object that gives even order and measure a unity, something that gives the Universal Mathematics a simple point, a convergence, something that imparts integrity to its several inner movements as a method, and comprehensiveness to its extension to "toutes les choses, qui peuvent tomber sous la connaissance des hommes"?[56] Yes, for order and measure are but varieties of proportion. Measure is the proportion for a magnitude, order for a multitude. Thus the *Regulae* and the *Discourse* can subsume both under the critical and universal object, proportion or relationship: "I saw that although the objects they discuss are different, all these [mathematical] branches are in agreement in limiting their considerations to diverse relationships or proportions which are found [*les divers rappors ou proportions qui s'y trouvent*]. I thought, consequently, that it would be better that I examine only those proportions in general [*ces proportions en general*]."[57] It is hard to exaggerate the methodological importance of this choice. Universal Mathematics can investigate whatever a human being can come to know by universalizing the method of mathematics—and the first thing to be universalized is its diverse objects. Figure, number, machine, and harmony can all be varieties of pure proportion or relationship. The Universal Mathematics, the true mathematics, is particularized or realized as the several kinds of pure or applied mathematics as these deal with different, less general objects which are related or in proportion to one another. Thus, the Universal Mathematics generates geometry or algebra, optics or music. Taking proportion or relation as its subject allows the Universal Mathematics to become pure method embodied in various ways, just as the specific proportions that it finds and that constitute the humanly knowable differ from one another. It is no wonder that in the *Meditations* this Universal or True Mathematics can take as one of its embodiments *mathesis pura et abstracta.*[58]

The Universal Mathematics is the science and the reality of pure, disembodied method, and the "simple nature" that is its object is proportion or relationship as such. L. J. Beck puts Descartes' discovery quite accurately: *Mathesis Universalis*, in distinction from other mathematical inquiries, "treats of proportions in complete abstraction from figure, number, or any other subject. Its object is proportions *ut sic*, and the nature of these proportions as such is identical in whatever subject matter it may be involved. Proportions as such are all expressible in terms of order, measure, and dimension and it is of these that the genuine science of *Mathesis Universalis* treats."[59] "Rapports ou proportion"—this pervasive subject leaves to the Universal Mathematics a method of inquiry and resolution which does not consider things simply in isolation (*naturas solitarias*), but always in connection or comparison with one another. Just as the sciences formed a concatenated whole, so do all things such that "some things can be known from the others." The emphasis upon series, upon chains of reasoning stretching back to first principles, comes out of the very subject of the Universal Mathematics.

This emphasis upon series in turn involves the critical distinction of the absolute from the relative. The absolute denotes those natures so pure and simple, so self-evident and intrinsically clear, that they are the objects and final resolutions of all scientific inquiry. The absolute is discovered whenever one finds a nature which can be designated as independent, as cause, or as universal; *equal, one, similar, straight* are all examples of such absolutes. The absolute is the most simple of natures. The relative, in contrast, only participates in some way either in the same nature or in something of the nature of the absolute—consequently, it can and must be referred to it (*secundum quod ad absolutum potest referri*) and can subsequently be deduced from it. Hence the name "relative." Its intelligibility and its justification are in terms of the absolute; the relative is and is known only through the absolute. The absolute is known reflexively, in terms only of itself. The relative is discovered whenever one finds a nature that is dependent, an effect, a composition of other elements; the particular, the many, the unequal are all examples of the relative.

Sometimes this distinction is a matter of perspective. The universal, for example, can be listed as an absolute because its nature is simple; from another viewpoint, it can be considered relative because it depends upon particulars for its existence. Any connected series will have its own absolute, but it may be an absolute just for that series. The only things which deserve the name "absolute" in an unqualified sense are those few very pure and simple natures which are understood simply in terms of themselves and not through a dependence upon something else. These absolutes can be known in themselves and in their correspondence to one another; relatives can be understood only through the absolute. Equals, for example, always correspond to and imply one another. Inequality, however, can be known only through equality. The relative indicates a dependency which bespeaks the absolute as the source of its intelligibility and its existence.

Proportion or relation can be found in all things, but differently in the absolute and in the relative. The absolute is the explanation of the relative in a reductive process and its ground in a process of synthetic deduction. Taking proportion or relation as the object of the Universal Mathematics allows this method to dispense with the Aristotelian categories as ultimate predicates of meaning and to divide all that is knowable into interlocking chains of causality and dependence in which "unae ex aliis cognoscantur."[60] Proportion and relation, the relative revealing the absolute in its very dependence, are critically important in the application of the Universal Mathematics to the questions of the divine existence.

Proportion or relation also dictate the pattern of the Universal Mathematics as well as supplying its object. The *mathesis universalis* must possess a double movement. One moves from the relative to the absolute, reducing complexities to the simples which are ultimate; the other builds from these simple natures by a chain of deductive implication to more complete and comprehensive knowledge. Make proportion the object of method, and the objects it can include are twofold: the simples which can be intuited clearly and distinctly, and the subsequent or dependent natures which can be deduced from these with certitude. Every mathematical process possesses this double movement, and the Universal Mathematics abstracts it as the pattern of its own procedures. The fifth rule of the *Regulae* formulates the process succinctly: "All method [*tota methodus*] consists in the order and the disposition of these things towards which our mental vision should be directed in order to discover some truth. We shall comply with this exactly if [1] we *reduce* involved and obscure propositions step by step [*gradatim*] to those which are more simple and [2] then, starting with the intuition of those things which are most simple we try to *ascend* by the same steps [*gradus*] to the knowledge of all others."[61] The double process of analysis and synthesis is reduction and ascension with reflexively self-justifying principles as the terminus of the first movement and the initiation of the second. In the first movement, the complex world of experiences and human opinions can and must be broken down progressively, and the criterion of the clear and distinct allows the solution of their complexities. Eventually one reaches that which is simple, but not simple like the atoms of Democritus, the ideas of Locke, or the terms of Russell. The simple for Descartes is both the terms that are "perfectly clear in themselves"—and that "of themselves give us no knowledge of anything that exists"—and the propositions whose truth is obtained the very moment their terms are understood. These latter are the *sponte obviae veritates*. It is critical to notice that Descartes' simples are reflexive, that is, self-explanatory or self-instantiating principles, not arbitrary units or elements of a subsequent system.[62] The second movement builds up from these, tracing their implications to reconstruct what had previously been reduced.

Descartes proposes the method of the Universal Mathematics not only as one that integrates with the issue of certitude those of the self, god, and the world, but as one that co-opts the skeptical method itself. The doubt with its consequent suspension of judgment that the Pyrrhonians counsel now becomes the initial step of an *ordo*, the movement of reduction and renunciation which eventually turns in on itself to discover the simplicity and certitude which even doubt and suspension embody. This method goes beyond the Third Academy and assumes that all probabilities are false. It concedes every antinomy to Sextus Empiricus. It beats the skeptics at their own game. Indeed, they find themselves enlisted in the process of clearing the ground. Skepticism has been moved from a hidden dogmatism to the initial, analytic moment of pure method.

Gilson, following Arnauld, noted that Augustine had also entered into the skeptical tradition in order to destroy it. Four times Augustine engaged the skeptics to reduce their doubt to the doubtless proposition that even if I am deceived, I am.[63] This is true, but Augustine had not done what Descartes insisted on doing: the integration of the skeptical method into a Universal

Mathematics. For Augustine, skepticism was a dialectical moment, which generated its own contradiction; for Descartes, it was a mathematical solvent, which reduced complexities to their simple and self-justifying constituents. In this way, Descartes could build a mathematical method whose principles were not arbitrary and whose referents were obvious. Mathematics could deal with existence and construct a metaphysics. If the double movement of the Universal Mathematics is understood, the pattern in which Cartesian metaphysics is attempted falls into an obvious outline: the analytic progression toward the reflexive simples, which are grasped by intuition; the synthetic progression from these simples to those conclusions that are obtained by deduction. Reduction leads to the intuition of the indubitable first principles; these in turn generate by deduction the implications that constitute the universal wisdom.

The Demonstrated Existence of God

Skeptical doubt was not only the initial dissolvent of accumulated propositions heretofore accepted as true or plausible or probable, an acid that burned through the years of teachings accepted by students and the great diversity of opinions and contrary customs observed by the spectator of the comedy of life.[64] Doubt was also, in spite of itself, evidence for its own reflexive transcendence. More than the first movement of method, doubt was the experiential embodiment of the critical principle that would terminate the comprehensive and destructive analysis of skepticism and furnish the metaphysical foundations of a true physics.[65]

Doubt is always an activity that exhibits the existence of the one doubting. It is a form of thinking, and thinking indicates as intuitively indubitable the thinking subject: "Je pense, donc je suis." Doubt might systematically dismantle sensible experience, all previous reasonings, even the apodictic assertion of any reality beyond the illusions of dreams—the way that an owner might have his house torn down to rebuild again on a firmer foundation—but doubt itself provides the new foundation: the existing ego emerges ineluctably from within the action of doubt.[66] Thus the doubt of the skeptics can be extended as far as Pyrrho, Cicero, Sanchez, or Montaigne draws it, and still be subsumed into a Universal Mathematics for which it is both the initial movement toward simple natures and the primary evidence for the first deductive moments. Its disintegrative procedure yields a simple intuition: "I am" is contained manifestly within "I doubt." The certitude that neither books nor the world are able to provide is reached through the "résolution d'estudier aussy en moymesme, et d'employer toutes les forces de mon esprit a choysir les chemins que ie devois suivre."[67] The subject is the self, the thinking self, isolated from the world and from the body by the renunciations imposed by skepticism; the paths are those of the Universal Mathematics which follow out the implications of the doubt as method and as evidence.

If the logistic method of the Universal Mathematics works skeptically, taking apart opinions proposition by proposition, it also reaches its reflexive, self-evident principle in the "je pense, donce je suis." This principle is not an inference; it is a proportion *per se notum*, grasped not by inference or science but by the simple intuition of the mind. Doubt contains its own contradiction. The existential interpretation gives Descartes his reason for both the skeptical moment of his method and the reflexive nature of his principles: the perspective of the knowing subject.

Doubt constitutes evidence for more than the existence of the subject; it also exposes the radical nature of the subject, what the subject is: "Sum autem res vera, et vere existens; sed qualis res? Dixi, cogitans."[68] The ego is a thinking thing, which includes doubt and affirmation and denial, knowledge and ignorance, love and hate, wish and rejection, imagination and sensation. *Cogito* comprises them all; it comprehends anything that is so much within the thinking subject that "we are immediately conscious of it."[69] The ego can be variously designated *mens, animus, intellectus,* or *ratio,* terms whose meaning is given only through the experience of thinking. However one hesitates metaphysically over the sensible contact with external reality, there is nothing easier for the ego to understand than that it is mind. All of this comes to the fore within the experience of doubt. One cannot claim that a bridge between the thinking subject and the external world is given indubitably. There are too many antinomies yet to be resolved. But one can claim one's own interior experiences, however they are connected with external reality; there is a reflexive certitude about them. To doubt is to hesitate between affirmation and denial—which presupposes some understanding of affirmation and denial and the awareness of their difference. To doubt is to pause between knowledge and ignorance, even between wish and rejection. These alternative experiences are given along with the hesitation which lies between them.

Doubt further discloses that something is lacking in the subject, that the subject is imperfect, limited, or finite. Just as doubt exhibits the existence and mental nature of the ego, so it manifests its imperfection. But this very sense of imperfection similarly contains within itself the prior notion of total perfection: "For how would it be possible for me to know that I doubt and that I desire—that is, that I lack something and am not all (*omnino*) perfect—if I did not have in myself any idea of a being more perfect than my own, by comparison with which I might recognize the defects of my own nature?"[70] As *je suis* is the condition for the possibility of *je pense,* so the idea of the all-perfect is the condition for the possibility of the idea of the imperfect. The intelligibility of the imperfect rests upon the prior intelligibility of that which is being negated, the perfect. In its understanding, in its clarity and distinctness, the perfect or infinite possesses a priority to the imperfect and finite which is revealed in doubt. The experience of one's own doubt allows the certitude of one's own existence to emerge; the experience of one's own imperfection allows the idea of the all-perfect to surface, an idea already nonthematically present and operative as the measure by which the limitations of the ego are understood.

If the unity and coherence of Cartesian methodology is to be grasped, it must be understood that the methodological doubt allows focally important and primary proportions or relationships to be asserted. The initial effort of the skeptical analysis establishes four indubitable proportions, and these relationships—the object of the Universal Mathematics—allow the employment of this *mathesis universalis* within metaphysics.[71]

First, there is the proportion between thinking and existing. Doubt uncovers the existence of the thinking subject because thinking is relative to or dependent upon existing. It is not enough to say that this is not an inference but an intuition. Of what is it an intuition? Of a necessary proportion, an ineluctable and undeniable dependency: "I existed if I was convinced or even if I thought of anything . . . I must finally conclude and maintain that this proposition: *I am, I exist* is necessarily true every time that I pronounce it or conceive it in my mind." The relative, for its own intelligibility, discloses the presence of its correlative absolute: "I am, I exist—that is certain; but for how long do I exist? For as long as I think. For it might happen if I totally ceased thinking, that I would at the same time cease to be."[72]

Second, there is the proportion between thinking and its agent, the "I" which exists—whatever its nature. Thinking is an attribute, and an attribute is relative to something. It makes no sense to speak of thinking without the concomitant note that "I" is the absolute by which this activity is done. This also is not an inference, but the intuition of a proportion. Just as there is no thinking without existence, so there is no thinking (or existence) without the subject; hence the "I" irreducibly given: "It is much more evident, it must be observed, that it is very manifest by the natural light which is in our souls, that no qualities or properties pertain to nothing; and that where some are perceived, there must be some thing or substance (*rem sive substantiam*) on which they depend."[73] Thing or substance is not a term to be analyzed as much as it is primary in experience, like thought itself: "What then am I? a *res cogitans*" simply translates *je pense* into its obvious implications.

Third, there is the proportion between kinds of thought and the thinking subject. Thought is doubt, affirmation, denial, or understanding. The same "I" causes all of these activities; the same ego imagines and perceives, desires and rejects. The diversity of kinds of thinking, the plurality of thinking, is relative to the unity of the ego. Multiplicity, it has been noted in the *Regulae*, is always relative to an absolute. The diversity of thoughts, for their very diversity, demand the unity of the ego.

Fourth, there is the proportion between the imperfect and the perfect. Doubt is incomplete, imperfect, limited—but the imperfect, like the unequal, is intelligible only through its absolute, the perfect. The imperfect, proportional to the perfect which is its measure, suggests at least a notion of the perfect. Eventually, to account for such a notion, one must find a proportional cause, and this necessity opens up the question of the divine existence.

Antecedent to the actual inferences with which the Universal Mathematics establishes the divine existence, the four proportions have been established which lie at its basis: (1) the proportion between thinking and existing; (2) the proportion between activity and nature, between property and thing; (3) the proportion between plurality and unity; (4) the proportion between the imperfect and the perfect. In each of these proportions, the absolutes are not deduced or inferred from the relatives; they are given in the relatives as their intelligiblity and cause. The cause is found within the effect. Existence is found within thinking; the ego within existence and thinking; the single ego within the plurality of its own thoughts; and the perfect within the experience of the imperfect.

The crucial axiom *je pense, donc je suis* or *cogito ergo sum* provides the matrix for each of the three demonstrations of the existence of God.[74] Each term of this axiom becomes a crucial commonplace (*topic*) under which a diverse demonstration can be located and constructed. *Cogito* founds a demonstration from the object of thought, the idea of perfection, to its cause, the all-perfect. *Sum* founds a demonstration from the limited existence of the thinking thing to its independent and infinite cause. But the fundamental and formal connection, *ergo*, between the content of perfection and the reality of its existence is the final, *a priori* demonstration that indicates that existence is an absolutely necessary attribute of the all-perfect. The three Cartesian proofs develop from the deduction from the content of an idea to its cause, in the first demonstration, to the final deduction, from the content of an idea to its necessary attribute. The first reflexive principle, *je pense, donc je suis*, provides the common foundation and the diverse terms that ground all three.

The resemblance between this and the subsequent Cartesian physics is striking. In the physics, the subjects to be treated are all determined in terms of light: the sun and the fixed stars as the source of light; the sky as the transparent medium of light; the planets, the comets, and the earth as they reflect light; the elements insofar as they emit, conduct, or reflect light;

finally, the human being "since he is the observer of it."[75] So in the metaphysics, the soul, god, and the external world are unified as objects of one inquiry insofar as they are illumined by the *res cogitans*, by the reflexivity and certitude of the axiom: *cogito ergo sum*.

Just as the source of light is fire, so the source of the *cogito* is the *sum* of the rational soul. Thus efficient causality is already given in the intuited axiom, *cogito ergo sum*. The *sum* is not demonstrated from the *cogito*; it is exhibited as necessarily with it, as proportionately imperative. One recognizes immediately that there could be no *cogito* if there were no *sum*, and in this recognition the principle of causality is irreducibly and intuitively given. One does not demonstrate causality—one does not deduce deduction. One discovers it as another proportion, immediate, clear, and distinct within this fundamental certitude of metaphysics. "Thus the light of nature certainly tells us that nothing exists about which the question, why it exists, cannot be asked, whether we enquire for its efficient cause, or, if it does not possess one, demand why it does not have one."[76]

This, in turn, allows two types of causes to be drawn from Aristotle and the Scholastics: the formal cause, if the reason for existence is derived from the essential nature itself; and the efficient cause, if the reason for existence is other than the result to be explained.[77] The movement of the Cartesian proofs is from god as the efficient cause of his idea in a human mind to god as the formal cause of his own existence. "For in every single case, we must inquire whether a thing is derived from itself or from something else. . . . What is self-derived comes, as it were, from a formal cause; it results from having an essential nature which renders it independent of an efficient cause."[78] Thus it is quite correct to formulate the principle of causality and then to extend it to all reality: there is nothing in the effect that has not existed in a similar or more eminent way in the cause; more simply, nothing can come from nothing.[79] God's existence is not an exception to this principle of proportional dependence. Rather, "intermediate between efficient cause, in the proper sense, and no cause, there is something else, viz. the positive essence of a thing, to which the concept of efficient cause can be extended in the way in which in Geometry we are wont to extend the concept of a circular line, that is as long as possible, to that of a straight line; or the concept of a rectilinear polygon with an indefinite number of sides to that of a circle."[80] The mathematical examples are instructive; efficient cause approaches formal cause as a limit and formal cause is to be understood through efficient cause. Thus the divine power will stand as the efficient cause of the finite. The causality is different, but in both cases it is divine power.

In the first demonstration, the object of the *cogito* must be explained: the idea of perfection or infinity. Ideas are images of things, not in the sense of sensible imaginations, but as those which the mind directly perceives and which represent something. The word "idea" comes from the medieval discussion of the divine ideas, the forms of perception in the divine mind. In Descartes the roles are reversed: the content of things conforms to the divine ideas; the content of human ideas conforms to their inciting cause. In some way, human ideas copy their cause. Ideas, then, are both the direct object of the *cogito* and the representative result of whatever their cause: "Among my thoughts, some are like images of things (*tanquam rerum imagines*), and it is to these the term 'idea' properly applies, as when I think (*cogito*) man or chimera or sky or angel or God."[81]

As a modification of the *cogito*, ideas do not differ among themselves, and they emerge from the thinking subject's causality; but as "one idea represents one thing and another represents another thing, it is obvious that they are very different among themselves."[82] If we ask about the origin of ideas, then, we may ask two questions. First, what is the source of the idea as an idea, that is, as a modification of the thinking subject? The answer is always the same: the *cogito*. Second, what is the source of the content (what Descartes calls the objective reality) of the idea? Here we must search for a cause proportional to or greater than the content: "In order that an idea should contain one particular objective reality rather than another, it should no doubt obtain it from some cause in which there is at least as much formal reality as the idea contains objective reality."[83] To deny this would be to deny what "the light of nature" makes one clearly recognize: that our ideas may fall short of their archetype or source—that which "models" them— but the archetype or source cannot be less than its effect upon the *cogito*. The cause must be proportional to its effect.

What is the originating cause, then, of the idea of god, that is, the infinite substance or all-perfect substance against which I measure myself? Nothing less than god can account for it. The idea of the infinite or perfect substance can be explained only by the existence and causal efficacy of a proportional archetype.

> There is no more probability that the imperfection of the human intellect is the cause of our possessing the idea of God, than that ignorance of mechanical science should be the cause of our imagining some machine showing highly intricate contrivance. . . . On the contrary, clearly, if one possesses the idea of a machine which involves every contrivance that ingenuity can devise, it will be absolutely right to infer that it is the product of some cause, in which that extreme pitch of mechanical ingenuity was actually embodied, although in the idea it existed only objectively. By the same reasoning, when we have in us the idea of God, in which all thinkable perfection is contained, the evident conclusion is, that

the idea depends upon some cause in which all the perfection also exists, to wit in the God who really exists."[84]

The question that occasions this demonstration might be: Where did that idea come from? Where did you get that idea—of total perfection? The line of argumentation is basically simple: the content of the idea is an effect, something caused, something to be accounted for. But the imperfect ego cannot account for it; it only knows its own imperfections in terms of this infinitely greater measure. Nothing finite can account for the notion of limitless perfection; there is an infinite distance between them. The Universal Mathematics is searching for a cause which, by its own proportionality, can account for this effect, one which must possess at least as much perfection as the representative idea. Such an infinite or all-perfect must therefore exist, the one whom we know under the title of "god."

Only god can explain what under various modalities and in various philosophies is a central problem in Western philosophy: How is it that the human, the finite or imperfect, is *capax infiniti*—if only as an idea?

From the *cogito* as radical evidence, the second demonstration moves to *sum*.[85] Just as the *cogito* can be divided into many different ideas as diverse objects, so the *sum* can be divided into the multiple moments over which its duration lasts. The infinite as qualitative perfection is the object for the *cogito* from which it deduces the existence of god; the infinite as indefinite multiplicity is the quantity into which human existence can be distinguished, and which necessitates the affirmation of the conserving god. The past cannot account for my present existence, because each moment is a discrete unit whose causal dependency cannot lie with the past moment which no longer exists. Nor do I find within my limited self the power to produce myself each succeeding moment. The effect that must be explained is not a past moment, an initial moment of existence that one could call creation. The effect that must be explained is the moment that is now, "so it does not follow from the fact that I have existed a short while before that I should exist now, unless at this very moment some cause produces and creates me, as it were, anew, or, more properly conserves me."[86] And what must that be? Once more the proportionality of the causal principle functions crucially: there must be at least as much reality in the cause as in the effect. The effect is a being which can think and which has the idea of the total perfection of the divine nature. This effect is either self-caused (*a se*) or derivative from another (*ab alia*). If from another, then the question of derivation must be placed again until one reaches that which is *a se*—and this is to arrive at god for "to have the power to exist *per se*, it doubtlessly must also have the power to possess actually all the perfections whose idea it has within itself, i.e., all the perfections which I conceive to be in God."[87] In the initial demonstration, the evidence for the divine existence is the idea of the divine perfection, the all-perfect substance. In the second one, the evidence for the divine existence is the existence of a mind possessing this idea. In contrast to Aristotle and Thomas Aquinas, "I prefer to use as the foundation of my proof my own existence (rather than sensible things), which is not dependent upon any series of causes, and is so plain to my intelligence that nothing can be plainer."[88] Even more critically different, this evidence is not personal existence or human nature insofar as it involves both the mind and the body; "I have limited myself definitely to my position insofar as I am merely a thing that thinks."[89] In both Aquinas and Descartes, existence is a result to be explained. In Descartes this existence is known and defined by the prior indubitability of the *cogito*. The *cogito* exhibits the *sum*.

The choice of the perfection of god as the idea that warrants the affirmation of his existence is a critical one. It founds the demonstration of a proportional efficient cause *a posteriori*, as indicated above. In addition, it serves as the basis of two crucial *a priori* inferences. From the perfection of god, one can argue first to his veracity and thus justify the assertions that the universe exists and that human contact with it is available. With the veracity of god, one can exorcise the malignant demon. Second, one can argue to his existence as intrinsically contained within the meaning of total perfection. Perfection, then, becomes the governing concept, whose objective reality must be accounted for through a movement back to a proportional efficient cause and whose implications as formal cause must be traced into the proportional affirmations of both the corporeal world and the necessity of the divine existence.

First, the perfect one cannot deceive, either in himself or in what he establishes. God, then, is intrinsically and necessarily veracious—and his truth allows one to trust the apperceptive powers and instincts which god has given to the human person and to believe in the world to which they bear testimony. The hypothesis of a continually deceiving, all-powerful spirit falls before the guarantee which the nature of god gives to what he has formed. Very simply: the perfection of god is the formal cause of his creative truth; his creative truth guarantees the possibility of authentic knowledge and the actuality of an existing world. To deny either of these would be to deny the perfection of god, to believe in a power that was ultimately malignant.

This is a revolutionary moment in Western philosophy. It is not the sensible universe that is the evidence for god, but the nature of god that is the warrant for the sensible universe. One is deducing the universe as a relative reality from the truth of the absolute.

Second, there is the formal demonstration of the divine existence. In causal explanation, efficient cause approaches formal cause as a limit, an approximation. Both of the two previous demonstrations of god's existence move from effect to efficient cause, and in this neither of them mirrors the causality that is proper to mathematics. Mathematics moves through formal cause. The triangle with which the geometrician works may or may not exist outside his mind, but it does have properties or attributes which in no way are determined by his mind, attributes which can be deduced with apodictic certitude. In mathematics it is necessary to begin with this simple nature and then to demonstrate that its three angles are equal to two right angles or that its greatest angle subtends the longest side. The deductions of mathematics are independent of human choice or human intention. They can be deduced or discovered. They cannot be made up out of whole cloth. The deductive derivation of propositional properties from natures is typical of mathematical method.

The idea of god is that of the *entis summe perfecti*, the most perfect being.[90] What attributes can be deduced from this besides veracity? Existence. A supremely perfect being who lacks existence is a contradiction in terms. Every mathematician knows that to say that something is contained in the nature or concept of a thing is to say that it is true of that thing. But necessary existence is contained in the concept of the all-perfect which is god. Thus god not only exists, he must exist. It would be a contradiction to assert that the supremely perfect nature did not exist. Its meaning would not be the supremely perfect nature if it did not necessarily exist. If one can argue from the incompatibility of a square circle that it cannot exist, can one not argue from the very concept of the supremely perfect that it cannot not-exist? There is no question here of arguing from any nature, any structure of meaning, that it must exist. Descartes is simply pointing out that any particular nature—whether it exists only conceptually or also outside of the mind—has its proportional attributes. If one speaks of a Euclidian triangle, one is led ineluctably to posit as proportionally necessary that its three angles are equal to two right angles. This is the pattern of the deductions in all of mathematics, that what one clearly and distinctly understands to belong to the nature of any thing can be accurately affirmed of that thing. But in the very meaning of the all-perfect being existence is contained, otherwise it would not be all-perfect.

Some would argue here that existence is not contained within any meaning; but that is obviously incorrect. In the understanding of anything, some form of existence is implicitly contained. If we understand something clearly and distinctly, we understand it as at least possible. Possibly what? Possibly existing. If, on the other hand, we understand something intrinsically contradictory, we say that it is impossible. Impossible to do what? Impossible to exist. In both cases, there is an implication about existence contained within the nature itself. And if these structures of meaning can indicate possible existence or necessary nonexistence, what is so extraordinary about extending the modality of this attribution from the negative to the positive? Is it not obvious that the very meaning of the all-perfect necessarily excludes non-existence? "After we have with sufficient accuracy investigated the nature of God, we clearly and distinctly understand that to exist belongs to His true and immutable nature."[91] It would be an intrinsic contradiction for the all-perfect not to exist.

The development of the *Meditations* is analytic, one of discovery, and one in which it is necessary to withdraw the mind as far as possible from *rebus corporeis* in order to obtain the primary notions of metaphysics.[92] The initial demonstrations of the existence of god are admittedly *a posteriori*, still lacking the conciseness and precision that geometry offered in its *ratio demonstrandi*, though necessarily first because analysis leads a person step by step down the path of discovery. But here, in the demonstration *a priori*, the deduction of the existence of god mirrors the deduction of mathematics: the notion or nature of the supremely perfect entails proportionately its own necessary existence. Metaphysics has reached the level of geometry: "It is at least as certain that God, who is this perfect being, is or exists, as any demonstration of geometry can possibly be."[93] No mean achievement for a Universal Mathematics!

"The Fable of My World"

But the project is not quite finished. In fact, it is only begun.[94] The self has been established as a thinking thing. God has been affirmed in three different ways, and in all of them, as Descartes promised the theologians of the Sorbonne, human inquiry does not need to find its evidence "from any other source than our own mind."[95] Metaphysics has become an analytic inquiry into the implications of thinking itself.

What, then, is left to be demonstrated? Nothing but the physical universe, beginning with our own bodies! The sixth meditation opens with the breathtaking line: "Nothing more remains for me to do except to examine whether corporeal things exist."[96] The theologians had handed the problem of the divine existence over to the philosophers; indeed, they had become philosophers in order to discuss the issue. Yet however divergent the philosophies they embodied, they had one thing in common: they argued from the world to the existence and nature of god, whether that world was located in the existence of the contingent universe, the nature of cosmic design, the structures of the human person, or the cultural persuasion of nations. The Universal Mathematics in its metaphysical moment agreed that the issue of the divine existence is more in the realm of philosophy than of theology, but it reversed the procedure of philosophy totally. It is not the world that gives warrant for god. God must give warrant for the existence of the world. One can no longer maintain that god exists because the world exists. The world can only be affirmed against a pervasive skepticism because one knows that god must exist.

What has led to this strangely novel natural theology? The conjunction with which the Universal Mathematics began: the conjunction of the issue of a corrosive skepticism with the issue of atheism. One could profitably co-opt the skeptical tradition, even enlarge its claim by the hypothesis of the malignant demon whose every effort is to deceive human intelligence and convictions; but one could not put this wariness about all assertions to rest until the existence of god was established, a god so perfect that he cannot and will not deceive human beings. One exorcises the demon only by demonstrating the existence of god. Now it is safe to assert the world.

By the strangest of coincidences, the metaphysical method follows the pattern and progress traditionally associated with medieval theology. Jacques Maritain makes this point very well: "Descartes often seems to conceive Philosophy on the pattern of Theology."[97] It is not just that the "simple natures" function like the articles of faith in a Thomistic scheme of theological implications or that the laws of physics will be deduced from the attributes of god. Most profoundly, the divine truth must be that which guarantees all subsequent affirmations, precisely as in theology the *veritas prima*, which is god, warrants even the articles of faith. It is only "after having recognized that there is a God, and having recognized at the same time that all things are dependent upon him and that he is not a deceiver, that I can infer as a consequence that everything which I conceive clearly and distinctly is necessarily true."[98] Whether this statement puts Cartesian metaphysics into a hopeless circularity or not is much debated in subsequent philosophic reflection, but that is not the point at issue here.[99] What is to the point is the profound reversal of roles as the inquiring intellect connects the existence of god with the existence of the world. One builds out from god to corporeal nature, "in so far as it can be the object of pure mathematics."[100]

The world is saved for mathematics—and through mathematics, physics. Indeed, after the demonstrations of the existence and veracity of god, the first thing one can affirm about the material universe is not that it exists, but that one directly imagines extension, the continuous quantity whose coordinates lie in the dimensions of length, breadth, and depth. Size, figure, number, situation, and locomotion follow upon extension. Extension and its modes provide the introit to material objects: "Certainly I at least know that these can exist in so far as they are considered as the object of pure mathematics [*purae Matheseos objectum*], since I perceive them clearly and distinctly."[101] The astonishing thing about this procedure is not only Descartes' attempt to demonstrate the corporeal universe, but the pivotal place of mathematics in this demonstration. He can argue from the veracity of god and the uses of the imagination to the *persuasio* that the material world may with great probability exist. But its content is—whether probable or certain—the objects of pure mathematics and the world that embodies them.

Intellection cannot guarantee the existence of this extramental world; imagination can only indicate its probability. But there is a passive capacity in the knowing subject of receiving "the ideas of sensible things." Now what is the active capacity of causing such sensation? Not myself—these sensations arise without my active consent or causation, even against my will. "It must necessarily exist in some substance different from myself, in which all of the reality which exists objectively in the ideas produced by this faculty is formally or eminently contained." If eminently, this cause is god. Malebranche later takes this option, but Descartes rejects it because it would mean that god is a deceiver, and that would be contradictory to his nature. If formally, the world of corporeal reality does exist.[102] Descartes proves the existence of the world in the same way in which he initially proved the existence of god—by the necessary proportion between effect and cause.

Proportion—the subject of the Universal Mathematics—functions crucially again. This time, it gives Descartes not himself nor god, but a universe: "Therefore we must conclude that corporeal things exist. Nevertheless, they are perhaps not entirely what our senses perceive them to be, for there are many ways in which this sense perception is very obscure and confused." Then comes the clincher: "But we must at least admit that all things are in them which I conceive clearly and distinctly in them, that is to say, all things which, speaking generally, are comprehended in the object of pure mathematics [*in purae Matheseos objecto*]."[103] Everything else admits of doubt, but with a hope that it too can be raised to the same clarity as mathematical objects. Sensation can guarantee the existence of my own body and the bodies that surround it, but the ultimate intelligibility is through extension and its direct modifications. Universal Mathematics gives a method for first philosophy and issues in the diversities of pure and applied mathematics. Pure mathematics gives the universe its content and constitutes objects for physics.

Corporeal realities are simply extended objects or, even more simply, matter. "In this way we shall ascertain that the nature of matter or of body does not consist in its being hard, or heavy, or coloured, or one that affects our senses in some other way, but solely in the fact that it is a substance extended in length, breadth and depth." One can place this contention in a simple principle: "The nature of body consists not in weight, nor in hardness, nor colour, and so on, but in extension alone."[104] The difference between number and what is numbered, between quantity and extended substance is not a real distinction, but only "in our conception."[105] It is no great leap to the merger of mathematics with physics. Nothing more is needed: "I do not accept or desire any other principle in Physics than in Geometry or abstract Mathematics, because all the phenomena of nature may be explained by their means, and a sure demonstration can be given of them."[106] By identifying matter with extension, Descartes provides a universe whose ultimate truth is mathematics and a physics whose embodiment is mechanics. Newton also has mathematical principles of physics, but by identifying matter with mass he authors an entirely different physics. Descartes makes bodies extensions and mathematics their key.

The divine truth is to guarantee this mathematicized physical universe. It is no wonder that all of philosophy is like a single tree. Metaphysics is its roots, physics is its trunk, and all the other sciences are its branches, which can be unified under the three principal sciences: medicine, mechanics, and morals.[107] Etienne Gilson maintains that the central concern in the Cartesian organization of the sciences is physics, of which metaphysical inquiry is the necessary basis and medicine, mechanics, and ethical reflection consequences.[108] As metaphysics finds its evidence within mind, so physics finds its evidence within matter, matter mathematicized. The organization is clear, and the labor neatly divided.

But at what a cost! Descartes has left the world godless. Nothing that the traditional natural theology employed as subject-matter is beyond the skeptical doubt. With a flanking movement, the Cartesian attack has allowed doubt its full rush into the center of philosophy and then destroyed it on its own grounds. Mind, not the universe, bears the evidence for the divine existence. Just as the divine truth guarantees the external physical world, so the divine infinity removes from this universe any discernible final order and purpose: "For, knowing by now that my nature is extremely weak and limited and that God's, on the contrary, is immense, incomprehensible, and infinite, I no longer have any difficulty in recognizing that there are an infinity of things within his power the causes of which lie beyond the powers of my mind. And this consideration alone is sufficient to persuade me that all causes of the type we are accustomed to call final are useless in physical [or natural] affairs."[109] Remove final causes from the universe, and what do we have? A mechanical universe whose entire composition can be explained simply by matter and the laws of nature. So adequate is such a mechanical explanation that "even if God had created several worlds, there would have been none where these laws were not observed."[110] Start with chaos rather than with creation, grant the continued divine concurrence, and "all material objects could have become, in time, such as we see them at present."[111]

The revolution in theism which Descartes has instigated lies precisely here: the world has become godless. Metaphysics treats of god through the inquiry into mind; physics treats of the world through the mathematical inquiry into matter. Descartes does not draw the corollary from his metaphysics, but succeeding ages will draw it very clearly. The Cartesian mathematics has not left us without a universe; it has strongly asserted one. Indeed, it has done what no metaphysician until this time thought to do: it has demonstrated it. Descartes has not failed to assert that this universe depends upon god. It depends upon god not merely for its existence and continuance, as traditional metaphysics argued, but even for the truth of its mathematical axioms. 1 and 2 would not be 3 unless god had freely chosen this equation.[112] You cannot get much more dependent than that! But the world does not assert or witness the existence of god. Just as the human person became a hazardous unity between the machine that is the body and the thinking thing that is the ego, so the unity of the sciences became a fragile concatenation of a metaphysics that inquires into thinking and a physics that examines the mathematical possibilities of extension. Wisdom lay in keeping them together.

But if there is one thing that the history of philosophy indicates, it is that dualisms, especially dualisms of independent but conjoined substances, exhibit a radical unintelligibility. In Descartes' terms, a multiplicity is only relative to a further absolute. Within a generation, subsequent thinkers would attempt to collapse the distinction. Spinoza would make both *cogitans* and *extensa* the two known attributes of nature, but nature as *Natura naturans*, that is, of the infinite and eternal god, the single substance, with the human being as the correlative final modal consequence of the divine nature. Both Leibniz and Malebranche would attempt to keep the Cartesian diremption between mind and matter within the human person, but subsequent generations would find neither a preestablished harmony nor an occasionalism very convincing. Berkeley and the later idealist traditions would resolve the dualism finally in favor of mind, dynamic, creative, and projectional. Aram Vartanian draws attention to this last development and makes it the fundamental impetus in the development of French materialism: "Diderot was well aware, on this point, of Hobbes' paraphrase of the crucial sentence that underlay Cartesian metaphysics: 'I think, therefore matter can think.'"[113] The intrinsic lack of unity in Cartesian philosophy proved to be a dialectical contradiction whose resolution lies at the heart of the development of modern Western philosophy.

For metaphysics cannot offer a principle of unity that justifies the duality of spirit and matter, and by making metaphysics deal with one and physics deal with the other it exiles metaphysical inquiry from extramental reality, whether in terms of process or in terms of being. One cannot ask directly about the real as such, and if the metaphysical foundation fails, one cannot turn back to the world for certitude or for the evidence which the Cartesian

Universal Mathematics has already yielded up to motion and the laws of nature. The world is now the field of mechanics; it can prove nothing about god's existence in a philosophy that must use god to prove the world.

The subsequent history of philosophic theology lends a certain irony to the confident reassurance with which Descartes (*Eudoxus*) introduces the Universal Mathematics with its skeptical solvents in his uncompleted dialogue, the *Search for Truth*: "I confess that it is not without great danger that one ventures without a guide when one does not know the ford, and many have lost their way in doing so; but you have no reason to fear if you follow after me."[114]

SECTION 2. God in the Discourse of a Universal Mechanics: Isaac Newton

If the central philosophical issue for Descartes was to distinguish between the certain and the doubtful, for Isaac Newton it was to discriminate between the real and the apparent.[1] For Descartes, the initial imperative for philosophic inquiry was to establish those proportions within metaphysics which could be intuitively and indubitably grasped. For Newton, the first necessity was to find the devices by which one could derive absolute and true mathematical motion, with its space and time. Descartes found his principle within the reflexive implications between thinking and being; Newton determined that his principle was the motive force whose properties, causes, and effects could establish true motion, and, consequently, true duration and extension. For Descartes, the fundamental examination was *dubitatio*, by which the indubitable principle could be exhibited and from which other proportions could be deduced. For Newton, the fundamental examination was the experiment with two globes connected by a cord and revolving longitudinally around a single axis perpendicular to the cord. Descartes, even when he was doing mechanics, was doing mathematics. Newton, even when he was doing mathematics, recognized that geometry is founded in mechanical practice and is nothing but that part of Universal Mechanics which accurately proposes and demonstrates the art of measuring.[2] Universal mechanics—*Mechanica universalis*. Perhaps no phrase better indicates how radically the intellectual enterprise changed with Isaac Newton.

A Visit from Edmond Halley

The great system of Newton began not with the doubts of others, but with their achievements, and nowhere were these achievements so ready to hand and so disposed to a comprehensive assimilation as in mechanics, perhaps especially in celestial mechanics. Descartes was struggling against Montaigne who in his turn was discrediting Raymond of Sebond. Newton was building upon Johannes Kepler who had built upon the painstaking observations of Tycho Brahe and the revolution of Nicolaus Copernicus. Indeed, in an uncharacteristically conciliatory letter to Robert Hooke, Newton wrote of his historic debts: "What Descartes did was a good step. You have added much several ways, and especially in taking ye colours of thin plates in philosophical consideration. If I have seen further it is by standing on ye sholders of Giants."[3] Newton did what Descartes would never have done— not merely in citing the medieval Bernard of Chartres, but in understanding his own work as a continuation of the work of others. He mentioned Christopher Wren, Edmond Halley, and the always contentious Hooke as contributing to the law of the inverse square, as well as "the excellent book of *De Horologio Oscillatorio*" of Christian Huygens.[4] He generously called Wren, John Wallis, and Huygens "the greatest geometers of our time."[5] But "the giants" for Newton were not his contemporaries but his predecessors: Copernicus, Tycho Brahe, Kepler, and Galileo. The project at hand for Newton was to build with the materials which the previous age had quarried, to bring to completion a Universal Mechanics which would construct the system of the world, and to open a line of inquiry which would "derive the rest of the phenomena of Nature, by the same kind of reasoning from mechanical principles."[6]

But to launch this project a visit from Edmond Halley was needed. In the preface to the first edition of the *Principia*, Newton alludes to the visit, in August, 1684. During the preceding year, Wren had been in conversation with Halley and Hooke and had promised a book worth forty shillings to the associate who produced within two months an adequate demonstration of the motion of the heavenly bodies by the law of the inverse square. Two years later, Halley recounted their failure in a letter to Newton: "I declared the ill success of my attempts. . . . Mr. Hook then said that he had it, but would conceale it for some time that others triing and failing might know how to value it, when he should make it publick; however I remember Sr. Christopher was little satisfied that he could do it, and tho Mr. Hook then promised to shew it him, I do not yet find that in that particular he had been as good as his word."[7]

In August of 1684, Halley went down to Cambridge to consult Newton, without then describing the situation which he would explain two years later. He simply put to Newton the question of the orbit of a planet if the gravitational attraction were to be calculated in inverse ratio to the square of the distance from the sun. Newton replied that is would be an ellipse. And how did he know? "Why, I have calculated it." Halley pressed him for the calculations, but Newton was unable to find them. The visit concluded with Newton's promise to send them.[8]

That September, Newton began to lecture during the Michaelmas Term *"de motu corporum."* He usually lectured one term a year, and each of his nine lectures lasted about half an hour. The previous lectures had been devoted to optics, arithmetic, and algebra. Now, in the fall of 1684, he was to lecture in mechanics. These lectures constitute the germ, as René Dugas notes, of the first book of the *Principia.* The definitions, the laws of motion, and the initial proposition succeeded one another in a manner which foreshadows the order and content of the completed work. The next year's lectures on the movement of bodies continued from where they had broken off the previous year. By 1687, the Michaelmas lectures had progressed into the matter of the third book, the system of the world.

Halley had visited again in November, 1684; the first public results emerged when Newton submitted to the Royal Society the *Propositiones de motu.* A letter from Newton to Aston, Secretary of the Royal Society, dated February 23, 1687, thanked Aston for having recorded his "notions concerning motions." The massive work was gradually taking shape during the seventeen months from December, 1684, to April, 1686.[9] The cost of publication seemed prohibitive to the Royal Society, but once again Halley appeared as the support behind the ponderous enterprise. In June, 1686, the Council of the Royal Society gave its decision that "Mr. Newton's book be printed," and indicated the critical help that had been given with the addendum "that E. Halley undertake the business of looking after it, and printing it at his own charge, which he engaged to do."[10] There was never an acknowledgement more merited than that which Newton delivered in the preface to the first edition: "In the publication of this work the most acute and universally learned Mr. Edmond Halley not only assisted me in correcting the errors of the press and preparing the geometrical figures, but it was through his solicitations that it came to be published; for when he had obtained of me my demonstrations of the figure of the celestial orbits, he continually pressed me to communicate the same to the Royal Society, who afterwards, by their kind encouragements and entreaties, engaged me to think of publishing them."[11]

Notice what interested Halley. It was not a new method of inquiry that would allow mathematical certitude in areas of investigation which until then had been only probable and whose conclusions had been habitually greeted with skepticism. It was not, in other words, anything like the problematic of Descartes. Halley was interested in the "demonstrations of the figures of the celestial orbits," the extraordinary unity which the law of the inverse square brought to the Copernican revolution, the observations of Tycho Brahe, and the geometry of Kepler. Newton had taken the work of his predecessors and systematized the universe in a synthesis of terrestrial motion (parabolic trajectories) and celestial motion (conic sections—ellipses and hyperbolae). The universality of this achievement underlies both the enthusiastic nagging of Halley and the inevitability of the theological question. And though the personal life of the historical Newton is not of final interest in the internal argument and effective history of his work, the *Principia* itself pays a multiform credit to the indefatigable Halley.

The comprehensive view of the sciences made the issue of god inevitable for Descartes; the comprehensive nature of mechanics made it inevitable for Newton. Newton wrote a mechanics of the world that also explained the world as a mechanical system. This ineluctably raised questions about the one whom Newton called "the Author of the system." As he wrote to Richard Bentley on December 10, 1692: "When I wrote my treatise about our Systeme, I had an eye upon such Principles as might work wth considering men for the beliefe of a Deity and nothing can rejoyce me more then to find it usefull for that purpose."[12] Copernicus, Tycho Brahe, Kepler, and the law of the inverse square led to the Newtonian system. The system led to god.

Tycho Brahe seems at first sight an odd choice to be among the giants of Newton. He is seldom mentioned in Newton's works, and he had been proven wrong about many things. He had fought the Copernican revolution of the earth around the sun and the diurnal rotation of the earth on its axis, while maintaining the sphere of the fixed stars and the finitude of the universe. On all of these points, the *Principia* sided with Tycho's adversaries. He had, however, provided the empirical foundations for the subsequent work of all celestial mechanics. His first recorded observation, dealing with the conjunction of Saturn with Jupiter, had found all of the almanacs, ephemerides, and even the Copernican tables seriously inaccurate. Tycho devoted almost the next forty years to the accurate observation of stellar positions, magnitudes, variations in the motion of the moon, and the great comet of 1577. From the Danish observatory on the island of Hven, Uraniborg, poured forth a cascade of astronomical observations, adjusted for the first time for atmospheric refraction. Tycho Brahe was of crucial importance not because of the system he elaborated—that would perish, along with other systems—but because of his assemblage of precise data and facts, which he left to his assistant to edit and interpret, a young man by the name of Johannes Kepler.[13]

In 1601, Kepler succeeded Tycho as imperial mathematician at Prague and continued his minute observations of the orbit of Mars. The data assembled finally dislodged both the uniform circular motion and the cycles and epicycles of Copernicus. None of these geometric forms inherited from Ptolemy could square with the precision of Tycho Brahe's facts. In place of the circular motion of Copernicus, Kepler used the *Conic Sections* of Apollonius of Perga to affirm that the orbit of Mars was an ellipse, with the sun at one of its two foci. In place of uniform motion, the traversing of equal arcs of a perimeter in equal intervals of time, Kepler found that the planet described equal areas of the ellipse in equal intervals of time. Kepler's first two laws were published in 1609 in *Astronomia nova*. The subtitle of this work, *Commentaries on the Motion of Mars*, gave away its observational basis. In 1619, Kepler published *Harmonices mundi*, with what has come to be termed his third or harmonic law, the sesquialteral proportion between the periodic times of the planets and their average distance from the sun. For any planet the cube of the mean distance from the sun is in a constant ratio to the square of the time required to complete its orbit. Kepler had taken the data provided by Tycho Brahe and reduced them to three geometrical descriptions of the cosmos. These three laws now demanded a single principle that would bring them into a systematic unity. Somehow or other Kepler himself looked forward to such a work: "I say that the veritable inclinations of the planets to a royal way, the causes, quantities and places of motion, the limits and the nodes, all these things and others unknown until now, are hidden in the Pandects of a future age, the book that the immortal God, arbiter of the centuries, will reveal to men."[14] When Halley made his first visit to Newton, he may well have thought that the time for the Pandects had come.

If the history of astronomy provided the resources for the "system, the world," it also provided the ambiguities of the problems to be resolved. For millenia, the motion of the sun around the earth had been taken for granted. Greek astronomy has been scored in contemporary textbooks for being based more on philosophical thinking than on observation. That is almost exactly wrong. Greek observers saw the sun rise in the east and set in the west. The sensory experience of every person suggested that there was a uniform circular motion of fixed stars around the earth, that the sky itself rotated westward, leaving these stars at rest among themselves to move as a unit. One could see the wandering of the planets and the irregular movements of the sun and the moon. An occasional genius like Aristarchus of Samos in the third century B.C. advocated the contradiction of direct sensory observation, insisting that despite all appearances the sun was the center of the planetary system, and the earth was not stationary but in annual revolution about the sun and in daily rotation on its axis. But Greek astronomical opinion and common sense were too strong for him, and the astronomies of Aristotle and Ptolemy were erected to "save these appearances." The Greeks were careful about their observations. Hipparchus of Bithynia in the second century B.C. did for Ptolemy what Tycho Brahe did for Kepler, and Ptolemy's *Almagest* provided geometrical interpretations of the observations which had been painstakingly recorded for centuries.

The startling thing about Copernius' theory was not that it relativized the earth by removing it from the center of the universe. For the Christian, there was no great honor in being the center of the universe. Any reader of Dante knew that the center of the universe was hell! Copernicus' *De revolutionibus orbium* was revolutionary because it contradicted the observations that were apparent to every human being. In the name of mathematics, it demanded that one no longer think of the sun rising and setting, but of the earth rotating and orbiting. Sensible experience gave no immediate reason to think of the earth rotating on its axis or in orbit around the sun. As anyone could plainly see, the earth remained at rest and the sun was obviously in motion. If an astronomical system was to be elaborated that proposed something other than the Aristotelian or Ptolemaic universe, it would have to be a system that did not make sensible experience apodictic in any immediate way. It would have to distinguish between the real and the apparent. It would have to free itself from the *praejudicia quaedam* that the merger of the apparent and the real had fathered. For the *vulgus*, the common people, conceive the quantities of motion, rest, space, and time "under no other notion than the relation they bear to sensible objects."[15]

Pappus of Alexandria in the *Synagoge* had indicated for Newton that the ancients took mechanics as of the greatest value (*maximi*) in the investigation of natural things. Recent thinkers (*recentiores*), freed from the Aristotelian explanations through substantial forms or occult qualities that had dominated later scholasticism, had returned to recall (*revocare*) the phenomena of nature to mathematical laws. This merger of mathematics and natural philosophy spelled out Newtonian mechanics. But this union was not consummated by making mathematics fundamental to mechanics, which constituted the possibility for Descartes' Universal Mathematics. In Newton, the opposite was the case: Geometry itself was grounded in mechanical practice: it was part of mechanics.[16] And here again it was necessary to distinguish between what was commonly held and what was actually the case.

The ancients distinguished rational mechanics from practical mechanics. Rational mechanics proceeded by geometric demonstrations, while practical mechanics proceeded through skill and by knack: "A Vulgar Mechanick can practice what he has been taught or seen done, but if he is in an error he knows not how to find it out and correct it, and if you put him out of his road, he is at a stand; Whereas he that is able to reason nimbly and judiciously about figure, force, and motion, is never at rest till he gets over every rub. Experience is necessary, but yet there is the same difference between a mere practical Mechanick and a rational one, as between a mere practical Survey or Guâger and a good Geometer, or between an Empirick in Physick and a learned and a rational Physitian."[17] Unfortunately, over the years "mechanical" had been applied simply to the "vulgar mechanick" and had been distinguished from "geometrical." Since human mechanics are

accustomed (*soleant*) to work with too little accuracy, the distinction between the geometrician and the mechanic came in time to be made in terms
of accuracy: "That which is perfectly accurate is called geometry; what is
less so is called mechanical."[18] It was only a short step to Descartes, who
took the accuracy of geometry and made it a guarantee of an indubitable
procedure and the criterion of those simple proportions which investigation
should take as its first objects.

But Newton would have none of it. Accuracy is a question of the human
person, not of the science or the art itself. One who works with less accuracy
is simply a less perfect mechanic or geometer. Newton separated himself not
only from Descartes but from the Aristotelian tradition with its substantial
forms and qualitative inquiries. In Aristotle, the subject-matter dictates the
accuracy possible, and to search in ethics for the same precision that is
obtained in physics marks an uneducated man.[19] In Newton, accuracy does
not distinguish either among the sciences or among their several subject-
matters. It specifies their practitioners, and nothing else. Newton's position
allows a mechanics that will eventually and profitably be brought to bear, as
the ancients' had been and Descartes himself had envisaged, on all of the
phenomena of nature.

An even stronger reason, however, prohibits a separation or adequate
distinction between geometry and mechanics. Mechanics lies at the foundation of geometry. "The description of right lines and circles, upon which
geometry is founded, belongs to mechanics." Here lies a radical reversal
from the mechanics of Descartes—even from the mechanics of Boyle. In
both, mechanics comes out of mathematics, not mathematics out of mechanics. Boyle also distinguished two senses of "mechanics." But even when
the term was understood in an extended sense it did not subsume geometry,
it applied it: "I do not here take the Term *Mechanicks* in that stricter and
more proper sense, wherein tis wont to be taken, when tis us'd onely to
signifie the Doctrine about the Moving Powers (as the Beam, the Leaver, the
Screws, and the Wedg,) and of framing Engines to multiply Force; but I here
understand the word Mechanicks in a larger sense, for those Disciplines that
consist in the Applications of pure Mathematicks to produce or modifie
Motion in inferior Bodies."[20]

Newton also takes mechanics "in a larger sense," indeed, in a universal
sense. But he does so by denying that geometry is a pure mathematics,
essentially uninvolved in mechanics. In order to do geometry, such figures as
right angles and circles must be described, and this is a problem for
mechanics: "Geometry does not teach us to draw these lines, but requires
them to be drawn, for it requires that the learner should first be taught to
describe these accurately before he enters upon geometry. . . . The solution
of these problems is required from mechanics, and by geometry the use of

them, when so solved, is shown. . . . Therefore geometry is founded in mechanical practice, and is nothing else than that part of universal mechanics which accurately proposes and demonstrates the art of measuring" (*fundatur igitur Geometria in praxi mechanica, et nihil aliud est quam Mechanicae universalis pars illa, quae artem mensurandi accurate proponit ac demonstrat*).[21] This sentence is crucial. Here, perhaps more than in any of his subsequent disagreements about gravity and vortices, Newton's disagreement with Descartes lies poised at its critical point. A Universal Mathematics that takes proportion for its subject could dictate both methodology and principle to first philosophy and extrapolate the nature of material things as geometric extensions. A Universal Mechanics will have to begin at the other point of departure: with material things and their careers, now articulated as mass, motion, and change, with force as the abiding and comprehensive cause, to build an all-inclusive science which must take up questions that Descartes had relegated to metaphysics. The fundamental and inclusive science, which will epistemologically give a method to the philosophy of Newton and architectonic unity to all the sciences with their subject-matter, is mechanics.

Startling as its enunciaton may have been at the time, this universal view of mechanics finds its tradition reaching back to Heron of Alexandria and Pappus of Alexandria. The first line of the *Principia* alludes to the eight book of Pappus' *Synagoge*, and it is here that this massive extension of mechanics can be located. Mechanical theory surpasses Aristotelian physics because it deals not just with the natural movements of bodies, but also with the propulsion of bodies by forces in directions contrary to their natural, "physical" tendencies. It further surpasses Aristotle because it treats the subject of physics itself mathematically. This enlargement of the subject and the mathematicizing of the method allowed the school of Heron to make mechanics a universal discipline, whose basic divisions—even as Newton later described them—were into rational (λογικόν) and manual (χειρουργικόν) sections: "The rational part is composed of geometry, arithmetic, astronomy and physics; the manual includes metal work, architecture, carpentering, painting, and anything which involves manual skill." Rational mechanics included almost all of those arts which would later constitute the medieval quadrivium; and manual mechanics, all of those dexterities which would be called, in the most narrow sense, the mechanical arts. Together, they bestowed a universality on mechanical theory that allowed it in the minds of philosophers and mathematicians to take "perhaps first place [σχεδὸν πρώτη] among the natural inquiries which deal with the matter of the elements in the world."[22]

Newton changed the ambiguous σχεδὸν πρώτη to the straightforward *maximi*, but the mechanical theory that frames the *Principia* allowed him to separate true motion from apparent—as the mechanics of Heron and Pappus allowed an inquiry into rest (στάσεως), the movement around the center of gravity (φορᾶς), and the locomotion of bodies in general (τῆς κατὰ τόπον κινήσεως ἐν τοῖς ὅλοις).[23] If such a science was to be true, motions and rests as well as the time in which they occurred and the space in which they took place would have to be absolute. And this means mathematical. Failure to distinguish the true from the apparent, to see the necessary distinction between a motion whose reality lay simply in the perspective of the observer and one that was absolute, actually in process whether observed or not, would hopelessly limit an astronomical system. Newtonian mechanics demands a distinction between those movements which are commonly held because commonly perceived (*vulgares*) and those whose foundations lie in mathematical demonstration (*mathematicas*). Consequently, mechanics allows identities to be drawn: true motion is absolute motion is mathematical motion; similarly, apparent motion is relative motion is commonly perceived motion. The same distinctions and equations can be determined for time, space, place, and rest. Mechanics allows each of these to be determined independently of immediate observation and sensible perception, perhaps even in seeming contradiction to them. The real does not identify with the phenomenal, it underlies it. So observation and experience are not the last word; they are the first word, and a word that needs further analysis to be understood.

In this division of the basic objects of mechanics into the real and the apparent, real time becomes duration and apparent time becomes the sensible measurement of that duration. Absolute space is always immovable and consequently always the same. It is eternal. Relative space is only the sensible measure of this space "which our senses determine by its position to bodies." Place constitutes that part of this space which a body (mass) occupies. Relative place is the sensible measure of place by perceptible objects. Such definitions of time, space, and place allow the critical distinction between real and apparent motions: "absolute motion is the translation of a body from one absolute place to another, and relative motion, the translation from one relative place to another." These absolutes constitute the object and coordinates of Universal Mechanics, whose purpose is to reach real motion and to determine its origins and characteristics. To accomplish this, one must forswear absolutizing sensible experience. Mechanics demands this abstraction from perception without a reversion either to Aristotelian occult qualities or to a simple relativizing of all physical knowledge. The critical methodological question is *how*? Mechanics focuses upon precisely this issue, which provides the problem for which the *Principia* was written: "How we are to obtain the true motions from their causes, effects, and apparent differences, and the converse shall be explained more at large in the following treatise. For to this end it was that I composed it."[24]

At this point the changes in astronomy intersect with the radical changes in dynamics itself. Motion, in the "New Science" of Galileo, dispensed with any need for simultaneous causes which all movement had demanded both in the physics of Aristotle and in some of the subsequent discussions in dynamics of the fourteenth and fifteenth centuries. It is obvious, Galileo maintained, that if a body is placed on an inclined plane and allowed to fall freely, its velocity will increase; if the same body is projected up the same inclined plane, its velocity will decrease: "From this it follows that motion along a horizontal plane is perpetual." Hence Galileo's statement that removes all causal influence from uniform motion: "We may remark that any velocity once imparted to a moving body will be rigidly maintained as long as the external causes of acceleration or retardation are removed, a condition which is found only on horizontal planes."[25] Motion in this mathematicized physics has become local motion and local motion has become velocity, a ratio of distance and time.

The first kind of motion is uniform motion, "one in which the distances traversed by the moving particle during any equal intervals of time, are themselves equal"—and it needs no cause or force for its explanation.[26] The second kind of motion is naturally accelerated motion, in which equal increments of speed are given during equal intervals of time.[27] The purpose of this "new science" is not to "investigate the *cause* of the acceleration of natural motion, concerning which various opinions have been expressed . . . but to investigate and to demonstrate some of the *properties* (whatever the cause of this acceleration may be)." Perhaps the critical property is given in the second theorem, that the spaces described by a body falling from rest with a uniformly accelerated motion are to each other as the squares of the time intervals employed in traversing these distances.[28] This allows the analysis of the third kind of motion, a compound of the other two, that is, of uniform velocity and uniform acceleration. It is the motion of the moving projectile. Its geometric description rests, Galileo wrote, on "this hypothesis, namely, that the horizontal motion remains uniform, that the vertical motion continues to be accelerated downwards in proportion to the square of the time, and that such motions and velocities as these *combine* without altering, disturbing, or hindering each other."[29] This "hypothesis" is, of course, "ideal." The actual event will always be disturbed by the resistance of the medium; but it approximates so closely Newton's second law of motion that he later wrote: "By the first two Laws [of the *Principia*] and the first two Corollaries, Galileo discovered that the descent of bodies varied as the square of time [*in duplicata ratione temporis*] and that the motion of projectiles was in the curve of a parabola."[30]

The mechanics of Galileo did more than provide Newton with his first two laws of motion, however; it also provided the complexity of the problem with which the *Principia* dealt. True motion must be distinguished from apparent motion. But motion as such, without acceleration or deceleration, does not have a proportional cause which accounts for its continuance. Only a change in motion has a proportional cause. How, then, can one get to true motion when it is neither the object of sensible observation nor the result of a corresponding cause? Without a solid establishment of true motion, instead of merely sensible displacements, any unified view of the universe is at best relative, provisional, and tenuous.

Newton's problem is not totally unlike Descartes'. The *Meditations* need a principle that would enable one to distinguish the certain from the uncertain and to build a metaphysics that would establish the self, god, and the world—a metaphysics that would found a physics. The *Principia* collapses this division between metaphysics and physics into a Universal Mechanics, for which it will be appropriate to inquire into the existence of god from the evidence offered by the appearance of things.[31]

This indicates something of the multiple problematic that Newton engaged and that emerged from the intertwining histories of astronomy and mechanics. Only a few years before, John Wilkins' *Mathematical Magic* had distinguished these sciences from one another: "*Astronomy* handles the quantity of heavenly motions, *Musick* of sounds, and *Mechanicks* of weights and powers."[32] Boyle would extend the meaning of the word "Mechanicks in a larger sense, for those Disciplines that consist in the Applications of pure Mathematicks to produce or modifie Motion in inferior Bodies."[33] Newton extended the meaning to universality. Through his reading of Pappus, he obtained a tradition from Heron that subsumed mathematics into a Universal Mechanics. But this left the *Principia* with two sequential problems. First, how to distinguish and chart true motion from apparent so that the mechanical descriptions would match real movement and not just that which was contingent upon perspective. Upon the resolution of this issue hung the truth or falsity of the mechanics in the *Principia*. Second, how to demonstrate from the principles of such a mechanics the movements so painstakingly noted by Tycho Brahe and so brilliantly geometrized by Kepler into a single system of the universe. The first issue deals with the mathematical principles that constitute the laws and conditions of absolute movements; the second with the demonstration from these principles of the entire *constitutionem systematis mundani*.[34] The first issue must be resolved in order to have a true mechanics; the second must be resolved in order that this mechanics be universal.

Out of these, the great theological issue of the existence and nature of god would emerge. Newton needed a principle to enable the *Principia* to distinguish appearance from reality and true movement from sensible displacement, a principle with which the world can become a system and the problem of god be discussed within this new natural philosophy. Only in this way can the Universal Mechanics unify into a single discipline the critical questions of dynamics, of astronomy, and of theology. All this was involved in the visit and question of Edmond Halley in that August of 1684, a question about the demonstration of the orbits of the heavenly bodies, if the gravitational attraction were to be calculated by the inverse ratio of the squares of their respective distances from the sun: "And how do you know?" "Why, I have calculated it."

The Derivation of the Real: Absolute Space and Absolute Time

The initial problem for the *Principia* was to get to the real. For Descartes, this had been a second problem, consequent upon the establishment of the certain. From the certitude about the existent, thinking self, the *Meditations* and the *Discourse on Method* had built out to the real, extramental world through the guarantees of the truthful god. The Cartesian theological assertion was imperative to a true statement in physics. In Newton's *Principia*, it was the reverse: theology followed from mechanical statements and a mechanical system. It did not sustain their validity antecedently. The principle from which the real could be deduced was not God. But if not god, then what?

Using the distinctions of the Heronians of Alexandria as related by Pappus, Newton defined his own enterprise within the ambit of rational, rather than practical, mechanics. His rational mechanics became within Universal Mechanics "the science of [1] motions which result from any forces whatsoever and of [2] forces which are required for whatsoever motions—accurately proposed and demonstrated."[35] This description of mechanics entails a causal relationship between the generation of movement and the influence of force. The sensible perception of movement, the observation of the translation of a body from one place to another, cannot distinguish between real movement and apparent. Therefore one must establish a principle apodictic enough to allow this differentiation to be asserted, a principle other than the sensible determination of one body by another. In no sense will bodies as such explain either themselves or their influence; that would be to resolve natural phenomena into physical hypotheses, substantial forms, and occult qualities, to trace phenomena back to *causamve aut rationem physicam*. Neither the perspectives of the skeptic nor the natures of the Aristotelian can function as an accurately discriminating principle. This differentiation will have to be derived somehow from that which effects motions and that to which motions can be resolved, that is, from forces. Thus the *Principia* inaugurates the subject of mechanics, real motions, with a series of eight definitions which build one upon the other until they reach motive force.

These definitions in the *Principia* accomplish two important tasks. First, they begin with the phenomenal and end with the underlying real. Second, they open with simple factors to build more complex concepts and then take a general conception to break it down into its component units. In other words, the argument through the series of definitions proceeds toward the real as that which sustains and explains the phenomenal, and it exhibits the basic Newtonian methods of composition and division. It is not simply a matter of taste, as Mach would have it, whether making explicit the concept of force is done in one or in several definitions.[36] It is a matter of methodology. The process of definition in Newton exhibits the influence both of his interpretation of what is real within human experience and of the methods by which the absolute is to be analyzed and established.

It had been otherwise. In *De motu corporum in gyrum*, the earliest version of those manuscripts that were to be embodied in the first sections of the *Principia*, Newton had used only three definitions, not eight. In *De motu corporum in mediis regulariter cedentibus*, the definitions had run into a series of eighteen. There are obvious changes and a decision was made that these eight should be prefixed to the *Principia*.[37] Why?

In the *De motu corporum in gyrum* the three definitions were those of centripetal force, inertia, and the resistance of the medium. In the *Principia*, resistance of the medium becomes another form of inertia, and inertial force itself is understood through the compositions of the previous definitions. Centripetal force, on the other hand, is broken down into its various quantities, whose subsequent composition results in motive force. In this series of definitions motive force becomes a comprehensive principle. Motive force is that by which all bodies and their inertias can be known and to which all impressed forces in the *Principia* can be reduced. In the *Principia*, motive force is the name of the game—and it takes the definitional sequence to begin to play it.

The definitional sequence underscores the contradiction which the Universal Mechanics poses to the mechanics of Descartes and to the physical doctrine of Leibniz. In both of these, the distinction between the apparent and the real is drawn as severely as it is in Newton. But the apparent for Leibniz and Descartes is force itself, whether gravitational or magnetic; the real is invisible particles—bodies—whose pressures and vortices cause the motions which were so mistakenly attributed to a distance force. The real for them is this underlying *plenum* with its swirling and endless movement; the merely apparent, what the English mechanist was so mysteriously calling forces. "To this Newton's thoughts were completely opposed; forces, he thought, were real and prior, though he recognized that there might be still deeper explanations of the way the force worked. The first thing was to find out the nature of the force itself, the laws it obeyed, not to imagine hypotheses about streams of invisible particles."[38] Newton's series of eight definitions is essential if bodies are not to be made absolute and force is to be asserted as comprehensive.

Thus the phenomenon with which the definitions begin is that of body, but body mathematicized as mass (*massa*). Mass is a quantity of matter, the product of its density and size, a quantity which is familiar to anyone as it is known (though not defined) through weight or as it is refined by such experiments as Boyle's investigations into the compression of gases. Nothing of this is to be predicated of a hypothetical medium which is alleged to pervade freely the spaces which intervene between bodies. For "body" is what everyone and anyone can perceive; that which has no weight and offers no resistance may be termed many things (as it has been in the history of physics), but it cannot be named mass or body. The perennial criticisms that have surrounded Newton's definition of mass have usually failed to perceive that it is an initial step toward the assimilation of body into inertial force. The great Ernst Mach calls it a "pseudo-definition"; he correlatively fails to grasp the internal dynamic of definitional movement toward principle.[39] René Dugas correctly remarks that with the exception of an incidental remark in Huygens' *De vi centrifuga*, "the concept of mass or 'quantity of matter' belongs properly to Newton."[40] Whatever its origins, mass does figure centrally in the *Principia* but only as subsumed into force. Without force, mass is simply and literally an unknown quantity, unable to be determined and inoperant in any dynamics. So the first three definitions build conceptually a dynamic understanding of body.

In the first definition, density and size are the simple factors whose product is mass (*massa*), the quantity of matter. The second definition adds mathematical movement, that is, velocity, to mass in order to get a quantity of motion (*motus*), which later writers call momentum. The third definition adds the external influence of another body to get change (*mutatio*). Change allows for a reconsideration of mass itself. For the power to resist this change is the *materiae vis insita*, the inherent force of matter, and it differs from "the inertia of the mass" itself only in its manner of conception. Mass was initially defined without qualities and without change. It reveals what it is, what this precise quantity of matter is, in its resistance to change. Thus there are two levels in the definition of mass: one is phenomenal in its perception and relative in its conceptualization; the other, in the third definition, is mathematical, absolute, and real, and is defined not in terms of density and volume but in terms of force. The mechanical intelligibility of mass lies in a force, an innate force, by which it tends to resist alien forces and to continue in its present state, whether at rest or in rectilinear movement.[41]

The inherent force of matter or inertial force which reveals the mass is itself evoked by impressed force. Innate force is a potency to resist; impressed force is an *actio* which is alien to the innate force and which has its effect in change or alteration. The fourth definition adds impressed force as the second kind of force, and the process of definition begins to break this general kind of force into its several parts. Impressed force can come either from percussion, from pressure, or from centripetal force. Percussion would end with a universe in random and chaotic movement, a billiard table in which everything would be the result of chance and thus finally unintelligible. Pressure would demand Cartesian vortices in an endless swirl to account for its efficacy. It would reduce mechanical inquiry to the "hypotheses" that have no place within it.[42] Furthermore, neither percussion nor pressure indicate a direction for movements, according to which motion could be charted and which would allow a system of the universe to emerge. From the possibilities of impressed forces, Universal Mechanics chooses centripetal force as the one best able to account for the kinematics of the solar system and least liable to the objections that its foundations are asserted rather than demonstrated. Just as Newton differs from Descartes in making forces prior to bodies, so he differs in making the primary impressed forces centripetal forces rather than pressure.

Centripetal force is any force, as the fifth definition has it, by which a body is either drawn or impelled or in any way tends towards a "point as towards a center." Gravity, magnetism, the fall of a projectile, and the orbit of the moon exhibit this force. It prevents either the moon or the projectile from continuing in "the rectilinear way which by inherent force it would pursue." Centripetal force impresses itself upon the innate force of the projectile to describe a parabola and upon the moon to describe an orbit. "If this force were too small, it would not be sufficient to turn the moon out of a rectilinear course; if it were too great, it would turn it too much and draw down the moon from its orbit towards the earth. It is necessary that the force be of a correct magnitude." The recognition of this *justae magnitudinis* reveals two sets of problems. First, the mathematician must determine the complicated forces necessary to hold a body in a given orbit with a given velocity, and, conversely, he must determine the path which a projectile will describe given the initial and the subsequent forces. Second, the recognition of the harmony of forces, innate and impressed, raises questions at the end of the inquiry regarding the one who calculated all this as being "not blind and fortuitous, but very well skilled in Mechanicks and Geometry."[43]

Just as impressed forces can be distinguished into percussion, pressure, and centripetal force, so centripetal force can be further analyzed into the three quantities of absolute, accelerative, and motive. These three quantities correspond to the inital definitions and the first two are joined to compose the last. In *De motu corporum in gyrum*, Newton was content to define centripetal force. Now he moves from this obvious and apparent force to its fundamental and underlying quantity. Absolute force is the quantity of centripetal force which is proportioned to the mass of the attracting body. This quantity is known according to the mass whose state is altered without consideration of velocity; some magnets can move bigger bodies than others. Accelerative force is the quantity of centripetal force which is proportioned to the velocity generated. From the legendary Pisa tower, the accelerative forces for all bodies in free fall near the earth would ideally be the same. Now put both definitions together and you have motive force: "The motive quantity of a centripetal force is the measure of the same, proportional to the motion which it generates in a given time." Just as momentum conjoined velocity and mass, so motive force combines accelerative and absolute force. And it does so in a manner which can unite the universe. Motive force looks toward the bodies which converge toward the unifying center; accelerative takes up the places in space over which and in which this movement is generated; absolute force looks to the center itself "as indued with some cause without which these motive forces would not be propagated through the spaces round about." The distinction of these three kinds of centripetal force allows the motive force of gravitation to be in direct proportion to the masses involved (absolute force) and in inverse proportion to the square of the distances from one another (accelerative force).

Mass is placed first as the quantity to be translated into inertial force; momentum is placed second as the quantity to be transformed into motive force. Seventeeth- and eighteenth-century mechanics tended to think of force as a characteristic of a body in motion. But the Newtonian mechanics offer "quite a different definition of force, an external action on a body producing a change in motion."[44] It is crucial to realize that with motive force, the Universal Mechanics has achieved a source comprehensive enough to deal with all of the locomotions that are the objects of Galileo's dynamics and Kepler's astronomy. It allows celestial and terrestial phenomena not only to be considered mathematically, but to be resolved by a single principle, a principle so pervasive as to make mechanics universal.

Before mechanics becomes universal, however, it must become true mechanics. And to do that, it must establish real motion, rest, time, and place. The first employment of the mechanical principle is to set up its own proper subject-matter. Real motion has been defined as the translation of a body from one absolute place to another, but absolute place does not fall under observation. Consequently, "motion and rest, as commonly conceived [*uti vulgo concipiuntur*], are only relatively distinguished; nor are those bodies always truly at rest, which commonly are taken to be so."[45] Absolute place enters definitionally into the understanding of absolute motion, but absolute place defies observational verification. Absolute rest is the opposite, the absence, of absolute motion, but true rest cannot be determined from the position of bodies in respect to one another.[46] Furthermore, if places are in motion, then these places are determined in their location by other places; they themselves are only relative. Take a ship at sea. While the ship is under sail, the individual parts or places of the ship are at relative rest; they would only be at absolute rest if the ship continued to occupy the same part of immobile space that contains the parts of the ship, the ship, and the cavity which the ship occupies, without movement. Hence "entire and absolute motions can be no otherwise defined except through immovable places."[47] If the places are movable, the motion can only be relative.

This understanding of the conditions of absolute motion is stark. It must occur in an absolute place, that is, in a part of absolute space. This space, to be absolute, must be *immota*, without movement. This can only be the case if this space lasts, perdures, stays the same from infinity to infinity without change. This infinite perduration, this absolute time, is eternal. In order to have true motion as its subject the Universal Mechanics needs changeless space which perdures eternally: "No other places are immovable [*immota*]; and do thereby constitute immovable space [*spacium immobile*]."[48] Absolute motion, then, implicates absolute space and this, in turn, implicates eternal time. But neither eternal time nor absolute place nor absolute motion falls under direct observation.

If the conditions for absolute motion are not open to observational verification, some of the causes and effects of this motion are. For the causes and effects are forces. True motion is generated or altered only by an impressed force. Conversely, true motion is always generated or altered by an impressed force. Futhermore, there is one effect which can distinguish absolute from relative motion: in real circular motion, there will be a force of receding from the axis of the circular motion. In both cases, force is the giveaway. Relative motion, on the contrary, can be generated or altered simply by the movement of another body, without any force exerted on the body in question that seems to move. Again, relative motion need not occur when impressed forces are exercised on a particular set of masses; these bodies may seem at rest because they do not change relative to one another. Finally, a purely relative circular motion does not generate a force of flying-off, of receding, from the axis of the movement.

This effect of real circular motion introduces the first experiment of the *Principia*. Hang a bucket filled with water by a long cord; twist the cord until it is tight; now let it go. The cord unwinds and untwists itself with greater and greater velocity. The bucket spins around. Is the water really moving? Initially, if you look at the surface of the water, it is still smooth. Gradually it begins to move up the sides of the bucket. Now bear in mind that in order to crawl up the sides of the bucket, the water has to overcome the pull of gravity. The centrifugal force becomes stronger and stronger; and up the sides it goes, "forming a concave figure (as I have experienced), and the swifter the motion becomes, the higher the water will rise, till at last, performing its revolution in the same time with the vessel, it becomes relatively at rest in it." What is this movement of the water up the sides of the bucket? An attempt to recede from the axis of the motion. How can we tell whether the water is in motion or not? Not by looking for it to change its position at the side of the pail. On the contrary. When the absolute motion of the water is at its greatest, the water clings to the sides of the bucket without any relative alteration. The real or absolute motion of the body actually effects that relative rest because it generates a *conatus recedendi ab axe* which forces the water into relative rest with the sides of the bucket. Notice, then, that real circular movement is not proved or determined by changes in relationship to circumambient bodies nor by the translation of one body from one relative location to another. Real circular movement is indicated by the force to move away from the axis of the circular motion, the force needed to overcome gravitation.

Force, then, is comprehensively indicative of real motion, either as its determining cause or as its symptomatic effect. With this principle, whose value has been experimentally verified, the Universal Mechanics can introduce the critical experiment of the two globes. Take two globes, connect them by a cord, revolve them around a common axis at some distance from one another. First, from the tension on the cord, it becomes apparent that there is a *conatus recedendi*, an attempt to fly off from the common axis of the circular motion. From this, one can compute the quantity of the circular movement, the momentum of absolute motion. Now impress equal forces on the opposite sides of each globe to augment or to decrease the quantity of this movement; again, from the decrease or the increase of the tension on the cord, one can compute the increase or decrease of the quantity of their movement. It would be easy enough to adjust these impressed forces until the greatest *conatus recedendi* had been achieved, that is, by having one impressed force augment another. In this way, the backs of each of the globes would be discovered. If you know the fronts of these revolving globes, you know the direction of their motion as they follow one another. Notice what has been achieved: We have established real motion, both its quantity and its direction, and we have achieved this without any attention to circumambient bodies by which these globes could be located. What was done was very simple. The connecting cord was observed and its tension was the very force which the revolving globes required for their motion. Thus it was concluded from the reduction of apparent motions to the real forces, impressed or recessive, that absolute, real, and mathematical motion existed. It was in the moving globes.[49]

But if there is absolute motion, there is absolute place—since real or absolute motion is nothing but the translation of a body from one absolute place to another. If there is absolute place, there is absolute space—since place is nothing but that part of absolute space which is occupied by a body. If there is absolute space, it must be infinite since it is contained by, hence limited by, nothing else. If there is absolute space, there must be absolute time—since absolute space is changeless, perduring from infinity to infinity.[50]

What Newton has done is not unlike what Archimedes promised, that given a place to stand on, he could move the earth.[51] Newton, in contrast, maintained: "But I [*Nos*] consider philosophy rather than arts and write not concerning manual but natural powers."[52] He used not the lever but the revolving globes, and his effort was not to move the world, but to establish within the universe absolute, real, and mathematical movements and the space and time in which they occurred. In the Scholium at the end of the eight definitions, that is precisely what the Universal Mechanics established, with an instrument as simple as a lever. One cannot and must not distinguish between the phenomenal and the real in Newton as if there were two different worlds; that is not the case. There is the real and its sensible measure. The phenomenon is never dismissed as unreal; it is examined for the reality that it possesses and indicates and of which it is the symbol. True motion gave Universal Mechanics a subject and a principle by which the subject could be determined, providing the entire problematic of the *Principia*: "But how we are to obtain the true motions from their causes, effects, and apparent difference, and the converse, shall be explained more at large in the following treatise. For to this end it was that I composed it."[53]

Not only was Universal Mechanics beginning its inquiry, it was also provoking a row—a row about theology at that. In 1710, George Berkeley, fellow and lecturer of Trinity College, launched his massive attack on the materialists, *A Treatise concerning the Principles of Human Knowledge*. The *Treatise* takes up the basic doctrine of the *Principia*, "a certain celebrated treatise of *mechanics*: in the entrance of which justly admired treatise, time, space, and motion, are distinguished into *absolute* and *relative, true* and *apparent, mathematical* and *vulgar*; which distinction, as it is at large explained by the author, doth suppose those quantities to have an existence without the mind; and that they are ordinarily conceived with relation to sensible things, to which nevertheless, in their own nature, they bear no relation at all."[54] Berkeley's reservations about these Newtonian coordinates issue both from his own philosophy and from the implications of Newton's. The "new principle" of Berkeley's treatise collapses the distinction between *esse* and *percipi*. Newton's distinction between the absolute and relative space then makes no sense. What is unperceivable has no reality. But theologically, the issue can be argued even on Newtonian terms. The *Principia* is left with a dangerous dilemma: "to wit, of thinking either that real space is God, or else that there is something beside God which is eternal, uncreated, infinite, indivisible, immutable. Both of which may just be thought pernicious and absurd notions."[55] Bishop Berkeley is saying this: If space is unchangeable and thus eternal, uncontained and thus infinite, it raises a radical theological issue. Either space is god, since it shares the predicates which are classically reserved to god, or there is something other than god that possesses these divine attributes.

For a true mechanics, there must be true motions, absolute movements whose causative forces can be analyzed and whose subsequent orbits can be charted. There must be absolute space in which these occur. Otherwise locomotion is a contradiction in terms, or is always simply relative to the perceiver. If this space is final and uncontained, then it is infinite; if it is immobile, then it is eternal. Then, Berkeley says, the condition for this Universal Mechanics is either god reduced to space or space exalted to god. This is the first theological issue to emerge from the Newtonian attempt to derive absolute movement as the subject-matter of a true mechanics.

Toward the Universal: The Importance of System

Universal Mechanics tendered not only a subject-matter that was real, absolute, and mathematical, as well as a principle of force by which it could be investigated, reducing mass to inertial forces and impressed forces to motive forces, but also a *genus argumentandi* a method by which issues could arise, evidence could be established, and solutions extracted from the evidence and verified by subsequent demonstrations. It offered, in refurbished form, the ancient methods of analysis and synthesis, which had found their classic genesis in the *Elements* of Euclid and early growth in the commentaries of Pappus. The thirteenth book of the *Elements* added a note to its first proposition: "Analysis is an assumption of that which is sought as if it were admitted [and the passage] through its consequences to something admitted to be true. Synthesis is an assumption of that which is admitted [and the passage] through its consequences to the finishing or attainment of what is sought." If this text is interpolated and if its actual author is, as Heiberg suggests, Heron of Alexandria, then the methodological connection between Newton and Heron is rich indeed!

Regardless of its author, the sentence is not exactly limpid in its clarity. Basically, as Pappus explains, "in analysis we assume that which is sought as if it were [already] done, and we inquire what it is from which this results, and again what is the antecedent cause of the latter, and so on, until by so retracing our steps we come upon something already known or belonging to the class of first principles." Euclid calls the reduction to antecedents a reduction to consequences because each step of the reduction must move through an inference in which the antecedent and consequent are convertible. When the antecedent and consequence are one, there is no chance of establishing a true conclusion from a false one. For this reason the Greek mathematicians insisted that synthesis follow and verify analysis. Thus Pappus: "But in synthesis, reversing the process, we take as already done that which was last arrived at in the analysis and, by arranging in their natural order as consequences what were before antecedents, and successively connecting them one with another, we arrive finally at the construction of what was sought." Analysis and synthesis were methods of mathematics. They were introduced into geometry, Pappus maintains, for those who had mastered the ordinary elements and were proceeding to consider the problems of the construction of lines, more specifically the problems of sections, leading into the problems of the five regular solids.[56] By the time the threads of this tradition wound their way into eighteenth-century England, analysis and synthesis had gone far beyond mathematical embodiment.

In 1704, John Harris composed the first alphabetical encyclopedia in English, the *Lexicon Technicum, or an Universal English Dictionary of the Arts and Sciences, explaining not only the terms of the arts, but the arts themselves.* It was a massive achievement, and a second edition was soon in demand. The second edition went beyond the one folio volume. The first volume was republished in 1708 and supplemented in 1710 by a second volume "in which the matter is entirely new and without any repetition . . . of anything in the former," as its introduction informs the reader. This second edition contained Newton's only treatise on a specifically chemical subject, *De natura acidorum.*[57]

Here, in his *Lexicon Technicum* of 1704, Harris defines analysis as a "Resolution of anything into its component Principles: Thus a Chymist is said to Analyze bodies, when he dissolves them by the Fire, and endeavours to find out their Constituent Parts." Algebra is called analysis "because it teaches us to solve Questions, and to demonstrate Theorems, by enquiring into the bottom, into the Fundamental Constitution and Nature of the Thing, which is, as it were, resolved into its Parts taken all to Pieces, and then put together again, that so we may see into the Reason and Nature of it. And in this Sense, Analytical Demonstrations are opposed to Synthetical ones." Following Vieta, analysis is ascribed to Plato with the definition actually taken from Euclid's *Elements*: "Assumpti Quaesiti tanquam concessi per consequentia ad verum concessum." On the other hand, "*Synthesis* is either the Frame and Structure of the whole Body; or more strictly, the composure of the bones. 'Tis also used in Mathematicks, in opposition to the

Word, Analysis: in which sense it signifies Composition, or the *Synthetical Method of Enquiry* or Demonstration in Mathematics, is [*sic*] when we pursue the Truth chiefly by Reasons drawn from Principles before established, and Propositions formerly proved, and proceed by a long regular Chain, till we come to the conclusion: As is done in the Elements of Euclid, and in almost all the Demonstrations of the Ancients. This is called *Composition*, and is opposed to the *Analytical Method*, which is called *Resolution*."[58]

Analysis comes into Newton's Universal Mechanics somewhat transformed. It consists of four heuristic moments: [1] the assessment of a phenomenon through either the immediacy of observation or the refinements of experimentation; [2] a derivative or deductive movement from this effect to its proximate causes; [3] an inductive or universalizing from these "particular Causes to more general ones, till the Argument end in the most general"; and finally, [4] the coordination of these conclusions with objections which may be taken from experiments or from propositions which have already been established. This last moment of verification is a continuation of the movement towards generality, for "if no Exception occur from Phaenomena, the Conclusion may be pronounced generally." Analysis is the resolution of effects into their causes, whether one is dealing with the solution of compounds into ingredients or of movements into their diverse and originating forces. Analysis is not a movement simply to particularities. It begins with particularity and it moves to particular causes; but it continues this causal resolution until it uncovers the general laws which are the reason that these particular causes act in this particular way.

Synthesis moves in precisely the opposite manner: from cause to effect. Granted the general laws of mass, distance, and force; granted further these particular forces inherent in this body and impressed by the agency of other influences; synthesis describes the career they will effect. Synthesis is a movement back to the phenomena, and it "consists in assuming the Causes discover'd and establish'd as Principles, and by them explaining the Phaenomena proceeding from them, and proving the Explanations."[59] Analysis proceeds from effect to cause and from particularity to generality, from phenomena to underlying and universal structure; synthesis proceeds from cause to demonstrate the effect, from general laws to show their instantiation in a particular event, from abstractions to explain and predict the phenomena.

The laws of motion, for example, are "deduced from Phaenomena" in various and particular observations or experiments; they are "made general by Induction: wch is the highest evidence that a Proposition can have in this philosophy."[60] Deduction moves from the phenomenon to its underlying, mathematical cause; induction performs this deduction or derivation often enough so that the cause can be generalized into a mathematical law. Two types of objections should be considered and these only: those that argue that the experiments are insufficient to warrant the causes or laws derived from them; and those that present other evidence or produce other experiments which render these conclusions doubtful.[61] These are, then, the four stages of analysis: observation, deduction of underlying causes, inductive generalization of these causes, responding to experimentally based objections. Synthesis reverses this procedure, as when Newton demonstrated for Halley the elliptical pattern of the planets from the law of inverse squares. Any explanation fabricated but not experientially inferred and confirmed is dismissed as a hypothesis: "Whatever is not deduced from the phenomena is to be called an hypothesis; and hypotheses, whether metaphysical or physical, whether of occult qualities or mechanical, have no place in experimental philosophy. In this philosophy particular propositions are inferred [*deducuntur*] from the phenomena, and afterwards rendered general by induction."[62]

Obviously, "hypothesis" can have and has had many meanings, some of them employed by Newton himself. In its unacceptable Cartesian sense, as Newton read it, it means anything that interrupts the progressive movement from phenomena through the method of analysis and back to phenomena through the method of synthesis. It is the introduction of foreign explanation, neither derived from the phenomena nor making a claim upon truth. This is fiction, for Newton, a basic failure in analysis, however much it was asserted by Descartes that "I desire that what I have written be only taken as a hypothesis, something that is perhaps far removed from the truth; but however that may be, I will believe myself to have really accomplished something if all the things which are deduced from it are entirely in conformity with experience."[63] Descartes maintains that success in the method of synthesis justifies the formation of a hypothesis that does not emerge from the method of analysis. This is precisely what Newton denies. Inquiry can entertain conjectures, questions whose solutions are not yet in, speculations upon the ultimate constitution of matter or the physical causes of gravity, but not in such a way that they interfere with the continuous movement provided by analysis and synthesis, or interrupt its derivative and inductive moments with explanations without a similar foundation in observation and experimentation. "For the whole burden of philosophy seems to consist in this—from the phenomena of motions to investigate the forces of nature [the analytic method], and from these forces to demonstrate the other phenomena [the synthetic method]."[64]

The *Principia* itself is offered as an embodiment of this method. Books 1 and 2 investigate the phenomena of motion in order to derive analytically the mathematical principles that are the laws and conditions of motions and forces, that is, the general causes of the subject of rational mechanics. These general laws, then, are not applied but synthetically instantiated in the third book. Celestial mechanics has both an analytic and a synthetic moment. The general motive quantity of centripetal force becomes gravity. The forces of gravity are derived analytically from the phenomena of the heavens. Then from these forces of gravity, the motions or elliptical orbits of the planets and comets, the movement of the tides, and the career of the moon are synthetically demonstrated. Newtonian method allows the whole to be broken into instances of phenomena or into controlled moments of experimentation; from this particularity one moves to general causes in terms of forces or, in celestial mechanics, to the universal law of gravitational force. With this general force, this comprehensive principle, one can return to the phenomenon and build it into a system, indeed, into a system of the entire cosmos. Universal Mechanics, with its processes of analysis, obtains a comprehensive principle, and then, with its processes of synthesis, composes the entire planetary system into a single structure. The Universal Mechanics can in this way establish a cosmos.

The Universal Mechanics begins, as discussed in the previous section, simply by defining two quantities, mass and what would later be called momentum. But if we are going to have a quantity, or a series of quantities, we are going to need a measure, something that will spell out the intelligibility of the quantities of mass and motion. In both cases, the measure proves to be force, either the resisting and impulsive force, which constitutes the measure for mass, or the motive force, which constitutes the measure for a change in momentum. Further, the measure for the inertial force will ultimately be motive force. Thus all masses and all movements can be determined by motive force. Force is both that which accounts for a change in motion and that into which every motion can be resolved. In Universal Mechanics, this comprehensive principle constitutes both the source of discovery and the source of demonstration, the possibility of analysis and the first principle of synthesis. One resolves finally not to atoms, as in Democritus, or into hypotheses, as in Descartes, but into motive force.[65]

And here lies the problem: How do we construct a universe out of force? The general analytic and synthetic methods of the Universal Mechanics embody themselves mechanically in the composition and resolutions of motions in terms of forces. Method is the crucial issue in the six corollaries which follow the axioms or the laws of motion.

The first corollary states that if any mass, any body, is acted upon by oblique forces, these forces combine in such a way that the resultant movement of the body describes the diagonal of a parallelogram in the same time in which it would describe either of the sides if acted upon by simply one or another of the forces. In other words, forces can combine to produce a single motion. The apparent simplicity of any motion may in reality, that is, mathematically, be a composite of diverse and component impressed forces. This in turn allows for the critical second corollary, in which these forces themselves can be further broken down into composing forces. A direct force can be explained as a composite of oblique forces, and this composition and resolution of forces lies at the heart of mechanics. Motions, however complicated, can be reduced to their originating forces. Similarly, one can build from component forces to simple and complicated movements. The classic examples all follow this composition and resolution: the wedge, lever, screw, winding-drum, and pulley. "Therefore the use of this corollary spreads far and wide, and by that diffusive extent the truth thereof is further confirmed. For on what has been said depends the whole doctrine of mechanics variously demonstrated by different authors. . . . *Cum pendeat ex jam dictis Mechanica tota.*"[66] *Resolutio* and *compositio* in mechanical practice and experience are identified with analysis and synthesis in rational mechanics. The practical and theoretic methods of Universal Mechanics are the same. The resolution of motions to fundamental forces is identified with the analysis of phenomena to first causes; the composition of forces to produce a resultant motion is identified with the synthesis of causes and laws to demonstrate phenomena. In both cases, what is examined or demonstrated is the real movement of bodies. What finally and apodictically explains or demonstrates is force.

Just as oblique forces can conjoin to form a single movement, so they can combine with each other to form a system. The third corollary allows conservation of the quantity of motion (momentum) among interacting bodies, where the actions of some are at odds with the actions of others. The effect of this interaction is that the group itself remains at equilibrium, even though the myriad forces, movements, and masses within it are in constant reinforcing and contradicting interplay. The fourth corollary allows this group to have a center and thus to be a system, for the common center of gravity of many bodies does not alter its state of motion or rest by the interaction of the bodies among themselves. Now, for the first time in the *Principia*, one can speak of a system. In such a system, all the mechanical actions of the bodies among themselves balance in a harmony. The composition and resolution of forces can be exhibited not only in rudimentary mechanical instruments, but in the most complex interacting congeries of bodies: "There is the same law in a system of many bodies as there is in a single body regarding its perseverance in a state of motion or of rest."[67]

Given the possibility of the composition of forces and their resolution, and given that this process can continue indefinitely until a system is realized, it is critical to note that only force can allow the determination of which motions in this system are true and which are only apparent. The fifth corollary provides for the relativity of all motions within an inertial system, that is, within a system that is either at rest or moving uniformly in a straight line. The sixth corollary maintains that if equal impressed forces are imparted to all the members of this system in the direction of parallel lines, their interactions with one another will be unimpaired. These last two corollaries underscore the catholic and necessary character of force, rather than observation of location, as the final explanation and guarantee of genuine mechanics. Through these corollaries mechanics can become universal. Now a comprehensive principle of explanation and demonstration possesses a method by which it can be applied both theoretically and practically to phenomena. With this, it is a short step to build the system of the world.

Only when the methodological insistences and directions of these initial corollaries are grasped can one also understand the theological issue which inescapably emerges. Many have maintained, like the gifted and insightful Edward Strong, that god was introduced into later editions of the *Principia* at the suggestion of Roger Cotes and that the scientific work of Newton exhibits a clear autonomy from any subsequent theological considerations. As such, "a scientist needs no knowledge of God to know the mechanism of things, but it would nonetheless be impious to suppose that the world could exist in its order without supervision of an intelligent Agent."[68]

As a matter of fact, however, Newton did not introduce the notion of god or divine providence only in later editions of the *Principia*. As early as the review of the first edition of the *Principia* in the *Acta Eruditorum* of June, 1688, an anonymous critic singled out Newton's introduction of god as responsible for the mathematical exactitude of the system of the universe: "From which he [Newton] concludes that God placed the Planets at different distances from the Sun, so that they would receive heat from the Sun according to the proportion of their densities."[69] Far from being a later introduction into the *Principia*, as Strong contends, or an interest evoked only in later life, as Laplace and J.-B. Biot assert, the theological issue was with the *Principia* from its first edition; it figured among Newton's interests as precisely appropriate within an elaboration of the system of the universe. It was of the first edition that Newton assured Bentley: "When I wrote my treatise about our Systeme, I had an eye upon such Principles as might work wth considering men for the beliefe of a Deity."[70] Whatever occurred by way of general scholium in the second edition or by way of queries in the *Optics*, the link between the system of the world and the theological interests of Newton had been established from the very beginning. However one responds to Strong's challenge that theology is an addendum, an unessential appendage to the Universal Mechanics, the response must register the importance of system.

Contemporary mechanics could draw the disparate lines of investigation into intelligibility, into a unity which made sense out of the diversity, in two different ways: either through a hypothesis that would explain the cause of gravity, or through a system that would demonstrate and universalize the laws of gravity to construct a single whole of all the masses in the universe. *System* and *hypothesis* had long and varied meanings in natural philosophy. One could speak of the Tychonian or Copernican or Ptolemaic "systems of the world" and mean not so much a physical description of the location of the planets as a hypothetical representation of their positions and movements, a "model" of the world. Indeed, the much-reissued work of Edward Phillips, *The New World of Words, or a Universal English Dictionary* (fifth edition, 1696) did precisely that, collapsing the antinomy between *system* and *hypothesis*. *System* is defined in the following way: "Among Astronomers, it is taken for the general Constitution, Fabrick, and Harmony of the Universe, or any orderly Representation thereof, according to some noted Hypothesis."[71] *Hypothesis*, however, in the sense that Newton rejected, is a gratuitous explanation, that is, one that terminates mechanical analysis in a cause which is neither phenomenal nor deduced from the phenomenon.[72] *System* is the mathematically realized structure of the phenomenon. System allows the forces and the laws with which they work and the absolute motions which they generate or alter to be brought into a single structure. System realizes a coincidence between the actual frame of the universe and the elaborate representation which is celestial mechanics. Newton might indeed have spoken of a Copernican hypothesis.[73] He spoke of his own celestial mechanics as the "System of the World." For Newton, *system* was both a real and an epistemological term. The "system of the world" indicated not only his celestial mechanics, but the mechanical way in which the sun, planets, and stars existed, moved, and mutually influenced one another.

The uses of *system* go back to the works of Plato and Hippocrates, and σύστημα always denotes some kind of order achieved within a multiplicity. This sense of the whole organized of many disparate parts, of the one out of the many, found its realization in such vastly divergent and complex organizations as the body of a literary composition, the constitution of a government, a confederacy of nations, a corps of soldiers, a college of priests or of magistrates, a system constituted according to musical intervals, an accumulation of sediment in medicine, and a union of several *versus nexi* in Greek meter.[74] So σύστημα passed into Latin and into the languages that Latin fathered. Everywhere it appeared, it represented a unity forged out of the diversity of elements or a whole whose divergent members found their intelligibility in the collectivity which they formed. System represented an attempt to frame the intelligibility of the many in terms of the one. Its introduction into celestial mechanics was inevitable. Out of the diversity of the heavenly planets, comets, stars, meteors, and the sun, out of their multiform interactions and divergent orbits, one attempted to form intelligibility: the whole that made sense out of the parts. So Galileo in 1632 titled his greatest and most fateful defense of the Copernican universe *Dialogo sopra i duo massimi sistemi del Mondo*, and John Locke's magisterial *Essay Concerning Human Understanding* of 1690 limited the discourse: "If we . . . confine our Thoughts to this little Canton, I mean this System of our Sun."[75]

It is not strange, then, that John Harris found the word so critically important in his *Lexicon Technicum*. He defined it under two headings. In music, it denotes "the Extent of a certain Number of Chords, having its bounds towards the Grave and Acute, which hath been differently determined by the different Progress made in musick, and according to the different Divisions of the *Monochord*. The *System* of the Ancients, was composed of four *Tetrachords*, and one *Supernumerary Chord*, the whole making Fifteen Chords." Properly, however, it denotes "a regular collection, or Composition of many things together. Thus the *Solar System*, is the Aggregate Union; or orderly Disposition of all those Planets which move round the sun as their Centre, in determined Orbits, and never deviate farther from him than their proper and usual Bounds. And a *System of Philosophy*, is a Regular Collection of the Principles and Parts of that Science into one body, and a treating of them Dogmatically, or in a Scholastic Method, which is called the *Systematical Way*, in contradistinction to the *Way of Essay* wherein a Writer delivers himself more loosely, easily, and modestly." In 1674, "the learned Dr. Hook" was known to "promise that he would explain a System of the World," which had three suppositions dealing with inertia, gravitation, and distance, "all which is abundantly confirmed in Mr. Isaac Newton's Admirable Principia Philosophae Mathematica."[76] For Harris, indeed for all of England, Hooke may have attempted or specified or promised a system of the world, but it was Isaac Newton who brought these promises to realization. The demonstrations were his.

The resolution and composition of forces function now in the methods of analysis and synthesis which give a system to the great third book of the *Principia*. They are the methods of investigation and demonstration. Investigation of what? Of the phenomena of the universe, the data turned gradually into kinematic facts from centuries of astronomic observation and calculation: the satellites of Jupiter, the satellites of Saturn, the "five primary planets" circling the sun, and the moon circling the earth. All of these exhibit the same kinematic proportions first formulated by Kepler: areas are described in proportion to time, and the square of the time is proportional to the cube of the mean distance from the center. The phases of Venus and Mercury, the quadratures of Mars, and the eclipses of the satellites about

Jupiter and Saturn—all support a heliocentric focus for these planets; this focus prescinds from the issue of the revolution of the earth, but a geocentric focus of the planets would not allow them to describe their areas in proportion to their time (Kepler's second law). Newton classified under "phenomena" six generalizations based on observation and framed in the mathematical patterns of Kepler.[77]

From these six phenomena the initial twelve propositions derive the force which underlies and accounts for their movements. This constitutes the analytic moments of deduction and the generalization of this deduction by induction. The force operating between Jupiter and its satellites, between the sun and the primary planets, and between the moon and the earth is proportional to the inverse square of the distance between their respective centers. This is a deduction of the mathematical cause for the orbital rather than the rectilinear movement of these bodies. Then, through induction, this force is generalized by identifying it with the force of gravity which has been so long observed on earth in falling bodies. The motive quantity of centripetal force now becomes gravity, and gravity has become universalized as a comprehensive principle operating in the movement of all bodies. It is the foundation for all regular descending movements, the *vis gravitatis*: "Gravity pertains to all bodies, and it is proportional to the quantity of matter in each . . . and inversely proportional to the square of the distance of places."[78] Universal Mechanics, then, can treat certain relationships among all bodies, whether earthly or celestial, as a phenomenon of gravity. The gravitational law is a mathematical principle that allows the investigations Pappus promised, one that is effective in all inquiries into natural phenomena. With the establishment of gravity, the true movement of the planets can be calculated and a system established that gives structure to each of its multiple elements. The mass directly proportioned to this force can be calculated directly from the center, whether one is talking about the weight of a body on the surface of the earth or the "weight of bodies revolving in circles around the planets" or the revolution of planets around the sun. On the hypothesis that the center of the system of the world is immovable, one obtains a gravitational center, which unites kinematically and dynamically the bodies that are gravitationally interacting. In twelve initial propositions and one hypothesis, the six phenomena are reduced to their fundamental principle and a systematic center.

The remainder of book 3 takes that principle and demonstrates *a priori* each of the phenomena which had emerged through astronomical observations over the prior two thousand years. It was a breathtaking moment in astronomy, drawing into a systematic unity the disparate facts that had been established: "Now that we know the principles upon which they [the initial phenomena] depend, from these principles we synthesize [*colligimus*] *a priori* the motions of the heavens."[79] The initial phenomena were the kinematic generalizations of Kepler. Now the phenomena comprised everything in the heavens: the annual orbits of the planets, the retrogression of the equinoctal points, the rotation of the earth, all the motions of the moon with their variations, the precession of the equinoxes, and the tidal movement of the seas. It all fitted together. It all made sense—not through hypothesis, but through system.

Gravity was paradoxically present. On the one hand, it was not affirmed as a property essential to bodies, inherent in matter, as were extension, mobility, hardness, impenetrability, and inertial power. These admit of neither intensification nor remission of degrees, but are always found to be present in all bodies "in reach of our experiments." In fact, so universal are these qualities that one can conclude their undiminished presence in the smallest unity of mass: "Hence we conclude the least particles of all bodies to be also all extended, and hard, and impenetrable, and movable, and endowed with their proper inertia. And this is the foundation of all philosophy (*et hoc est fundamentum Philosophiae totius*)."[80] Yet gravity is more given by the phenomena than impenetrability. No one can experience the impenetrability of the celestial bodies, but both experiment and astronomical observation indicate "that all bodies about the earth gravitate toward the earth, and that in proportion to the quantity of matter which they severally contain; that the moon likewise according to the quantity of its matter, gravitates towards the other; that, on the other hand, our sea gravitates towards the moon, and all the planets one towards another; and the comets in like manner towards the sun: we must, in consequence of this rule, universally allow that all bodies whatever gravitate mutually one towards another." That gravity is universal is affirmed. That it is inherent or essential to bodies is *not* affirmed. Its physical cause remains unknown. "It is enough that gravity really does exist and that it does act according to the laws which we have explained, and that it is adequate for all the motions of the celestial bodies, and our sea."[81]

On the other hand, is the mechanical force of gravity able to account for the system which it continuously effects and to which it gives unity and coherence? The universal presence of gravity reveals the systematic nature of all astronomical bodies and all bodies of terrestrial experience. But this answer only poses the question more severely. Granted such a geometrically precise relationship, is there another force which must be introduced in order that the system itself not be absurd? In other words, if the meaning of gravity, its impact and the extent of its presence, is revealed in the system which it controls, is it adequate to account for this system? And if not, does this make the system itself finally unintelligible? This question remains to be answered if the entire enterprise of a universal mechanics is not to founder.

"Thus Far of God . . . "

It fell to Samuel Clarke to defend Newtonian mechanics against the insistent attacks of Gottfried Wilhelm Leibniz in a polemical exchange that enjoyed the services of Caroline, Princess of Wales, as intermediary, and whose terminus was written only with the death of Leibniz in 1716. Clarke protested stoutly that this new philosophy, done with mathematical principles, was diametrically opposed to the materialism with which Leibniz had tarred it. In fact, only Newton put matter in its place, so to speak: "the mathematical principles of philosophy . . . alone, prove matter, or body, to be the smallest and most inconsiderable part of the universe."[82] Who then are the real materialists, those who deserve the strictures of the gifted Leibniz and the rejection they have won in England? They are obviously those who "suppose the frame of nature to be such as could have arisen from mere mechanical principles of matter and motion, of necessity and fate."[83] The assault from the Continent had included much more in its arraignment than this putative coincidence between Newton and an organic god, but materialism was the first salvo in a series of barrages. It was answered by repudiating the identification and by reversing the charge. Newton is not fielding a mechanics that is materialistic. That adjective belongs rather to the philosophy that makes matter all-pervasive and projects a universe whose system is the inevitable result of matter and the laws of motion. It is, by your leave, Mr. Descartes, not Mr. Newton, who should be called to account! By elaborating a distinct metaphysics, Descartes had sectioned off theological inquiry from any evidence in the world studied by the sciences. By rejecting metaphysics with its purported occult qualities and dubious procedures, the Universal Mechanics had brought the issue of the existence of god back to its proper location within the serious considerations of the physical sciences.

Certainly the coordination between scientific inquiry and religious belief was part of the air that England breathed. "Who can better magnify the arm that expanded the heavens," asked Christopher Wren in his inaugural oration as Professor of Astronomy at Gresham College, London, "than he who tells you that seven thousand miles will fall short of the diameter of this earth, and yet that this diameter repeated a thousand times will not reach the sun, or this distance between the sun and us repeated a thousand times reach the nearest fixed star?"[84] In his *Discourse Concerning a New Planet*, John Wilkins urged that the positive religious value of astronomy be understood: "It proves a God and a providence and incites our hearts to a greater admiration and fear of His omnipotency."[85] Perhaps even busier about this issue than any of his colleagues, if that were possible, the great Robert Boyle insisted that the scientific and religious intellect were one: "the knowledge of the works of God proportions our admiration of them, they participating and disclosing so much of the unexhausted perfection of their Author, that the further we contemplate them, the more footsteps and impressions we discover of the perfections of their Creator; and our utmost can but give us a just veneration of His omniscience."[86] It was a heady time in England, in which "footsteps and impressions" were imprinted deeply on all natural phenomena, but on none so emphatically and irresistibly as on the heavens. Leibniz's charge to the Princess of Wales was then doubly galling: to assert that "Natural Religion itself, seems to decay (in England) very much," and to couple this charge with a line directed against John Locke and the remainder of the paragraphs against Isaac Newton![87] Of all people, Newton seemed least open to these charges. He, above all, seemed to have given substance and direction to the universal convictions of his colleagues: "I am compelled to ascribe the frame of this Systeme to an intelligent Agent."[88]

The third book of the *Principia* had brought the astronomical embodiment of the Universal Mechanics to an end, but not to completion. Two critical problems still pressed for treatment: One emerged from the structure or pattern that marked Newtonian method and with which a system of the universe had been logistically constructed; the other was born with the mechanical enterprise itself, the imperative of differentiating true from false motions within their conditions of absolute space and absolute time. The first of these problems appeared only after the system of the world had been established. The second presented itself as prior, lying at the basis of any true mechanics and antecedent to any systematization of celestial mechanics. The first was a problem of system; the second was one of space and time. The two together spelled out the problem of the general scholium that was appended to the second and third editions of the *Principia*.

The Universal Mechanics had distinguished two types of force: the inertial force, which was identified with mass, and the impressed force, which effected change. Inertial force was the power of resisting change. It was the power by which a body persevered (*perseverat*) in its state of rest or moving uniformly in a straight line. Impressed forces were those actions that told upon inertial forces, that compelled an alteration in velocity or direction. What was more, inertial force only revealed itself as it resisted impressed force. Force was the key to all movement.

The parallelogram of forces provided the means by which this key could be used. Complex motions could be broken down into simple motions. These motions, in turn, could be understood only by reducing them to the impressed or motive forces which gave them birth. Inertial forces explained continuance; impressed forces explained the momentum that inertial force conserved and the direction that it kept. Furthermore, the composition of forces allowed a self-sustaining system of bodies to emerge, in which the momentum was constant and a common center of gravity existed around which the units of mass revolved. This center of gravity gave such unity to these masses with their varied movements that "est igitur systematis corporum plurium lex eadem, quae corporis solitarii, quoad perseverantiam in statu motus vel quietis" (there is the same law in a system of many bodies as there is in a single body, regarding its perseverance in a state of motion or of rest)."[89] In a system, all of the forces that keep the structure in its present state, whether of rest or of rectilinear motion, are now inertial forces.

Thus the forces that constituted impressed or motive forces within the Newtonian system now become inertial forces that sustain the system as a whole from outside and alien impressed forces. The gravitational attraction of the sun, for example, is a motive force on the planets, consistently pulling the great masses into an orbit around it. But when the solar system is looked at as a whole, gravitational attractions as well as the inertial forces of each of the planets are all assimilated into the inertial forces which sustain the system in its continuance. Therefore, the question a system poses is the same as the problem that any movement of any body raises: what lies at the origin of its compound movements?

When Strong maintained that the theological inquiry indicated a shift from the scientific mechanics of Newton to an acceptable but essentially different concern, he failed to reckon that the consistency of the mechanical methodology is involved.[90] The intelligibility of a compound movement is found through analytic resolution into its causes; these causes or forces are generalized through induction. Newtonian mechanics never maintained that mechanics had to reduce everything to mechanical causes. It did demand a coherence of procedure, that one should not cut off the analytic method arbitrarily through hypotheses. In fact, for Newton, these two inconsistencies coalesce: the arbitrary termination of analysis and synthesis and the elaboration of simple mechanical causes. The only way that one can arbitrarily terminate the process of mechanical analysis is by fabricating a gratuitous mechanical cause. Newton understood this to be the cardinal sin of Cartesian mechanics. The ancients allowed atoms, the void, and the gravity of atoms as the principles of their physics, while "tacitly attributing Gravity to some other Cause than dense Matter. Later Philosophers banished the Consideration of such a Cause out of natural Philosophy, *feigning Hypotheses for explaining all things mechanically*, and referring other Causes to Metaphysicks." These later philosophers are the Continental Cartesians, and they are wrong on both counts: "the main Business of natural Philosophy is to argue from Phaenomena without feigning Hypotheses, and to deduce Causes from Effects, till we come to the very first Cause, which certainly is not Mechanical."[91] This assertion is repeated too many times during the discussions Newton entertains about the proper methodology of experimental philosophy for its authenticity to be doubted. Mechanics, for Newton, does not end finally in a mechanical principle, but in one "very well skilled in Mechanicks and Geometry."[92] This is not an arbitrary statement. It issues from the intrinsic need of consistent method and an absolute space. Strong fails to notice that the theological concern arises in Newtonian mechanics from two inherent problems. What are the forces that account for this system of motions, which can be treated as if it were one body? How is it possible to talk about true, absolute, and mathematical space and not be doing theology? The first problem involves the explanation of the system; the second involves the issue of whether mechanics has been treating of god from the beginning.

The position that mechanics must reduce all phenomena to mechanical principles is certainly legitimate. Indeed, it is the opinion of Descartes and of many of the later Newtonians. But it is not the position of Newton, and to assert that it is the only opinion possible is unwarranted.

System, then, is the first of the problems that the general scholium engages. System is a problem of the one and the many. The many are the diverse masses, their individual locations, the velocity of their movements; the unity comes from the common center of gravity, some geometric focus, and the laws of gravitation by which this focus gives structure to the diversity. When system becomes the "system of the world," the objects of mass become the sun, the six primary planets, the ten moons that revolve around the earth, Jupiter, and Saturn, and the comets that range eccentrically over all parts of the heavens. Their locations are such that the planets move almost in the same plane in their revolutions, and the moons almost in the planes of their planets. The comets pass through extended ellipses with the sun as one focus; at their aphelions, they proceed most slowly as they move at the greatest distance from it. The larger orbits of Jupiter and Saturn prevent these greater bodies from significantly disturbing the movement of the lesser. The mathematical balance among them is such as to form "this most beautiful system of the sun, planets, and comets."[93] This is the phenomenon that demands explanation.

Masses, location, and velocity also figure in Newton's further specification of the factors within this system whose intelligibility looks for a cause beyond the mechanical ones. Bentley had posed the classical Epicurean hypothesis: an even distribution of matter throughout space and a descending movement by which these particles, endowed with gravity, came together to form the masses and the motions that compose the solar system. If the space were finite, countered Newton, the internal gravitational pull would have collapsed one body into another until there was left only one great spherical mass. But if the space were infinite and matter evenly disposed throughout infinite space, some of the particles would have formed one body and others would have composed another, "so as to make an infinite number of great masses scattered at great distances from one to another throughout all of infinite space." But even with this assumption, one would have to account for the formation and the content of these great masses: how these elemental units coalesced to make up the huge, light-giving sun, and those other elements came together to form the many opaque planets. This composition and division of primordial matter "I do not think explicable by mere natural causes but am forced to ascribe it to ye counsel and contrivance of a voluntary Agent." Further, one must account for the fact that these masses were placed at such locations that the Sun could give system to the others by its massive gravity, and light and heat because of its composition. Jupiter and Saturn revolve last among the planets, so that their great masses would not seriously perturb the orbits of the lesser bodies. The intricate balance of the objects of mass and the careful correlation of their composition, their distances, and their gravitational attractions would have been impossible "had this cause been a blind one without contrivance."[94]

If we move the consideration further, from the objects and their distances to the kinematics of motion and the dynamics of their velocity, the evidence increases proportionally. The comets descend into the area of the planets and move among them in vastly different ways; some move in the same manner as the planets, some cross their planes, while the solar system is undamaged by these eccentric visitors. The primary planets and their moons move in the same way and in the same plane without any considerable variation, a phenomenon so exact in its multiple proportions that "no natural cause" can reasonably explain it.

Take the degree of velocity of each of the planets and comets. If the planets had been as swift as the comets, they would have described not concentric orbits around the sun but such eccentric ones that a life-supporting solar system would have been impossible. Were all the planets as swift as Mercury or as slow as Saturn; or were their velocities much different from what they are now; or had their velocities remained what they are now and their distances from the sun changed; or had their velocities and distances been what they are now and their masses significantly different, with proportional changes in their mutual gravitational attractions—in any of these cases, the present system could not exist. The mass objects would have described hyperbolic, parabolic, or very eccentric elliptical movement. Everything that Universal Mechanics found essential for its investigations and specified in its initial definitions had to be harmonized to form the system which now exists. This very complicated, mathematically intricate structure demands to be explained, if any motion demands explanation: "To make this systeme therefore with all its motions, required a Cause which understood and compared together [1] the quantities of matter in ye several bodies of ye Sun and Planets and [2] ye gravitating powers resulting from thence, [3] the several distances of the primary Planets from ye Sun and secondary ones from Saturn, Jupiter and ye earth, and [4] ye velocities with which these Planets could revolve at those distances about those quantities of matter in ye central bodies." These factors, which make up the "harmony of ye systeme," are the same factors that made up its primitive definitions: mass, the velocity added to mass that gives the quantity of motion, the gravitational powers that now translate motive force, and the distances through which they operate. But these initial abstract concepts are now concretized in this massive "harmony of ye systeme." Their concrete realization makes the theological question one that was native to the Universal Mechanics: "And to compare and adjust all these things together in so great a variety of bodies argues that cause to be not blind and fortuitous, but very well skilled in Mechanicks and Geometry."[95]

Just as masses can be broken down into composition and size, so each of the velocities of the planets, moons, and comets can be resolved into the gravitational attraction and the inertial force which give them a transverse motion. The delicate balance of these two forces gives the planets their orbits and the moons their revolutions around their several planets. As the parallelogram of forces indicates that mechanics should resolve compound movements into original forces, so the orbit of each of these masses demands a similar analysis. Gravity accounts for the decline or divergence of the body from rectilinear movement, but it cannot account for its balancing transverse motion. "Gravity may put ye planets into motion but without ye divine power it could never put them into such a Circulating motion as they have about ye Sun, and therefore for this as well as other reasons I am compelled to ascribe ye frame of this Systeme to an intelligent agent."[96] The compound movement of the earth in its orbit originates in the balancing of gravity with a transverse motion which will be conserved by inertia. The mathematical adjustment of these two forces indicates the presence of a calculating intelligence.

But this annual movement about the sun is only one of the three motions of the earth. There is also the diurnal movement on its axis, which yields night and day, and the precession of the equinoxes. The diurnal movements of the planets are not caused by gravity. The earth rotates on its axis such that the surface velocity at the equator is about a thousand miles per hour. If, for example, it turned at one hundred miles per hour, day and night would each be ten times as long. The hot sun would annihilate vegetation, and in the long nights any surviving living thing would freeze. Conserved by inertial force, these movements "required a divine power to impress them."[97] The inclination of the axis of the earth may be urged "as a contrivance for winter and summer and for making the earth habitable towards ye poles, and that ye diurnal rotations of ye Sun and Planets as they could hardly arise from any cause purely mechanical, so by being determined all the same way with the annual and menstrual motions they seem to make up that harmony of ye systeme wch . . . was the effect of choice rather than of chance."[98] The axis of the earth is tilted at an angle of 23.5 degrees to the plane of its motion around the sun. Not only does this ensure the rhythm of the seasons, but, were it not so tilted, vapors from the ocean would move north and south, piling up into continents of ice. Everything within the structure of the system of the world is a function of everything else: masses, gravitational attractions, distances, and velocities. Each of these can be broken down further to its component units. In the presence of these units and in their combination, a mathematical exactitude was discovered which drove Universal Mechanics to a cause that was not mechanical. This was not a new step in physics: Aristotelian inquiry into nature uncovered an eternality of movement, which indicated the causality of some principle that was beyond nature. A similar path was being traced by Universal Mechanics.

But the phenomenon at hand was more than the system of the world. There was the universe with the fixed stars, and the possibility that each of these was the center of another such system. Each of these stars possesses a unity with the other stars, since the light from one passes into the light of another. But while they mutually illumine each other, the stars do not draw one another into a single mass by their gravity. Their immense distances from one another prevent this, as they also hinder their coalescence with the sun of this solar system. The universe is a system of systems.

Granted this phenomenon, that is, so many exacting conditions for human life to exist on this planet or even for this system to emerge, what does it indicate for the inquiry of mechanics? Another kind of force, one not mechanical, one that can compare and dispose of great masses, immense distances, gravitational attractions, velocities, diurnal and annual revolutions. In the early work in mechanics, impressed force had been counted a motive force; in the system of the world, this motive force became gravity. Now all of these forces that compose and conserve the universe are equivalently inertial forces, continuing the structure of the multiple units. What, then, is the force that gave it origin and structure, a force that must be both intelligent and powerful?

It is dominion. *Vis impressa* is now *dominium* or *dominatio*. It is critical to note that Newton does not have to go beyond the notion of force in order to account for the universe, any more than he had to transcend the notion of motive force in order to grasp gravity. Gravity is a particular form of motive force. Dominion is the primordial form of impressed force.

It is dominion which makes god to be god. The researches of Edward Pococke, the English orientalist and biblical scholar who introduced the study of Arabic at Oxford and served as the University's first professor of

Arabic, had convinced Newton that the Latin word *Deus* comes from the Arabic *du*, which means "lord," as in Latin *dominus*. *Deus* is a relative word, relative to that which is ruled by the *dominus*, and this rule is his *dominium* or *dominatio*. What makes god to be god, his *deitas*, is this *dominium*: "Deitas est dominatio Dei." Dominion constitutes the crucial attribute for Universal Mechanics. Dominion holds a position in Newtonian theological inference similar to the infinite or perfect in Descartes: dominion is that out of which all of the divine attributes will be inferred and by which their intelligibility will be governed. In fact, even here Newton makes his disagreement with Descartes sharp: "The supreme God is a being eternal, infinite, absolutely perfect; but a being, *even a perfect one*, without dominion is not the Lord God [*Dominus Deus*]." The relativity of the word *god* emerges in ordinary speech. It makes sense and is common practice to speak of "my god" or "your god." It makes no sense nor is it anyone's practice to speak of "my Eternal" or "my Infinite" or "my Perfect." Just as force is known and designated by the change it can author and in this way is a relative word, so god is known and designated by the rule he exercises. There are many lords, and the title is given them in accordance with the area of their rule. There is only one lord god, and the dominion (*dominatio*) of the spiritual being constitutes god to be what he is. As his dominion, so is his divinity. "A true, supreme, or imaginary dominion makes a true, supreme, or imaginary God."[99]

The system of the universe has yielded the existence and power of god, but this handles only one of the problems with which the *Principia* ends. There was a prior problem, which had been with the mechanics from its beginning, and which Bishop Berkeley had pointed out as an inescapable dilemma: "to wit, of thinking either that real space is God, or else that there is something beside God which is eternal, uncreated, infinite, indivisible, immutable. Both of which may justly be thought pernicious and absurd notions."[100] Absolute space, unchangeable and consequently eternal, was essential for Newtonian mechanics. Without this, there would be no true or absolute motion, which was by definition the movement of a body from one absolute place to another. Descartes' relative motion did not necessitate absolute space and time. In fact, it denied them. Newtonian absolute movement did necessitate absolute space and time, and the theological problem which inescapably emerged—not as an addendum, but at the heart of mechanics—was to prove that space and time were not already divinized, that one had not been doing theology from the beginning of the *Principia*. Berkeley's dilemma was an essential question within Newton's mechanics.

The establishment of the existence and dominion of god allows Berkeley's problem to be handled synthetically. The system of the world, which functions as the phenomenon for theological analysis, has been reduced finally "to a first cause, which certainly is not mechanical."[101] Now one can assume this cause as established and by it handle the data or facts of mechanics which remain unexplained.

From the domination that marks god to be god and by which the system of the world is explained, it follows that he is intelligent and powerful and living. Indeed, these three attributes simply spell out what intrinsically constitutes *dominatio*. If he is dominant, then he is supreme or most perfect (*summe perfectum*). In *summe perfectum* are contained the assertions that he is eternal and infinite, omnipotent and omniscient, "that is, he continues [*durat*] from age to age, and is present [*adest*] from infinity to infinity; he rules all things, and he knows what happens and what is able to happen."

Now Newton can deal with Berkeley. God is not eternity or infinity, but eternal and infinite. By existing eternally, he constitutes the absolute duration that is real time. By being everywhere, he constitutes the infinite extension that is absolute space. It is not so extraordinary to say this of god. A particle of space is always, and a moment of time is everywhere. If the supreme being were not both always and everywhere, he would be less than either. Again, in a line that echoes in the discussions with the materialists: "It is allowed by all that the Supreme God exists necessarily; and by the same necessity, He exists always and everywhere."[102]

What, then, is this eternal space—if it is not god, but that which is constituted as an infinite extension by the omnipresence of god? Descartes had made extension substantial, equating it with matter; Spinoza had made it accidental, one of the two known attributes of the single eternal substance. The fundamental error of both, according to Newton, was to insist that space must fit within the ancient division of all being into substance and accident. It was neither. In his *De gravitatione et a equipondio fluidorum*, which Westfall places at the very end of the 1660s, Newton insisted that space had "its own manner of existing which fitted neither substances nor accidents."[103] It is not a substance because it does not exist absolutely by itself. It is not god, nor is it an accident of god, for god has no accidents.[104] It is an effect, but a necessary effect, of the divine existence. It issues not from his choice, but from his existence everywhere. Newton, following Gassendi, reaches back to the Neoplatonists for the vocabulary and distinction he wanted: Space is an *effectus emanativus*, an effect that emanates or issues from the divine omnipresence, one which is neither independent of god nor simply a creature produced by the divine choice.[105] Thus it becomes "a disposition of being *qua* being. No being exists or can exist which is not related to space in some way. God is everywhere, created minds are somewhere, and body is in the space it occupies; and whatever is neither everywhere nor anywhere does not exist. And hence it follows that space is an effect arising from the first existence of being, because when any being is postulated, space is postulated."[106] Thus god, by being present, constitutes as a necessary and emanant effect an infinite space, and by being everlasting constitutes an eternal time. It is not that god acts to create space and time. He is, and that constitutes space and time. What is necessary must exist always and everywhere, must constitute time and space, must realize the Pauline allusion to Epimenides of Cnossos, which Newton rephrases. "In Him all things are contained and moved, but without affecting one another."[107] God constitutes space and time in which all that moves occurs.

What, then, does the Universal Mechanics tell us about god? This question presupposes a position on a prior question: What can we know about anything? What do we know about bodies? "We see only their figure and colors, we hear only the sounds, we touch only their outward surfaces, we smell only the smells, and taste the savors; but their inward substances are not to be known either by the senses or by a reflex act of our mind." Universal Mechanics cannot deliver any different knowledge about god. One can know that he exists, that he is characterized by *dominatio*, that his attributes are such, and that these exclude others which would be proper to masses or bodily reality. Beyond this, we cannot go: "Much less, have we any idea of the substance of God. We know Him only through his properties and attributes. We know him only by the most wise and excellent structures [*structuras*] of things and final causes. We are in wonder because of his perfections, but we reverence and adore him because of his dominion [*dominium*]."[108] Just as gravity cannot be traced to the inner structure of matter, nor the cause of its laws determined with certitude, so also the divine dominion cannot be reduced to a grasp of the divine nature itself. It is enough that gravity does exist and that it acts in this way. It is enough that god does exist, a god whose dominion reveals his living presence always and everywhere.

The alternative to the divine dominion, for Newton, is not that the Universal Mechanics would stop its inquiry with mechanical laws. The alternative is that it would end with fate and nature (*Fatum et Natura*), that is, with a blind metaphysical necessity (*caeca necessitate metaphysica*), which under the guise of preserving the autonomy of science would posit rather another kind of god, one without dominion, providence, and purpose. This would not only be scripturally false, it would fail to account for the diversity seen everywhere in things, whether different masses and their conjunctions, different velocities and their composing forces, or different geometric configurations and the complicated unities they form. Whatever is necessary must exist always and everywhere. If this necessity is blind and without choice, it will act, like the laws of gravitation, always and everywhere the same. Diversity comes from ideas and will. The issue, then, for the Universal Mechanics is not whether or not it will terminate in god. God in the sense of the dominion or the force from which the world issues is obvious for Newton and inescapable as the rational consequence of a system of the world. The crucial inference is that this dominion is intelligent as well as powerful, that is, that it is personal. The mathematical coordination within the system of the world, the structure of unity with such enormous diversity, is the best warrant for this conclusion. It is the evidence that this god is personal. "And thus much, concerning God: to discourse of whom from the phenomena certainly does belong to Natural Philosophy."[109]

Does this leave Newton with the distant god, who constructed the watch but now leaves it to run on its own? The previous issues of systems and space both function in the response to this question. First, god constitutes the space and time in which all takes place by his omnipresence. He is in no sense distant; his presence makes possible the existence and movement of all things. Second, the system of the world is not of itself an eternal system. Granted that once formed, it "may continue by these Laws for many Ages," but it is inevitable that the mutual actions of the planets one upon the other will give rise to "some inconsiderable irregularities . . . which will be apt to increase, till this System wants a Reformation."[110] Newton conceived of something like a gradual enervation of motion: "It appears that Motion may be got or lost. But by reason of the Tenacity of Fluids, and Attrition of their Parts, and the Weakness of Elasticity in Solids, Motion is much more apt to be lost than got, and is always upon the Decay."[111] There are active principles such as gravity, magnetism, electricity, and fermentation (heat-producing reactions) which continue to reinvigorate the system, but even with these the system would eventually need reformation. Leibniz was scandalized by this assertion. Clarke, or Newton through Clarke, used it as a mechanical indication of the presence of a continual providence so that "nothing is done without his continued government."[112] For a god without providence would be mere blind fate or nature.[113] David Kubrin details the various conjectures Newton entertained about the manner of this periodic reformation, including etherial hypotheses of a perpetual circulation of matter and the conjecture that the comets were the instruments with which god perpetually reconstituted the universe.[114] These remained hypotheses for Newton, though the latter was allowed a place in the system of the world: "So fixed stars, that gradually waste away [*expirant*] into light and vapors, can be renewed by comets that fall upon them; and from this new nourishment those old stars, acquiring new splendor, can pass for new stars."[115]

Whatever the manner in which this reformation of the system of the world was to occur, whatever the actual manner in which the harmony of the system itself was achieved through the balancing of the myriad factors which composed it, that it occurred was an important indication of the steady influence of divine intelligence and power. Reformation warranted belief in a continuous providence, just as formation gave evidence of an all-powerful understanding and choice. Neither was magic, but both manifested the divine dominion of the one who "rules over all things, not as the world soul, but as the Lord of all things."[116]

If the *Principia* allowed a universe to emerge that gave system and consequent intelligibility to the heavens, the *Opticks* proceeded in almost the opposite direction. It began with that which was as universal as motion and as phenomenal as bodies. It began with light. Light was passed on from the stars, transmitted from the sun, reflected by the planets and by the moons. Light pervaded the entire system of the universe and touched all its parts in one way or another. The *Opticks* proposed an investigation of light, but the final product is not a system of the world, but the inner structure of natural bodies. The developing line of investigation in the *Opticks* is not toward the comprehensive assemblage of everything; it is toward the internal makeup of each thing. Yet this inquiry discloses an arrangement similar to the universe itself; both are read through mathematical proportions of masses and forces. The parallelism between movement and light had been noted early in the *Principia*, emphatically enough so that either could be the subject of Universal Mechanics: "Because of the analogy which exists between the propagation of the rays of light and the motion of bodies, I thought it not amiss to add the following Propositions for optical use; not at all considering the nature of the rays of light or inquiring whether they are bodies or not; but only determining the curves of bodies which are extremely like the curves of rays."[117] The emission of light paralleled the movement of masses. The motions of bodies allowed one to build to a system of the universe; the light from bodies, whether refracted or reflected, allowed one to discover something of their inner depth and internal constitution.

Optical inquiry focused initially on the broad questions of its subject-matter: light and its consistent property, color. Color can be analytically reduced through the two mechanical operations which account for it: refraction and reflection. Refraction further reduces compound or heterogeneous color into its simple or primary components. Thus, white light can be analyzed into its component colors just as compound motions can be resolved into simple motions; or, again parallel with the procedures of the *Principia*, simple colors can be conjoined into a compound or heterogeneous light. Color itself, in any of its forms, is the result of either refraction or reflection.

This pushes the examination of light one step further: What is the nature of transparent and opaque bodies? Like white light itself, each of these visible bodies is a compound, a porous composite of least particles or corpuscles and many empty spaces. The connection between the internal composition of bodies and the basic properties of light is firmly established by the discovery that the opacity of bodies is in indirect relationship to their density. "That this discontinuity of parts is the principal Cause of the opacity of Bodies, will appear by considering, that opake Substances become transparent by filling their Pores with any Substance of equal or almost equal density with their parts. Thus Paper dipped in Water or Oil, the *Oculus Mundi* Stone steep'd in Water, Linnen Cloth oiled or varnish'd, and many other Substances soaked in such Liquors as will intimately pervade their little Pores, become by that means more transparent than otherwise."[118] And the conclusion emerges: "Hence we may understand that bodies are much more rare and porous than is commonly believed."[119] Just as the free movement of the planets and their moons indicate that the universe is empty of matter with the exception of some very thin vapors or steam or effluvia which rise from the atmosphere of the earth, and possibly of a medium so rare as to register no resistance, so the refraction and reflection of light indicates myriad spaces among the particles by which the visible bodies are composed.

Thus the phenomenon of color allows the mechanical activities of refraction and reflection, and these powers have their location in the internal structure as well as the surfaces of each body. Each of these bodies is itself a composite of least particles, interstices, and the powers of attraction, cohesion, and repulsion. Each body is then a structure, a system. The queries appended to the *Opticks* continue this reductive analysis. They analyze light into the bodies from which it comes and the corpuscles by which even the rays of light are formed. This is a section of questions, essential questions if the phenomenon of light is to be brought under Universal Mechanics. The reduction of bodies to least parts and of light to corpuscles allows this integration. The *Lexicon Technicum* of John Harris had already identified the corpuscular philosophy with the mechanical philosophy.[120] The queries of Newton allow light and color to be subsumed into mechanics because through light one reaches into the corpuscular construction of things.

The corpuscular composition of masses introduces new phenomena into the theological considerations Newton thought appropriate to mechanics. To the order and beauty of the heavenly composition can be added questions such as: "How came the Bodies of Animals to be contrived with so much Art, and for what ends were their several Parts? Was the Eye contrived without Skill in Opticks, and the Ear without Knowledge of Sounds? How do the Motions of the Body follow from the Will and whence is the Instinct in Animals[?] . . . And these things being rightly dispatch'd, does it not appear from Phaenomena that there is a Being incorporeal, living, intelligent, omnipresent."[121] The divine attributes here are similar to those in the

Principia, but with two notable differences. First, dominion does not figure as yet. The comprehensive principle of force has still to be worked into the optical discussion. Second, space is now seen not simply as the extension that emanates from god and allows for real motion. The citation continues: ". . . who in Infinite Space, *as it were in his Sensory*, sees the things themselves intimately, and thoroughly perceives them, and comprehends them wholly by their immediate presence to himself." The previous discussion about seeing now allows a parallel predication about space. Space analytically is the condition for the possibility of movement; space in the synthetic moment of the *Opticks* is that in which god is present to all things consciously. Newton is comparing the sensorium of human beings with the space of god. In his representative theory of perception, what human beings perceive directly are not things, but the images of things, brought into the human interiority through sensible experience. In this interiority—the interior senses or the phantasm—these images "are there seen and beheld by that which in us perceives and thinks."[122] Space is that in which god perceives and thinks, and is present not to images, but to things.

This was the first point of Leibniz's attack on Newtonian mechanical theology: as if god needed an organ, through which he could perceive what is. Clarke's reply was short and to the point: "The word *sensory* does not properly signify the organ, but the place of sensation. The eye, the ear, etc., are organs, but not sensoria. Besides, Sir Isaac Newton does not say, that space is the sensory; but that it is, by way of similitude only, *as it were the sensory*."[123] Just as the soul perceives the images by which things are present to it in its sensory, that is, in its interior sense in which they are represented, so god is present to things directly and hence perceives them in themselves, in the way and place that they are, that is, in space.

But the theological argument from the corpuscular composition is basically the same as from the system of the world: compound bodies are porous, they consist of parts "which are only laid together," and these parts are conjunctions of similarly smaller parts until one comes to the "simple Particles." What holds the great masses of the system of the universe together is the force of gravitation "which intercedes those Bodies, and almost all the small ones of their Particles." The theological argument can be basically the same because "thus Nature will be very conformable to herself and very simple."[124] In the universe and in any compound body, inertial forces will only account for the perduration in existence. They will not account for the origin and composition of structures. The active forces in the universe—such as magnetism, gravity, fermentation, and electricity—can account for some of the composition. But the structure of movements in the universe and the system of relationships that make up a body demand intelligence and power in the ultimate force: "Such a wonderful Uniformity in the Planetary System must be allowed the Effect of Choice. And so must the Uniformity in the Bodies of Animals," that is, the symmetry of right and left sides, the location of the arms and legs, the relationship between shoulders and neck and backbone and head. Or analyze the body still further into each of its parts and its organic composition. Any and all of these "can be the effect of nothing else than the Wisdom and Skill of a powerful ever-living Agent, who being in all Places, is more able by his Will to move the Bodies within his boundless uniform Sensorium, and thereby to form and reform the Parts of the Universe, than we are by our Will to move the Parts of our own bodies."[125]

The last query links the theological reflections of the *Principia* with those of the *Opticks*, for the power that joins the least particles together to constitute a more complex body elicits a consideration of the power by which the structure has come together. This power operates in space, and Newton conjectures a "probable" scenario by which the divine *dominatio* constructed the bodies, minuscule, planetary, and astral: "God in the beginning form'd matter in solid, massy, hard, impenetrable, moveable Particles, of such Sizes and Figures, and with such other Properties, and in such Proportion to Space, as most conduced to the End for which he form'd them; and that these primitive Particles being Solids, are incomparably harder than any porous Bodies compounded of them; even so very hard, as never to wear or break into pieces; no ordinary Power being able to divide what God himself made one in the first Creation. . . . And therefore, that nature may be lasting, the Changes of corporeal Things are to be placed only in the various Separations and new Associations and Motions of these permanent Particles."[126] These particles, then, were the original and perduring building blocks of all corporeal things, and things themselves are associations of these particles.

What was "system" for the universe is now "association" for each body in it, and both demand an intelligent cause: "Now by the help of these Principles, all material Things seem to have been composed of the hard and solid Particles above-mention'd, variously associated in the first Creation by the Counsel of an intelligent Agent. For it became him who created them to set them in order."[127] This last sentence summarizes Newtonian natural theology: where there is an order of masses and gravitational attractions, of orbits and proportional distances, or of the design of bodies and their functions, a proportional force is required to account for so carefully constructed an order, whether it is a system or an association.

All the data of mechanics and of an optics reduced to the principles of mechanics pointed to this intelligent force: "Atheism is so senseless and odious to mankind, that is never had many professors. . . . Whence arises this uniformity in all their outward shapes but from the counsel and contrivance of an Author."[128] This author was an inescapable object of inquiry for a Universal Mechanics that both demanded absolute space and absolute time as the conditions for its subject-matter and analyzed any system back to its original forces.

The Assimilation of Theology into the New Philosophic Consciousness

SECTION 1. The Mystical Theology of Controversy: Nicolas Malebranche

When Father Yves de l'Isle André, the Jesuit biographer and disciple of Nicolas Malebranche, came to determine the date of the great Oratorian's conversion—the word is not too strong—to the philosophic guidance of Descartes, he chose the famous visit to a bookstore. The walk that afternoon was all under the governance of god, "who had destined Father Malebranche to humble the pride of pseudo-intellectuals before the feet of truth." The place was Paris, more precisely a bookstore which André located appropriately on "le quai des Augustins." The year was 1664, the year of his ordination, and the young Malebranche asked the bookseller for something recently published. He was given Clerselier's edition of Descartes' *Traité de l'Homme*. Malebranche had heard of Descartes' closeness to the founder of the Oratory in France, Cardinal de Bérulle. But thirty-six years had passed since that November conference between Descartes and Bérulle, and the climate of the French Oratory had not encouraged Cartesianism. Malebranche had entered the Oratory only four years before, at the age of twenty-two, and during his preparation for the priesthood was "extrêmement prévenu contre ce nouveau philosophe." Then, in an Augustinian drama of *tolle et lege*, Malebranche took up the volume of Descartes and began to read. The effect was electric. Let Father André describe this first encounter: "The joy of learning so vast a number of new discoveries caused him such violent palpitations of the heart that he had to stop reading in order to breathe easily once more." One cannot but comment with Monsieur de Fontenelle that invisible, purely speculative truth does not find such a delicate sensibility among the common run of men and women. But Father André does not wonder at the response. Descartes was very simply the greatest and the most original genius the world had ever witnessed, allowing for the single exception of Saint Augustine.[1] Augustine, Descartes, and Malebranche. It was a unity of tradition and of variations within a tradition that would bring Cartesianism directly into the apologetic fray against the atheists.

It was not that Malebranche had never cracked a philosophic text before. On the contrary, at the Collège de La Marche, from 1654 to 1656, he had given himself to the study of what passed for Aristotelianism. Henri Gouhier, in his classic *La vocation de Malebranche*, maintains that this philosophy curriculum ran through a series of commentaries on the works of Aristotle. From La Marche, Malebranche passed to the Sorbonne for three years of study of scholastic theology, and thence to the Oratory. In these years, theology was pursued with the text of Saint Thomas as the central and organizing intellectual tradition, a Thomism, maintains Gouhier, that was "très voisin du thomisme des Pères Dominicains."[2] It was astonishing, Malebranche reflected later in his inaugural masterpiece, *Recherche de la vérité* (1674–1676), that such an education should have been offered, in which the pagan philosopher's emphasis upon the union of the soul and the body took precedence over the Augustinian emphasis upon the union between the soul and God; it was astonishing especially for Christian philosophers who should prefer "Moses to Aristotle, Saint Augustine to some wretched commentator on a pagan philosopher, considering the soul more as the form of the body than as that which is made in-and-for the image of God, that is, according to Saint Augustine, for the Truth with which alone it is immediately united."[3] The curriculum that preceded the seminarian's entrance into the bookstore was all wrong: Aristotle instead of Descartes in philosophy, Thomas instead of Augustine in theology. The central issue which exposed its limitations was that of the soul united in some way—even substantially—with matter.

It is certainly true that the soul is one with the body, as Descartes had insisted. He had attempted to make his peace with the scholastics in allowing the soul even to be called the form, but it was form in a sense Aristotle would never have recognized, a form as distinct from its matter as one substance from another.[4] Malebranche also granted that usage. But he emphasized that the human soul was united with god "d'une manière bien plus étroite, & bien plus essentielle."[5] This is an extraordinary statement. That god was more united, more intimate with the soul than the soul with itself was a commonplace in the Augustinian *intimior intimo meo*. But to assert that the soul was "more essentially" united with god than with the body turned the whole world around. Whatever one said subsequently about a unity which the soul formed with the body would never get them back together as one substance. Just as the soul could be infinitely distinct from god, infinitely other than god, and still essentially one with him, so also gradations of unity could be forged to include that of the soul and the body, but never a unity in which the body could act upon the human spirit or the senses account for some of the content of an idea. That the soul is more naturally united with god than with the body is evident, Malebranche maintained. Pure thought can distinguish them completely. One can think about the human spirit without a body, and, further, the immortality of the soul demands that the human spirit continue to exist without a body. But the soul can neither be thought about nor exist separated from god. *Ergo, stat thesis.*

This is why Malebranche became an occasionalist; it is also, more immediately, why he remained fundamentally a theologian. How can one account for the pervasive and spontaneous distortions of experience and perception with which every human being lives? The average person thinks more of his body than of his god. There is a vividness about the world that god himself does not usually enjoy in human consciousness. Human experience is fundamentally deflected in the wrong direction—toward the world and toward the body—and human perception of sensible interactions is fundamentally misleading. It is no wonder that the history of philosophy, pagan philosophy, has led inevitably to skepticism. Until one recognizes that the instrument is faulty, the disorder in the apperception of what is real or unreal will never be recognized. To grasp how deeply misplaced is our primitive focus upon sensibilia, sense objects, and the world of sensations, it "would be necessary to destroy the principal foundations of pagan philosophy [read: Aristotle], to explicate the disorders that issue from sin [read: Augustine], to battle against that which one falsely calls experience and to reason against the prejudices and the illusions of the senses [read: Descartes]."[6] It is not that philosophic reasoning does not have its place with its rigor of mathematical method and autonomy of evidence. But its foundations must be laid in the theological awareness of the destructive influence of sin and the cancerous malformation of human perception, experience, and pagan philosophy.

One cannot understand Malebranche without understanding the central role that the doctrine of original sin plays in his system. This aboriginal distortion, established and reckoned in every judgment, accounts for the seemingly bizarre positions of occasionalism and spiritualism. Father Malebranche would be among the first to acknowledge their strangeness to the ordinary person, to the theologically untutored, to the pagans. But this alienation of experience from reality is an ineluctable consequence of the events revealed in Genesis, the Wisdom of Solomon, and Paul's Letter to the Romans. The very first page of the very first chapter of the *Recherche de la vérité* explains human misery through the teachings of the biblical authors: "Sacred Scripture teaches us that human beings are only wretched because they are sinners and criminals, that they would be neither sinners nor criminals if they had not made themselves slaves of sin by consenting to an error."[7] Malebranche is at pains to distinguish his understanding of original sin from that of his Jansenist critic, Antoine Arnauld. Human nature is not totally corrupt, but it has been distorted and damaged.[8] "The soul after [Original] Sin has become, as it were, *corporeal by inclinations*. Its love for sensible things constantly diminishes its union with or relation to intelligible things."[9] The entire seventh chapter of Romans details the inner alienations which original sin insinuated into human experience, into the desires and capacities within human life. Unless a person grasps how profoundly deviant the world has become, a naive reliance upon sensible experience and everyday common sense will corrupt philosophy from its beginnings. This is the burden of the question that Aristes puts to Malebranche in the guise of Theodore:

> ARISTES: I find a disorder which is very great and which seems to me unworthy of the wisdom and the goodness of our God. For, after all, for us unhappy creatures this order is a fruitful source of errors and the inevitable cause of the greatest evils of life. The tip of my finger is pricked, and I suffer, I am unhappy, I am incapable of thinking of the true good. My soul can attend to nothing but my injured finger and is entirely filled with pain. What a strange misfortune! A mind to depend upon a body and because of it to lose the sight of truth! To have one's attention divided, indeed to be more occupied with one's finger than with the real end of one's being! What disorder, Theodore! There is assuredly some mystery in all this. I beseech you to unravel it for me.

> THEODORE: Yes, without a doubt there is some mystery in this. *How much philosophers are indebted to religion, my dear Aristes, for it alone can help them out of the perplexity in which they find themselves!* Everything in the procedure of God seems to be self-contradictory . . . sin brings it about that God, without effecting any change in His laws, becomes for all sinners the just avenger of their crimes. . . . [Thus] experience convinces me that my mind depends on my body. I suffer, I am unhappy, I am incapable of thought when I am pricked, of this there can be no doubt. We have, then, here *a flagrant contradiction between the certainty of experience and the evidence of reason.* See, however, the solution. The mind of man has lost its worth and its excellence in the eyes of God. We are no longer such as god originally made us. We are born in sin and corruption.[10]

Descartes had been satisfied to trace this misplaced reliance upon sensible experience to habits ingrained from childhood—and so Descartes remained essentially a philosopher.[11] Nicholas Malebranche was not content to leave it there. Seven years of theological studies had more than left their mark. They had given him resources and a cast of mind within which he would always do his philosophy. They had formed him essentially as a theologian, who would trace the origins of errors in perception to the primordial disaster inherent in a fundamental choice of evil, original sin and its consequences. Much of the difficulty in attempting to understand and appreciate Malebranche stems from a basic failure to grasp that he was a theologian, an Augustinian theologian, whose philosophy was always an attempt to overcome the effects of original sin. The radical and irredeemable fault in pagan philosophies was theological. The pagans had no way of assessing how profoundly misguided their experience of reality was. Doing philosophy among them and using their texts is possible, but it is like reasoned discourse in an institution whose members are slightly mad. Malebranche can do philosophy, indeed, so well that he is frequently cited as the greatest French metaphysician after Descartes, his master. But it is philosophy as a moment within theology, as dependent upon revelation and faith for its fundamental outlook on the world. It is philosophy done by an Augustinian theologian.

If original sin made Malebranche skeptical of philosophic reasoning based on sensible experience, it made him even more wary of pagan philosophers. Aristotle remained unregenerate after so many centuries of attempts to incorporate him into scholastic theology. It is not difficult to imagine, then, how Malebranche greeted the claims of some Jesuit missionaries that Chinese culture possessed a profoundly authentic, albeit limited, conception of the transcendent god. This claim struck at the very heart of his view of the ravages of sin.

To Correct the Chinese

There was another encounter, much later in the life of Malebranche, after his philosophic fame had diffused throughout Europe and one of his theological tractates, the *Traité de la nature et de la grâce*, had reached the giddy heights of the Roman Index. The confrontation was occasioned by a series of conversations between Malebranche and the exiled French missionary bishop, Artus de Lyonne, bishop of Rosalie and one of the vicars apostolic who returned to Europe in 1706.

The disastrous embassy of Carlo Tomasso Maillard de Tournon to the court of China (1705–1706) had concluded with the legate's condemnation of the Chinese Rites and the expulsion of three vicars apostolic from the country by the enraged K'ang-hsi Emperor. Back in France, the literature for and against this and the Roman condemnations roared around in a vacuum of understanding. Very few of the intellectuals of Europe could read or speak Chinese; fewer had visited the Middle Kingdom. The condemnation of the Holy Office (1704) and Maillard de Tournon's own condemnation were followed by an edict of Clement XI, backing the actions of his envoy, newly created Cardinal, demanding compliance from the maligned and harassed Jesuits left in China, and culminating in the brief *Ex illa die* of March 19, 1715, in which the Rites were again condemned, an oath of obedience exacted from the remaining missionaries, and the end of the great and tragic experiment drawn.[12]

It was in this decade that Malebranche was asked by Artus de Lyonne to address himself to the atheism contained in Chinese thought, which lay at the heart of Chinese philosophy. So Malebranche set to work "to rectify the false idea they [the Chinese] have of the nature of God."[13] Chinese philosophy is seen by Malebranche through the classic neo-Confucianism of Chu-Hsi, which was correct enough, but neo-Confucianism as understood by the bishop of Rosalie, who unfortunately did not seem to know what he was talking about.

Neo-Confucianism had added the concept of *li* (Principle) to the tradition it was reviving. *Li* came not so much from the occasional references in great classics, the *Book of Changes* and the *Book of Mencius*, but through the influence of the neo-Taoists of the third and fourth centuries who established a doctrine that Principle (*li*) governs all things. In the centuries that followed, the Buddhists also employed the concept of *li* in their teachings on the harmony of principle and fact. This incited the rising neo-Confucianists to take the various statements about *li* from their own historical books, reinterpret them, and build an entire system with this as its metaphysical basis. So thoroughly did they accomplish their task that, by the end of the thirteenth century, neo-Confucianism was called the School of Principle.[14] This was the school whose great masters had been synthesized by Chu-Hsi (1130–1200), "probably the greatest synthesizer in the history of Chinese thought."[15] This synthesis remained the orthodox version of Confucianism from the imperial decree of 1313 until the termination of the civil service examinations in 1905.[16]

It is notoriously difficult to render Chinese terms into English, and *li* provides no exception to this harsh experience. Wing-Tsit Chan documents the various choices which have been made: law, reason, order, organization, principle of organization. Each has its limitations. "Reason" implies consciousness or personality; "law" involves a sense of rules and of formula. Though "organization" and "order" keep the original meaning of *li*, they fail to express the basic meaning of a fundamental truth. "*Li* is not only a principle of organization, but also a principle of being, nature, etc."[17] Chan settles for "principle," as do the majority of Chinese philosophers. The translation is critical, because the interpretation of the term depends on the translation of the word.

It is of paramount importance to understand that *li*—like the Platonic idea of the Good—is a highly analogical conception. It has, like Platonic and Neoplatonic reality, both a transcendent and an immanent meaning. It subsists in itself, antecedent to any single physical object: "in the beginning, when no single physical object yet existed, there was then nothing but Principle [*li*]."[18] Yet this form or principle possessed a multiplicity within itself, the archetypes of those physical things that could exist. Each thing that comes into physical existence possesses its own nature, a nature which is formed by its own *li*: "*Question*: 'How is it that dried up withered things also possess the nature [*hsing*]?' *Answer*: 'For them there has been from the beginning such a Principle [*li*]. . . . The bricks of these steps have within them the Principle [*li*] that pertains to bricks. . . . This bamboo chair has within it the Principle pertaining to bamboo chairs.'"[19]

Father Malebranche found in all of this tradition the doctrine of Spinoza! He would have been better advised to look to Alexandria rather than to Amsterdam, not for an identical philosophy—philosophies seldom simply repeat others—but for a similar spirit of philosophizing or world view. Each temporal object has its own structure of intelligibility and existence, but this is a formal participation in the single and ultimate reality, which in Chu-Hsi is called the Supreme Ultimate (*t'ai chi*): "Chaing Yüan-chin remarked: 'The benevolence of the ruler and the reverence of the subject are, then, such Ultimates?' The Master replied: 'These are the Ultimates of a single thing or a single object. But the Principles [*li*] of *all* the myriad things within the universe, brought into one whole, constitute the Supreme Ultimate [*t'ai chi*]. The Supreme Ultimate did not originally have this name. It is simply an appellation applied to it.'"[20] Thus Chu-Hsi can speak of the Supreme Ultimate as the supreme archetype for all that is, much as the Platonic idea of the Good radiates the archetypal forms of the individual participants. In Neoplatonism, these forms become the ideas contained in the *nous*; in neo-Confucianism, they are the myriad *li* contained in the single *li*. In neither philosophy is there a question of a pantheism or a materialism. In Plotinus, the process of emanation is compared to the radiations of the sun, using the metaphorical terms *perilampsis* and *ellampsis*, with the prior principle remaining the same.[21] And in Chu-Hsi one reads: "Originally there is only one Supreme Ultimate; yet each of the myriad things partakes of it, so that each in itself contains the Supreme Ultimate in its entirety. This is like the moon, of which there is but one in the sky, and yet by scattering (its reflection) upon the rivers and lakes, it is to be seen everywhere. But one cannot say from this that the moon itself has been divided."[22] Like the space of Plato (χώρα) or the darkness of Plotinus (στέρησις), there is a material *ch'i* into which *li* radiates order. "Men or things, at the moment of their production, must receive this *li* in order that they may have a nature [*hsing*] of their own; they must receive this *ch'i* in order that they may have form."[23] Of these two components of each individual, one can predicate a certain sempiternality. Of *li*, it can be predicated as a changeless eternality; of *ch'i*, it can be predicated as something endless, formless in itself, given the structure of a nature and of movement through the influence of *li*. "Before Heaven and Earth existed, there was only Principle. There being this Principle, this Heaven and Earth then came to exist. If there were no Principle, there would also be no Heaven and Earth, no human beings, and no things. None of these would have any place on which to stand. There being Principle, there is then the Ether, which flows into movement to produce the myriad things."[24]

The similarities between Chu-Hsi and the Neoplatonic tradition are striking. The single *li* is participatively present in the *li* of each thing as the moon is present in its reflection. Like the One of Plotinus, the *li* subsists above limited existence and nonexistence. "Before the Heaven and Earth 'existed,' it already was as it is."[25]

Unfortunately, all of these subtleties escape Father Malebranche. As a matter of fact, in using the Chinese as a foil for the debate of Western ideas, Malebranche was employing a literary device quite common in the seventeenth and eighteenth centuries. It was enough that the bishop of Rosalie had spoken with *les Chinois lettrez*. They had taught him of *deux genres d'êtres* which were eternal: *li* and matter. They had also taught him that "le *Ly* ne subsiste point en lui-même, & indépendament de la matiere. Apparament ils le regardent comme une forme, ou comme une qualité répanduë dans la matiere." Artus de Lyonne and Malebranche have collapsed the distinction between the transcendent and the immanent *li*, wiped out any theory of participative reflection or emanation, and made of *li* and *ch'i* coordinate sources in the composition of material reality. *Li*, in Malebranche's reading, is the order inherent in things, the wisdom embodied in their structures or the justice incarnate in their actions. Consequently, it renders all things intelligent, wise, or just, though it is neither personal nor transcendent itself. In this sense, Malebranche can adopt from the prologue of the Gospel of John a line to describe the *li*: The Chinese philosophers agree "que le *Ly* est la lumiere qui éclaire tous les hommes, & que c'est en lui que nous voyons toutes choses."[26] Malebranche has managed to do precisely the opposite of what the early Church did with a comparable situation of Neoplatonism. The early Christians read pagan philosophers at great length and with cautious respect and sympathy, and through so lengthy an acquaintance learned which elements were supportive of Christian revelation and which could be reinterpreted in terms of that revelation; they then used these elements to construct so profound a system as that of the great Augustine and so religious a synthesis as that of the Alexandrian mystics. Malebranche took up the neo-Confucian ideas during his vacation conversation with the exiled bishop of Lyonne, after a series of interchanges felt himself master enough of the six errors about the existence and nature of god which that ancient culture embraced, and set himself "to rectify the false idea they have of the nature of God." Few things exhibit the casual arrogance of the Western clerical world more than the events of that sad and needless time: Maillard de Tournon sent to the Middle Kingdom with no knowledge of its language or respect for its culture; Malebranche confident of his crusade against the neo-Confucianists because "it seems to me that there are many correspondences between the impieties of Spinoza and those of the Chinese philosopher."[27] Never mind the Jesuits' protest in the *Mémoires de Trévoux*, or the attempts of centuries of cultural interchange reaching one of their finest expressions in Leibniz! The matter can be handled in a short essay whose data is culled from the conversations of a vacation.[28] In 1707, the *Entretien d'un philosophe chrétien et d'un philosophe chinois sur l'existence et la nature de Dieu* was written.

From Idea to Existence

As it is applied polemically to the issues of the existence and nature of god, the methodology of Malebranche functions in four stages. Perhaps a contrast with Euclid's great paradigm of geometrical method will illumine the unique features of the procedures traced in the reflections of Malebranche.

Initially, the definition of god is established as an idea, precisely as a definition. Euclid's classic treatise placed its twenty-three definitions first in order to supply the elements with which to build and combine. In Malebranche, three definitions are laid out as a set of possibilities, a matrix within which the discourse will move. In the second moment of Euclidian method, the issues of existence are introduced, not as statements of facts but as postulated activities, taking the elements given by definition and drawing the lines or describing the circles. In Euclid, one moves from definition to existence by production. In Malebranche's dialogue, existence is a matter neither of assumption nor of production, but of demonstration. One moves from the idea of god to his existence through proof. In the third moment of the *Elements*, "common notions" are elaborated and problems, theorems, and porisms are advanced through thirteen books. What these have in common is that they all make a claim to truth. The common notions are general statements about quantities whose evidence lies within the statement itself; the others, figures to be constructed, theorems to be demonstrated, or possibilities to be investigated, are all assertions whose establishment lies within the processes of construction and demonstration. In contrast, Malebranche's third stage enters immediately into theorem or statement: what are the assertions that can be made about the god whose idea and whose existence have been established. This movement is a progressive definition through the gradual accretion of predicates, moving from the infinitely perfect until the adjectives become primarily personal. Finally, in a fourth step which indicates the fragmentary nature of any single dialogue, the results of this inquiry are made coordinate with the results of others without an attempt to construct an entire system. Two corollaries emerge which must be handled if the previous statements are to be coordinate with what is known of life: how is evil present within such a theological understanding of reality, and how does matter emerge from nothing? Both of these questions are a matter of context or verification: how does what has been asserted fit in with what else one knows about the universe?

The Christian and the Chinese begin their dialogue with the definitions that circumscribe the common subject-matter: what are we talking about? The dialogue begins with a common word, god, and outlines three meanings that this word can possess. These definitions do not offer three coordinate units to be built variously into a synthetic whole, but a matrix of theological possibilities, one of which will exclude the others. "God" can denote another thing in the universe, another reality alongside others, like Jupiter for the Romans, or "Lord of Heaven and Earth" conceived as a powerful emperor writ large. Religious adherence to such an idea is idolatry. "God" can also be understood as the *Li*, in Malebranche's transposition of this concept, that is, a form inherent in each thing and the universal order within all things, a structure immanent within the universe and forming with matter the objects one sees. Religious attachment to such a metaphysics can be called atheism, neither the idolatry of the pagan Greeks nor the authentic theism which the Jesuits mistakenly read into Chinese beliefs. Finally, "god" can denote the transcendent one, immanent because transcendent, not because it is a part in the composition of anything. This is the god of Exodus, "He who is," and Malebranche merges with this the Cartesian insistence or emphasis upon infinitude. He who is is "the Being who contains in his essence all there is of reality or of perfection in all beings, the Being infinite in every sense, in a word, Being."[29] Only this idea offers the religious affiliation that the Christian could recognize as valid theism.

These three ideas which give definitional limits to the dialogue come out of the fundamental Cartesian dichotomy of finite/infinite. The god of the idolaters is essentially finite, limited quantitatively by space and time, and limited qualitatively in his perfections. The *Li* of the atheist, like the substance of Spinoza with its twofold attributes, is essentially and quantitatively infinite, coextensive with the extension that can be studied in mathematics. The god who is Being is essentially and qualitatively infinite, limitless in his endowments and in his perfections, containing in an "eminent way" the perfection of all things.

The simplicity of these formulae, however, obscures the inherent ambiguity of essential terms. The dialogue opens with the problem about definition, posed by the Chinese philosopher, but it is framed in terminology which means one thing to the prophet Isaiah and a radically different thing to the long Chinese tradition: "Who is this Lord of Heaven which you have come from a distance to proclaim to us? We do not recognize him at all."[30] The entire dialogue is an attempt to answer this question. As the question is initially stated, the Chinese reads the Christians as idolaters and rejects their primitive idea of god. On the other hand, the Christian understands the Chinese as revering only "le *Ly* cette souveraine Verité, Sagesse, Justice, qui subsiste éternellement dans la matiere, qui la forme et la range dans ce bel ordre que nous voyons."[31] To the Christian, this is equivalent to atheism, an atheism he has met before, that of Spinoza. Spinoza functions in this dialogue—besides simply as someone woefully misunderstood—in two ways: Malebranche's Spinoza becomes the pattern of the neo-Confucian metaphysics, and the antecedent presence of Spinoza in Europe makes it even more likely that atheism could arise in China. Malebranche's Spinoza furnishes both the paradigm by which Chu-Hsi and his followers are to be understood and the likelihood that such a godless metaphysics could find its place in countries that had never been exposed to Christianity.

The Jesuits had argued that Chinese philosophy and Chinese culture condemned atheism. But what does that prove, even if it were true, responds Malebranche. Europe also condemns atheism. "And does that prevent me from believing that there are some Spinozists and keep me from producing a dialogue between a Christian and a Spinozist in order to combat the strange paradoxes of this impious person? If some persons instructed in the truths of religion are capable of falling into atheism, what must one think of the Chinese who have not been enlightened, as we have been, by the light of the Gospel?"[32] The *Ethics* of Spinoza in Western philosophy not only provided a set of coordinates that could be used to chart Chinese philosophy, but made the atheism of this philosophy seem more likely. If Europe produced atheists, how much more China! Once the distinction between the transcendent *Li* and the individual *li* was erased and matter was interpreted in terms of the extension of the Cartesians, it is easy enough to see how Chu-Hsi and Spinoza were one for Malebranche.

The god who is another finite thing in the universe is never seriously considered. Both the Chinese and the Christian have gone beyond such a construct. "Your *Li*, your supreme justice, approaches infinitely closer (*infiniment plus*) the idea of our God than that of this powerful emperor."[33] Why? Because *Li* is infinite. "Infinity" leaves this form of atheism closer to authentic theism than to idolatry. Malebranche titles the position he was attacking "le libertinage," and qualifies the sense in which one could charge the Chinese interlocutor with atheism: "I do not place atheism in the mouth of the Chinese, unless one means by atheism the refusal to recognize the existence of the true God, of being infinitely perfect in every manner."[34] He cites the witness of the Jesuits themselves to confirm his view, for the word "atheism" was used frequently in the works to which he refers. The great Matteo Ricci had indicated that a number of Chinese thinkers, as they abstained from the worship of false gods, had fallen into atheism ("Il y en a peu de ceux là qui d'une cheute plus grande ne tombent dans l'Athéisme"); Nicolo Longobardo cited this opinion of Ricci's and added his evaluation of its general acceptance: "In qua sententia omnes absque differentia concordamus." Martin Martini, who had represented the missionaries before the Holy Office to obtain the decree of March 23, 1656, giving permission for the Chinese Rites under the explanations and conditions indicated by the Jesuits, maintained that some learned Chinese held that things come from chance and that there obtained among them "de summo ac primo rerum principio mirum apud omnes silentium." Alvarô Semedo, Jacques LeFavre, and Louis Le Comte are all quoted with various degrees of accuracy to substantiate Malebranche's contention that atheism was rampant in educated China. None of these citations accomplishes, however, the liaison Malebranche makes, the identification of the classic School of Principle with the atheism of which the missionaries spoke. None of the missionaries, whatever their learning and levels of insight, ever drew an equation between Chu-Hsi and Baruch de Spinoza.[35]

The issue between these two ideas of god is the issue between design and the infinite author of the design. The Christian does not deny *li* within the universe, the order, justice, and wisdom embodied and exhibited in each thing and in the universe as a whole. The question the Christian wishes to pose goes further: Is there a Being unrestricted and unlimited, one infinite in his perfections and consequently incomprehensible to any finite mind, one without the nonbeing which necessarily goes with the space-and-time limitation of material things? The issue between the neo-Confucianist and the Christian lies in the nature of the infinite and the meaning of matter.

Matter by its very nature bespeaks qualitative limitation. Matter is "the least and most contemptible substance."[36] It carries with it what it is not. The hand is not the head; my chair is not my room. But the infinite Being contains all perfections in itself, not in a comprehensible way but in a necessary way. The infinite is another word for the all-perfect. It is always and everywhere what it is. It exists as the simple which is perfect in every way. The infinite can only demonstrate *that* it must be; *what* it is is beyond any finite mind. The contrast cannot be sharper: anything material always contains the nonbeing of what it does not possess or of what it is not; it can always be more. The infinite is that greater than which nothing can exist or be conceived.

In the second stage of Malebranche's argument, the question turns from idea to existence. The Chinese philosopher agrees that "this idea which you present to me of your God is the most excellent of all, for there is nothing greater than what is infinite in every manner. But we deny that this infinite exists (*cet infini existe*). It is a fiction, fancy, without reality."[37] The issue shifts from idea to existence. How can one demonstrate the existence of the infinite?

The question is classically Cartesian. From the idea of the infinite, Descartes' metaphysics had demonstrated a proportional cause. In the *Meditations*, the idea of the infinite implicates the existence of its efficient cause, and of an infinite cause because of the coordination that must exist between an effect and its cause. Again and again in various arguments Descartes used this idea to move the thinking subject outside its own mind to affirm the existence of the truthful god. It was enough to know that the thinking subject possessed the idea of the infinitely perfect. The idea was the evidence. From this, one could and must infer the reality of that which the idea represented.

This is not the move that Malebranche makes. Like Descartes, he begins with the thinking subject. Like Descartes, he begins with a thinking of the infinite. But, unlike Descartes, "the infinite" is not an idea that belongs in any way to the thinking subject. Unlike Descartes, the inference is no inference at all: "De cela seul que nous appercevons l'infini, il faut qu'il soit."[38] How so? Let us begin, as good Cartesians, with the phenomenon of consciousness:

1. To-think-of-nothing and not-to-think-at-all are two different phrases for exactly the same reality. To-perceive-nothing and not-to-perceive-at-all are likewise two different phrases expressing the same experience. Even in ordinary language, "I am not thinking at all" and "I am thinking of nothing" are the same assertion. One cannot think or perceive and have that activity terminate in nothing.

2. Consequently, whatever the mind thinks of or perceives is not nothing; that is, whatever the mind immediately or directly perceives is something that in some way exists. Otherwise, there would be no perception or thought going on. This is not to assert that these objects must exist outside the mind. They may or may not so exist. Extramental things in general are not the immediate objects of the thinking subject. Our ideas and impressions are the immediate objects of our minds. As with Descartes, what we know

or perceive are our ideas; things we infer from them. Just as Malebranche's philosophy begins like Descartes' with the thinking subject, so it accepts the representational nature of its ideas: the direct objects of consciousness are the mind's own ideas.

3. But among the objects that I perceive and think immediately and directly, rather than infer, is the infinite. It is not, as Descartes would have it, that I have a clear and distinct idea of the infinite. But the infinite is certainly present as an object of consciousness. I can think about the infinite and insist that to be thus, it must contain all perfections "eminently" within it. What is more, I can perceive the infinite, perceive everything else within it—in fact, this perception of the infinite indicates immediately how finite everything else in my experience is. The infinite is the background against which I perceive everything else. Everything else is measured within it. What is the reality of this infinite which I indubitably perceive?

4. It is itself nothing finite. There is not sufficient reality in anything finite to represent the infinite. Nothing finite can offer an awareness of the infinite. Where there are only two realities, one cannot sanely perceive four. Where there is only finite reality, the mind cannot perceive or think infinitude.

For example, contrast the idea of the sky with that of space. No matter how vast one makes the sky, the infinite extension of space surpasses it. The sky can be used as an image of the infinite space—but as an image of something it is not. One needs the finite metaphor to carry the symbolism of something that completely surpasses it. So also for that which is "infinite in the full sense of being, being infinitely perfect, in a word, Being"[39]

5. One is continuously in the presence, then, of what is infinite and thus of what is not of the human mind, since the human mind is finite. Philosophical theology is not a matter of finding the idea of the infinite within us and looking for a proportional cause. It is rather a matter of finding the infinite within our consciousness and recognizing that it is no human idea. One can call this perception of the infinite an idea or not, depending upon the precision with which one is speaking. For example, the Christian can begin his apologia to the neo-Confucianist with the words: "The God whom we proclaim to you is the same one whose idea is imprinted within you and within all human beings."[40] On the other hand, in the more labored *Entretiens sur la métaphysique et la religion*, Theodore can say: "But above all you must note that God or the Infinite is not visible by an idea representative of Him. The Infinite is its own idea. It has no Archetype."[41]

6. To perceive the infinite, then, is to perceive not an idea but a reality. Nothing finite can represent it. The contrast cannot be sharper. Any finite thing may be known, may exist as an idea, and yet not exist outside the thinking subject. "We can see its essence without its existence, its idea without itself. But we cannot see the essence of the Infinite without its

existence, or the idea of Being without Being. For Being can have no idea representative of it. There is no archetype which could comprise all its intelligible reality."[42]

7. Thus, unlike Descartes, but continually reaffirmed in Malebranche, is the statement that to perceive or to think of god necessarily entails the truth that god exists. He is his own idea within us. Thus the proposition that god exists is as certain as the Cartesian *cogito ergo sum*. Neither is an inference; both are proportions. In the Cartesian *cogito*, the proportion is between the being and the consciousness of the subject; in Malebranche the proportion is between the perception of the infinite god and the necessity of his existence, for he can be represented by nothing else.

Very simply, the idea of god is that of the infinite, of Being in all of its perfections. The existence of the infinite is given by the very act of perceiving the infinite, for there can be no finite, hence created, idea of the infinite. "Ainsi il n'y a que Dieu, que l'infini, que l'être indeterminé, ou que l'infini infiniment infini, qui puisse contenir la réalité infiniment infinie que je voi quand je pense à l'être, & non à tels & tels êtres, ou à tels & tels infinis."[43] As opposed to the idea of indefinite quantitative extension, which is the archetype of the material world and of all possible material worlds, god is the "infinite, infinitely infinite." Such a reality can only be represented to our consciousness by itself. One can only perceive the infinite in the infinite.

Malebranche has significantly altered Descartes. Descartes used a mathematical method to subtract analytically one proposition after another in order to obtain those basic proportions which would be the objects of the Universal Mathematics. With these, one could build gradually, adding those propositions that were causally implicated in the proportions that were self-justifying. In other words, Descartes used a logistic method founded on a reflexive set of principles. Malebranche came out of this mathematical master, but his method was first to erect a matrix of definitions and then to bring that to bear upon the phenomenon of consciousness. The distinction that Descartes maintained between the divine idea and the divine reality is eliminated; god is his own idea. Just as all causal activity in Malebranche's occasionalism is reduced to the activity of god, so all intelligibility of the infinite is reduced to the presence of the divine infinite itself. In other words, Malebranche brings Cartesianism into theology by changing Descartes' reflexive principles into the single, comprehensive principle that explains all things and exercises an immediate self-disclosure to the human intellect. Malebranche has expanded Descartes' "infinite substance" or "supremely perfect Being" into "the infinite, infinitely infinite," and by transforming Descartes' methodology into an operational method he has erected a structure of possibilities and moved to the demonstration of existence. Malebranche is the faithful disciple of Descartes, who "in thirty years has discovered more truths than all other philosophers" in the centuries before him.[44] But, like most faithful disciples, he has significantly transformed the appearance of the master.

The All-Encompassing God

The third stage of Malebranche's argument with the neo-Confucianist is the progressive delimitation of the idea whose referent or existence has been demonstrated, that is, demonstrated as self-evident. What can one say about infinite Being? Perhaps first and most important of all, that everything one can say will come as a deduction precisely from this idea.

From the Buddhist tradition in China comes the first objection: "When I think of the infinite, I think of nothing [*je ne pense à rien*]." A twofold response to this objection is indicated, one dealing with the truth of its assertion and the other explaining the human experience out of which the assertion issues and which it attempts to capture.

Take extension or its synonym, matter, as an example: a foot (*pied*) of extension is not nothing. Add a hundred or a thousand such feet and you have more reality, not less. Now extend this to infinite space, and we will see that whoever thinks of the infinite, even in its quantitative dimensions, "is infinitely removed from thinking nothing, since what you will be thinking of is greater than everything you have thought of." It is not that we get the infinite by adding to the finite. Rather, by this imaginary experiment we recognize that the infinite is limitlessly more real than anything finite. It is the contradiction of nothing.

At the heart of the objection is the failure to distinguish, as Descartes himself distinguished, between the content of an idea and the vividness of its perception. The infinite Being that is god is the immediate object of human perception, but it lacks the vividness of the piercing pain inflicted by a thorn prick or the suffusing color of a room. The paradox of the human experience of god comes through in these comparisons: the reality of god is infinite Being, but the human perception of this reality is "as feeble as it is vast, and consequently, infinitely feeble, for it is infinite." The first assertion that can be made about infinite Being is that in contrast to the vagueness of its impression it is not nothing.[45]

Is it then a particular being (*un être particulier*)? The infinite rules this out. A particular being would make god one more thing in the universe, a finite reality. Because god is Being, he is not nothing. Because god is infinite, he is not particular. "He is rather all being [*tout être*]," and all the realities that human beings know, "ne sont que des participations, (*je ne dis pas des parties*) infiniment limitées, que des imitations infiniment imparfaites de son essence."[46]

The first two objections with their correlative theorems take up the dilemma that any natural theology of an infinite god must face. Either the infinite is everything because it is being, or it is nothing because it is infinite. If there is something besides Being, then god becomes a particular. If there is something other than the infinite, then the infinite becomes finite, for it is limited by what is other than itself.

It is essential to see through these objections that the infinite Being is not composed of a limitless series of finite beings. It is a radically different order of reality, which possesses all reality as its infinite source. Finite realities do not constitute the infinite, nor do they add to it. The infinite Being and the theologian Malebranche do not add up to two! But all the perfection that Malebranche attains and possesses mirrors in a finite way what is limitlessly identified with the divine infinity. Things are not parts of god nor modes of god; they are participations, limited and distinct sharings, in a reality that is limitless, perfectly simple or integral, without any composition of parts. The difficulties encountered in Malebranche's elaboration of the nature of god are not regrettable failures in the system. To say that god is infinite Being is to speak of a reality that is incomprehensible. For a finite mind to comprehend what it means to be infinite Being is a contradiction in terms. There is nothing in terms of which the finite can delimit, coordinate, or grasp the infinite. Such a mind can, however, deduce that it is so: Being is beyond nothing and the infinite is beyond particularity. The first two theorems, then, establish the absolute transcendence of god. The idea of infinite Being, defined by the Christian philosopher, but the object of immediate and direct experience by anyone who will attend to it, functions as the middle term, the *raison d'être*, that denies the nothingness of the Buddhists and the particularity of the idolaters.

It is imperative, however, to establish that god acts. Existence without activity is only an abstraction, the Chinese philosopher maintains. The Christian counters with the assertion that there is nothing created that will not serve as evidence for the existence of the acting god. As in the *Entretiens sur la métaphysique*, the philosophic procedure is much more like a meditation, an appropriation of one's own experience step by step, than a dialogue. The Christian offers "points" for this meditation, "provided that you observe this condition—take note—to follow me and not to reply to anything unless you conceive it distinctly."[47]

For Descartes, the "composition of place" for such a meditation was the "serene retreat in peaceful solitude," shut in by winter in a heated room near Ulm, "where I had plenty of leisure to examine my ideas."[48] For Malebranche, at this point in his dialogue, the place is an open field. One opens his eyes deliberately. At that instant one's vision is flooded by "a very large number of objects, each according to its size, its shape, its movement or its rest, its nearness or distance; and you discover all these objects by the perceptions of entirely different colors."[49] This experience anyone can have. Most people have had it. The question is: What is the cause of this comprehensive and rapid perception?

The matrix of possible causes contains five items: the objects themselves; the organs of the body; the human soul; the *Li* of the neo-Confucianists; the god of the Christians. The objects themselves only reflect the light into our eyes; they do not see. The framework of the eye simply collects these rays and stimulates the brain, but "the diverse disturbances of the brain and of the animal spirits which are modifications of matter agree in nothing with the thoughts of the mind, which are certainly modifications of another substance."[50] In this, Malebranche is faithfully following the master.

One is confronted with two different substances in treating of the human person; the distinction between them is established by the fact that we can think of one without the other. One can think of extension without thinking of perception—consequently, extension and perception are two different realities. But one cannot, on the contrary, think of figure or movement or rest without thinking of extension—these, then, are modifications of matter. The intelligibility of matter does not include joy, pleasure, sadness, or pain, nor does this intelligibility include anything but a thinking, rather than an extended, substance. The modifications of matter are mechanical, and since the brain and the organs of sensation are material, "it is clear that our perceptions are not modifications of our brain, which is but diversely configured extension, but uniquely of our mind, the only substance capable of thought." Mind is a different substance, united with the brain, certainly, but never such that it composes one substance with it. Perception, feelings, thoughts are modifications of the mind, not arrangements of the extension that is the brain.[51]

Is the soul, then, the cause of perception? The soul knows its own ideas, but how could it know that there are projections of the optic nerve from an external source? Furthermore, how could it know enough optics and geometry to reckon the true sizes and distances of objects from the image cast on the retina? Finally, how could it make all of the million inferences necessary to account for the instantaneous perception of the things in that field? The soul does not know any of these things. It does not know of the reflection within the eye or the rules of optical projections, nor has it any experience that it is moving inferentially to determine the accurate place and size of the myriad things that surround it. Whatever does this, it is neither the object seen nor the organs of sight nor the human soul.

What is it, then? What is the cause of my perception in the field? There is a unique aspect of this experience of perception to which we should more often advert because it contains a clue to the truth about perception: "Nous avons *sentiment interieur* que toutes nos perceptions des objects se sont *en nous sans nous, & même malgré nous*, lorsque nos yeux sont ouverts & que nous les regardons." Our perceptions of the sun, for example, may vary as the sun moves across the sky or dips into the west, but the sun is judged to be the same size. The image of the earth in my eye is greater than that of the sun, but I know that the sun is a million times larger. I see someone at a distance and perceive his image grow larger as he approaches, but I know that his size remains the same. I do not consciously infer that this is the case, knowing and making allowance for the geometric proportions. We do it "within ourselves, without ourselves, and even in spite of ourselves." How can we account for this? Only two possibilities remain. Human perception is caused either by the *Li* or by god; neither the object known nor the knowing substance can explain it. The human person is profoundly passive in sensation.[52]

The cause must be one, like Newton's god, who "knows perfectly both Geometry and Optics." The cause must be infinitely aware of how the various organs of perception work and the diversity of modifications that can ensue second after second. Its skills in reasoning must be so inferentially accurate that space and distance, size and movement are immediately grasped and registered: "This cause reasons so rightly and quickly that one sees clearly that it is infinitely intelligent, a quality that you refuse to the *Li*, and that it reveals [*découvre*] immediately the most remote consequences of principles according to which it acts unceasingly in all human beings and in an instant." In Newton, the design within things indicates the presence and creative domination of god. In Malebranche, the experience of perception indicates the more startling assertion that the only agency in the perception itself is that of god. God not only acts; he is the only one who acts. The perception of the knowing subject, which Descartes had established as completely other than extension, depends upon a cause that grasps the full intricacies of optics and geometry, which the soul itself does not possess. For "it is evident that if I do not know exactly the size of the projections which are traced on the optic nerve, the situation and the movement of my body, and know divinely so to speak, Optics and Geometry, when it should depend on me to form within myself the perceptions of objects, I could never perceive the distance, shape, situation and movement of any body. Therefore, it necessarily follows that the cause of all the perceptions that I have when I open my eyes in the middle of a field knows exactly all that, since all our perceptions are regulated only by that cause."[53] Design does not function in Malebranche as in Newton to found an inference from the nature of things to the force that is god. Design is found in human perception, the activity of the knowing subject, and the agent out of which this pattern of movement issues can only be the infinite Being previously grasped in thought and perception. The object of perception indicates his existence; the patterns of perception indicate the comprehensive nature of his activity.

The example of perception is peculiarly appropriate because it touches the nature of what it is to be a human being. Like Descartes, Malebranche has long since established: "I think, therefore I am. But what am I, I that think during the time that I am thinking . . . I am something that thinks."[54] That means for Malebranche, as for Descartes, that he is other than his body. The body is an extended reality. Is there anything in the nature of extension that includes the processes of thought? Certainly not. It is obviously possible to have extended things that do not think. Even further, while the body and all extended reality occupy space, the intelligible dimensions of ideas occupy no space. The difference between the body and the thinking substance is mirrored in the difference between the figure of a circle, drawn on a particular page, and the intelligibility of a circle, which is eternal, immutable, and necessary, equally applicable to the figure of a particular size and to one that is a million times larger. "My soul is not material. It is not a modification of my body. It is a substance which thinks and which has no resemblance to the extended substance of which my body is made up. . . . The distinction of the body and the soul is the basis of the main tenets of philosophy."[55] In such a philosophy, it is not strange to discover that perception is the action of god; there is no way in which the extensions of matter can account for an object or an activity of the soul.

There is no real relationship between a soul and a body. But Malebranche cannot leave it at that, startling as that may be to those who cannot meditate with him and transcend the baleful influence of original sin. There is one further step, which Malebranche will take and David Hume will follow with delight: "What I am saying? That there is no relation between a mind and a body. I am saying more. There is no real relation between one body and another, between one mind and another. In a word, no created thing can act upon another by an activity which is its own."[56] One is in the billiard room with Hume as the great Oratorian explains the totality of the action of his comprehensive god. "Suppose that this ball is set in motion, and that in the line of its motion it meets with another ball at rest. Experience teaches us that this other ball will move without fail, and according to a certain velocity always exactly observed." So far, so good. "Now, it is not the first ball which sets the second in motion. This is clear from our principle, for a body cannot move another without communicating to it its moving force. But the moving force of a body in motion is nothing but the will of the Creator who keeps it successively in different places. It is not a quality which belongs to the body itself. Nothing belongs to it but its own modifications; and modifications are inseparable from substances. Hence bodies cannot move one another, and their encounter or shock is merely an occasional cause for the distribution of their movement."[57] What the comprehensive principle does in Malebranche is infinitely more pervasive and efficacious than anything seen in Catholic thought up to this time. It accounts for all causality, both the influence between mind and matter and the influence between two units of matter. God not only acts; he is the only one who acts. As James Collins has noted, the occasionalism classically associated with the philosophy of Malebranche consists essentially in his denial of all secondary or finite causality and of intrinsic relationships of things within the world, and his insistence that all real causality belongs to god.[58] The infinite Being has become the comprehensive and sole agent.

What, then, can one say about infinite Being? God emerges as Supreme Truth. As the infinite Being, he contains within himself all the perfections and all the ideas that are embodied participatively in things. In him the truth of all things resides, since "truths are only the relations between ideas."[59] He is truth also in the sense that he alone reveals or discloses what is. Things cannot affect the human mind. One human person cannot influence the thinking of another. Only god can influence what is, and on the occasion of its position or action affect the mind of another to understand what is taking place. God is truth, not only in possessing all relationships within himself, but in revealing (*découvre*) them to me. The intuition or constant perception of god by the thinking subject has this continuous revelation as its affect. Take an example that Malebranche offers. Take a look at a plain, whitewashed wall near you. Suppose that it actually were able to act upon your mind. Notice that it has triangles and curves written on it, lines and circles. Now allow the wall itself to become perfectly transparent. You see the triangles and the curves, the lines and the circles, but not the wall. This is how god implants in the human mind the ideas of what is going on in the extended universe. What we see directly are the ideas that he implants and the relationships among them. Whatever we see or understand we see quite literally in god.[60]

Finally, god is true in the sense that was crucial for Descartes: he cannot deceive us or break his promises. The ontologism of Malebranche has transferred the scholastic threefold kind of truth to god. "The sovereign Truth or Supreme Relation" possesses formal truth in the relations among his ideas. He possesses ontological truth or intelligibility because he can act upon the mind to implant the proper relationship among the ideas, ideas that correspond to the way things are. He possesses moral truth, since deception or false dealings are essentially foreign to him.

The concept of Infinite Being clinches the Christian's contention that god subsists in himself and does not exist as a modification of matter, that he is intelligent and not just a wiser order of things. Very simply: he is infinitely perfect. It is more perfect to subsist; it is more perfect to be understanding.

Just as in Newton, the attributes of god issued from the divine *dominatio*, so in Malebranche, they issue from primordial human experience: the intuition into the presence and nature of the infinitely perfect Being.[61]

The influence of Descartes on theology was never more profound than when it furnished Father Malebranche with his evidence for the existence and meaning of god. Malebranche merged the Cartesian idea with its efficient cause to found his theology on the basis laid by one whom he celebrated as the greatest of the Christian philosophers. Descartes' idea had become the divine reality itself, and this was what any theology was all about.

SECTION 2. The Logistic Theology from Mechanics: Samuel Clarke

There was no question that Cambridge at the end of the seventeenth century exulted in the achievements of its Newton, so recently knighted by England's Anne. There was also no question that the great university continued to study its physics under Descartes. Newton had published his *Principia* in 1686, and would wait patiently until 1713 to see its second edition. So many years before, René Descartes had departed this life, on February 11, 1650, his health shattered by the stern winter of Sweden and the even sterner demand of its extravagant Queen Christina that lessons begin in her library at five in the morning. Descartes' philosophy had awakened and taken wing with lengthy hours of morning reflection spent by the master stretched out in bed; it terminated with early risings in Scandinavian darkness. But, while the French philosopher had not been unmitigatedly advanced by the royal favor of the "Minerva of the North," he was blessed with a coterie which would insure a more lasting academic immortality. His progress through European thought was swelled by the writers of textbooks in great throngs. Devoted disciples included not only such inventive theologians as Father Malebranche, whose *Recherche de la vérité* appeared in 1674–1675, but, more important, perhaps, a bevy of journeymen, the hewers of tradition and the drawers of manuals. Their textbooks could fit the university's term like a glove its hand in a way that the massive *Principia* could not. Cartesian physics, thus, came to settle over the lecture halls and dominate the tutorial sessions of the colleges clustered by the river Cam. And premier among the manuals that ensured this occupation was the *Traité de physique* by Jacques Rohault.

Rohault had captured physics in Cambridge. Published in French in 1671, his book was quickly turned into faulty Latin by Théophile Bonnet three years later. A cascade of French and Latin editions poured into the European universities, and London printed its own proud copies of Bonnet's translation in 1682. Bishop Benjamin Hoadly recalled the rule of the French: "The

Philosophy of Des Cartes was then the Established Philosophy of that University; and the System of Nature hardly allowed to be explained any otherwise than by His Principles: Which, at best, were evidently no more than the Inventions of a very Ingenious and Luxuriant Fancy; having no Foundation in the Reality of Things, nor any Correspondency to the Certainty of Facts."[1] But, while Newton's natural philosophy engaged the Royal Society and the few scholars who had followed his lectures, even his most enthusiastic followers at the university conceded with William Whiston, Newton's deputy and successor as Lucasian Professor of Mathematics, that an alternative course had to be charted at Cambridge: "Since the Youth of the University must have, at present, some System of Natural Philosophy for their Studies and Exercises; and since the true System of Sir Isaac Newton was not yet made easy enough for the Purpose, it was not improper, for their Sakes, yet to translate and use the System of Rohault."[2] Whiston had no more illusions than Benjamin Hoadly about the educational value of these manuals: "we at Cambridge, poor Wretches, were ignominiously studying the fictitious Hypotheses of the Cartesian."[3] The "poor wretches" deserved better, but the need for a manual was pressing and immediate. Newton himself had studied Rohault, and not even the great John Locke could pick up the *Principia* and make much headway with its mathematics. The situation was vexed and intolerable, and demanded some redress.

"Propero ad Class. Newtoni Theoriam"

Relief came gradually—in a very English manner, one is tempted to say. A new translation of Rohault's *Traité de physique* would be made by a young fellow of Gonville and Caius College, Samuel Clarke. But it was to echo an event of the previous century in France. At the urging of his enthusiastic father, Montaigne had translated Raymond of Sebond's *Theologia naturalis* into French, and then promptly destroyed Raymond's arguments in the apology appended to the work. At the urging of his tutor, John Ellis, heart and soul a Cartesian, Samuel Clarke translated the *Traité de physique* into Latin, and then gradually undermined its Cartesian physics in the Newtonian notes that he attached to the volumes. The first edition of this academic Trojan horse, in 1697, carried only a few such sorties into the enemy camp under the unimpressive flag of "annotatiunculae," brief annotations joined to the end of the two volumes. By the second edition, these had grown to a fifth of Rohault's manual and graduated to the more solemn rubric of "annotata." When the translation was published again, in Amsterdam in 1708, the treacherous notes had moved from the back to lodge as footnotes beneath the text itself.[4] "By this means," delighted Hoadly, "the True

Philosophy has without any Noise prevailed: and to this Day, His Translation of Rohault is, generally speaking, the Standing Text for Lectures; and
His Notes, the first Direction to Those who are willing to receive the Reality
and Truth of Things in the place of Invention and Romance."[5] In the
meantime, Newton's *Opticks* had appeared in 1704, and the indefatigable
Samuel Clarke rendered the book into Latin in 1706. The situation had
become protean enough for any author. The major texts of the warring
parties had emerged to do battle in the translations of the same man. But by
this time, his position was unmistakable: his notes on the Cartesian text had
evolved into "a systematic refutation of the text."[6] The text remained the
text of Rohault, but the voice that surrounded it was Newton's. Who was
this amazing Samuel Clarke?

Samuel Clarke arrived at Cambridge from Norwich in 1690, enrolled as a
pensioner at Gonville and Caius College, and became a scholar there the
next year. Still not quite fifteen that August 19, 1690, the young student was
given over to the charge of John Ellis, "that eminent and careful Tutor," as
William Whiston later complimented him.[7] Careful indeed was John Ellis,
whom Hoadly termed a "zealot" for Descartes. Clarke received his B.A. in
1695 and was elected a fellow of the college in the year that followed.[8]

1697 was an *annus mirabilis* for Clarke. It saw the publication of his
translation of Rohault, the beginning of his theological studies, and the
chance meeting with the great William Whiston, whose own career as a
mathematician and a theologian strikingly prefigured Clarke's. Malebranche's philosophic career had turned on an event in a Parisian bookstore,
his first encounter with the inspiration of Descartes. Clarke met Whiston in
a Norwich coffeehouse. He approached Whiston, presently serving as chaplain
to the bishop of Norwich, John Moore, and known only at a respectful
distance by most serious students in Cambridge. With some diffidence he
introduced the subject of his translation of Rohault to this distinguished
friend and disciple of Newton, elaborating upon his project of notes which
would provide the transition to the *Principia*. Whiston approved the program, citing the need for the kind of comprehensive system in physics that
Newton had yet to provide. Many years later, Whiston recalled that meeting
in his *Memoirs*, and even then remembered how deeply impressed he was
with Clarke's grasp of the work of Newton. Whiston "was greatly surprised
that so young a man as Mr. Clarke then was, not much I think above
twenty-two years of age, should know so much of those sublime discoveries
which were then almost a secret to all, but a few particular mathematicians."
Whiston had been one of the few who sat for Newton's original lectures, out
of which the *Principia* came, and one of the even fewer who managed to
understand them. The discovery that this young scholar had assimilated so
much from the master grappled him to Whiston with hoops of steel.

Clarke's career received the advancement of a friend. Whiston returned to the episcopal palace to relate the conversation to Bishop Moore. The bishop invited Clarke and his father, an alderman of Norwich, to dinner; that meal "proved the happy Occasion of that great Favour and Friendship which was ever afterward shewed him by the Bishop."[9] Within a year and a half, Clarke had been ordained to the priesthood and established as chaplain to the bishop, receiving his M.A. the same year from Cambridge. In another few years Clarke was settled as rector in Drayton near Norwich and beneficed with a small parish in Norwich itself.

The Rohault translation was followed by serious studies in divinity "which he proposed to make the peculiar Study and Profession of his Life."[10] Clarke gave himself to theological studies with a brilliance that matched his earlier attendance on the *Principia*. The Old Testament was studied in Hebrew, the New Testament in Greek, and a program carefully followed in which the Fathers of the Church were painstakingly read and analyzed. Out of this regimen of study came his first tractate on baptism, confirmation, and repentance (1699), and hard on its heels a second dealing with the Fathers of the Church and the canon of sacred scripture. The next few years saw *A Paraphrase on the Four Evangelists. Wherein for the clearer understanding of the Sacred History, the whole text and paraphrases are printed in separate columns against each other. With critical notes on the more difficult passages. Very useful for families.* All of this was mere prelude to his theological bombshell, published in 1712: *The Scripture-Doctrine of the Trinity: wherein every text in the New Testament relating to that doctrine is distinctly considered, and the Divinity of our blessed Saviour, according to the Scriptures, proved and explained.* Twelve hundred and fifty-one texts from the New Testament are examined. These yield fifty-five propositions, all of which are combined to attack the assertions of the Athanasian Creed of the co-equality of the Son and the Spirit with the Father. The Father alone is self-existent and absolute; the Son and Spirit, derivative and subordinate. In his attacks on the Athanasian Creed, Clarke was aligning himself with the private position of Newton and the public contention of Whiston, and over his head a theological polemic would break that would last until the end of his life.[11] But in the lull between his battles with the Cartesians and the Athanasians, Clarke turned to engage a still more fundamental foe, the atheists. He had been invited to deliver the Boyle lectures for 1704.

Robert Boyle had led the seventeenth century in the insistence that science and religion bore finally upon a single object, the existence and actions of god. He had conducted fundamental experiments in gases and given the resultant discoveries his own name. He lived the life of an ascetic and gave away many of his possessions to charity. His physical science, his natural theology, and the quality of his life all issued from the radical commitment of his conscience to god, and his will provided on his death for a series of public lectures "to prove the truth of the Christian religion against infidels, without descending to any controversies among Christians." He gave one of his houses in London to provide a foundation for the series, and Thomas Tenison, bishop of Lincoln and later archbishop of Canterbury, increased the foundation from a farm in the parish of Brill in Buckinghamshire. Tenison, besides being generous, was also influential as one of the trustees of the lectureship; he invited the young Clarke to deliver the Boyle lectures at St. Paul's Cathedral in 1704, which he did so successfully, as it turned out, that he was invited again the next year.[12]

Richard Bentley—the redoubtable discoverer of the lost digamma—had begun the series and set its tone the year after Boyle's death, with his straightforward *Confutation of Atheism*. His lectures had elicited from Newton the classic correspondence which he entertained with Bentley about the bearing of his natural philosophy upon the existence and nature of god. Now, some twelve years later, Clarke took up a similar battle with the atheists, once more merging Newtonian natural philosophy with the theological issue. The 1704 series bore its project in its title: *A Demonstration of the Being and Attributes of God, More Particularly in Answer to Mr. Hobbs, Spinoza and their Followers*. In the subsequent year, he delivered: *A Discourse Concerning the Unchangeable Obligations of Natural Religion, and the Truth and Certainty of the Christian Revelation*. In 1711, both series were published together in a single volume which reached its tenth edition by the year 1749.[13] The reception and influence of the work was enormous. As Malebranche was considered the great French métaphysician after Descartes, so Clarke was ranked among English philosophers second only to Locke. The challenge that Artus de Lyonne had set before the aged Malebranche Thomas Tenison of Canterbury provided for the young Clarke. In both cases, theologians took up philosophy to execute the tasks given them by bishops, but in these philosophies they differed profoundly. Malebranche brought Cartesianism to bear upon the issue; Clarke's approach was generated out of Newton. Both turned to philosophy from theology, and so successfully did Clarke make the transition that Voltaire ranked him first among the English philosophers: "Parmi ces philosophes, Clarke est peut-être le plus profond ensemble et le plus clair, le plus méthodique et le plus fort, de tous ceux qui ont parlé de l'Etre supreme."[14]

Voltaire had arrived in England in 1726, too late to meet the great Isaac Newton but fortunate enough to witness with astonishment his coffin carried with the pomp of England into its resting place in Westminster Abbey, followed by dukes and earls. He had called upon Clarke, to find him "d'une vertu rigide, et d'un caractère doux, plus amateur de ses opinions que passioné pour faire des prosélytes, uniquement occupé de calculs et de démonstrations, aveugle et sourd pour tout le rest, une vraie machine à raisonnements."[15] This reasoning machine impressed Voltaire mightily, who cited three works as its issue. There was the great tome on the Trinity, which won him partisans all over England, but lost him an appointment to the see of Canterbury. The story was told that when the queen wished to confer this office on Clarke, Gibson of London informed her that Clarke was the wisest and the most honest man in her kingdom, but that he lacked one qualification for the position: he was not a Christian![16] The story is a witty one, but it sounds much too much like Voltaire to be more than clever. Bishop Benjamin Hoadly, who, truth to tell, might have been accused of the same Trinitarian persuasions, puts the history more mysteriously: "He had Reasons within his own Breast, which hinder'd Him either from seeking after, or accepting any such Promotion."[17] Whatever Clarke's views on the Trinity and the influence of *The Scripture-Doctrine of the Trinity* on his career, there were two other works which Voltaire was at pains to single out. For Clarke "est l'auteur d'un livre assez peu entendu, mais estimé, sur l'existence de Dieu, et d'un autre, plus intelligible, mais assez méprisé, sur la vérité de la Religion chrétienne."[18] Voltaire was not about to subscribe to the Christian religion, however ably the learned Dr. Clarke might defend it, but the existence of god was another story. In a letter to his former professor at the Collége Louis-le-Grand, Father René-Joseph Tournemine, S.J., he pays Clarke's first Boyle lectures the ultimate compliment: they changed his mind. "My very dear Father, this, I swear to you, is the way I conduct myself. For a very long time, I thought the existence of God could only be proved by *a posteriori* reasons because I had not yet applied my mind to the few metaphysical truths that can be demonstrated. Reading Dr. Clarke's excellent book showed me my error, and I found in his demonstrations a clarification I had been unable to obtain elsewhere."[19] Voltaire might later mock the whole tribe of English metaphysicians, and, indeed, of metaphysicians in general. But this did not erase those years when he was under the spell of Samuel Clarke, a situation he shared with most of England and with much of Europe. Clarke never reached wider and more deeply than in the lectures in which he battled atheism to defend the existence of god.

If the atheists, for Malebranche, were the hapless Chinese, who were they for Clarke of Norwich? Strangely enough, neither Hobbes nor Spinoza, though the subtitle of the lectures gives them pride of place as the principal adversaries. "Atheists" are defined in abstract terms, rather than by concrete referents, and the devices by which the definition is constructed come to the *Demonstration* from the Universal Mechanics.

Newton distinguished his subject and its attendant characteristics into the apparent and the underlying real. Clarke similarly distinguishes between apparent and real atheism, naming "all those who either are or pretend to be Atheists."[20] Universal Mechanics maintained that human knowledge is limited to the existence and attributes of what it grasped, "but what the real substance of anything is we know not."[21] For Clarke, then, denial can focus upon either of these. Atheists are those who deny either the being or the principal attributes of god, those by which god is personal. These distinctions yield a fourfold meaning for the word "atheism," but the two "apparent" atheisms can be dismissed. What remains to be treated are the two forms of real atheism; hence the title of these sermons, *A Demonstration of the Being and the Attributes of God.*

Newton established his subject-matter not only through the distinction between the real and the apparent, but also through the investigation of its properties, causes, and effects. Atheism can be similarly determined. Three possible "accounts" or "causes" can be adduced for it: real atheism can issue from ignorance and stupidity, from immorality and degeneracy, or from "Speculative Reasoning, and upon the Principles of Philosophy." The first characterizes those who have never "made any just use of their natural Reason, to discover even the plainest and most obvious Truths." The second characterizes those who "by vicious and degenerate Life, corrupted the Principles of their Nature . . . [and] are resolved not to hearken to any Reasoning which would oblige them to forsake their beloved Vices." Those characterized by the third are both reasonable and moral, and their own speculations have convinced them that the atheistic position is "more strong and conclusive." These distinctions further narrow the subject of these lectures. The *Demonstration* does not attempt to argue with those deficient in intelligence or morality, the "enemies of reason" and the "enemies of religion." The third group "are the only Atheistical Persons, to whom my present Discourse can be supposed to be directed, or indeed who are capable of being reasoned with at all."[22] Atheism, then, is to be defined in a manner very similar to real motion, and it allows for a treatment or a method kindred to that which Newton used so successfully in the *Principia.*

The scholastic procedures have already been discredited; the skeptical meditations of Descartes' progressive doubt actually introduced hypotheses or fantasies into physics. What Newton did for physics was to collapse the distinction between natural philosophy and mathematics to allow a Universal Mechanics to emerge. This also provided Clarke with a paradigm for his own demonstration, "One only Method or continued Thread of Arguing; which I have endeavoured should be as near to Mathematical, as the Nature of such a Discourse would allow."[23] Clarke is not doing mathematics; he does not possess a Universal Mathematics. But he employs a logistic method which emulates on its own terms the careful additions and subtractions, the step-by-step constructions of mathematics. The contrast between his methodology and that of the Cartesians lies not in the exemplary nature of mathematics, but in its universality. For Descartes, all scientific method is finally mathematics; for Newton, mathematics is a part of mechanics and used to measure and demonstrate. In Clarke, natural theology does not become mathematics, but imitates it as an "endeavour by One clear and plain Series of Propositions necessarily connected and following one from another, to demonstrate the Certainty of the Being of God, and to deduce in order the Necessary Attributes of his Nature."[24]

Scholastic occult forms had already been exposed as useless, but the Newtonian rejection extended also to the Cartesian use of hypotheses. Thus Clarke's choice and the concatenation of argument must omit any reliance upon the hypothetical. "It seems not to be at any time for the real Advantage of Truth, to use Arguments in its behalf founded only on such Hypotheses, as the Adversaries apprehend they cannot be compelled to grant." But while neither the scholastic forms nor the Cartesian hypotheses will serve, Clarke will not simply debate against them. The progress of his simple proof is neither dialogue nor debate. There is no effort in these sermons to engage continually variant metaphysics or alternative natural philosophies, unlike the annotations on Rohault. Here, the effort is to demonstrate logistically the being and the attributes of god, not erect a system like the system of the world. For this purpose "every Man ought to use such Arguments only, as appear to Him to be clear and strong; and the Reader must judge whether they truly prove the Conclusion." The method is to be as mathematical as possible, but the foundations are not to be hypothetical. In a further contradistinction to the methodology from the Continent, the criterion is the "clear and strong" argument, not the clear and distinct idea.[25] The concatenation of argument establishes the suasiveness of the conclusion, not the reflexive self-justification of the idea and its definition.

Any Cartesian could recognize that another methodology is involved, one that had risen long since to challenge the master. It is the voice and the influence of Newton in the theology of Clarke.

Clarke was not the first to take Newton's natural philosophy and construct a systematic natural theology. But he was probably the best. And he did not build this natural theology out of the data of the conscious subject, as did Descartes and his theological heir, Malebranche. He built it directly out of the world that confronted the subject, the world that had been given principles and system by Isaac Newton. The phrase he had appended to his very first edition of Rohault could well stand for his natural theology, and, indeed, for his entire life: "Propero ad Class. Newtoni Theoriam."[26] Newton had written extensively on natural theology, but had left these writings in the form of almost random reflections. The issue that confronted Clarke was how this natural philosophy and these reflections could be coordinated into a single natural theology, one in which each step followed from the previous conclusion, one that resembled the procedures of mathematics, one "as near to Mathematical, as the Nature of such a Discourse would allow."

Newtonian method was a twofold *derivatio*. Beginning with the phenomena of nature, one derived the underlying causes or forces of nature; then, from these principles, one could demonstrate the phenomena of nature. These were the moments of analysis and synthesis that constituted the methodology of the Universal Mechanics. Roger Cotes, in his celebrated preface to the second edition, promised that "Newton's distinguished work will be the safest protection against the attacks of atheists, and nowhere more surely than from this quiver can one draw forth missiles against the hand of godless men."[27] The "missiles" were twelve propositions in Clarke's *Demonstration of the Being and Attributes of God*, twelve statements that first established analytically the being of god and then deduced his necessary attributes. The title of the lectures indicated the twofold movement of the demonstration. Analysis of phenomena back to original forces led to the establishment of the being of god; synthesis conjoined the divine existence with the personal attributes, so that at the end of the concatenated propositions one had established the god of providence, the foundation of all religion.

This analytic and synthetic movement, however, must occur twice: once to establish the being of god and demonstrate his impersonal attributes; again, to establish the intelligence and freedom of god and demonstrate his consequent power, wisdom, and providence. In both of these distinct but coordinate movements, one begins with the phenomenon and progresses analytically to the cause or force behind it; one then demonstrates synthetically the attributes which necessarily follow. Since this twofold structure is pivotal both for understanding of Clarke's argument and for its subsequent uses by Baron d'Holbach, the twelve propositions of the *Demonstration* that form it should be seen as a whole within the methodology of the argument.

I. THE BEING OF GOD:

    A. *Analytic Movement*:
        Proposition 1. That Something has existed from Eternity.
        Proposition 2. That there has existed from Eternity some one Immutable and Independent Being.
        Proposition 3. That that Immutable and Independent Being, which has existed from Eternity, without any External Cause of its Existence; must be Self-Existent, that is, Necessarily-Existing.

    B. *Synthetic Movement*:
        Proposition 4. What the Substance or Essence of that Being,

which is Self-Existent or Necessarily-Existent, is: we have no Idea, neither is it at all possible for us to comprehend it.

Proposition 5. That though the Substance or Essence of the Self-Existent Being, is itself absolutely incomprehensible to us: Yet many of the Essential Attributes of his Nature are strictly Demonstrable, as well as his Existence. As in the First Place, that He must of Necessity be Eternal.

Proposition 6. That the Self-Existent Being, must of Necessity be Infinite and Omnipresent.

Proposition 7. That the Self-Existent Being, must of Necessity be but One.

II. THE PRINCIPAL ATTRIBUTES OF THE DIVINE NATURE:

A. *Analytic Movement*:

Proposition 8. That the Self-Existent and Original Cause of all Things, must be an Intelligent Being. This, the main Question between us and the Atheists.

Proposition 9. That the Self-Existent and Original Cause of all Things, is not a Necessary Agent, but a Being imbued with Liberty and Choice.

B. *Synthetic Movement*:

Proposition 10. That the Self-Existent Being, the Supreme Cause of all Things, must of Necessity have Infinite Power.

Proposition 11. That the Supreme Cause and Author of all Things, must of Necessity be Infinitely Wise.

Proposition 12. That the Supreme Cause and Author of all Things, must of Necessity be a Being of Infinite Goodness, Justice and Truth, and all other Moral Perfections; such as become the Supreme Governour and Judge of the World.

Clarke took from the Universal Mechanics both its distinction between the apparent and the real and its logistic methodology of analysis and synthesis. The "thesis method" still in use in the English universities was adapted to provide propositions that were theorems whose conjunction created "One only Method or continued Thread of Arguing; which I have endeavoured should be as near to Mathematical as the Nature of such a Discourse would allow."[28]

To Establish the Necessary Being of the One God

To ground his demonstration of the existence of god, Father Malebranche adduced as initial evidence the idea of god. In sharp contrast, Samuel Clarke begins with the datum: "Something now is." Malebranche opened with an idea; Clarke calls to the stand an existent thing. The idea is of the infinite; the thing is of the temporal, is "now." For Malebranche, the idea of the infinite was necessarily identified with the existence of the infinite. For Clarke, the existence of some concrete thing necessarily implies the existence of something eternal. "For since Something now Is, 'tis evident that Something always Was; Otherwise the Things that Now Are, must have been produced out of Nothing, absolutely and without Cause." Hence the initial proposition of the *Demonstration*, which serves as the foundation for the subsequent eleven: "It is Absolutely and Undeniably certain, that Something has existed from Eternity."[29]

This difference in the choice of initial evidence marks the radical difference between the philosophical constituencies these theologians represented and whose mandate they were carrying so confidently into theology. The Cartesian meditations inaugurated the proof of the divine existence with the idea of the infinite, and Malebranche supported this initiative though he denied that this idea was clear and distinct. Newtonian real motion involved the eternality of duration and the infinity of extension. Both figure in Clarke, but his *Demonstration* begins with the eternal because time entails both the causal principle and the causal chain, allowing inference from the phenomenon to the underlying cause.

A cause is a reason, a ground, a foundation: "Whatever Exists, has a Cause, a Reason, a Ground of its Existence; (a Foundation on which its Existence relies; a Ground or Reason why it doth exist, rather than not exist)." A cause accounts for the fact that something is so. It is not simply an explanation, a hypothesis which can account for a fact; it is a reason or influence that does *de facto* account for a fact. There are two kinds of such causes, of reasons that something is so: internal and external. Internal causes reflexively account for the properties or even for the existence of themselves. External causes act on something else, and their action is responsible for whatever change they effect. An example of the contrast: The reason a Euclidian triangle possesses angles whose sum is 180 degrees is that it is such a triangle; the reason this piece of dough or this cookie is triangular is the choice of the pastry cook and the shape of the cookie cutter. Reflexive causes, however, explain themselves by what they are. They are simultaneous with their effects. External (actional) causes influence their effects by their will or action, and they "must, at least in the order of Nature and Causality, have Existed before it."[30]

The distinction the *Demonstration* draws between two types of causes parallels that which the *Principia* drew between two types of forces, inertial forces and impressed forces. The inertial force is inherent to matter itself and differs in no way from its mass except in conception. The impressed force is an external force, an *actio*, which comes from outside and generates a change. Inertial forces and impressed forces easily translate in the *Demonstration* into the intrinsic causes, which in no way differ from nature and possess the same necessity, and the extrinsic causes, which operate upon another being and produce a change in existence.

The *Demonstration* opens, then, with the existence of something now, and the fundamental judgment that something prior must account for it. But this prior object itself did not issue from nothing. To be produced out of nothing, absolutely and without cause, is simply a contradiction in terms. "To say a Thing is produced, and yet that there is no Cause at all of that Production, is to say that Something is Effected, when it is Effected by Nothing; that is, at the same time when it is not Effected at all."[31] The principle of noncontradiction figures pivotally in both Malebranche and Clarke, but its applications diverge radically. For Malebranche, to be thinking and to be thinking of nothing is a flat contradiction. In excluding that contradiction, one can infer that whatever the mind immediately perceives really exists. For Clarke, to come into being is to be produced. To be produced by no "producer" is intrinsically contradictory. Thus, the assertion that something has existed from all eternity can be drawn from the single evidence that something exists now. The temporal stands as warrant for the eternal.

Now there are two possibilities for this eternal. It is either one (at least) unchangeable and independent being, which accounts for other beings, or it is an infinite series of changeable and dependent beings, one produced from another in endless progression. But this second alternative is unacceptable: it does not account for the series itself. There is nothing in the nature of anything in the series that would account for its infinite progression; that is, nothing that would account for the existence of the series, that would answer the question why it exists rather than not. The infinite series of dependent, temporally existing units does not explicate itself. If each unit is produced by the prior unit, the question remains: What keeps the whole series going? "To suppose an infinite Succession of changeable and dependent Beings produced one from another in an endless Progression, without any Original Cause at all; is only a driving back from one step to another, and (as it were) removing out of Sight, the Question concerning the Ground or Reason of the Existence of Things."[32] Why reject an infinite series of dependent beings as a final account? Because there is nothing independent in the series to account for its existence. It is equally possible that such a series should never have existed at all. But it does exist, by hypothesis. If so, what grounds it? Why is it that it exists rather than not? "What is it that has from Eternity determined such a Succession of Beings to exist, rather than that from Eternity, there should never have existed any thing at all?" As long as the cause is external (actional) the question can and, indeed, must be raised: what accounts for the existence of this very cause? As long as each of these causes is produced, that is, changeable, and dependent, nothing has been answered—the question is simply postponed. Unless one posits at least one reality that is not changeable and dependent, that is, a reality that is unchangeable and independent, the question remains to be answered. The *Demonstration* puts the issue in almost Heideggerian terms: "Of two equally possible things (viz. whether anything or nothing should from Eternity have existed,) the one is determined, rather than the other, absolutely by Nothing: Which is an express Contradiction."[33]

The line of reasoning runs like the addition of ciphers. Something exists now; something has eternally existed; something independent has eternally existed. Only the independent can account for the eternal; only the eternal can account for the temporal. The first proposition establishes two types of causes, reflexive and actional. The second proposition establishes that actional causes cannot function as an adequate explanation of the eternal. Thus the third proposition follows: the independent and eternal cause must be self-existent, that is, necessarily existing. For what comes into being must come out of the agency of something. If that something is itself produced, if it is an external or actional cause, it still depends upon something else. The only cause that can account for the existence of such actional causes is one that is reflexive, one whose existence issues not from another but from the necessities of its own nature, one that accounts for its own existence simply by what it is. Reality is found to be temporal by experience; therefore, it must be eternal; therefore, it must be independent; therefore, it must be self-existent; therefore, it must be necessary. The causal chain does not terminate until such a reflexive cause is asserted. External or actional causes are only intelligible in terms of the self-existent.

What does "self-existent" mean? "Now to be Self-existent, is not, to be Produced by itself; for that is an express Contradiction. But it is, (which is the only idea we can frame of Self-existence; and without which, the word seems to have no Signification at all:) It is, I say, to exist by an Absolute Necessity originally in the Nature of the Thing itself."[34] This "absolute necessity" means that something does not just happen to exist and make its existence known by its effects; it means that to suppose its nonexistence would involve a contradiction in terms.

Elmer Sprague criticizes Clarke's argumentation for his third proposition, which, Sprague recognizes, was "meant to be the clinching step in the demonstration." He questions whether the self-existent must be necessarily existent, and he frames Clarke's argument as follows: "It looks as though self-existence might be an interesting fact about this being, and Clarke argued that it follows from his account of this being, as having existed from eternity without any external cause, that this being is self-existent." Clarke equated, Sprague maintains, the notions of "self-existent" and "necessarily existent," "but we need to have the equation of self-existent and necessarily existent clarified. Why is it that a self-existent being must necessarily exist? . . . On this transition from self-existence to necessary existence, Clarke's natural theology appears to founder."[35]

Sprague's judgment itself may be questioned. The transition from self-existent to necessarily existent is neither arbitrary nor sudden. It is founded on the original description of a reflexive cause as one that has the ground of its existence not in another but "in the Necessity of its own Nature."[36] The self is the nature. Whatever issues not by the choice of the self, but as a necessity that it be what it is, is necessary for the self. So, for example, a student must be a human being, a circle must be extended, and time must be progressive. Without these predicates, there is no subject. The reason—the cause—for each of these predicates is the nature of the subject. They so enter into its definition that to assert one and not to assert the other would be a contradiction in terms. In this lies their necessity.

If existence, then, issues from the very nature of the thing in question, that is, if it enters into the definition or internal constitution of the self, then it is necessary in order for the self to be what it is, that is, for both the reality and the definition of the self. One cannot grasp the nature of that reality without realizing simultaneously not only that it is, but that by its very nature it must be. One cannot understand the nature of that reality and think of it as nonexistent without intrinsic contradiction.

The *Demonstration* does not maintain that one comes to the existence of the self-existent through its definition. Clarke asserts emphatically that human beings cannot understand the nature of god, that his definition is beyond human comprehension. One comes to the existence of the self-existent *a posteriori*, by the "Demonstration of Something being Self-existent, from the Impossibility of every Thing's being dependent."[37] If the reason for the existence lies with the nature of the reality itself, if it is intrinsic to its nature, then it is no illegitimate transition to affirm it as necessarily existing. Sprague's question, "Why is it an absolute contradiction to think of a self-existent being as not existing?" is misstated. Clarke does not maintain this. He states that "the only true *Idea* of a Self-existent or Necessarily Existing Being, is the *Idea* of a Being, the Supposition of whose Not-existing is an express Contradiction."[38] It is not the proposition "There is no such thing as a self-existing being" that is contradictory. Clarke's assertion might read something like this: "If there is a Self-existing being, it would be one the supposition of whose nonexistence would be intrinsically contradictory." Sprague fails to give the order of the propositions (which he lists as eight rather than twelve) any great weight. The *Demonstration* begins with the concrete, temporal existent. From this, it concludes that something must be eternal. From the existence of the eternal, it follows that something must have the reason of its existence in its own nature, in what it is, not in the choice or action of another. If its reason for existence is its own nature, then it exists as a necessity of this nature, as something that "goes with it" or characterizes it because of what it is. This is what is meant by "absolute necessity" or by necessarily existing. Clarke is not a formalist; he uses words with the ease of ordinary language; but there is no question of a sloppy transition or of a failure to provide clarity for such critical terms. "Now a Necessity, not relatively or consequently, but absolutely such in its own Nature; is nothing else, but its being a plain Impossibility or implying a Contradiction to suppose the contrary. For Instance: The Relation of Equality between twice two and four, is an absolute Necessity; only because 'tis an immediate Contradiction in Terms to suppose them unequal."[39] One does not argue to the existence of the necessarily existing because of the definition of the terms. One argues to the existence of the self-existing because of the evidence of a concrete existent. But if there is a self-existent, then it exists necessarily—because it exists not as dependent upon another, but as a necessity of being what it is. From a single temporal existent, one can conclude cogently the existence of the self-existent, or that which necessarily is.

What one does not begin with, however, is the idea or the definition of god—however dear this point of departure to the Cartesians. Directly against the fifth meditation of the French master, Clarke wrote: "Our first Certainty of the Existence of God, does not arise from this, that in the Idea our Minds frame of him, (or rather in the Definition that we make of the word, God, as signifying a Being of all possible Perfections,) we include Self-Existence."[40] The idea of god is not his first evidence, not even the idea of the self-existent. His Newtonian natural theology remains faithful to the analysis of phenomena back to their primordial forces. Any form of the ontological argument, the argument from definition to existence, must be resisted, even if the definition be Clarke's own: "The bare having an Idea of the Proposition, There is a Self-Existent Being, proves indeed the Thing not to be impossible. . . . But that it actually Is, cannot be proved from the Idea." Many learned men have argued the contrary of this, and there may be much in their attempts to prove that the actual existence of a necessarily existing being follows from the possibility of such an existent, that is, from its definition. "And their subtil Arguings upon this Head, as sufficient to raise a Cloud not very easy to be seen through." But Clarke will have no part of it, whatever the genius of an Anselm, of a Descartes, and of a Leibniz. "But it is a much Clearer and more Convincing way of Arguing, to demonstrate that there does actually exist without us a Being, whose Existence is necessary and of it self; by showing the evident Contradiction contained in the contrary Supposition, (as I have before done) and at the same time the absolute Impossibility of destroying or removing some Ideas, as of Eternity and Immensity [space], which therefore must needs be Modes of Attributes of a necessary Being actually Existing."[41] The human experience of the material universe warrants the assertion that there must be a self-existing, that is, a necessarily existing, being.

But the idea of such a being, its intrinsic intelligibility, functions critically in Clarke's debates with the materialists. The idea of the self-existing, of the necessarily existing, is the "idea of a Being" the supposition of whose not-existing is an express contradiction. The material universe is a warrant that such a being exists. The question now becomes, can it be identified with the material universe itself? Granted that this idea can be predicated of something real, can it be predicated of matter itself? Here the adversaries become the Cartesians and Spinoza.

The Cartesians make matter necessary because they have confused it with space. That space or immensity is unchangeable or eternal, any Newtonian will grant; it is a necessity if motion is to be absolute. But to have "supposed the Idea of Immensity to be the Idea of Matter," is simply absurd.[42] Matter in the Universal Mechanics is identified with mass and measured by inertial force. It occurs and moves within space; it is not identified with it. The necessity of space and eternality is a derivative attribute or mode of existence of the necessary being.

Could the material universe itself be the necessary being? Here, the enemy is "Spinoza, the most celebrated Patron of Atheism in our Time."[43] Clarke reads him to say: "The Material World Exists Necessarily by an Absolute Necessity in its own Nature, so that it must be an Express Contradiction to suppose it not to Exist."[44] Absolute necessity of existing and the possibility of not existing are contradictory ideas. Consequently, "absolute necessity" cannot be predicated of the material world, if it is possible to conceive it either as nonexistent or as other than it is. But this is obviously possible, whether one speaks of the world in either of two ways: the form of the world, that is, the way it is composed and the movement of its parts, or the matter of which it is composed.

To assert that the form of the universe is necessary would be to assert that it is contradictory to suppose that any section of the universe could be other than it is—that there could be more stars or fewer planets, or that their movements and figures and sizes could be other than they are. It would be contradictory to suppose more and different plants and animals, varied in size and shapes. Whatever one says about the wisdom of the present form of the world, no contradiction is implied in supposing its contrary.[45]

To say that the movement of all matter is necessary would be to assert that it is contradictory to suppose any matter to be at rest, "which is so absurd and ridiculous that I hardly think any Atheists, either Ancient or Modern, have presumed directly to suppose it." Further, whatever the movement of a particular particle, one must explain why its tendency, its *conatus*, is to go in one determined way rather than another—since it is not contradictory to suppose either. Both motion and rest, then, as well as the determination necessary for a particular movement, indicate the presence of an external cause.

But the battle with the materialists is joined not so much on the form or on the movement of all matter as on the necessity of matter itself. Here, the Newtonian quiver supplies more missiles. If matter cannot be identified with Cartesian space, it can be known by its tangibility or resistance. "Tangibility or Resistence, (which is what Mathematicians very properly call *Vis iner-tiae*,) is essential to Matter. Otherwise the word, Matter, will have no determinate Signification. Tangibility therefore, or Resistence, belonging to All Matter; it follows evidently, that if All Space were filled with Matter, the Resistence of All Fluids (for the Resistence of the Parts of Hard Bodies arises from Another Cause) would necessarily be Equal." But experience indicates that the resistance of all fluids is not equal, "there being large Spaces, in which no sensible Resistence at all is made to the swiftest and most lasting Motion of the solidest Bodies. Therefore, All Space is not filled with Matter; but, of necessary Consequence, there must be a Vacuum."[46] Various resistances to movement, the kinds of variations the Second Book of the *Principia* had explored, and the same void that had allowed the calculations of the third book, entail that there are vacua or places in the universe void of matter. Experiments with both the pendulum and the acceleration of falling bodies confirm these "Spaces void of sensible Resistence." And since matter or mass is known by resistance, these places are known to be void of matter. The Universal Mechanics, both in its astronomy and in its atomic construction of bodies, has demonstrated that the universe is porous.

If there are vacua, "it follows plainly, that Matter is not a Necessary Being. For if a Vacuum actually be, then 'tis evidently more than possible for matter not to Be." If there are vacua, matter is here but not there. One part of space is occupied, but another empty. It is obviously possible for matter not to exist; in fact, there are places in which it does not exist. There is, then, nothing absolutely necessary about it. "For absolute Necessity, is absolute Necessity every where alike. And if it be no Impossibility for Matter to be absent from one Place, 'tis no Impossibility (absolutely in the Nature of the

Thing; For no Relative or Consequential Necessity, can have any Room in this Argument:) 'Tis no absolute Impossibility, I say, in the Nature of the Thing, that Matter should be absent from any other Place or from every Place."[47] This is one of the most critical junctures in the battle between Cartesians and Newtonians. Matter is to be identified with extension, and the universe is a *plenum*; or matter is to be identified with mass and made known through inertial force, and the universe is in many places a vacuum. The existence of voids allows Clarke to argue that matter is absolutely necessary neither in itself nor in any of its dispositions. The line of reasoning from the temporal to the eternal, from the eternal to the independent, from the independent to the self-existent or the necessary, does not terminate in anything material. The reflexive principle of all things cannot be matter.

If the predicate "self-existing" or "necessarily existing" cannot be attached to the material world, what can it be attached to? The causal chain from an actual temporal existent implicates the existence of such a reality. But what is it, if not the material world or the matter out of which it is composed? What can one say about the subject of which "necessarily existing" is the predicate?

This question moves the "One only Method" from analysis to synthesis, from the establishment of the existence of that which necessarily exists to the demonstration of the attributes which this ineluctably entails.

It is not a question about the substance of such a being. "We are utterly ignorant of the Substance or Essence of all other things; even of those things which we converse most familiarly with, and think we understand best."[48] The *Demonstration* repeats the abstention of the Universal Mechanics from any statement about the nature of things. As with things, so with god: "We have ideas of his attributes, but what the real substance of anything is we know not."[49] The basic Newtonian division between the apparent and the real shifts to the distinction between the attributes and the substance. This allows an incorporation of the classic Thomistic distinction between knowing that god is (*An sit*) and what he is (*Quid sit*), but the Universal Mechanics makes this not a special statement about god but a general statement of all human knowledge: "That there is such a Being actually Existing without us, we are sure (as I have already shown) by strict and undeniable Demonstration. Also what it is not; that is, that the Material World is not it, as Modern Atheists would have it; has been already Demonstrated. But what it is, I mean as to its Substance and Essence; this we are infinitely unable to comprehend."[50] But just as one can, from the forces of gravity, demonstrate the career of a planet, so from the being of what is necessarily being "many of the Essential Attributes of his Nature, are strictly Demonstrable."[51] Some of these have been discovered in the reductive movement toward the self-existent; others emerge only in the process of demonstration itself. Among the former are eternality, independence, and self-existence. Among the latter must of necessity be infinity and omnipresence.[52] In the Universal Mechanics, space is infinite, and in the *Opticks* it becomes *tamquam sensorium Dei*. The self-existent, then, must be independently infinite in a manner distinct from space, otherwise its effect (space) would be more perfect than the cause. But the infinity of the self-existent flows immediately from the necessity of his existence. If the self-existent is intrinsically necessary, if it cannot be otherwise, then "it must be every where, as well as always, unalterably the same. For a Necessity which is not every where the same, is plainly a Consequential Necessity only, depending upon some External Cause" by which it is altered or dispensed. If something is intrinsically necessary, if it cannot not-be, then there is no place where it *can* not-be. Necessity requires immensity and immensity requires omnipresence.[53]

This repeats the *Demonstration*'s fundamental attack on the materialists, those who predicate "necessarily existing" of the material universe or of its matter. Matter is only in some places; it is not every place. It is no contradiction to have place and find matter absent. The Universal Mechanics established precisely this. For Clarke, as he later wrote to Leibniz, unlike the mechanics from the Continent, "the mathematical principles of philosophy . . . alone, prove matter, or body, to be the smallest and most inconsiderable part of the universe."[54] The infinity of god means not that god is extended, but that god is everywhere that extension is; indeed, that he constitutes extension by his omnipresence. It means, furthermore, "that the Infinity of the Self-Existent Being, must be an Infinity of Fullness as well as of Immensity."[55] This introduces the distinction, made strongly since the Middle Ages, between quantitative and qualitative infinity, between the infinity and the perfection of the self-existent. Fullness means, not that the self-existent is a material *plenum*, but that it is "without Diversity, Defect, or Interruption." The self-existent must not only be everywhere. It must be complete; it must exist everywhere and must everywhere be fully present. If either of these is not realized, then the self-existent is not necessary. Its presence and its fullness of presence would depend upon factors other than itself. No material objects, nothing composed of parts, can fit that bill. Infinity as omnipresence rules out atomic matter with its void as the necessary being. Infinity as fullness rules out anything with parts or anything that changes, for "Parts, Figure, Motion, Divisibility, or any such Properties as we find in Matter . . . do plainly and necessarily imply Finiteness in their very Notion." The necessary entails omnipresence and fullness, being everywhere and fully everywhere. Both of these eliminate matter from the self-existent. Both of these involve necessarily utter simplicity, lack of change, and incorruptibility.

Finally, this self-existent must of necessity be but one, rather than plural.

For necessity is always simple and uniform and universal. If there were two such beings, they would have within them that by which they differed. Their diversity would indicate a factor which depended upon some causal factor, other than the simple necessity of the self-existent. But the simplicity of the necessary being precludes such a factor and hence such a diversity of beings. Furthermore, it would be a contradiction to suppose the nonexistence of the necessary being, if it exists. But if there were two, it would be no contradiction to suppose that there was only one. If either of them could be supposed not to exist, neither would meet the definition of the necessary being.

The uniqueness of the self-existent, then, follows directly from its simplicity, which follows from its necessity. "Because in absolute Necessity there can be no Difference, or Diversity of Existence . . . no Other Being can be Self-Existent, because so it would be individually the same, at the same time that it is supposed to be different."[56] The *Demonstration* has established, not unlike Spinoza's *Ethics*, that from the necessary existence of god, "it follows with the greatest clearness, firstly, that God is one." But Spinoza equates this statement with the assertion that "besides God no substance can be nor can be conceived."[57] Clarke comments that the folly of Spinoza's proposition "is entirely built [on] that absurd Definition of Substance." The *Demonstration* does not begin with definitions, postulates, and axioms; it begins with the existent thing. This allows a variety of substances, whose essences remain hidden but whose attributes manifest their variety. From these one concludes the existence of the necessary being. The existence of a variety of things entails the necessarily existent. Spinoza's *Causa Sui*—similar in so many ways to the self-existent—cannot explain this variety, or the experienced arbitrariness within the universe and within the more immediate appropriations of human freedom. All is ultimately necessary with Spinoza. All points to necessity in Clarke, but necessity is not the last word. The first seven propositions have led to the One, Infinite, Necessary, Self-Existent. But this only prepares the ground for Clarke's more significant battle with his adversaries.

The First Foundation of Religion

The principal issue between the *Demonstration* and atheism does not lie in the assertion of the self-existent, the one being which necessarily and eternally exists. The principal issue lies in the eighth proposition: "The Self-Existent and Original Cause of all Things, must be an Intelligent Being. In this Proposition lies the main Question between us and the Atheists."[58] Most atheists could rest easy with a metaphysics of matter as the ultimate and generative reality. But when matter is denied and intelligence affirmed as this reality, the issue is engaged.

Intelligence introduces not only the characteristic of personality, but more particularly that of freedom. The battle rages through both the ancients and the moderns. The ancients asserted the self-existent to be matter and denied intelligence; "Spinoza and some Moderns" assert intelligence but remove choice, which "is the very same thing as no Intelligence at all." Irrespective of vocabulary, they have in common the generation of all reality from such a principle by "Blind and Unintelligent Necessity." Both contradict freedom and choice in the self-existent, a freedom that issues from intelligence and a choice that is the foundation of providence and religion. To establish religion, one must first establish that the self-existent is intelligent.

Just as in the third book of the *Principia* the analytic method is resumed to discover within celestial mechanics the phenomena of the planetary motions and their resolution to the law of the inverse square, so at this juncture the *Demonstration* again takes up analytic, rather than synthetic, considerations. Intelligence is to be established within the self-existent not *a priori*, by a demonstration from the attributes of the self-existent, but *a posteriori*, by a reconsideration of the phenomena and reduction to their underlying cause. Clarke rejects the method of Aquinas. The *Summa theologiae* answers the question of whether there is knowledge in god through this deduction: "Thus, since God is immaterial in the highest degree, it is evident from what said above, that He possesses knowledge in the highest degree."[59] Saint Thomas argues *a priori* from one of the divine attributes; Clarke, on the other hand, argues *a posteriori* from the evidence of the phenomena of nature. The way was already traced out by the master at Cambridge: "We know him only by his most wise and excellent contrivances of things, and final causes."[60] In the *Demonstration*, this becomes the statement that "almost every thing in the World, demonstrates to us this great Truth; and affords undeniable Arguments, to prove that the World, and all Things therein, are the Effects of an Intelligent and Knowing Cause."[61]

The first of the phenomena which point toward intelligence in the self-existent is that of finite intelligence in the world. To say that knowledge and understanding are in the world, and not in the being upon which the world is causally dependent, is to postulate that the effect is greater than the cause, that something can come from nothing. A god who is unintelligent is less than his world—even if one asserts that intelligence is a combination of factors—for there is certainly intelligent life in the world. The second phenomenon is simply a particularization of the first "since in Men in particular there is undeniably that Power which we call Thought, Intelligence, Perception or Knowledge." What is the source or cause of such a phenomenon? Either an endless succession of human beings—but this would deny all necessity; or an emergence of intelligent beings out of that which has no consciousness—but this would deny the distinctive quality of consciousness and knowledge; or the influence of an intelligent and superior being—ultimately an intelligent self-existent."[62]

The third phenomenon is design in the unintelligent things within the universe. Like Newton before him, Clarke finds within the universe "Variety, Order, Beauty, and Wonderful Contrivance, and Fitness of all Things in the World to their proper and respective Ends." This shifts the area of evidence from intelligent things to phenomena that exhibit the influence of intelligence. The argument is admittedly old; but it is also notably new. One has only to consult the work of Robert Boyle on final causes, that of John Ray on the *Wisdom of God in the Creation*, or that of William Derham, so suggestively called *Physico-Theology*, to find the contributions that contemporary science makes to this argument. The adversaries here are both ancestral and modern: the Epicureans, who have the world originate in chance, and Descartes, whose "most impossible and ridiculous Account" hypothesizes "how the World might be formed by the Necessary Laws of Motion alone."[63] Fourth, even if one maintains that the final design—its order and beauty and the configurations of variety toward a single function—and intelligence itself could both be the effects of unintelligent matter, mere figure and motion, these so-called ultimate principles of figure and motion still demand an intelligent cause. Why? Because each demands for its existence a determination of one possibility out of many. If either were necessarily what it is, then motion and figure would be always and ineluctably so. But motion's direction is one out of many possibilities, and the determination of which possibility presupposes that which can impose design, namely, intelligence.[64]

The phenomena which the *Demonstration* adduces as evidence for a supreme intelligence begin with the most obvious; intelligent life on this planet. They progress to one part of this life, human life; then to the objects of intelligence, design in the variations and unity of things; and finally to the underlying principles of material things: motion, figure, and matter.[65] At each of these levels, the phenomena indicate the presence of causative intelligence. First, because nothing can be in the effect which is not in the cause; second, because intelligence could not have arisen from figure and motion; third, because design indicates an antecedent purpose and an orientation of matter toward function and purpose; finally, because even the underlying principles of a putative design and/or intelligence presuppose their own unique determinations, whether temporal or configural.

The Universal Mechanics provides the basic axiom of this analysis: there is nothing in the effect which is not in the cause. If the cause is external, then it must possess all of the perfections or positive attributes found in its effect. If the cause is a component, internal to its effect, then the final product will be nothing more than the sum of its parts. The major intellectual failure of the materialists is the failure to see this axiom, which works so pervasively and powerfully in Newtonian mechanics through the parallelogram of forces. They "imagine Compounds, to be somewhat really different from That of which they are Compounded: Which is a very great Mistake."[66] Divide or compose any figures, they are still figures; analyze or compose any motion, it is still motion. Whoever will show intelligence or design in the effect must find it in the determinant causes.

Intelligence leads the discussion to freedom, to the assertion that "the Self-Existent and Original Cause of all Things, is not a Necessary Agent, but a Being imbued with Liberty and Choice." The issues of personality and the origins of the movements studied in the Universal Mechanics devolve upon the question of freedom, whether human or divine. Intelligence without freedom becomes mere consciousness, unable to act, capable only of recognizing that it is determined or moved to whatever it influences. This is to say, as Spinoza says, that the self-existent, the *Causa sui*, moves only by the necessity of its nature, that "from the supreme power of God, or from His infinite nature, infinite things in infinite ways, that is to say, all things, have necessarily flowed, or continually follow by the same necessity, in the same way as it follows from the nature of a triangle, from eternity and to eternity, that its three angles are equal to two right angles."[67] To assert causality or agency of such a necessity would make as much sense "as if a Man should say, that a Stone, by the Necessity of its Nature, is the Cause of its own falling and striking the Ground."[68] Whatever influences the stone causes its movement; whatever implants the necessity is responsible for its consequences. To speak of god as agent or cause of anything and to deny him freedom is a contradiction in terms. The agent would be that which authored his nature.

To remove freedom from god is also to assert necessity of whatever depends upon him, that is, that nothing can be other than it is, was, or will be. Spinoza accepts the consequence, that all things are determined out of the necessity of the divine nature and there is nothing that can be styled "contingens."[69] The *Demonstration* brings as refutation the "Experience and Nature of Things, and . . . the most obvious and common Reason of Mankind." For all things in the world, whether given in immediate experience or analyzed in Newtonian natural philosophy, "appear plainly to be the most Arbitrary that can be imagined."[70] The list is one that any Newtonian would immediately recognize: motion and its quantities and directions; the laws of gravitation; the number and movements of the heavenly bodies; everything on earth, the number and kinds of animals and plants. For none of these, as their attributes are disclosed, does one find a contradiction in supposing either its nonexistence or some alteration in its composition and movement. The Newtonian focus on the phenomena of nature discloses two aspects of the physical world: the intricacy of its design and the arbitrariness of its existence and modality. Intricacy of design shows intelligence in the self-existent. Arbitrariness manifests his freedom.

What is more, the design discovered is that of final cause, of purpose realized by the designation of organs and material conditions by which it is brought about. The argument from final causes, from realized purpose and proportionally developed matter, can be traced to Galen's *De usu partium* and Cicero's *De natura deorum*; but, like Lessius before him, Clarke finds that "the larger the Improvements and Discoveries are, which are daily made in Astronomy and Natural Philosophy; the more clearly is this Question continually determined, to the Shame and Confusion of Atheists."[71] The analytic observation of human experience indicates it arbitrary and purposeful; it also indicates the human as finite. But if all things emerge from the necessity of their principle, that is, if the self-existent cannot govern or direct its own actions, then there is nothing to check or direct or alter the immensity, indeed the infinity, of its effect. Only infinite things can emerge from an infinite and necessary being. Spinoza saw this, but limited the infinity to number and mode, "but whoever reads his Demonstration of this Proposition, can hardly fail to observe, (if he be at all used to such Speculations,) that if it proved any thing at all, it would equally prove, that from the Necessity of the Divine Nature, only Infinite Things (meaning Infinite in Extension) can possibly arise."[72]

Newtonian celestial mechanics provides the basis for affirming that each new discovery indicates intelligence and choice in the self-existent. But the Newtonian concern with real, as opposed to apparent, movement also leads back to divine freedom. Liberty is an active principle; it begins movement. Mass objects only continue the movement once begun. Without liberty in the first cause, "every thing in the Universe must be Passive, and nothing Active: Every thing Moved, and no Mover: Every thing Effect, and nothing Cause."[73] In this statement Clarke extraordinarily merges Newtonian mechanics with something of a Cartesian physics. Newton acknowledged active principles within the universe: magnetism, fermentation, and the cause of gravitation. Descartes acknowledged only bodies with an initial endowment of motion. Clarke argues that this initial endowment could not have taken place without freedom. The argument is a classic one, but it is Descartes rather than Newton who is speaking. This unconscious subsumption of Descartes under a Newtonian natural philosophy is a brief harbinger of the synthesis which awaits the Universal Mechanics on the Continent. For the time being, it appears only as the fifth reason drawn from the phenomena of nature that the self-existent is free, that it "can govern and direct its own Actions."

From the confluence of intelligence and liberty comes the reflexive power of the self-existent over its actions. The reflexivity which was established in the first analytic movement, reflexivity of self-existence, now is established in terms of personality and operations. The self-existent not only accounts for its own existence, but for its action, and thus for the existence and nature of its effects.

The synthetic demonstration of personal attributes follows from this. Infinite power can be attributed to the self-existent because he alone is self-existent; thus all things are dependent upon him; thus the powers of all things depend upon him. What comes under such power? Whatever is intrinsically possible, that is, whatever does not imply internal contradiction. For a contradiction is nonexistent, necessarily nothing, and the power to do nothing is no power at all. A contradiction is understood as either that which would be self-contradictory or that which would contradict the nature of the self-existent. It is crucial to understand that matter and the creature with intelligence and freedom of will, namely the human being, fall within his power. Human freedom, like divine, lies in choosing between alternatives, in "having a continual Power of choosing, whether he shall Act, or whether he shall forbear Acting. Which Power of Agency or Free Choice, (for These are precisely identical Terms, and a Necessary Agent is an express Contradiction,) is not at all prevented by Chains or Prisons."[74] Here both Hobbes and Spinoza are encountered: Spinoza, in his identification of freedom with necessity; Hobbes, in his identification of freedom with unhindered movement. For Clarke, the first is a contradiction and the second is a consequence. Freedom lies in choice, and its highest form is found in god. Both god and the human being are necessarily free: they must choose. Freedom lies in the power to choose among alternatives without a necessary determination to one or the other. From the freedom of god come all other things. From the freedom of the human person comes not only good, but the moral evil that is the finite alternative to the good.

Evil is always at issue in the debates between the theists and the atheists, and the *Demonstration* locates the problem here. "All that we call Evil, is either an Evil of Imperfection, as the Want of certain Faculties and Excellencies which other Creatures have; or Natural Evil, as Pain, Death, and the like; or Moral Evil, as all kinds of Vice."[75] The distinction between real and apparent tells in the divisions of the kinds of evil. Imperfection simply goes with being a finite reality; the only alternative to this state would be infinity itself. Natural evil issues in some way from the first or third kind. Death is only the dissolution to which any material compound is liable; the experiences of suffering that good people undergo yield a peculiar deepening of their lives and a sensitivity to others which otherwise would not be possible; punishment and ruin inescapably follow moral evil. This third kind of evil is genuine evil, the abuse of human freedom in the choice of the immoral.

Imperfections are only apparent evils; moral evil is absolute evil; natural evil results from either form. If human beings are to exist, imperfections must be necessary and moral evil must be a possibility. In such a context, natural evil follows in causal chain. The alternative to moral evil is the elimination of human beings with their freedom.

As the power of god follows synthetically from his discovered attributes, so does the assertion of his wisdom. "For nothing is more evident, than that an Infinite, Omnipresent, Intelligent Being, must know perfectly all Things that are; And that He who alone is Self-Existent and Eternal, the sole Cause and Author of all Things; from whom alone all the Powers of all Things are derived, and on whom they continually depend; must also know perfectly all the Consequences of those Powers, that is, all the Possibilities of Things to come, and what in every respect is Best and Wisest to be done: And that, having infinite Power, he can never be controuled or prevented from doing what he so knows to be Fittest."[76] God in this synthetic demonstration becomes "Infinite Mind or Intelligence," and this allows a unity to be found both in the universe and in the progress of science. Like Galen and Cicero, so Ray and Derham now find confirmation of the wisdom of god. The design in the human body or in the celestial mechanics which Newtonian natural philosophy insists upon forces one to acknowledge his wisdom.

If Galen so many Ages since, could find in the Construction and Constitution of the parts of a Human Body, such undeniable marks of Contrivance and Design, as forced him Then to acknowledge and admire the Wisdom of its Author; What would he have said, if he had known the Late Discoveries in Anatomy and Physick, the Circulation of the Blood, the exact Structure of the Heart and Brain, the Uses of Numberless Glands and Valves for the Secretion and Motion of the Juices in the Body; besides several Veins and other Vessels and Receptacles not at all known, or so much as imagined to have any Existence.[77]

What gives the lie to Lucretius and Epicurus as they find fault in the nature of things is not religion but contemporary science. Not religion, but anti-religion, has ignorance at its base.

Here the discoveries of astronomy are made to tell. The third book of the *Principia* can be resumed theologically under this proposition on the wisdom of god: the immense greatness of the world, the "Exquisite Regularity of all the Planets Motions, without Epicycles, Stations, Retrogradations, or any other Deviation or Confusion whatever"; the "inexpressible Nicety of the Adjustment of the Primary Velocity and Original Direction of the Annual Motion of the Planets, with their distance from the Central Body and their force of Gravitation towards it." One after another, the elements and findings of celestial mechanics are listed in their proportions, balance, and central gravitational unity.[78] Newton gives the theologian grounds to assert what Scripture has maintained for millennia, perhaps expressed best in Ecclesiasticus (43:32): "There are yet hid greater things than these, and we have seen but a few of his Works."[79]

The use of the sciences instanced and continued in the works of Lessius and Mersenne has reached full term. Atheism has become a philosophic issue and the evidence for its discussion is philosophic. Philosophy has become the natural philosophy of Newton. Now this philosophy serves as evidence not only against the atheists, but to establish the credibility of Scripture. Science now grounds not only philosophy but theology.

The final step of the *Demonstration* is obvious. One must move from the wisdom of god exhibited in the physical universe to the infinite moral virtues of god which constitute him "Supreme Governour and Judge of the World." This movement from wisdom to providence establishes the first foundations of religion itself. The moral perfections of infinite goodness, justice, and truth can be demonstrated as following necessarily from the infinite knowledge and wisdom of god, from the independence of god from all evil influences, and from the infinite power of god. These necessitate that god knows what is fitting in the relation among things and that he possesses the rectitude of will to choose freely what is fit and wise and good.

Clarke argues against those who make the moral law issue simply from the arbitrary choice of god, the nominalists descended from English William of Ockham who maintain that the freedom of god means that there is no intrinsical morality, that god could have created a universe whose entire purpose was to hate him.[80] The *Demonstration* takes as its initial moral insight this principle: "That there are different Relations of Things one towards another, is as certain as that there are Different Things in the World. That from these Different Relations of Different Things, there necessarily arises an Agreement or Disagreement of some things to others, of a Fitness or Unfitness of the Application of Different Things or Different Relations, one to another; is likewise as certain, as that there is any Difference in the Nature of Things, or that Different Things do Exist."[81] The knowledge of this fitness or unfitness is the basis of all morality, and it exists perfectly in god.

Clarke also argues against Spinoza, who would make creation issue from a necessity of the divine nature. Eliminate freedom from god, Clarke contends, and you eliminate the "Ground of all our Prayers and Thanksgivings." Human beings do not pray for god to be omnipotent or omnipresent or omniscient. They do "pray to him to be good to us and gracious, and thank him for being just and merciful." Prayer responds to an unspoken recognition that certain attributes of god follow necessarily from the divine nature, but that in his gracious actions "the Divine Nature is under no

Necessity, but such as is consistent with the most perfect Liberty and Choice."[82] The assertion of the moral attributes of god allows the link to be forged between the demonstrated characteristics of god and the usages of religion. It permits two central religious insights: the freedom and the goodness of god. And these, in their turn, found the moral life directly upon the nature of the things which god has freely chosen to create. The *Demonstration* does not enter into the question about the relationship between these things, with their relations, and the divine nature; it has no doctrine of the divine ideas. Consequently, the question is never raised whether god is morally coerced by something other than himself.

Clarke has, however, met the atheists on their own terms and laid "the First Foundations of Religion." "They desire it should be thought, that, in the Fabrick of the World, God has left himself wholly without Witness; and that all the Arguments of Nature, are on the side of Atheism and Irreligion."[83] The opposite is the case. The Universal Mechanics has furnished both the evidence and the methodology with which the existence and attributes of god can be demonstrated: the constitution of the world and the structure of the human body. There were others which could have been used, Clarke wrote, but they were not so integrated into the natural philosophy that gave structure and direction to his theology: such evidence as "the unavoidable Apprehensions of our own Minds," which stood Malebranche in such good stead, and "the common Consent of all other Men," which played so important a role in Montaigne and Lessius. The "Notices" of god are finally "every thing within us, and every thing without us."[84]

The Atheistic
Transformation of
Denis Diderot

René Descartes had sat as a student of the Jesuits during those years when the glory of the early seventeenth century unfolded in France, and much of his later philosophic development can be traced in the letters occasioned by their criticisms or in the manual which he composed for their classrooms. Denis Diderot was also their pupil and their correspondent, and the passion and the scorn he heaped upon them in his subsequent history mirrored in its intensity the strength of his earlier involvement. For, unlike the student of La Fléche, Diderot, in the Collège de Langres, had proposed to enter the Society of Jesus.

The Hôtel du Breuil, the museum of Langres, still exhibits the solemn certificate from the Jesuit prefect of studies, attesting that Denis—"ingeniosum adolescentem"—had publicly read, translated, and interpreted the poet Horace and the historian Quintus Curtius Rufus "cum laude plausuque omnium" during one of the many *academiae* beloved by the instructors of the *Ratio studiorum*. Langres rivaled neither the La Fléche of Descartes and Mersenne nor the proud Louis-le-Grand on the Left Bank of Paris which educated François-Marie Arouet, better known as Voltaire, but its two hundred students entered into the same humanistic traditions and were inspired by the same pattern of academic advancements. Young Denis' triumphs in Latin verse and translation won him two quarto volumes of some twelve hundred pages, a history of the Catholic Church in Japan by Father Grasset, S.J.; many years later, Diderot described to his mistress, Sophie Vollard, the elation of such academic success: "One of the sweetest moments of my life—it happened more than thirty years ago, though I remember it as though it were yesterday—was when my father saw me coming home from school with my arms laden with the prizes I had won and around my neck the academic crowns that I had been given and which, too large for my brow, had let my head pass through. From the farthest distance that he saw me, he left his work, came to the door, and began to weep."[1] Those thirty years had seen Diderot turn to nagging and bitter conflict with the Jesuits and had replaced Grasset's heavy volumes with his own more massive *Encyclopédie*, but they had not dimmed the memories or the tenderness in which he held his early education. Vergil, Horace, Terence, Anacreon, Plato, and Euripides were always to occupy niches in his pantheon, and as for Homer: "Let me be pardoned for the little grain of incense I burn before the statue of a master to whom I owe what I am worth, if I am worth anything."[2]

It was not strange, then, that this "adolescens multiplici nomine commendandus," at the age of thirteen, on August 22, 1726, received the tonsure from the Bishop of Langres, inducting him into clerical ranks. The town was pervasively and piously Catholic. Many members of his family had followed religious vocations. His sister entered the Ursuline cloister, and his brother became a canon in the cathedral, though neither were to speak peace to their talented sibling. Diderot maintained that Angelique's insanity and early death came from overwork in the convent, and his ecclesiastical brother found the religious disaffiliation of Denis to be among his greatest sufferings. Tonsure obliged its recipient to wear the clerical collar with its white tabs, but it entitled the young student to the title of "abbé" and—more important—conferred the right to ecclesiastical benefice. Many young men in the declining France of Louis XV accepted the title in order to obtain the benefice, without intent or inspiration to proceed to priestly ordination. The clerical state had mammon written deep into its possibilities, and the great crowds of these demi-clerics darkened the history of the French Church and wrote the progression of its debilitation.

No benefice materialized for Denis. Sickness came instead, bringing with it a certain momentary sobering. He began to fast, to wear a hairshirt, to sleep on straw. He decided to become a Jesuit. Religious fervor lasted about half a year. Arthur M. Wilson suggests that Diderot composed the following passage in his novel *James the Fatalist* (1773) out of his youthful experience with a religious vocation: "There comes a moment during which almost every girl or boy falls into melancholy; they are tormented by a vague inquietude which rests on everything and finds nothing to calm it. They seek solitude; they weep; the silence to be found in cloisters attracts them; the image of peace that seems to reign in religious houses seduces them. They mistake the first manifestations of a developing 'tempérament' for the voice of God calling them to Himself; and it is precisely when nature is inciting them that they embrace a fashion of life contrary to nature's wish."[3] The error does not last; the expression of nature becomes clearer. *Tempérament* will become crucially important in Diderot's discussions of religious affirmations. Wilson records with great skepticism the story of Diderot's attempt to creep down the stairs of the family home and leave Langres for Paris and the Jesuits. This dramatic flight to religion evokes the same incredulity as Diderot's claim that his grandmother had had twenty-two children by the time she was thirty-three. Diderot was never "the sort of man to mar a tale in the telling."[4]

Whatever the truth about the midnight staircase, Langres did give way to Paris, the religious vocation to a clandestine marriage, the tutelage of the Jesuits to the influence of Voltaire and Rousseau, Descartes and Newton, Toland and Clarke, Bacon and Boyle, and the achievements in the classroom to translations of Temple Stanyan's *Grecian History* (1793), Lord Shaftesbury's *Inquiry concerning Virtue and Merit* (1745), and Robert James' *Medicinal Dictionary* (1746–1748). The translations were auguries. Shaftesbury indicated how far Diderot had moved from a clerical prospect; James nourished the profound orientation of his interests toward biology, physiology, and medicine. The company of the ancient authors would always stay with Diderot, the impressions of a world which the Church had replaced and which the Enlightenment would apotheosize as a lost paradise. Civilization and Church need not commingle. Shaftesbury's great contribution was to divorce morality from any necessary connection with religious belief, insisting with the skeptical Pierre Bayle that each had its own internal authority and autonomy. Voltaire, and much of Europe with him, feared that moral anarchy would follow a denial of God. Bayle and his disciple Shaftesbury contested this thesis and advocated the possibility, which Diderot would later espouse, that the persuasions of atheism need not threaten ethical convictions and political stability. Under the influence of the English lord, Diderot passed from the intellectual chaos of his bohemian twenties to the reflective career of the French philosophe. Robert James' three-volume *Medicinal Dictionary* did not give him philosophic doctrine as much as it bespoke the focus and outlines of a life's work. The *Dictionary* included "Anatomy, Chymistry, and Botany, in all their Branches relative to Medicine," as well as "tracing the Progress of Physic, and explaining the Theories which have principally prevail'd in all Ages of the World." So Diderot's vastly divergent enterprises would reach through the natural sciences of the time, especially biology, to converge upon the human; the knowledge attained would be ordered and made available through the alphabetical listings and divisions of his life's most significant work, the *Encyclopédie*. To support his first exuberance in Paris, Diderot translated, or, in the case of Shaftesbury, paraphrased, but this working over the tractates of others set the lines of his own development.[5]

Setting the Stage

By 1746, it was time to move beyond translations and write for himself. He was ready to begin the *Pensées philosophiques*, which would draw the strands of his reflections together and set the stage for the great drama of his philosophy. For a philosophy that was later identified with theater, "setting the stage" is not an inappropriate metaphor. The *Pensées philosophiques* would not offer the conclusions of the drama, but would form the matrix within which all his subsequent philosophical reflection is done. Positions which remain in conflict in all of Diderot's philosophic reflections are introduced, characterized, and argued briefly. Each major profession obtains a place, a hearing, and a brief determination of its meaning and direction. A decision is rendered about the argument and the evidence which seems most telling. But there is no interchange among them. It is a dialogue without dialogue—but it forms the critical set within which all subsequent dialogues occur.

The philosophic method that governs this novice work, the later, more mature, reflections, and the great opus that was the *Encylopédie* is the interplay of many perspectives. Human knowledge invites many serious perspectives, outlooks which differ radically in their premises, their patterns of inquiry, and their conclusions. These perspectives are not the last skeptical word, as for Montaigne, but the first critical moment of method. Each prospect gathers into a group those who pretend to knowledge, and each must be tested against the others in debate and weighed finally for its likelihood. Diderot describes himself here, not as a protagonist, but as an umpire: "I was the umpire [*juge*], and held the balance between the adversaries. It rose or fell in sympathy with the weight thrown into the scales. After long hesitation, the balance dipped in favour of the Christian, but simply by way of reaction to the weights placed on the opposing side [*sur la résistance du côté opposé*]. I can bear witness to my own impartiality."[6] Eventually the *juge* would change his conclusions radically, but not his method. Utterly unlike the Newtonian method, which abhorred the distraction of dissension and debate, the methodology Diderot often employs for his physics—in which he claimed Newton would function only in the discrimination of points of view, of positions, and experimentation—is the debate, in which they fight for primacy.

Even the announcement of the subject-matter is arresting. Probably very few works in any language are written to obtain money for the author's mistress and open with the legend: "J'écris de Dieu."[7] Irrespective of the uniqueness of this combination, the question of the existence of god generated denials throughout its history, and debate is appropriately the method employed. But prior to the argument it is imperative to introduce and describe the various positions, positions not to be assimilated into some higher doctrine or perspective, positions to be announced, defended, and espoused or rejected.

Each of these perspectives and its convictions about god involves immediately the question of evidence: what warrants any statement about the divine existence or attributes? What are the resources for any theistic assertion? Where are the foundations for valid religious judgment and discourse? Each viewpoint advances its own evidence. In the history of theological discussion charted by the *Pensées philosphiques*, the reality of the divine has disclosed itself either phenomenologically, in the religious experiences and passions of the knower; ontologically, in the speculations which bear upon propositions whose truth transcends immediate experience; or entitatively, in the discovery of patterns in matter, underlying the chaos of the phenomenal that indicate design and intellect. If one is to "write about god," the first task is to decide among these three, to determine what constitutes the evidence for god.

Religious experiences or *tempérament* embody the passions which had led the young Diderot to consider a future with the Jesuits. The choice of passions as the determinant of religious convictions and decisions is an easy one, for "it is passions alone, and strong passions, that can elevate the soul to great things. Without them, there is no sublime."[8] But passions demand balance. Allow the longings of hope, the desire for honor, or the love of pleasure to dominate life, and you destroy life; you tear it to pieces. "It would be fortunate, people will say to me, for a man to have strong passions? Certainly, if they are in harmony. Establish a just harmony among them, and you need fear no convulsions and disorders."[9] "Disorders" erupt violently in the convulsions of the enthusiasts who have dominated the history of religious fanaticism in France. Radically different experiences were claimed by the Jansenists and the Pietists and, more concretely, by the surpassing but dark genius of Pascal and his Jesuit critics. If religious experience constitutes theological evidence, all assertions depend on idiosyncratic perspective and all religious claims are reduced to superstition. The convictions of the Jansenists differ from those of the Jesuits; *les idées sombres* of the first clash with the second whose *dévotion est enjouée* and whose *sagesse est fort humaine*. But this irreconcilable differentiation of persuasions soon makes skeptics of us all, undermining for the reflective intellect any reliance upon religious experience as a basis for theism: "Whence comes this difference in sentiment between people who prostrate themselves before the same altars? Does piety follow the law of this wretched temperament [*de ce maudit tempérament*]? Alas. It must be so. Its influence is only too apparent in the same devotee: he sees, in accordance with its variations, a jealous or a merciful God, and hell or heaven opening before him, he trembles with fear or burns with love; it is a fever [*une fièvre*] with its hot and cold fits."[10] Base your reflections upon immediate religious experience, and the norm which actually governs your judgment and constitutes the criterion for your assertion is nothing but your *tempérament*. Since temperaments differ so radically, the lineaments of god change as various enthusiasts draw them. Contradicting voices come from contradicting experiences, which depend on contradicting temperaments. As these contradictions emerge, skepticism about any theological assertions rises with them.

The eruptions of temperament tell us nothing of the nature of god; in fact, the god they fabricate is often a monster. His irrational rages, the implacable vengeance he wreaks on human beings, the *massa damnata* of Augustinian theology—these notions, which rot at the heart of superstition, tempt the upright to wish for a godless reality and drive others from skepticism to atheism. An ultimate paradox rules the absolute reliance upon religious experiences and passions: Such a religious attitude moves through superstition and skepticism and finally terminates in atheism.[11] Indeed, superstition offends human sensibility far more than atheism. The *Pensées philosophiques* reach back to Plutarch for a formulation of this opinion: "I should prefer that men should say about me that I have never been born at all, and there is not Plutarch, rather than that they should say 'Plutarch is an inconstant fickle person, quick-tempered, vindictive over little accidents, pained at trifles.'"[12] Plutarch's preference lies behind Diderot's conviction that superstition's final moment is atheism: "The atheist has no part in causing superstition, but superstition provides the seed from which atheism springs, and when atheism has taken root, superstition supplies it with a defense, not a true one or a fair one, but one not destitute of some speciousness."[13] One has only to attend to the terror of god that religion has elicited, or the resentments enkindled against other human beings, or the somber record of religious wars, to know that any evidence adduced from purported revelations and from religious experiences is ultimately and decisively its own fatal contradiction. All its notions of god emerge from an unknown sea of fathomless subjectivity, and what surfaces in this appeal to pretended immediacy is so inhumane as to generate atheism.

There is a second possibility to be considered: the evidence for god is transcendent. Descartes wrote in this vein to the theologians of the Sorbonne, as he made a claim for the proper location of the question of god: "I have always considered that the two questions respecting God and the Soul were the chief of those that ought to be demonstrated by philosophical rather than theological arguments."[14] Not immediate religious experience, but philosophical reflection, furnishes a warrant for god. Descartes' demand is at bottom polemic: by no other means can one deal with the "infidels of any religion." Philosophy under his guidance siphoned off such theological interests into metaphysics, leaving physics to become mechanics with no final causes or grounds for theological inquiry. Metaphysics, however, in the readings of Diderot, was simply *billevesée*, variously rendered into English as "an empty tale" or "nonsense." Descartes thought the metaphysical job done, the *Meditations* so carefully framed and defended that one could get on with the task of physics. Diderot, and the Enlightenment whose debates he mediated, revisited the Cartesian tree whose roots were metaphysics, whose trunk was physics, and whose limbs were the other sciences. The roots were rotten! These foundations of philosophy were not even rhetorically suasive. "None of the vain speculations of metaphysics have the cogency of an argument *ad hominem*."[15] Diderot's dismissal ranges further than the Ambrosian "non in dialectica complacuit Deo salvum facere populum suum."[16] He dismisses all transcendent evidence with its appropriate arguments.

Religion appeals to experience, to distorted passions, and ends either with the relativity that such perspectives make inevitable or with superstition and fanaticism. The metaphysics of Descartes attempted to move beyond experience and perspective to a series of proportions independent of conditioning and of sensible perception, proportions whose knowledge inevitably entails assent. The unhappy product of this Cartesian assent is skepticism, just as religious enthusiasms terminate in atheism. "The subtleties of ontology have at best made skeptics."[17] Neither the passions of religion nor the metaphysics of the Universal Mathematics can furnish evidence for one whose opening declaration is: "I am writing about god."

If not Pascal or Descartes, then who shall supply such evidence? One must turn to *la physique experimentale*: "It is not from the metaphysician that atheism has received its most vital attack. The sublime meditations of Malebranche and Descartes were less calculated to shake materialism than a single observation of Malpighi's. If this dangerous hypothesis [of atheism] is tottering at the present day, it is to experimental physics that the result is due. It is only in the works of Newton, of Musschenbroek, of Hartsoeker, and of Nieuwentijt that satisfactory proofs have been found of the existence of a reign of sovereign intelligence."[18] Newton is identified with the deist in Diderot, and "only the deist can oppose the atheist. The superstitious man is not so strong an opponent. His God is only a creature of the imagination." The English deists Cudworth and Shaftesbury constitute a far more serious challenge to the atheism of Vanini than do Nicole and Pascal.[19]

Experimental physics alone supplies theological evidence, since neither religious experience nor indubitable metaphysical proportions are serviceable. *La connaissance de la nature*! The evidence for the divine existence is nature. But what does "nature" mean? That which can be observed and whose interior structure can be discovered. It is a double-decker nature, susceptible to "une observation de Malpighi," and to the mechanical investigation which reveals that the world is "une machine qui a ses roues, ses cordes, ses poulies, ses ressorts et ses poids."[20] Religious warrant is furnished by mechanics. One must leave Pascal and Descartes for the genius whom Voltaire's *Lettres philosophiques ou lettres anglaises* had done so much to celebrate: Isaac Newton.

Newton proposed that "the rest of the phenomena of Nature" could be investigated and finally derived "by the same kind of reasoning from mechanical principles."[21] Unlike Descartes, he skeptically shunned metaphysical inquiry, contending that to discourse about God "from the appearances of things, does certainly belong to Natural Philosophy."[22] This enterprise of Newton gathered to itself the intellectual energies already at work in England and swept onto the Continent, summoning the enthusiasm and the scientific investigations that had preceded it into a single *sentiment physique*. Diderot's citation of Malpighi discloses this *sentiment*.

In 1628, Harvey had inferred the capillary circulation of the blood and had published *De motu cordis*. Descartes defended Harvey's conclusions, but changed them in order to fit them into his mechanical biology. Gilson comments: "The learned world was then called upon to witness that surprising spectacle: Descartes, who had not discovered the circulation of the blood, explaining it to Harvey, who had made the discovery, and adding to it as many mistakes as he was adding explanations. Yet, Descartes was so sure of himself that he made public his wrong theory in the fifth part of his *Discourse*, where it is expounded at length as a perfect instance of mathematical demonstration in biology. A more blindly trusted method never took anybody to more consistently wrong conclusions."[23] This was precisely Diderot's point. The whole Cartesian project was not as good as one observation of Malpighi.

What did Malpighi observe? Marcello Malpighi was the founder of microscopic anatomy. While Harvey had accurately argued to the capillary circulation of the blood, he had never seen it. Four years after Harvey's death, Malpighi saw by means of microscopic techniques the blood coursing through a system of small tubes on the surface of the lung and the distended urinary bladder of a frog. In 1661, he published his findings in two letters, *De pulmonibus*, containing also his findings on the vesicular structure of the human lungs. His observations of the capillaries confirmed Harvey's theory of the circulation of the blood and redressed Descartes' errors.

Observation and investigation. Newton's *Principia* and *Opticks* lay at the basis of Bernard Nieuwentijt's *L'existence de Dieu, démonstrée par les merveilles de la nature*, in which biology is reduced to physics and the structures of nature used as evidence for the divine reality and providence.

The work appeared in Amsterdam in 1714 and was translated four years later into English as *The Religious Philosopher, on the Right Use of Contemplating the Works of the Creator: (I) In the Wonderful Structure of Animal Bodies, (II) In the Formation of the Elements, (III) In the Structure of the Heavens, Designed for the Conviction of Atheists*. J. Chamberlayne had translated this review of almost the whole of natural science into three volumes totaling about a thousand pages. The basic argument for the divine existence was that of Newtonian design, but never before had it been tried on such a scale. "None among Nieuwentijt's numerous imitators equaled his completeness."[24] Normally, the argument from design was dispatched either as Lessius had sketched it, a number of examples from which the major point could be induced, or as Newton had built it, to demonstrate the universality of the system of the world. In Nieuwentijt, however, the evidence of all the sciences pointed to the same conclusion, leading to Diderot's estimation that the materialist hypothesis was tottering (*chancelle*).[25] This major tractate of observation and investigation had been translated into French by P. Noguez in 1728 as the work in experimental physics that classically embodied the Newtonian theological method extended throughout natural phenomena.

The Universal Mechanics delivered a method to Europe as the critical contribution from the Newtonians. It became a flag of many nations. Petrus van Musschenbroek's inaugural address, *Oratio de certa methodo philosophiae experimentalis*, given when he assumed the chair of natural philosophy and mathematics at the University of Utrecht in 1732, mustered under the standard of Newton not only Galileo and Torricelli but also Christiaan Huygens and René-Antoine de Ferchant de Réaumur. Musschenbroek, later to invent the Leyden jar, insisted upon the painstaking care demanded for his experiments and observations—not so surprising when one realizes that his family had for generations invented and constructed scientific apparatus. Mathematics keeps the place, both descriptive and demonstrative, that Newton had allotted it within this general investigation of nature, and the climax of this scientific inquiry is the discovery of the divine intelligence at the basis of the laws of the universe.[26]

Religious experience leads to superstition, which leads to atheism. Metaphysics leads to contradicting systems, which lead to skepticism. Experimental physics, in contrast, leads to the "true knowledge of nature," which leads to deism. Nature, not experience or speculative ideas, constitutes the only evidence in the universe that can support theistic commitments. Diderot's *Pensées* exhibit in miniature the development of natural theology since the days of Lessius and Mersenne. Theology gives way to Cartesianism, which gives way to Newtonian mechanics. The great argument, the only evidence for theism, is design, and experimental physics reveals that design.

Design is both mechanical and organic. Newton found no contradiction between these; Descartes did. Indeed, Newton spoke not only of "this most beautiful system of the sun, planets, and comets," but of "the excellent contrivances of things and, final causes."[27] Descartes, on the contrary, identified final causes with the purposes of god, confessed that he found them all hidden, and decreed for his followers that "the species of cause termed final, finds no useful employment in physical [or natural] things."[28] Diderot continued to follow Newton, but extended the method, as the master had suggested, into biological realities as well.

It was not enough to say that the world exhibited system as the *Iliad* exhibited poetic structure and from either to argue demonstratively to intelligence. Rivard, professor of philosophy at the Collège de Beauvais, had made precisely that argument, but it was open to the kind of analysis that Jacques Bernoulli had made possible, the calculus of probabilities detailed in the *Ars conjectandi* (1713). The discussions of Pascal and Fermat about the nature of a game of chance had given rise to the notion of mathematical probability. Pascal had seen the issue as one of the arrangements or combinations of given elements and of the mathematical method for calculating those arrangements. Jacques Bernoulli brought their work into a systematic whole. For Diderot, this meant that the Newtonian argument from design needed to be radically rethought.

Granted an eternal time and a consequently infinite number of possible combinations of characters, it is not irrational to suppose that Voltaire's *Henriade* could have issued from the fortuitous conjunctions of these characters. So also with the world. If one grants that matter has been eternally in movement, and that the multitude of atoms is infinite, and that the possible combinations that would compose a system are infinite, there is nothing so strange in the possibility that one of these combinations has occurred. Eternal time, an infinite number of throws of the dice—throws in which motion recombines the elements—and an infinite number of systematic possibilities: it would be far more astonishing if one of the many systematic possibilities were not realized.[29]

What one has in nature is not indifferent dice, however, but organic orientation. The phenomena of nature result not from a throw of the dice, but from seeds whose development is internally charted to form "le méchanisme de l'insecte," whose structure is expressed again and again through a pattern of evolvement into organs, functions, and purpose. "The discovery of seeds [*germes*] alone has destroyed one of the most powerful arguments of atheism."[30] Francesco Redi's *Esperienze intorno alla generazione degli insetti* (1668) had disproven the Aristotelian doctrine of spontaneous generation, and through careful microscopic analysis had detailed both the internal organization and the egg-producing functions of insects. Antoni van Leeuwenhoek had similarly used microscopy to refute the doctrine of the spontaneous generation of insects from decaying matter and had charted the fertilization process in the origins of all new animal life. The Aristotelians had taught that small animals such as insects and intestinal worms issued from the putrefaction of organic matter, since their structures were so primitive. "Leeuwenhoek demonstrated the complete structure of mites, lice, and fleas and described their copulation and life cycles."[31] Both Redi and Leeuwenhoek allowed Diderot to see the organic pattern in seed, development, and subsequent organization, and to write that "I can allow that the mechanism of the vilest insect [*le mécanisme de l'insecte le plus vil*] is not less marvellous than that of man; and I am not afraid of the inference that as an intestinal agitation of molecules is able to produce the one, it is probable that it has produced the other. If an atheist had maintained, two hundred years ago, that some day perhaps people would see men spring full-formed from the bowels of the earth just as we see a mass of insects swarm in putrefying flesh, I would like to know what a metaphysician would have had to say to him."[32] The metaphysician would have had nothing to say to him—especially in his Cartesian guise. Experimental physics had made Diderot find, not chance, but purpose and organic connection at the origin of all life.

The issue of spontaneous generation figured critically in Diderot's later works, in which he decided the question differently. For the time being, however, the discoveries of Redi and Malpighi and Leeuwenhoek were taken as decisive. Animal life does not emerge from organic corruption; it emerges from seeds. Thus the chance occurrence of higher forms of reality does not figure as a real possibility. The issue is a question of principle: what is the source of life? The probability calculus has disproved, in the reckoning of Diderot, any argument from design that would depend simply on internal elements or arbitrary actions. Either of these, given enough or indeed an infinite time, would coalesce into some system such as confronts the reflective person in the phenomena of nature. There must be a shift in principle. The principle must be such as to indicate an internal possession of its end in some form or another; it must show that conjunction of seminal beginning and end which is organic life. The principle must be reflexive. The *Pensées* saves the classical argument of design from Lessius through Newton by this insistence upon a different kind of principle, one not unlike that of Descartes' *cogito* or self-evident principles. But now the reflexivity is found in the underlying, organic material which emerges as biological life.

The *Pensées philosophiques* opt thus for reflexive principles, seeds that grow into full living things, and the career that matter and motion take is that of development, of organic growth: "Whether motion be essential or accidental to matter, I am now convinced that its effects are limited to developments [*ses effets se terminent à des développements*]."[33] Settling for reflexive principles at this juncture, a settlement which microscopic analysis had grounded, allows autonomous levels of reality whose entities develop from seed to full maturation. The relationship between the completely developed entity and its beginnings indicates not only the mechanics of related parts, but an organic purposiveness that needs to be explained.

The reason that a "butterfly's wing shows me traces of an intelligence a thousand times more distinct than the indications you have that another human being thinks," is not simply, as for Newton, the structure of this organic reality. It is also its purposive development from the first instance of its conception. How does one human being know that another human being thinks, that there is recognition, awareness, cognition, and choice behind human gestures? One does not see the thinking going on. One sees only external behavior. For many of these things one could train an animal or construct a machine. It is "by the continuity of ideas, the connection between propositions, and the links of the argument that one must judge if a creature thinks. If there was a parrot which could answer every question, I should say at once that it was a thinking being." But has one ever observed in human beings the kind of intelligent results that one observes in nature? Are not continuity, connections, links as apparent in the "mechanism of an insect? Is not the Deity as clearly apparent in the eye of a flesh-worm as in the works of the great Newton? What, does the formation of the world [*le monde formé*] afford less proof of intelligence than its explanation?" One reads the *Principia* and recognizes the mind behind it. If one only looks at the formation of the butterfly's wing or at the development of a flesh-worm's eye—"when I could crush you with the weight of the entire universe"—is not a much more precise and calculating intelligence revealed? "Is not the intelligence of a first cause more conclusively proved in nature by his works than the faculty of reasoning in a philosopher by his writings?"[34]

The evidence for theological assertion, then, is entitative, the structure that underlies phenomena as well as the phenomena themselves. The evidence is "nature," whose internal formations are suggested by observation and experimentation, which are themselves made possible by the integration of mathematics into science. But in order to justify this interpretation of reality, the principle must change from the comprehensive force of Newton to the reflexive principles, such as the seed, by which these structures are begun and ultimately explained. Reflexive principles provide for the unity of the entire process of development. Diderot has continued Newton's inquiry, but only by radically shifting one of its coordinates.

Once the issue of evidence is settled, however, a second critical issue must be decided: what is the method to be employed when one talks about god? What is the pattern of discourse in which one will use the underlying evidence?

A major section of this question has already been settled. It would have been impossible to deal with the issue of evidence without the practice of a definite method. The methodology praised in the *Pensées philosophiques* is that of experimental physics; the methodology concretely employed in the definition of evidence is that of a matrix of possibilities and perspectives, articulated and examined one against the other to elaborate and criticize ideas. *Les pensées philosophiques* does not respond to the issue of evidence nor determine the principle coordinate with this kind of inquiry by the use of Newtonian analysis and synthesis. It isolates various perspectives and examines each. The method is operational—it discovers reality by constructing a matrix of possibilities and bringing it to bear upon the subject under consideration. But this is not an adequate description of Diderot's method. It is broadened and made a far more flexible instrument through the incorporation of skepticism.

The kinds of evidence have changed coordinately from those given by Lord Shaftesbury. Diderot distinguishes three levels of religious evidence: religious experience, metaphysical ideas, and the phenomena and underlying structure of nature. Those who rely on religious experience generate a correlative atheism as they discredit theism with their superstition. Those who elaborate vast systems of metaphysical inquiry only lead into a further skepticism. Only experimental physics provides both the multileveled data and the developmental principles that can ground theistic or deistic assertions. But these levels of theological evidence can be rephrased in terms of the basic question of the *Pensées philosophiques*, and they become the three kinds of atheism.

There are first *les fanfarons*, those who for one reason or another pretend to have eliminated the possibility of god's existence and whose life mirrors their pretensions. But their public posture comes from an internal terror of god; they "wish that there were no God." Second, there are those who can come to no decision, the skeptics; they do not know what to think. Finally, there are the *vrais athées*, "those who will tell you there is no God." *Les fanfarons* lack honesty, and no rational discourse can possibly move them beyond the decision that their desires have established. The skeptics "lack knowledge" and could perhaps profit from further inquiry and analysis. The genuine atheists lack all consolation in this life. "I pity genuine atheists."[35] One can dismiss the swaggerers and braggarts, but the skeptics and the true atheists merit further consideration by one who writes of god. This is even more important because skepticism and genuine atheism are the ineluctable products of metaphysics and superstition in one form or another. They remain viable and serious religious options. Perhaps most important, skepticism has a critical role to play in the elaboration of a method.

The fundamental distinction between the real and the apparent provides the basic device for the classification of skepticism. There are those who doubt, but doubt only because they have not examined with any serious methodology the grounds of credibility (*les raison de crédibilité*). Just as one dismissed an entire class of atheists as braggarts, so one can dismiss this level of atheism as ignorant. "The true skeptic has counted and weighed his reasons," and the central problem he must deal with is that of the reduction of all arguments to perspectives. "Out of a hundred proofs of the same truth, each one will have its partisans. Every mind has its own telescope. An objection which is invisible to you is a colossus to my eyes, and you find an argument trivial that to me is crushing in its efficacy. If we dispute about their intrinsic value, how shall we agree upon their relative? . . . Are my spectacles in fault, or yours?" The figure of Montaigne looms large before any commitments. We live in a world in which probabilities are foisted upon one as infallibilities, and in which our propositions should be softened into modesty by such additions as "*à l'adventure, aulcunement, quelquefois, on dict, ie pense.*" The unassuming stance of the skeptic recommends itself spontaneously to the cultivated intellect. The skeptic has not looked or reasoned too little. He has reasoned so much that perspective after perspective swims before his eyes.[36]

Any number of reasons explain religious skepticism. We teach children about God—something far beyond their capacities—at the same time that they are learning about ghosts and goblins. We confine the presence of god to churches, and so teach people to live in a world from which he is habitually absent. "Men have banished God from their company and have hidden him in a sanctuary; the walls of a temple shut him in, he has no existence beyond."[37] Two sources combine in experimental physics to produce theorems and convictions: reason and sensible experience. God is taught at a time and in a way that makes him inaccessible to either.

A methodological value lies in skepticism, however. It contributes enormously if it is the first stance and not the last word. The search for truth demands that one question all that is believed. To fail to do this is to build upon religious experiences and temperament. "What has never been put in question has not been demonstrated. What people have not examined without prepossession has never been examined thoroughly. Skepticism is thus the first step toward truth. It must be applied generally, for it is the touchstone."[38] The *Pensées'* repudiation of the Cartesian *Meditations* does not extend to a total denial of Descartes. Descartes' response to Montaigne is strikingly similar to Diderot's. Montaigne is not rejected out of hand, though "vigorous minds and ardent imaginations do not take kindly to the indolence of skepticism."[39] Assimilate him, however, into one's method; make skepticism the initiation of inquiry; and one has an investigation that moves toward demonstration. Skepticism provides the deist's only defense against either atheism or superstition. The arbiter among the three is finally and definitively and solely reason. Thus runs the creed of the Enlightenment: "If the religion that you announce to me is true, its truth can be demonstrated by unanswerable arguments. Find these arguments. Why pursue me with prodigies, when a syllogism serves to convince me? Do you find it easier to make a cripple stand upright than to enlighten me?"[40] The value of skepticism is that of an acid; it burns through inconclusive argument and insubstantial evidence. It lays bare the demonstrations and the unanswerable arguments. Just as seeds are the reflexive principle of self-generation and self-development, so reason is the appropriate, reflexive principle of any conviction.

The alternative is superstition, and the evidence to which it appeals is revelation, prodigy, and miracle. Witnesses breathlessly assured France that the churchyard of Saint-Médard had for years been the scene of miracles. Crowds gave themselves to religious enthusiasm and hysteria from 1728 to 1732. The shrine of the miracles was the grave of the Deacon François de Pâris, and its prodigies were doubly welcome, for Pâris was not only a deacon, he was a Jansenist. The wonders around his tomb were taken as confirmation of that beleaguered group. Carré de Montgeron, a *conseiller* to the Parisian *parlement*, had been converted from the life of a libertine to a life of piety by one of Pâris' miracles, and had spent much of his life collecting and recording similar divine interventions. His *Vérité des miracles opérés par l'intercession de M. de Pâris, démonstrée contre M. L'archevêque de Sens* appeared in 1737, published safely in Utrecht though dedicated to Louis XV. Diderot was not buying. "A certain street resounds with acclamations; the ashes of one of the elect work more miracles in one day than Jesus Christ during his whole life. . . . I would wager that all who have seen spirits are afraid of them beforehand, and that all those who saw miracles there had made up their minds to see them."[41]

First, as the famous Jansenist Antoine Arnauld emphasized in the great *La logique, ou l'art de penser* (1662): "Things known by the mind are more certain than those known by senses."[42] When the evidence presented by the senses is inconsistent with that of reason, one should obviously prefer the demonstrations or the inclinations of reason. Ideally, they would operate together, as they do in experimental physics. The central error in metaphysics and in superstition lies in their disjunction. Metaphysics cultivates reason in separation from sensible experience; religious fanaticism and superstition play upon sensible experience in contradiction to reason. It is not enough to appeal to the testimonies of eyewitnesses or the written collections of history. Fables have always swarmed to circle and protect religions as different from Christianity as Roman divinations and the cult of Romulus. Cicero's response to his credulous brother, Quintus, in the *De divinatione* remains perpetually valid: "Hoc ego philosophi non esse arbitror testibus uti, qui aut casu veri aut malitia falsi fictique esse possunt; argumentis et rationibus oportet, quare quidque ita sit, docere, non eventis, eis praesertim quibus mihi liceat non credere."[43] And what falls under the rubric of "events, especially those which I am unable to credit?" Such stories as the superstitious use to ground religious experience or convictions. "Every nation has stories like this, which would be miraculous if true; which are never proved, but which serve to prove everything; which it were impious to deny, and folly to believe."[44] Why refuse belief in the face of so much testimony? Because the calculus of probabilities tells against it. The same mathematics that undermines the static argument from design renders revelation and miracles incredible.

If Jonah were to wander through Paris, as through Nineveh, crying out that in three days Paris would be no more, the Parisians would not rush for sackcloth and ashes. They would hurry the poor wretch off to the lunatic asylum. Even if he were to work "miracles" to substantiate his claim to divine guidance, the real miracle would be for anyone to pay attention to him.[45] But what if an entire nation claims to have witnessed miraculous intervention? "The less probability a fact has the more does the testimony of history lose its weight. I should make no difficulty in believing a single honest man who should tell me that His Majesty had just won a complete victory over the allies; but if all Paris were to assure me that a dead man had come to life again at Passy, I should not believe a word of it. That a historian should impose upon us, or that a whole nation should be deluded—there is no miracle in that."[46] The apostle Paul had warned against any gospel that was preached, even by the miraculous intervention of an angel, which would be contrary to his. Christianity does not rest upon prodigies taken away from argument and content. "It is not, therefore, by miracles that a man's mission is to be judged, but by the conformity of his doctrine with that of the people to whom he declares himself sent, especially when the doctrine of that people is proved to be true."[47] The foundation of religion is not religious experience, nor is it miraculous events. The foundation of religion is reason, tested by the rules of demonstration. One demonstration is worth fifty historical events, and reason alone safeguards human beings from the *saltimbanques* that swarm around religion.[48]

The *Pensées philosophiques* are moving to establish a position similar to Clarke's premise in the first series of Boyle lectures, that the natural philosophy of experimental physics could constitute "the First Foundations of Religion."[49] The fundamental error of the appeal to religious experiences and to the tales of miracles is the priority given to sense experience over the claims of probability and reasonableness. The fundamental error of the Cartesian metaphysicians is the priority given to reason existing in tension with sense experience. The value of the *Pensées* lies in the conjunction between reason and sense experience, a conjunction that is fundamentally human, with reason the final arbiter over sense and passion.[50] "Example, prodigies and authority may make dupes or hypocrites; reason alone can make believers."[51] And reason, brought to bear upon proper evidence, makes belief. If reason comes upon the enthusiasm of the fanatic, it ends in atheism; if it follows the winding arguments of Malebranche and Descartes, it comes to skepticism. But if it enters into an experimental physics that follows the developing designs within organisms, as with Malpighi or Nieuwentijt, both evidence and argument lead to a deism that can call itself Christian. Diderot has no trouble accepting the title of "deist" along with the confession that he is a Christian, although he knows that "deist" in the mouth of an adversary is incompatible with "Christian." "If they only call me a deist and a wretch, I shall get off lightly. They have long since damned Descartes, Montaigne, Locke and Bayle. . . . I was born in the Roman, Catholic, and Apostolic Church, and I whole-heartedly submit to its decisions. I wish to die in the faith of my fathers, and I respect it as far as is possible for a man who has never held immediate intercourse with the Deity, and has never witnessed a miracle. That is my confession of faith, and I am persuaded that they will find fault with it, though perhaps not a man among them can make a better."[52] The *Pensées philosophiques* have assimilated enough of the skeptical method to dismiss all other means of establishing the existence of god. For one who opens with "I am writing about god," the quest is to find a level of evidence, a method, and a principle that will allow him to accomplish that task. The skeptical method clears away the other claimants, and leaves the field to the evidence of organic development and the designs studied in experimental physics. Various positions are compared and the more probable chosen, and a principle that will be reflexively coordinate with the conclusions reached. For "every proof ought to produce in me a certainty proportionate to its conclusiveness, and the effect of geometrical, moral, and physical proofs upon my mind must be different, or else this distinction is a frivolous one."[53] It is not strange that the consideration of evidence and the construction of method both terminate in the establishment or assertion of reflexive principles, namely, seeds for the biological world and reason for the conscious world of conviction and statement. In both Descartes' *Discourse* and Newton's *Principia*, principle was the critical issue. The value of the Cartesian method was that it could uncover an indubitable proportion which could serve as a principle for subsequent argument. The value of all the definitions of Newton and of the phenomena discovered and mathematicized by his predecessors was that they pointed to a comprehensive principle—force in the earlier books, gravity in the system of the universe, and God as the *dominatio*—that both made infinite and eternal coordinates possible and established the mathematical structure of the visible universe. Diderot's *Pensées* are also a coordinate search for principle, first in the physical universe and then in the reflective, scientific intellect. In both cases, the principle is reflexive.

Les Pensées philosophiques have determined the coordinates of Diderot's investigations and the meaning of the deism which answers atheism. It would seem that the issue was settled and the answer nailed to the question. Nature has provided the evidence for the assertions of the deist, and the reflexive principle has justified the establishment of this evidence. But what if that principle should change?

"La matière se mouvoir et le chaos se débrouiller"

On Tuesday, November 20, 1711, Nicholas Saunderson succeeded William Whiston as Lucasian Professor of Mathematics at Cambridge. He was fourth of a line that numbered Isaac Barrow and Isaac Newton. Barrow was dead; Newton had been knighted and appointed master of the Mint; Whiston had been expelled from the university because "he sides wth ye Arrians." Saunderson delivered his inaugural lecture in "very elegant Latin and a style truly Ciceronian," and set about the business of teaching. He devoted seven hours a day to this task, an astonishing record, in which he covered such subjects as Newtonian natural philosophy, hydrostatics, mechanics, sounds, astronomy, tides, algebra, and fluxions.[54] With enormous admiration, Diderot records Saunderson's lectures on optics, the nature of light and colors, the characteristics of lenses, the various phenomena of the rainbow, the nature of vision, and "many other subjects connected with sight and its organ."[55] It was a breathtaking accomplishment. For Nicholas Saunderson was completely blind. Before he was a year old, smallpox had robbed him not only of his vision, but of his eyes.

That Diderot would celebrate the eminence of Saunderson is, at first blush, almost as surprising as the remarkable achievements of the great Cambridge mathematician. In his unpublished *Promenade de sceptique*, Diderot named the irrational, fanatical representative of religion "l'aveugle"; this unhappy figure enters into dialogue "en marchant toujours les yeux bandés." In contrast, the various philosophic types, irrespective of their persuasions and of their schools, engage the arguments "sans bandeau et les yeux tout ouverts."[56] But believers have covered their own eyes. They have chosen their darkness. They are not those, like Saunderson, without the power of sight whose other senses have compensated for this loss. Whatever their inabilities to see, these religious enthusiasts have deliberately courted ignorance. Privation has not driven them down different paths in the sensible search for truth.

What is more, Saunderson was not only blind. He was intelligent and educated. When the great René-Antoine Ferchaut de Réaumur contracted with the Prussian oculist Hilmer to couch the cataracts of the young daughter of M. Simoneau, both Diderot and his mistress, Madame de Puisieux, applied for permission to witness the event. Such an operation was only four years old, and it riveted the attention of the philosophes. For a philosophy that built everything upon sensation, the variation of perceptions and judgments consequent upon the introduction of one of the senses after its privation offered critical data for inquiry into the formation of ideas. But to no avail. Réaumur welcomed the eager presence of neither Diderot nor Madame de Puisieux. No invitations were forthcoming to observe either the displacement of the cataracts or the subsequent removal of the bandages.

Diderot subsequently professed himself less than sanguine about the philosophic import of the experiment. Philosophic method involved more than a doctor's operating upon the blind and reporting his findings. Philosophic method was the concourse of perspectives, and the perspectives of the blind girl comprised the most important element of all. But if these perspectives were untutored and naive, if the subject lacked education and reflective talents, then the scientific findings were inevitably of the same character. Madame de Puisieux may have thought the experiment philosophically promising; her lover thought it "an experiment in which I saw little profit." To understand the formation of ideas among the blind and to extract both the data and its correct interpretation, it would be necessary to find one both blind and educated.[57] Thus enter Saunderson!

Saunderson, after all, was magnificent in his achievements, but not unique. In his *Elements of Algebra*, he memorialized those whose condition was like his and whose success in life was similar.[58] Didymus of Alexandria, St. Jerome related, was blind from infancy, but learned both "logic and geometry to perfection." Cassiodorus credited Didymus with a classic exposition of the *Book of Proverbs* and was astonished to discover the number of *disciplinae* he had mastered. Cassiodorus gave credence to Didymus' story only after meeting Eusebius of Asia, because Eusebius himself also combined immense education and total blindness. Finally, Trithemius' *De scriptoribus ecclesiasticis* commemorated the brilliant legal ability of the blind Nicaise de Voerde, while Diderot adds to the list a "Hollander, and some others, whom blindness did not hinder from excelling in mathematical learning."[59] Saunderson placed himself within a tradition of the learned blind; Diderot honored that tradition and credited its members with unique abilities to learn mathematics and to grasp speculative matters.

In 1749, two years after Diderot constructed the matrix for the discussion of the divine existence in the *Pensées philosophiques*, his inquiry could proceed further with electrifying results through the introduction of new perspectives, those of the learned and gifted blind. His *Lettre sur les aveugles à l'usage de ceux qui voient* investigates two questions: What is the validity of ideas formed by the blind? and, What is the correct answer to Molyneux's problem? Since John Locke had introduced this problem into the philosophic commerce of the time, let him describe it as he himself had received it in a letter from Molyneux: "Suppose a man born blind, and now adult, and taught by his touch to distinguish between a cube and a sphere of the same metal, and nighly of the same bigness, so as to tell, when he felt one and the other, which is the cube, which the sphere. Suppose then the cube and sphere placed on a table, and the blind man be made to see: *quaere*, whether by his sight, before he touched them, he could now distinguish and tell which is the globe, which is the cube?" In answer, Locke joins Molyneux in denying that the blind man could so distinguish, because, "though he has obtained the experience of how a globe, how a cube affects his touch, yet he has not yet obtained the experience, that what affects his touch so or so, must affect his sight so or so; or that a protuberant angle in the cube, that pressed his hand unequally, shall appear to his eye as it does in the cube."[60] Despite, or because of, the presentation in *An Essay Concerning Human Understanding*, the issue continued to be debated in academic Europe, Berkeley agreeing with Locke's solution and the Abbé Etienne Bonnot de Condillac's *Essai sur l'origine des connaissances humaines* (1746) contesting their answers.

The problem of Molyneux enters the inquiry of the *Lettre sur les aveugles* as a subissue of the first and far more fundamental problem: How do the blind form ideas and what is their validity? Until this issue is resolved, Molyneux's problem will remain, but both questions will only be solved through a more appropriate method. Any failure of Locke or of Condillac is essentially a failure of method. Both reduce complex wholes to simples in the logistic manner which characterized Newtonian mechanics, building the complexities again only when the simple constituents are analytically established. Both mathematics and metaphysics move toward such simple principles, Diderot maintained, but metaphysics is basically misguided and mathematics does not deal with existents. "An infallible secret for obtaining incorrect results in *physico-mathématique* is to suppose objects *moins composée* than they usually are."[61] If logistic analysis and synthesis ineluctably lead to results that are *défectueux*, what is the process or pattern of discourse to which the two questions must be submitted?

Intelligibility is generated through perspectives, ideally through perspectives in conflict. Thus it is critically important to get the perspectives of the blind on the issues through the questions raised in conversation. Madame de Puisieux cannot attend the experiment of Réaumur upon the blind girl. No matter. What she can obtain from Diderot is better: *le récit d'un de nos entretiens.*[62] To answer the first question, that of the formation and validity of the ideas of the blind, one must move through increasingly intelligent perspectives, first in a conversation with the man from Puiseaux, then in a similar report on the enormously talented Saunderson, and finally in a debate between Saunderson and Holmes through which Diderot actually engages Newton and Clarke. The question of the formation of ideas concludes only with the clash of two hypotheses on the formation of the universe. Similarly, Molyneux's problems can be resolved only by first investigating the possibility of any perception at all, and then differentiating the various perspectives of the subjects of the experiment: "In order to treat the question in the manner you will appreciate—for you like method [*la méthode*]—I will classify the persons on whom the experiment might be made."[63] For both questions, the method is radically the same, in its introduction of hypothesis into physics and in its insistence that the blind should be consulted and that experiments will differ as their agents differ.

Diderot's method, on which he insists, is to situate divergent claims in their appropriate frames of reference and then bring them into conflict to test their validity. The method is operational rather than logistic; intelligibility is not discovered ready-made, as Réaumur's naiveté might suggest, but generated by the various perspectives at work. The first question uses this method to establish a fundamentally new principle and to destroy the claims of Newtonian natural theology; the second question confirms the values of this universal method by bringing it to bear upon a problem critical to the discussions of the time.

The first question deals immediately with the problem of god, and its resolution develops in three successive stages. The first stage is to establish the importance of the reflections of the educated blind. For this, a visit and a conversation, "nous allâmes interroger l'aveugle-né du Puiseaux." Philosophy becomes the recitation of a narrative. The attainments of the man from Puiseaux must be listed. He does not lack that *bon sens* which both Montaigne and Descartes after him had celebrated. Beyond this, he has some knowledge of chemistry and botany, and was raised by a father who was a distinguished professor of philosophy at the University of Paris. "We arrived at our blind man's house about five o'clock in the afternoon, and we found him busy teaching his son to read with raised letters." Touch is his means of reading. From touch his world derives its intelligibility. He has come to understand beauty because of the order in which he must keep his things, because of his acute sense of symmetry; and he understands beauty as Diderot himself understood it, as utility or good. It is only an instance of the unique philosophic superiority open to the blind: "The only compensation for their loss is that their ideas of beauty, though less extensive, are more definite [*plus nettes*] than those of many keen-sighted philosophers who have written prolix treatises on the subject." This point constitutes the credibility of the blind: their very deprivation enhances their speculative abilities. Touch provides the basis in sensation for analogies that are not only intelligible, but illuminative. The blind man's definition of a mirror was such that "had Descartes been born blind, he might, I think, have hugged himself for such a definition," and his understanding of sight such that "Descartes, and all the later writers, have not been able to give us clearer ideas of vision."[64]

Not only does this blind man equal Descartes in abstract conceptions, but his compensatory sensations of hearing and of touch are far more developed than they are in those who see. Jarring as it was, the report of the man from Puiseaux read: "He would have thought himself a pitiable object in wanting those advantages which we enjoy, and he would even have been inclined to consider us as superior beings if he had not a hundred times found us very much inferior to him in other respects."[65] Just as human beings invented terms to represent ideas for which there are no sensible referents by a "number of ingenious and profound analogies observed between them and the ideas they suggest," so the blind are forced to live more profoundly by analogy and by abstraction. This allows them to question the bias of those who so easily accept conclusions as given, needing no proof. The argument from the wonders of nature, the Newtonian argument for god's existence in all its celestial magnificence, "falls flat upon the blind." They demand something more at hand, and "as they see matter in a more abstract manner than we do, they are less indisposed to believe that it thinks."[66] The man from Puiseaux not only has a sensitive life in many ways superior to his sighted compatriots, but in abstract thought he can move beyond their prejudices and challenge their most cherished conclusions.

For abstraction comes as the culmination of sensation for all. The blind, like the sighted, form their ideas from sensations, but primarily from touch and hearing. These in turn give way to connected memories of past sensations, while imagination can both recall these memories and combine them into analogies of straight lines and perfect curves. Abstraction, the final development of ideas from sensations either external or internal, "consists in separating in thought the perceptible qualities of a body, either from one another, or from the body itself in which they are inherent." But the blind have already begun this process. Imagination has already separated the visual discourse which surrounds it in order to form analogies. Thus the critical conclusion from the conversation with the blind man of Puiseaux: "The person born blind consequently perceives things in a much more abstract manner than we; and in questions purely speculative, he is perhaps less liable to be deceived." In abstract thought, the blind are privileged! Jean-Jacques Rousseau constituted for Emile an ideal tutor and an ideal preacher. Diderot has created an entire class who can tutor the metaphysicians: the blind. And who from this group had greater credentials than Nicholas Saunderson? In the inquiry into the fundamental principles of the formation of the universe, his should be a perspective of unique value.

The conversation with the man from Puiseaux has established the nature of the principle that this inquiry into the formation of ideas is looking for. Error arises when abstractions are done in the wrong way: "There is perhaps one certain method of falling into error in metaphysics, and that is, not sufficiently to simplify the subject under investigation; and an infallible secret for obtaining incorrect results in *physico-mathématique* is to suppose objects less compounded than they usually are." Descartes and Malebranche are the metaphysicians, and their errors lie in their failure to obtain samples. Nor is their appeal to a universal mathematics of any help. That is "one kind of abstraction of which so few are capable that it seems reserved for purely intellectual beings, and that is that by which everything would be reduced to numerical units." Such a mathematics might be able to represent everything, but it would approach divine knowledge and could only be done by angels! "Units pure and simple are too vague and general symbols for us." What one does, then, in the investigation of the formation of ideas and their validity is neither metaphysics nor mathematics; it is much more like mechanics and medicine. You may call it metaphysics at times, if you will, but it is leagues away from the angelic discipline to which the French gave that name.[67] It would have to be metaphysics integrated with mechanics and its subdisciplines: "C'est qu'il est bien difficile de faire de la bonne métaphysique et de la bonne morale sans être anatomiste, naturaliste, physiologiste et médecin."[68]

What kind of principle does such a synthetic discipline look for? One that is *composé*. Diderot goes to his engagements with Saunderson, looking not for a simple principle but for a compound principle, which will lie at the basis of speculation on the formation and validity of ideas because it lies at the basis of the formation of the universe.

What the first stage of investigation established as general possibilities for the blind has been realized in Saunderson. The report of his success moves Diderot's inquiry into its second stage, to obtain the actual achievements of the blind. "Wonderful stories, indeed, are told of him, and yet there is not one to which, from his attainments in literature and his skill in mathematics, we may not safely give credit."[69] He invented, from the sheer necessity of his own genius, *une arithmétique palpable*, a machine which could be used by the blind both for algebraic calculation and the formation of rectilinear figures. The machine was a board composed of carefully placed squares, each square representing a different number by the location of large or small pins. The board could be as large and the constituent squares as numerous as need dictated. "We only know that his fingers moved over his tablet with astonishing rapidity; that he made the longest calculations successfully; that he could interrupt them, and recognise when he was in error; that he could verify them with ease."[70] So complete was his *Elements of Algebra* that the only indication of blindness lay in demonstrations that would have occurred only to a blind man. His skill in teaching mathematics stemmed directly from his blindness, "for he taught his pupils as if they could not see, and a blind man who makes himself clear to the blind must be doubly lucid to the sighted."[71] Blindness did not inhibit his abilities to engage in abstract mathematics, it enhanced them, and enabled him to assume the major chair of mathematics in England. The necessity that blindness imposes on the use of analogy doubled the effectiveness of his communication, as metaphor sheds a double light upon any subject.

Diderot's operational method allows a similar translation of physics into the perspective of mathematics. There are three distinct moments in mechanics, or in any question in which physics and mathematics enter. There is first the phenomenon to be explained; second, the supposition or the hypothesis of the geometer; third, the resultant calculation and its conclusion. The centrality of "hypothesis" in this threefold schema of mechanical method indicates that Diderot has moved to a different world from that of Newton. The actual phenomena of optics, light and color, could not fall immediately within Saunderson's experience. But he can accept from those scientists gifted with sight the physical hypothesis by which they can be understood: light can be either a succession of bodies or a ray like a "fine and elastic thread." Physical hypotheses make it possible to move from one level of sensation to another. Unlike Newton, Diderot can translate the phenomena to be studied into geometry through the creation of physical-mathematical hypotheses. "The transition is made from physics to geometry, and the question becomes purely mathematical."[72] Finally, in Diderot's reading of the method of experimental physics, the mathematical methodology of the Cartesian heritage subsumes Newtonian mechanics. Hypothesis once more has a place in its inquiries, and the function of mathematics is not simply to describe and to calculate, but to translate and to confirm suppositions which do not emerge from analysis. Clarke's notes introduced Newtonianism into Cambridge through a Cartesian textbook; Diderot is now returning the compliment with a vengeance!

Calculation confirms hypothesis. This function, perhaps more than any other, indicates the shift that Diderot is reading into Saunderson; it also indicates the need for a corresponding shift in principle. For these preliminary hypotheses can be either single or complicated. "When the calculation is based on a simple hypothesis, the conclusions have the force of geometrical proofs." When the hypotheses are many, the situation becomes more complicated and defective. Many false hypotheses can be mutually corrective, leading to a materially correct conclusion. The greater the number of hypotheses, however, the greater probability of error. Take a very common example. If one wants to determine the curvature of a ray of light, a number of hypotheses must be taken into account: the density of the atmosphere, the laws of refraction, the nature and form of light (corpuscular or wave), and so on. "If the actual curve agrees with that of his calculation, there are two alternatives: first that his hypotheses were mutually corrective, secondly that they were correct. But which is true? He does not know, and yet that is all the certitude to which he can attain."[73] The conclusion this Cartesian rendering of mechanics yields is very straightforward: it is very advantageous to have a single hypothesis, a single principle. If one wants a certitude that has the force of geometric proof—and what Cartesian does not?—then one must push his physical inquiry back, not to a simple principle, but to a single hypothesis.

The failures previously registered of Locke and Condillac were failures of method. The failures now to be noted of Berkeley and Condillac are those of principle. Both have the same principles, according to Diderot's reading: one's own existence and the succession of external sensations or thoughts. So many hypotheses can offer no certitude of final judgment nor constrain philosophic discourse: "We never get beyond ourselves, and it is only our own thoughts that we perceive."[74]

The report of the blind man of Puiseaux discovered the need for compound principles in the investigations of nature. The success of Saunderson's reduction of mechanical methodology to mathematics indicates that this compound principle must be single. Underneath the charm of Diderot's narrative, there is a deadly serious argument, and it reaches its climax—as one would expect—in the third stage of his inquiry into the formation and validity of the ideas of the blind, the debate between Gervase Holmes and Nicholas Saunderson.

Holmes was "un ministre fort habile," summoned to the side of the dying Saunderson to offer whatever comforts religion could afford. "They held," Diderot wrote, "a discussion upon the existence of God, some fragments of which are extant, and which I will translate to the best of my ability, for they are well worth it." A noble enterprise, indeed, which would rock intellectual France back on its heels, land the collector of these "fragments" a few months in the prison of Vincennes, and prevent his ever being numbered, like d'Alembert, among the fellows of the Royal Society. For the conversation never took place, the fragments never existed, and the theological opinions of Saunderson are made up out of whole cloth![75] The dialogues of Cicero were contrived, but they expressed the positions of those whom they named. It is quite another thing to place the convictions of Diderot in the mouth of the distinguished Lucasian Professor of Mathematics. Diderot has already made him a Cartesian; now he makes him an atheist. The dialogue has gone some distance from consulting the blind! It has become drama, rather than history, but a drama of surpassing moment in the history of the issue debated.

The *Pensées philosophiques* reduced all valid arguments to those from organic design. Holmes represents that position, *les merveilles de la nature*, only to find it immediately countered by the perspectives of the blind man. The celestial mechanics of Newton are quite beyond him; he has spent his entire life in darkness. Holmes must bring the argument closer to his abilities: "If you are to make me believe in God, you must make me touch Him." But this only shifts the Newtonian design into the biological frame of reference in which the *Pensées philosophiques* had cast it. "'Sir,' the clergy-man appositely returns, 'touch yourself, and you will recognize the Deity *dans le mécanisme admirable de vos organes.*'" So far, so predictable! What was the mechanism of the insect and the observations of Malpighi in the previous work is open to the blind man in his own body. But it is precisely here that the revolt takes place.

What seems so marvelous to the revised Newtonian is simply mechanical to this revivified Cartesian. The physical universe, however its component relations are construed, cannot bear the weight that the Newtonian is giving it: "What relation is there between such mechanism and a supremely intelligent Being?" What is so miraculous to the inexperienced dims to the commonplace to those with more acquaintance. Let Saunderson use himself as an example. His accomplishments are incomprehensible to those who hear of them for the first time, but he knows that each step along this long way resulted from human ingenuity and human cultivation. There is nothing miraculous about his grasp of mathematics, however wonderful it may appear at first announcement. In fact, "I have been myself so often an object of admiration to you, that I have not a very high idea of your idea of the miraculous. . . . We think a certain phenomenon beyond human power and we cry out at once: ''Tis the handiwork of a god.'" The three stages of experimental physics structure the debate. The first stage is the selection of a mechanical or organic phenomenon. The second stage, the hypothesis or the principle by which it is finally to be explained, is the sticking point. Holmes, with Newton and Clarke behind him, states the hypothesis: god. Saunderson, within the hidden autonomy of Cartesian mechanics, sees no need to invoke that hypothesis. "Mr. Holmes availed himself of his good opinion of his probity and of the abilities of Newton, Leibniz, Clarke, and some of his fellow country-men, men of the highest genius, who had all been impressed by the wonders of nature and recognized an intelligent being as its creator. This was certainly the clergyman's strongest argument." Saunderson accepts the phenomenon, but refuses to resolve the issue by the hypothesis advanced or by faith in the word of Newton.[76]

What hypothesis can he advance in its place? *La matière se mouvoir et le chaos se débrouiller.*[77] Accept the order of the universe, either physical or biological, but push the question back to its origins. Consider how such design and such order first came into being, and "here you will have no witnesses to confront me with, and your eyes are quite useless."[78] The Newtonians never gave serious consideration to the possibilities Lucretius' *De rerum natura* suggested in the first century. They are content to take design as they see it and postulate a divine intelligence. The *Pensées philosophiques* particularize the design in the organic relationship between seed and its final product, in a reflexive principle which contained its terminus within itself. Now Saunderson wishes to introduce the issue of the origin of all design, to return to a time before there were animal bodies or plants, and ask the question: How did design come to be? He also introduces the phenomena that have always embarrassed those who argue from design. Part of the data to be explained are monsters, the deformed, the blind—people like himself whose "design" is faulty and whose privations are obvious. If God is given the credit for the marvels of nature, must he not assume the burden of physical evils and the horrors of nature? Or must the experimental scientist look for a more comprehensive cause, one that will explain both the marvels and the horrors with equal ease? Would not such a principle be a hypothesis "more conformed to nature?"[79] Let us, then, explain present design by a return *à la naissance des choses et des temps.*[80]

If we were to go back to the origin of things and the beginnings of time, what would we perceive? Precisely what Descartes has suggested in his mechanics: matter in motion. But in this scenario there is no need for god to establish matter and the laws of nature. Descartes only goes halfway, artificially deriving his mechanics from the divine attributes. Saunderson's real master is Titus Lucretius Carus. Newton's natural theology is to be refuted by the hypothesis drawn from the great Epicurean poet.

Let us go back to origins, Saunderson, urges. We may well find creatures whom chance has grotesquely misarranged:

> I may ask you and Leibniz and Clarke and Newton, who told you that in the first instances of the formation of animals some were not headless and others footless? I might affirm that such an one had no stomach, another no intestines, that some which seemed to deserve a long duration from their possession of a stomach, palate, and teeth came to an end owing to some defect in the heart or lungs; that monsters mutually destroyed one another; that all the defective combinations of matter [*toutes les combinaisons vicieuses de la matière*] disappeared, and that those only survived whose mechanism was not defective in any important particular and who were able to support and perpetuate themselves.

Men born with closed larynxes died off; those born with open larynxes, finding suitable food, possessing adequate organs for generation, had a chance for life. It is not surprising that we find design in the physical universe. Beings with no design or inadequate design simply perished. But even today, enough monstrosities come briefly into existence to remind us that both design and defective design are the work of chance and of the survival of those which alone can survive. No other premise or supposition will explain both order and chaos, both organic perfection and biological deficiency. The blind can put the argument with great poignancy: "Look at me, Mr. Holmes. I have no eyes. What have we done, you and I, to God, that one of us has this organ while the other has not?"[81] Newton's methodology traced motions to their original forces. The operational method changes this to explain phenomena by the most adequate hypothesis, single but compound. The phenomena include organic life, its history, and its monstrous deviations; here the unique perspective of the blind is made to tell. Why go to the blind for the argument from design? The blind can insistently introduce what they actually embody: disorder, privation, physical evil, useless human suffering—phenomena which are often omitted and always discomfiting to such as the Newtonians. They introduce data for which god is now less than adequate as an explanation. A far more satisfying hypothesis is primordial matter in motion.

Diderot has stripped Descartes of his theological metaphysics, and, in insisting upon the autonomy of mechanics, restates Lucretius. For the Roman poet also found this at the formation of the biological universe, as he had found the chance combination of atoms at the basis of the physical universe. "Many monsters too earth then essayed to create, born with strange face and strange limbs . . . all in vain, since nature forbade their increase, nor could they reach the coveted bloom of age nor find food nor be joined in the work of Venus. . . . And it must needs be that many races of living things then perished and could not beget and propagate their offspring."[82] Lucretius finds the origin of animal life in the state of the world: "For much heat and moisture abounded then in the fields; thereby, wherever a suitable spot or place was afforded, there grew up wombs, clinging to the earth by their roots."[83] When Diderot's Saunderson retrieves this tradition, he specifies it through his own blindness: "In the beginning, when matter in a state of ferment brought this world into being [*la matière en fermentation faisait éclore l'univers*], creatures like myself were of very common occurrence."[84] What is the hypothesis that takes the place of god? It is matter in a state of ferment, matter to which motion is not an arbitrary addition but an intrinsic necessity. For Descartes, god had to create matter, establish its laws, and give it movement because matter is geometric extension and only obtained motion from without. For Lucretius, on the contrary, motion belongs aboriginally to the descending atoms and brings about their initial combinations and the ceaselessly cyclic movements of decomposition and recomposition: "Omnia commutat natura et vergere cogit . . . sic igitur mundi naturam totius aetas mutat et ex alio terram status excipit alter, quod tulit ut nequeat, possit quod non tulit ante."[85] Thus Saunderson: "Motion continues and will continue to combine masses of matter, until they have found some arrangement in which they may finally persevere. . . . What is this world, Mr. Holmes, but a complex, subject to cycles of change, all of which show a continual tendency to destruction; a rapid succession of beings that appear one by one, flourish and disappear; a merely transitory symmetry and a momentary appearance of order."[86]

Diderot thus obtains a new principle, a new hypothesis, not simply a different explanation but a radically different kind of principle. Previously, his work insisted upon a reflexive principle, seeds coordinate with product and reason coordinate with rational conviction. Now these reflexive principles are all instances of a single yet compound hypothesis, a comprehensive principle, to which all reality may be finally reduced and by which it may be explained. It can be variously designated *la matière se mouvoir* or *la matière en fermentation*. Dynamic matter generates the various forms of inorganic and organic existence and continually dissolves them once generated.

Diderot has taken something from both Newton and Descartes and turned these weapons against their forgers. From Newton, he takes the universality of physics and its adequacy to handle theological issues; from Descartes, he takes a mechanics that is artificially construed to depend upon the divine attributes but cannot demonstrate the existence of god, and whose physical hypothesis, compound but single, is dynamic matter. With such an understanding of experimental physics, a science universal and self-contained, any metaphysical introduction of a "god hypothesis" is simply an attempt to cover ignorance. It is pride and not philosophy, Saunderson contends, that calls for a transcendent explanation of the problems we cannot immediately resolve. Instead of resorting either to the Cartesian metaphysics or to the Newtonian god of the gaps, "my good friend, Mr. Holmes, confess your ignorance."[87] Diderot's Saunderson introduces a critical transition in Western thought with his dismissal of transcendence and assertion of the virtualities of dynamic matter. He introduces atheism.

It is an atheism not denied but heightened by the sequel. The debate proves too much for the dying Saunderson, and he passes into delirium. At the close of the narrative, the blind mathematician cries out, "O thou God of Clarke and Newton, have mercy on me!" and then expires.[88] The cry is filled with a thousand ironies. For Diderot, it sounds the sardonic repudiation of the going natural theologies. For the history of theology, it indicates the last and inevitable stage of religion become philosophy.

In putting the doctrine of a dynamic materialism in the mouth of Saunderson, Diderot was indeed being historically untruthful about the Cambridge mathematician, but loyal to a philosophic spirit which was arising in France. The importance of the *Lettre sur les aveugles* is precisely that it was not the isolated hypothesis of a single French philosophe. Its premise was being half-formulated or hesitantly articulated through a circle which comprised biology, microscopy, natural history, zoology, geology, oceanography, and cosmogony. Like the great insights of the calculus, the hypothesis of generative matter was born in a number of places, and it would be hard to ascertain its first parents. When Diderot switched so soon from his reflexive principle to an all-encompassing matter, he spoke for a generation.

In March, 1741, the Académie Royale des Sciences in Paris received an astonishing communication which was read in its entirety to the members during two official sessions. The letter, addressed to Réaumur and communicated by him to the Académie, detailed with great precision the work of a thirty-year-old Swiss zoologist, Abraham Trembley. Trembley had written to Réaumur in search of reassurance that he had not made an error. In June of the previous year, Trembley had taken to his room some ditchwater containing aquatic plants.

> He noticed a green hydra (*Chlorohydra viridissima*) attached to one of the plants, and at first took it to be itself a plant. He noticed, however, that the tentacles moved, and soon found that organisms of this species could change their positions; but he still hesitated to call them animals. He decided to determine the matter by cutting one of them in two, on the supposition that if both parts survived, the organism would clearly be classifiable as a plant. The cut was made in such a way that one of the parts possessed all the tentacles. He watched the regeneration of both fragments during the following days until regeneration was complete, when both parts were tentaculate; they were indistinguishable from one another. Nevertheless, the apparent spontaneity of the hydra's movements made it difficult for him to accept the conclusions that these were in fact plants.

Hence the astonishment of the Academy. Réaumur did in fact confirm Trembley's work. What did it mean to organic finalism, to seeds, and to biological design if an animal could be regenerated simply by cutting it in half? Voltaire refused to accept it. "Long afterwards he still persisted in denying the possibility and dismissed the subject contemptuously, describing the animal in print as a 'kind of small rush.'" It seems that not only Galileo's Aristotelians refused to look through telescopes. No matter; experiments followed, one hard on the heels of another, until Trembley

capped the whole history by transforming two hydras into a single hydra
with two tails. His monumental work, *Mémoires, pour servir à l'histoire
d'un genre de polypes d'eau douce, à bras en forme de cornes*, appeared in
1740 and led many to think that inquiry would have to move beyond the
arrangement of parts or the organic development of seeds in order to
account for living matter.[89] Perhaps there was something vital, something
dynamic, in matter itself. Perhaps matter held a principle that was not
captured by equating it either with extension, as Descartes, or with mass, as
Newton; perhaps it had internal forces beyond the inertial.

Boiled mutton gravy figured next in this accumulation of evidence, and
with it an English Catholic priest, John Turberville Needham. Needham
boiled the gravy until he thought all life was dead within the sealed jar.
Microscopic analysis, however, discovered infinitesimally small living creatures, apparently generated from the putrefying mass. Needham reintroduced what Malpighi amd Remi had exorcised as "my system of spontaneous
generation and epigenesis." Experiment followed experiment; various forms
of decaying vegetable and animal matter were employed. Needham's *Account of Some New Microscopic Discoveries* appeared in 1745, indicating that
small wormlike microorganisms issued from putrefying matter,[90] and re-
storing spontaneous generation briefly to academic respectability. However
mistaken this position, and however fiercely contested by the abbé Spallanzani, Needham's finding not only influenced Buffon's hypothesis of "organic molecules" but added to the weight of evidence which made Diderot
rethink his original repudiation of spontaneous generation. His Saunderson
accepted it, and it pointed beyond seeds and their products to a creative
matter that underlay them both.

The possibilities for life were not just in seeds, nor immediately to be
attributed to some divine intervention. The possibilities for life were within
matter itself. Aram Vartanian accurately comments upon the effect of these
discoveries in altering the thinking of Diderot: "In the *Lettre sur les
aveugles*, the notion of spontaneous generation, fused with a transformistic
hypothesis, was promptly magnified by Diderot to cosmic proportions, and
the focal point of his entire vision of nature became the question of how, 'in
the beginning . . . matter in fermentation caused the world to take shape.'"[91]
Small wonder that Diderot took Buffon's *Histoire naturelle* with him into
imprisonment and spent the months at Vincenne glossing the text. There is
no question that the developments in biological speculation parallel Diderot's own turn to a new principle: "*la matière se mouvoir et le chaos se
débrouiller.*"

What is one to make of Diderot's response to Voltaire's admonition about
the *Lettre sur les aveugles* and his arguments for the existence of the deist's
god? "The sentiment of Saunderson is not any more my sentiment than it is
yours. . . . I believe in God, although I live very well with the atheists."

Diderot's statement is probably as true as many of the assertions he made, coordinate with the opinion of those whom he either admired or feared. At philosophical issue is not his private opinion, but the public argument of his *Lettre sur les aveugles*; Voltaire and the Parisian police read its message in similar fashion. Perhaps even more telling is that Diderot has rendered the question insignificant. Religion has long since been dismissed. The god of the philosophers has nothing to do with the universe which experimental physics treats. In any case, whether god exists or not no longer matters: "It is ... very important not to mistake hemlock for parsley; but to believe or not believe in God, is not important at all."[92] Earlier investigation reduced all religious argumentation to superstition and all philosophic demonstration to reliance upon organic design. Now even this is swept away. What emerges as comprehensively significant is dynamic matter, lying beneath the various and transient forms in the phenomenal universe, obeying its own laws and ultimately responsible for whatever happens within the world. Any discussion of the existence of a god whose reality cannot be proven and who does not interfere in the life of the universe is idle. At best, the one god has become *deus otiosus*. Henceforth, all serious inquiry will resolve its issues by appeal to matter and its properties. Montaigne had long since given up on any knowledge about the world. So he had handed over the question, like a tennis ball which the philosophers could bat back and forth, endlessly and fruitlessly. "And I," Diderot wrote, "have said almost as much about God himself. Whether God exists or doesn't exist, He has come to rank among *ces très sublimes et très inutiles vérités*."[93]

Oddly enough, this position synthesizes what has gone before. Like Newton, it rejects metaphysics and relies upon a physics or a mechanics which is 'universal. Like Descartes, it reduces all mechanics to matter in motion and eliminates any treatment of final causes, whether mechanical or organic. The two greatest thinkers of the seventeenth century are not only still serviceable, but mutually corrective. Newton pried Descartes' progeny loose from his theological premises and metaphysical foundation. Descartes corrected the Newtonian acceptance of the argument from design, and eventually furnished something far more serviceable and less occult than force as the comprehensive principle to which natural phenomena were resolved. The happy result is an autonomous and universal natural philosophy which explains all reality as physical and all its various forms through matter in motion.

The Dream of d'Alembert

In the centuries that culminated in the Enlightenment, philosophic reflection assumed many forms. Europe was profoundly influenced by monumental, labored tractates, by the *Principia* and the *Recherche de la vérité*. More popular modes of inquiry and debate—letters, satires, dialogues, and conversations—also flowed into the tributaries of its consciousness and convictions. Religion contributed its own peculiar modes of expression to swell this philosophic current. Mersenne wrote philosophy as a commentary on Genesis; Descartes' greatest work was meditations, Clarke argued the existence of god in sermons. It was the glory of Denis Diderot to sponsor still another genre: philosophy in the form of drama.

In drama, the conversations no longer had to mediate those of history. The characters were free to advance opinions as the argument dictated without the nagging need to adhere to the actual programs of the persons represented. For a philosophic method whose movement and productivity consisted in the introduction of perspectives, drama offers obvious advantages. It allows one to move beyond discussing various positions and permits these positions, embodied in the characters, to present and argue themselves. A whole philosophic tradition can take flesh in a single actor. What is more, the movement of a drama mirrors the movement of nature. As the truth of biology or of cosmology emerges from an inquiry into the origins of natural forms and the attentive observation of their development into their final patterns and products, so the play or spectacle can exhibit the principle and the inner logic of a philosophic doctrine, trace its strengths and weaknesses in its interaction with others, and chart its consequences. Drama can debate with an immediacy that no other form commands; it draws the observer into the subject as it is being explored. From his earliest writings, Diderot had recognized that "la perfection d'un spectacle consiste dans l'imitation si exacte d'une action, que le spectateur trompé sans interruption, s'imagine assister à l'action même."[94] So Diderot counted it against Corneille that each of his characters, Cinna, Sertorius, Maxime, and Emile, were nothing but Corneille's mouthpieces (*sarbacanes*), for in better drama each person speaks out of a unique and determined character. The perspectives or the dialogues fail, not if all the characters do not represent the playwright, but if they are "à mille lieues de la nature."[95] Drama incarnates the diversity of perspectives in its characters and in their dialogue, and it forges this diversity into the single argument that is its plot. Drama need be nothing more than good drama to be good philosophy, the faithful presentation of nature: "On n'y représente l'événement de la manière la plus naturelle."[96]

The dramatist, then, must be a philosopher. To write well about human beings, he must have meditated profoundly upon what it means to be a human being, to possess mind and soul as well as body, and to live within social interactions and political systems.[97] Philosophy degenerates in its effectiveness when it separates itself from eloquence, and the arts become similarly debased when they lose the insights and the moral guidance of philosophy. "How mankind would be benefited were all the arts of imitation to seek a common end, and come together with laws forcing us to love virtue and despise vice! It is the philosopher's place to invite them."[98] The union can be even more emphatic in a philosophic drama such as that of the death of Socrates, taking what Plato has left us and creating a one-act play in five scenes: "What eloquence is required! What profound philosophy! What truth to nature! What essential truth!"[99] As the various forms of drama differ, so their coordination with philosophy varies. But all drama demands fidelity to nature, and like all philosophic inquiry into nature, all drama entails a concern about causes. The difference between the phenomena of nature and the anatomy of drama lies here: "In nature we see only a vast succession of events, the causes of which are unknown to us, whereas the march of events in a play are revealed to us, or if the poet conceals a sufficient number of causes for a while, he finally initiates us into his secrets and satisfies our curiosity."[100] Conformity with nature gives drama credibility and awakens philosophic interest; insistence upon clear causal relations gives drama a depth beyond simple history and identifies it with philosophy. It is philosophy quite literally in action.

The objects of philosophic inquiry are the phenomena of nature, and these phenomena may be either "donné par la nature, ou imaginé à l'imitation de nature."[101] Phenomena are "given by nature" through the operations of observation, thought, and experimentation. Observation collects the facts, thought combines them, and experiment verifies the results of these experiences. These constitute the three moments of any method which deals with nature. The verification of the hypotheses by which data are selected and phenomena explained lies in the final adequation between the conclusions of thought and the observed or predicted natural phenomena.[102] Phenomena are created or invented through "the imitation of nature." What does one do when one imitates nature in serious drama? What does Diderot do—and implicitly all those who have the abilities which he commands? "There is one method [*manière*] I have adopted of going about work, a successful one to which I turn whenever habit or novelty obscures my judgment—both produce this effect—and it is to seize the very thought of certain objects, transport them bodily from nature to my canvas, and examine them from a point where they are neither too far from me, nor too near."[103] Imitation of nature, then, can be described in terms not totally foreign to those by which abstraction is defined. In both cases, an object is determined in nature. In abstraction, its sensible properties are reduced or eliminated; in imitation, its sensible situation or context is eliminated. The transformed object is then examined by bringing the perspective of the scientist or the artist to bear. The effect of both is didactic, the presentation of truth, for in drama as well as in philosophy one comes to see things the way they really are. "There they will see mankind as it really is, and they will become reconciled with it."[104] Imitation as well as abstraction offers new and fruitful perspectives on nature.

The didactic purpose of drama dictates that its plot should be as simple as possible. A plot once known, however intricate, fascinates no longer. What lingers in the memory and insures an enduring presence for the drama in the ages to come? The ideas. "One good scene contains more ideas [*plus d'idées*] than is possible in a whole play of incident; and it is to ideas that we return, that we listen to and never grow tired of; these affect us in every age." [105] And where does one find these ideas? Not in the plot, but in the discourse. One cannot forget the reflections of Roland waiting for the faithless Angélique or the words of Clytemnestra to Agamemnon. If one complicates the plot with subplots and minor intrigues, the discourse in which ideas emerge and are developed is necessarily impoverished. "There is no middle way: you will always lose in one place what you have gained in another. If you gain interest and rapidity by a number of incidents, you will have no discourses, for your characters will have no time to speak: they will merely act instead of develop."[106] In its development of character and its discourse, drama exhibits nature most. The plot, for all its ingenuity, is ultimately the product of the creative imagination of the playwright, but "good dialogue comes from the observing of nature." To a philosophic method whose strength lies with the introduction of clashing perspectives, testing plausibility in debate, there corresponds a poetics of theater whose depth consists in the development of characters and their appropriate discourse. "You can formulate any number of plots on the same subject and with the same characters; but, given the characters, there is only one way in which they may speak [*la manière de faire parler est une*]. These will say such and such things according to the situations in which you place them, but since they are always the same people, in any situation, they must be consistent."[107] Philosophic perspectives originate ideas which are tested in discourse; dramatic characters originate ideas which are developed in discourse.

The analogy between drama and philosophic reflection presents a new literary form for philosophy. For if drama can be philosophic, philosophy can be dramatic. The dramatic mode offers new possibilities for the unity and coherence of argument without the straightjacket of system.

Systems had fallen on hard days. In 1749, the abbé de Condillac had launched his concentrated attack on the great systematizers of the Cartesian tradition, *Traité des systèmes*. Condillac did not condemn all systems. His great hero, Isaac Newton, had advanced a system of the world as the climax of the *Principia*. But systems not built upon observation of phenomena are misleading and useless. What was fatally wrong with Descartes, Spinoza, and Leibniz was not the desire for systematic unity, but the principles with which they attempted this unity, either abstract principles of thought or hypotheses about the nature of the real. Neither would serve, and both had so permeated the idea of the systematic as to make it suspect in the new world in which innate ideas and abstract notions alone inspired little conviction. Diderot seized the critique of Condillac and extended it to cover not only those systems whose principles were abstract or hypothetical but those whose method was too tightly knit and logistic.

Facts, of whatever kind, are the genuine riches of philosophy. The painful work of the philosopher consists in gathering these facts and in tying them together. One can distinguish philosophers fundamentally by the task they principally undertake. The experimental philosophers foster the empirical discovery and collection of facts, observations, and experiments. The others, "orgueilleux architectes, s'empressent à les mettre en oeuvre." Time inexorably destroys all of these "edifices de la philosophie rationnelle," but the empirical data, the critical observations about human conduct and the phenomena of nature, remain as the raw material for subsequent constructions.[108] Nature is the source of any permanence that philosophy can claim—not ideas, not suppositions—and nature is not only so endlessly fecund but so ceaselessly varied in its apparitions that it can never model the careful deductive concatenations with which the great systemizers rivet their work. Diderot does not inveigh against an order or method of philosophizing. He protests against a tight deductive system whose effect is "étouffer le génie."[109] The *Encyclopédie* is described as "le système général" for gathering the various sciences, arts, and mechanical skills into one coherent pattern of presentation, one point of view which provides freedom of exposition and clarity of relation.[110] In striking contrast to the order of knowledge diagrammed by Peter Ramus, in which the various sciences are deduced from the three operations of the intellect, the order of the *Encyclopedia* is alphabetical, an arrangement which is simple, available, and utterly arbitrary in the connections drawn among the articles. Diderot himself notes: "L'ordre alphabétique donnerait à tout moment des contrastes burlesques; un article de théologie se trouverait relégué tout au travers des arts mécaniques."[111] But this order, with its systematic crossreferences, allows each subject to be explored with the maximum of freedom without artificially forcing all knowledge into some grand plan. Each contributor develops his topic as he will, conjoining this piece of knowledge with that as his own perspectives dictate and employing whatever methods of analysis and exposition he thinks appropriate. The *Encyclopédie*'s alphabetical order is ideal for understanding philosophic method as a congress of points of view. It promotes pattern, but with freedom and diversity.

Drama offers something of the same fecundity and liberty to philosophic reflection itself. The habitual irregularity in the characters and in their discourse catches something of the chaotic flux and reflux of eternally changing nature, with its designs and its accidents, its moments of almost perfect symmetry and of unrelieved disorder. The method of philosophizing should suit the objects about which one is reflecting, and the comprehensive nature of Diderot's principle tells in his selection of a dramatic method. "It is of nature that I am going to write." And how can one write of nature, of this matter continuously in motion, continuously creating and destroying in an endless ocean of new forms and chance occurences? "I shall allow the thoughts to follow one another from my pen, in the same order in which the objects offer themselves to my reflection because these best represent the movements and the advance of my mind or spirit." Nature lies at the basis of both *les objects* and *les movements et la marche de mon esprit.* [112] Things and thoughts contain the same dynamism as nature. It is imperative to discover a discourse that can mirror this dynamism.

Various forms had been tried, especially fragmentary *pensées* and the free-flowing letter. Both allowed spontaneity in the reflections, in the point of view being expressed, without the hindrances of an antecedent, predetermined pattern. Both lacked a central coherence and the testing of prolonged debate. Both contained the rudiments of a conversation. It was not strange, then, that they both developed into drama, in which convictions could be embodied in characters and expressed and defended in conversation. Conversation, rather than logistic analysis or synthesis, provides a philosophic discourse which mirrors the endless flow of objects and the clash of reflecting minds. The dramatic form allows conversation this freedom while giving it a unity or an internal coherence far more appropriate than an abstract system. Philosophy becomes more than the debates of Cicero or the careful dialogues of Plato; it becomes even chatty, and chatty enough to register the wild pace of reflection and the swirling alterations of matter in motion.

There is another, perhaps more profound, advantage in the dramatic form: it allows the philosopher to talk to himself. The perspectives engaged in the drama need not be those of others; they may well be contradicting attitudes and positions which seem variously more plausible as mood and sentiment change. Ever-restless nature, matter whose motion is inherent and essential, is mirrored in the oceanic mutations within the reflective mind itself. This understanding of the dramatic form of philosophic reflection provides one analysis of *Rameau's Nephew*—and also an explanation of the vastly different positions found in Diderot's unpublished papers. The rejection of system may well represent not just the repudiation of an internal unity of coherent discourse but the denial of coherence at the heart of the philosopher himself. System is false, not simply because it does not mirror objects, but because it does not mirror the *esprit* of the philosophe; the method of perspectival discrimination is most accurate, not only because it represents the world of various and external persuasions but because it expresses the internal dialogue which is the mind and the endless discussion within the thinker himself.[113]

The line of argument that runs—the word is utterly appropriate—through the trilogy of conversations with d'Alembert and his mistress, the somewhat frenetic Mademoiselle de L'Espinasse, imitates its subject in its pattern. Three distinct pieces form the framework which Leonard Tancock has appositely called "a kind of play in three acts," *Entretien entre d'Alembert et Diderot, Le rêve de d'Alembert,* and *Suite de l'entretien.*[114] The dramatic conflict is the struggle of giants, the continuous battle that had bloodied European science and natural theology over the past century, the hostilities between Newton and Descartes. Newton and Descartes are now hardly recognizable, sobered and maimed by the wars into which they had been carried by their own armies. D'Alembert carries the escutcheon of the god of mechanics, the Newtonian coat of arms, but with quarterings that indicate geometry's autonomy from mechanical practice and denote allegiance to a god who is at best the best of possible hypotheses. Diderot declares a Cartesian heritage, but he has abandoned metaphysics as a first philosophy and enlarged Descartes' mechanics into a universal experimental philosophy. In many ways, the struggle of the drama continues the battle between Holmes and Saunderson, but d'Alembert argues skeptically and without the passionate conviction of Holmes, and Diderot takes Saunderson's first argument far beyond its initial statement. Indeed, one could maintain that the *Lettre sur les aveugles* sets the stage for the trilogy as the *Pensées philosophiques* introduces the *Lettre.* The literary form changes each time, but the argument deepens in focus, intensity, and consequences. The *Pensées* eliminate all evidence for the existence of god except organic design; the *Lettre* disposes of organic design through a calculus of probabilities over sempiternal time and infinite elements, and it substitutes for god the alternative hypothesis of dynamic matter, endlessly creative and essentially in motion. Our play opens with these two hypotheses center stage, borne by Jean d'Alembert and Denis Diderot.

But the two hypotheses have altered in a manner commensurate with the alteration in their traditions. It is all very well to have the greatest geometer in Europe represent the god of mechanics, but even as he postulates a divine causality to explain the universe, he discovers his greatest difficulties to be with the inner coherence of the concept of god itself. The problem lies not with his postulate, but more radically with the very definition of god; "un être d'une nature aussi contradictoire est difficile à admettre." What are those contradictions? They are framed in terms of the space, motion, and providence of Newtonian mechanics, and the problem is to reconcile them into a definition consistent enough to be used as if it were a Cartesian hypothesis: "I confess that a Being which is unextended, yet which occupies extension and which is present in its entirety in each part of that extension; which differs essentially from matter, but is one with it; which attends matter and moves matter, without being moved itself; which acts upon matter, yet is subject to none of its alterations; a Being about which I can form no idea; a Being of so contradictory a nature is difficult to accept. But other difficulties [*obscurités*] await the one who rejects this Being."[115] D'Alembert will defend the Newtonian god, but with the skeptical realization that he is working with a definition that does not make much sense.

Descartes' initial postulate of matter continually in motion, for which Diderot argues, has undergone a parallel reworking. All the attributes of spirit, of *res cogitans*, which had served as the basis for the demonstration of the divine existence, must now be traced back to the underlying *res extensa*. If the Newtonian hopes of a Universal Mechanics were ever to be realized, it would be only by admitting no other than mechanical hypotheses, more specifically hypotheses of matter in movement. The Cartesian mechanical principle must be universalized, freed from its metaphysical grounding. This matter-in-motion must be more than matter and motion because it must account not only for the physical world—for which it had been formulated by Descartes—but for the mental world of human beings, since there is no god to create a distinctly different substance from matter. The intellectual world must necessarily be an epiphenomenon of matter. Not only motion, then, is inherent to matter, as Diderot's Saunderson had demanded; *sensibilité* must also be a general and essential quality of all matter.

In the article on *sensibilité* in the *Encyclopédie*, Théophile de Bordeu and Jean Fouquet use this term to designate sensible perception and the reactions that follow upon it, "to perceive the impressions of external objects and to produce as a consequence movements which are proportioned to the degree of intensity of this perception." Diderot must extend "sensibility" both in meaning and in application. In meaning, it will cover every perception, sensation, and intellectual awareness; in application, it resides in everything that is material, everything that exists: elements and material bodies as well as plants, animals, and human beings. Matter is universal; motion is universal, because inherent in matter; now sensibility is universal, because inherent in matter.

Several years before, Diderot had made this claim in an argument with the Marquis de Ximénès and reported it to Charles Pineau Duclos: "Sensibility is a universal property of matter, an inert property in inorganic or senseless bodies . . . a property rendered active in the same bodies by their assimilation into an animal substance, one that is living. . . . The animal is the laboratory where sensibility changes from being inert to being active."[116] In Spinoza, extension and thought could never be reduced to one another, though both could enter constitutively into the divine essence as subject and render it available to understanding. This reduction is precisely Diderot's project. Sensibility is simply a quality of matter, as essential to it as motion.

Motion provides the analogy with which the seeming absurdity can be resolved. Descartes had already asserted that there was a determined quantity of motion in the universe, a quantity which always remained the same irrespective of its various realizations in different parts of the universe.[117] Leibniz corrected this to make a law of perfect equality between the complete cause and the whole effect, and then used motion to discriminate between two kinds of forces: "Force is twin. The elementary force, which I call dead because motion does not yet exist in it, but only a solicitation to motion, is like that of a sphere in a rotating tube or a stone in a sling. The other is the ordinary force associated with actual motion, and I call it living."[118] Diderot accepted this Leibnizian correction. The universal motion can exist either as *force vive*, in the movement of a body from one place to another, or as *force morte*, in the pressure or tendency to movement. "Motion exists equally in the body displaced and in the body that remains stationary." If one removes the hidden surrounding pressures which keep a body stable, movement will immediately ensue. Rarefy the atmosphere surrounding a huge tree and the "water contained in it, suddenly expanding, will burst into a hundred thousand fragments. I say the same of your own body.[119]

Rest is either an abstraction or a relative phenomenon: an abstraction when one treats a mass as if it were unalterable, not resistant to pressures and moving toward its own dissolution; a relative phenomenon when one considers the location of one compound relative to another to be unchanging. "Absolute rest is an abstract concept which does not exist in nature, and motion is a quality as real as length, breadth, and depth."[120] Even the smallest unit of matter possesses three kinds of movement: weight or gravity; the action proper to its own nature; and its resistance or response to the actions of all other units of matter upon it.[121] Consequently, matter is filled with motion and is inconceivable without it by sciences like physics and chemistry which deal with the real. If one makes the Newtonian distinction between appearance and reality, rest can be consigned to the level of appearance, and motion understood to be inherent to matter on both the level of appearance and the deeper, underlying level of the real:

But I fix my gaze on the general mass of bodies; I see everything in action and reaction, everything destroying itself under one form, recomposing itself under another; sublimations, dissolutions, combination of all kinds, phenomena incompatible with the homogeneity of matter; and therefore I conclude that matter is heterogeneous, that an infinity of diverse elements exist in nature, that each of these elements, by its diversity, has its own particular force, innate, immutable, eternal, indestructible; and that these forces contained in bodies have their action outside the bodies; whence comes the motion, or rather the general fermentation of the universe.[122]

Diderot distinguished between an active and a dead force just as contemporary high school students learn to distinguish between kinetic and potential energy. He used this analogy to characterize sensibility as active or inert. Inert sensibility lies in the chemicals of the earth which are assimilated by plants; active sensibility marks the same chemicals after the plant is eaten by animals. Eating is the transmutation of matter from inert to active sensibility. One can even trace a similar but more complicated process in changing a marble statue into a human being: grinding it to powder, mixing it with humus, planting it with seeds, etc. Matter moves through many different forms just as motion does. Motion is active or dead force; matter is active or inert sensibility. Flesh and the soul are nothing else than "une matière activement sensible."[123]

But this does not satisfy d'Alembert, for the basic question is not answered: How do we derive a being that can think from a being that can sense? For this problem, the operational method draws a second analogy: the original generation of animal life is analogous to the generation of an individual animal. Once can trace the present being of d'Alembert himself back to the small elemental bodies found in "les jeunes et frêles machines" that were his parents. So one can trace the origins of all life, as Needham's retrieval of spontaneous generation had suggested, back to "le vermisseau imperceptible qui s'agite dans la fange," infinitesimal beginnings of life in abiogenic matter, life from nonlife. Diderot's analogy of the elemental bodies which eventually form the seed which eventually becomes d'Alembert permits a doctrine of the genesis of life from nonlife through a construction which is purely mechanical, that is, done purely through successive additions and their resultant organization. As in the poetry of Lucretius, heat plays the central causal role in bringing the elements together and in their subsequent union and development. By the same token, all life will perish when the sun expires and the earth's heat dies away.[124]

If "everything is connected in nature," then intelligent life itself must emerge from the single principle of matter in motion, matter with inert or active sensibility. Feelings and sensations are given permanence through that organization of the present and past which we call memory. Out of memory, a person organizes "a history which is that of his life and so acquires a consciousness of himself: he denies, he affirms, he concludes, and he thinks."[125] Thinking is only possible after one has acquired a series of sensations and a consequent memory of the external world, and in the resultant permanence found the identity of oneself. This perspective, this sense of oneself, allows one to think: to contrast and to compare, to organize, to combine, and to separate.

The mind can be understood by another analogy, that of the vibrating string which accepts an impulse, oscillates, and continues to vibrate long after the impulse has ceased. An object stimulates thought; thinking, like oscillation, keeps the original object of thought present and its vibrations call up sympathetic vibrations in other "strings" of the thinking subject, "so that there is no limit to the ideas awakened and interconnected in the mind of the philosopher, as he meditates and hearkens to himself amid silence and darkness." Thinking is the addition and sympathy or subtraction and disharmony of ideas, and the thinking philosopher is both the musician and the harpsichord:

> As he can feel, he is immediately conscious of the sound he gives forth; as he is an animal, he retains the memory of it. *Cette faculté organique*, by connecting the sound within him, produces and keeps the melody there. Just suppose that your harpsichord has the power to feel and to remember, and tell me if it will not know and repeat of its own accord the airs that you have played upon its keys. We are instruments endowed with feeling and memory; our senses are so many keys that are struck by surrounding nature, and that often strike themselves. This is all, in my opinion, that happens in a harpsichord which is organized like you or me.[126]

And if this is all so evident in a machine, in matter which is inert, how much more possible in a living being. It is crucial to see the structural analogy between the harpsichord and the person, and the dynamic analogy between the genesis of one living being and the epigenesis of life. Once both of these analogies are grasped, matter in motion can be supposed the single comprehensive principle of all reality, "une cause qui est et qui explique tout."[127]

Diderot's mechanics or experimental physics is universal because this comprehensive principle allows him to eliminate the distinction which Descartes had drawn between the two substances of matter and thinking, the distinction that lies at the basis of Spinoza's two divine attributes. Inert matter becomes living matter, sensitive matter, thinking matter through obvious human mechanical experiences like eating and generation. "Do you see this egg? *With this you can overthrow all the schools of theology, all the churches of the earth.* What is this egg? An insensible mass before the seed [*germe*] is introduced into it; and after the seed is introduced, what is it then? Still only an unperceiving mass, for this seed itself is only a crude, inert fluid. How will this mass develop into a different organization, to sensitiveness, to life? By means of heat. And what will produce the heat? Motion." The example is available to everyone, the development of the embryo from the egg under the influence of heat, which is itself the result of the motion of matter. "From inert matter, organized in a certain way and impregnated with other inert matter, and given heat and motion, there results the faculty of sensation, life, memory, consciousness, passion and thought."[128] The two original hypotheses that opened the first act have become the only two hypotheses in embryology: either a dualism in which god injects some new element into the fetus during its development, or a monism in which hidden elements, like sensitivity, emerge as the fetus itself evolves; that is, "une supposition simple qui explique tout, la sensibilité, propriété générale de la matière, ou produit de l'organisation."[129]

D'Alembert's initial skepticism about the definition of god comes from the internal contradiction of its attributes; his questions issue directly from philosophic coordinates which contradict those of Diderot. His phenomenal interpretation dictates the first question: How can we say that sensibility is in all matter?—a question that Diderot answers in terms of the entitative Newtonian discrimination between the apparent and the underlying reality, that is, by distinguishing active from inert sensibility. His second question—how do we derive a being that can think from one that can sense—probes after principle, and Diderot responds by tracing all things to the endless movement of eternal matter. The question that ends the first act deals with the issue of method, the pattern of thinking and of discourse: Is the process of thinking essentially other than the movement of matter? Thinking is essentially a simple process, indivisible, while matter is an extended substratum and its movement is essentially divisible. Granted that the action of eating can indicate the *sensibilité inerte* within all matter and that the analogy of individual generation can disclose the purely mechanical nature of the generation of all life from nonlife, is there not still an unaccounted-for remainder? Is not sensibility a pattern of activity essentially other than the motion of matter, as the indivisible is the opposite of the divisible?

Not if every sensible form, every organization of matter, is essentially indivisible! A block of marble is either impenetrable or it is not—there is no quarter-impenetrability. If one cuts a round body in half, one doesn't have half a roundness. Motion can be either faster or slower, but one can't cut motion in half and get half a motion. Whether one is talking about those qualities by which a body is perceived or those forms by which it is organized, one is always talking about the indivisible.

But there is an activity in thinking, in the construction of a syllogism and the drawing of an inference, that is different from sensation and perception. The operational method celebrates this activity of the intellect. The very pattern of this method consists in actively formulating hypotheses or discriminating various positions, and bringing these matrices to bear either upon the subject, through experimentation, or upon each other, through debate, to obtain probable or profitable conclusions. How are these reflective and active moments of intellect to be rooted in matter? The answer is uncompromising: "C'est que nous n'en tirons point: elles sont toutes tirées par la nature."[130] Intellectual activity is but another epiphenomenon of the single fundamental active principle of all things, matter in endless movement: "We only state the existence of connected phenomena whose connection is either necessary or contingent, phenomena which are known by us through experience: necessary, in the case of mathematics and physics and other rigorous sciences; contingent, in ethics, politics and other conjectural sciences."[131] Diderot's method is not less active; but the universal character of "nature" makes both the activity of the knower and the pace of the conversation instances of that dynamic matter which is comprehensive of both.

Does this mean that phenomena themselves are more necessary in some cases and less necessary in others? No. Rather, in some cases the causal chain is clear while in others the influence of alien causes escapes human observation. The connections of nature are not intrinsically random or free; rather, human experience and observation are clumsy and limited. Even argument from analogy, as obviously useful as it is, can lead to the fantasies of the poet unless one examines nature itself. Fantasies are fine for the poet—they lie at the basis of plot—but "it is otherwise with the philosopher; he must proceed to examine nature, which often shows him a phenomenon quite different from what he had supposed, and then he perceives that he had been seduced by an analogy."[132]

D'Alembert's attempt to switch the operational method into an existentialist interpretation, that is, to understand all the conclusions of the conversation within the context of skepticism, falls before the calculus of probabilities. It is not necessary to have certitude to escape skepticism; human life is lived according to probabilities. The most probable explanation for everything in human thinking and human life can be given to him as a final talisman: "Good night, my friend, and remember that 'dust thou art, to dust thou shalt return.'"[133] The admonition from the Ash Wednesday liturgy is transferred to a deterministic materialism which derives everything from the endless movement of matter. The alternative to such a hypothesis is a god who is a definitional contradiction, whose internal inconsistency is repeated like a leitmotiv through the first act whenever the choice confronting the characters rises in their struggle: "Be a physicist, and acknowledge the produced character of an effect when you see it produced, even if you cannot explain all the steps that led from the cause to the effect. Be logical, and do not substitute for a cause which exists and explains everything, another cause which cannot be comprehended, whose connection with the effect is even more difficult to grasp, which engenders an infinite number of difficulties and solves not one of them."[134] The conflict of the first act is resolved with the establishment of matter ceaselessly in motion and endowed with sensibility as the hypothesis most adquate to explain all the phenomena of nature. The first act does not create a system, but it constitutes a synthesis: all things are connected together and rooted in a single principle.

The first act accomplishes brilliantly what Diderot considered fundamental for any successful philosophy or scientific inquiry: it concatenates all phenomena. "If phenomena are not linked together [*enchaînés*], each one to another, there can be no philosophy. Phenomena may be totally linked together, so that the state of each one would still be able to exist without permanence."[135] The *Entretien entre d'Alembert et Diderot* builds that concatenation, progressing through the three developing stages marked by d'Alembert's questions. Sensibility is obtained from matter; thought is obtained from sensibility; and thinking is disclosed as another modification or motion of matter. The effect on the great geometer was shattering. After all, he had assured the first readers of the *Encyclopédie* that "it is not necessary to probe deeply into the nature of our body and the idea we have of it to recognize that . . . the properties we observe in matter have nothing in common with the faculty of willing and thinking."[136] The *Entretien* leaves this easy assurance in ruins.

The second act opens the morning of the next day in d'Alembert's apartment in the Rue de Bellechasse. D'Alembert sleeps after a restless, dream-filled night, the object of the anxious observation of his mistress, Mademoiselle de L'Espinasse. Mlle. de L'Espinasse, perhaps the most celebrated *salonière* in Paris, has every reason to be worried. D'Alembert continually talked during his sleep, and "it seemed so crazy to me that I resolved not to leave him alone all night, and not knowing what else to do I drew up a little table to the foot of his bed, and began to write down all I could make out of his ramblings."[137] The scene opens as the distinguished Parisian physician Theophile de Bordeu enters to attend d'Alembert, a doubly appropriate visit, since Bordeu had coauthored the article in the *Encyclopédie* on *sensibilité*.

Diderot could call this second act an *éclairissement au premier*, one in which the devices of conversation are extended to include dream and its report. If conversation allows a flexibility of argument and a fluidity of demonstration, dream does so even more emphatically: "It is of the highest extravagance, and yet at the same time contains most profound philosophy. There is some skill in having put my ideas into the mouth of a dreaming man."[138] *Le Rêve de d'Alembert* illumines the previous *Entretien* both by introducing new characters, whose perspectives test the conclusions of the *Entretien*, and by employing new devices by which these conclusions can be expanded beyond the rigors of deduction or verification. A logical sequence or a careful inquiry is vulnerable to the questions of evidence and coherence. Dreams also possess their own consistency, but one expects less logical rigor; missing connectives and wild guesses draw more sympathy. At one moment "it isn't possible to be more profound and more mad [*fou*]."[139] But if the *Rêve* is madness, yet there is serious method in it. It is not simply that "it is sometimes necessary to give wisdom an air of madness in order to procure a hearing." The Cartesian hypothesis, unlike the Newtonian system, does not claim to be grounded in irrefutable evidence; it claims to be a profitable assumption whose acceptance permits progress in scientific investigation. The *Entretien* has advanced matter in endless movement, endowed with inherent sensibility, as the most likely of hypotheses, significantly more intelligible and productive than the hypothesis of an existent god.

This leaves d'Alembert with the immediate and pressing problem of making sense out of Diderot's hypothesis. The alternatives are a supreme intelligence or comprehensive, generative matter, and one cannot "come to a decision about the Supreme Intelligence without knowing what opinion to hold as to the eternity of matter, its properties, the distinction between the two substances, the nature of man and the production of animals."[140] This means that each *sujet grave* must be considered: [a] "la sensibilité générale, [b] la formation de l'être sentant, [c] son unité, [d] l'origine des animaux, [e] leur durée, [f] et toutes les questions auxquelles cela tient."[141] The *Entretien* established the first of these. The *Rêve* considers successively each of the remaining topics. The movement of the second act follows Bordeu's classification of the serious subjects which he characterized as essential to the consideration of an alternative to theism. Each of these topics [b-f] contains its own cluster of issues and, allowing for the scattered behavior of conversation and dream, the *Rêve* considers them in the order Bordeu provided as a matrix. The discussion considers issues which fall under the general subject of formation [b]; those which deal directly with the resultant unities [c]; then those which inquire into the origins of animal life [d]; and those presented by the duration of life and its interchange with death [e]. Lastly, d'Alembert himself raises four or five problems necessarily involved in the *Rêve*. Bordeu observes that "we skim the surface of everything and go into nothing deeply," to be met by the Mlle. de L'Espinasse's contented, "What does that matter? We are only chatting, we are not composing a thesis [*nous ne composons pas*]."[142]

The operational method allows both the elaboration of hypotheses and settings as fruitful perspectives on the subject and the construction of analogies by which an issue may be argued. The interplay between these two allows d'Alembert, whether speaking in Diderot's dream or interpreted in conversation by Bordeu, to build his case. D'Alembert must translate the doctrine of the *Entretien* into the logistic procedure which marks the methodological heritage of Newton. D'Alembert presents an odd form of the logistic method, one done in an operational framework, one which is itself yet another standpoint within the greater, operational pattern of discussion. Through hypotheses and analogies, the Newtonian method becomes another realization of the introduction of new perspectives. It must make sense of the hypothesis of endless matter in continual motion as the universal principle of all things. Diderot accomplishes this translation by shifting the interpretation, that is, the area of evidence, from the underlying entitative interpretation of the *Entretien* to the existential discrimination of the perspectives of the *Rêve*. The comprehensive principle remains the same, but in the *Rêve* the operational method presents a logistic d'Alembert whose sense of reality is reduced to a set of perspectives.

The Newtonian distinction between the apparent and the real now becomes a distinction between *la fait* and *la raison du fait*, between a fact or a state of affairs and an explanation that makes that fact intelligible.[143] Each *sujet grave* begins with such a fact, established by observation or experiment; each of these facts demands a hypothesis by which it can be explained. This is a more difficult problem than its statement might indicate because Diderot has already championed the position that the universal *raison du fait* is matter in endless motion. The dramatic struggle in the *Rêve* is to take up each of the subjects essential to philosophy and to show that its facts can be made intelligible and its questions answered by reduction to this comprehensive principle.

Under the general topic of formation [b], three issues are clustered: how does one trace the emergence of a personal unity; how does one trace the emergence of a cosmic unity; and how does one identify the causality involved in either process and in the process of formation in general?

D'Alembert, like Descartes, begins with a fact that he is unable to doubt. Unlike Descartes, he chooses not his personal existence but his personal unity. D'Alembert begins his translation of Diderot into a Newtonian perspective with a unit, himself. "Car je suis bien un, je n'en saurais douter. . . . Mais comment cette unité s'est-elle faite?"[144] How did this complex unity occur? It is not enough to say that it came about by successive increment or to assert that each increment makes for continuity, not just contiguity. That much is obvious. As early as 1751, Maupertuis had addressed his Latin thesis to this subject at Erlangen; he reinforced that thesis in 1754 with his *Essay on the Formation of Organic Bodies*. The alternative he proposed to thinking simply as a result of an arrangement of matter (thus just another movement or configuration of matter) was to place consciousness at the very earliest stages of matter and to obtain a sensate or thinking being by the successive addition of these conscious units. Adding units of matter together was adding things that already possessed consciousness.[145] Initially, Diderot rejected this hypothesis, but the discrimination in the *Entretien* of a universal sensibility existing in all matter, either inert or active, allowed its incorporation into a theory of organic emergence. Unity is obtained by coalescence, on the analogy of one drop of mercury coalescing with another; now, however, the mercury is inertly sensible and organization will translate this into active sensibility. Organic life can also be understood by the analogy of a swarm of bees clustered together on the branch of a tree. "Would you like to transform the cluster of bees into one single animal? Modify a little the feet by which they cling together; make them continuous instead of contiguous." The experiment by which the feet are removed and the bees made into one animal rather than a collection of animals is rather like Einstein's falling elevator, an idealized or imagined experiment, more likely in a dream than in a conversation, but it allows one to understand the formation of large organic unities by addition, and even to argue that all human organs "are just separate animals held together by the law of continuity in a general sympathy, unity and identity."[146]

If material units can combine synthetically to form higher conscious units, perhaps the converse is also the case, that one can divide organic beings into parts like Trembley's hydras or polyps which would regenerate themselves. If consciousness is inertly present in each unit, perhaps the separation of the parts of the larger unit could be executed in such a way that, like worms, serpents, or hydras, each part would grow again to full stature and organic completeness. The suggestion raises issues which two centuries later would be discussed under the problems of cloning and fundamental genetics. Needham's revival of spontaneous generation allows life to arise from nonlife. Cannot life also be generated by the appropriate divisions of that which is already living? Is there some way in which complicated organisms, analytically like human beings, can be treated as hydras and polyps, and the native dynamism of matter unleashed to generate others of the same kind from these divided units? "If a human being does not split up into an infinite number of other human beings, at any rate a human being does split up into an infinite number of animalcules, whose metamorphoses and whose future and final organization cannot be foreseen."[147] D'Alembert's dream and its interpretation translate Diderot's doctrine by employing the classic logistic movements of analysis and synthesis—just as it assimilates the distinction between the fact and the reasoned fact into the distinction between phenomenon and underlying cause—and in either pattern dynamic matter can account for the formulation of a single, organic unity.

What happens now to the Newtonian system of the universe with its god who gives the plurality within the cosmos an origin and constitutes the eternality and infinity of time and space? Now, it is not god who constitutes eternality and infinity; it is this "vast ocean of matter." Needham's microscopic examination of a single drop of water indicated a whole world of living things, which come into being and pass away in a few moments. That drop of water is a microcosm of our world, d'Alembert maintains. The life of the universe is mirrored proportionately in its infinitely smaller dimensions.[148] In our world, things have somewhat more permanence, but are still part of this endless, infinite flux. "Everything changes and everything passes away, only the whole endures. The world begins and ends ceaselessly; it is in each moment at its beginning and at its end." Its unity does not lie in a perduring order. On the contrary, *"rerum novus nascitur ordo* is eternally inscribed upon it."[149] When the Epicurean philosopher Lucretius proposed that earth contained the seeds of everything and that the animal species were the product of fermentation, he was simply perceiving in microcosm what has taken place in the universe in all times. What forms have preceeded these and what forms are to succeed, we do not know. "Maybe the same huge animal that we know to-day, maybe an atom—both are equally possible; you need assume only motion and the varied properties of matter."[150] The unity of the world is in matter in motion; the systems that this principle can generate are numberless in successive time and in endless space.

The final problem of formation, whether it explains personal or universal unity, is that of causality. Matter is comprehensive of all reality and the underlying source of all of its forms, and its acts endlessly, relentlessly, and necessarily. D'Alembert asserts what lies behind his and all formation: "So I am what I am, because I had to be so. Change the whole, and you will necessarily change me; but the whole is constantly changing. . . . Man is merely a common product, the monster an uncommon product; both equally natural, equally necessary, equally part of the universal and general order of things. . . . Everything is connected in nature, and it is impossible that there should be a missing link in the chain."[151] The formation of any of these phenomena emerges from the mass and returns eventually to the mass. There are no final causes. In this, Cartesian mechanics reasserts itself definitely over Newtonian philosophy. There is action and reaction, cause and necessary effect. The great "individual" is the whole. The other things whose unity we recognize or experience are its parts and products, as necessary in their generation and formation as the organic parts of a single animal. One can give a name to a part of an animal or a machine, but to fail to see that it is necessarily derived from a chain of causes is to fail to grasp its underlying reality. So also to give the term "individual" absolutely to any of the parts of the whole would be as serious and pervasive an error as to apply it to the wing of a bird or to the feather of that wing. "Voyez la masse générale, ou si, pour l'embrasser, vous avez l'imagination trop étroite, voyez votre première origine et votre fin dernière."[152] In the consideration of origins and termination one obtains some grasp of all-encompassing reality that is the source and end of all formation.

The second group of questions addresses the unity within various phenomena [c]. Again, they touch the phenomena of the personal self and the universe. What constitutes each of these and all of these as a unit—not what brought them about, but what gives them *now* their consistency and coherence? This is the second *éclairissement* offered by the *Rêve*.

A cluster of bees exemplifies incremental addition. Now "imagine a spider in the center of its web"; consider what would be the case "if the thread that the insect draws out of its intestines, and draws back thither when it pleases, were a sensitive part of itself." This web, this network, constitutes the personal unity with the spider as the self, the living point. This spider generates from within itself all the other parts of the body. These parts are "only the gross developments of a network that forms itself, increases, extends, throws out a multitude of imperceptible threads." Now locate this spider within the meninges of the brain and its web everywhere throughout the body and we have the analogy through which we can understand the unity and diversity that is the personal self.[153]

Can one extend this analogy to the cosmos, with god as the spider and the universe as his web? This is Spinoza's god, Bordeu maintains, the only kind of god that is conceivable, but he will not measure up to the god who is the alternative to eternal matter in motion. The god of Spinoza, who generates, like a spider, the forms of the universe from within himself and dwells in some part of infinite space, is comprehended within matter itself. With Fenelon and Bayle, Bordeu dismisses such a hypothesis as a halfway house. The god who dwells within the universe would be only "a material part of the material universe, subject to vicissitudes, he would grow old and die." If this "spirit"—a combination of intelligence and very active matter— were everywhere, then one would have to allow for a vast number of marvels or spirits. Devils and angels, ghosts and disembodied intelligences generated by such a "spiritual" spider would range throughout our universe, interfering with all its workings, disrupting the chain of cause and effect, and making science and philosophy impossible.[154] The spider analogy cannot explain cosmic unity; it would destroy it. The present unity of the world is the unity of contiguous bodies—neither continuous, as in Spinoza, nor separated by a void, as in Newton. Matter in eternal time brings the present cosmos into existence; matter in the infinite contiguity of diverse bodies constitutes whatever unity this universe presently enjoys. Even for d'Alembert, as much as he would represent a Newtonian method, the basic understanding of the universe is the Cartesian *plenum*.

In this context of utter materiality, the issue of the origin of animal life [d] arises as it did in the *Entretien*. Bordeu retrieves its argument in the stages by which *un point imperceptible* becomes *un fil délié*, then *un faisceau de fils*. The "bundle of threads" follows the analogy of the spider's network as the network followed the cluster of bees. The early stages of embryonic growth is the evolution through nutrition of this bundle, each thread of which contains fibers (*brins*) whose development terminates in a particular organ. The ear or eye or palate concludes the growth of the fiber and introduces various sensations, each of which is a variation of touch. These sensations themselves give rise to memory and memory to those comparisons and differentiations which constitute the activity of reasoning. Life emerges from nonlife through the formation of these threads and fibers, and the difference between a normal child and a monster lies with the number and kinds of fibers in the initial bundle. "Do in your mind what nature sometimes does actually; deprive the bundle of one of its fibers, for instance of the fiber which should form the eyes; what do you think will happen? . . . It would be a Cyclops." Or duplicate the fibers, again in an idealized experiment, and you have a child with six fingers or two heads. The difference between the normal and the freak lies simply in the addition or subtraction of fibers from the whole. The proper quantity and kind results in the normal; any addition or deduction from this amount results in the abnormal.[155]

Now the bundle of threads can be combined with the spider and its network to answer the question of unity more fully. The organs and the fibers refer all impressions to the center of this web, the common origin and seat of all sensation. "It is the constant and unvarying communication of all impressions to this common origin which constitutes the unity of the animal." Here memory conserves and recollects the successive impressions communicated by sensation, and "memory and the process of comparison . . . form thought and reasoning power."[156] This center, the judge of all sensations and memories and the locus of the self-consciousness and self-government of the person, can make mistakes as well as certify truth. Mistakes issue from previous habits, the lack of experience, the limitation of coordinate sensations, or physical changes within the body. But correctly or incorrectly, it is always this center, this spider at the origin of the web, that is judging.

The subject of duration, *leur durée* [e], takes on a peculiar urgency in the order of topics to be considered. The formation of things [b], their internal unity [c], and the genetic origin of animals [d] all deal with the question of beginnings. The progress of life to its termination in death classically involves a consideration of the soul and its loss. Diderot changes this into a deeper reflection upon the center of the web and the alternation of life and death within it. For the medical experiments of the time indicated that life could be lost and restored through the reactivation of this center, of the spider. The *Mémoires de l'Académie royale de chirugie* records such a case, which, as Paul Vernière comments, Diderot obviously interprets in accordance with his central thesis.

Peyronie had trepanned a patient who had suffered a violent blow on the head. An abscess had formed on the brain, with the attendant pus. Peyronie removed the abscess with a syringe. "When he drove the injection into the abscess, the sick man closed his eyes; his limbs remained inactive, motionless, without the slightest sign of life; when the injection was pumped out again, and the origin of the bundle relieved of the weight and pressure of the injected fluid, the sick man opened his eyes again, moved, spoke, felt, was reborn and lived."[157] *La Gazette de France* of September 4, 1769, recorded the even stranger case of two female children born back to back, joined at the lower part of their trunk, their buttocks, and their lowest lumbar vertebrae. Their "existence [*la durée*] lasted for two days, which they shared equally and alternately, so that each had for its portion one day of life and one of death." When one began to exhibit the signs of life, the other began to die; while one was reviving, the other was expiring; when one was conscious, the other was unconscious. How could one explain such an anomaly? When the center of the network of one became dominant, the first was modified and temporarily lost its life. Mlle. de L'Espinasse suggests that two souls were linked together. Bordeu corrects her. The time for "souls" has passed. What we have here is "un animal avec le principe de deux sens et de deux consciences."[158] The question of *durée* bears upon the principle of all things in this manner: the alternation of life and death, their virtual interchange under the additions and subtractions disclosed by observation and experiment, indicates that no spiritual soul through its presence or absence is responsible for rational life. Only the condition of the brain is critical. Furthermore, the change from life to death is not irreversible, death inevitably and irrevocably replacing life through the soul; life and death can alternate as the brain itself is affected. Even rational life issues from a material unit.

This position engages a host of corollary issues, each of which is raised by d'Alembert [f]. First, personal identity is preserved, not by the perdurance of a rational soul, but by the addition of memories and by the slowness of changes. This personal identity can be that of either self-consciousness or self-government. In the first case, memory conserves successive sensations so that they form the unbroken unit by which self-awareness is constituted. In the second case, the center of the bundle of fibers can maintain its authority only if the fibers stay subordinate to their origin. In the fury of passion or the collapse of naked terror, the fibers revolt against this central authority and the result is personal anarchy. "One is strong, if, through habit or through one's organization, the origin of the bundle dominates the fibres; weak if, on the contrary, it is dominated by them."[159]

Everything in education, then, points to the strengthening of this center, and the Enlightenment ideal is reinforced by this psychology, which insists upon the dominance of intellect. It is not sensibility or deep emotional attachments which make for wisdom, but the preeminence of the mind. Not the sentimentalist or the romantic—whatever Rousseau might write—but the enlightened and disciplined have the right to declare what is true or good or beautiful.

Second, sleep occurs when the entire network becomes slack and the center is left to the various subjects that have infiltrated its consciousness or dominated its sensible experience. Its movement depends on the strength of these subjects and the energy native to the one who sleeps. For this reason the sleep and dream of d'Alembert prove so philosophically valuable. The subjects which the *Entretien* introduced are left to develop under their own natural impetus and according to the pattern of thought of the greatest mathematician of the time. The evolution of these subjects and their transformation by the logistic procedure introduces a perspective upon Diderot's central hypothesis which expands its range of applications and counters the objections of inadequacy. The *Rêve* clarifies the *Entretien* by revealing the spontaneous fecundity of the material hypothesis and by reducing all interjected phenomena and alternative philosophies to the comprehensive causality of matter in endless motion.

Third are the inevitable questions of will and liberty. Here, sleeping or waking makes no difference. The human will and its supposed self-determination are actually "the latest impulse of desire and aversion, the last result of all that one has been from birth to the actual moment." What is true of the formation and causality of the cosmos is true of each human will. Freedom is the necessary effect of the causality which has preceeded it; "one is irresistibly carried away by the general torrent that brings one man to glory and another to disgrace."[160] All foundations for praise or blame, for self-esteem and self-reproach, are hereby removed. They emerge only when one is ignorant that whatever one does, whether by instinct or by choice, is determined by the unbreakable chain of cause and effect.

Lastly, d'Alembert advances the questions of imagination and abstract ideas. In the logistic method, imagination becomes the talent to subtract various forms and colors, animal parts and historical episodes, and to recombine them in a new and different manner. Abstract ideas do not exist. They are actually "only habitual omissions, ellipses, that make propositions more general and speech swifter and more convenient. It is the symbols of speech that have given rise to the abstract sciences. . . . An abstraction is merely a symbol emptied of its idea. The idea has been excluded by separating the symbol from the physical object, and it is only when the symbol is attached once more to the physical object that science becomes a science of ideas again."[161] Poor d'Alembert! He has translated Diderot into the coordinates of his own method only to discover his previous assurance in the *Preliminary Discourse* destroyed. The very assertion with which that work began is denied as the second act comes to an end. Four subjects have confirmed the material hypothesis. Four corollary questions of d'Alembert have applied this hypothesis directly to the understanding of the human being. The initial hypothesis about matter or the existent god terminates in a comprehensive understanding of the human being: his possession of identity in change, his loss of unity in sleep, the determinism of his actions, and the emptiness of all abstractions.

The revolution Diderot urges is universal. The denial of god dictates a profound reinterpretation of the universe and of what it means to be a human being. It is little wonder that Bordeu sweeps out of the apartment in a great hurry. He has left much of Western philosophy and all of its theology in ruins.

Diderot dropped out of the second act to allow his material hypothesis free play in the world of d'Alembert. Now d'Alembert drops out of the third act, the *Suite de l'entretien*, to leave the further implications of this premise to the lodging and the liberty of the world of Mlle. de L'Espinasse. Under d'Alembert's influence, the second act conducted dreams and discussions which expanded the initial hypothesis and tested it against Newton's method. Under that of Mlle. de L'Espinasse, the third act becomes a satyr play and to no one's surprise draws out the sexual implications of Diderot's revolution. Bordeu is dining with Mlle. de L'Espinasse, whose first question indicates the area to be explored: "What do you think of the intermingling of species?"[162] The question has moral, poetic, and physical aspects; the moral aspect sets the criteria by which the advisability of the other two can be judged.

The materialism of Diderot takes much from the materialism of Lucretius framed in the *Ars poetica* of Horace. "*Omne tulit punctum qui miscuit utile dulci* [He has deservedly received every approbation who has mingled the useful with the pleasant]."[163] From this formula, Bordeu constructs a hierarchy of the morally good. At the top are actions that combine pleasure and utility, followed by those which are only useful, those which are only pleasant, and those which are neither—in which class Mlle. de L'Espinasse is willing to enter both chastity and celibacy, although her acquaintance with either seems somewhat limited. *Actiones solitaires*, homosexuality, and bestiality fall under the third heading, and Bordeu raises the question of the usefulness of sexual liaisons between goats and human beings, for thus "we should produce a vigorous, swift, intelligent and indefatigable race of beings, of whom we could make excellent servants."[164]

The tittering consequences suggested in this interchange found enthusiastic, if pornographic, developments in the decades which lay ahead. In July, 1782, the Marquis de Sade opened his literary career with an argument between a dying man and a Christian minister attempting to convince him of the divine existence, the *Dialogue entre un prêtre et un moribund*, composed in the celebrated prison of Vincennes. Sade was made of much sterner stuff than Diderot. He was a man who knew a conclusion when he saw one. The *Dialogue* allowed him to pronounce his atheism and have the dying man and the converted priest abandon the theological conversation for sexual orgy. Atheism and polymorphic sexual experiences defined much of Sade's life; his later four-page poem, *La vérité*, advanced the former far beyond the dismissals of Diderot into a concentrated hatred:

> Yes, vain illusion, my soul detests you,
> And I protest that, in order to further convince you,
> I wish that for a moment you could exist
> To have the pleasure to better insult you.

As he furthered the atheism, so he extended the sexual liaison into the possibilities offered by promiscuity, perversions, misogyny, and cruelty. *Le philosophe dans le boudoir*, published in 1795, drags the fifteen-year-old Eugénie de Mistival out of the convent, teaches her to eliminate religion and virtue from her language, and inducts her into incest, sodomy, flagellation, and orgiastic sexual promiscuity: "It was for this that you were brought into the world; no other limit to your pleasure than those of your strength and will, no place, time, or person excluded." How many of Dr. Bordeu's principles find their ineluctable consequences in Sade's polyvalent perversions?[165]

The *Ensuite* spells out something of the revolution which the two previous acts sponsor. The human good in this brave new world is defined by utility and pleasure; the application of this principle is made possible by the presence of Mlle. de L'Espinasse and Bordeu's grateful recognition that "you are not a prude." Whose utility and whose pleasure are not spelled out; but two centuries are waiting in which these questions will occupy the struggles and the agony of human beings.

What Hath Diderot Wrought?

It was a common opinion in the eighteenth century that it would take centuries for the human race to appreciate the genius of Diderot: he was an encyclopedist, novelist, dramatist, mathematician, natural philosopher, ethician, psychologist—and above all, their synthesis, a philosophe. His *Encyclopédie* set the form by which available knowledge would be represented, classified, and made available to an educated public for the centuries that followed. His theories about the theater rescued drama from rhetorical declamation and reappeared in the method of Stanislavski. Above all, however, Diderot introduced into philosophic consciousness a dynamic materialism as the alternative to a supreme intelligence. As a gradually evolving hypothesis within his own world view, Diderot developed the principle of Cartesian mechanics into a metaphysical explanation of all reality. In many of the reaches of his genius, he stands with the two other great figures of the Enlightenment, Voltaire and Rousseau, but in this he stands alone. Passing through Catholicism, deism, and skepticism, he finally recognized his principal adversary to be, not the Jesuits or the Church, but belief in god itself. This stood in the way of the ethics, the science, the political freedom, and the thousand possibilities that issue from nature. The beginning of all things was not the Spinozan *Deus sive Natura*; it was *aut Deus aut Natura*. Diderot's own works indicated the increasing sharpness of this antinomy and the emphatic nature of his choice.

In many ways, Diderot is the first of the atheists, not simply in chronological reckoning but as an initial and premier advocate and influence. He argued his case not by repudiating the mathematical physics of Descartes or the universal mechanics of Newton but by bringing them, as he contended, to fulfillment. He expanded the principles of Descartes and freed them from an unwarranted metaphysics. In so doing, he realized his own Universal Mechanics, the dream of Newton, but it was a science which did not point beyond itself to nonmechanical principles. In the outline that he sketched he united the natural history of Buffon, the experiments and observations of Trembley, and the errors of Needham, and all in the most vigorous retrieval of Lucretius and the Epicurean heritage.

But there is much more here than simply a revival of the atoms of Epicurus. For in the place of god, Diderot not only offers matter, but radically redefines it in the union he forges between the natural philosophies of the period. Matter is no longer the inert, geometric extension of Descartes, nor the Newtonian mass identified with inertia and known only through its resistance to change. Now matter is the creative source of all change. What Spinoza attempted with god as *causa sui* Diderot achieves through this comprehensive, dynamic matter which moves itself, a pervasive reality inseparable from its endless becoming. Western thought has been challenged to a profound advance beyond Malebranche's "least and most contemptible substance" or Clarke's "smallest and most inconsiderable part of the universe." Matter now emerges as the ceaseless cause of all things, and in its causality Diderot fathers a revolution. The stone that the builders so long rejected has become the cornerstone.

It is little wonder that August Comte hailed Diderot as "the supreme genius of that exciting age" or that Karl Marx declared him to be his favorite prose writer.[166] Diderot had made the initial but definitive statement of the conviction that lies at the basis of both positivism and Marxist humanism: there is no god; the principle of everything is creative nature, matter in its self-activity eternally productive of all change and all design.

5 Atheism as the System of Nature: Baron Paul Henri d'Holbach

With processions, exhortations, and liturgy, the Assemblée générale du Clergé de France inaugurated its solemn quinquennial convocation in March of 1770. Summoned to Paris with the permission of the monarch, each French province was represented in the Assembly by two bishops and two deputies from its lesser clergy. To the feckless, extravagant Louis XV, the clergy as its first order of business voted the customary *don gratuit*, an annual subsidy whose amount had swollen over the centuries to sixteen million livres in 1755. That done, the convocation turned to engage the issue which had converted the capital of France into an increasingly savage religious battleground. No longer were Jansenists taking up arms against Jesuits. The Jesuits had been suppressed and banished from the kingdom. The conflict had grown more elemental, more raw than when theologians debated grace and casuistry. An invasion of skeptical, mocking literature placed Christianity itself under siege. Tracts, poetry, drama, and public letters repudiated the basic beliefs of previous centuries and mobilized the resources of the French intellect against any confessional adherence. Christianity was to be "unmasked" or "erased" and supplanted by a natural religion which was modest in its assertions, universal in its consensus, and tolerant in its practice. Yet even this crusade against institutional Christianity was itself yielding before something far more radical.

Diderot's own *Rêve de d'Alembert*, proposing creative matter in place even of the deist's god, had been completed in the previous year, but its circulation remained discreetly clandestine, threatening neither the redoubts of the clergy nor the reputation of Mlle. de L'Espinasse. Neither Diderot nor Doctor Bordeu figured in the Assembly's calculation of the atheistic array. But the same year saw the most comprehensive repudiation of all religious theories and convictions of the century appear: *Le Système de la nature ou des loix du monde physique et du monde moral*. Not even Voltaire had ever seen anything like it, a veritable "recueil organique de toutes les thèses matérialistes et athéistes du xviiiᵉ siècle." Many, if not all, of its theses had been formulated before, principally by Diderot, but never had they been so radically or defiantly stated and so rigorously argued.[1]

The *Système* was reckoned the major effort of the antireligious infestations. Its title page ascribed this massive broadside to the late Jean-Baptiste de Mirabaud, the distinguished former secretary of the Académie française, now ten years in his grave, but few in Paris considered this attribution more than a prudent cover. In vain the French police had searched to establish the real author, but he was no more to be discovered than his publication stopped. Its first year saw four printings, and in the second month of its appearance, the abbé Bergier recorded that two hundred copies had already been sold in Paris at two louis each, a sizable cost. But the price did not stem its popularity. The religious circles of the city were alarmed, the country scandalized, and the salons febrile with delight. The *Système* now led the invasion, taking honor of place despite its late arrival at arms, and in April, the Assembly gathered its own forces to repulse "les arguments les plus témeraires et sacrilèges."[2]

Since 1755, the Assemblée générale du Clergé had warned of the danger to France if censorship and punishments did not protect religion against this avalanche of hostility. Now it convened in an atmosphere charged with the recent suppression of the Society of Jesus despite appeals from the bishops of France, and heavy with the proliferation of attacks on any religious convictions as well as the most anciently embattled confessional beliefs. Loménie de Brienne, the youthful archbishop of Toulouse, delivered an extensive evaluation of the challenge as its features had emerged over the previous fifteen years. The Assembly voted to include his report in a direct appeal to the throne, *Le Mémoire au Roi*, begging for royal intervention. In a response, the clerical delegation to Versailles received from the deteriorating monarchy "quelques lignes fort roides," but no one took the languid indolence of the palace to be a match for the dangers before them.[3]

To the faithful of France, then, the Assembly addressed itself directly, formulating an *Avertissement du clergé de France assemblé à Paris par permission du Roi, aux Fidèles du royaume, sur les dangers de l'incrédulité*. Each prelate in the kingdom was to publish this pastoral admonition in his diocese, either as it had been framed in Paris or with an accompanying episcopal letter to stress its urgency and to buttress its authority. Naturally, the doctors of theology at the Sorbonne would add their own denunciations, but as Friedrich-Melchior Grimm had sardonically observed: "It's a shame that the thunder of the Sorbonne resembles the thunder of the Opéra, which no longer frightens anyone, not even children."[4]

Finally, Antoine Louis Séguier, the *avocat-général*, denounced to the Parliament of Paris a list of seven antireligious works, six of which had been edited or translated by Paul Henri d'Holbach and Jacques-André Naigeon. The highest court in France responded strongly to the impassioned, detailed *réquisitoire* of Séguier. Séguier's brief painted the picture of religious collapse in France so darkly, quoting extensively from the very works he denounced, that the government prohibited its publication as scandalous. But it carried its effect, however thwarted in its own printing. On August 18, 1770, seven books were ordered publicly torn to pieces and burned by the official executioner. Some of these seven have passed into oblivion, their one moment of fame attained in being singled out for so dramatic an exit. Others lent a macabre distinction to this proscription and pyre of the Parliament: *L'Examen critique des Apologistes de la religion chrétienne*, attributed to Nicolas Fréret (actually by Levesque de Burigny), Voltaire's *Dieu et les hommes*, and three pseudonymous works by Baron Paul Henri d'Holbach, *Christianisme dévoilé*, *Contagion sacrée*, and, latest and most inflammatory, *Le Système de la nature*.[5] The last held its place of horror because the clergy feared above all neither the historical scholarship of Fréret nor the skeptical deism of Voltaire, but the positive union worked out in the *Système* between the emergent mechanics and atheism. The *Système*, if successful, could take the arguments of Descartes and Newton, of Malebranche and Clarke, and stand them on their heads, co-opting for its universal materialism the very evidence that centuries of physicotheology had used to demonstrate the existence and attributes of god. The Fathers of the Assemblée générale du Clergé de France saw in the gathering assault a transmogrification of everything that centuries of natural theology had utilized. The guns of the defense were being seized and turned against them. The *Système* urged not simply a rejection of belief, but another total world system in its place, built upon the same foundations and concluding to an absolute materialism. P. Charbonnel underlined this menace: "Il ne s'agit plus seulement de dire aux hommes de ne pas croire en Dieu, il s'agit de leur proposer un système philosophique qui a la prétention d'apprendre aux hommes à vivre dans un monde sans Dieu, la prétention de pouvoir remplacer la religion dans toutes ses fonctions, intellectuelles, morales, sociales, et politiques. Par conséquent, le poids principal de toutes les contre-attaques porte sur le *Système de la Nature*."[6] Nature, which had insistently depended upon god, either for the certitude of its existence, as in Descartes, or for the pattern of its existence, as among the Newtonians, is now not only to be absolved from this dependence, but to replace what was once its master.

The Assembly was keenly aware that appeal, denunciation, proscription, and an occasional zealous bonfire would not settle the conflict; it would have to argue as well. In the abbé Nicolas-Sylvain Bergier it had just the man to call to its colors. After graduating as a doctor in theology from the

Université de Besançon in 1744 and completing several years of theological studies at the Sorbonne, Bergier had served as parish priest of Flangebouche in the diocese of Besançon, and, after the expulsion of the Jesuits, had taken over the leadership of the Collège de Besançon. In 1765, he leveled against deism such as that of Rousseau's Savoyard Curate his *Déisme réfuté par lui même*, a riposte that later served in sorties against Voltaire himself. Two years later, he moved against the *Examen critique* with his *Certitude des preuves du Christianisme*. Congratulated by Clement XIII and Clement XIV and attacked by Voltaire, he responded with his *Réponse aux Conseils raisonnables* in 1771. In the meantime, he left Besançon for Paris to become a canon of the Cathedral and eventually confessor to the daughters of Louis XV, the "Mesdames de France." Versailles undoubtedly needed whatever spiritual direction this gentle, learned priest could provide. The Assembly seized upon him, voted him a pension of two thousand livres a year, and commissioned him to write against the rising infidelity. In 1771, to fulfill his mandate from the Assembly, he trained on the *Système* his two-volume *Examen du matérialisme*, "one of the best pieces of critical writing of the century."[7] The editors of the *Encyclopédie*, recognizing the mettle of their adversary, invited him to write for subsequent editions of this great work, which was to be transformed into the mammoth *Encyclopédie méthodique* under the editorship of Charles-Joseph Panckoucke. Bergier agreed, with the provision that he would revise or rewrite all the theological articles. These writings became the *Dictionnaire Theologique*, some twelve volumes in the reprinted Paris edition of the next century. Leaders of the Catholic revival of the nineteenth century hailed him, as did the brilliant, tragic Felicité de Lemennais: "Le plus grand apologiste des siècles passés, et peut-être de tous les siècles."[8]

It was a measure of the rising tide of disbelief that the Assembly continued in its next convocation to trouble the same topic, having involved the throne, the judicial system, the Catholic populace as a whole, and one of the finest of contemporary apologists as support and stay against it. Even more symptomatic was the insistence upon the ground where the battle against atheism should be waged. It was to be fought on the evidence of physics! "As soon as it is evidently proven," Bergier wrote, "that movement is not essential to matter, that the latter is purely passive by its nature and without any activity, we are forced to believe that there is in the universe a substance of a different nature, an active being to which movement must be attributed as it is to the first cause, a Motor that is not itself matter."[9] It is astonishing to see that theology itself remains silent on this subject. One continues to accept the area of evidence that has been there since Lessius and has been developed by mechanics. The existence of god hangs from a theory of motion and matter.

Bergier represented what was most acceptable both within the Church and among its major apologists. The great Benedictine scholar Louis-Mayeul Chaudon explicitly agreed with Bergier that the conflict must be over a reading of nature. He concluded with an axiom of this tradition: "The study of Physics is quite properly the cure of the two extremes, Atheism and Superstition. . . . It proves that there is an intelligent first cause, and it makes known the particular mechanical causes of this and that effect. Physics augments admiration and diminishes astonishment."[10] The theologians had become more than philosophers to counter the rising atheism. They had become physicists, and they wagered the game on their ability to do physics better than their opponents.

Catholic France did not stand alone in its battle against the universal materialism being formulated in Paris. Skeptical England also registered rejections. David Hume found himself bemused at the dogmatism of the atheism he encountered in the City of Lights, its *a priori* character, and its ridicule of his own reluctance to move down a more radical path.[11] Edward Gibbon judged as paradoxical "the intolerant zeal of the friends of d'Holbach and Helvétius, who preached the tenets of scepticism with the bigotry of dogmatists, and rashly pronounced that every man must be either an Atheist or a fool."[12] Horace Walpole, fourth earl of Oxford, man of letters and indefatigable correspondent, recorded an urbane distaste in comments from Paris: "The *philosophes*—are insupportable, superficial, overbearing, and fanatic: they preach incessantly, and their avowed doctrine is atheism; you would not believe how openly—Don't wonder, therefore, if I should return a Jesuit." Walpole may have had many avocations, but religious life was not among them, whatever his contempt for the philosophes: "I sometimes go to Baron d'Olbach's [*sic*]; but I have left off his dinners, as there was no bearing the authors, and philosophers, and savants, of which he has a pigeon-house full. . . . Nonsense for nonsense, I like the Jesuits better than the philosophers."[13] Finally, Joseph Priestly, a pioneer in chemistry and the discoverer of oxygen, found Paris dirty, Parisians impolite, and the philosophes unbelievers. His visit led him "to find all the philosophical persons to whom I was introduced at Paris, unbelievers in Christianity, and even professed Atheists. As I chose on all occasions to appear as a Christian, I was told by some of them, that I was the only person they had ever met with, of whose understanding they had any opinion, who professed to believe Christianity."[14] It is remarkable that a leading English philosopher, historian, scientist, and litterateur read the currents of Parisian intellectual life in a manner not unlike that of the Assembly. All of these individual judgments finally led, knowingly or unknowingly, to the Rue Royale, Butte St. Roche, to the house and the conversations it fostered, the tractates it nourished, of Baron Paul Henri d'Holbach. Here one found what Jean-Jacques Rousseau stigmatized as the *coterie holbachique*. Rousseau cursed with equal breath both the Society of Jesus and "my colleagues' unbelief. For fanatical atheism and fanatical belief, having intolerance in common, can even unite, as they have done in China and they do against me."[15] Rousseau laid the "fanatical atheism," which the Assembly fought and the English despised, at the door of the group which clustered around the baron d'Holbach.

Jean-Jacques Rousseau may well have coined the term "coterie holbachique," but Diderot's letter to his mistress, Sophie Volland, related the previously cited anecdote that embodied everything that roiled these Englishmen and aroused the Assembly. Hume was attending his first dinner at the Rue Royale. In conversation with the baron, "The English philosopher took it into his head to remark to the Baron that he did not believe in atheists, that he had never seen any. The Baron said to him: 'Count how many we are here.' We are eighteen. The Baron added: 'It isn't too bad a showing to be able to point out to you fifteen at once: the three others haven't made up their minds.'"[16] Rousseau's epithet was meant for Diderot, Grimm, and d'Holbach and their personal friends, but it has come to stand for a much larger group of savants who gathered for discussion and dinner every Thursday and Sunday during the thirty-five years that Baron d'Holbach entertained at the Rue Royale as the "maitre d'Hotel de la Philosophie."

D'Holbach's great wealth made both the company and their conversations possible, and the reputation of this coterie was spread by the judgments and reports of English visitors and French devotees and adversaries. What was remarkable about the coterie was not that there was a salon in Paris; Paris teemed with salons. It was somewhat remarkable to find a salon not presided over by a woman, as were those of Mme. Geoffrin (whom Gibbon found intolerable), Mme. du Deffand, Mlle. de L'Espinasse (whom Diderot celebrated in his *Rêve*), and Mme. Necker. Even more remarkable was that its conversation was not inhibited by the elegant limits which those polite and elegant societies wordlessly imposed. As Kors remarked about the usual Parisian salon:

> The rules of that society posed definite limits to the liberty of saying what one thought. It was impolite to challenge the vague religiosity of the ladies; it was impolite to be pessimistic; it was impolite to offer in the midst of a pleasant afternoon or evening a view of man and the universe that was without inherent charm, inherent warmth, inherent light. In addition, there were limits to the *forms* of expression tolerated at these gatherings; it was impolite to quarrel and, above all, to quarrel sincerely and doggedly. Pervading the society of these assemblies was the need to say things well—not in the sense of saying them as rigorously and as thoughtfully as one might, but in the sense of saying them wittily, of delighting one's listeners, of making the discussion pleasurable less by its content than its mood.[17]

The Rue Royale provided philosophic relief for those who would speak their minds. The baron did not impose or even welcome such limitations as were current in Paris, and his salon generously admitted not only Diderot and Naigeon but Morellet, who despised their views, and even the abbé Bergier, who struck against them for all of France to read. Arguments, endless and heady quarrels, open conflict on any subject—for this, one came to the Rue Royale.

Perhaps no single episode so well vignettes both the freedom enjoyed in the *coterie holbachique* and the anonymity of the author of *Le Système de la nature* as that described by the abbé Bergier to the abbé Trouillet. The year was 1770. Bergier had accepted the invitation and the pension of the Assembly and was preparing his *Examen du matérialisme* against the *Système*. "I will ask permission to dedicate the refutation of the *Système de la nature* to the Clergé; I am two-thirds finished with it. Diderot and d'Holbach have seen the first, and the most essential section; they answered that this work would be considered victorious in my camp, but that I did not understand their language, and that there were not fifty people in Paris who were capable of understanding it. So much the better; it is a proof that their language is not that of common sense." Diderot in his turn attempted to reassure his clerical brother that whatever his views, he lived in friendship with Bergier and counted him among the learned people with whom he could discuss religion without insult or bitterness.[18] The members of the *coterie holbachique* could disagree with passion, and there were few places in Paris that allowed discussion so free a flow. The English thought them dogmatic atheists and Rousseau thought them fanatical atheists. So be it. But contrary to both beliefs, atheism was not present without question.

For over a century, since Charles Avezac-Lavigne's *Diderot et la société du Baron d'Holbach* (1875), it has been an unquestionable persuasion that "the Holbachian clique felt it necessary to be so ferocious and so tireless in its impiety." Peter Gay advances the argument even further, bringing all of the philosophes into consensus at least with the baron's negative criticism, caviling only at the positive doctrine he advanced: "They opposed what he opposed, but while they agreed with him about what was false, they were by no means as certain as he was about what was true."[19] This putative accord squares with Gay's thesis that by the end of the century the leaders among the philosophes had become atheists.[20] Unfortunately, neither Gay's general contention nor his reading of negative agreement into the group around d'Holbach is accurate. Atheists there certainly were, important they certainly were, but they were few—even in the circle that surrounded the baron. The critical contribution of the work of Alan Kors, as Daniel Roche has pointed out, is his "démystification des clichés hérités de Rousseau et de l'émigration, repris par Avezac et pratiquement jamais discutés depuis."[21] The coterie was not a club only of atheists.

Let us agree with Kors that legend and scholarship have exaggerated the homogeneity and the atheism of the *coterie holbachique*; still all the English and all the enemies and all the scholars could not have been homogeneously wrong! There was more than something of the truth about their tales, their witticisms, and their footnotes. If they were not all in agreement, who were the atheists? Lessius' list from antiquity and Mersenne's codex of contemporary skeptics, naturalists, and pantheists will no longer satisfy. Atheism is no longer a charge hurled at another. From invective, "atheist" has become a badge of honor, asserted, argued, and claimed for oneself. But by how many was it claimed?

In all of that group, only three took the title in some way for themselves: Diderot, d'Holbach, and Jacques-André Naigeon. If the list were expanded by including those "who, on circumstantial evidence alone, possibly should be placed beneath this rubric," one could add three more names: the physician Augustin Roux; the soldier, poet, and philosopher Jean-François de Saint-Lambert; and, perhaps most important, Claude-Adrien Helvétius, whose *De l'esprit* (1758) had caused an uproar second only to what the *Système* excited in 1770. These men are styled atheists by others, but all three "chose to refrain from explicitly communicating this side of their thought to the reading public, even through the medium of posthumous publication."[22] As is frequently the case with these ascriptions, the charge or the boast about these three is problematic at best. Roux's only published work, the *Nouvelle encyclopédie portative*, not only explicitly argues for the existence of god, but attacks the central contention of Diderot and d'Holbach, that motion is an essential attribute of matter. The salonière Mme. d'Epinay identifies Saint-Lambert as an atheist, but nothing in his public writings or in the judgments of others who knew him in private discussion seconds that identification. Helvétius, even in his most materialistic moments, allows the possibility of the deistic god who is both "the still unknown cause of order and movement" and one who wants human beings to attain their happiness by the use of their reason.[23] As the unknown cause of order and movement, Helvétius' god is still closer to Newton's and even Descartes' than to the endlessly recombining matter of Diderot and d'Holbach. Whatever weight one assigns to memoirs and gossip, the public register and the common discussion do not allow for an unambiguous conscription of these three within the ranks of the atheists.

Finally, there was Friedrich-Melchoir Grimm, who asserted neither deism or atheism. His was a Pyrrhonian skepticism, which prescinded rigorously not only from any statement about the existence and nature of god, but also from any apodictic propositions about the nature of matter, space, movement, and time. With d'Holbach and Diderot, Grimm attacked a natural theology built upon physics; with Bergier, he equally attacked anything that his friends would put in its place. Theology was "the absurd science," but in natural science as well "the facts are everywhere missing, and everywhere the philosophers have substituted their false systems for them."[24] Grimm was a latter-day Montaigne, but one without faith. His stance did not allow for theism, but neither did it allow for the rising, confident atheism of the new materialism. Grimm remained, both in physics and in theology, distant and agnostic.

Certainly, as available evidence indicates, the issues of belief and nonbelief, of theism, deism, atheism, and agnosticism, ranked high as subjects of debate during the baron's receptions, but the perennial conventional story that a dogmatic atheism united this group of some twenty or thirty philosophes will not wash. The only dogma that they held in common was the value of discussion; the only general belief was that the testing of discussion would bring all points of view into conflict and disclose the probabilities, certitudes, and implausibilities in each system and argument.

The baron's coterie revived the Ciceronian dialogues, in a form less organized, of course, more disparate in its representations, and remaining a conversation rather than emerging as a coherent series of reports. The positions and arguments of Lessius and Mersenne retrieved the perspectives of the Stoics, the Epicureans, and the Academics as they appeared in Cicero's *De natura deorum*. In the gradual transition into atheism, however, the Western world witnessed another kind of retrieval of Cicero, of discussion and debate as the universal philosophic and scientific method. D'Holbach's coterie was an embodiment of Cicero's *controversia*: "If it is a great accomplishment to master each discipline, how much greater is it to be competent in them all! But this is necessary for those who propose, for the sake of discovering the truth, to argue for and against all philosophers. I do not maintain that I have attained success in a matter so very difficult, but I do claim that I have attempted it."[25] The Ciceronian debate is not the two-voice dialectic of Plato, in which oppositions are uncovered and the discussion moves toward their resolution in a higher truth; much less is it the logistic catechism, styled a dialogue, of Mersenne, in which one admission after another is wrested from the reluctant opponent and added, part by part, into a composite conclusion. Cicero's debates and d'Holbach's discussions at the Rue Royale begin and end with perspectival discriminations. All the points of view are brought together, and the debate terminates only when one side or any auditor adopts one of the positions advocated as the more probable. The "maitre d'Hotel de la Philosophie" could make the same boast to his friends that Cicero made to his readers: "I place in your midst the opinions [*sententias*] of the philosophers."[26] Discussion, not atheism, was the unifying form of the coterie—and out of the discussions came the work that was called the bible of atheistic materialism. But this was still one perspective out of many, albeit perhaps the dominant one.

There are no written records of the controversies, the quarrels, and the agreements of the Rue Royale; there are only reports about them. But these reports furnish the historian of ideas with enough evidence to catch echoes in the bombinations of the *coterie holbachique* from the garden of Epicurus, the library at Alexandria, and those medieval *studia generalia* in which questions were endlessly investigated and various kinds of philosophy formulated. The Rue Royale differed from both the garden and a contemporary lecture hall in that there was no master and no disciples. There were a host and his guests. In this the Rue Royale resembled the lyceum of Aristotle or the academy of Plato less than the Tuscan villa and the conversations recorded by Cicero, where hospitality and freedom fostered those controversies which constituted philosophic method. It is unfortunate that these discussions were never even artificially reconstructed except in anecdote, for there are few philosophic or theological conflicts that could encourage works so vastly different in their conclusions as Bergier's *Examen du matérialisme* and the book it was intended to refute, *Le Système de la nature*.

If the *Système* emerged from the conversations that swirled about its author, it also gathered to itself both in its evidence and in its conclusions many threads of development which extended far beyond Paris. The *coterie holbachique* was a microcosm of conversations that were being entertained and published throughout France, Italy, and England. The *Système* came at the climax or crisis of such conversations, but it came as their synthesis, not their creator. It assimilated and transposed the ideas of the most critical figures of the decades that preceded it.

The major conjunction it made was between the two greatest figures of the seventeenth century, Descartes and Newton. Their union was effected through doctrines which neither of them would have accepted and through a project which the masters themselves would have thought reprehensible in its intention and impossible in its execution: a universal materialism that would eradicate or replace the notion of god. The job d'Holbach and Diderot proposed was thought by Descartes and Newton to be absurd: to destroy any dualism between matter and spirit, between *res extensa* or mass and *res cogitans* or spiritual reality. This job was to be accomplished by mingling the method of Newton with the issues and principles posed by Descartes. Through Newton's Universal Mechanics, Descartes could be corrected in his physics, and his proposal for mechanics developed into a more unified total philosophy.

A critical stage in this development lay with the abbé Etienne Bonnot de Condillac. He praised metaphysics in the opening sentence of his first work, *Essai sur l'orgine des connoissances humaines.* He was determined to rescue this science which more than any other rendered "l'esprit lumineux, précis et étendu" from the negligence and contempt that covered it in France.[27] And how would he rescue it? By doing what Descartes had never done and what

Locke had never completed: "Il faut remonter à l'origine de nos idées, en développer la génération, les suivre jusqu'aux limites que la nature leur a prescrites, par-là fixer l'étendue et les bornes de nos connoissances et renouveler tout l'entendement humain."[28] Descartes had established the thinking subject as given in the very process of doubting, as reflexively present and self-justifying. Metaphysics focuses upon the ideas that such a subject has. To account for the idea of infinite substance one must infer an infinite god. From his infiniteness one deduces his truthfulness as well as his other perfections. In his truthfulness one possesses an ironclad guarantee against the most radically skeptical hypotheses about the existence of the extramental world, since god would not allow the knowing powers of a human being to be essentially and pathologically deceived. With god as guarantee, one can then—and only then—justify sensations as a source of knowledge and accept a world as a subject for physics. In other words, from the *res cogitans*, one can deduce a defense for the human sensations of a *res extensa*.

Condillac collapses the distinction between thinking and sensation. This reintroduces a tradition from the much-repudiated Aristotelians, "que toutes nos connoissances viennent des sens," but those Peripatetics never understood the truth in what they asserted and could never expose it successfully. Bacon was probably the first to understand this principle, using it as the foundation for the *Novum Organum*. John Locke had the honor of not only articulating this principle and using it, but of demonstrating its truth with his plain and historical method. But Locke never carried this principle to its inherent conclusions.[29] Like Aristotle, he still insisted upon the distinction between sense and intellect, between sensation and understanding. This is precisely what Condillac denies. Condillac introduces to this tradition a single comprehensive principle that will account for everything that concerns human understanding. And that principle is sensation. Just as Newton introduced force into the universal mechanics as the comprehensive principle of all change, either inertial force which resisted change or motive force which effected change, so Condillac proposes a similar universal principle: "My purpose therefore is to reduce to a single principle [à un seul principe] whatever relates to the human understanding, and this principle shall neither be a vague proposition, nor an abstract maxim, nor a gratuitous supposition, but a constant experience [une expérience constante], all the consequences of which shall be confirmed by new observations [expériences]."[30] In sensation Condillac has found something, a fact or an experience, that allows analysis of all intellectual and volitional activity to a single comprehensive principle, something analogous to force in Newton but on the psychic level.

Sensation as this universal physical source and stuff allows Condillac to differentiate his true system from the abstract systems of Descartes, Malebranche, Spinoza, and Leibniz, which begin or end with formal definition and hypotheses. Sensation, perception, or the sensible consciousness of an internal motivation by an external object begins all knowledge. It exists as attention when that object is the sole subject of sensible consciousness or as reminiscence when consciousness attends to a perception of the past. Imagination, memory, and even contemplation are combinations of sensations and the objects or circumstances to which they are bound. What is true of ideas in general is true of each of these once-distinguished powers of the soul. All of them are at root simply transformed sensations.[31] This moves Locke far beyond empiricism into sensationalism. As in so many other cases, when the loyal disciple adjusts the master, he changes him radically. Locke's mistake was not in method, but in principle. Condillac corrects the *Essay Concerning Human Understanding* by making its principle comprehensive: "Locke distingue deux sources de nos idées, les sens et la réflexion. Il seroit plus exact de n'en reconnoître qu'une, soit parce que la réflexion n'est dans son principe que la sensation même, soit parce qu'elle est moins la source des idées, que le canal par lequel elles découlent des sens."[32] Thus a human being is without innate ideas and also without innate powers other than those acquired and developed through the onrush of sensations: "Elle [a statue] n'est donc rien qu'autant qu'elle a acquis. Pourquoi n'en seroit-il pas de même de l'homme?"[33] Why not, indeed! These are the last words of Condillac's great tractate on sensations, and they bear the total weight of a unification of all human psychic activity in sensation.

As sensations in their most primitive stage are the passive impressions made on the knowing subject by external objects, the guarantee of their veracity, that is, of the existence of this extramental world, is not god but touch. Touch teaches the other senses to judge of external objects. One emerging into human life learns to know his body not by sight or hearing, but by running his hand over his body and recognizing *c'est moi, c'est moi encore*; similarly, by touching another body, "le *moi*, qui se sent modifié dans la main, ne se sent pas modifié dans ce corps. Si le main dit *moi*, elle ne reçoit pas le même réponse."[34] This is Condillac's response to the question implied in his earlier statement that "nous ne sortons point de nous-mêmes; et ce n'est jamais que notre propre pensée que nous apercevons."[35] We are now outside ourselves and guaranteed an external world—and sensation has done it all, through touch. Without touch, we would have gone the way of Berkeley.

Condillac does not extend his ideas of sensation to a universal materialism. Quite the contrary. He posits god as the supreme cause and the spiritual soul as the center of human unity, and answers as impossible Locke's query whether god can endow matter with sensibility and thought.[36] But the revolution in his introduction of sensation as comprehensive of all psychic events does not end with Condillac. It is only a step in a longer journey which he does not take, but which—as is so often the case—is walked by others. Someone was bound to ask: If reflection can be reduced to sensation, can we not go further and reduce mind to body?

This is precisely what Claude-Adrien Helvétius asked in 1758 in *De l'esprit*, a book that shook intellectual Paris to its foundation. Like Condillac, he analyzes all psychic activity into various stages of sensation; unlike Condillac, he grants a spiritual soul neither as a principle of unity nor as a source of ethical action. Like Condillac, his method continues the tradition that repudiated the deductive Cartesians: "C'est par les fait que j'ai remonté aux causes." But unlike Condillac, and fulfilling the pattern of Newton far beyond Newton, the next sentence indicates what this analysis means: "J'ai cru qu'on devait traiter la morale comme toutes les autres sciences, et faire une morale comme une physique expérimentale."[37] How can ethics or moral science take on a method that parallels or even reproduces that of physics or mechanics? Only if the subjects of these sciences are parallel in their necessity and movement can the dream of a universal mechanics be generally realized. *L'esprit* reduces human psychic life to two faculties: memory and physical sensibility. Thus one can say that "sensibility produces all of our ideas." As in Condillac, everything is to be explained by "le principe qui sent en nous . . . tout se réduit donc à sentir."[38] Unlike Condillac, however, there is no reason to posit a spiritual soul as the basis for *sentir*. What is established about the human being can equally well be explained by the hypothesis of a human unity which is either spiritual or material; there is no evidence open to all which would convince one of the spirituality so insisted upon by Descartes.[39]

One can take even the most complicated and scientific judgments, those which relate to philosophic method and procedures, and resolve them into simple sensations, just as mechanics can take the most composite movements and break them into composing motions evoked by simple forces.[40] When one recognizes that this not only eliminates a distinct power of forming judgments, but also takes as universal a sensibility which is *physique*, one sees that the mechanical method has found in human actions a principle as tangible and observable as the movements of the planets. Helvétius' *De l'esprit* does not insist upon the material nature of all that was once *res cogitans*, but it is more than just present between the lines of this early text. While Condillac denies that matter can be endowed with the power of thought, Helvétius leaves the issue open in such a way as to affirm it, and he builds both a psychology and an ethics on the axiom that corporeal sensibility is the sole mover of the human person.[41] This advances the coincidence of matter and reality in a way vigorously furthered by Diderot. If all ideas can be reduced to sensations, then the second stage of this developing argument removes any necessity for a spiritual soul as the basis for sensations or perceptions. Diderot carries this one step further by a doctrine of the latent sensibility of matter. Helvétius also contributes to the coherence of matter by advocating the doctrine—again one repudiated by Condillac—that all human events are universally determined, as fixed in their actions by environment and education as the motion of a projectile or the orbits of planets.

Newton had hoped that his method could be extended to all the phenomena of nature. Condillac and Helvétius have applied it to the human person, the *res cogitans*, as *cogitare* can be reduced to sensations and sensations are suggested of matter. Neither of these philosophers rejects the Cartesian idea that first philosophy should study the ideas given in the mind, but by the use of the Newtonian method they effectively destroy the distinction between the *res cogitans* and the *res extensa*, and the analysis that Condillac's own *Logic* so highly treasures contributes significantly to the reduction of all things to matter and its motions.

If the intellectual inquiries of Condillac and Helvétius can be understood as the gradual and proleptic reduction of all reality to matter, a reduction which is an extension of the Newtonian mechanical analysis, the work of Julien Offroy de La Mettrie is perhaps best understood as a progression in Newtonian synthesis. In 1748, in the safety of Leyden, La Mettrie published *L'Homme machine*. Condillac and Helvétius analyzed the *res cogitans* further and further into the possibility that it was not essentially different from the *res extensa*. La Mettrie goes in the opposite direction, augmenting what Descartes had written about animals as automata in order to apply it to human beings. In either case, Newtonian mechanics is universalized to overcome the Cartesian diremption between spirit and matter. In his earlier *Histoire naturelle de l'ame* (1745), La Mettrie traced the active principle that is in matter from its earliest elemental forms until it reaches sensibility in animal life and the thinking brain of human beings. Now, in his great work of synthesis, every form of life is to be understood as an organization of matter.

Synthesis constitutes no random persuasion of La Mettrie. Synthesis or organization is the key to many of the questions which metaphysicians had posed but were unable to answer or to whose answers they were unable to win converts. Take Locke's question on which Condillac and Helvétius differ: Could matter be endowed with a capacity for thought? The question by itself makes no sense, La Mettrie remarks. It is just as inadequate as the question of whether matter can tell time. Matter has to be organized into a watch; a similar organization allows one to speak about thinking and judgment.[42] The synthesis explains the particular operations and properties of each of the parts. To correct Locke, Condillac, and Helvétius, La Mettrie uses a principle quite different from simple ideas or comprehensive sensation. He introduces a reflexive principle, one which will explain its own data and operations, without assimilating all reality into a single principle or reducing all thought to its composite elements. A similar synthesis is the function of reason: "If there is a God, He is the Author of nature as well as of revelation. He has given us the one to explain the other, and reason to make them agree."[43] The agreement, the organization, the complex structure alone can account for the operations and agencies of individual parts and powers. This is true of matter; this is true of philosophic reflections; this is true of the human being.

The major influence here is Descartes. Strange, for Descartes erred so influentially in insisting upon the essential difference between the *res extensa* and the *res cogitans*, but he provided the basis for understanding all animal nature and left subsequent philosophers only the challenge of extending this understanding. "This celebrated philosopher, it is true, was much deceived, and no one denies that. But at any rate he understood animal nature, he was the first to prove completely that animals are pure machines [*pures machines*]." Descartes' distinction between the spiritual and the bodily in human beings was only a ruse to make the theologians accept his mechanical interpretation of corporeal life. Once accepted, the analogy needed only time to work its way into the interpretation of human life.[44] This progress in understanding waited for La Mettrie to recognize through experience and observation that "all the faculties of the soul depend to such a degree on the proper organization of the brain and of the whole body, that apparently they are but this organization itself, the soul is clearly an enlightened machine." That mysterious word *soul* should only be used for that part of the mechanism which thinks.[45] It is not that one knows the nature of matter and of motion and thus can build this synthesis out of the knowledge of what produces it. La Mettrie professes himself a skeptic, a Pyrrhonist— though his Pyrrho belongs in reality to the third Academy! This skepticism does not allow the certain knowledge of anything. It allows probabilities for the superimpositions of a structure of meaning upon phenomena to see if this structure explains what is there and permits prediction of the future. The analogy of the machine is such an intellectual structure. It explains animals for Descartes and human beings for La Mettrie. The riddles of substances are really riddles of diverse organizations of matter. The human being "is to the ape, and to the most intelligent animals, as the planetary pendulum of Huyghens is to a watch of Julien Leroy. More instruments, more wheels and more springs were necessary to mark the movements of the planets than to mark or strike the hours; and Vaucanson, who needed more skill for making his flute player than for making his duck, would have needed still more to make a talking man, a mechanism no longer to be regarded as impossible, especially in the hands of another Prometheus." Making such a machine is all a question of degrees and of complications and of more elaborate art. But in the end, the human being is best understood by analogy with a very elaborate watch: "The human body is a watch, a large watch constructed with such skill and ingenuity, that if the wheel which marks the seconds happens to stop, the minute wheel turns and keeps on going its rounds. . . . Is it not for a similar reason that the stoppage of a few blood vessels is not enough to destroy or suspend the strength of the movement which is in the heart as in the mainspring of the machine?"[46] This synthetic analogy also gives organization to the vision that characterizes the materialist. It leads him to pardon wrongs as faults in the operation of the clockwork and to recognize in animals a degree of kindredness that inspires sympathy and kindness in their treatment.[47]

This does not call into question the existence of god. "On the contrary it seems to me that the greatest degree of probability is in favor of this belief. But since the existence of this being goes no further than that of any other toward proving the need of worship, it is a theoretic truth with very little practical value."[48] But whatever the probability, the existence of god is at best a distraction for those who were not made for an understanding of the ultimate causes of things—as philosophers from the time of Aristotle have insisted. All the physicotheology and astro-theology of the Newtonian William Derham and all the attempts of the mitigated Cartesian mathematician Bernard Nieuwentijt to demonstrate the existence of god "par les merveilles de la nature" come up against the skepticism of the Academy and such counterevidence as Trembly's demonstrations of the ability of polyps to regenerate themselves. "Why then would it be absurd to think that there are physical causes by reason of which everything has been made, and to which the whole chain of this vast universe is so necessarily bound and held that nothing which happens, could have failed to happen,—causes, of which we are so invincibly ignorant that we have had recourse to a God, who, as some aver, is not so much as a logical entity?"[49] La Mettrie's explicit position is neither to deny nor to affirm. He grants the weight of probability to the theists, but it is only that. *L'Homme machine* adopts from Vergil's third eclogue the motto that carefully measures its operational method: "Non nostrum inter vos tantas componere lites."[50]

La Mettrie may draw back before an explicit repudiation of all theistic convictions, may content himself and his inquiry with the statement that they cannot be resolved by human beings with certitude, and may insist that his synthesis of all human reality through the machine analogy stands unshakably before either hypothesis about ultimate reality. But *L'Homme machine* relates a story that takes the whole issue to another level of discussion:

> This is what I said to one of my friends, a Frenchman, as frank a Pyrrhonian as I, a man of much merit, and worthy of a better fate. He gave me a very singular answer in regard to the matter. "It is true," he told me, "that the *pro* and *con* should not disturb at all the soul of a philosopher, who sees that nothing is proved with clearness enough to force his consent, and that the arguments offered on one side are neutralized by those of the other." "However," he continued, "the universe will never be happy, unless it is atheistic." Here are this wretch's reasons. If atheism, said he, were generally accepted, all the forms of religion would then be destroyed and cut off at the roots. No more theological wars, no more soldiers of religion—such terrible soldiers! Nature infected with sacred poison, would regain its rights and its purity. Deaf to all other voices, tranquil mortals would follow only the spontaneous dictates of their own being, the only commands which can never be despised with impunity and which alone can lead us to happiness through the pleasant paths of virtue.[51]

One cannot but wonder if this friend was not at the Rue Royale; if it was not La Mettrie himself, perhaps it was the baron d'Holbach. For La Mettrie's theological discussion concludes with the suggestion that begins the *Système*, that human happiness is contingent upon the development of atheistic consciousness. La Mettrie himself does not explicitly identify with this position, but his work provides a synthesis for a universe that is simply the single reality of matter, one substance in different kinds of organization.[52] The operational method allows such a synthesis to be imposed as the intelligibility of the phenomena, as the logistic methods of Condillac and Helvétius allow them to build gradually from sensation to a composite grammar of the higher psychic operations of a human being. Condillac, however, explicitly repudiates the doctrine that is the central contention of La Mettrie, that animals and human beings are pure machines, and insists both upon a natural theology that establishes the existence of god and upon an understanding of the universe that discloses final causes within it. Helvétius leaves open the possibility that reasoning may be an activity of a spiritual soul, but finds no evidence to support it. La Mettrie closes off this possibility entirely. The analyses of Condillac and Helvétius do not yet square with the prior synthesis of Helvétius; both await the genius of *Le Système de la nature* to accomplish precisely that conjunction of two schools of materialism in France through a radical fulfillment that rejects any spirituality of the human person and the existence of god.

But neither d'Holbach nor Diderot before him was the first to espouse atheism. Prior to either by several decades looms indistinctly the remarkable, anomalous figure of the abbé Jean Meslier. His story is as brief as it is extraordinary; he was a parish curé who moved beyond Christian belief, skepticism, and agnosticism to champion atheism, indeed to champion it with passion if only from his grave. Though still ignored by the editors of the *Encyclopedia Britannica* and the *New Catholic Encyclopedia*, his anonymously authored life was circulated by Voltaire, and his posthumously published *Mémoire* was tirelessly recommended by that philosophe from the safety of Ferney. Letters of 1762 to d'Alembert, to the Count d'Argental, to Damilaville, and to Helvétius extolled this country pastor and urged what Voltaire titled his *Testament* upon these correspondents: "Read and read again Jean Meslier; he is a good curate."[53] This from Voltaire might seem a strange message indeed, but it was all of a piece with the *Mémoire* of Jean Meslier and the *Abrégé de la vie de l'auteur.*

Jean Meslier was born in 1664, directed into the seminary by his parents from their village of Mazerny, and, after ordination, assigned as curate to Etrépigny in Champagne, in the diocese of Rheims. In his seminary years he devoted lengthy hours of study to Descartes, remaining all of his life under the influence of the Cartesians, "les plus sensés, et les plus judicieux d'entre tous les philosophes deicoles."[54] His life as a priest was exemplary in its austerities and virtues; on one occasion he courageously denounced the local squire for his oppression of the peasants. The *Abrégé de la vie* relates the general belief that he died "disgusted with life" and refusing the "food necessary to sustain it, because he did not want to take anything, not even a glass of wine."[55] To his parishioners he left his meager possessions. To France he left one of the strangest literary legacies the nation with its philosophes would ever receive. In the rectory, his parishioners found three complete copies of a manuscript entitled *Mémoire des pensées et sentiments de Jean Meslier*, wrapped in gray paper on which the author had written: "I have seen and recognized the errors and the abuses, the vanities, the follies, and the wickedness of human beings. I have hated and detested them. I did not dare to say it during my life, but I will say it at least in dying and after my death."[56] What had the parish pastor not dared to say during his life, but would communicate to his flock now? That not only Christianity, but all religious belief, was exploitation and hoax! His own years of ordained ministry had begun in obedience to his parents and were lived out in a double life because he could not safely enlighten others. But when death did come at the age of 65, in 1729, fear had no more power over him and from his sepulcher his *Mémoire* spoke.

Meslier's *Mémoire* became part of the clandestine literature circulating throughout the country and pouring into the nation's capital, not to be published openly and in full until the middle of the nineteenth century. Voltaire published an *Extrait des sentiments de Jean Meslier* in 1762, but removed the atheism and reformed the curé of Etrépigny into an ally in his anti-Christian crusade against *l'infâme*. From the eight proofs that composed the *Mémoire*, Voltaire selected from the first five, leaving Meslier a deist.[57] Diderot also read the entire text of the *Mémoire* and transposed a citation from it into his poem "Eleutéromanes," never mentioning the name of the atheistic abbé.[58] Baron d'Holbach did just the opposite of Voltaire. He used the name of Meslier, attached it to *Le Bon Sens, ou Idées naturelles opposées aux idées surnaturelles*, and floated it into the market in 1772 as the genuine *Mémoire* of Meslier. Actually, *Bon Sens* was a popular condensation of the baron's *Système de la nature*, made more accessible in its briefer form and more romantic by its clerical attribution. It was one of the most astonishingly successful frauds in the history of letters.[59] While Peter Gay is inaccurate in maintaining that "Voltaire's abstract, published in 1762, follows Meslier faithfully," Will and Ariel Durant take their entire analysis of Meslier from this bogus product of d'Holbach.[60] In the enthusiasm of the philosophes, Meslier was celebrated, adapted, and used for whatever propaganda purposes a particular philosophe desired. It is all very well for Jean Delumeau to remark how unrepresentative a figure Meslier was.[61] One was quite enough for the philosophes, and they made the most out of him. For all of that, d'Holbach was closer to the mark than Voltaire. Meslier did not die, as Voltaire so cleverly and so repeatedly asserted, asking "God's pardon for having taught Christianity."[62] He did not ask god's pardon for anything. He did not believe in god. The parish priest, unlike Voltaire, was an atheist.

Meslier's *Mémoire* carries the marks of his Cartesian masters, who corrected Descartes with the teachings of Malebranche. The clear and distinct are still the characteristics of valid ideas, ideas whose truth does not admit of doubt. The first of these ideas is the assertion of being itself: "Nous connoissons naturellement que l'être est, nous ne sçaurions l'ignorer. La raison naturelle nous fait clairement voir qu'il faut nécessairement qu'il ait tousjours été."[63] What is the characteristic attribute of being? Infinity. As with Descartes and Malebranche, the infinite becomes the critical note of the supremely real, but Meslier finds a triple embodiment of this infinity. There is the infinite of extension, the infinite of time or duration, and the infinite of number.[64] Meslier can agree even further with Malebranche that the infinite being must necessarily exist—the illation of the ontological proof. But this infinity is not one of spirit, but of matter. What is unrestricted, and hence necessary, is matter: "L'être et la matiere ne sont qu'une même chose."[65] Meslier takes from the Cartesians the primacy of the infinite, but reinterprets this infinite in quantitative terms. Plotinus gave infinity a qualitative meaning, rather than continuing the various quantitative understandings of the infinite from prior Greek philosophy and mathematics. In the Middle Ages, this sense of the infinite as unlimited perfection reached a crest in such thinkers as Henry of Ghent and John Duns Scotus and the scholastics who followed them. It was this sense of the infinite that Descartes took for granted and that functioned so centrally in Malebranche. Descartes used "perfect" in the *Discourse* and "infinite" in the *Meditations* to denote the same meaning predicated. Malebranche summarized his demonstration "that the infinitely perfect being exists, because I perceive it, and because nothing cannot be perceived, nor consequently can the infinite be perceived in the finite."[66] The fundamental shift which Meslier makes in this tradition is not to deny that one perceives the infinite, but to interpret that infinity as the Newtonian extensions of space and time and as the mathematical considerations of number. Infinity is returned to its quantitative meaning. Since, for the Cartesian, extension is the primary significance of matter, it is an easy turn to take the entire tradition into a radical and universal materialism. Matter and being are the same.

One of the more significant events in the history of atheism is a nonevent. Something did not happen, and the absence allowed the Enlightenment to take a particular cast. Meslier never achieved his own voice. His central thought with its array of eight proofs gained only surreptitious readers; it obtained a presence in their discussions only as they quarried his *Mémoire* to build their own monuments, very much as the great houses of Rome had plundered the pagan grandeur of the ancient city to erect their own baroque constructions. In the extracts of Voltaire, he became a deist; in the transformations of Diderot, his curse took the form of poetry; in the ascriptions of d'Holbach, his work became a primer for those who could not work their way through the whole of the *Système*. But Meslier himself was not published, and his absence from the public discussion allowed the major lines of the argument to continue in terms of physics as philosophy. For Meslier wrote primarily as a theologian. The line of his argument and the place of philosophy within it are essentially theological. The eight demonstrations follow the path of topics marked out by centuries of apologetics: the nature of religion, the fact of revelation, and the evidence for a natural theology. The commonplaces for such an argument are not from Descartes; they are much more like those of Pascal. But Pascal died leaving the *Pensées* unfinished, and Meslier's *Mémoire* was never published in complete form until the Enlightenment had run its course. The consideration of these two works for a theologian remains a haunting essay in what might have been.

The *Mémoire* subsumes religion into politics among the human artifices to subjugate the masses, founded upon the stratagems and arrogance of the great and the ignorance of the small. In the first four demonstrations, an examination of the pretended foundations of religions discloses nothing but errors, illusions, and impostures, while an inquiry into the actual consequences of religion finds them the source of political and social alienation. Even the gospels are a tissue of corrupt texts and internal contradictions. Each of the classic confirmations of revelation undergoes inquiry and repudiation: visions, revelation, sacrifices, prophecies, and any of the four senses of scripture that would render them palatable. The fifth demonstration moves from the foundations of the Christian religion to its doctrinal and moral content, scoring the principal absurdities in Christian teaching: the trinity, the incarnation, the eucharistic presence, the creation out of nothing, and commission of sins. Again these doctrines are refuted both in terms of the basic weakness in their justification and in terms of the social and political consequences to which they lead: oppressive nobility, parasitic monks and religious, private property, and the tyrannical rule of monarchs. Only in the seventh demonstration are the philosophic issues as such introduced and the grounds for any assertion of the divine existence repudiated. The argument from universal consent evanesces before the discovery that the wise have historically either doubted or denied the existence of god, while the masses have adored gods in abundance. The beauty or the order of the perfection that is found in the physical universe can be attributed to matter that moves itself. If one espouses the physics of Newton, it is internally contradictory to assert that either time or space has been created, as contradictory as it would be to assert that being or the eternal truths have been created. Finally, the positive conclusion of the philosophic demonstration: "L'être ou la matiere qui ne sont qu'une même chose, ne peut avoir que de lui même son existence et son movement."[67] Every other explanation refutes itself, leaving only this principle of singular plausibility, which can explicate equally the existence of evil, the quantity of false prophecies, and the invalidity of the arguments of Descartes, Fenelon, and Malebranche.

The outline of the eight demonstrations does not do them justice, but it indicates the location of philosophy within theology and the identification of religion within politics. It suggests how different a discussion might have occurred if Meslier's *Mémoire* had set up the problem for the theologians. While theologians were engaged in each of these subjects, the central line of argument was elsewhere; the pivotal issues in the discussion of god were those of motion and matter, not religious consciousness or the teaching and figure of Christ. There might be excursions in either of these directions, but the preponderance of the battle lay in physics and philosophy.

Around this major assault swirled the general and undisciplined currents of discussion and debate, of circuitous satire and comfortably fashionable opinions, the talk in the café, the gossip in the salon, and the whispers at the court—never committed to paper or print, but forming a climate of opinion in which presuppositions could crystallize and exist without searching internal criticism. Such criticism always came from the outside, dowdy and irrelevant, lacking crispness, smartness, and even good taste. Increasingly, as Nietzsche later wrote, it was not only reason but taste which decided against the beliefs of what had been a Christian Europe. For there were still scandals which could not be hushed—the intolerance that broke the body of Jean Calas before his public strangulation and condemned Jean François Lefebre de la Barre to be tortured and beheaded for blasphemy—scandals that reinforced a rising horror at religion and at the cruel blindness that it spread. The early poetry of Voltaire lashed out against all the various confessions and sects of Europe:

> Je veux aimer ce Dieu, je cherche en lui mon père:
> On me montre un tyran que nous devons haïr.[68]

The tyranny of the church, the tyranny of the nation-state, the tyranny of their god, the oppression by the clergy and the nobles and the monarch—all of these formed the unquestioned presuppositions of the "enlightened"; their identity in institutional despotism roused frustration, rage, and the kind of fury embodied in Diderot's transformation of Meslier into those famous lines:

> Et ses mains ourdiraient les entrailles du prêtre:
> Au défaut d'un cordon pour étrangler les rois.[69]

These verses were cited by Naigeon after the Revolution had given them a bloody and somber realization. They expressed the great bitterness of an age. While their hatred did not enter into the formal structure of the atheistic argument that was evolving, it formed the condition that made this argument possible and the passion with which it lived. To all of this, Baron Paul Henri d'Holbach was heir and host.

Paul Hazard says of d'Holbach what many historians of philosophy have also said about Cicero: "It must not be supposed that the Baron was a genius, or that there was anything strikingly original about his ideas; he appropriated them from others right and left."[70] This is true enough. The baron's coterie opened upon his salon and his salon opened upon all of Europe. What Cicero accomplished by his *quaestiones* and dialogues, d'Holbach achieved in receptions and discussions. From these, each drew his own conclusions, persuaded by arguments of endless duration and complicated lineage. D'Holbach had loved the far-ranging conversations of his student days at the University of Leyden, and when he moved to Paris shortly after those years he brought with him both the interest and the wealth with which to continue them. Gradually the group gathered around him. Gradually and anonymously he began to publish his own tractates and translate those of others.

Jacques-André Naigeon was the only one who habitually "helped d'Holbach in the editing and publishing of some of the Baron's own manuscripts, and who worked with him in the rewriting of several anti-Christian texts by other thinkers."[71]

And Diderot? The question is much debated. Virgil W. Topazio urges that Diderot not only did not directly collaborate with d'Holbach in his anti-religious writings, but was probably unaware of their scope in the 1760s, and, further, that the major works of the baron "were as much the thought and work of d'Holbach alone, as any work could have been the product of any member of that eighteenth-century society."[72] Roland Mortier finds Topazio's conclusions "trop catégorique, qui ne tient pas assez compte de la complexité de la matière et des servitudes de la littérature d'opposition sous l'ancien Régime." Exposing the various theses in the works of both d'Holbach and Diderot, Mortier prefers the term "innutrition" to indicate the dialectic of mutual influence.[73] Their differences, Mortier insists, were not as much those of doctrine as of style or method (*un mode de penser*): d'Holbach "est un penseur systématique, dogmatique," while Diderot possesses "une méthode plus sinueuse, mieux adaptée à la complexité de l'homme."[74] Alan Kors judges that "Diderot helped d'Holbach infuse a certain style and rhetorical flourish into some of his works, but his contribution, aside from the question of his general intellectual influence, was limited to that extent."[75]

Finally, Jeroom Vercruyesse, while admitting that "la collaboration exacte de Diderot n'a pas encore été étudiée de manière approfondie," points out both the parallels in the style of the last chapter of the *Système* and the *Rêve de d'Alembert* and the very close bond in doctrine between the *Rêve* and "certaines thèses du *Système*." His conclusion leaves the issue still imprecise in its resolution: "Il est donc bien admis à l'heure actuelle que l'auteur principal de ce livre incendiaire est le baron d'Holbach et qu'il a reçu une collaboration non négligeable de Naigeon et de Diderot."[76]

Fortunately, the question of intellectual parentage is not pressing here. No one doubts the *Système*'s masterly summary of the cresting atheism, and as a single work "it remained until about the second quarter of the twentieth century—the most important demonstration of materialism and atheism, and consequently, the center of attacks by both 'philosophes' and theologians."[77] *Le Système de la nature* was not only the culmination of d'Holbach's career, but the culmination of a mode of thought that stretches far behind him into decisions that were taken when atheism was only invective.

"Ce livre effraie tout le monde, et tout le monde veut le lire"

The revolution that Denis Diderot effected in the plausibility of any theistic affirmation carried in its circuit a concomitant inversion in the understanding of everything else in the universe. Metaphysics, physics, and mechanics, optics, medicine, and history had not waited upon revulsions in convictions about god and religion. In many ways, the influences were reciprocal, and a shift in one area brought about massive upheavals in the others. But scattered through these moving, inconstant patterns, not only god, but nature, motion, matter, animal life, and human beings with all their private morals and social interactions progressed through critique and reevaluation into new understandings. Each was part of a piece, a spoke reaching from hub to rim, and with the revolutions of the wheel, the parts groaned, turned, and advanced into new locations and a different world.

Nature had long since traveled from the Aristotelian substantial form to Descartes' "la Matiere mesme, entant que je la considere avec toutes les qualitez que je luy ay attribuées, comprises toutes ensemble, et sous cette condition que Dieu continuë de la conserver en la mesme façon qu'il l'a crée."[78] Change in its turn had become the locomotion of material bodies, measured out mathematically in terms of space and time. Matter itself had become either the extension of the Universal Mathematics or the mass of the Universal Mechanics or the creative potentiality of elements whose inherent attributes were self-locomotion and latent sensibility. Animals had become automata, not unlike the hydraulically powered statues in the Francini Gardens. Most recently, human beings themselves had become, in La Mettrie's writings, similar machines, fixed in their organization and totally determined in their operations and choices.

The central paradox of the Enlightenment gradually assumed its ironic shape through each of these removals to new meaning, drawn perhaps most sharply in the claims staked out for nature and culture. Diderot had effectively reduced culture to nature, leaving the age with as strong an internal contradiction as any that civilization had borne. The philosophes urged a gospel of unhampered human liberty, a gospel that should have had a telling effect on private morality and on social structures. At the same time, often within the same exhortations, they formulated a rigorously mechanical doctrine of nature and of human beings enclosed within this nature. Every form of nature, each of its movements and resultant organizations, emerged necessarily, completely determined by the interaction of its particles and by the iron rule of their invariant laws. The rhetoric of human freedom registered a sharp, if unnoticed, dissonance with this undeviating causal determinacy. Education, morality, and the understanding of human happiness had to be recast but recast in such a way that they could treat these incoherences between nature and culture. The Enlightenment had forged as severe an internal inconsistency as previous generations had found between faith and reason, grace and nature, or predestination and freedom. Only when this irony was unraveled could one deal with the theistic issue as such. Without the establishment of consistency between nature and culture, all these revolutions against god would remain palace revolts, stigmatized cynically by Voltaire: "Voylà une guerre civile entre les incrédules."[79]

Coherence was the first order of business. Coherence is only possible through system. System cannot be the abstract structures of Descartes and Spinoza, webs spun from definitions and axioms whose refinement contrasted sharply with their poverty of experience and observation and whose credibility had been savaged by the abbé Condillac's *Traité des systèmes*. One must bring nature, movement, matter, the modes of matter in movement, chance—the classic topics that had been in discussion since the new mathematics and Newtonian mechanics arose—together with the human person, the body and soul, the intellectual capacities and their moral uses, the origin of ideas and the possibilities of freedom—the elements of culture to which mechanics was being applied. These topics form the table of contents of *Le Système de la nature*'s first volume. Only out of the unification of these can the new education, the reformed sense of human happiness, and such projects as the elimination of god emerge.

All of these elements had already entered into the redetermination of the reality of god, but it remained to reduce them to system. Diderot had done much through aphorism, debate, and drama, but the mechanics and mathematics that dominated the intellect of the age could not be satisfied with a form so at odds with its scientific content. System was in critical demand. A book that systematized the product of the centuries would stand as a *summa* of the sciences in their growing alienation from theological concerns. The time was mature for such a work as that of d'Holbach, a tract which would merit the judgment of Robert Sasso: "On peut considérer le *Système de la nature* comme le recueil organique de toutes les thèses matérialistes et athéistes du xviiie siècle."[80]

It was not remarkable, then, that the *Système* had first to draw together the new lines of nature and human culture and only then to follow their logical sequels into atheism. Atheism was not the system; nature was. Since culture was only the human epiphenomenon of nature, to systematize nature was to unify culture and to eliminate the antinatural chimera of religious belief.

Nature, then, rather than the uses of the imagination which resulted in theology or the verbal skills which resulted in skepticism, must furnish the horizon of philosophic inquiry and the area from which the categorical units of meaning and lesser terms can be drawn. Nature must continue to function in this way as it had for much of the last two centuries, the fundamental focus of whatever philosophy was to be taken as first. In d'Holbach, nature is not only this elemental selection; it is the all-encompassing whole. Nature is the source from which all things issue; it is the context in which they exist; it is the subject which their individual organizations modify; it is the legislative *centrum* by which they act, move, and are governed. What is universally true of all things is true also of the human person. "Man is the work of Nature: he exists in Nature: he is submitted to her laws: he cannot deliver himself from them; nor can he step beyond them even in thought."[81] Nature is the total concrete universal. Experience, rather than imagination, assumes a correspondingly irreplaceable authority. Experience alone forms the apperceptive link between the reason of the individual human subject and this universal nature.

Human beings can be classified as they relate noetically to this great, all-comprehending reality. "Savage" denotes human beings impotent or untutored in their resistance to immediate impulse, while the civilized human being is the one "whom experience and social life have enabled to draw from nature the means of his own happiness."[82] The enlightened human, the self-congratulatory ideal of the period, is the one who has learned to examine universal nature and to think for himself. Human happiness comes from learning to enjoy the benefits that nature prodigiously yields, while the unhappy person lives in a world constructed by the imagination and peopled with chimeras. These various categories of human life are specified by the selection of the *Système*, a selection which dictates both the epistemological priority of experience and the disciplinary hegemony of natural philosophy. First philosophy is natural philosophy. "It necessarily results, that the human person ought always in his researches to fall back upon physics and experience. These are what he should consult in his religion—in his morals—in his legislation—in his political government—in the arts—in the sciences—in his pleasures—in his misfortunes."[83] One contacts universal nature only through experience, and experience itself is the result of sense perception. The axis of truth runs from sense perception, through experience and reason, to universal nature, generating a revolving but advancing solid of scientific inquiry and poised in absolute opposition to the constant sources of error: imagination, enthusiasm, habit, prejudice, and authority.

Nature, in its primary sense, denotes the vast assembly of all that exists; it is coextensive with reality. This universal nature comprises "the great whole that results from the assemblage of different matters under their various combinations, with that diversity of motions which the universe offers to our view." One can also speak, however, of individual or particular natures as well, but only in the sense of diminutive assemblages. Just as universal nature, or nature in its most proper sense, is the whole composed of all of these lesser material combinations and their appropriate movements, so these individual natures are not the forms of Aristotle but smaller mixtures of material components. Each of these individual natures is only "the properties, the combinations, the movements, or the modes of action, by which it is discriminated from other beings."[84] Each sense of nature denotes a system: either the particular system that combines the lesser elements to make up an individual thing, or the general system of all of these individual natures that constitute the single, greater whole. Nature is always a whole of parts, of individual bodies and the laws of motion by which they are governed. "Natural" correspondingly denotes what is coordinate with these individuals, with these modalities of movements, or with the universe they systematically form.

There is no disagreement between d'Holbach and the various philosophic currents which he counts as tributaries to the stream of philosophic discourse. The area for basic philosophic inquiry must be nature or the nature of things. D'Holbach's divergence from the general consensus of philosophy occurs both with the identification of nature with general or particular assemblages and their fundamental variant elements—though there are many in the history of philosophy who could be counted in his corner even here—and with the arbitrary exclusion of anything beyond nature from intellectual respectability. In the last position, he stands among the pioneers.

Descartes had begun with ideas and established god as a guarantor of nature. Newton had begun with the phenomena of nature and established god as a force by which the phenomena were structured so that they could interact. In both systems, god entered as a casual necessity. In both physics, god gave movement or design to nature. Diderot had eliminated this inferred necessity by positing movement not as an effect upon matter, but as an effect of matter. Matter was reflexively responsible for its own movement. The *Système* followed suit. Both Cartesian and Newtonian physics had posed the question: granted that the natural universe was a combination of matter and movement, how was it that inert or static matter possessed movement? This question involved the nature of movement, the understanding of cause and effect, and the fundamental attributes of matter.

Motion retains in d'Holbach the character it has acquired over the centuries of mathematical and mechanical study. "Motion is an effort by which a body either changes, or has a tendency to change its position: that is to say, by which it successively corresponds with different parts of space, or changes its relative distance to other bodies."[85] Motion is either actual local motion or the pressure to move locally. Both Newtonian and Cartesian mechanics figure in this definition. Relative or measurable motion is no longer simply the insubstantial phenomenon and measure of true motion; it is a variety of true motion. The occupation of successive locations in space is no longer the only mathematical or real motion; it is the first of the two kinds of movement. While nature as selection has been interpreted to eliminate any transcendent realm, motion as one of the critical elements of this nature has eliminated any underlying areas as "the really real." Descartes might warn human inquiry against too much reliance upon the sensible and the imagination, and Newton differentiates between the real and the apparent. The *Système* insists upon sense perception and experience as sources for reason and differentiates motions according to changes in phenomena.

Motion provides the link both within universal nature itself and with the noetic involvement of the knowing subject. Universal nature is an assemblage of various bodies, and these bodies are themselves assemblages of various elemental bodies, brought together or separated only by movement. All the links within universal nature are seen in terms of movement. Cause and effect—the generic bonds among all natures and bodies—are not Aristotelian variant relationships to a single event. They are distinct mechanical units, connecting through the movement that is engendered: "A cause is a being which puts another in motion, or which produces some change in it. The effect is the change produced in one body by the motion or presence of another."[86] One has only to compare this understanding of motion and cause with that of Thomistic metaphysics to see how far the *Système* has traveled down the road to an entirely mechanical view of the universe, to a philosophy of nature become a universal mechanics and functioning as a metaphysics. The problematic procedures of Aquinas distinguish three types of motion in contrast to change, in its strict sense of the generation and corruption of substances. D'Holbach breaks down all of these distinctions and reduces all motion or change to locomotion. All natures and their modifications are brought about by the disintegration and recombination of the component bodies.

Locomotion, rather than existence, actualizes either the universal or the particular natures; so cause and effect are defined as the generator of locomotion and as its result. Again, Aquinas distinguishes with Aristotle four types of causes and assimilates into Aristotle's "moving cause" the efficient cause whose formulation lies in the Moslem philosophy of Ibn Sina. But Aquinas ultimately defines causality not in terms of movement, as did d'Holbach, but in terms of being or existence: "*Causa importat influxum quemdam in esse causati*. A cause conveys the notion of some sort of influence upon the being of the effect."[87] In d'Holbach's universe, there is no consideration of existence as such, but of the movements which constitute this universe: a cause is that thing which produces locomotion in another; an effect is the locomotion produced. A more mechanical horizon for the universe would be impossible to imagine.

This theory of causality allows an initial understanding both of universal nature and of the epistemological framework by which it can be comprehended. Cause and effect both translate the action and reaction of universal mechanics and give the perspective in terms of which reality can be asserted or denied of any element within it. If a thing does not act upon our senses in some causal fashion, either directly or indirectly, it does not exist for us; conversely, human beings can have no additional knowledge of anything beyond this change. Cause and effect allow universal nature to be spelled out as an objective unity and as a noetic system. From the continual action and reaction of all of these beings that comprise nature results a series of causes and effects, or a "chain of motion, guided by the constant and invariable laws peculiar to each being."[88] Universal nature is now an iron sequence of necessity. This means not only that any compound motion can be reduced fully to its component simple motions, but that intellectual control of the simple motions gives one a comprehensive mastery of all future combinations. Descartes distinguished between acquired and spontaneous motion. Motion is acquired when it is impressed by one body on another; it is spontaneous when it is spiritual, self-caused, as when a man decides to take a journey. The *Système* reduces all motions to acquired motion; spontaneous motion is fiction. Even the will of a human being is equally "determined by some exterior causes producing a change in it: we believe it moves of itself, because we neither see the cause that determined it, the mode in which it acted, nor the organ that it put in motion."[89] The fact of the matter is, however, that the laws that govern the movement of human beings are as unvarying as the constants that govern all bodies, and their laws not only dictate how they move, but that they move necessarily.

Neither Descartes nor Newton sought the origin of movement in matter itself. Descartes posited an initial endowment of motion by god, which the universe conserved and conveyed in its mutual interactions. Newton allowed some active principles such as fermentation and gravitation within the phenomena of nature, but insisted that mass of itself was inert. That gravitation was an innate attribute, essential to matter, was for him an absurdity. But the eighteenth century did not find it as unthinkable. Toland's *Letters to Serena* opened up this possibility again and Diderot seized upon it to exclude any divine intervention in the movement of things. For Diderot, matter moved itself and possessed this self-movement inherently. The *Système* finds this material principle of Diderot satisfactory enough, but insists upon extending its heterogeneity, to make its activity and variety the final explanation of all subsequent assertions and affirmations about the nature of things. Motion itself has become locomotion, differing only in the perspectives brought to bear upon it. Now motion springs inexorably from active and heterogenous units of matter: "Every thing in the universe is in motion; the essence of nature is to act: if we consider its parts attentively, we shall discover that not a particle enjoys absolute repose."[90]

D'Holbach's existential interpretation of motion allows him to eliminate the Newtonian distinction between absolute and relative, true and apparent, mathematical and common. The logistic methodology of his natural philosophy and the generically comprehensive nature of matter allows a parallel elimination of the Cartesian distinction between acquired and spontaneous motion. All motion is relative; all motion is acquired, impressed necessarily by another. Now the reflexivity between motion and matter, writ as large as the universal nature, eliminates the distinction between motion and rest. All rest is only relative or apparent, a perspective, but a perspective negated by the higher perspective of science and physics: "All beings are continually breeding, increasing, decreasing, or dispersing, with more or less tardiness or rapidity."[91] Natural philosophy indicates that even for massive pillars apparently at rest and for monuments that seem immobile, there is a *nisus*, a continuous resisting action, incessantly reacting to the pressures and impacts upon it. In those bodies which appear at rest, there is "continual action and reaction, constant efforts, uninterrupted impulse, and continued resistance." One does not need to canonize a final distinction between the real and the perceptible, as did Newton, in order to deal with this fact: observation and reflection ought to convince us that everything in nature is in continual motion. Where there is matter, there is necessarily movement.

With rest eliminated from nature, the issue treated by Descartes and Newton and used as evidence by Newton and Clarke to establish the existence of god comes into sharper focus. Whence this continual movement, change, motion? D'Holbach sharpens the response of Diderot: "The idea of Nature necessarily includes that of motion. But, it will be asked, from whence did she receive her motion? Our reply is, from herself, since she is the great whole, out of which, consequently, nothing can exist. We say this motion is a manner of existence, that flows, necessarily, out of the essence of matter; that matter moves by its own peculiar energies; that its motions are to be attributed to the force which is inherent in itself."[92] Universal nature is reduced to the material integers that compose it. These units are in turn the assemblages of lesser elements brought about by movement. All movement is local movement. All local movement comes out of matter, is nothing but "a manner of existence," that flows necessarily out of the essence of matter. What observations and reflections, what natural philosophy, indicate this dynamic, creative nature of matter? The natural philosophy of Isaac Newton, the microscopy of Father Needham, and the art of gunpowder.

Newton's system of the world, the unification of all celestial phenomena as the effect of the gravitation of celestial bodies toward each other, introduced gravity as it overthrew the Cartesian attempts to explain celestial movements as the clashing of one body against another. The subtle matter that Descartes postulated could never account for the massive movement of the planets, and the prejudices of the Cartesians blinded them to the obvious truth of the *Principia*. Newton himself needs some adjustments by d'Holbach, however; the Universal Mechanics fails to make the necessary link between gravitation and matter, and to recognize that all locomotion is relative gravitation and that every motion in the universe results from gravitation. Newtonian mechanics will serve the *Système* as method only when corrected in its principle, only when force and motion and matter are merged. Likewise, the Cartesian mechanics will serve the *Système* as principle, but only when its principle becomes the heterogeneous matter for which motion is not an endowment from outside but a mode of existence.

The microscopic observations and the claims of the English priest John Turberville Needham confirm for d'Holbach the existence of spontaneous generation—as they did for Diderot. Never mind its earlier rejections by Remi and Leeuwenhoek and subsequent refutations by the abbé Spallanzani; the scientific matter is quite clear and in the name of natural philosophy the *Système* makes this counter against superstition and prejudice: "If flour be wetted with water, and the mixture closed up, it will be found, after some little lapse of time, by the aid of a microscope, to have produced organized beings that enjoy life."[93] If insects can issue from inanimate matter, one can reason analogically that human beings have a similar origin for we have here the principle; and with proper materials, principles can always be brought into action. And as final philippic: "That generation which is styled *equivocal*, is only so for those who do not reflect, or who do not permit themselves attentively to observe the operations of Nature."[94] Such confident scientific judgment, tucked within the context of a flour-and-water origin of animal life and salted with contempt for its opponents' failures in observation, is not without its own quiet irony.

There are any number of observations or experiments in which seemingly inert matter generates movement. Usually these combinations are those of fire, water, and air, "the most volatile, the most fugitive of beings." Thunder, earthquakes, and volcanoes are ascribed to their intermixture. Anyone can observe the astonishing effect of gunpowder, a seemingly inert compound, when it comes into contact with fire. What is operative in this example is neither the comprehensive nature of matter nor the latent existence of sensibility in matter, but modalities of violent motions issuing from nothing more than the combination of the basic elements of matter. The first observation and reflection lay in the use and correction of Newton; the second, that of John Needham; the third, however, goes back to

Empedocles and Chinese gunpowder. But whatever their ancestry, "these facts incontestably prove, that motion is produced, is augmented, is accelerated in matter, without the concurrence of any exterior agent: it is, therefore, necessary to conclude, that motion is the necessary consequence of immutable laws, resulting from the essence, from the properties inherent in the different elements, and the various combinations of these elements."[95] These "facts" undermine the natural theology of the Universal Mechanics of Newton and the divine principle which confers movement on matter in Descartes. They assert an axiom that will close off the universal nature from any appeal beyond it: "There is no necessity to have recourse to supernatural powers to account for the formation of things [such as design in Newton], and those phenomena which we see [such as in Descartes' first philosophy]."[96] Motion as a result or inherent attribute of matter gives natural philosophy its own enclosed world, its own principle, and eliminates the natural theologies of either the religious believer or the deist. Matter carries the attributes of god. It is the necessary being. It is contradictory, inconceivable, to imagine a moment when it did not exist. And since motion is a necessary property of matter, it is coeval with matter.

"To form the universe *Descartes* asked but matter and motion." The *Système* gives an answer far beyond what he requested: "Motion is a manner [of being], which matter derives from its own proper existence."[97]

Universal nature breaks down logistically into individual natures; these natures decompose into their parts, these parts into their heterogeneous elements. As these parts are different, so "the elements, or primitive matters which enter the composition of bodies, are not of the same nature, and consequently, can neither have the same properties, nor the same modifications; and if so, they cannot have the same mode of moving, and acting." What are these actional elements to which the natural philosophy of the Enlightenment appeals as the root sources of all the phenomena of nature? The answer is astonishing: air, earth, fire, and water. Fire becomes the principle of the motion or the activity of matter; earth, of its solidity or impenetrability; water, the condition for their combination; and air, a fluid which constitutes space, the space necessary for the movement of the other elements. Human observation never comes across these elements in a pure form. They are "continually and reciprocally set in motion by each other; which are always acting and reacting; combining and separating; attracting and repelling; are sufficient to explain to us the formation of all of the beings we behold. Their motion is uninterruptedly, and reciprocally, produced from each other; they are alternately causes and effects. Thus, they form a vast circle of generation and destruction of combination and decomposition, which could never have had a beginning, and which can never have an end." This ultimate resolution of universal nature into the four elements and their native motions allows a final precision in the understanding of universal nature: "Nature is but an immense chain of causes and effects, which unceasingly flow from each other."[98] Anything else is an abridgement of our sense, a denial of our experience, and a negation of that precision of experience that is natural philosophy.

There is nothing shocking in such a doctrine, the *Système* maintains. Philosophers in every age have maintained it, and one can even find theologians who have upheld it. François Vatable, the great Renaissance Hebraist, and Hugo Grotius are enlisted to deny that Genesis indicates a beginning to matter. Jerome can be found to have given *creare* the same meaning as *condere*, to found or to build. Both the ancient Tertullian and the great Jesuit patristic theologian, Petavius, admit the *creatio ex nihilo* to be a doctrine better established from reason than from sacred Scripture. Justin Martyr can be read to hold that matter is eternal; Justin praises Plato's *Timaeus* for asserting that the divine creation meant, not the making of something from nothing, but the formation of the world through design. Lastly, appeal can be made to the prayer of the Church, the "Gloria Patri" with which each psalm and many prayers reach their conclusion: "sicut erat in principio, et nunc, et semper, et in saecula saeculorum. Amen." The theological demonstration of the *Système* runs through some of the major *loci theologii* in the manner of the scholastic manuals of the time: Scripture, the Fathers, the approved *orationes* of the Church.[99]

But it is an essay in window-dressing. The theological underpinnings are not in this pastiche of exegetes and patristic authorities. The real theological influence occurred many centuries before the Enlightenment, with the surrender to natural philosophy of the foundations of religion. What had been given away could not be recalled, and it was eventually made to tell against the giver. Lessius had wanted evidence for the fundamental theological assertion which was neither immediately theological nor metaphysical. Descartes and Newton, Malebranche and Clarke had followed that direction insofar as it had denied theology any proper place in the discussion of the existence of god. This ended in the Enlightenment with the combinations and corrections of Cartesian and Newtonian mechanics: "Let us, therefore, content ourselves with saying that matter has always existed; it moves by virtue of its essence; that all the phenomena of Nature is ascribable to the diversified motion of the variety of matter she contains; and which, like the phoenix, is continually regenerating out of her own ashes."[100] The theologians appealed to natural philosophy, now let them live with it!

If d'Holbach's selection makes universal nature the horizon of inquiry; if his logistic method allows this nature to be broken down into heterogenous elements of matter, each with its inherent locomotion; if these actional principles, that always were and always will be, demand that every phenomenon of nature be understood ultimately in terms of distinct kinds of matter, each with its inherent movement; his existential interpretation makes any definition of these principles generically impossible. We do not know matter in itself; we know it only by its effect upon ourselves. These effects are not the *signa quibus* of the scholastics, the alteration of the apperceptive powers of the human person through which the actual subject is related to and knows the actual thing. In scholastic terms, they are the *signa quae*: the things which are actually known are only the alterations of our apperception. The *Système* has taken the method from Newton and the principle from Descartes, but the conclusion sounds remarkably like Montaigne: "We know nothing of the elements of bodies, but we know some of their properties or qualities; and we distinguish their various matters by the effects or changes produced on our senses; that is to say, by the different motions their presence excites in us. . . . Thus, relative to us, matter in general is that which affects our senses, in any manner whatever; the various properties we attribute to matter, are founded on the different impressions we receive, on the changes they produce in us."[101] This allows a modification in the question entertained for centuries on the primary and secondary qualities of matter, a question whose classic treatment began with Galileo. If philosophers want to talk about matter and yet have no idea what "matter in itself" is—if that question is even to be intelligible—then the centuries that made matter of focal interest must find another way of talking about it.

Galileo made a distinction between the use of logic and the use of geometry in the mastery of nature. Logic allows the scientist or philosopher to test the coherence of any argument or demonstration once discovered; but it does not encourage or allow discovery. Geometry, on the other hand, becomes the instrument of discovery and the means of constructing demonstrations. Mathematics, not logic, is the means for the investigation of nature.[102] From this comes the critical distinction between those properties or qualities of matter which are mathematical (number, motion, rest, figure, position, size, contact) and those which are not immediately mathematical but sensible, those which are actually the impressions made upon the perceiving subject, which were called secondary qualities (taste, odor, color, heat, and sound). Make mathematics the truth of nature, and such a distinction is inescapable. The tool for discovery is not indifferently related to what is discovered. It is the condition for the possibility of what is discovered. In *Il Saggiatore* the great Florentine master elaborated this distinction and its occasion and so set in motion a way of thinking that would deeply influence the Enlightenment:

> As soon as I conceive a piece of matter or corporeal substance, I feel myself impelled by necessity to conceive: that in its own nature, it is bounded and figured in such and such a figure; that in relation to others, it

is large or small; that it is in this or that place, in this or that time; that it is in motion or remains at rest; that it touches or does not touch another body; that it is single, few or many. In short, by no imagination can a body be separated from such conditions. But that it must be white or red, bitter or sweet, sounding or mute, of a pleasant or unpleasant odor—I do not perceive my mind forced to acknowledge it necessarily accompanied by such conditions. So if the senses were not the escorts, perhaps the reason or the imagination by itself would never have arrived at them. Hence I think that these tastes, odors, colors, etc., on the side of the object in which they seem to exist, are nothing else than mere names [*puri nomi*], but hold their residence solely in the sensitive body."[103]

Galileo's employment of mathematics as the truth of nature led inevitably to his reading of the human subject out of nature, a spectator whose sensitive interactions with nature distorts its mechanical reality and generates endless illusions.

While Galileo used mathematical imagination and conception as the criteria to distinguish the purely mathematical qualities from those of sensible perception, Descartes employed purely intellectual insight. The *Meditations* offer the commonest example, that of a piece of wax newly taken from the hive. Remark its sweetness, odor, color, shape, and size; note how hard it is, how cold, how it rings upon being struck. Now bring this piece of wax close enough to the fire, and all of these qualities change: the taste and odor vanish, the color changes, and the shape is altered; it melts into a greater size, emits no sound upon being struck, and becomes so hot that it is difficult to handle. Yet it is the same piece of wax. What makes it the same when all of its qualities that could appeal to sense perception or imagination have altered? What remains throughout the change? *Mentis inspectio* finds only something extended, flexible, and movable. The primary qualities are reduced to three: extension as the essential attribute of matter, and figure and movement as its two modes.[104]

Newton's third rule of philosophizing expanded the Cartesian list. The universal qualities of a body, that is, of mass as such, are those which admit neither of intensification nor of remission of degree. The extension and mobility of Cartesian physics are there, but so are hardness, impenetrability, and inertia. The Universal Mechanics, unlike the Universal Mathematics, did not dismiss the evidence of sense perception as inherently doubtful, and registering these universal qualities of mass-objects on the level of phenomena allowed the extrapolation of these wholes of experience to their constituents: "Hence we conclude the least particles of all bodies to be also extended, and hard and impenetrable, and movable, and endowed with their proper inertia. And this is the foundation of all philosophy."[105] Gravitation is also universal to all bodies. They attract one another in proportion to their masses. But gravity is not numbered as one of the primary qualities, because it admits of intensification and remission of degree, but also and more critically because Newton would not admit it to be innate or inherent in matter.

> That gravity should be innate inherent and essential to matter so yt one body may act upon another at a distance through a vacuum wthout the mediation of anything else by and through wch their action or force may be conveyed from one to another is to me so great an absurdity that I believe no man who has in philosophical matters any competent faculty of thinking can ever fall into it. Gravity must be caused by an agent acting constantly according to certain laws, but whether this agent be material or immaterial is a question I have left to the consideration of my readers."[106]

Epicurus and his followers were among those incompetent enough in physics to consider gravity an innate property of matter, and Newton wrote as if their day had passed. But the obituary for this opinion was written somewhat prematurely.

Against this background, the *Système* takes up that to which nature and movement have ultimately been reduced, matter—not what it is, but what its attributes are. Despite the *Système*'s high praise of Newton, the primary properties of body now include precisely what he was at pains to term a philosophic absurdity. "We discover in them [bodies], extent, mobility, divisibility, solidity, gravity, and inert force."[107] Gravity is a property of matter. The merger of motion with matter as the actional principle of universal nature has its correlative expression in the crucial assertion that gravity is an inherent and primary property of matter, primary in contrast with the secondary attributes which result from these primitive characteristics of matter, namely, density, figure, color, weight, and so on. The *Système* corrects both Descartes and Newton in their central and common failure, their understanding of matter as inert and passive. While no satisfactory definition can be given of matter, the natural philosopher "ought to have contemplated it as a *genus* of beings."[108] Whatever is is but an individual material thing. This genus is differentiated into species by the various motions proper to its elements or to their compounds. Gravity insures that contact whereby the movement proper to one element will always intermingle with the actions proper to another. Fire, for example, can excite the sensations of heat and light and communicate them to the iron with which it combines.

All of the phenomena of nature are drawn into interaction by the gravity generically common to them all, and all of the various gradations of nature—mineral, vegetable, and animal—are established by the massive circulation, interchange, and circuit of the elements and particles of matter.

This constant building and decomposing of all things mirrors in the universal nature the philosophic method by which that nature is studied. In the motion of the inquiring mind and in the motion of universal nature, there is the logistic analysis and synthesis of thought and of things, a parallelism made possible by the comprehensive principle of both: matter in endless motion, creating and destroying bodies and propositions about bodies, with the variety of movements resulting from the heterogeneity of the actional elements and their compounds. Gravity makes it possible to reduce all motions to matter, to action and reaction, and to the resulting interactions of various forces: "Such is the invariable course of Nature: such is the eternal circle, which all that exists is obliged to describe. It is thus that motion generates, preserves for a time, and successively destroys one part of the universe by the other; although the sum of existence remains eternally the same."[109] In an analysis which resembles the Newtonian parallelogram of motions and forces, d'Holbach has reduced everything to the properties, generic and specific, of the forms of matter. "We shall find in the formation, in the growth, in the instantaneous life of animals, vegetables and minerals, nothing but matter."[110] As in any analysis to a first principle, the value of this analysis lies with the subsequent synthesis or system that it makes possible.

Nature provides the *Système* with its horizon of conscious focus, its selection which continues the long revolt against Montaigne by taking its categories of terms and its simples of analysis directly from the philosophical or scientific consideration of the nature of things, rather than from the processes of thought or the meaning of statements. Nature also provides the possibility of system because nature is not only the general subject of inquiry, but the comprehensive context of everything. The noetic unity of a system is possible because each thing is itself an assemblage, which is universal nature.

Each of these combinations is a combination of matter. Dynamic heterogeneous matter serves as the fundamental explanation of all nature because, through the movement which is its inescapable mode, it accounts both for the ingredients of each assemblage and for the organization that they are given. System occurs within d'Holbach's philosophic inquiry only because the pattern of his inquiry mirrors in its analysis and synthesis the pattern by which material things themselves are broken down into their elements and recombined into alternative units. Universal nature is the great whole of coordinate parts and causal chains; system is a whole of coordinate propositions whose causal interconnections are traced to matter and the endless concatenations that its motion effects.

System is possible because of the generic principles that constitute nature; system is necessary because of the hidden nature of matter. The existential interpretation of d'Holbach dictates that radical intelligibility comes out of the work of the knowing subject. It is not things that we know, but the manner in which they affect us, that is, their modes and properties. Changes produced in our senses dictate our reading of the world, and the variety in nature is disclosed or asserted because of the variety of motions that these properties and qualities evoke in us. The reaction of the knowing subject endows universal nature with intelligible structure, and this reaction reaches its climax in system. To speak of the "system of nature" is to speak of the final intelligibility of nature—not that one ever analytically reaches a definition of matter, but one does reach a synthetic whole which includes all of the elements of the human experience of nature. System is not the immediate work of analysis; it is the work of synthesis. Synthesis is possible because of the concatenation of nature in causes and effects and, more immediately, the laws of motion. Newton built a cosmos from these laws; d'Holbach builds all of reality, that is, universal nature. And the source of all of this is "nothing but matter."

System results logistically from both kinds of mechanics contained in the *Système*, statics and dynamics. Natural things and the entire universal nature can be broken down into material elements and then reframed synthetically. Complex movements can be analyzed back to the simple motions by which they are initiated and then recombined synthetically. In either case, "we have only to decompose and analyze them, in order to discover those of which they are combined." In moving toward the formulation of a synthesis, "experience teaches us the effects we are to expect. Thus it is clear, the simplest motion causes that necessary junction of different matters of which all bodies are composed: these matters varied in essence, in properties, have each its several modes of action, or motion, peculiar to itself: the whole motion of a body is consequently the sum total of each particular motion that is combined."[111] What the existentialist interpretation does to the logistic method, however, is to insist that the first actional principles or simple motions are in themselves "impenetrable mysteries"; that Newton did not make a statement about the fundamental nature of either, but had to be content to discover "the laws by which heavy bodies fall, by which they communicate to others their peculiar motions."[112] From such a system, in either its analytic or synthetic stage of formulation, one expects the recognition of regularities and the insistence that one remain within the concatenation of natural causes.

As will be explored in much greater detail, the alternative to such a system is religion. Both serious philosophy and religion have a similar origin: inquietude and fear. An unusual effect is noticed; this leaves the mind unsettled. So inquiry begins. Often nothing is learned through sense perception, observation, or experiment. So human beings resort to the imagination:

"This disturbed with alarm, enervated by fear, becomes a suspicious, a fallacious guide."[113] And where does it guide? To religious beliefs. Religious adherence issues from an imagination driven to create gods because it despairs of a natural explanation of the phenomena that terrify it. Belief in the supernatural is a gesture of human despair of the mind's own analytic powers. God is always "of the gaps."

Religion is not disposed of simply by analysis, since in the final moment the nature of causes remains an impenetrable mystery. Religion is destroyed by an alternative synthesis, made possible by the recognition and description of the invariant laws of motion. Nothing in nature justifies the hypothesis that this chain of cause and effect is broken; everything points to its regularity and determination. "In spite of our ignorance of the meanderings of Nature, of the essence of beings, of their properties, their elements, their combinations, their proportions, we yet know the simple and general laws according to which bodies move, and we see clearly, that some of these laws, common to all beings, never contradict themselves."[114] Human beings have often enough seen the mysteries of phenomena resolved into such interactions of natural causes; the rest can be argued to by analogy.

The laws are those of attraction and repulsion, read by d'Holbach as lying at the heart of Newtonian mechanics but reaching back in their earliest formulation to Empedocles' φιλία and νεῖκος as the cosmic principles responsible for union and separation. Physicists term these attraction and repulsion, sympathy and antipathy, or affinities and relations, while moralists speak about human love and hatred or friendship and aversion. But the actional nature of matter discloses that the physical and the moral are really all the same. The motions excited in a human being are more concealed and differ only in this respect from the movements of the elements or of the planets. From matter diversely combined, in proportions varied almost infinitely, all physical and moral bodies result. Thus solids result from the union of homogeneous particles, and families or friendships result from the common attraction of human beings.[115]

As Newton, in d'Holbach's reading, formulated the laws of attraction and repulsion, so did he author the law of self-conservation, which he called inertial force. Self-conservation is the common direction to which all motions are directed, even attraction and repulsion: to attract that which supports and to repel that which is injurious. This law of physics exists in morals, as severely and inevitably as it does in unthinking objects, as the law of self-love. The law of conservation and the primacy of motion allow a redefinition of existence itself in these terms: "To exist, is to experience the motion peculiar to a determinate essence: to preserve this existence, is to give and receive the motions from which results the maintenance of its existence:—it is to attract matters suitable to corroborate its being,—to avoid that by which it may be either endangered or enfeebled."[116]

The universality of matter and the inherent nature of its movement thus allow the laws of motion to become axiomatic of all reality. The axioms which in Aristotle's *Metaphysics* were true of being as being find a parallel in the mechanics of d'Holbach. Motion and matter are true of all reality as such; now, the question is: What is true of motion, what are its laws? They are three: attraction or repulsion, conservation, and necessity.

Necessity exists because there can be no cause that does not produce its correlative effect, and there can be no effect that does not issue from its correlative cause. "Necessity is the constant and infallible connexion of causes with their effects." However hidden the cause or concealed the effect, it is there, for "impulse is always followed by some motion more or less sensible, by some change more or less remarkable in the body which receives it." This irrefragable necessity founds the unbroken chain of cause and effect that constitutes the universe, a whole which has an iron connection with its parts, and parts which connect inexorably with their whole. The universe "is itself but an immense chain of causes and effects, which flow without ceasing one from the other. If we reflect a little, we shall be obliged to acknowledge, that every thing we see is necessary."[117]

Observation may not be able to prove such a law, but examples can clarify how strenuously and how universally it is asserted. Take a whirlwind of dust: a geometer who knew the forces and positions of each particle could demonstrate that what looks so chaotic possesses internal coherence, each part of which is moved only as it must be. Take a revolution that shakes a political society to its foundations: "There is not a single action, a single word, a single thought, a single will, a single passion in the agents, whether they act as destroyers or as victims, that is not necessary; that does not act as of necessity it must act from the peculiar situation these agents occupy in the moral whirlwind." It is all one. The storm that is rising on the Libyan desert is amassing those elements which will alter the modes and the passions of men now living in Paris.[118]

Attraction or repulsion, conservation, and necessity: with these laws, the *Système* can do more than build the physical cosmos of Newton. It can build a cosmos that identifies the physical and moral worlds, nature and culture, through single laws by which everything is to be explained and active, diverse material principles to which everything is to be reduced. According to these laws universal nature is ceaselessly formed and reformed *au grand tout* by causes inevitable in their activity and irresistible in their efficacy. The *énergie générale* of nature is only a consequence of this interaction. The origin of religion lies with the activity of the terrified imagination, separating this *énergie* from the intractable movements of natural necessity and hypostatizing it as an agency distinct in itself. But understand nature either in terms of composition and decomposition of parts and whole, or understand it as mechanical cause and effect; it comes to the same autonomous and necessary whole.

To reach such a system, either of thought or of nature, it is necessary only to generalize the Newtonian method and to diversify Descartes' reflective principles for mechanics into a variety of actional principles which constitute dynamic matter. This system of nature allows a discussion of the origins of religious belief and the validity of theological argument, which will allow d'Holbach's work to present a coherent alternative to religious conviction. The *Système* becomes, quite literally, another world, one that awakens fear and hypnotic fascination with the systematic sweep of its comprehension. As Voltaire wrote to his niece: "Ce livre effraie tout le monde, et tout le monde veut le lire."[119]

Weakness, Ignorance, and Superstition

A system of nature that attempts to replace the patterns of religion must do more than explain nature. It must explain religion as well. It is not enough for such a doctrine to analyze all reality back to dynamic matter and to synthesize the universe into coherence through the laws of motion. The advancement of materialism must include an exploration of what has been either the alternative to science or a critical principle within science until the emergence of this new and autonomous first philosophy. The double sources of the divine existence must be analyzed, namely, the human processes through which religious convictions have arisen and the philosophical arguments by which they have been justified. The *Système* possesses its power not only as it elaborates an internally consistent natural philosophy, but as that doctrine is able to dissolve the mistakes of earlier cultures and previous philosophers. Systematic integrity, then, demands that a double examination take place: first, of the emergence of the idea of the divine within human consciousness; and second, of the argumentation by which this idea was so confidently advanced and made to figure so pivotally in the intellectual inquiries that preceded the late eighteenth century. The system must explain two histories: the evolvement of religious convictions within the general history of human understanding and the progress of this conviction within the intellectual history of science and philosophy. How could human beings, either in their natural operations or in the advancement of their methodological reflections, be so pathologically wrong?

In order to understand the evolvement of the god of religion, it is essential to understand something of the human being that gives religion birth.

Like other organic things, the human person is, to put it bluntly, a machine, an organization of matter generated without either innate ideas or a spiritual soul. A human being is born into the natural world possessing nothing except the aptitude for feeling or sensation (*l'aptitude à sentir*).[120] The human subject progressively admits the world through sensation. Sensations, in their turn, distinguish this world into two massive, sensible categories: that which is agreeable, or coordinate with the human machine; and that which is disagreeable, or painfully disproportionate. The first kind of sensation leaves a human being happy; the second, miserable. Both experiences are inevitable: "A sensible being placed in a nature where every part is in motion, has various feelings [*il sentira diversement*], in consequence of the agreeable or disagreeable effects which he is obliged to experience [*éprover*]." As these experiences occasion happiness or pain, so they evoke love or fear; in these two fundamental desires all movement in human life originates. Love and fear realize in human form the general physical laws of attraction and repulsion. Just as attraction and repulsion explain the generation for all motions and change within the universe, so love and desire explain all human movement and history. The human person's reactions are as thoroughly mechanical as the interaction of the planets, dictated by all of the surrounding objects as putative causes of happiness or pain.[121]

Underlying both love and fear is the pervasive single law of self-conservation. Pain and happiness indicate what will further or hinder self-preservation. The very first impulses (*instans*) within the human subject are dictated by needs (*besoins*) either to assimilate or to reject what is perceived—with this absolute law of conservation acting as criterion. As coordination or disproportion generates love or fear, so those wants or needs that lie at the heart of human existence and urge self-preservation reveal themselves by an internal experience of "disorder, a weakness, an apathy in his machine which gives him the sensation of pain."[122] This pain or restless lack of tranquillity persists and grows in intensity until the cause requisite for its removal comes to reestablish the order appropriate to the human machine. Unsatisfied needs are perceived as a threat to the human persistence in being. The experience of needs is the primordial human experience of evil.

The irony of the human condition is inescapable. "Want or need [*le besoin*] is the first of those evils which a human being experiences, and yet this evil is necessary in order to conserve his being. . . . Without needs or wants, we would be nothing but insensible machines." The human being would exist like vegetable life, incapable both of self-conservation and of acting on the attractions or repulsions which indicate the means for continued life and growth. Human wants transcend nutrition, development, and reproduction. Human needs involve passions, desires, and the play of our bodily and intellectual faculties. "These are our needs, and they force us to think, to wish, and to act. It is to satisfy these, or rather to put an end to the painful sensations that they cause in us, that following our natural sensibility and the energy which is peculiar to us, we exert the forces, either of our body or of our spirit.[123] The equation between human wants and human evil makes evil fundamental to the human machine, essential to its conservation, and at the basis of all human experience and activity. Human history, individual actions as well as the ponderous agencies of empires, results from this primordial experience of evil. The good reveals itself only as a cessation of evil.

Evil also provides the energy behind human inquiry. If nature did not press upon human beings with pain as well as with pleasure, nothing would induce them to search out the causes of the nature in which they found themselves. Nothing would drive them to a life of reflection if basic human experience were of a world luxurious in its riches and utterly satisfying every immediate need. The land of the Lotus-eaters did not produce philosophers. "Méditer est une peine!" Nothing brings human beings to struggle toward a reflective grasp of universal nature except the threat of greater pain. Paradoxically, a life always and immediately pleasant would destroy human life.

But the human being is a driven thing. Love and fear are various ways to escape from evil. Without that whip, the human person would remain "un automate insensible, il ne seroit plus un homme."[124] Pain and fear—these are the mechanical powers urging human beings to inquiry and philosophy. They lie at the basis of all human advancement. Everything is an attempt to escape them. It is critical to note about this doctrine that philosophy does not come out of a native desire to know, as Aristotle asserts at the beginning of his own first philosophy. It issues from a prior and radical attempt to escape the sensibly painful.

Human wants play this prodding part not only in the organic development of the human machine, but in its historically conditioned surroundings. Human life *in concreto* comprises an endless multitude of evils: poverty and epidemics, wars and famine. These in their dreadful turn awaken relentless and abiding fears. Terror drives human beings to search out the causes of these events, to control them, and to restore the harmonies of human existence. The labored, progressive stages of science and philosophy extend these reflective attempts to eliminate fear and pain by regulating human existence and its total context. All of these form in their histories "a long succession of causes and effects, which are nothing more than the development of the first impulse given [humans] by nature."[125] Human progress results from the evils naturally internal to the human machine and historically characteristic of its surroundings.

This development, however, can proceed by different, even contradictory, paths. There is the path of philosophic inquiry: observation, experience, and rational judgment, whose product is knowledge. Human fear disappears when one obtains an understanding of the universal nature in which human beings live. But this way is not always open. Events of cosmic and disastrous consequences continually intervene, implacably oppressing human life, rendering the present unendurably painful and the future ominous. Exacting observation and experience are powerless to alleviate these events, and reason stands impotent to shed light upon them.

There is another way, one conceived in ignorance and chaotic passion and given structure and direction by the imagination. Human beings can fashion a powerful, personal agency, either identified with the elements of nature or behind them. They can endow this agency with angry, but approachable, characteristics. They can then use means analogous to those of human relationships to entreat and placate it. "Making an analogy between [this agency] and those terrific objects with whom he is already acquainted, he suggests to himself the means he usually takes to mitigate their anger; he employs similar measures to soften the anger and to disarm the power of the concealed cause which gives birth to his inquietudes, and alarms his fears. It is thus his weakness, aided by ignorance, renders him superstitious."[126] The introduction of the divine or the supernatural can be explained by the same laws of attraction or repulsion and of self-conservation, and the movement from ignorance through need and fear to an imaginative construct can be traced in the same mechanical way as the career of the planets. This is the aboriginal source of the first notion of god and of the enthusiastic or frantic practices of religion. Even today, the *Système* notes, when disasters or catastrophes force upon human beings the recognition of their ignorance and deepen the experience of their terror, gods are adapted, returned to favor, or created anew. The cradle of religion is ignorance and terror, and the model on which the imagination fashions its creations is the human person writ large. Once fashioned, this chimerical agent is open to prayers and sacrifices, appeals of penitence and self-denial, which will disarm his anger and control the outrages of nature. Religion is the magical way of controlling the causes of human tragedy.[127]

The history of religions follows in its development those agencies that human beings have deified. Initially, they conferred this honor on the elements and natures themselves. Everything in universal nature became the object of reverence and worship, as it had earlier preempted the attention of fear. The second stage consisted in a logistic subtraction: the agents were differentiated from the material natures themselves. They became the genii or the heroes or the pluralistic gods behind the phenomena. The last stage coalesced all of these gods into one, adding all of their attributes into the single god and further subtracting this one from the various natural things which were his tutelary origin. "By dint of reflection, the human person believed that one simplified the thing in submitting the entire of nature to a single agent—to a sovereign intelligence—to a spirit—to a universal soul, which put this nature and its parts in motion."[128]

D'Holbach's analysis of religious development parallels the stages that Freud outlines a hundred years later in *The Future of an Illusion*, which he terms animism, polytheism, and monotheism. As in Freud, the energy behind religious assertion is a mixture of fear and magic. However, its contours are not taken from the model of the father figure nor its aboriginal experience from an early oedipal event. In d'Holbach, the parallels used by the imagination are taken from the human person himself as a model, more precisely from the division between the powerful and the weak; the generating experiences are those of want, fear, and personal despair. In both d'Holbach and Freud, religion is a product of ignorance, a substitute for science, ultimately to be destroyed by the advance of enlightened, scientific thinking.[129] This analysis of religion and of its future gives the *Système* not only a theoretic motivation for its inquiry, but a practical one as well. It is an effort not just of speculation but of exorcism, not merely atheistic but antitheistic as well: "If the ignorance of nature gave birth to the Gods, the knowledge of nature is calculated to destroy them."[130]

This hopeful return to nature is not a contradiction of the origins of religion, but a basic and more accurate recovery of its originating experience: the observation of nature. There was something profoundly true in the initial divinization of the elements. The savage and the nations as yet uncivilized did not suppose that the events that happen around human beings had some cause other than themselves. They did not look to transcendence in order to explain what was immanent in their experience. This kind of human being "never wandered to seek out of visible nature the source either of what happened to himself, or of those phenomena to which he was a witness. As he everywhere saw only material effects, he attributed them to causes of the same genus." Not only did these primitive peoples possess a generic truth in the absence of transcendence, but they were basically right about the source of material movement: "It was natural for them to believe that those beings they saw move of themselves, acted by their own peculiar energies."[131] The fatal error came when these peculiar energies were personalized.

There is no need in d'Holbach's analysis to recreate the aboriginal state of human beings. There are several reasonable hypotheses about such a state. Human beings may have always been on this earth, "but at different periods they may have been nearly annihilated, together with their monuments, their sciences, and their arts; those who outlived these periodical revolutions, each time formed a new race of human beings." Alternative possibilities are that the larger animals were originally derived from the smaller microscopic ones, or that human beings were originally hermaphrodites who produced sexual differentiation after some generations.[132] One can allow any of these perspectives, an epochal history, a myth of the eternal return, or an evolutionary history in which forms emerge as the organization of matter becomes more complicated. It makes no difference because "it is extremely easy to recur to the origin of many existing nations: we shall find them always in the savage state; that is to say, composed of wandering hordes."[133] The perspective taken on the question of whether human beings have always existed on this earth or were produced by nature only recently does not alter the question of the origins of religion. Why not? Because d'Holbach merges the distinction between the prehistoric and the primitive; one is the same as the other. Even today, human beings have enough data on the origins of religion among the primitives.

Primitive human beings existed in "wandering hordes" until called into a stable society, that is, until collected together "at the voice of some missionary or legislator, from whom they received benefits, who gave them Gods, opinions, and laws." What France saw in the New World among the savages of North and South America is paradigmatic of the action and influence of Bacchus and Orpheus, of Moses and Numa Pompilius. To the societies they formed, they gave instruction in agriculture and jurisprudence and indoctrination in religion. Their command of natural observation gave them skills which the savages respected, bending them to confidence in their judgments, and as these primitive peoples found their inventions useful, so they hoped to profit from their religious calendars, their cultic institutions, and their hierarchical guidance, whether these developed a natural animism, an abundant polytheism, or a subtle, even metaphysical, monotheism. The guides, whether priests or monarchs or both, possessed the leisure to observe nature and to cull from this observation a knowledge which made them "masters of these infant societies." This very inchoate natural philosophy was combined with poetry to form such religious beliefs as these nations possessed. Both spoke to the imagination of the savage and drew him into civilization. "Thus, the entire of nature, as well as all its parts, was personified."[134]

Nature, which had given such power to individual leaders, was worshiped in a manner appropriate to the development of its devotees. The wise worshiped universal nature, the great whole, the macrocosm which included each individual thing as a part. The ignorant adored each of the factors: winds under the name of Juno, time which devours all things under the name of Saturn, the sun as Apollo. "The igneous matter, the ethereal electric fluid, that invisible fire which vivifies nature, that penetrates all beings, that fertilizes the earth, which is the great principle of motion, the source of heat, was deified under the name of Jupiter." Each element, each natural thing of passionate force, was personified and its divinity recognized in worship. So mythology was "the daughter of natural philosophy, embellished by poetry, and only destined to describe nature and its parts."[135]

As religion progressed, it insisted upon mysteries, to cover its own ignorance, and upon obedience to its power. Personification was succeeded by a polytheism marked by political interests, frenetic imagination, and fraud. Finally, monotheism came. Natures had been the first gods; then the gods moved above nature; then the god gained in his simplicity the attributes of all, but at the expense of irreconcilable contradiction. During this elaborate process "natural philosophers and poets were transformed by leisure and by vain researches into metaphysicians and theologians."[136]

In each stage of religious progression, d'Holbach's existential interpretation tells. Human beings, as Feuerbach later insists, were worshiping nothing but themselves. They had added human consciousness to the elements of nature; they then added human personalities and individuation to separate the gods from these elements and natural things; then, they did "nothing more than make a gigantic, exaggerated man, whom they will render illusory by dint of heaping together incompatible qualities. Human beings will never see in God, but a being of the human species, in whom they will strive to aggrandize the proportions, until they have formed a being totally inconceivable."[137] Human beings cannot get beyond the human perspective unless they allow this perspective to be purified by submission to nature and by the higher perspective of the resulting philosophic system. Monotheism is so filled with self-contradicting assertions about god that, although it seems to be religion in its triumph over nature, it is the last stage before its dissolution. The projection of the human person by the imagination in an endlessly exaggerated manner introduces not only the personal god, but the personal god whose central mark is infinity. The god of monotheism possesses all the human qualities, but possesses them infinitely: infinite power, infinite goodness, infinite wisdom, and even the infinite time which is called eternity. By the use of infinity, the theologians hope to overcome the contradictions that lie within the assertion of the one god. Infinity for the theologians makes of god a comprehensive principle of all that is, and the contrast between the infinite and the finite allows them both to assert the incomprehensibility of god and to free their statements from the criteria of the clear and distinct. Thus theology obtains the point of persuading the human being that one must believe that which cannot be conceived. "It had made mortals implicitly believe that they were not formed to comprehend the thing of all others the most important to themselves."[138] Infinity actually introduces the irresolvable contradiction between the metaphysical and the moral attributes of god. At the height of religious evolution religion perishes at its own hand.

The progress of religion was a successive personalization of the causes of natural events, whether ordinary or marvelous. The theological god comes at the end of this process, as mythology gives way to metaphysics. But the metaphysical attributes of god are "nothing but pure negations of the qualities found in the human person, or in those beings of which one has knowledge."[139] Theology finds itself denying the very things that religious history labored to establish. Infinity, for example, does not mean that reality is found in its completion in the divine essence; it means that, unlike anything human, god is not circumscribed or hemmed in by space or by anything human beings know. The combination of these metaphysical (negative) qualities with the moral (religious) qualities is to square the circle. The metaphysical attributes place god beyond all understanding, an inexplicable chimera; the moral attributes make him accessible to human beings, like them by analogy and available to prayer and worship. Theologians attempt to remove this contradiction by asserting the moral qualities, purified by the metaphysical, as "eminently" possessed by god, "although they every moment contradicted each other."[140]

Take, for example, the attribute "goodness." Theologians call god "good," and human beings have some idea what is contained in that predicate. Then realize that this god is also omnipotent. Try to combine these two predicates in the face of human pain, the desolation of war, the destruction of earthquakes and disease. It makes no sense to say that this omnipotent god is good in an "eminent way." If he is omnipotent, then god is "sporting with his creatures." If he is good, then all of the metaphysical attributes fall away and god is left as helpless before calamity as human beings. But the combination makes no sense. What is more, while this "feeble monarch" explains nothing, nature moving itself by necessity explains evil and good with equal facility. The goodness of an omnipotent god is contradicted at every turn of human history; the necessity of an impersonal nature is confirmed both by human happiness and by human destruction. The only god that theologians can elaborate is riddled with such contradictions.[141]

The metaphysical contradicts the moral. This contradiction is resolved not by some transcendent way of "eminence" but by a system of nature that reduces the moral itself to the physical. The distinction so long drawn between the physical and moral is shown to be radically false. The human being "is a being purely physical: the moral human being is nothing more than this physical being considered under a certain point of view, that is to say, with relation to some of his modes of action, arising out of his particular organization. But is not this organization itself the work of Nature?"[142] So also for the causes of the movement of natures and the happiness of human beings. Nothing is gained by making these causes ultimately moral; everything is explained if these causes are the active units of an exhaustive, dynamic matter.

The logistic addition of personality to nature and the amalgamation of these personalities into a single personality introduce an internal contradiction so profound that nothing can save it but the recognition that personality itself is a product of impersonal nature. Religion cannot return to the mythologies of polytheism. Theology was a necessary development, but theology involves its own contradiction. In that contradiction, philosophers can find the confirmation of the universal materialism which the previous analysis of nature, matter, and motion disclosed, and which the subsequent synthesis by the laws of motion drew into a system. Now into this synthesis or system religion itself easily fits, for "in whatever manner we view the theological system, it destroys itself."[143] The weakness and terror of human beings gave rein to the steady advance of religious consciousness, situated in ignorance and directed by the imagination; this process, like any extended illusion, eventually comes up against the contradictions implicit from its beginning. Superstition reaches levels of self-disclosure in theology that cannot be disguised. It is one of the glories of the Enlightenment that it brings the human to this moment of a revolutionary change in perspective, when human beings can finally "fall back on experience, and natural philosophy."[144]

This is as glorious in its promise as in its rhetoric. But what can one say about those who also took a rational view, whose inquiries did not refuse "experience and natural philosophy," but in fact advanced the scientific understanding of nature far more impressively and influentially than d'Holbach or Naigeon or even Diderot? What is to be said for them and their persistence in finding god at the beginning or at the end of their labors? This question turns the *Système* to the second part of its confirmation, from a consideration of the emergence of religious consciousness to an evaluation of religious philosophies. D'Holbach's materialism had to explain the human processes through which religious convictions arose. It did so both in terms of their origin and in terms of the logical resolution of their inescapable contradiction in materialism. Now he must turn to those philosophies that have mounted the attacks against atheism. It is time to show that the *Système* justifies what is true in their evidence, corrects their errors in physics about matter and motion, and gives their meditations, dialogues, systems, and even sermons a realization in universal nature.

"Nouveaux champions de la divinité"

Voltaire had celebrated Samuel Clarke as the clearest and most profound among those philosophers who had attempted a natural theology.[145] D'Holbach recognized that Clarke's *Demonstration of the Being and Attributes of God* "passe pour en avoir parlé de la façon la plus convaincante," and that those

who followed Clarke had been content to repeat what his twelve propositions had already established as evidence and as argument.[146] The *Système*,
however, took Clarke's structure less as a challenge than as an opportunity.
Both Clarke and d'Holbach employ a logistic method, which allows an easy
transfer of reflective patterns from one to the other. But Clarke is found to
be wrong in his interpretation of the data with which he works and even
more in the principle by which his demonstration is grounded. Clarke, like
Newton before him, gives an entitative interpretation to reality, distinguishing sharply between the phenomena and the real that lies beneath, while
d'Holbach's interpretation is existential, distinguishing not between the
apparent and the real but between various appearances or perspectives.
Twice Clarke argues analytically to god as a reflexive principle, that is, a
principle which is self-existent and self-conscious. D'Holbach corrects this
by making matter generically comprehensive, but composed of active and
divergent fundamental units which are radically responsible for all that is
and acts. Make universal matter so diverse and so dynamic, and refuse to
distinguish between levels of reality, and the total materialism of d'Holbach is
inevitable. Clarke's demonstration offers a logistic structure by which this
reinterpretation and analysis can be verified. The twelve propositions become a method of exhibiting the universality of the material principles.

Clarke's first three theorems demonstrate three successive predicates
about reality. There is a being that is (1) eternal, (2) immutable and independent, and (3) self-existent or necessary. D'Holbach concurs in these attributes, but counters that they inhere in nature or matter. Clarke is right about
his predicates; he is wrong about their subject.

Matter is eternal; only its various organizations are evanescent. Experience indicates that everything in universal nature is material; the first volume
of the *Système* analyzes that experience and justifies this interpretation.
Matter is the generic common denominator of that which is. If matter exists
now, it must have always existed. "Ce qui existe, ne suppose-t-il point, dès
lors même, que l'existence lui est essentielle?" "That which exists," for
millennia the name of god, belongs better to matter, something that human
beings experience daily and know from causal argumentation must always
have existed. Furthermore, one cannot annihilate matter; one can only
change its forms. Now that which cannot be annihilated not only exists, it
exists necessarily. It cannot not be. Unlike Clarke, d'Holbach can move
immediately to infer the necessity of the eternal being, and do so from an
experiential awareness that matter is never destroyed. Human experience, or
the perspectives that come from it, delivers two facts: matter is the genus of
everything that exists; matter is never annihilated. From the first, one can
infer that matter has always existed; from the second, that matter always will
exist. From both, one can infer that matter is necessary. This reverses

Clarke's order of inference. That matter is necessary, that is, indestructible, becomes the ground for asserting that it is eternal.

Immutability and independence are ambiguous predicates, but they amplify the sense of the necessary. Matter is necessary not only in its existence (indestructible), but in its movements and activity (independent). "Nature is obliged to act in the manner set by her essence; everything which takes place in her is necessary." Matter is immutable in the sense that it cannot become something else; it changes only its forms; it necessarily is what it is. Matter is independent in the sense that it is and acts independently of the influence of anything else. It dictates what is to be; it is not dictated to. Since it acts with this unhindered necessity, each thing cannot be other than it is. What happens happens inevitably and necessarily. The second proposition of Clarke, then, is made to become a statement as much about all natural things as about matter, for matter enters determinately into their constitution. Immutability can be predicated not only of matter but also of universal nature, predicated quantitatively. Universal nature maintains itself as a whole by its interior movements and mutual causality. The sum of the fundamental elements that act in it is always the same. "Nature is not more to be accused of mutability, on account of the succession of its forms, than the eternal being is by the theologians, by the diversity of his decrees."

The analytic movement by which Clarke discloses the necessary, self-existent being has actually confirmed eternal and necessary dynamic matter. "Ainsi nous dirons à Mr. Clarke que c'est la matière, que c'est la nature agissante par sa propre énergie, dont aucune partie n'est jamais dans un repos absolu, qui a toujours existé."[147]

From his third proposition, Clarke moves to engage the materialist. A corollary of this proposition is that the material universe cannot be this necessary being. Something exists with "absolute necessity" whose nonexistence would be a contradiction in terms and impossible to conceive. Neither in its various forms nor in its atomic elements is this the case with matter. One can imagine it in a thousand different ways. Furthermore, the Newtonian vacuum indicates that matter can either be or not be, that it depends upon something else for the resolution of its ambivalence in existence. In d'Holbach's translation, this definition makes the whole demonstration *a priori*, equivalent to the procedures of the ontological proof and of the same invalidity. This *a priori* method was rejected even by the major theologians of the Middle Ages and "by the greater part of the moderns, with the exception of Suarez." Such an evaluation allows the *Système* to dismiss all the arguments against its principle drawn from the Newtonian analysis of matter. The statements about mass are not necessarily false. Rather, the middle term of the inference, the definition of the necessary being, is hopelessly *a priori*.[148]

The synthesis that Clarke formulates with the self-existent being as principle, that is, the demonstration of its attributes, is equally susceptible to a materialistic interpretation. Like Clarke's god, the essence of matter is "incomprehensible, or at least, we conceive it very feebly by the manner in which we are affected by it." Human beings know their own perceptions and the mode of change within them, and they gauge the particular natures of various things by what they effect within the human person. "When a being does not act upon any part of our organic structure, it does not exist for us." For both Clarke and d'Holbach, the ultimate reality is incomprehensible: for Clarke, because what really exists lies beneath the epiphenomena of its appearances and attributes; for d'Holbach, because human beings cannot get beyond their own perspectives.[149]

Each of the synthetic and metaphysical predicates of Clarke's god receives a similar transformation. Infinite, omnipresent, and one: each broadens the description of matter. Matter cannot be limited by anything outside itself, for there is nothing outside itself, and it stands, in this negative sense, as infinite. Matter, and only matter, can be omnipresent, because to penetrate all things presupposes extension, and extension is a mark of matter. Matter is one in the sense of being unique, because there is nothing beyond or outside it.[150]

The second series of Clarke's analysis-synthesis investigations, propositions eight to twelve, moves toward the establishment of god as intelligent and volitional, and from these deduces his power, wisdom, and moral goodness. In assigning intelligence to the necessary being, one projects human qualities into it instead of dynamic energies into matter. Cognition reveals that thinking results from ideas, ideas result from sensation, and sensation presupposes matter. Matter as the necessary being "produces animated beings, contains, includes, and produces intelligence." Nature is not intelligent like a human being, but it ceaselessly composes those organizations which do think, just as the earth spontaneously generates worms without itself being a living thing. All the *a posteriori* indications of a superior intelligence are contradicted by the evil in the universe and rendered otiose by dynamic, growing matter.[151]

Human freedom in the *Système* is both positive and negative: positive, insofar as human beings find within themselves motives that determine their wills to action (*motifs qui le déterminent à l'action*); negative, insofar as no obstacles inhibit the will from putting into practice that which has been dictated by its motives. There is no question here of a self-determination or of a prior indeterminacy before a series of motivations. Freedom is interior determination by motives and the unhampered external realization of this determination. It is a logistic freedom, one that begins with the necessity of the interior cause, the motive, and finds its realization in the external world because nothing interferes with the chain of cause and effect until it has reached completion. Freedom is as much a statement about the external world as it is about the interior determination. This makes Clarke's assertion of the freedom of god patently fallacious. The existence of evil indicates that god does not possess that kind of unimpeded accomplishment. If the chain of causality stretched from the determinations of the divine nature to the unimpeded realization of the divine will in the world, how could one possibly explain evil and sin? The contradiction within divine freedom is evident: "Either he wants evil to cease or he cannot prevent it: In this latter case, he is not free, and the will meets with continual obstacles; or else we must say, he consents to the commission of sin . . . he suffers human beings to restrain his liberty and derange his projects. How will the theologians draw themselves out of this perplexing intricacy?"

Predicate this freedom of active units of matter, however, and all contradictions cease. The movements of matter have nothing external that determines them. All movements are necessary, but none of them lack freedom, for they proceed from the inner directions of matter and encounter no resistance external to it. The material elements are the actional principles of all that is. The two central, personal attributes of Clarke's god involve irresolvable contradictions when predicated of this chimera; they make perfectly good sense when understood of self-determining and productive matter. The reflexivity defended in the first analytic movement, the necessity of the self-existent being, is now seconded by the reflexivity of the self-determination and inexorable external freedom of matter.[152]

The synthetic demonstration of other personal or moral attributes of Clarke's god continues to entangle his natural theology in implacable contradiction. A divine infinite power could and would have dictated that human beings could not act against it, could not sin—but sin is the bread and butter of religious discourse! A divine infinite wisdom could and would have insured that god's plans for the universe be fulfilled, but both sin and the wretchedness of so many human lives gives this the lie—or else end with a monstrous god. Divine moral perfection is contradicted by the radical defects in his works and in his government, and by the metaphysical attributes which isolate him in his impassibility from all relations with the creatures he has supposedly made. "The more we consider the theological God, the more impossible and contradictory will he appear; theology seems only to have formed him, immediately to destroy him."[153] D'Holbach is not maintaining a theological version of Gödel's theorem; he is not asserting that any comprehensive logistic scheme ends in contradiction. His conclusion is more modest and more radical. Take the god of Christianity—or any similar god, for that matter; reason rigorously, with a consistency that resembles a mathematical addition of each new proposition to what has been established before. With the reasoning that is valid, one obtains eternal, dynamic matter; if one insists upon sustaining the Christian god, one obtains hopeless and irreconcilable contradiction, "and *infinite nothing*, since the idea of this Divinity is the *absolute negation of all ideas*."[154] The fatal flaw is ultimately a mistake in physics. "Doctor Clarke, as well as all other theologians, found the existence of their God upon the necessity of a power that may have the ability to begin motion. But if matter has always existed, it has always had motion, which as we have proved, is as essential to it as extent, and flows from its primitive properties."[155] Clarke's twelve theorems, rigorously analyzed and properly interpreted, come to nothing more than a clarification of the fundamental contribution of Toland, Diderot, and d'Holbach: motion is as essential to matter as extension.

The twelve propositions of Samuel Clarke allow full play to the principles of *Le Système de la nature*, units of dynamic matter as the ultimate explanation of all things. But if Clarke's Boyle lectures provide this schema for the exhibition of an actional principle, the initial argument of Leonard Lessius serves as a foil for the existential interpretation. D'Holbach does not mention Lessius. There is no need for such a reference. The argument from the universality of the conviction that the divine exists, which appears first in *De providentia numinis*, was classic in the history of natural theology and figures, for example, in three different manners in Cicero's *De natura deorum*.[156] Lessius merely supplements it with additional evidence. Consent was found to be even more universal than previously imagined as European explorations discovered the New World and made tentative contacts with Japan and China, as well as extending their knowledge of India and the Spice Islands. Everywhere and in every people was the conviction that a divine reality governed the material and spiritual universe.

If Lessius took up the argument from Cicero's Balbus, d'Holbach's existentialist interpretation makes him sound like a latter-day Cotta. Lessius had placed this argument before all others in his register, and d'Holbach agrees that "the unanimity of human beings in acknowledging a god has been commonly accepted as the strongest proof of the existence of that being."[157] But an examination of the god acknowledged and of the universality with which he is acknowledged discloses how fraudulent such evidence is. Lessius cited Balbus to the effect that universal consent indicates that nature—in the translation now of d'Holbach—"a pris soin de graver la notion dans l'esprit de tous les hommes."[158] From the Stoics to Descartes, this universality supported an innate idea of god, but this conviction only took its shape because they failed to note how culturally conditioned and perspectivally dependent every notion of god was. If the idea were innate, its essential contours would be prior to historic experience and not show the differences that come from divergent experiences and persuasions. That is not the case.

A survey of its variations in different times and civilizations does more than eliminate any persuasion that the idea of god is innate. The correlation between culture and religion indicates that "each made himself a God after his own manner. . . . Thus the God of one human being, or of one nation, was hardly ever that of another." The notion of god is not only acquired; it is a human creation that bears the mark of its creator. Any universality divinity has in the beliefs of human beings simply manifests the common human experiences of terror and dread and the attempt of the victims to imagine some means of escape. "The theological God, although incomprehensible, is the last effort of the human imagination."[159] The theologians have worked out a theology because they have no need to labor like other human beings. "Theology, although a science so much vaunted, considered so important to the interests of people, is only useful to those who live at the expense of others; or of those who arrogate to themselves the privilege of thinking for all those who labor."[160] What looks as if it were a progressive refinement of perspective is actually the fixation of human projections by a parasitic class for its own advantage. Their leisure has alienated them from the world as well as from the work of human beings, and the cultural effect of the perspective of this alienated class is this self-contradictory god.

Granted that god is perspectivally determined, what can one say about the universality of the conviction that there is a divinity that governs human life? First, such a universal belief proves nothing. Other general beliefs have given way before more adequate hypotheses for the interpretation of reality. We have recently seen an obvious and universal belief in the geocentric universe yield before the more adequate explanation of the heliocentric universe of Copernicus and Galileo. Second, it claims more universality than history will allow: "There have been many intelligent human beings who have said, there is no god."[161] There is no need to list the classic atheists. They have been cited everywhere, and those of d'Holbach's time will swell their ranks. But the point is not that there is one here or there, but that they are "many" and that they are "*sensés*." Ignorance and superstition has a way of limiting their numbers, and political fear has a way of muting their voices. But they are there, and they give the lie to this unbroken universality claimed so often by the apologists.

The god of Clarke proceeds from a radical failure in principle; the god of universal consent, from a parallel neglect of cultural differences and interpretations. The weakest of all the theologians' retorts is an attack on d'Holbach's method. "They will, without doubt, tell us, that God has made himself known by revelation."[162] Their greatest champion and their most persuasive evidence having been defeated, the theologians fall back upon the claim that they alone make. Theological statements have their basis, not in evidence open to all, but in a revelation proffered to some and received in faith. Theology has its own methodological autonomy. D'Holbach counters this with its history. From Lessius to Clarke, theologians habitually set revelation aside as inappropriate to a discussion that must range over a wider, more common field. The discussion of revelation and the figure of Christ had no place in their works on atheism. They made it an issue of natural philosophy as metaphysics; and as metaphysics gradually lost its adherents, natural philosophy became physics. This shift in disciplines was an effort to deal with persons who "must be supposed not to believe any Revelation, nor acknowledge any Authority which they will submit to, but only the bare force of Reasoning."[163] Consequently, any discussion of the person, teaching, or witness of Christ was ruled out in these efforts to demonstrate "the First Foundations of Religion."[164] D'Holbach's reply, then, is quite in keeping with the problematic and the method, which have been set for centuries: "But does not this revelation suppose the existence of the God we dispute?"[165] If the theological champions have found revelation insufficient for their purposes and have relied rather upon the physical universe as the foundation of religious assent, then they cannot recall their intellectual commitments when the battle seems lost, when the paradoxes in nature for which they summoned up the figure of god are more easily satisfied by a new concept of matter.

Lessius deliberately chose a form of natural philosophy that skirted metaphysics as too obscure, and Clarke selected a line of reasoning that incorporated Newtonian mechanics, but there was another tradition which was not so squeamish about first philosophy, which had revolutionized metaphysics in order to make it more serviceable both to physics and to the demonstration of the existence of god. Here one finds Descartes and his great theologian, Malebranche. They also fail profoundly in the tasks they have set themselves, for "the most sublime geniuses have been obliged to run aground against this rock."[166]

Descartes, "le restaurateur de la philosphie parmi nous," fielded his major argument, not with the classic ontological proof of the fifth meditation, but with the initial *a posteriori* demonstration of the third meditation. True, the *Meditations* proposed three proofs of the divine existence. The *a priori* character of the argument from definition has already lost any right to serious mention, however, and the second argument can be reduced to the first. This second argument is based upon the existence of the thinking subject. But existence itself never poses a serious datum for the *Système*. One never argues from existence. Existence is not a proper subject for natural philosophy, as are nature or matter, motion, and their attendant modifications. But ideas are data for the *Système* because what human beings know about nature is determined by the manner in which they are affected. Ideas are perspectives on nature. Natural philosophy, then, can deal with the content of ideas and their implications. From this content the third meditation first infers the existence of god: "Il faut nécessairement conclure que de cela seul que j'existe, et que l'idée d'un être souverainement parfait (c'est à dire de Dieu) est en moi, l'existence de Dieu est très évidenment démonstrée."[167] But d'Holbach finds Descartes patently wrong about both the use and the character of his evidence.

One cannot infer the existence of a referent from the existence of its idea. No idea stands as warrant for its extramental reality, and Descartes is mistaken in his use of such a reflexive principle, one that would be its own proof. The idea of a hippogriff guarantees nothing about its existence in nature.

Descartes also errs about the content of this idea of god. There is no positive meaning in the term. Material beings cannot even imagine spirit, a substance without matter, mass, or extension. The very "hautes perfections" from which Descartes argues are equally devoid of any real content: perfection, infinity, and immensity are easily disclosed as empty or self-contradictory. The titles of some Descartes' greatest works, *Meditations on First Philosophy* and *The Principles of Philosophy*, ring ironically at this point. His reflexive principle is basically misguided, for no idea can deliver its own referent, and his first philosophy allows an illegitimate and inappropriate meaning to sterile concepts actually barren of content.

But the active material principles of d'Holbach can be derived by following Descartes' reasoning more consistently than the Cartesians have done. For Descartes is not only wrong about his principle, but inconsistent in his conclusions. All the thought and perfections of his god depend upon a subject of which they are predicated. What is this subject? God is a power that applies itself successively to the parts of the universe. God, then, is by his very nature extended throughout universal nature. But, and this is the crucial twist, the divine nature does not possess any extension in itself; it depends upon nature in order to be extended: "God cannot be said to be extended except in the sense: as we say of the fire contained in a piece of iron which has no other extension, properly speaking, than that of the iron itself." This gives the game away. God must be everywhere, but his presence is derivative—it depends upon universal nature. Descartes' god depends upon nature in order to be god. What is in itself successively present throughout everything is nature or matter.

In 1663 the Roman Curia had placed the works of Descartes on the index "donec corrigantur" because—among other reasons—his doctrine of extension led logically to a denial of transubstantiation. The *Système* urges that the same doctrine of extension leads logically to atheism. It needs only Spinoza to take the next step and maintain that "there is no God other than nature." This, in its turn, needs only the *Système* to take the final step: there is no nature but generic matter and its individual or essential organizations.

"We might, then, with great reason, accuse Descartes of atheism, seeing that he destroys in a very effectual manner, the feeble proofs which he gives of the existence of a God." The first of the modern philosophers has provided reflections whose logical terminus is with d'Holbach! While Clarke formulated a structure that discloses the pervasive presence of matter, Descartes provided the dynamism that proves this matter to be inevitable.[168]

The faithful Malebranche contributes to this dynamic. If Descartes is fundamentally wrong in his principle, Malebranche seems mad in his interpretation of reality. The classic doctrines of Malebranche—that human beings see everything in god, that they cannot be affected by natural things but only by god on the occasion of a change in the external world, and that they can only know this external world by faith—make sense to d'Holbach only by being assimilated into Spinoza. They are "the principles of the celebrated Father Malebranche, which, if considered with the slightest attention, appear to conduct us directly to Spinosism." But in the ninth dialogue of his *Dialogues on Metaphysics and on Religion*, Malebranche had been at great pains to distinguish his position from Spinoza's. Spinoza was represented by Aristes and the assertion to be refuted by Theodore was: "We are, but we are not made. Our nature is eternal. We are a necessary emanation from the Divine."[169] The proposition made to represent Malebranche's theology in d'Holbach is: "The universe is only an emanation from God." D'Holbach introduces this with the comment: "What indeed could be more conformable to the language of Spinoza." But "emanation" has classically been used for creation in Catholic theology.[170] Only by transposing Malebranche's god into the universal nature proposed by the *Système* can one come up with Spinoza.

Nevertheless, this transposition remains the only way that the *Système* can make sense of Malebranche. It makes sense to say that everything is an emanation of nature, that we see everything in nature, that all that we see is only nature, and so on. The comprehensive principle of Malebranche is not at fault; in fact, it is generically true. Malebranche's ontological interpretation is radically misleading. Everything, for Malebranche, is ultimately real in the transcendent realm; it is the phenomenal that one has to prove or accept on faith. This is totally the reverse of the truth for d'Holbach: the only reality is the phenomenal universe as given to human beings through experience and reason; the transcendent is chimerical. Malebranche thinks that the first thing known is god; d'Holbach thinks that the first thing known is nature. Malebranche maintains that one must take the existence of the physical universe on faith; d'Holbach, that the physical universe is the only thing that one does know. If one defines god as the creator of heaven and earth, as Malebranche certainly did, and then say with Malebranche that one must accept on faith that there is a heaven and an earth, d'Holbach can only retort that it is just the opposite. Everyone agrees that god's existence must first be known through reason before one can believe anything: "After these notions [of the creator of a material universe], it is evident, that according to Father Malebranche, human beings have only their faith to guaranty the existence of God; but faith itself supposes this existence; if it be not certain that God exists, how shall we be persuaded that we must believe what he is reported to say?"

If some of Malebranche's mystical theology needs to be shifted into natural philosophy in order to be salvaged, nothing can be done with the remainder. It destroys itself. What is left between occasionalism and human liberty but contradiction? If god does everything to human thought that creatures are believed to do, what is there but utter determination and fictitious choices? God does everything; creatures are ultimately passive. The only thing real and really effective is this transcendence. What shall one say, then, about either virtue or sin, about merit or blameworthy actions? The contradictions seen in Clarke are even more manifest in Malebranche. His ontological interpretation highlights what has been the history of theology: "This is what annihilates all religion. It is thus that theology is perpetually occupied with destroying itself."[171] Metaphysics, whether as first philosophy or integrated into theology, makes very little sense. One does not have to look beyond theology's own inner incoherence for its annihilation.

There is one figure, however, who cannot be dismissed in a few paragraphs. Towering over anything that French philosophy or theology had fashioned stood the peerless *Principia mathematica philosphiae naturalis*, whose influence dominated the scientific direction of the century and whose own structure realized the promise that universal mechanics offered. Just as Clarke was the greatest of the theologians, so Newton was the greatest of the natural philosophers. Descartes had introduced modern philosophy, Malebranche was "célèbre," but Newton was "l'immortel Newton." Nothing rivaled his inquiries into nature and its laws. No one could claim parity with his leadership in natural philosophy. Newton employed a logistic method that d'Holbach himself imitated, breaking all movements down into their composing motions and tracing these effects back to their originating forces.

D'Holbach recognized Newton as a "man whose extensive genius has unravelled nature and its laws." But even so great a philosopher became "a slave to the prejudices of his infancy" as soon as he left the phenomenal world. Newton's massive blunder lay in his interpretation of reality, his insistence upon distinguishing the apparent from the real. As long as the *Principia* stayed with phenomena, his work was faultless; but when his physics moved to an ontic level that eventually involved theology, the same method and principle produced opinions that were puerile. Newton's interpretation was a fundamental failure in inquiry, a refusal to submit religious foundations to the same enlightened investigation to which he subjected nature: "In short, the sublime Newton is no more than an infant, when he quits physics and evidence to lose himself in the imaginary regions of theology." Nevertheless, no matter how childish Newton's theological attempts, they are Newton's—and they must be reckoned with. Unlike Descartes and Malebranche, these Englishmen knew natural philosophy and correct demonstration, and their fallacies are only to be determined if the pattern of their argument is carefully followed. Newton was "le Père de la Physique moderne," and his theological claims must be submitted to that same logistic analysis that the parallelogram of forces indicates for every physical motion. Clarke's demonstration had been traced through its twelve propositions step by step. So his master's General Scholium would be divided into eleven stages, each of which is marked off by a citation from this central text.[172]

These eleven propositions are divided into two basic arguments, as Newtonian mechanics had come to deal with the existence of god because of two problems: one, the problem of space; the other, the problem of system. How is it possible to speak of true, absolute, and even everlasting space and not to be speaking of god? How is it possible to account for the system of motions that make up the cosmos? These two problems are inherent in Newtonian mechanics, and they constitute the two issues that d'Holbach engages as he corrects Newton's interpretation of reality. What does the god of Newton actually amount to?

God is a composite of two oblique influences which he synthesizes. One of these proceeds from dominion as the central characteristic of god, while the other proceeds from god's more general attributes. Taking dominion as the central characteristic of god and following d'Holbach's first five citations from the General Scholium, one ends with a different answer to Newton's first problem; Newton's god is actually the void divinized by the imagination. Taking the more general attributes of god, and following the next six citations from the General Scholium, one finds a different answer to Newton's second problem; Newton's god is really nature acting according to necessary laws, but personalized by the imagination. The eleven propositions or citations selected from the General Scholium allow d'Holbach to reinterpret Newton radically, and this correction of Newton's interpretation of his own work is imperative because "it appears evident that here the author does not understand himself."[173]

Newton insists in the first proposition that dominion comprises the major trait of god: "La Déité est la domination ou la souveraineté de Dieu." What is this sovereignty or dominion over? It is "sur des esclaves." Sovereignty has been added as synonym of dominion and Newton's *servi*—usually rendered by his translators as "servants"—have become slaves. Nothing could indicate more tellingly what Newton is doing. His god is an infantile projection: the all-powerful monarch who rules over slaves, a deified despot, "un homme puissant," evidence that Newton had never overcome "the prejudices of his infancy," that he "is no more than an infant" when he comes to theology. The dominion Newton attributes to god throws into sharp relief what has been variously alleged again and again in the *Système*: the god of theology is simply the projected figure of a powerful man.[174]

The second proposition maintains that "sovereignty" is so central as the divine characteristic that the other attributes follow: living and intelligent, powerful and perfect, eternal and omniscient. Translated from the ontic interpretation of Newton into the existential interpretation of d'Holbach, these make no sense at all. They involve an irreducible clash of perspectives. The contrast here runs through all of the contradictions that the *Système* has already underlined. In this clash "we see nothing but incredible efforts to reconcile the theological attributes or the abstract qualities with the human qualities given to the deified monarch." The first proposition establishes this deified monarch; the second adds a series of irreconcilable attributes. The sovereign actually depends upon slaves in order to be a monarch; he is master of his subjects who have the freedom to revolt against him; this perfect monarch is continually having his empire overthrown by the devil. How can god endure these repudiations and still be happy? How can he fill all without corresponding or relating to various parts of space?[175]

In the third proposition, Newton adds to these attributes the manner in which the monarch dominates his kingdom: always the same, but present to everything "non seulement par sa seule vertu ou son énergie, mais encore par sa substance." All of this vocabulary, however much it attempts to describe god as motive force, is vague or meaningless. An existential interpretation knows nothing of unmoved movers. To this, Newton conjoins yet another and still more formless attribute. The monarch contains all things; they exist and move within him, but without reciprocal action. God experiences nothing from things, and they experience nothing from his omnipresence.

For d'Holbach, the fourth proposition betrays the real features of god in the *Principia* and divulges how Newton actually deals with the problem of eternal space: "It would appear that Newton gives to the Divinity characters which are suitable only to the *void* and to nothing [*au vuide et au néant*]."[176] Only in the void—the phenomenal interpretation of absolute space—could those substances exist and act in one another and not be related.

Fifth, Newton insists that "Dieu existe nécessairement"—insists but does not prove. This failure in demonstration testifies to the debility in his natural theology. The critical point for a natural theology, as even Clarke under-stood, was to prove the existence of a necessary being. Newton only asserts it. "It is this existence which it is necessary to have verified by proofs as clear, and demonstration as strong, as gravitation and attraction. . . . But, O man! so great and so powerful, when you were a geometrician; so little and so weak, when you became a theologian!" Natural philosophy differs from theology in subject and in method. Theology's subject cannot be submitted to experience nor to the methodological types of reflection that give physics its texture: Newton himself admitted that discourse about god was like a blind man talking about colors. Nevertheless, he still deserted nature and reason "to seek in imaginary spaces, those causes, those powers, and that energy, which nature would have shown you in itself." The transition that Newton has made in the *Principia* stunningly indicates how strong a hold religious prejudice had on him.[177] He left nature for chimeras, experience and reason for imagination, and a calculation and demonstration for groundless assertions. What he actually obtained as divine is absolute space.

Composition is the method of the *Système*'s first line of reasoning, division is the method of the second. It begins with the attributes of god and ticks them off one after another until only nature as dynamic matter remains. The sixth proposition from the General Scholium asserts that god is incorporeal. D'Holbach can dismis that with the obvious evaluation that it makes no sense from a phenomenal perspective, either as an idea or as a religious belief. As an idea, god would possess nothing that human beings know; as a religious belief, this metaphysical spirituality would deny any relation between god and us. Much better for religion to preserve him as the divinized monarch! At least this figure would be open to adoration and homage, flattery and gifts.[178]

The seventh proposition takes even more away. We cannot know the substance of god, Newton maintains, but we can know his attributes. There is nothing extraordinary about this statement; it can be made of anything that human beings know. "We have still less ideas of God." For d'Holbach, these moral attributes themselves have over and over again manifested themselves to belong, not to a putative god, but to human beings. Human beings take their own characteristics, aggrandize them beyond limit, and then mistakenly believe that they still have some idea what they are talking about. But "infinite good" means nothing, though in its origins and in its model it bespeaks a human quality.

If spirituality and moral attributes must be removed from god, even more must the final causes which the eight proposition asserts. The wise disposition of things and their final causes that Newton takes as evidence provides even more reason to accuse him of projection. Dispositions are called wise when human beings find them favorable; otherwise, they complain about their fate and puzzle out the problem of evil. "Thus it is always in ourselves, that is in our peculiar mode of feeling, that we draw up the ideas of order, the attributes of wisdom, of excellence, and of perfection, which we give to

God." If Newton's perspective explains his continual personalizations, still his mechanics should have inhibited him from speaking of final causes. What happens to things is a consequence of the mechanical forces working upon them. In d'Holbach's translation of the Universal Mechanics: "All the good and all the evil which happen in the world, are the necessary consequences of the essences of things, and of the general laws of matter, in short, of the gravity, of the attraction, and of the repulsion, and of the laws of motion, which Newton himself has so well developed, but which he dared not apply."[179]

This *divisio*, the progressive separation of spirituality and moral attributes, dispositions and purposes, from god, leaves religion without justification. The ninth proposition of Newton provides the transition to the true cause of movement and the unifying center of system: "Nous lui rendons un culte comme ses esclaves; un Dieu destitué de souveraineté, de Providence et de causes finales ne seroit que la nature et le destin." Both statements, the *Système* agrees, are correct. It is disgusting but accurate to describe present religious practice as the worship of god by slaves. It is of critical importance to see what Newton suggests as the only alternative to his view of god: nature and destiny. His image of God is unacceptable, but his alternative squares perfectly with the convictions of d'Holbach's natural philosophy. "This God is nothing more than nature acting by necessary laws necessarily personified, or destiny, to which the name of God is given."[180] The separation from god of spirituality, attributes, and final causes has left natural philosophy with the generic and dynamic matter of d'Holbach. Newton's force, variously realized in motive force, gravitation, and divine dominion, gives way to d'Holbach's matter and its essentially different active units. The system of the world in its final moment yields to the system of nature.

Two questions remain. How does one explain diversity within the world and the emergence of religious claims to knowledge? Diversity in the universe would be impossible, Newton maintains, if nature were ultimately ruled by such "blind necessity" as d'Holbach demands. One must find the causes for this variety on some intelligent level beyond the phenomenal. But this is needless. Ordinary phenomenal factors mingle to form something quite different from themselves, and they combine with necessity. Flour, yeast, and water form bread, a new organization of matter that emerges necessarily from these ingredients with properties distinctly its own. Diversity occurs because of the various combinations of diverse elements within nature. D'Holbach's actional principles allow diversity in any effect because there is a fundamental material diversity in the basic principles. Furthermore, the claims even to analogical knowledge of god are the best that human beings have been able to do "for want of being better acquainted with nature." Ignorant and terrified, they personalized an ontic interpreta-

tion of reality because they could not handle the phenomenal. They manu-
factured gods because they could not manipulate the causes around them. As
control of the phenomenal increases, the reliance upon transcendence will
correspondingly decrease.[181] The alternatives continue to be the same ones,
that Newton himself had set: either a providential god or nature acting by
necessary laws. The first fails before the growing philosophies of nature;
only the second remains.

D'Holbach's selections from Newton follow the text of the General
Scholium fairly closely with two exceptions. First, Newton's discussion of
geometric design in the planetary system is left for the *Système*'s more
general debate with the deists. Second, the very last line of Newton's natural
theology is omitted: "This much concerning God: To discourse of whom
from the appearances of things, does certainly belong to Natural Philosophy."[182] D'Holbach omits it because he has stated it already, at the very
beginning of the *Système*. Since human beings are defined by the attitude
they take toward nature, "a human being in all of his or her researches,
ought always to fall back on experience and natural philosophy. These
are what they should consult in their religion."[183] For Newton, natural
philosophy and especially Universal Mechanics foster religious belief; for
d'Holbach, these purge religious belief away. For one, physics is the
foundation of religion; for the other, it is the foundation of atheism. In
either case, the existence of god is fundamentally an issue of natural philosophy. This is also the general position of the deists.

When theologians turned to philosophy to supply the foundations of
religion in their counterattacks against the supposed atheism around them,
they looked either to the metaphysicians or to the natural philosophers.
Those who chose natural philosophy did so for a variety of reasons. Either
metaphysics was too obscure, as for Lessius; or all natural phenomena had
to be investigated by Universal Mechanics, as for Newton; or metaphysical
considerations needed a basis in the current physics, as for Clarke. Lessius'
problematic method insisted upon the distinction between theology and
philosophy, between metaphysics and other philosophical procedures.
Newton's comprehensive principle dictated that everything be ultimately
explained in terms of force and through the science that examines forces.
Clarke's reflexive principle allowed theology to be sectioned off from
philosophy, but philosophy for him is basically one and as much like
mathematical mechanics as possible. The distinctions that theologians elaborated, either among the sciences or among themselves, can be traced to
any one of the coordinates of their discourse, but usually it was a question of
method or of principle. They stood in agreement, however, on the ontic
nature of their interpretation, a distinction between the apparent and the
real. For Lessius and Mersenne, the real transcended the phenomenon (an

ontological interpretation); for Newton and Clarke, the apparent was the epiphenomenon of the underlying real (an entitative interpretation). In either of its modes, the ontic interpretation stresses that the structures given in the world of perception and experience are the effects of either transcendent of underlying causes; the apparent world is an expression of this unseen ontic reality.

Turned to theological uses, the ontic interpretation stresses the argument from design. Most of Lessius' and Newton's arguments are elaborations of this one, and it provides Clarke's evidence for the inference to the intelligence, personality, and providence of god. In a very different way, Mersenne builds his initial arguments from the pattern found in the universe.

A phenomenal interpretation will have none of it. The structure of the real does not derive from the divine ideas, as in Aquinas' ontological interpretation, nor does an underlying pattern exhibit itself in the movements of human history, as in the entitative interpretation of Hegel. Either the structure of the real comes only from the essences of things, from natures which manifest themselves in their functions, as in the essentialist interpretation of Aristotle; or the knowing subject confers a structure and hence an intelligibility on phenomena through the perspectives he takes, the matrix of distinctions he brings to bear, or the aspects he selects, as in the existentialist interpretation of Mill. In either case, there is no place for a theology built upon a pattern in nature whose "real truth" or intelligibility lies with an ontic dimension of reality.

The clash, then, between the argument from design and the *Système* is mortal. D'Holbach has insistently used an existentialist interpretation. We do not know things in themselves. "We only know the effects which they produce on us, and according to which we assign them qualities."[184] Neither higher ideas nor an underlying pattern are being played out. To the existentialist interpretation, these appeals are just the posturing and argumentation that cloak nonsense. The numberless tracts on human anatomy and botany which theologians sponsor or even compose demonstrate nothing about an ontic intelligence, just as the regular motions of the cosmic system touted in astro-theologies are only the inevitable consequences of movement and the laws that govern matter. Endlessly elaborate as all of these tractates are, their evidence is only a repetitious insistence upon an argument that does not gather strength from reiteration. D'Holbach's existentialist interpretation allows two serious counters to any argument from design.

First: there is no order or disorder in the universe as such. Everything happens by necessity in universal nature, and cannot be other than it is once the integers and forces act upon one another. Order and disorder are different human perspectives. "Order, as we have elsewhere shown, is only the effect which results *to us* from a series of motions. . . . The order of nature may be contradicted or destroyed, *relatively to us*, but never is it contradicted relatively *to itself*, since it cannot act otherwise."[185] Order is not a pattern in nature; it is a perspective taken on nature.

Second: if order is considered to manifest a divine intelligence, the corresponding disorder must equally manifest a divine neglect and malice. If god is to account for one, then he must account for both. When Lessius confronts the atheist with the *Commentaries* of Livy, and Mersenne uses the examples of a house, a town, and the *Aeneid* of Vergil, they are reaching for something prior to any evidence: the intuitive certitude that order bespeaks intelligence. The order that they describe is different. In Lessius, it is the orientation of things toward their functions; in Mersenne, it is the fitting relationship between part and whole. But the intuition that they attempt to disclose is the same, and it pervades all the arguments of Newton and Clarke. D'Holbach counters that this must entail a parallel intuition: where there is no order, there is either no intelligence or malicious intelligence. If design manifests god, disorder must equally count against him. The relative nature of order and the telling force of disorder must figure in any discussion of this evidence for the existence of god. This allows the *Système* to admit all the evidence that Lessius and Mersenne, Newton and Clarke have been at pains to describe—and read it quite differently.

Nature can account for the complex design in animals, but it can equally well account for their disintegration and destruction. The god of design can account for the first, but not the second. "If this God cannot do otherwise, he is neither free nor omnipotent. If he changes his will, he is not immutable. If he permits those machines, which he has rendered sensible, to experience pain, he wants goodness. If he has not been able to render his works more solid, it is that he wants the ability." What is true of all life is especially true of human beings, announced to be the greatest of god's works. In the human being "who forms his God after his own peculiar model, we only see a more inconstant, more brittle machine, which is more subject to derange itself, by its great complication, than the grosser beings."[186] Beasts do not reach the glory of the human being; but they also do not know the range of human sorrow and superstitious fear. Both glory and terror make up human life; both must be accounted for in any causal analysis of the human person. If you would celebrate human intelligence and will, then remember also the afflictions of memory and guilt and the anxiety before the future and before death. One must endlessly wrestle with the notion of the Christian god to get a justification for what happens in human experience.

In any careful assessment of the evidence, the actional principles of matter are a better hypothesis than god. Nature is not an effect of that which is, but its cause and encompassing whole.

Nature is not a work; she has always been self-existent; it is in her bosom that everything is operated; she is an immense laboratory, provided with materials, and who makes the instruments of which she avails herself to act: all her works are the effects of her own energy, and of those *agents* or *causes* which she *makes*, which she *contains*, which she *puts in action*. *Eternal, uncreated, indestructible elements, always in motion*, in combining themselves variously, give birth to all the beings and to all the phenomena which our eyes behold; to all the effects, good or bad, which we feel; to the order or the confusion which we never distinguish but by the different modes in which we are affected; in short, to all those wonderful phenomena upon which we meditate and reason. For that purpose, these elements have occasion only for their properties, whether particular or united, and the motion which is essential to them, without its being necessary to recur to an unknown workman to arrange, fashion, combine, conserve, and dissolve them.[187]

This paragraph stands for the whole of the *Système de la nature* and its atheistic manifesto.

What does the *Système* do with the governing intuition of its adversaries, that order bespeaks intelligence, even if that order is only perspectival? Lessius had Livy, Mersenne Vergil; d'Holbach anticipates Paley—some thirty-five years before the great archdeacon of Carlisle published his *Natural Theology, or Evidences of the Existence and Attributes of the Deity collected from the Appearances of Nature*. D'Holbach is quite willing to work with the analogy: what would happen if a watch were shown to a savage? The example was not original with d'Holbach, much less with Paley; both may have had as their immediate source Bernard Nieuwentijt. Whatever, its source, there was the watch and there was the savage and what was d'Holbach going to do about them?

The case proposed by d'Holbach allowed more than the radical intuition of the relationship between order and intelligence to be discussed. It exhibited in its own fashion the issue basic to the quarrel between the theists and the atheists. Was the material universe the result of nature or of art? The alternatives had been formulated by Aristotle's *Physics* centuries before: nature, art, chance, and fortune. A natural thing has within itself the specifications of its existence, its movement, and its product. For an artistic thing, what it is to be, how it is to change, and what it is to produce are within the reasoning and skill of another. In nature, the moving and final cause are identified as different aspects of the natural form; in art, the moving cause is always other than the form of the thing and its purpose. These distinctions can be doubled through their privations, chance or fortune. By chance are those things which could have resulted from nature, but did not; there is no natural orientation toward them, though they are produced by natural functions and processes. By fortune are those things which could have been produced by planning, but are not. Nature and art are essential sources of movement and change; chance and fortune are accidental and derivative sources of movement and change, dependent upon nature and art.[188]

The theists maintain that the world is the result of art, and the atheistic criticism is that they leave too much fortune unaccounted for. The atheists, on the other hand, maintain that the world is a result of nature, and the theists claim that they are leaving the product to blind chance. D'Holbach's actional principles reduce art and fortune to nature and chance. The necessity found in every aspect of nature further reduces all chance to natures of whose inner determinants human beings are ignorant. For d'Holbach, there are only these dynamic units of nature which act by necessity. Intelligence is a product of nature, not a cause of natural things.

What, then, does he do with the watch and its savage? Three things: the first with the watch. The next with the watch and the savage. The last with the watch and the savage after a bit of education. And all are done within a philosophical *retorqueo*, turning the argument back upon its authors.

The watch indicates how projectional our creation of god is. Human beings admire nature, compare its wonders to themselves, and then conclude that it must be the product of intelligence just as their artifacts are. Our narrow perspective clouds our ignorance. "We no more understand how she [nature] has been capable of producing a stone or a metal, than a head organized like that of Newton." To disguise our ignorance, we homologize the production of natural things to the human production of art objects. As there is intelligence at work in the latter, we presume that intelligence is at work in the massive arena of the former. The very example of the watch itself indicates the degree to which human beings have proportioned everything to their own perspective.[189]

The savage who first sees a watch may have a prior idea of human resources. If he does, he will understand this strange object to be the product of another, more skillful, human being. If he does not, he might well think it an animal and attribute it to a spiritual force, to god. God is the occult quality which explains whatever his experience does not explain. This does not prove that there is a god; it indicates that the agent is a savage. This primitive process lies at the basis of the apologetics of the theologians. "It is thus that theologians solve all difficulties in attributing to God everything of which they are ignorant, or of which they are not willing that human beings should understand the true causes." The procedures of the ignorant savage and the methods of theology are radically the same, conceived in ignorance and projecting causes beyond their experience.[190]

The more the savage examines the watch—now a metaphor for nature—the more he will see what its actual cause is. The more the human causality is recognized, the less tendency there will be to attribute the watch to a spiritual, unknown being. Gradually, education will accustom the savage to recognize the universe as containing its own explanations and justifications: "In seeing the world, we acknowledge a material cause of those phenomena which take place in it; and this cause is nature, of whom the energy is shown to those who study her." Does this not reduce everything in the universe to chance rather than to nature, to the accidental intersections of atomic or elemental forces? Not at all. Chance is a statement about the human perspective, not about the state of things. "We call *fortuitous* those effects of whose causes we are ignorant, and which our ignorance and inexperience prevent us from foreseeing. We attribute to chance, all those effects of which we do not see the necessary connextion with their causes."[191] Nothing that nature does is by chance; everything is by a necessity that is identified with nature. As one comes to grasp the actual chain of successive causes and effects, the word "chance" disappears. Its presence only indicts those who employ it for ignorance.

D'Holbach's selection of his adversaries allowed the basic errors of theism to be exhibited, criticized, and replaced. The issue of the foundations of religion was engaged a fundamental premise, not of religion or theology, but of physics: "All the proofs upon which theology pretends to found the existence of its God, have their origin in the false principle that matter is not self-existent, and is, by its nature, in an impossibility of moving itself; and, consequently, is incapable of producing those phenomena which attract our wondering eyes in the wide expanse of the universe."[192] The theologians had for centuries appealed to philosophy to ground their reflections, to demonstrate the existence of god. So thoroughly successful had this appeal been that the two groups are indistinguishable: Clarke and Newton, Descartes and Malebranche—they are all theologians! Their fundamental error is an error in principle: they have failed to see the actional nature of heterogeneous matter. Matter is not only reflexive, in that it accounts for its own existence and for its own movement; it is comprehensive, in that it is the basic category for everything that is. D'Holbach has taken the comprehensive principle from Newton and changed it into actional elements, whose movement is the all-inclusive source of explanation. All these "theologians" failed to see that this transposition was either possible or necessary.

The second pervasive error of the theologians followed from the first. It was an error in interpretation. They failed to grasp that dynamic matter, this phenomenal reality pervading everything in their experience, could account for all its forms or designs. There was no need to ascend above it or descend beneath it to posit an overarching providence or an immanent, spiritual force in order to explain the material world. Universal nature is quite capable of

explicating itself without assistance from either the underlying or the transcendent. The only error in method itself that some theologians made was to
insist that the divine existence could have some other justification than
physics. After all, faith had to be based upon reason, and reason had become
identified with physics or natural philosophy.

Many influences conspired in the great synthesis of d'Holbach, influences
he hardly mentioned while devoting chapter after chapter to his adversaries.
Congenial to the intellectual tradition he could call his own were such lesser
figures as Anthony Collins, Thomas Woolston, Peter Annet, and Matthew
Tindal, but they remained unmentioned in his greatest work. More telling
was the weight of Hobbes and Locke, and the major advance of John
Toland.[193]

In many ways, Toland's fifth letter in *Letters to Serena* had made it
possible for both Diderot and d'Holbach to move in the direction in which
they went. He corrected both the extension of Descartes and the mass of
Newton by making motion essential to matter. Toland established, as
Giordano Bruno had argued long before him, the principle which all of the
theologians had missed: matter is essentially in movement. But neither gets
more than a footnote in the *Système*, while pages are spent on the theologians. The baron does not oppose the presence of others within his own
tradition; his work often insists upon its historical antecedents in a most
general way. But they get comparatively little consideration, while the
theologians occupy a major portion of the inquiry. Why?

These theologians formulated the intellectual matrix of Europe. One
might study physics dominated by the Universal Mathematics of Descartes
or the Universal Mechanics of Newton; but the choice was between Descartes and Newton, not between Bruno and Toland. Descartes was the
restorer of philosophy and Newton was the father of physics in the records
of d'Holbach. One might despise Clarke or Malebranche, but one could not
deny that Clarke was the greatest of the natural theologians and Malebranche the only Frenchman of comparable originality and influence. The
Système proposed more than a refutation of them; it proposed to demonstrate that atheism was their secret. A change in the coordinates of their
discourse would remove the contradictions in which they were enmeshed
and make their work come out right. Even the structure of their argument
and the fundamental intuition that lay beneath it could be purged of error
through the actional principles of universal matter, endlessly active in the
ebb and flow of all things. D'Holbach did not find Descartes totally false
and Newton completely ill-considered. He found that Descartes could
actually be accused of atheism, once the disguise was removed, and that
Newton only needed the consistency of his own mechanics to come out
godless. Change the infinite god into infinite matter for Malebranche, and

his emanations make perfect sense. Take Clarke's necessary reflexive being as the active, necessary nature, and everything he has said about his principle can be saved.

D'Holbach's purpose and his power are basically dialectical, assimilating into his generic principle the most articulate positions against it. The strength of his work is not that it completes Toland, but that it completes Newton. It is so devastating a reply to Clarke because it uses Clarke's own outline and so obtains a presence in Europe that Anthony Collins did not have. The security of the *Système*'s universal materialism lies in this dialectic: it purifies and then confirms as its own what should have been its contradiction.

The Dialectical Origins of Atheism

Although neither Diderot with his drama nor d'Holbach with his system presided over the culmination of the denial of god, they introduced this denial into the intellectual culture of the West with such strength that its presence was permanently secured. Atheism increasingly asserted its negations in the intellectual and social evolution of the great nations of Europe. The massive shadow that Nietzsche and Newman watched descending upon Europe had its origin and shaping during the termination of the French Enlightenment.

The End of the Beginning

The decade before the Revolution witnessed the deaths of Diderot and d'Holbach, but lesser figures had already joined them in overshadowing religious belief and in lending continuity to what they had begun. Principal among them was, of course, Jacques-André Naigeon. Since 1766, he had collaborated with the baron in the surge of pamphlets engulfing Paris. An early tract, *Le militaire philosophe*, had taken up the attack against Father Malebranche, summoning society from creeds of human invention to a religion so obvious and so natural that even the atheist could not deprecate its validity. Whatever the conviction and cooperation standing behind this earlier work, Naigeon's later "Discours preliminaire" affixed to *Le Système de la nature* linked him with d'Holbach's unconditional atheism. With Diderot, they ranged as musketeers, aligned not against a cardinal but against the Church and its religious convictions. Naigeon's militant atheism drove him to work with d'Holbach while the baron lived and then to edit the gargantuan literary yield of Diderot after the great encyclopedist's death.

Naigeon was the sole spirit from the circle closely surrounding the baron to support the destruction of the French throne, only to become wretchedly disillusioned with the rule of Robespierre. Naigeon was, after all, the man who d'Holbach said was "so proud not to believe in God." Many years later, Jean Philibert Damiron relates, "at the height of the terror, friends who saw him believed his life to be in danger, given his troubled and shaken air, and asked him if he were on the list of victims: 'It's worse than that,' he cried. 'What then?' 'This monster Robespierre has just decreed the Supreme Being.'"[1] The Terror had become pious! Well could Paul Hazard call this faithful fanatic both the successor of Diderot and the literary ghost of baron d'Holbach. He clung to the doctrines of his colleagues with uncompromising orthodoxy.[2]

The Revolution saw Naigeon bring forth the third volume of his *Philosophie ancienne et moderne*, which denied any middle path between baptism and atheism, and asserted that of all religious convictions the deism preached by Voltaire and swallowed whole by the Revolution disclosed itself to be the most savage and the most intolerant.[3] Naigeon's was the "dogmatic atheism" which Morellet attacked, in his later *Mémoires* recalling that their passage at arms had begun during those years when they were "in the society of Baron d'Holbach." That society Naigeon also recalled with nostalgia. In his monumental edition of Diderot's works, he appended to a description of the conversation and life of that brilliant coterie the poignant epigraph, "Et in Arcadia ego."[4] Naigeon's fifteen-volume compilation of Diderot's *Oeuvres* was complemented by his own *Mémoires historiques et philosophiques sur la vie et les ouvrages de D. Diderot*, a last attempt to carry the heritage he honored into the next century. Carrying the heritage was indeed what Naigeon accomplished: he added little to its content, convinced that the definitive word about reality had been written with the ultimate principle of dynamic matter.

At the beginning of the nineteenth century, Sylvain Marechal, a friend and fellow nonbeliever of Naigeon, published his *Dictionnaire des athées*, five hundred pages which recruited an astonishing series of thinkers to the colors. Bayle, Spinoza, and d'Alembert found themselves marching beside Naigeon, Cabanis, and Volney, and in the ranks were numbered Abelard and Zoroaster, Berkeley and Gregory of Nazianzus, while whole countries—England, Brazil, Chile, and the United States—lined up behind them. "It was," Hazard judges "the work of a maniac pure and simple."

Marechal may well have been a maniac, but since 1801 the Marquis de Sade had been the one confined to an insane asylum. Much of his stream of literary efforts purchased publication only in the twentieth century. He stood, in the opinion of Apollinaire, as a man who would count for little in the nineteenth century, but "pourrait bien dominer le vingtième." The meaninglessness of life carried to its logical conclusions, was the judgment laid upon him by Aldous Huxley; Albert Camus saw him as the beginning of the tragedy of the contemporary world. The early nineteenth century saw him writing and directing dramas for the inmates of Charenton until his death in 1814. He bequeathed to the twentieth century a series of strange paradoxes and a reputation for horrors that remain unresolved.[5]

During these troubled decades in which the ancien régime gave way to the Revolution, which in its turn yielded to Napoleon, someone far more substantial than either Naigeon or Marechal was furthering the system of Newton rather than denying its theological conclusions. Pierre Simon de Laplace established the dynamic stability of the Newtonian universe. First he resolved the "great inequality" between the orbit of Jupiter and that of Saturn, proving that over a period of 929 years the mean motion of the two planets is very nearly commensurable. Then he demonstrated that the eccentricities and inclinations of all the planetary orbits to each other remain always small, constant, and self-correcting. In 1787 he presented the final memoir on the secular acceleration of the mean motion of the moon, explaining its average angular velocity by the changes in the eccentricity of the earth's orbit caused by the perturbations from the other planets. Laplace had established the permanent stability of the solar system, a dynamic stability that needed no intervention from god to correct its mechanical errors and mount "a reformation." Laplace responded to the Newton of the *Queries* whose god prevented the fixed stars from collapsing onto each other and could readjust the solar system when its irregularities threatened its continuity. No matter that this divine intervention had never figured in the *Principia*. It had been dealt with substantially in the Leibniz-Clarke correspondence and marked the later natural theologians who counted Newton as their master. Laplace corrected, or rather eliminated, the theology by improving the celestial mechanics which formed its basis. The solar system could and would stand forever on its own; there would be no call upon a divine interference.

After the Terror, in 1796, Laplace published his *Exposition du système du monde*. In the seventh and last note to this elegant as well as influential work, he took up the question which Newton had addressed in the General Scholium, the origin of this system. For Newton, everything in the system pointed to intelligence. For Laplace, everything could be explained by nature, more specifically, by "une nébulosité tellement diffuse, que l'on pourrait à peine, en soupçonner l'existence."[6] Laplace was writing, not against Newton, but against the Comte de Buffon, who had attributed the beginnings of the solar system neither to art nor to nature, but to chance—the accident of a comet colliding with the sun and tearing materials from it which coalesced at great distances. Such a hypothesis could never explain "le peu d'excentricité des orbes planétaires." The nebular hypothesis could. Originally, a fluid circled the sun as its atmosphere, heated to unimaginable temperatures and extending from the sun even beyond the present orbits of the farthest planets. The sun constituted the core of this original cloud. The condensation of the matter of the cloud in various zones around the cooling sun formed the planets. The solar system did not need the artifice of Newton or the violence of Buffon to explain its presence. Beginning with a massive, heated cloud, and the rest was a gradual, necessary working out of mechanical laws.[7]

The story is often told of the interchange between Napoleon and Laplace, an event which, as Roger Hahn perceptively notes, "deserves to be taken seriously, not merely because it happened, but for its symbolic meaning as well." William Herschel recorded the visit of Napoleon, first consul of France, to Malmaison on August 8, 1802. After a discussion with Herschel, Napoleon "also addressed himself to M. Laplace on the same subject and held a considerable argument with him in which he differed from that eminent mathematician. The difference was occasioned by an exclamation of the First Consul's, who asked in a tone of exclamation or admiration (when we were speaking of the extent of the sidereal heavens), 'and who is the author of all this?' M. de LaPlace wished to shew that a chain of natural causes would account for the construction and preservation of the wonderful system; this the First Consul rather opposed."[8] The story has been simplified in the retelling by having Laplace reply to Napoleon's Newtonian theology, "Je n'avais pas besoin de cette hypothèse-là." Neither, of course, did Descartes. Granted matter and motion, the universe must have inevitably arranged itself as it did. Laplace is not asserting an atheism, as his thesis has been often and mistakenly interpreted to assert. He insists with Descartes and against Newton that the principles of mechanics must be mechanical. Laplace had assisted Newtonian celestial mechanics as no other figure in French astronomy had done, but his aid consisted in the extension of Newton's method, the correction of his principle, and the termination of his theology.

Ernst Mach also registered the remarkable elimination of theology from physics that occurred as the Enlightenment neared the political upheaval of the Revolution, though he awards the palm to Lagrange rather than to Laplace. Mechanics had been used to demonstrate the existence of god; mechanics had been used to deny it; now mechanics separated itself from the theological questions entirely.

After an attempt in a youthful work to found mechanics on Euler's principle of least action, Lagrange, in a subsequent treatment of the subject, declared his intention of utterly disregarding theological and metaphysical speculations, as in their nature precarious and foreign to science. He erected a new mechanical system on entirely different foundations, and no one conversant with the subject will dispute its excellences. *All subsequent scientists of eminence* accepted Lagrange's view, and the present attitude of physics to theology was thus substantially determined. The idea that theology and physics are two distinct branches of knowledge, thus took from its first germination in Copernicus till its final promulgation by Lagrange, almost two centuries to attain clearness in the minds of investigators.[9]

Whether the lead belongs to Laplace or to Lagrange, there was no doubt that the physical scientists had grown weary of theological conflict and tedious physicotheology. After the work of Diderot and d'Holbach, the theological explanation had become a hypothesis and not a very useful one at that. It was better to discard the issues that gave it birth; better for physics, in concern for its own integrity, to cut it loose.

To assert that the universe is an intrinsically stable physical reality would hardly count as a theological perturbation for Newton. He had never argued from the instability of the solar system to the existence and attributes of god. To go further and say that "mere mechanical causes could give birth to so many regular motions," however, does strike at the heart of Newton's argument that this "most beautiful system of the sun, planets, and comets could only proceed from the counsel and dominion of an intelligent and powerful being." It is to say that Newton was wrong in his argument. But to advance even further and assert that the discourse about god from the appearances of things in no way belongs to natural philosophy denies any legitimacy to the theological enterprise within physics. Lagrange and Laplace demanded a physics like Descartes' in its autonomy, while at the same time denying the need to found its fundamental assertions on the nature or actions of god. Physics was to be theological neither in its final reaches, as in Newton, nor in its foundational moments, as in Descartes. This odd marriage of two different physics denies the theological in-laws of either. Physics, in its mechanical usages and expectations, insists that this is not the place for theological quarrels either for or against the existence of god, and it would prefer that these battles be mounted elsewhere.

Concomitant with this development in mechanics a revolution in philosophical thinking occurred, a profound reversal that made this insistence of Laplace and Lagrange no longer merely a preferred option for an autonomous science, but the only status appropriate for all theoretical knowledge. There was a strange sort of kinship between this advance in mechanics and this radical shift in philosophy. For Laplace was not the first to introduce the nebular hypothesis into cosmogony. Immanuel Kant had formulated this explanation in 1755 with his *General Natural History and Theology of the Heavens*. Like Laplace, Kant was heart and soul a Newtonian, but whereas Laplace saved Newton by correcting his celestial mechanics, Kant rescued him from the dogmatism of his presuppositions. Laplace demanded—with Descartes—mechanical principles for mechanical issues; Kant demanded empirical limitations on all theoretical knowledge. Laplace insisted that mechanics proceed no further, that it not attempt a natural theology; Kant insisted that no physics or natural philosophy, no theoretic knowledge of any stamp, could form the basis for any natural theology. The theological renunciations of Laplace were expanded and grounded by the critiques of Kant. And while Kant eliminated the theology based upon nature, he equally attacked that which Descartes and Malebranche had built upon the *res cogitans*. The illation from the *cogito* to the substantial ego involved inevitable paralogisms, just as the arguments from nature spawned antinomies that two thousand years of philosophy had not been able to resolve. In the transcendental dialectic, the *Critique of Pure Reason* brought together the two kinds of natural theology, the one which came out of the Universal Mathematics and the other which formed part of the Universal Mechanics. But they converged only for their mutual destruction, only for the disclosure that both were transcendental illusions. The two massive streams of natural theology fed into this first *Critique* only to disappear into its ocean, their waters mingling and corrupted in the logic of illusion.[10]

The attack of the *Critique of Pure Reason* upon natural theology proceeds systematically in three stages. The paralogisms of pure reason destroy the self-knowledge which grounds the initial Cartesian inferences to the existence of god. The antinomies of pure reason destroy with their skeptical method the knowledge of nature which secures the Newtonian inferences to the existence of god. Finally, the ideal of pure reason combines the arguments of both, reduces those of Newton to the ontological argument of Descartes, and discloses the inherent error in treating *Sein* as though it were a predicate. Kant reduces all to Descartes, and "the attempt to establish the existence of a supreme being by means of the famous ontological argument of Descartes is merely so much labor and effort lost."[11] The first *Critique* saves the synthetic *a priori* propositions of pure mathematics and pure science, and while doing so shows that any metaphysics can only inventory pure reason. The natural theologies always collapse because their reach exceeds their grasp, because they attempt to employ pure concepts beyond the manifold of experience. Unlike mathematics and physics, metaphysics in its prior forms—openly in the Universal Mathematics of Descartes, or even disguised in the Universal Mechanics of Newton—removes its concepts from their necessary connection with sensuous intuition, and it reaches not what can be known but only what can be thought.

The Kantian critique of the employment of pure reason spells the end of an era, but not the end of the employment of reason in theology. Kant offers no comfort to the atheists, for he insists that the area of evidence for theism has been wrongly selected. His philosophy calls for a revolution, not in the assertions of the divine existence, but in the area from which terms and evidence are to be drawn. What is necessary for theological concepts is an *Übergang*, a transition from the theoretical or scientific enterprise to the practical as their proper location.[12] This radical transition itself issues from the more fundamental Kantian revolution: the shifting of the ground of all philosophical statements from a metaphysical to an epistemological selection. The primary focus is no longer on the nature of things as the foundation; it is on the processes of thought. This in turn shifts the area of theological statements from the theoretical to the practical enterprise. Freedom, immortality, and god obtain "stability and objective reality" through inquiry into the condition for the possibility of the interior moral law.[13] Speculation could never find unquestionable grounds or adequate guarantee for theological possibility; a critique of ethics can supply both. The *Übergang* of Kant is part of a general transition in primacy from metaphysics to epistemology, a necessary transition, "for these concepts of reason are now seen in transition to an altogether different use from that made of them in the first *Critique*. Such a transition makes necessary a comparison of their old and new employment in order to distinguish clearly the new path from the previous one."[14] Kant traced this new path, not merely for himself but for the whole of the nineteenth century. It gives a primacy to pure practical reason and transfers the traditional subject of metaphysics to ethics. God, in the Kantian *Übergang*, becomes a necessary postulate of the human ethical life.

A brief outline of his argument: a human being lives an ethical, a moral, life if he follows the commands of obligation, the self-legislation of the will, action motivated simply by the command of duty. But the object of duty, that which duty commands, is to seek above all the highest good. This is the synthetic connection between complete human morality and complete human happiness. The connection is synthetic because human morality cannot guarantee human happiness in this life, nor does human happiness necessarily produce a moral life. One of the strongest arguments against the existence of god has always been: why do the good suffer? Everyone recognizes that the good should be happy. Moral goodness is not identifiable with happiness, but it is identifiable with this worthiness or this appropriateness to be happy. The objective *summum bonum* is the realization of this synthetic completeness.

Now if the human duty to seek the highest good is to make any sense at all, if it is not to be an essay in absurdity, its object must be possible. There must be a cause that can bring this *summum bonum* about, that can effect the conjunction between morality and happiness. Otherwise what is appropriate to morality will never be achieved, or will occur only by happenstance or accident. The intrinsic connection between morality and happiness, the highest good, would then depend upon historical chance for its achievement or frustration. If the commands of duty are to be more than absurd, there must be a cause adequate to guarantee that the connection between morality—both in actions and in intentions—and happiness will be achieved. This demands a god of intelligence and will who is the supreme cause of nature.

The Kantian *Übergang* turns the argument from evil against itself. If the good suffer, it has been argued for centuries, the existence of god can be called into question. If the good suffer, Kant argues, the intrinsic validity of the ethical commitment demands that there be a god who will rectify this intrinsic disorder; otherwise, not only does the existence of god become questionable, but human ethical life itself becomes absurd. A human being would be commanded by duty to do or seek the impossible. Kant does not argue what was so often advanced in the past, namely, that belief in god provides a sanction for the ethical life—exactly the opposite. The prior conviction that the ethical life makes sense, that the imperatives of duty do not lead into intrinsic contradiction and frustration, makes the existence of god a necessary postulate. "Postulate" does not indicate a viable hypothesis, temporarily useful until its truth has been demonstrated, but "an inseparable corollary of an *a priori* unconditionally valid practical law."[15] If duty commands something, its conditions must inescapably exist. God becomes a condition for the possibility of the human ethical life. Kant's *Übergang* is from the god of mathematics and science—the god who either guarantees things or is guaranteed by them—to the god who is an inevitable corollary if human life is to be ethical. Previously, god was a condition for the world; now he is a necessary condition for the human.

The moral imperative serves as the grounds not only for the existence of god, but for the predicates once reserved for the religious. "Holiness," for example, no longer designates a union with god or a special relationship with god, but the "complete fitness of the will to the moral law."[16] Human history and its continuation through the endless progression that is eternity now take on an importance which previous natural theologies did not give them. They provide the arena for the practical progress of that complete fitness of human will and law that is human holiness. Thus immortality becomes the first postulate of practical reason, as human history alone does not provide time enough for such a coincidence between law and will. God becomes the second postulate since neither nature nor morality can secure the coincidence between ethical goodness and human happiness.

The Kantian *Übergang* took the topics of speculative metaphysics and placed them as postulates of practical reasoning, but this transition occurred only within the more massive Kantian revolution to establish all assertions about objects upon a previous criticism of the powers of the human subject. This profound change in philosophical selection found its ethical principle in the self-legislation of the will. This same shift toward the inner powers of human awareness found its parallel realization in the Protestant theologian Friedrich Schleiermacher. In both, the self-apprehensions of the knowing powers of the subject founded any subsequent statements of the object.

Friedrich Schleiermacher "may justifiably be called the Kant of modern Protestantism," Richard R. Niebuhr wrote in his introduction to the *Glaubenslehre*. Schleiermacher, like Kant, set "the basic problems for the succeeding nineteenth century and the greater part of the twentieth."[17] But even more fundamentally, Schleiermacher shifted the evidence for religion and for religious assertions to the human processes of awareness. His summons to the German nation, superior to the crassness of the English and to the Gallic combination of the barbarism of the people with the witty or cold frivolity of their elite, was not to a consideration of the nature of the world as a foundation for judgments about religion. Religion was not to be rooted in the cosmos; it was to be rooted in the interiority of the human person. "I would conduct you," he wrote to the cultured despisers of religion, "into the profoundest depths whence every feeling and conception receives its form, I would show you from *what human tendency* religion proceeds and how it belongs to what is for you highest and dearest."[18] The sources of religion are neither what passed for natural theology or natural religion nor god's self-revelation in Christ. The sources of religion are the processes and experience interior to the human person. This is its center. Thus, "considered from the centre outwards, that is according to its inner quality, it is an expression of human nature, based in one of its necessary modes of acting or impulses." Schleiermacher invites his readers "to seek in it the true and eternal, and to unite your efforts to ours to *free human nature from the injustice which it always suffers when aught in it is misunderstood or misdirected*."[19] His effort is "to free human nature."

As Kant turns philosophic focus from nature to human ethical life in order to found religious assertion, so Schleiermacher turns the defense of religion from dogmas and religious practices, from systems of theology and promises of immortality, to that unity of intuition and feeling that lies deep in the human. Whatever value these ideas and this information possess comes from this interior depth, from that feeling of the infinite which the *Glaubenslehre* sharpens even more as *das schlecthinige Abhängigkeitsgefühl*, the feeling of utter or unqualified dependence. For the self-consciousness of any human being always involves two factors: the consciousness of the subject knowing or doing or feeling, and the consciousness of something besides the human ego. These can be otherwise categorized as activity and receptivity. In every experience of receptivity, there is a feeling of dependence, just as every experience of spontaneous activity or movement is the feeling of freedom. Both of these enter into the constitution of self-consciousness. They form a reciprocity between the subject and the corresponding other of which the subject is aware. Now if one inquires into these diverse feelings, that is, of dependence and freedom, it is clear that there cannot be a feeling of unqualified freedom. For freedom always demands an object which has been given to self-consciousness. Neither the object of our choices nor the entirety of our existence presents itself to our self-consciousness as the result of our spontaneous interior activity. On the other hand, there is present to self-consciousness the feeling of unqualified dependence—not in this or that moment, as if resulting from an external object now and then impinging upon consciousness. "It is the consciousness that the whole of our spontaneous activity (of our freedom) comes from a source outside of us in just the same sense in which anything towards which we should have a feeling of absolute freedom must have proceeded entirely from ourselves."[20]

This human feeling of utter dependence is the primordial source of all religion and of religious affirmations. God is fundamentally experienced and identified as the Whence of this feeling: "God signifies for us simply that which is the co-determinant in this feeling and to which we trace our being in such a state; and any further content of the idea must be evolved out of this fundamental import assigned to it." The subsequent predicates of god, even the idea of god itself, are nothing more than expressions of this feeling of unqualified dependence or the direct reflections upon it. Hence the formula that lies at the basis of all religious propositions and all theological systems: "To feel oneself absolutely dependent and to be conscious of being in relation with God are one and the same thing; and the reason is that absolute dependence is the fundamental relation which must include all others in itself."[21] This experience of absolute dependence, then, is not to be identified with moments of religious mysticism or with the self-transcendence of peak experience. It is given with self-consciousness itself, though it emerges into clarity only as reflection and self-appropriation move primordial feeling into the realm of idea.

Schleiermacher's revolution consists of shifting the metaphysical doctrine of the contingency of all things to the epistemological doctrine of the human feeling of unqualified dependence. Dependence is not a statement immediately about the nature of things, but about human self-consciousness. God is given to human beings, not fundamentally through the universe, but through and with self-consciousness: "In this sense it can indeed be said that God is given to us in feeling in an original way; and if we speak of an original revelation of God to human beings or in human beings, the meaning will always be just this, that, along with the absolute dependence which characterizes not only human beings but all temporal existence, there is given to human beings also the immediate self-consciousness of it, which becomes a consciousness of God."[22] In Kant, god is a necessity of consistent ethical doctrine; in Schleiermacher, god is an inescapable attendant of all human self-consciousness. For both, and for the generations that follow them, god is a necessity for the human enterprise itself. What Laplace and Lagrange had done for mechanics was incorporated into the new philosophy and theology. The evidence for god is no longer nature. It is to be human nature. The human is the basis for the affirmation of the divine.

This revolution in theological foundations elicited and fashioned its own correlative atheism. This is not the place to trace the schema and institutions that followed hard on the heels of these revolutionaries in philosophy and theology. One point alone demands to be emphasized: this shift in theological foundations evoked, carried, and even shaped its corresponding atheisms. If nature was not at issue, human nature was. And for every philosopher or theologian who asserted god as a necessity if human life were to be consistent, appropriated, or "freed from the injustice which it always suffers when aught in it is misunderstood or misdirected," another rose up who argued just the opposite: that human life was not enhanced but infantilized by god; that god was not part of human appropriation but of human projection; that human beings could only be free when religious belief had been superseded. The area of evidence advanced by the great upheavals of Kant and Schleiermacher became, not the final moment, but a formative influence in the evolution of atheistic consciousness. Human nature, the processes of awareness—even when identified with the dialectical movement of all reality, as by Hegel—did not end the battle; they rather prompted a new series of appeals by which the conflict was waged. The new works in German philosophy and theology meant to eliminate the atheistic fires lighted in France did not quench their flames; they fed them and gave them an increase and direction which lasted through the twentieth century. Whereas the theological appeals to nature had generated an atheism founded upon the adequacy of nature, similar calls upon human nature for theological assertions now generated the demands of Feuerbach, that human nature be recognized as infinite, of Marx, that it be freed from the social alienation wrought by religion, and of Freud, that it be free to live without these theological illusions.

The atheism evolved in the eighteenth century was thus not to be denied by the strategies elaborated in the revolutions of Kant and Schleiermacher: it was only to be transposed into a different key. Argue god as the presupposition or as the corollary of nature; eventually natural philosophy would dispose of god. Argue god as the presupposition or as the corollary of human nature; eventually the denial of god would become an absolute necessity for human existence. With Diderot and d'Holbach, a pattern had been completed. A beginning had been finished. The nineteenth century would renew the question and reformulate the basis for argument as human nature, but it would repeat the pattern.

To discuss the pattern of the twentieth century is beyond the scope of this book, as is any extensive exploration of the nineteenth century. It is enough to note that a structure evolved that terminated in the atheism of Diderot and d'Holback, a structure of antecedent and even necessary influences which they recognized and assimilated, and this pattern lived in their efforts with such intellectual depth and tenacity that their arguments and conclusions might be translated by the nineteenth century into a different philosophical idiom but never erased. These Enlightenment figures effected a movement whose inner dynamism and persuasive abilities gathered strength from each succeeding century. So extraordinary a phenomenon in intellectual history demands an explanation. Could its increasing and cumulative strength lie with the pattern of which it was the issue?

The Demonstration of History: A Methodological Retrieval

When Hegel justified the history of philosophy as a properly philosophic discipline, he contended that the same necessity that exists within philosophic arguments subsists also within their history. The various stages of the history of philosophy must not be reduced to contingent events, an accumulation of opinions, or freaks of thought. They are inexorable developments: "I maintain that the sequence in the systems of philosophy in history is similar to the sequence in the logical deduction of the Notion-determinations in the Idea. . . . The whole of the history of philosophy is a progression impelled by an inherent necessity, and one which is implicitly rational and *a priori* determined through its Idea; and this the history of philosophy has to exemplify." The "logical deduction" running through this history was not that of Euclid's *Elements*, an external and static demonstration. It was rather the "inner dialectic of the forms." No finite concept was either complete or what it was to become, and that incompletion or contradiction worked itself out through its history: "This same contradiction appears in all development. The development of the tree is the negation of the germ, and the blossom that of the leaves, in so far as that they show that these do not form the highest and truest existence of the tree."[23] Internal contradiction generates history, certainly the history of ideas, while the converse is equally true: intellectual history is the manifestation of prior internal contradiction. The history of philosophy as a philosophic discipline has as its purpose the manifestation of this inner and organic necessity.

One need not espouse Hegelian speculative logic to recognize how much truth clusters in these statements. Much more may be involved in such a progress of ideas than their own internal necessity, but internal necessity remains and governs inherently. Given enough time, intrinsic contradiction and ineluctable implications will out. The origin and choice of particular philosophic ideas may be free; their exploration may be voluntary; but their consequences are necessary. To trace this internal necessity is to grasp an idea in its fullness.

Theological ideas similarly possess their own iron logic. Depositions of the Calvinists, or the Jansenists, and the Banezians have always pleaded their predestination as a faithful reading of the later Augustine. Virginia planters derived their defense of slavery from an exegetical fundamentalism: "Slaves, obey your masters."[24] Decisions about hermeneutics forced the interdiction of Copernicus, Galileo, and Darwin, while fierce persuasions in sacramentology sanctioned theories of conquest to make baptism available to the hapless Africans even at the cost of eradicating their freedom. Theology should find a profound value in tracing the historical logic of its concepts. The sequel to which a doctrine or a method leads often opens the only path to its full meaning, and the absurdity of an unavoidable implication may give the first signal of the falseness of its premise. Attention to the historical experience of theological ideas, the consciousness of their intellectual roots, growth, and full flower, constitutes an indispensable prerequisite for their assessment. This awareness expects from the evolving process of an idea something analogous to what Herodotus fixed as the character of his writings: ἱστορίης ἀπόδεξις—the demonstration of history.[25]

Herodotus allowed ἱστορίη—now transliterated "history"—a generous range of related meanings that are still productive today in the analysis of ideas. The term primarily designated the process of intellectual inquiry or investigation; then, by metonymy, the results of this investigation, that is, the knowledge acquired; and only once, very much as "history" would be used today, the written and interpreted record of the deeds and actions of human beings. "History" was alternately for Herodotus the process of inquiry, the knowledge attained, and its record. And the ἀπόδεξις it offered was equally rich in its kindred possibilities: exposition, demonstration, or proof; the manifestation, display, or performance of actions; and, again by metonymy, the actions performed. Ἀπόδεξις—whence our word *apodictic*—denotes an exposition either of meaning, of action, or of truth.[26] Herodotus' "demonstration of history" carries with it all of this complex potentiality and promise of meaning, a potentiality that can be drawn from events or from language or from ideas. And the habit of mind or the attitude of culture which searches for this potentiality in the course of its development bears the contemporary name of "historical consciousness."

Historical consciousness may well constitute a major contribution that nineteenth-century German philosophy has made to the contemporary assessment of ideas.[27] Ideas take their moment and reveal their implications over time, through the processes out of which they come, the modifications they undergo, and the sequences they in their turn further. Ideas can only be understood in their history. This does not mean simply that changes take place and are registered, are differently perceived and differently evaluated, and eventually are productive of new sciences and new arts. This is certainly true, but it hardly constitutes a nineteenth-century renaissance or innovation in thought. It means, rather, that history itself incarnates the ongoing realization of the significance and validity of any idea, of all ideas. The process of history is itself "demonstration"—in two of the senses Herodotus offered: an exposition of meaning and a presentation of truth. The sequence of consequences exhibits the inner virtuality of ideas. The pattern of their histories discloses the necessity with which both the content and the form of ideas work their way inexorably through incompleteness or through internal contradiction to spell out their truth.

Historical consciousness does not entail an epistemological relativism that reduces all assertions to perspectival discriminations. This ancient skepticism looks to history, not for the truth it discloses, but for the absorption and annihilation of any claim to truth. Historicism finds itself in the embarrassing position of axiomatically insisting that all judgments are only the shifting persuasions operative at a particular time, historical relativism asserts absolutely that all assertions are relative. Nor is historical consciousness unaware that true propositions and valid actions can issue from false premises, that the soundness of consequences does not guarantee the soundness of antecedents. Apodictic demonstrations belong to another moment of any discipline that claims them. Still, tracing out the entailments of ideas and charting the influence of the forms in which they are proposed exhibits their fullness of meaning and the capacities conferred upon them by the modes in which they are specified. The falsity of consequences exposes the fallacies of an initial idea, the equivocations of its language, or the paralogisms inherent in the form by which its content is explored and its conclusions reached. In this way, history demonstrates the meaning and truth of ideas. In reflecting upon their history, one can enter into their truth. For these reasons, the history of theological ideas is not external to theology, but an essential moment within it.

What has frequently made philosophers and theologians restive with a steady study of the histories of their disciplines is its manner of prosecution. The history of ideas may be allotted a presence in the study of theology, but it is often a tolerated presence, possessing neither the concretion of the history of the Church nor the illumination of the history of dogma. Often the history of philosophic or theological ideas narrates only a bewildering variety of contradicting opinions, necessary perhaps for erudition, but hopelessly confused one with another, opinions that are irresolvable and finally of little importance. What the student or the reader remembers is that a galaxy of opinions and quarrels came to light, one often in violent opposition to another, that their genesis owed more to contingent factors in politics, economics, and geography than to any internal necessity, and that they spawned endless battles resolved by the weariness eventually induced by time rather than by inherent modulations, correction, or synthesis. What one remembers above all in the history of ideas is contradiction, endless contradiction. And this has often discredited the entire process.

But it need not. Contradictions, if given time and if pursued beneath a superficial variety of opinions, can begin the process of fruitful, serious thought. Ideas may possess their own inherent possibilities of resolution. The generation and resolution of contradictions in Hegel constituted the only appropriate and organic demonstration of the concept. The contradiction between potentiality and privation formed the necessary conditions in Aristotle for any movement toward the actualization of a natural subject-matter, just as the contradiction innate to "problem" was the initiation of inquiry. For both Hegel and Aristotle, contradiction in a multitude of forms lies at the heart of movement, whether that movement takes place in things, in ideas, or in language. Contradiction generates movement. Contradiction does not threaten ideas, but it suggests unrealized potentiality, the inadequacy of a present formulation, or the becoming which is their actual form of being. Contradiction indicates that a process has yet to be undergone or must be continued, and it discloses that its own resolution demands a harmony or a synthesis not yet in evidence. Contradiction is the condition for the possibility of the history of ideas.

Contradiction can mean many things. In Plato, it can be the contradiction between a valid word and a false instance, or between a true instance and a false definition, or between a true instance and a false word. The Platonic dialectic was the gradual working through these contradictions to their correction and internal harmony. In Hegel, contradiction can denote an inner incoherence within content or between content and its form—or an inexhaustible series of antithetical tendencies in which the incompleteness of the concept is manifested and the demands of a further historical process underscored.[28] Conversely, any movement or process will itself demonstrate that contradiction is latent within the factors that are operative—within things, within ideas, or within language. The movement of the content or the form to the progressive resolution of its latent contradictions cannot be classified only as a useful instrument for the historian of ideas, imposing an artificial matrix of successive negations in order to control the subject. Nor does such an internal necessity ignore or discredit the vagaries, the idiosyncratic and even arbitrary spontaneities, that issue from so many social, cultural, and heteronomous influences. The progress of ideas is neither an operational matrix nor a mathematical necessity nor total chance. But thoughts do have consequences and cogency, and in that they exhibit their own rigorous necessity. Thoughts are also thought by a thinker, and in that they exhibit all the fortunes and interests to which human beings are heir. In either case, contradiction will out as movement, and contradiction writ linguistically is ambiguity.

This book began with the ambiguity of the term *atheist*: its meaning as a designation of the first Christians, its truth as a charge against Socrates, its appropriateness as a classification of Akhenaten. This ambiguity was augmented when attention was taken from the possibilities of the term itself and concentrated upon the variety of thinkers to whom the classical world applied it: Diogenes of Apollonia, Hippon of Rhegium, Protagoras of Abdera, Prodicus, Critias, Diagoras of Melos, Theodore of Cyrene, Bion of Borysthenes, Euhemerus, and Epicurus. The word's profound ambiguity could only be clarified by that specification of vocabulary, meaning, and embodiments which Plato's *Seventh Epistle* advanced as the origin of any dialectical inquiry into reality. The *Seventh Epistle* provided the first hint for reading the history of ideas, for mounting a demonstration of "history." It not only insisted upon a grasp of language, meaning, and thing, but it introduced the various modes of thought that can be identified as this mastery: science or intuition or true opinion—such as one might find in works of art—can differently resolve into unity ambiguous vocabulary, indeterminate meanings, and questionable instances.

It was critical to recognize that "atheism" was parasitic. The word, its significance, and its application were derived from what was denied. How one used the word "god," how one formulated its meaning, and how one applied it determined its multiple negations in language, significance, and thinkers. And this sixfold ambiguity involved the further questions about the kind of knowledge by which the existence or denial of god was asserted—whether in a moment of intuition, in the labored arguments of science, or in the opinions that come in the cultural atmosphere of an epoch or the common sense judgments of reflective human beings. Since atheism did not stand on its own, it could only be understood through the theism of which it was the denial. A history of atheism could never achieve the determinacy necessary for inquiry unless it was also a history of theism.

The first imperative for this essay in the history of ideas was to determine whether its subject could be definite enough so that one could speak of authentic affirmations and denials. For that purpose, this inquiry—to use Herodotus' word—framed certain parameters by which the massive ambiguity of its topic might take on some specification, consistency, and coherence. This allowed an indeterminate problematic situation to attain the consistency of a problem.

The first of such parameters was deceptively simple: that the central meaning of any atheism is to be found, not in atheism, but in the theism of which it is the denial. The name, the definition, and the referent for atheism are set by the going theism. The *meaning* of atheism, then, is always dialectical, that is, it emerges from its contradiction. But in this dialectical generation of meaning, more is involved. Each decision about the significance of *god* also settles new meanings on such systematically plastic terms as *matter, world,* and *human being.* These loose and inherently ambiguous terms whirl kaleidoscopically around the central term and then settle into a new and coherent pattern. The term *god* collects and defines a host of words around itself. A determination about god and about atheism invariably involved the conferral of meaning on everything else, either as presupposition or as consequent.

The first parameter permitted a second, one which set the central problem for this study. If the meaning of atheism is shaped by the going theism, is this also true of its *existence*? Is there a similar dialectical dependence? Is atheism called into being not primarily by elements and forces distinct from it—epiphenomena of political or psychological independence and the development of science—but by the going theism? If theism is responsible for the patterns of atheism, did it also generate its actual birth? More particularly, since this book proposed an inquiry in the modern period: did modern theism lie at the root of modern atheism? Is atheism, as Feuerbach repeatedly insisted, the secret of religion? Is atheism an immanent progression out of modern theism? Both the assertion of the first parameter and the question that was the second dictated that this work would be a study of a transition, that as much attention be given to the theists as to the atheists, in an attempt to trace the origins of modern atheism. Atheism that is not a dialectical transition could only be an abstraction.

The *Seventh Epistle* directed attention not only to the essence and the existence of the content, but to the *form* in which this content emerged into knowledge. The third parameter registered a determination of the content by the form or manner in which this content is derived, argued, or expressed. Dialectic moves not only toward a resolution of the internal contradictions within its content, but toward an appropriate synthesis of the content with its form. For the content covers everything from the initial evidence to the final conclusion. The form, the third parameter, involved considerations of all of the modes of thought—from beginning to end—by which theism and atheism formulated their problems, articulated their meanings, established their evidence, argued from evidence to conclusions, and verified their conclusions. Just as the first and second parameters dictated that atheism be treated as a transition from theism, so the third parameter demanded a careful analysis and retrieval of the actual working context in which this content is treated and conclusions advanced. For the form in which something is asserted or denied functions just as critically as the content itself. The first two parameters demanded that atheism be treated symbiotically with theism; the third necessitated both that major working inquiries be carefully analyzed and that these working inquiries be sequenced within their "effective histories"(*Wirkungsgeschichte*), within their tradition of influence, debate, acceptance, and rejection. Each of these intersections involved a "fusion of horizons," as one work picked up the resources, the latent possibilities, and the consequences of another.[29] The transition from one to another was a study in interpretation.

Each of these working inquiries to be studied was not only a form or structure of thought; it was thought embodied in discourse. They all possessed language, discourse in its patterns of development. This permitted a fourth parameter for their individual and collective interpretation, for the tracing of their effective histories. Discourse can be calibrated by a philosophic semantics which isolates and relates vastly divergent systems through the coordinates of selection, interpretation, method, and principle. These four coordinates allow questions to be leveled at each text, questions which probe for the constants necessarily present in all significant discourse: (1) What is the area, the source of subject-matter and basic terms, absolutely fundamental to this reflective inquiry? (2) What is the "really real" that permits a predicate to be affixed truly to a subject? (3) What is the pattern or structure of the discourse? (4) What is the source of its unity or of its value or of its truth? A philosophic semantics whose components are selection, interpretation, method, and principle provides an instrument neutral enough to allow the working inquiries of the most divergent thinkers to be charted and coordinated one with another—without the reduction of all the forms of thought to one true form or all the modes of philosophy to one true philosophy. This parameter of discourse attends to the unity of all working inquiries; the coordinates of discourse it embodies acknowledge and respect their diversity.

These four parameters, then, enabled the indeterminate situation of modern atheism to take on a determinacy which it would otherwise not possess, a determinacy which registered in its own fashion the factors urged in the *Seventh Epistle*. The first parameter provided the content of this book: the transition from theism to atheism. The second parameter posed the question which this content elicited: Did theism internally generate atheism, as well as give it its meanings? The third parameter supplied those labored forms of inquiry in which meaning is asserted, systems built, and the resultant theological assertions and influences specified. The fourth parameter accepted the omnipresence of discourse through which the most divergent inquiries could be united, and it furnished the coordinates of discourse through which their differences could be recognized and related to one another.

There could be no fixed priority in which these parameters or the coordinates of discourse were brought into play. They could and must operate in various patterns according to the demands of the text under consideration or the needs of the inquiry being advanced. Neither the parameters nor the coordinates constitute an ordered method of hermeneutics; they are constants that are present in any hermeneutical attempt to deal with the problem of atheism. It was important that they be present and function; the order in which they functioned was necessarily flexible and adjusted to a working inquiry and its argument.

No effort, then, was made to repeat in every way the dialectic suggested by the *Seventh Epistle*, even in a Hegelian transposition. Rather, this *Epistle* and the dialectical tradition suggested the devices with which the indeterminacy of the situation of modern atheism could be given some determination and its inner consistencies discovered. It was important that one learn what this historical experience had to teach. The tradition that came from Plato made it easier to respond to the methodological demands that came from John Dewey. Plato and Dewey made it that much easier to deal with the question leveled at our culture by Nietzsche's Madman: "How did we do this? How could we drink up the sea? Who gave us the sponge to wipe away the entire horizon?"[30]

It would have been misguided to grapple with this question by constructing a single internal cogency, from the multiple forces prior to the Enlightenment, by building a world in which each thinker and each tract moved inevitably through a system of conceptual necessity to produce the outcome that was atheism. The complexity of human motivation and interests, the pluralism of alien developments, and the endless potential of ideas could have admitted such an exhaustive internal logic only by the most arbitrary and subjective selection. Through a series of examples and a choice of "typical thinkers," one can prove almost anything. It was Aristotle who wrote that the use of examples is the induction of the rhetorician.[31] But among the very tangled lines that come together in d'Holbach and Diderot, there were those whose beginnings stretched back into a twilight past; those rambling, twisting fibers eventually formed a web in which nature could become its own system. If thinking exhibits chance, thought—whether as intuition, science, or opinion—exhibits the inward conceptual continuity of unfolding determinations and necessity. In this way, the demonstrations of history, of the cogency, power, and sequence of an idea as it works out its inner meaning and implications over time, is self-demonstration, "immanently formative, which is to say that it continues to form itself out of itself."[32] This immanent formation generates its own pattern, a pattern whose inherent source is the contradiction found within the *content* of the reflection and the *form* in which this content assumes its career. The strength of the development is always determined by the depth of the contradiction.

The Self-Alienation of Religion

A critical self-contradiction developed within theology out of a decision about form. Leonard Lessius had counted heavily in the Thomistic revival in Louvain, supplanting Lombard's *Liber sententiarum* with the *Summa theologiae* in a textbook revolution. He had paralleled Aquinas' philosophical demonstrations of the existence of god, the *quinque viae*, with his own *rationes philosophicae*. The *rationes* of Lessius owed more to the *De natura deorum* of Cicero than to any particular medieval theologian, but Lessius took from the Thomistic tradition an abrogation, the persuasion that the existence of god was essentially a philosophical problem rather than a theological or religious one. He did not excuse himself from referring to Christology or to properly religious experience; it seems never to have occurred to him. He excused his work from the *Metaphysics* of Aristotle, not because it would be intrinsically inappropriate but because it would make too heavy a demand upon his readers. Philosophy was the proper form for the issue of god, a philosophy that would think through its arguments in abstraction from any common religious tradition or particular experiences.

Neither the first nor the last Thomist to insist upon this form for the question about the existence of god, Lessius confirmed his heritage at a critical junction in the history of Western thought. That confirmation has been repeated over the centuries that followed. Etienne Gilson, one of its most eminent representatives in the twentieth century, endorsed a similar procedure in his own comments upon the *Summa theologiae*: "It is natural that [Thomas'] first question should be about the existence of God. On this problem, however, *a theologian cannot do much more than apply to the philosophers for philosophical information. The existence of God is a philosophical problem.*"[33] Lessius had assumed—rather than argued—precisely this thesis some four centuries before. Gilson modified, but did not deny, his own methodological assertions through his inclusion of "philosophical problem" within *sacra doctrina*: "Practically speaking, this means that the problem of the existence of God, for instance, will be treated by Thomas Aquinas using the method of philosophy, but at its theological place."[34]

Centuries have rendered this critical choice of the Thomists common enough—expected, ordinary, self-evident, and bearing a major influence on the history of ideas. By implication, Gilson and Lessius are asserting that

↳ new form of implication!!

religious experience or Christianity as such possesses nothing with which to engage this issue of the existence of god, that there are no specifically religious resources upon which theology might reflect and with which it might respond to the atheistic question. The theologian as such is to say that he has nothing to say. He must "apply to the philosophers for philosophic information." The forum or form for such a question is philosophy. Since the issue does not comprehend all of theology, but only the divine existence, Lessius could abstract the problem from its "theological place" and bring to bear simply "the method of philosophy."

Two crucial premises were fundamental to Lessuis' decision, one historical and the other methodological. Historically, his philosophical location of the question bespoke the inability to recognize that atheism in the sixteenth century was not simply a formal retrieval of classical authors. It was intrinsically and inescapably a religious judgment. The putative denial of god pivoted much more on a rejection of the meaning and reality of Christology and of the religious experiences carried within the Judeo-Christian tradition, of church and synagogue, than on a theorem in philosophy which one might come across in the debates of Cicero. Methodologically, Lessius relegated theology to the moments which followed the commitment of faith. Religion and theology could only speak within faith. These strategies devised against the atheists adopted a peculiar understanding of Anselm's *fides quaerens intellectum*: there could be no appeal to religious experience or to Christology until the grace of faith had been accepted. Philosophy had to become the apologetic counter, a tool to deal with this profound religious rejection.

Perhaps the contradiction inherent in this procedure can be discerned in its origins through an inspection of two programmatic statements in the *Summa theologiae* itself. As prologue to the third part, where he initiates his exploration of Christology, Aquinas wrote: "Our Savior, the Lord Jesus Christ—'saving his people from their sins,' according to the witness of the angel—demonstrated in himself the way of truth for us [*viam veritatis nobis in seipso demonstravit*], through which we could come to the happiness of immortal life."[35] In the third part, there is but one *via*, one way of truth through which the human being must move: this is the person and the reality of Jesus. *Demonstrare* covers the same range as Herodotus' ἀπόδεξις: exposition, manifestation, proof. Here it obviously means "to manifest," but to manifest as a convincing exposition of the truth. Now turn to the early questions of this same *Summa*, to the third article of the second question of the first part, where the question is raised: "Whether god is?" The response returns: "It should be said *that God is* can be proved in five ways [*Dicendum quod Deum esse quinque viis probari potest*]."[36] *Demonstravit* may not mean exactly the same thing as *probari potest*, but they both include a convincing manifestation of the truth. It is puzzling that Aquinas speaks of Christ as the *via veritatis* in the third part and does not number him among the *quinque viae* in the first. Only philosophic inference figures here.

[handwritten marginalia: This is ignorant + stupid]

There are many reasons advanced to explain this anomaly, perhaps the principal one being that the whole of the *Summa theologiae* must be taken as an inquiry into the reality of god—his existence, his nature, and his activity—an inquiry effected through his works, the greatest of which is the Incarnation. The *Summa* must be taken as an integral whole in order to obtain a demonstration of the personal god proportional to his effects within creation. One part of the *Summa* explains, augments, and completes what has gone before. Even the *quinque viae*, it is crucial to note, are only schematic, to be argued and amplifed in the articles that succeed them. But if the whole of the *Summa* is not seen as a continuous *demonstratio*, as it was not by the time of Lessius, but as autonomous units which could be abstracted and commented upon at great length in isolation; and if this single article from the second question of the first part is from its theological location untimely ripped; then the tension between the *via veritatis* and the *quinque viae* develops into a contradiction. It is an intrinsic contradiction between the religious or theological nature of the question with its evidence and the philosophic form in which it is pursued.

The contradiction between form and content in Lessius was homologized by a similar contradiction within content itself, between the evidence and its conclusion. Lessius' problematic method allowed him to distinguish the content appropriate to revelation from that appropriate to philosophy; in the latter he distinguished the inquiries whose evidence rested upon a universality of opinion from the arguments relying upon the design found in the nature of things. That he came down on the philosophical side can be traced to his Thomistic allegiances; that he came down in this way indicates the profound influence of Cicero's Stoics. The content, then, from which he argued was the structure of nature. His Ciceronian heritage would permit him to bring in prophecies and miracles, but as the unexpected alterations within the knowledge and the uses of the nature of things. Basically, the warrant for the personal god was the impersonal world: the strongest evidence for the personal god was the design within nature.

Each inquiry into nature revealed inherent structure, and each structure indicated the action of a providential *numen*. In place of a religious tradition in which the personal god was known primarily by personal communication, Lessius returned to the Stoic choice of nature while removing from that nature the intrinsic rationality asserted by the Stoics. This dialectical contradiction in content transformed the theologian into the natural theologian, a philosopher as independent of Aquinas' *sacra doctrina* as were the Stoics from whom the topics of argumentation were selected.

Marin Mersenne's logistic method pursued the same differentiations as Lessius and made the contradictions in form and content more rigorous. Both employed particular methods to distinguish various kinds of science. Lessius differentiated the sciences according to the types of problems engaged; Mersenne, according to the various components that were added or substracted, composed or divided in the process of building a case. For both Lessius and Mersenne, a strong sense of the transcendent reality as the "really real" allowed for some retrieval of the ontological argument, but both insisted upon philosophy as the form appropriate for the question of the existence of god. If anything, Mersenne's coordinates of inquiry further purified the question from any intrusion of religion such as miracles or prophecies and further permitted an absolute form of philosophy alienated from any theological place or evidence.

For all of Lessius' celebration of the *fistula dioptrica*, Mersenne lived closer to the world of the rising mechanics. Lessius' actional and intelligent *numen* allowed him to merge the questions of the existence of god with those about providence. Mersenne's god is the comprehensive, transcendent, and pervasive explanation of all phenomena, and is reached by inquiry only when philosophy has established the *plenum* and the infinite. Here also Mersenne bore an elective affinity to the French philosophy that followed. While the infinite functioned as a conclusion in Mersenne, it constituted the central evidence around which the systems of Descartes and Malebranche turned. Lessius' evidence lay with the design specified through a problematic method, namely, the orientation of parts to their organic unity and of the whole to its functions. Mersenne's logistic method also relied upon design, but an Epicurean design, in which the mechanical parts of a whole form a unity which is nothing more than the sum and the arrangement of its components. These great mechanical structures in which each element contributes to the harmonious movement of the whole were the ultimate witness to "un souveraine Architecte." The highest evidence for god was still an impersonal nature.

The philosophical options in both content and form that Lessius and Mersenne represented in Catholic theology did not take their motives from the crudely mistaken notion that human beings are governed by logical processes, nor even from an evaluation that the theistic apologetic should avail itself of the best arguments available, which were philosophic in form and physical in content. Their position was more self-conscious and more pervasive. Following what seemed to be the clear line mapped out by past centuries and by the great tractates of the late Renaissance theologians *de analysi fidei*, they mounted their debate with atheism in a profound abstraction, in which neither Christology nor religious experience played much of a role. Christ was not totally excluded by Lessius, but he became one more instance of miracles and prophecies. By the time of Mersenne, this minor part would be written out of the script. The theists and the putative atheists had to find a common ground, and that ground was neither the person of Jesus nor the individual or communal experiences of religion. Common ground was provided by the cosmos; the world bore witness to god. Let nature, then, whether in the inner orientation of things or in the ontological structure of ideas, constitute the evidence for the existence of god; let philosophy be the discipline by which this evidence is analyzed.

It is not remarkable that neither Lessius nor Mersenne appealed to participative religious experience. This had already been relegated to the practices of piety, to the private progress of contemplative development, and to the tractates in spirituality that abounded in the Netherlands and in France. It is not remarkable, but it is ironic and paradoxical. For in these centuries was written a brilliant page in the history of spirituality with its accompanying descriptions and analyses of religious experience. But the discipline and study of religious experience presumably had nothing to say to the rising sense of atheism. "Natural theology" and "mystical theology" never intersected except in a genius such as Blaise Pascal, even though a theologian like Lessius could write insightfully in both fields. These fields were kept abstracted one from another, each allowed its own evidence, cultivation, and growth; natural theology was given the privileged position of the spectator over the participant. Nor is it remarkable, on the other hand, that Christology had nothing to contribute to the debate about the Christian god. In an effort to avoid a developing fideism, associated either with Montaigne or with Calvin, and to lay a common basis for rational discussion, any appeal to the witness of a person—which is fundamental to Christianity—became inadmissible. The theologians followed the Thomistic lead, or what they understood as the Thomistic lead, and consigned Christology with its endless refinements to a more remote phase of theology. It is not without some sense of wonder that one records that the theologians bracketed religion in order to defend religion.

The unrecognized violence of this contradiction thus lay not only between the religious content and the philosophic form but also between the Christian god and the impersonal content that was counted as his primary evidence. The contradiction lay also between European religious culture whose god was warranted and defined through Jesus Christ and the reaching of the theologians to a providential *numen* or a great architect as if sixteen hundred years of religious history had never occurred. The Christian culture of Europe within which these theological apologetics were launched incarnated a sense of divinity which was both intimately personal and present, a god whose tangible religious atmosphere could be found in the village churches and local monasteries as well as with the crucifix on the walls of taverns and the great celebrations which punctuated the year, a god whose interventions were the stuff of prayer and mysticism, ritual and rural superstition. This transcendence was woven into the texture of the culture, and Christ defined the meaning and the truth about god. Daily patterns of speech bespoke this permeating influence, and the success or failure of life was judged by it. Precisely this determination of life as a whole precluded a fundamental return to the Stoic and Epicurean philosophies. The providential *numen* and the sovereign architect lay at too great a distance from what this religious culture recognized as god, against whom a putative atheism was purported to be antagonistic. The determinations of Lessius and Mersenne abstracted god from Christ as either definition or manifestation. The Christian god was to be justified without Christ.

This contradiction in the conception of god was coordinate with the intellectual world emerging from these choices of the theologians. Participative religious experience was only "pieties" and was excised from the evidence, going the irrelevant way of Christology. The world that was emerging is confessionally irreligious. It can be common to Christian and pagan, atheist and believer, because it is untouched by anything which either Jew or Christian would recognize as religious challenge, religious belief, religious practice, or religious experience. The form of knowledge was philosophy, and the content that constituted its evidence was nature. "Natural theology" synthesized the Schoolmen and Cicero; and Christianity, in order to defend its god, transmuted itself into theism.

These determinations, represented by preeminent theologians of unquestionable orthodoxy, placed a double and unrecognized contradiction within any further discussion of the atheistic issue—a discussion that had begun before the "atheists" had appeared. There was a contradiction within the content of the theists: impersonal nature was made the primary warrant for a profoundly personal Christian god. There was a contradiction between this content and the form in which it was advanced: philosophic inference was the fundamental form for the defense of religious knowledge or awareness. Religion was treated as if it were theism. Negatively, this twofold contradiction can be put into a single assertion: Religion has neither the evidence, nor the kinds of reflective inquiries, nor the participative awareness to establish its own cognitive claims. Impersonal nature is the evidence for a personal god; philosophic inference is the foundational form for religious assertions. One is convinced or informed about god "from the outside." In this process of self-alienation, religion denied itself both a proper form to reflect upon this issue and commensurate evidence by which it could be resolved—and all of this before the question had even been raised by the intellectual culture in which the theologians wrote.

This twofold inner contradiction generated much of the dialectical history that followed. The new philosophies accepted their mandate with the same unquestioned sense of entitlement with which the theologians proffered it. Theologians were not to do this task. Philosophers would do philosophy themselves. Serious philosophy then took its selection directly from the nature of things, rather than from the processes of judgment or the use of words. Both Descartes and Newton registered their recognition of the theological office fallen to them, and both honed a logistic method to construct either a first philosophy with the procedures of a Universal Mathematics, or a natural philosophy within the ideal of a Universal Mechanics, that would assume the mantle. Descartes employed this method to demonstrate the existence of god analytically as the efficient cause of the idea of infinite or perfect substance, and then synthetically to prove that existence was a necessary attribute of god. Newton realized this method in constructing a universe whose movements could be traced back to gravity and to impressed inertial forces whose program, initiation, and continuation could then be analyzed back to divine dominion. Descartes' existential interpretation needed god as an initial factor within his system; otherwise, all assertions would melt before Montaigne. God was the condition for the possibility of doing physics with certitude. Newton's entitative interpretation needed god to carry out the last moments of the mechanical method, when the Universal Mechanics finally resolved movement back to a nonmechanical principle, to a dominion that both underlay the universe and synthetically sustained the coordinates of space and time. For Descartes, god was a presupposition for physics; for Newton, god was a corollary. Nothing manifests more the difference between the two philosophies that inaugurated modernity than the location of their natural theologies.

How ironic it is to read in popular histories of the "antagonisms of religion and the rising science." That was precisely what the problem was not! These sciences did not oppose religious convictions, they supported them. Indeed, they subsumed theology, and theologians accepted with relief and gratitude this assumption of religious foundations by Cartesian first philosophy and Newtonian mechanics. If, after all, "a theologian cannot do much more than apply to the philosophers" on the problem of the existence of god, what more prominent or influential philosophers could the seventeenth century put forward? And how willing they were to take on the job! Descartes to the Sorbonne, Newton to Bentley, indicated this theological apologetic as a subject meet for their métier. First philosophy and natural philosophy moved to comprise the foundations of religion, and no one—least of all the theologians—sensed the formal contradiction entailed in this hegemony.

Discordant as the methods and the systems of Descartes and Newton might be on so many issues, it is crucial to notice that they both continued to demonstrate a god known only by inference. One neither experienced anything of god nor discerned within oneself a pervasive orientation that could tell as theological evidence. One was informed about god from the outside—as one might be informed about the existence of the New World or deduce the corpuscular theory of matter. The conceptual, the objectifying, the reflexive deductions that lead to the assertion of god to account for any particular effect—all of these were not taken as secondary and reflexive objectifications of a prior and personal involvement either in orientation or in experience. They were taken as the primordial and responsible religious awareness itself. While religion presupposes personal engagement as the permeating and fundamental relationship with god, philosophic inference introduces a third term or warrant other than this involvement, namely, the evidence through which one is informed about god and from which god is deduced. In one way or another, religion involves god as a living presence; philosophic inference demonstrates that there is a god as "a friend behind the phenomena." Descartes and Newton omit any experiential transcendental or religious orientation and the personal involvements that issue from either; they sustain an inferential form of knowledge as original and essential.

The absence of the specifically religious within the intellectual makeup of either the Universal Mathematics or the Universal Mechanics made such a surrogation as inevitable for the philosophers as it was acceptable to the theologians. Heidegger's protests against the Cartesian-Spinozan tradition tells equally against Newton and discloses the inherent contradiction, unseen and unsuspected, in the subsumption of the grounds of religion by the new philosophies: "Man can neither pray nor sacrifice to this god. Before the *causa sui*, man can neither fall to his knees in awe nor can he play music and dance before this god."[37] The formal contradictions inherent in the Cartesian and Newtonian substitutions made profoundly misleading their promise of the stable defense of religious belief. Actually, this subsumption embodied a further stage in its developing self-alienation. To gauge how profound the contradiction was in each system, it is necessary to assess not only the form of knowledge, but the developing content which was employed as its evidence.

The evidence was now particular factors given in experience: How do I account for this particular idea? How do I account for this singular structure of the universe, with each of its particular and individual motions? Even the ontological argument becomes one idea justifying itself. Descartes and Newton shared the exclusion of any effect total enough to be proportional in some way to a universal and utterly transcendent cause. Accepting these two philosophers, as this book does, as the most influential thinkers at the dawn of modernity, we will not find better examples of what Martin Heidegger characterizes as the malaise of our world: *Seinsvergessenheit*—a forgetfulness of being, with its concomitant inability to ask the question of god at the depth which alone can give any theological sense to the content of the answer.[38] Their evidence is always particular. Neither took up being as the actualization of all things, the actualization of the possible, which cried out for explanation. The only existence that Descartes could advance as evidence was his own, this individual *res cogitans*, a particular existent to be explained not as an actualization but as a single fact, to be discriminated from the existence of sensible things as certain because it is given in the very process of doubting. The evidence for both was not the realization of everything, but particular facts about something.

Both Descartes and Newton achieved a god commensurate with the evidence they explored. God was the efficient cause proportional to his own idea and its formal justification; god was the geometric artisan who arranged the mechanical structures of things and who sustains by his own existence infinite space and sempiternal time. In both of these philosophies, god functioned as an explanatory factor in a larger, more complete system. God was the ultimate condition for the possibility of knowing nature in Descartes, and mechanical nature was the ultimate condition for the possibility of knowing god in Newton. Both moved inexorably to a final dualism that posited the difference between god and nature as between members of a coordinate duality that made up a larger whole. Not only did the inferential, philosophical form in which the content was embodied constitute a hidden but formidable stage in this self-alienation of religion; there was also the dualistic polarity in each philosophy. Individual things needed explanation—ideas or individual facts—and god provided that explanation.

This hidden alienation told also upon their worlds. In Newton, everything led to god; in Descartes, everything proceeded from god. The world of Newton was mechanically free from all confessional religion, as was that of Lessius and Mersenne, but Newton carried this freedom one step further. Lessius and Mersenne abstracted from religious experience as an initial and apologetic moment; Newton made mechanics universal and confined all demonstration to a commensurate god. The world, according to the General Scholium, disclosed god's "most wise and excellent contrivances of things and final causes." But the *Principia* itself had formulated a world in which final causes played no part, a world of geometric patterns and mass-objects, of quantified movements and motive forces. It was not easy to see how these two worlds could be resolved into a unity. But if the world of Newton was contradictory, that of Descartes was simply godless. The self-enclosed physics of Descartes was established as autonomous, however much it might find its roots in first philosophy. Once launched, it was on its own with matter in movement inevitably finding its predetermined contours. With the

Universal Mathematics, Descartes removed any final causes, any *notae* or *vestigia* of god, from the world. The world did not bear witness to god: god bore witness to the world. Descartes presented to the opening of modernity a world that was intrinsically and methodologically secular, yet, paradoxically, utterly dependent upon god before its first laws of movement could be formulated. His world was as godless as his physics was autonomous—not because god was not necessary for either, but because the world gave no convincing evidence of his presence or even of his existence. Physics presupposed the theological issue settled. Descartes' world was secular, but not his total system. God was an integral factor in that system.

There was an unrecognized progressive movement in this ongoing dialectic of content. In their search for proof of the divine existence, the theologians had shifted from the god defined by and disclosed in Christ and religious experience to the god disclosed in impersonal nature. The philosophers took this displacement of content one step further. Now the content that functions as evidence is irreducibly impersonal and particular: the god that is inferred is personal only as a deduction from the idea of his perfection or from the mechanical workmanship that shows his dominion. The contradiction between the religious content and the philosophic form grew similarly. The theologians had insisted that the issue was philosophic. Now the philosophers said that it was only philosophic, that there was a correlation between god and philosophic system. If philosophy was necessary for theism, theism was also necessary for philosophy. For Descartes, god functions as a linchpin for a Universal Mathematics that would draw all of the sciences into their unity with first philosophy and make any science epistemologically possible. For Newton, the whole enterprise of tracing movements to their originating causes would falter if one could not analyze complex structures of motions back to their original sources or find that which synthetically sustains the mathematical coordinates of nature by a constitution of space and time. *Manus manum lavat!* God and nature were mutually implicated in both philosophies.

If anyone could have reversed this inexorable dialectic, it would have been Nicolas Malebranche. Henri Bremond, in his magisterial eleven-volume *Histoire littéraire du sentiment religieux en France depuis la fin des guerres de religion jusqu'a nos jours*, avowed that "the philosophy of Malebranche propagated, more or less disfiguring it in the process, Bérulle's spiritual doctrine." Bremond wrote more truly than he knew. But two influences extended into the history of thought from the great cardinal. One represented in brilliant idiom the rich tradition that reached back to Bonaventure and Augustine, and within this observance Malebranche could assert: "Religion is the true philosophy." Even more emphatically, he urged in an exhortation that might have come directly from Bonaventure's *In Hexaemeron* or his inaugural lecture, *Christus, unus omnium magister*: "Let us value nothing save in relation to Jesus Christ; let us not look on ourselves save as in Jesus Christ."[39] But there was another Bérulle, as there had been another Lessius, the spiritual guide to Descartes, and his influence also told upon Father Malebranche. For when the issue of atheism arose and the shadows of the Chinese fell across his path, the profound Christology and spirituality of his other works fell away, and only Cartesian philosophy remained. It is simply astonishing to see Malebranche, of whom Maurice Blondel acutely wrote that "the Word Incarnate is the only intelligible explanation . . . there is no reality but in Him, no Truth but He"—it is astonishing to see him assume so entirely different a stance.[40] The abstraction of philosophy from theology which Descartes had defended now disclosed the options available, and the Chinese were to be engaged not with religious figures or experience but with philosophy as an autonomous discipline, as the critical apologetic for a barren religion that could not defend itself. Here Malebranche most emphatically looked at himself "save as in Christ."

Perhaps no figure in this struggle of Christianity for its soul so exhibits the contradictions into which it fell and the dialectical development in which it was caught as the theologian Malebranche. On the question of the existence of god, he fully accepted the Cartesian division of labor—but he accepted Descartes by altering almost every one of his coordinates of inquiry. Malebranche transposed the logistic, mathematical methodology of Descartes to an operational mode, to a pattern of discursive processes whose beginning lies in the interpretation of arbitrary formulations. The term *god* possesses a fourfold ambiguity, and the initial moment of the debate—the manner of discourse most suited to this method—proposes to remove this ambiguity. His debate not only changes the method of Descartes, it also formulates a principle far more comprehensive than anything in the Cartesian self-instantiating principles. He accepts as the critical designation of god the qualitatively infinite, agreeing with Descartes that this is present to consciousness, but contending against Descartes that this presence is immediate. The infinite is present to human consciousness not as an idea, but as itself—as god! The infinite must not only account for its own idea, as in Cartesian first philosophy; the infinite must be its own idea. But it is one idea among many, not totally unlike space in Newton. There is no reflexivity between the infinite substance and its idea; there is identity. Rather than the existentialist interpretation of Descartes, which reduced reality to the perspectives of the subject, Malebranche works with an ontological interpretation that locates all reality and all evidence with the transcendent: the trace of god has to be god himself. One does not so much infer the existence of god as deduce that what already occupies one's consciousness is divine: "the infinite, infinitely infinite." Through the shift in the coordinates of inquiry,

Malebranche expands philosophic inquiry to include what was once the climax and fulfillment of theology: the intuitive vision of god, kept from being beatific only by the feebleness of its perception and the vagueness of its impression.

That god himself becomes the *forma intelligibilis* of the human mind was not a novel doctrine. The medieval theologians had formulated this teaching and advanced its justification as an explanation of the evangelical promise of the beatific vision, the supreme triumph of revelation and grace. Malebranche adapts this doctrine and locates it at the heart of philosophy. True, one does not know god absolutely, but one can see his essence insofar as it is relative to created and possible beings (the divine ideas). This is not the fullness of the beatific vision promised to the blessed, but it is far beyond what Descartes had allowed to human experience and to philosophic inquiry. The question of the existence of god remains properly philosophic, but Malebranche extends its empire to include god as imitable and imitated by all things. Just as Christ was not necessary to establish the existence of the Christian god, so now the Logos is not necessary to communicate the vision of god. Christians need Christ neither for the existence nor for the perception of god. As the philosophic form was expanded to handle further questions about god, so this all-comprehensive god who initiates all philosophical reflection will further drive the content comprehended under this form to its own inner alienation.

Despite the promise inherent in the intuition of Malebranche and the correlations between the infinitely perfect and being, this comprehensive god is still known as one reality among many. This point is critical because it continues Malebranche in a line from which he would fain extricate himself. Neither being nor the world bespeak god. God bears witness to himself in the form of an idea, as one subjective modification of the mind among many. In this Malebranche follows Descartes. But he pushes this particularity further. God is not only this subjective modification of human consciousness; his causality is placed in polar opposition to that of individual things. With Descartes, Malebranche does not allow a world that witnesses to god; god guarantees the world. But he goes further—much further: god carries the world into human consciousness through the divine ideas. The world not only stands in its Cartesian inability to manifest god; it is incapable of acting on a human being at all. In fact, it is intrinsically incapable of any causality at all. Descartes' world was secular; before the all-devouring god of Malebranche, the world is not only secular, but impotent. Descartes had introduced the *res extensa* and the *res cogitans* as two different substances. Malebranche posed them in such alienation one from another that one could not act upon the other. What is more, material things could not act upon one another: "There is a contradiction in saying that one body can move another." All causality is god's, extending even to the last syllable of local motion: "The moving force of a body in motion is nothing but the will of the Creator, who keeps it successively in different places."[41] Nature is not only alienated from human nature; nature is alienated from its own causality, alienated from itself.

This alienation was inevitable with a comprehensive principle that had waxed so powerful. The infinite does everything, and the divine causality among things becomes the occasion for the divine causality upon the human soul. Malebranche's world is not only secular; it is sterile. Nature had become mechanical for Descartes, and his mechanics had excluded all final causality. Nature remained mechanical for Malebranche, but his philosophy religiously excluded all causality from the world. And nature did nothing because god did everything. God's greatness was reflected in nature's impotence. This extraordinary opposition between nature and god in the doctrine of Malebranche was not that sensible things needed divine ideas to exist and divine causality to act—this was part of a Christian patrimony. The extraordinary thing was that this divine presence and activity was placed in contradiction to rather than in support of the activity of material things. God became great at the expense of nature. God alienated nature from itself.

Malebranche's philosophy thus presents a threefold alienation: human beings from sensible things through their consciousness of god; nature from god in its secular character; nature from itself because god comprehends all real causality. The dignity of god consisted in two things: the abrogation of all secondary causality in nature, and the dominance of all human consciousness.

Thus, in Malebranche's philosophy, the inner contradictions of the traditions he so carefully developed have reached a crisis. Either god engulfs consciousness by this dominant presence or the divine existence cannot be asserted. Either god causes all human perceptions or the mind is nothing else than matter. Either all activity is really god's or things act in godless isolation. Either philosophy can manifest the existence of god or nothing can manifest that existence. The alternatives are clear. No matter where one touches the questions of content—human beings, god, the sensible world—one finds a pitch of inner alienation and contradiction. Malebranche answered each of these antinomies with the first alternative, but his was only a moment in an ongoing dialectic that his writings had radicalized.

What Malebranche was to Descartes, Samuel Clarke was to Newton. Both theologians, however varied their intellectual engagements and opposed their confessions, kept one policy in common: they accepted the philosophic settlements of which they were heirs. Malebranche transposed the Universal Mathematics to an operational matrix, brought to bear upon experience to disclose the vision of god within human consciousness. Clarke kept the

logistic method of Newton, but translated the theology contained in fragments throughout the Universal Mechanics into a carefully crafted Euclidian
structure of analysis and synthesis. This complete movement takes place
twice. Through analysis, contingent being is reduced to necessary being and
through synthesis, this being is conjoined with the eternal, infinite, omnipresent, and unique as predicates proper only to it. Then this self-existent is
analyzed into personal attributes and these are synthesized with power,
wisdom, and all moral perfections. Malebranche and Clarke both accepted a
mathematicized philosophy as the proper location for the problem of god.
Clarke engaged the atheists with a method as much like mathematics as
possible because only in this way could he lay "the First Foundations of
Religion" in philosophy. Lessius and the tradition that stemmed from his
writings insisted that the question of the existence of god should be handled
philosophically. Clarke developed this dependence of religion or theology
upon philosophy until the true philosophy constituted and defended the
ground of all religion.[42] That Christology or religious experience received no
mention stirs nary a tremor. The young Clarke had devoted fifty-five
propositions to a massive attack on the Athanasian Creed with all its
presumed divinization of the Logos. No Christology is needed. The Universal Mechanics of Newton could entertain these theological issues quite
adequately. Now Clarke advanced its competency further. The mechanical
natural philosophy grounded all religion; religion became a corollary of
mechanics.

With Newton, Clarke found the real underlying the phenomenal; an
entitative interpretation runs through his works. Appearances are reduced to
the movement and conjunction of atoms in a void, and god to that which
underpins this whole by causality and necessity, constituting the space and
time in which all things take place. But Clarke changes the nature of
Newtonian principles, from the comprehensive force that explains all things to
the reflexive principles in which the subject and the object necessarily involve
each other. The *Principia* had distinguished two types of forces, inertial and
impressed. Clarke translated these into causes, internal and external, and then
reduced all external causes to the internal reflexive principles that could
formally explain themselves. Reflexive principles explain themselves by what
they are, and all other types of causal influences must ultimately lead to these
self-instantiating explanations. Something exists now; something eternally
exists; only the independent being can intrinsically be eternal; only a
reflexive self-existent can be independent; this is the necessary being, god.
God is demonstrated by inference, an implication of what is directly known;
god is never the object of orientation or experience, let alone intuition, nor
does god achieve personal witness in the world. The reflexive principles
allow the necessary being to emerge within a philosophic system, and this in
turn significantly furthers the contradictions within content as well.

The difference in evidence between Malebranche and Clarke bespoke the mechanical coordinates of the seventeenth century: the infinite and the eternal. Descartes began with the idea of infinite substance; Malebranche, with its perception. Newton began with the phenomenon, entailing infinite space and eternal duration. Clarke simplified this for theological purposes to an immediate inference to the eternal: if something exists now, it is absolutely certain that something has existed from all eternity. But these differences are more apparent than real. The tradition of the Universal Mathematics makes appropriate a focus upon the infinite. The tradition of the Universal Mechanics makes appropriate a focus upon the eternal. The Cartesian infinite was limitless perfection; the Newtonian eternity was limitless time. For both theologians, the evidence was a philosophical appropriation of a basis congenial to the mathematical or mechanical traditions from which they came.

Clarke has reached a god commensurate with existence, but by eliminating anything that indicated religion, either by experience or in tradition. The highest and most successful theistic warrant is atomic nature, the personal being inferred from the impersonal, as in Newton. A central question for Clarke must be whether this necessary being was matter. This question could not arise in the Cartesian tradition; the dualism in that first philosophy insured that the *res cogitans* and the *res extensa* would never be confused. The issue emerged inevitably in the Newtonian mechanics when the principle became reflexive, when evidence should reflect its cause.

Yet both Malebranche and Clarke linked their glorification of god to the denigration of matter. Malebranche removed from material bodies any causality of their own. Clarke insisted against Leibniz that the Universal Mechanics could alone "prove matter, or body, to be the smallest and most inconsiderable part of the universe."[43] What Malebranche accomplished by identifying matter with inert and ultimately impotent extension, Clarke accomplished by identifying matter with mass, isolated in an infinite void. Hydrodynamics, the pendulum, and celestial mechanics had given evidence of this void; the void meant that there are places where there is no matter; this absence of matter indicates that it does not have to be, that it is not necessary. Coming from different traditions, both Malebranche and Clarke brought the tension between god and matter to a profound dialectical antagonism. Matter as extension was in every way ineffectual; matter as mass was ultimately inconsiderable. The time was soon to come when this despised matter would wreak a terrible revenge on both theologians and their god. Christology, with its doctrine of the Incarnation, would have read matter religiously in a very different manner.

If the Universal Mechanics was to ground religion, it has to justify a necessary being who was preeminently personal. Here the world comes together as evidence, from the rational processes of human beings to the design discovered in inanimate nature, terminating in the underlying origins of all material life in motion, figure, and mass. While the design within all things manifests his intelligence, the arbitrary choice of these things rather than of others manifests his freedom. This intelligence and this freedom grounds all of those virtues that the Christian insists upon in his god: power, wisdom, and the other moral perfections. Universal Mechanics can comprehend it all and justify the one who is "Ground of all our Prayers and Thanksgivings."[44] One needs no other source of religious affirmation. The logistic structure of mathematicized argument brought to bear upon the data discovered or determined by mechanics is enough. With this structure even metaphysics could be done, a disciplined argument constructed "partly by metaphysical reasoning, and partly from the Discoveries (principally those that have been lately made) in Natural Philosophy."[45] The god that emerges from these carefully constructed arguments is quite adequate to the needs of Christianity. The god of these theologians is Christian in the absence of Christ and religious in the absence of religious experience.

The impetus of a Universal Mathematics led to the comprehensive god of Malebranche, to be established before one began a physics that possessed no theological content, a god whose assertion was the impoverishment of matter. The impetus of a Universal Mechanics led to a god quite independent of religious teaching and experience, a god whose assertion was also the impoverishment of matter. In France, the mechanics was independent and its world was secular, leaving theological issues to another science and satisfied with its own internal principles of matter and impressed motion. In England, mechanics was universal and the world was warrant both for its subsumption of theological issues and for its exploration of the corollaries of existence and design in passage to the existence and attributes of god. In both cases, philosophy was the form of grounded religious assertions, as adequate to these questions as it was alienated from any attempt to introduce religious density.

A subsequent dialectical negation of each of these movements brought them into an internal and concrete unity. From Newton was accepted the universality and adequacy of mechanics. The program he had envisaged became the dream of the century, that all the phenomena of nature would be resolved by procedures similar to those of the *Principia*. From Descartes was accepted the autonomy of mechanics from all alien principles, from any causes which were not mechanical. Newton was denied his theology, but his mechanics were admitted as universal; Descartes was denied his first philosophy, but the mechanical character of his principles eliminated the contradiction inherent in Newton. The synthesis of these movements left the hegemony to a natural philosophy become mechanics. The contradictions inherent in both were resolved in this new unity, a mechanics with only mechanical principles.

The alienation in the previous conjunction of religious content with philosophic form was reduced by the disclosure that what had been thought religious was actually dynamic matter. Religion had entrusted itself to philosophy. Philosophy first subsumed this task, then became the only grounds for religion, then denied religion in order to be true to its mechanical nature. The very appeal of religion had generated its own denial. Religion protested that it could not speak for itself, that only philosophy could argue for it. Philosophy spoke, and its final word was no. In failing to assert its own competence, in commissioning philosophy with its defense, religion shaped its own eventual negation.

Just as the formal contradiction was resolved by the universality of the new mechanics, so the concrete content was brought into unity by the emergence of dynamic matter. Descartes had allowed everything to develop from the principles of matter in motion, but motion had first to be conferred upon inert matter. Newton had allowed everything to develop from various kinds of forces, but the only force intrinsic to matter was inertial. About gravity's origins he would not hypothesize, and he insisted that all mechanical forces eventually pointed to the dominion or force that was god. The next stage of the dialectical development of this content was to negate the alienation of matter from motion, to insist that not only inertial force was *vis insita* but creative self-moving force as well, that just as local motion entailed material bodies so material bodies necessarily entailed local motion. Take matter and motion from Descartes as adequate to all physical phenomena, collapse the distinction between them, and one has dynamic matter. Take the comprehensive principle from Newton, deny any nonmechanical force, and one not only restores the integrity of mechanics, but has in dynamic matter something as comprehensive as the Universal Mechanics could demand. By asserting this universality of mechanics with mechanical principles, one has given absolute autonomy and comprehensiveness to mechanics. By asserting dynamic matter as ultimately comprehending all mechanical principles, one has at last a content integral to the form in which it is articulated. By resolving the alienation of form from content and evidence from principles, philosophy has reached a new integration; it is reached by eliminating religion as a form and god as a content. The resolution of the contradictions has been achieved by the negation of their alienation, by the denial of god. In reasserting the positivity of matter, god has been eliminated; just as in asserting the emancipation of natural philosophy, theology had been left bereft of foundation and evidence and naked to its enemies.

The young Karl Marx noted this dialectical pattern of emancipation and the atheism which it entailed, though he read the cast of characters somewhat differently, and within this pattern he located his own efforts in politics and economic theory:

Philosophy has done nothing in politics that physics, mathematics, medicine, every science, has not done within its own sphere. Bacon of Verulam declared theological physics a virgin vowed to God and barren; he emancipated physics from theology and she became fruitful. You have no more to ask the politician if he has faith than the doctor. Immediately before and after the time of Copernicus' great discoveries on the true solar system the law of gravitation of the state was discovered: the centre of gravity of the state was found within the state itself. As various European governments tried to apply this result with the initial superficiality of practice to the system of the equilibrium of states, similarly Macchiavelli and Campanella began before them and Hobbes, Spinoza, and Hugo Grotius afterwards down to Rousseau, Fichte and Hegel, to consider the state with the eye of man and to develop its natural laws from reason and experience, not from theology, any more than Copernicus did.[46]

Francis Bacon had indeed protested against the corruption of philosophy by theology, but his protests were against founding a system of natural philosophy on the first chapter of Genesis. "From this unwholesome mixture of things human and divine there arises not only a fantastic philosophy but also a heretical religion."[47] But the history of ideas had followed precisely the opposite career. Instead of founding philosophy on religion, it founded religion on philosophy. Its effect was not heretical religion but an emancipated philosophy which eventually negated all religion. Over the centuries, "physics, mathematics, medicine, every science" asserted their own autonomy from physicotheologies, and the theologians who had deposited all their coin with them found themselves bankrupt. These sciences moved into atheism with Diderot and d'Holbach only because theology had made them the primary area of its evidence and of its argument. They could only establish their own autonomy by the denial of this theological character. Theology alienated its own nature by generating a philosophy that functioned as apologetics. Philosophy eventually developed into natural philosophy, which became mechanics. And mechanics established its own nature by denying that its evidence possessed any theological significance and by negating any theological interest.

By the heady age of the Enlightenment, the tensions and contradictions within the various forms of natural theology had reached such a point that the next stage of dialectical development was inevitable. As theology generated apologetic philosophy and philosophy generated Universal Mathematics and Universal Mechanics, and as these in their turn co-opted theology to become the foundations of theistic assertions, theology itself became a *disciplina otiosa* in the justification or establishment of its own subject-matter. When the contradictions between Cartesian and Newtonian mechanics were further negated by a mechanics like Newton's that resolved all its data, evidence, and explanations into mechanical principles, god became a *deus otiosus*. The Enlightenment simply had to synthesize Newtonian mechanics as universal with Cartesian principles as reflexively mechanical. Natural theology itself disappeared along with the god it had for centuries defended. In following the form of thought, one internal mode of reflection gave way to another until a synthesis was reached in an autonomous physics—"godless" only because the theologians had insisted that it ground theology. In following the content, impersonal nature eventually moved through its theological denials to reassert itself as dynamic with the predicates once reserved for god, "eternal" and "infinite."

The tracing of these complex dialectical lines of development allows some response to the question that generated their study. Modern atheism took not only its meaning but its existence from the self-alienation of religion. In an effort to secure its basis, religion unknowingly fathered its own estrangement.

Christianity would not accept the skepticism of the fifteenth and sixteenth centuries as its canonical appraisal of the human intellect, and then affirm the divine existence through an irrational faith glorying over epistemological ruins. Certainly such a strategy existed; certainly it engaged intellects of the highest quality and religious influence; but it did not prevail. It did not specify the culture. What later generations would title "fideism" was always present, but never definitive. But if Christianity would not guarantee its god through an attack on reason, it must give an account of its assertion of the divine existence. In response to this need, religion as a reality distinct in itself—religious experience, event, and personal witness—was relegated to the realm of faith, and the preambles or the foundations of such a faith were to be sought elsewhere. Religion abandoned the justification intrinsic to its own nature and experience, and insisted that its vindication would be found in philosophy, become natural philosophy, become mechanics. This decision was not always and everywhere; but it determined the progress of the religious culture in its most profoundly apologetic moment.

Atheism is not the secret of religion, as Feuerbach would have it, but it is the secret contradiction within a religion that denies its own abilities to deal cognitively with what is central to its nature. Atheism is the secret of that religious reflection which justifies the sacred and its access to the sacred primarily through its own transmogrification into another form of human knowledge or practice, as though the only alternative to fideism were such an alienation, as though religion had to become philosophy to remain religion. The unique character of religious knowledge does not survive this reduction. Another discipline cannot be made more fundamental and religion its corollary or its epiphenomenon. Religion, with all of its intersubjec-

[margin note:] Buckley's apparent favorite

tivities, cannot but be destroyed if dissolved into some other human experience in order to justify its most critical cognitive claims. Eventually, such a dissolution will out as atheism.

This self-alienation of religion or of its theological reflection lies at the heart of the atheistic transition in the modern world. The strength of the transition is derived from its dialectical pattern: religion itself, to defend itself, is denying itself. This strength became irresistible because of the very enthusiasm with which the theologians turned to philosophic inference from the sensible universe and to the philosophic denigration of matter as the foundation upon which to establish the existence of god. For if religion itself has no inherent grounds upon which to base its assertion, it is only a question of time until its inner emptiness emerges as positive denial. The pattern that has been traced in the seventeenth and eighteenth centuries and glimpsed in its transposition into the nineteenth possesses its own logic. Eventually the self-denial of religion becomes the more radical, but consistent, denial that is atheism. If religion has no intrinsic justification, it cannot be justified from the outside. The very forces mustered against atheism will dialectically generate it, just as the northern tribes enlisted to defend Rome and its empire eventually occupied the city and swept the empire away.

What else can theology learn from this repeated and repeatable pattern in the history of ideas? Not that the metaphysical enterprise becomes false when it comes to deal with the reality of god. This is not true of the great metaphysicians from Plato and Aristotle to Pierce and Whitehead. The philosophical investigation of the world has not found it godless in all the thousands of years of human wisdom. To insist that such reflection can not substitute for the interpersonal experience of the sacred characteristic of religion is not to assert that a doctrine of god that is formally and explicitly philosophical is secretly and inevitably atheistic. The dynamism of the inquiring mind inevitably moves toward a transcendence that makes sense out of that which does not explain or justify itself. A doctrine of god can arise within such an inquiry when the namelessly transcendent is approached as its asymptotic horizon, or as the never-comprehended "lure of transcendence," or as that which essentially is, giving context and intelligibility to everything else encountered and understood but remaining endlessly other. God has emerged again and again in the history of wisdom as the direction toward which wonder progresses. The project of natural theology need not stand deficient or "idolatrous" as it discloses or objectifies the stages of human transcendence or the implications of the universe given in human experience. It is neither deluded nor simpleminded to discover with Augustine that everything within human scope, especially the human person, points beyond itself.

Perhaps theology can learn further that the question about the existence of god is so profoundly and pervasively human that it inescapably involves a circle in which all of the human disciplines figure and condition one another. There is a depth at which human beings confront the great issues of life that lies beneath the formal separation of the sciences and of the sciences from the humanities. Indeed, the various disciplines emerge from this experience. They respond with calibrated study to aspects of the issues that this experience embodies, and it is to this experience that they return as they minister to the unity of the human person and the integrity of human life. Here the question of god is posed most radically. It has engaged reflections that are philosophical and theological, psychological and phenomenological, humanistic and scientific. Often only partial answers can be given to the question. But the question, as it emerges out of human existence, formulates a context that is irreducibly religious. *God* is not a neutral term. It denotes one who calls and lays the absolute claim upon human life and practice that is religious. The commensurate evidence with which the divine existence is asserted or denied must include both the external presence of the saints of religious culture, or of Jesus, and the internal orientation of human beings toward the ultimate, the sacred, or the absolute. As the question is primarily religious, so the religious experience of human beings provides evidence that cannot be supplanted by something else.

The history that has been followed indicates that the god of the religious culture of the West cannot be asserted either by bracketing the religious phenomena, history, and experiences that enter into god's intelligibility or by neglecting the religious warrant and its cognitive claims by which this divine existence is maintained. Religion has too long recognized in god a personal density, a weight of intersubjective relationships, that neither inference nor external information can sustain by themselves. The god who is so personal must have the personal as the foundation of his human assertion, and all other reflection that bears upon the existence of this god must have the personal as its critical context.

The Christian god cannot have a more fundamental witness than Jesus Christ, even antecedent to the commitments of faith; Christian theology cannot abstract from Christology in order to shift the challenge for this foundational warrant onto philosophy. Within the context of a Christology and a Pneumatology of both communal and personal religious experience, one can locate and give its own philosophical integrity to metaphysics, but Christology and Pneumatology are fundamental. If one abrogates this evidence, one abrogates this god. For the Christian, Jesus belongs to the intelligibility and to the truth of god. What god is, and even that god is, has its primordial evidence in the person and in the event that is Jesus Christ. This person and this event make claims about god. These claims take precedence if one is to establish the truth of any conclusion that such a god exists. Wolfhart Pannenberg has put this contention very accurately: "Who and what God is becomes defined only by the Christ event. . . . Jesus belongs to the definition of God."[48] Without the modification and development of human subjectivity through religious influence, experience, and contents, and without the confrontation with the person and history of Jesus to which this subjectivity responds, neither impersonal evidence nor philosophic inference can sustain the god sacred within a Christian religious culture.

What is true of Christianity finds its striking parallel in Judaism. Julius Guttmann has written of Israel's

> idea of God, not the fruit of philosophic speculation but the product of the immediacy of the religious consciousness. . . . The decisive feature of monotheism is that it is not grounded in an abstract idea of God, but in an intensely powerful divine will which rules history. This ethical voluntarism implies a thoroughly personalistic conception of God, and determines the specific character of the relationship between God and man. This relationship is an ethical-voluntaristic one between two moral personalities, between an "I" and a "Thou." As God imposes his will upon that of man, so man becomes aware of the nature of his relationship to God.[49]

However one reads this "voluntarism," the personal lies at the heart of this confession. Nothing can substitute for it and still sustain the affirmations of the great monotheistic religions.

Metaphysics and philosophy, the common-sense inferences from obvious phenomena and the implications of the dynamic orientation of the human spirit, the witness of conscience and even the arguments from evidence available in the sciences—all can second the god of such confessions, but they cannot substitute for personal disclosures and their witness. The god defined in religion cannot be affirmed or supported adequately over time without the unique reality that is religion.

For the pattern described here has not only happened but will inevitably recur when two things coincide as internal contradictions. First, when the culture insists that god is preeminently personal, intimately involved with human subjectivity and history, and the argument takes as its fundamental evidence for this assertion something impersonal. Second, when religion attempts to maintain the god of religion without any reference to religious experience or personal witness, history, or event, and the argument becomes irreducibly inferential. Both the intrinsic contradiction within content and the concomitant contradiction between content and form will eventually tell. To insist that god is personal, and to insist as well that human beings have no basic experience or personal manifestation of this personality such as would engage the cognitive claims of religion itself, leaves too great a gulf between experience and reason. In that conflict, reason inevitably gives way

who insisted on this?

to experience. This history adds one more lesson to that of dialectical contradiction: if an antimony is posed between nature or human nature and god, the glory of one in conflict with the glory of the other, this alienation will eventually be resolved in favor of the natural and the human. Any implicit, unspoken enmity between god and creation will issue in atheism.

In the centuries in which these lessons were being driven home to the Christian culture of Europe, there was at least one figure who weighed religious reflection and found it moving unknowingly and progressively into its own estrangement. The troubled, sensitive Blaise Pascal framed prophetically the sweep of such a movement, the outcome of which the history of ideas has substantiated: "All of those who seek God apart from Christ, and who go no further than nature, either find no light to satisfy them or come to devise a means of knowing and serving God without a mediator, thus falling into either atheism or deism, two things almost equally abhorrent to Christianity."[50] The origin of atheism in the intellectual culture of the West lies thus with the self-alienation of religion itself.

This book is an incoherent attack on a straw man!

Abbreviations

ANET	*Ancient Near Eastern Texts*, ed. James B. Pritchard. Princeton: Princeton University Press, 1955.
AT	*Oeuvres de Descartes*, ed. Charles Adam and Paul Tannery. Paris: Cerf, 1887–1909.
CDD	*Conversation Between D'Alembert and Diderot*, in Kemp.
DEPW	*Diderot's Early Philosophical Works*, ed. M. Jourdain. Chicago: Open Court, 1916.
DBAG	Samuel Clarke, *A Demonstration of the Being and Attributes of God*. Ninth edition. London: Botham/Knapton, 1738.
DIN	Denis Diderot, *De L'Interpretation de la nature*, in *OP*.
DND	Cicero, *De natura deorum*. Loeb edition. London: Heinemann, 1933.
DNR	Samuel Clarke, *A Discourse Concerning the Unchangeable Obligations of Natural Religion, and the Truth and Certainty of the Christian Revelation*. Ninth Edition. London: Botham/Knapton, 1738.
DPN	L. Lessius, *De providentia Numinis et Animi immortalitate*. Paris: Lethielleus, 1880.
EDD	Denis Diderot, *Entretien entre D'Alembert et Diderot*, in *OP*.
Enc.	*Encyclopédie ou dictionnaire raisonné des sciences, des arts et des métiers*, ed. Denis Diderot and M. D'Alembert. Paris: Briasson, 1751–1780.
H-R	*The Philosophical Works of Descartes*, trans. E. S. Haldane and G. R. T. Ross. Cambridge: Cambridge University Press, 1931.
K-C	Isaac Newton, *Philosophiae Naturalis Principia Mathematica*, ed. A. Koyré and I. B. Cohen. Cambridge: Harvard University Press, 1972.
Kemp	*Diderot. Interpreter of Nature: Selected Writings*, ed. J. Kemp. New York: International, 1963.
LA	Denis Diderot, *Lettre sur les aveugles à l'usage de ceux qui voient*, in *OP*.

LB	Denis Diderot, *Letter on the Blind for the Use of Those Who See*, in *DEPW*.
LBI	*Les Bijoux indiscrets*, ed. Jean Macary et al. Paris: Hermann, 1978.
L-C	*Leibniz-Clarke Correspondence*, ed. H. G. Alexander. Manchester: Manchester University Press, 1956.
NS	Norman Kemp Smith, *New Studies in the Philosophy of Descartes*. London: Macmillan, 1952.
OCD	Denis Diderot, *Oeuvres complètes*, ed. J. Assézat. Paris: Garnier, 1875.
OCJM	*Oeuvres complètes de Jean Meslier*, ed. Deprun Desné and Albert Soboul. Paris: Antropos, 1970–1972.
OCM	*Oeuvres complètes de Malebranche*, ed. A. Robinet. Paris: Vrin, 1962– .
ODP	Denis Diderot, "On Dramatic Poetry," in *European Theories of Drama*, ed. B. H. Clark. New York: Appleton, 1929.
OP	Denis Diderot, *Oeuvres philosophiques*, ed. P. Vennière. Paris: Garnier, 1961.
OPC	*Oeuvres philosophiques de Condillac*, ed. G. Le Roy. Paris: Presses Universitaires de France, 1947.
PD	*Discours de la poésie dramatique à M. Grimm*, in *OCD*.
PL	*Patrologiae cursus completus*, ed. J. P. Migne. Paris: Series latina, Migne, 1844–55.
PP	Denis Diderot, *Pensées philosophiques*, in *OP*.
PPSMM	Denis Diderot, *Principes philosophiques sur la matière et le mouvement*, in *OCD*.
PPMM	Denis Diderot, *Philosophic Principles on Matter and Motion*, in Kemp.
RG	L. Lessius, *Rawleigh His Ghost*. English Recusant Literature, 1558–1640, vol. 349. London: Scholar Press, 1977.
SV	Denis Diderot, *Lettres à Sophie Volland*, ed. A. Babelon. Paris: Gallimard, 1930.

Notes

Introduction

1 Cyril Aldred, *Akhenaten: Pharaoh of Egypt—A New Story* (London: Thames and Hudson, 1968), p. 256. Sir Alan Gardiner, *Egypt of the Pharaohs. An Introduction* (New York: Oxford University Press, 1966), pp. 233–235.

2 Stela inscription n. 34183 in the Cairo Museum, originally erected in the Temple of Amun at Karnak by Tutankhamun. The stela was later usurped by Horemheb who replaced the name of Tutankhamun with his own, since the former was tainted by his relationship to Akhenaten. The stela inscription has been edited and translated in James B. Pritchard, ed., *Ancient Near Eastern Texts* (Princeton: Princeton University Press, 1955), pp. 251–252. In the restoration and translation of the text, square brackets have been used for restoration; parentheses indicate interpolations made by the translator; a lacuna is indicated with an ellipsis; and italics indicate a doubtful translation.

3 Aldred, *Akhenaten*, pp. 245–246, 66–67; Gardiner, *Egypt*, pp. 214ff.

4 "The Hymn to the Aton," Pritchard, *ANET*, pp. 369–371. The solar disk is variously transliterated into English as "Aten" or "Aton."

5 Stela inscription n. 34183, Pritchard, *ANET*, p. 251 n. 2.

6 Plutarch, "Life of Pericles," in *Plutarch's Lives*, English translation by Bernadotte Perrin. Loeb Classical Library (London: William Heinemann, 1915), 32. There are variant and contradictory accounts of this trial; see Diogenes Laertius, *Lives of Eminent Philosophers*, English translation: by R. D. Hicks. Loeb Classical Library (London: William Heinemann, 1925), 2.12ff. For a critical evaluation of this history, see G. S. Kirk and J. E. Raven, *The Presocratic Philosophers: A Critical History with a Selection of Texts* (Cambridge: Cambridge University Press, 1957), p. 364: "Fortunately too, the most important facts of his life are not in dispute. There can be no question that he spent a large part of his active life in Athens, that he was fairly intimately associated with Pericles, that he was prosecuted on a charge (at least among others) of impiety, and that he thereupon withdrew to Lampsacus."

7 The story is given under "Diagoras the Melesian" in *Suidae Lexicon*, ed. Thomas Gaisford with annotations by Godfrey Bernhardy (Halle and Braunschweig: Sumptibus Schwetschkiorum, 1853), vol. 1, cols. 1272–1273. The Lexicon cites this story also from Aristophanes, "The Birds," 11. 1071ff. For an assessment of

this legend, see A. B. Drachmann, *Atheism in Pagan Antiquity*, trans. Ingebord Anderson (London: Gyldendal, 1922), pp. 31–34.

8 Eusebius, *Praeparatio evangelica* 14, 3, 7. See Hermann Diels, *Die Fragmente der Vorsokratiker*. 10th edition, ed. Walther Kranz (Berlin: Weidmannsche Verlagsbuchhandlung, 1960), 80 B 4 (II 265, 6–8) (M). When a standard translation is modified by a comparison with the original text, this will be indicated by (m); if the translation is my own, this will be indicated by (M). Drachmann, *Atheism*, pp. 39–42, 156. See Joseph Owens, *A History of Ancient Western Philosophy* (New York: Appleton-Century-Crofts, 1959), pp. 158–160. Owens comments upon this text: "This seems to be merely a practical statement of the difficulties encountered in proving anything rationally either for or against the gods. The further context and development of the theme are not known."

9 Plato, *Apology of Socrates*, 26b–e. The Greek text is found in John Burnet, *Plato's Euthyphro, Apology of Socrates and Crito* (Oxford: Clarendon Press, 1924). For the English translation, see Thomas G. West, *Plato's Apology of Socrates* (Ithaca: Cornell University Press, 1979), pp. 31–32.

10 *Apology* 28e; West, *Plato's Apology*, p. 35.

11 Justin Martyr, *First Apology*, 6. For English translation, see Thomas B. Falls, *Writings of Saint Justin Martyr* (New York: Christian Heritage, 1948), pp. 38–39 (m).

12 Justin Martyr, *First Apology*, 13; Falls, *Justin Martyr*, p. 45.

13 Irenaeus, *Adversus haereses*, 2.14.2. Diels, *Fragmente*, 59 A 113 (II 31, 18–19). Aurelius Augustinus, *De civitate Dei contra paganos*, 8.2. For the English translation, see *Concerning the City of God Against the Pagans*, trans. Henry Bettenson (London: Penguin, 1972), pp. 300–301.

14 Cicero's own list is short: "Most thinkers have affirmed that the gods exist, and this is the most probable view and the one to which we are all led by nature's guidance; but Protagoras declared himself uncertain, and Diagoras of Melos and Theodorus of Cyrene held that there are no gods at all [nullos esse omnino]." To these is added a third group: "There are and have been philosophers [the Epicureans] who hold that the gods exercise no control over human affairs whatever. But if their opinion is the true one, how can piety, reverence, or religion exist?" *De natura deorum* 1. 1. 2–3. The text of *DND*, the English translation, and the system of references are taken from Cicero, *De natura deorum*, with an English translation by H. Rackham, Loeb Classical Library (London: William Heinemann, 1933). Cotta, as a representative of the New Academy, cites the same listing of Protagoras as undecided and of Diagoras and Theodore as atheistic in order to undermine the Epicurean argument for the existence of the gods which used as its evidence the universal agreement of all peoples; See *DND* 1. 23. 63. Sextus Empiricus gives a similar index in his *Outlines of Pyrrhonism*: "While the majority declare that the gods exist, some deny their existence, like those who follow Diagoras of Melos and also Theodore and Critias the Athenian." Sextus Empiricus, *Outlines of Pyrrhonism*, English translation by R. G. Bury, Loeb Classical Library (London: William Heinemann, 1933) 3. 218 (m). This list is expanded in his *Adversus mathematicos* 9. 50–59 and includes Euhemerus, Diagoras of Melos, Prodicus of Ceos, Theodore of Cyrene, and Critias. The agnosticism of Protagoras is noted and Epicurus' name is listed because "according to some in his popular exposition, Epicurus allows the existence of God, but in expounding the real nature of things he does not allow for it." And finally, Sextus includes the skeptics who hold that the arguments for

and against the existence of god balance each other. Sextus Empiricus, *Against the Physicists*, English translation by R. G. Bury, Loeb Classical Library (Cambridge, Mass.: Harvard University Press, 1936) 1. 50–59. (In the Loeb edition, the ninth and tenth books of *Adversus mathematicos* are taken as a separate work and entitled *Against the Physicists*.) Claudius Aelianus contrasts the reverence which the mice on an island in the Black Sea proffer the gods with the irreverence of Hippon and Diagoras and adds the name of Herostratus of Ephesus because he was responsible for the burning of the temple of Artemis in 356 B.C. These he numbers within what he calls "the register of the enemies of the gods" (ὁ λοιπὸς τῶν θεοῖς ἐχθρῶν κατάλογος). Aelian, *On the Characteristics of Animals*, English translation by A. F. Scholfield, Loeb Classical Library (London: William Heinemann, 1959), 6. 40. Finally, in his *historia*, Aelianus contrasts the universal consensus among the barbarians, that is the Indians, the Celts, and the Egyptians, about the existence and providential care of the gods with those Greeks who have fallen into atheism (εἰς ἀθεότητα): "Euhemerus of Messene or Diogenes the Phrygian or Hippon or Diagoras or Sosias or Epicurus, not an Indian or Celt or Egyptian. For these Barbarians attest that there are gods and that they have a providential care for us, and that they presignify events by birds, omens, entrails, and other observations and rules, which teach men the providence of God towards them." Claudii Aeliani, *Varia historia*, ed. Mervin R. Dilts, *Bibliotheca Scriptorum Graecorum et Romanorum Teubneriana* (Leipzig: B. G. Teubner Verlagsgesellschaft, 1974) 2. 31 (M). An English translation is found in Thomas Stanley, *Claudius Aelianus, His Various History* (London: Thomas Dring, 1665), p. 51. For Clement's reversal of this general assessment, see. *Protrepticos* 24, Diels, *Fragmente*, 38 A 8 (I 385–386, 32–1): "I cannot help wondering how Euhemerus of Agrigentum, and Nicanor of Cyprus, and Hippon and Diagoras of Melos, and besides these, that Cyrenian by the name of Theodorus, and numbers of others, who lived a sober life, and had a clearer insight than the rest of the world into the prevailing error respecting those gods, were called Atheists; for if they did not arrive at the knowledge of the truth, they certainly suspected the error of the common opinion; which suspicion is no insignificant seed, and becomes the germ of true wisdom." See also Clement of Alexandria, *Exhortation to the Heathens*, ch. 2 in *The Writings of Clement of Alexandria*, trans. William Weston, Ante-Nicene Christian Library, ed. Alexander Roberts and James Donaldson (Edinburgh: T. and T. Clark, 1880), p. 33 (m).

15 In his commentary on Aristotle's *Physics*, Simplicius associates Hippon with the opinion of Thales that water is the source of all things, but adds the qualification that he "seems to have become even an atheist." Diels, *Fragmente*, 11 A 13 (I 77, 16) (M). Joannes Diaconus, in his allegorical interpretation of Hesiod's *Theogony*, refers to him simply as "Hippon the Atheist," Diels, *Fragmente*, 38 A 6 (I 385 29), as does Alexander of Aphrodisias in his commentary on Aristotle's *Metaphysics*, Diels, *Fragmente*, 38 A 9 (I 386, 5). See also Diels, *Fragmente*, 38 B 2 (I 389, 3). Though he is listed by Aelianus among the atheists, Diogenes of Apollonia insisted that the order of things within the world would have been impossible without an active, directing intelligence. Diels, *Fragmente*, 64 B 3 (II 60, 12–16). For the identification of "that which has intelligence" with air, and this in turn with god: "It seems to me that that which has intelligence (νόησιν) is that which is called Air by humankind; and further, that by this, all creatures are guided, and that it rules everything; for this seems to me to be God and to reach everywhere and to arrange everything and to be in everything." Diels, *Fragmente*,

64 B 5 (II 61, 4–8). For the English translation, see Kathleen Freeman, *Ancilla to the Pre-Socrates Philosophers*, p. 88 (m).

16 Thus Philodemus of Gadara writes of Prodicus in his *De pietate*: "Persaeus [of Ceos] is clear . . . obliterating the divine or knowing nothing about it, when in the [treatise] about the gods he relates things which do not seem to be unpersuasive, namely that those things which nourish and are beneficial are held to be gods and are honored and [that this opinion occurs] first in the writings of Prodicus. According to these [writings] the discoverers and nurses and shelters and the other arts just as Demeter and Dionysus and the . . ." (100. 9. 7). Again, in Sextus Empiricus' *Adversus mathematicos*: "Prodicus of Ceos says that the sun and the moon and the rivers and the springs and in general all the things which benefit our life, the Ancients held as gods because of the benefit which issues from them, just as the Egyptians [did] the Nile; and because of this, bread was held to be Demeter while wine was held to be Dionysus and water Poseidon and fire Haephestus and each of the things which were serviceable" (9. 18). "Those who say that there is no god are called atheists as Euhemerus . . . and Diagoras of Melos and Prodicus of Ceos and Theodore. . . . Prodicus [said] that that which was beneficial for life [τὸ ὠφελοῦν τὸν βίον] was supposed to be a god, as the sun and the moon and the rivers and harbors and meadows and fruits and all other such things" (9. 51–52). Diels, *Fragmente*, 84 B 5 (II 317, 2–7, 12–20) (M).

17 Diels, *Fragmente*, 88 B 25 (II 386–389, 21–5); Freeman, *Ancilla*, pp. 157–158.

18 Drachmann, *Atheism*, pp. 45–48.

19 For Euhemerus, see Sextus Empiricus, *Adversus mathematicos* 9. 17, 51. For a collection of the texts relating to Euhemerus, see Geyza Némethy, *Euhemeri reliquiae* (Budapest: Kiadja a Magyar Tud. Akadémia, 1889). Némethy maintains that in a section of Euhemerus' Ἱερὰ Ἀναγραφή excerpted by Diodorus Siculus and cited by Eusebius in his *Praeparatio evangelica* 2. 2. 8. 9, one obtains an overview of Euhemerus' theology: "Thereafter he said that Uranus was the first to become king, an appropriate man and one disposed to do good and knowledgeable in the movement of the stars, who [he said] was the first to honor the heavenly gods with sacrifices and consequently was also called Uranus [οὐρανός means "heavens"]. He has sons by his wife Hestia [Vesta?], Titan and Kronos, and his daughters were Rhea and Demeter." Némethy, *Euhemeri*, p. 53 (M).

20 Epicurus to Menoeceus: "First of all believe that god is a being immortal and blessed, even as the common idea of a god is engraved on the minds of human beings, and do not assign to him anything alien to his immortality or ill-suited to his blessedness: but believe about him everything that can uphold his blessedness and immortality. For gods there are, since the knowledge of them is clear. But they are not such as the many believe them to be: for indeed they do not consistently represent them as they recognize them to be. And the impious man is not he who denies the gods of the many, but who attaches to the gods the beliefs of the many." *Epicurus: The Extant Remains*, trans. Cyril Bailey (Oxford: Clarendon Press, 1926), #123–124, pp. 82–85 (m). It is this happiness or perfect beatitude of the gods which excludes all care, anger, or kindness for the world. See Epicurus to Herodotus, ibid., #76–77, pp. 48–49.

21 Diagoras of Melos is almost lost in legend. Sextus Empiricus relates the tale of loss of conviction about the existence of the divine: "And Diagoras of Melos, the dithyrambic poet, was at first, they say, godfearing above all others: for he began his poem in this fashion—'By Heaven's will and Fortune all things are accomplished': but when he had been wronged by a man who had sworn falsely and

suffered no punishment for it he changed round and asserted that God does not exist [μὴ εἶναι θεόν]." *Adversus mathematicos* 9. 53. Suidas gives the title of his work against the existence of the gods as ᾿Αποπυργίζουτες Λόλοι. *Suidae Lexicon*, 1, cols. 1271–1274. For the discussion of the two Diagorases and their possible identity as Diagoras of Melos, see Drachmann, *Atheism*, pp. 31–34, 39, 50.

22 Diogenes Laertius makes Theodore's atheism seem absolute: "Theodore was one who utterly rejected the opinions about the gods (τὰς περὶ θεῶν δοξας). And I have come across a book of his entitled *Concerning the Gods*, which is not to be despised. It is said that Epicurus took most of what he wrote from this work." *Lives of Eminent Philosophers* 2. 97 (M). Still, "opinions" could mean the current religious persuasions, and Epicurus did not deny the existence of the gods. Sextus Empiricus calls him simply θεόδωρος ὁ ἄθεος and maintains that his work *Concerning the Gods* demolished the theological beliefs of the Greeks with a number of various arguments. *Adversus mathematicos* 9. 55. Diogenes Laertius relates of Bion of Borysthenes that he became a disciple of Theodore of Cyrene after hearing him lecture and that "in his familiar talk he would often vehemently assail belief in the gods, a taste which he had derived from Theodore. Afterwards, when he fell ill (so it was said by the people of Chalcis where he died), he was persuaded to wear an amulet and to repent of his offences against religion." *Lives of Eminent Philosophers* 4. 52–54.

23 Plato, *Epistle VII*, 342a–d, in *Timaeus, Critias, Cleitophon, Menexenus, and Epistles*, ed. R. G. Bury. Loeb Classical Library (London: William Heinemann, 1929), pp. 532–535 (m).

24 Plato, *Sophist*, 263e. Unless otherwise noted, the English translation of Plato is taken from Edith Hamilton and Huntington Cairns, eds., *The Collected Dialogues of Plato Including the Letters*, Bollingen Series 71. (New York: Random House, 1963), p. 1011. See *Theaetetus*, 189e: "Socrates: And do you accept my description of the process of thinking? Theaetetus: How do you describe it? Socrates: As a discourse that the mind carries on with itself about any subject it is considering." Hamilton and Cairns, *Collected Dialogues*, p. 895.

25 Hans-Georg Gadamer, *Truth and Method*, trans. Garrett Barden and John Cumming (New York: Seabury Press, 1975), pp. 378–387.

26 Plato, *Republic*, 2. 368c–369c, in Hamilton and Cairns, *Collected Dialogues*, pp. 614–615.

27 George T. Buckley, *Atheism in the English Renaissance* (New York: Russell and Russell, 1965), p. 64. For the background of Cheke's work, see pp. 15–16, 36–37. John Strype related that Cheke's essay "hath lyen for ought I know this hundred and fifty years and more in Obscurity; but lately discovered in the Library of University College, Oxon by the Reverend Mr. W. Elstob, then a Fellow of that House. Who did not only courteously transcribe it for me, but hath now voluntarily taken the Pains to translate it out of Cheke's Elegant Latin into English, for the more common Benefit." *The Life of Sir John Cheke, Kt., First Instructer Afterwards Secretary of State to King Edward VI* (London: John Wyat, 1705), "Advertisement."

28 C. W. King, ed., *Plutarch's Morals: Theosophical Essays*. Bond's Classical Library (London: George Bell and Son, 1898), pp. 272–273. See also G. Buckley, *Atheism in the English Renaissance*, pp. 15–16.

29 G. Buckley, *Atheism in the English Renaissance*, p. 71n.

30 G. Buckley, *Atheism in the English Renaissance*, p. 50. The irony of Walter

Devereux's anxious denunciation is not lost on Buckley, who comments dryly about Essex's "concern for religion that one would have thought incompatible with his character."

31 Thomas Nashe, "Christs Teares over Jerusalem," Q 1, *The Works of Thomas Nashe*, edited from the original text by Ronald B. McKerron (Oxford: Basil Blackwell, 1958), vol. 2, pp. 121–122. Nashe speaks of the atheist as a person who has been "Diagoriz'd"—after Diagoras of Melos—and urges that all the theological forces in England should concentrate upon this godlessness: "University men that are called to preache at the Crosse and the Court, Arme your selves against nothing but Atheisme, meddle not so much with Sects and forraine opinions, but let Atheisme be the onely string you beate on." Ibid., p. 121. The ambiguity of "atheism" and its indefinite application are realized also in the life of Thomas Nashe, accused by his fellow Cambridge Whit, Gabriel Harvey, of similarities to Pliny and Lucian and given the name of Aretine, the author of *De tribus impostoribus*; see G. Buckley, *Atheism in the English Renaissance*, pp. 83–86.

32 G. Buckley, *Atheism in the English Renaissance*, pp. 29–30, 64–68.

33 Joseph McCabe, *Life and Letters of George Jacob Holyoake* (London: Watts, 1908) 1:199–202, 2:55–59, 265–269.

34 For Huxley's account of his invention of the term "agnostic," see Thomas H. Huxley, "Agnosticism," in *Science and Christian Tradition: Essays* (New York: D. Appleton and Company, 1896), especially p. 239.

35 For the debate between Holyoake and Bradlaugh, see Hypatia Bradlaugh Bonner, *Charles Bradlaugh: A Record of His Life and Work by His Daughter* (London: Adelphi Terrace, 1908), 1:332–336. To this work is appended as part 2 the seventh edition of John H. Robertson's *Account of His Parliamentary Struggle, Politics, and Teaching* in which the events of February 1882 are related (pp. 298ff). See also Walter L. Arnstein, *The Bradlaugh Case* (Oxford: Clarendon Press, 1965), pp. 130ff.

36 McCabe, *Holyoake*, 1:62–87; Bonner, *Bradlaugh*, 1:137ff.

37 Benedict de Spinoza, *Ethics*, bk. 4, appendix, #4. ed. James Gutmann, based on the translation by William Hale White as revised by Amelia Hutchinson Stirling, Hafner Library of Classics (New York: Hafner, 1963), p. 242. See ibid., bk. 5, prop. 36, note: "our salvation, or blessedness, or freedom consists in a constant and eternal love toward God, or in the love of God toward men." p. 275.

38 Pierre Bayle, "Spinoza," *Historical and Critical Dictionary*, selections trans. Richard H. Popkin. Library of the Liberal Arts (Indianapolis: Bobbs-Merrill, 1965), p. 288.

39 Johannes Colerus [Köhler], *The Life of Benedict de Spinoza*, was written in 1706 and translated into English the same year. It is added as an appendix to Frederick Pollock, *Spinoza: His Life and Philosophy* (London: Duckworth, 1889), p. 404.

40 David Hume, *A Treatise of Human Nature*, bk. 1, pt. 4, sec. 5, ed. L. A. Selby-Bigge, 2d. ed., rev. P. H. Nidditch (Oxford: Clarendon Press, 1978), p. 240. See "Spinosa" and "Spinosiste" in *Encyclopédie ou dictionnaire raisonné des sciences, des arts et des métiers, par une société de gens de lettres. mis en ordre et publié par M. Diderot; et quant à la Partie mathématique, par M. D'Alembert* (Paris: Briasson, 1751–1780) 15:463–474. Colerus' own judgment was that "the God of Spinoza is a meer Phantom, an imaginary God." Colerus, *Spinoza*, p. 430.

41 "X," "Athéisme," *Enc.* 1:815–817, "X" was the identifying code of L'Abbé Claude Yvon. For the expansion of this article, see the third edition of *Enc.* (Geneva: Pellet, 1779), 3:806–829.

42 Novalis [Friederich Leopold von Hardenberg], "Fragmente der letzten Jahre, 1799–1800," *Schriften*, ed. Paul Kluckholm in collaboration with Richard Samuel (Leipzig: Bibliographisches Institute A.G., 1892), 3:318, #253. R. H. M. Elwes in his introduction to his own translation of *The Chief Works of Benedict de Spinoza* (New York: Dover, 1955), pp. v–xxxiii traces the reevaluation of Spinoza from the recognition given him by Lessing and from the indebtedness to his writings which Goethe confessed.

43 See Heinrich Scholz, ed., *Die Hauptschriften zum Pantheismusstreit zwischen Jacobi und Mendelssohn* (Berlin: Verlag von Reuther und Reichard, 1916). The statement of Ernest Renan comes from his commemorative address on Spinoza as translated by Santayana. See T. M. Forsyth, "Spinoza's Doctrine of God in Relation to His Conception of Causality," in *Studies in Spinoza: Critical and Interpretative Essays*, ed. S. Paul Kashap (Berkeley and Los Angeles: University of California Press, 1972), p. 3.

44 Nietzsche to Overbeck in a postcard dated July 30, 1881. Walter Kaufmann, *Nietzsche: Philosopher, Psychologist, Antichrist*, 4th ed. (Princeton: Princeton University Press, 1974), p. 140. For a summary of Nietzsche's estimation of Spinoza, see pp. 246–247n19. Vladimer Sergeyevich Solovyov [Solovyev], "The Concept of God: In Defense of the Philosophy of Spinoza," *Collected Works*, [*Sobranie Sochinenii*] 2d ed. (St. Petersburg: Prosvieshchenie, 1911; photographic edition, Brussels: Foyer Oriental Chrétien, 1966) 9:19. For Solovyov's early involvement with the writings of Spinoza and his indebtedness to him, "not only in regard to philosophy, but also in regard to religion," see the bibliographical sketch in the *Collected Works*, 10. I am indebted to Father Frederick Copleston, S.J., for the suggestion of Solovyov and for this translation of the Russian text.

45 Harry Austryn Wolfson, *Religious Philosophy: A Group of Essays* (Cambridge, Mass.: Harvard University Press, 1961), p. 271.

46 Paul Tillich, *Shaking the Foundations* (New York: Charles Scribner's Sons, 1948), p. 63.

47 Friedrich Jodl, "Wissenschaft und Religion," *Von Lebenswege*, art. 67 (Stuttgart and Berlin: J. G. Cotta'sche Buchhandlung Nachfolger, 1916–1917), 2:370. "Nur der Mensch ohne Ideal ist der wahre Atheist; und der Mensch ohne Glauben an die Vervollkommung seiner selbst und der Gattung der wahrhaft Ungläubige."

48 Sigmund Freud, *Civilization and Its Discontents*, ch. 2, *The Standard Edition of the Complete Psychological Works of Sigmund Freud*, ed. James Strachey (London: Hogarth, 1961) (hereafter cited as *SE*) 21:74. See *Future of an Illusion*, ch. 8, *SE* 21:42–45; *Leonardo da Vinci and a Memory of His Childhood*, ch. 5, *SE* 11:119; *Totem and Taboo*, ch. 4.6, *SE* 13:148ff. See also Paul Ricoeur, *Freud and Philosophy: An Essay on Interpretation* (New Haven: Yale University Press, 1977), pp. 541, 203n, and 238n; Ludwig Feuerbach, *The Essence of Christianity* (New York: Harper and Row, 1957), pp. 3–32.

49 John Dewey, *Logic: The Theory of Inquiry* (New York: Henry Holt, 1938), pp. 104–119.

50 Bonner, *Bradlaugh*, p. 337. For Justin Martyr's principle, see *First Apology*, 6. 13: "ὁμολογοῦμεν τῶν τοιούτων νομιζομένων θεῶν ἄθεοι εἶναι" (we confess that we are atheists of those purported gods).

51 Bonner, *Bradlaugh*, p. 87.

52 Augustinus, *De civitate Dei* 4.27; Bettenson, ed., *City of God*, p. 169.

53 Feuerbach, *Essence of Christianity*, pp. 185–278.

54 Thomas Aquinas, *Commentary on the Metaphysics of Aristotle*, trans. John P.

Rowan (Chicago: Regnery, 1961) 1, lect. 10, #167. For a discussion of the origin of this axiom and its bearing on the mystical theology of John of the Cross as well as on the theories of projection in Feuerbach and Freud, see Michael J. Buckley, "Atheism and Contemplation," *Theological Studies* 40, no. 4 (December 1979): 693–699.

55 Georg Wilhelm Friedrich Hegel, *The Science of Logic*, English translation by W. H. Johnson and L. G. Struthers (London: Allen and Unwin, 1961), 2:478. "Method at first may appear as the mere manner and fashion of cognition, and indeed such is its nature. But manner and fashion as method are not only a modality of Being, determined in and for itself, but are posited as modality of cognition as determined by the Notion, and form in so far as form is the soul of all objectivity and every content otherwise determined has its truth in form alone" (pp. 467–468). P. F. Strawson's failure to recognize the profound interconnection between the content and the form, framed as the invariant central subject-matter of descriptive metaphysics and the impermanent, changing idiom in which it is expressed, is severely criticized by James Collins in *Interpreting Modern Philosophy* (Princeton: Princeton University Press, 1972), pp. 16–18. In contrast with Strawson, Collins insists that the philosopher "aims at a radical reconstruction affecting both the old and new methods of inquiry, the basic concepts, and the descriptive analyses. The practice of philosophical minds reveals that all these factors are concretely coadapted and deeply modified by any general reinterpretation."

56 Gadamer, *Truth and Method*, p. 358.

57 Gadamer, *Truth and Method*, p. 401.

58 Richard P. McKeon, "Philosophic Semantics and Philosophic Inquiry," (Mimeographed, Chicago, 1966). For a use of these coordinates of discourse in a previous work, see Michael J. Buckley, S.J., *Motion and Motion's God: Thematic Variations in Aristotle, Cicero, Newton, and Hegel* (Princeton: Princeton University Press, 1971).

59 Richard Robinson, *Plato's Earlier Dialectic* (Oxford: Clarendon Press, 1962), pp. 67–69.

60 Plato, *Republic* 7. 533b, in Hamilton and Cairns, *Collected Dialogues*, p. 765.

61 M. Buckley, *Motion and Motion's God*, p. 9.

62 Magni Aurelii Cassiodori Senatoris, *Variarum libri XII*, ed. C. Fornerius (Paris: apud Sebastianum Nivellium, 1589), 4:51. "Antiquorum diligentissimus imitator, Modernorum nobilissimus institutor, mores tuos fabricae loquuntur: quia nemo in illis diligens agnoscitur, nisi qui et in suis sensibus ornatissimus invenitur." See *Harper's Latin Dictionary: A New Latin Dictionary*, founded on the translation of Freund's *Latin-German Lexicon*, edited by Ethan A. Andrews, revised, enlarged and in great part rewritten by Charlton T. Lewis and Charles Short (New York: American Book, 1907), s. v. "moderna."

63 Etienne Gilson, *History of Christian Philosophy in the Middle Ages* (New York: Random House, 1955), pp. 487, 499.

64 Nicholas Nicholay, Daulphinois, Lord of Arseuile, *The Navigations, peregrinations and voyages, made into Turkie by Nicholas Nicholay*, trans. Thomas Washington (London: Thomas Dawson, 1585) 1. 15, p. 16b. Francis Bacon, Letter to Tobie Matthew, June 1623, in *The Letters and the Life of Francis Bacon, Including All His Occasional Works*, ed. James Spedding, (London: Longmans, Green, Reader and Dyer, 1874), 7:429. It was for this reason that Bacon was having his works translated into Latin!

65 For the ambiguity of "ancient" and "modern" as these terms were transposed and used in the problems of Roman culture by Cato the Censor, in the issue of the principles of science in the fourteenth century, in the battle of the neoterics in the sixteenth and seventeenth centuries, and in the opposition between Swift and Richard Bentley, see Richard P. McKeon, "The Battle of the Books," in *The Knowledge Most Worth Having*, ed. Wayne C. Booth (Chicago: University of Chicago Press, 1967), pp. 173–202. For Swift's *Full and True Account of the Battle Fought Last Friday Between the Ancient and the Modern Books in St. James's Library*, see *The Works of the Rev. Jonathan Swift*, ed. John Nichols (London: Nichols and Son, 1801), 2:207–246.

66 *Oxford English Dictionary*, s. v. "modern."

67 James Collins, *God in Modern Philosophy* (Chicago: Regnery, 1959), p. ix. Idem, *A History of Modern European Philosophy* (Milwaukee: Bruce, 1954), p. 7. See also idem, *Interpreting Modern Philosophy*, pp. 28–29.

68 Ernest Campbell Mossner, *The Life of David Hume*, 2d ed. (Oxford: Clarendon Press, 1980), p. 483. Mossner cites and translates a letter from Diderot to Sophie Volland: "The first time that M. Hume found himself at the table of the Baron, he was seated beside him. I don't know for what purpose the English philosopher took it into his head to remark to the Baron that he did not believe in atheists, that he had never seen any. The Baron said to him: 'Count how many we are here. We are eighteen.' The Baron added: 'It isn't too bad a showing to be able to point out to you fifteen at once: the three others haven't made up their minds.'" Mossner notes that many years later, Samuel Romilly heard the same story with slight variations also from Diderot. Again, Boswell and Samuel Rogers repeat slightly different versions.

69 Georg Wilhelm Friedrich Hegel, *Lectures on the History of Philosophy*, trans. E. S. Haldane and Frances H. Simson (Atlantic Highlands, N. J.: Humanities Press, 1983), 3:387.

70 David B. Barrett, *World Christian Encyclopedia. A Comparative Study of Churches and Religions in the Modern World AD 1900–2000* (Nairobi: Oxford University Press, 1982), p. 6. "Non-religious" is defined as "professing no religion, or professing unbelief or non-belief, non-believers, agnostics, freethinkers, liberal thinkers, non-religious humanists, indifference to both religion and atheism, apathetic, opposed on principle neither to religion nor to atheism; sometimes termed secularists or materialists; also post-Christian, dechristianized or de-religionized populations. Global adherents: (1970) 543,065,300, (1980) 715,901,400 in 177 countries, (1985) 805,784,900" (p. 836). "Atheists" are defined as "persons professing atheism, scepticism, impiety, disbelief or irreligion, or Marxist-Leninist Communism regarded as a political faith, or other quasi-religions, and who abstain from religious activities and have severed all religious affiliation; and others opposed, hostile or militantly opposed to all religion (anti-religious); dialectical materialists, militant non-believers, anti-religious humanists, sceptics. Global adherents: (1970) 165,288,500, (1980) 195,119,400 in 113 countries, (1985) 210,643,500" (p. 817). Allowing for this distinction, Barrett projects that by the turn of the century atheists will be 4.2 percent of the world population (262,447,550) and the non-religious 17.1 percent (1,071,888,370) (p. 6).

71 Schubert M. Ogden, *The Reality of God* (New York: Harper and Row, 1966), p. 13. See Gerhard Ebeling, "The Message of God to the Age of Atheism," *Oberlin College Bulletin* (January 1964): 3–14; interview with Karl Rahner by

Gwendoline Jarczyk, *France Catholique* (June 12, 1981): 3–4; address of Pope John Paul II at the Urbaniana University (October 10, 1980), *L'Osservatore Romano* CXX:236 (October 11, 1980): 1–2.

72 Friedrich Nietzsche, *The Gay Science*, trans. Walter Kaufmann (New York: Random House, 1974), bk. 5, fr. 343, p. 279.

73 John Henry Cardinal Newman, *Apologia Pro Vita Sua* (New York: Norton, 1968), p. 188.

74 Ibid., p. 188.

75 Nietzsche, *The Gay Science*, bk. 3, #125, pp. 181–182 (m).

76 Alasdair MacIntyre and Paul Ricoeur, *The Religious Significance of Atheism* (New York: Columbia University Press, 1969), pp. 5, 17–20, 29.

77 Nietzsche, *The Gay Science*, bk. 3, #125, pp. 181–182.

78 Ibid., bk. 5, #343, p. 279.

79 Henri de Lubac, *The Discovery of God*, trans. Alexander Dru (New York: P. J. Kenedy and Sons, 1960), pp. 18–38.

80 Owen Chadwick, *The Secularization of the European Mind in the Nineteenth Century* (Cambridge: Cambridge University Press, 1977), p. 5.

81 Henri Lion, "Essai sur les oeuvres politiques et morales du Baron d'Holbach," *Annales révolutionnaires* (1922), 14:89. Cited in Virgil W. Topazio, "D'Holbach, Apostle of Atheism," *Modern Language Quarterly* 17:3 (September 1965): 260.

82 Nietzsche, *The Gay Science*, bk. 3, #125, p. 181.

83 Aristotle, *Politics* 1. 2. 1252a. 24–25. The citations from Aristotle, unless otherwise noted, will be taken from *The Basic Works of Aristotle*, ed. Richard McKeon (New York: Random House, 1941) (m).

Chapter 1

1 Peter Gay, *The Enlightenment: An Interpretation*, vol. 1, *The Rise of Modern Paganism* (New York: Norton, 1966), p. 18.

2 Gay, *Enlightenment*, 1:141.

3 Ernst Cassirer, *The Philosophy of the Enlightenment*, trans. Fritz C. A. Koelln and James P. Pettegrove (Princeton: Princeton University Press, 1951), pp. 135–136.

4 Cassirer, *Philosophy of the Enlightenment*, pp. 169–171.

5 "*Un jour tout sera bien*, voilà notre espérance; *Tout est bien aujourd'hui*, voilà l'illusion." Voltaire, "Poëme sur le Desastre de Lisbonne," *Oeuvres Complètes de Voltaire* (Paris: Garnier Frères, 1877), 9:478.

6 Cassirer, *Philosophy of the Enlightenment*, p. 169.

7 Francis Bacon, "On Atheism," *The Essays* (New York: A. L. Burt, 1883), p. 103.

8 Jefferson to John Adams, April 11, 1823, *The Writings of Thomas Jefferson*, ed. A. Bergh (Washington, D.C.: Thomas Jefferson Memorial Association, 1903), 15:425.

9 Thomas Paine, *The Age of Reason, Being an Investigation of True and Fabulous Theology* (New York: Peter Eckler, n.d.), p. 34. [In some editions, this is cited as Part 1, Chapter 17.]

10 Gay, *Enlightenment*, 1:388.

11 Gotthold Ephraim Lessing, *The Education of the Human Race*, in *The Enlightenment: A Comprehensive Anthology*, ed. Peter Gay (New York: Simon & Schuster, 1973), p. 365.

12 Gay, *Enlightenment*, 1:381.

13 Jefferson to Benjamin Rush, April 21, 1803, *The Writings of Thomas Jefferson*, ed. P. L. Ford (New York: Putnam, 1892–1899), 8:223.

14 Ibid., p. 227.

15 Paine, *Age of Reason*, p. 10 [Part 1; Chapter 3].

16 Jefferson to John Adams, April 11, 1823, Ford *Writings of Jefferson*, 15:428ff.

17 Newton to the Reverend Dr. Richard Bentley, *Isaaci Newtoni Opera quae exstant omnia*, commentariis illustrabat Samuel Horsley (London: Excudebat Joannes Nichols, 1779–1785), 4:429.

18 See Daniel Brewster, *Memoirs of the Life, Writings, and Discoveries of Sir Isaac Newton* (Edinburgh: T. Constable, 1850), 2:347–348.

19 Lessing, *Education*, p. 365.

20 *Rawleigh His Ghost. Or, A Feigned Apparition of Syr Walter Rawleigh, to a friend of his, for the translating into English, the Booke of Leonard Lessius (that most learned man) entitled, De providentia Numinis, et Animi immortalitate; written against Atheists, Polititians of these days*, trans. A.B. (1621), in vol. 349, *English Recusant Literature, 1558–1640*, ed. D. M. Rogers (London: Scholar Press, 1977), p. 2 (henceforth cited as *RG*).

21 *RG*, pp. 2–3.

22 Leonard Lessius, S.J., *De providentia numinis et animi immortalitate. Libri duo adversus atheos et Politicos*, in the *Opuscula Leon. Lessii, S.J.* (Paris: P. Lethielleus, 1880), 3:312ff. (henceforth cited as *DPN*).

23 For the biographical outline of Lessius' life, see C. Chamberlain, "Leonard Lessius," in *Jesuit Thinkers of the Renaissance*, ed. Gerald Smith, S.J. (Milwaukee: Bruce, 1939), pp. 133–135.

24 See Ricardo G. Villoslada, S.J., *La Universidad de Paris durante los estudios de Francisco de Vitoria. Analecta Gregoriana XIV*. (Rome: Apud aedes Universitatis Gregorianae, 1938), especially pp. 261ff. Arnaldo M. Lanza, "Lessio Leonardo," *Enciclopedia Cattolica*, 7:1203–1204. See V. Betran de Heredia, "La eneñanza de Santo Tomás en la compañia de Jesús durante el primo siglo de su existencia," *La Ciencia Tomista* 11 (1915):388–408. See also R. Guelluy, "L'évolution des méthodes théologiques à Louvain d'Erasme a Jansénius," *Revue d'histoire ecclésiastique* 37 (1941):31–144. For the beginnings of this revolutionary change from the *Sentences* to the *Summa theologiae*, see Villoslada, pp. 279–307.

25 For the interchange between Aquaviva and Lessius, see X. M. Le Bachelet, "Le Décret d' Aquaviva sur la Grâce Efficace," in *Recherches de Science Religieuse*, (Paris: Bureaux de la revue, 1924), 11B:46–60, 134–159. Lessius eventually carried the day but had to wait upon another General, Mutius Vitelleschi. Two years after this virtual reversal of Aquaviva's decree, the gentle Francis de Sales wrote of his delight in coming across his book containing the opinion of which Francis could say: "J'ai toujours regardé cette opinion comme plus vraie et plus aimable, en tant que plus digne de la grâce et de la miséricorde divine." Bachelet, "Décret," p. 157.

26 Chamberlain, "Lessius," p. 143.

27 *DPN*, preface, pp. 317–318.

28 *RG*, preface, unpaginated. The seventeenth-century translation is often used in this paper because of the fine quality and vigor of its English.

29 Niccolo Machiavelli, *The Prince and the Discourses*, ed. Max Lerner (New York: Random House, 1950), p. 65.

30 *DPN*, 1.1., p. 320; *RG*, 1.1., p. 6: "These men be commonly called Polititians, in that they subject all religion to policy, and consequently by how much the more

any religion is conducing to the bettering of their political and temporall estate; by so much it is by them more esteemed and practised. Among these men Nicholas Machiavel hath gained the chiefest place."

31 *DPN*, 1.1., 1–3, pp. 319–321.

32 *RG*, 1.1., p. 5.

33 *RG*, 1.1., pp. 5–6. Mersenne would read this atheistic presence somewhat differently from Lessius, as will be indicated below. The epithet "atheist" was hurled as freely as "communist" in the middle of the twentieth century, and was used to fix enemies, real or imagined. Lessius' own moderation here, with precise definitions and careful delimitations, contrasts sharply with the abandon with which the term was employed. That great atheist hunter of England, Thomas Nashe, saw them everywhere; see "Christs Teares over Jerusalem," *The Works*, Q1, 2:121–122. See G. Buckley, *Atheism in the English Renaissance*, p. 83. For a similar reading of the social historical context on the European continent, see Lucien Febvre, *Le problème de l'incroyance au XVIe siècle: La religion de Rabelais* (Paris: Edition Ablin Michel, 1962).

34 Ibid., 10, p. 323.

35 *DPN*, 1.2. 9, p. 322.

36 Ibid., 9, p. 323.

37 Ibid., 8, p. 322.

38 *DND*, 2.2.4, p. 124. For an analysis of this dialogue, see M. Buckley, *Motion and Motion's God*, pp. 89–156.

39 *DPN*, 1.1. 4–7, pp. 321–322; *RG*, 1.1., pp. 6–11.

40 *DND*, 1.17. 45.

41 Ibid., 20. 53.

42 Ibid. See ibid., 3.9.24–11.29.

43 Ibid., 1.20.54.

44 Ibid., 9.23. See ibid., 3.31.76–39.93.

45 It is only upon the completion of the argument from universal consensus that Lessius writes: "Adferam nunc aliquot rationes philosophicas, sed perspicuas, omissis obscurioribus, quae ex metaphysica peti possent." *DPN*, 1.2.16, pp. 325–326. The problematic tradition, as represented, for example, in Aristotle, distinguishes those arguments whose principles lie in the thoughts and opinions of human beings from those whose principles lie in the nature of things. For Aristotle, it is the difference between dialectic or rhetoric, and the theoretical, practical, and poetic sciences. Lessius seems to be employing some similar distinction here.

46 See *DND*, 2.4.12. The actual statement of Lucilius Balbus is: "Omnibus enim innatus est et in animo quasi insculptum esse deos."

47 *DPN*, 1.2.10–11, pp. 323–324. *RG*, 1.3., pp. 13–15. There are many different ways in which this argument from universal consent can be argued. The Stoic attributed it to nature, the Epicurean to a preconception (*prolepsis*) in the human intelligence, the skeptic to the national acceptance of a certain time. All of these explanations would reappear at the time of Lessius, with Gassendi adopting the preconception as one of his two demonstrations of the divine existence and Montaigne accepting the universal belief within the body politic. For Gassendi, see Pietri Gassendi, *Syntagma Philosophiae Epicuri, cum refutationibus dogmatum, quae contra fidem christianum ab eo asserta sunt, oppositis*, pt. 2, 1.4.2–8, in *Opera Omnia* (Lyons: Annison and De Venet, 1658), 1:287–326. For Montaigne, see "We are Christians by the same title that we are Perigordians or Germans,"

"Apology for Raymond Sebond," "First Objection: Defense" in *The Complete Essays of Montaigne*, trans. Donald M. Frame (Stanford: Stanford University Press, 1958), p. 325.

48 *DPN*, 1.2.12, p. 324. *RG*, 1.3., pp. 15–16.

49 *DPN*, 1.2.14, p. 325. *RG*, 1.3., p. 18. Mersenne refers to the same work: "Je ne veux pas vous rapporter une infinité de passages de Platon, d'Aristote, et des autres Philosophes, pour vous monstrer la cognoissance qu'ils on euë d'une divinité, et l'estat qu'ils en ont fait, de peur d' estre trop long en ce discours, voyez seulement Eugubin au livre qu'il a composé sur ce suiect." Marin Mersenne, *L'Impiété des Déistes, Athées, et Libertins de ce temps* (Paris: Pierre Bilaine, 1624, reproduced in photostat, Stuttgart-Bad Cannstatt: Friedrich Frommann Verlag, 1975), p. 139. Augustinus Steuco, known both to Lessius and Mersenne as Augustinus Eugubinus, seems to have coined the term which titled his work, *De perenni philosophia*. See also Charles B. Schmitt, "Perennial Philosophy: From Agostino Steuco to Leibniz," *Journal of the History of Ideas* 27, no. 4 (October–December 1966): 505–532.

50 See the similar judgment of the Stoic argument in Cicero's Balbus: "Quod nisi cognitum conprehensumque animis haberemus, non tam stabilis opinio permaneret nec confirmaretur diuturnitate temporis nec una cum saeculis aetatibusque hominum inveterari potuisset. . . . Opinionis enim commenta delet dies, naturae iudicia confirmat." *DND*, 2.2.5.

51 *RG*, 1.4, p. 26. See *DPN*, 1.2.20, p. 328.

52 Newton to Bentley, January 17, 1692/3, *Opera*, 4:435–437: "I do not know any power in nature which would cause this transverse motion without the divine arm. . . . So, then, gravity may put the planets into motion, but without the divine power it could never put them into such a circulating motion as they have about the sun; and, therefore, for this as well as other reasons, I am compelled to ascribe the frame of this system to an intelligent Agent."

53 *DPN*, 1.2.16–19, pp. 325–328; *RG*; 1.3, p. 19–26. When one considers that Galileo had built and begun to use his own telescope in 1609, after learning that it had been invented in 1608 by the Hollander Hans Lippershey, and that January and February of the next year saw his discovery of the moons of Jupiter, as well as the appearance later in that same year of the work *Siderius Nuncius*, Lessius' grasp and incorporation of contemporary astronomy is even more astonishing. The determination in the subsequent year of the phases of Venus seemed to give the death blow to Aristotelian celestial mechanics. The argument from the movement of the heavenly bodies had been the first and favorite of the Stoics; see *DND*, 2.2.4: "Quid enim potest esse tam apertum, tamque perspicuum, cum caelum suspeximus caelestiaque contemplate summus, quam esse aliquod numen praestantissimae mentis quo haecregatur?" See *DND*, 2.5.15, 6.16.

54 *DND*, 2.6.17.

55 *DPN*, 1.2.21–25, pp. 328–329; *RG*, 1.5, pp. 27–32.

56 *DPN*, 1.2.25, p. 330.

57 *DND*, 2.2.6, 7, 2.5.13–14.

58 *DPN*, 1.2.113–138, pp. 373–395; *RG*, 1.11–12., pp. 153–206.

59 *DND*, 2.2.4.

60 Collins, *God in Modern Philosophy*, p. 45.

61 From "Quatrains de Déiste" in Robert Lenoble, *Mersenne ou la Naissance du Mécanisme* (Paris: Librairie Philosophique J. Vrin, 1943), pp. 182–188.

62 Mersenne, *L'Impiété*, preface, unnumbered page 4.

63 Robert Lenoble, "Le Père Mersenne," *Giornale di Metafisica* 3, no. 4 (15 July–August 1948): 311.

64 Collins, *God in Modern Philosophy*, p. 51.

65 Richard H. Popkin, *The History of Scepticism from Erasmus to Descartes* (Assen, Netherlands: Koninklijke Van Gorcum, 1960), p. 131.

66 Collins, *God in Modern Philosophy*, p. 51.

67 Lenoble, *Mersenne*, pp. 15–27.

68 Marin Mersenne, *Quaestiones celeberrimae in Genesim, cum accurata textus explicatione. In hoc volumine Athei, et Deistae impugnantur, et expugnantur, et Vulgatae editio ab haeriticorum calumnijs vindicatur. Graecorum, et Hebraeorum Musica instauratur. Francisci Georgii Veneti cabalistica dogmata fuse refelluntur, quae passim in illius problematibus habentur. Opus Theologicis, Philosophicis, Medicis, Jurisconsultis, Mathematicis, Musicis vero,·et Catoptricis praesertim utile* (Paris: Sebastiani Cramoisy, 1623). See Lenoble, *Mersenne*, p. 26.

69 Mersenne, *L'Impiété*.

70 Mersenne, *Quaestiones in Genesim*, cols. 669–674. For the population of Paris, see Leon Bernard, *The Emerging City: Paris in the Age of Louis XIV* (Durham, N.C.: Duke University Press, 1970), pp. 284–285. See also Roland Mousnier, *Paris au XVIIᵉ Siècle* (Paris: Centre de Documentation Universitaire, 1961) pp. 22–23.

71 Lenoble, *Mersenne*, p. 26.

72 Collins, *God in Modern Philosophy*, p. 417 n. 32.

73 Mersenne, *L'Impiété*, preface, unnumbered page 12: "I'ay aussi combatu l'Atheisme & découvert les erreurs de Charron, de Cardan, & de Iordan Brun, à ce que ce livre puisse servir de bouclier contre toutes les impietez de ce siecle."

74 Popkin, *Scepticism*, p. 57 ff.; Collins, *God and Modern Philosophy*, pp. 42–45; Lenoble, *Mersenne*, p. 185; for Mersenne's reading of Charron, see *L'Impiété*, pp. 180–204.

75 Lenoble, *Mersenne*, p. 121ff; on Mersenne's reading of Cardano, see *L'Impiété*, pp. 211–228; see also G. Buckley, *Atheism in the English Renaissance*, pp. 20–30.

76 Mersenne, *L'Impiété*, pp. 229–235. Mersenne attaches to his treatment of Giordano Bruno a brief consideration of Machiavelli, Vanini, and a series of others who figure importantly, but in a secondary fashion, in his discussion of atheism.

77 Mersenne, *L'Impiété*, pp. 1–71.

78 M. Buckley, *Motion and Motion's God*, pp. 159–170.

79 Collins, *God in Modern Philosophy*, p. 417 n. 33.

80 M. Buckley, *Motion and Motion's God*, pp. 105–111.

81 Mersenne, *L'Impiété*, p. 71.

82 Ibid., p. 72.

83 Ibid., pp. 73–75.

84 *DND* 1.19.45–20. 56; M. Buckley, *Motion and Motion's God*, pp. 124–128.

85 Mersenne, *L'Impiété*, pp. 75–76.

86 Ibid., pp. 76–78.

87 Ibid., pp. 78–81.

88 Ibid., pp. 81–94.

89 Ibid., pp. 96–111.

90 Ibid., pp. 114–120.

91 Collins, *God in Modern Philosophy*, pp. 45–50; Lenoble, *Mersenne*, p. 328.

92 Galileo Galilei, *Les Méchaniques de Galilée, Mathematicien et Ingenieur du Duc de Florence. Avec plusieurs additions rares, et nouvelles, utiles aux Architectes,*

Ingenieurs, Fonteniers, Philosophes, et Artisans, trans. from the Italian by L.P.M.M. [Mersenne] (Paris: Jacques Guénon, 1634); *Les Nouvelles pensées de Galilée, Mathematicien et ingenieur du Duc de Florence. Où il est traité de la proportion des mouvements naturels et violents, et de tout ce qu'il y a de plus subtil dans les Méchaniques at dans la Physique. Où l'on verra d'admirables Inventions, et Demonstrations, inconnuës iusqu'à present.* (Paris: Henry Guénon, 1639).

93 *Petri Gassendi theologie epistolica exercitatio, in qua Principia Philosophiae Roberti Fluddi Medici reteguntur; et ad recentes illius Libros, adversus R.P.F. Marinum Mersennum Ordinis Minimorum Sancti Francisci de Paula scriptos respondetur. Cum appendice aliquot Observationum Coelestium* (Paris: Sebastianum Cramoisy, 1630).

94 *Encyclopaedia Britannica*, Micropaedia, 15th ed., s.v. "Mersenne, Marin."

95 Chamberlain, "Lessius," pp. 143–144.

96 For Lessius, see *DPN*, 1, pp. 321–322; *RG*, 1.1. pp. 5–9; for Mersenne, see *Quaestiones in Genesim*, cols. 226–233. Lenoble assembles these citations, among which figures one whose influence on succeeding generations is obvious: "18. le désir de ne rien admettre qui ne soit établi *more geometrico.*" See Lenoble, *Mersenne*, pp. 174–175.

97 Popkin, *Scepticism*. The citation is from Montaigne, "Apologie de Raimond Sebond," in *Les Essais de Michel de Montaigne*, ed. Pierre Villey (Paris: F. Alcan, 1922), 2:279. Popkin summarizes the position which Montaigne elaborated and which had so many subsequent supporters: "The complete sceptic was in the ideal state for receiving Revelation, if God so willed. The marriage of the cross of Christ and the doubts of Pyrrho was the perfect combination to provide the ideology of the French Counter-Reformation." Popkin, *Scepticism*, p. 49.

98 Popkin, *Scepticism*, p. 59.

Chapter 2: Section 1.

1 René Descartes, *Meditationes de prima philosophia*, preface, in *Oeuvres de Descartes*, ed. Charles Adam and Paul Tannery (Paris: Léopold Cerf, 1897–1909) (henceforth cited as AT) 7:8–9. A standard English translation is René Descartes, *Meditations on First Philosophy*, trans. Laurence J. Lafleur (Indianapolis: Bobbs-Merrill, 1978). When this translation is used, it will be cited as *Meditations*, Lafleur.

2 Popkin, *Scepticism*, p. 18.

3 Michel de Montaigne, *Essays*, 2, 12: "Apology for Raymond Sebond," in *The Complete Essays of Montaigne*, trans. Donald M. Frame (Stanford: Stanford University Press, 1958), pp. 392–393.

4 Etienne Gilson and Thomas Langan, *Modern Philosophy: Descartes to Kant* (New York: Random House, 1963), pp. 5–15.

5 Etienne Gilson, *The Unity of Philosophical Experience* (New York: Charles Scribner's Sons, 1937), p. 127.

6 René Descartes, *Notes Directed Against a Certain Programme*, in *The Philosophical Works of Descartes*, trans. Elizabeth S. Haldane and G. R. T. Ross, reprinted with corrections (Cambridge: Cambridge University Press, 1931) (henceforth cited as H-R), 1:449. The full title of the *Meditations* is *Meditationes de prima philosophia, In quibus Dei existentia, et animae humanae à corpore distinctio, demonstrantur.*

7 Raymondus de Sabunde, *Theologia naturalis sive liber creaturarum* (Strasbourg:

Martin Flach, 1496). This edition is available on film; the original is in the Vatican library. A facsimile of the Sulzbach edition of 1852 is available in book form (Stuttgart-Bad Cannstatt: F. Frommann, 1966). "Sebond" wanders through many different spellings. Raymond himself took degrees in art, medicine, and theology and ended his days teaching theology at the University of Toulouse. The *Theologia naturalis* was written two years before his death, between 1434 and 1436. See the *New Catholic Encyclopedia* (New York: McGraw-Hill, 1966), s.v. "Raymond of Sabunde."

8 Cited in Clement C. J. Webb, *Studies in the History of Natural Theology* (Oxford: Clarendon Press, 1970), p. 294.

9 Webb, *Studies*, p. 295.

10 Montaigne, "Apology," p. 320.

11 Ibid., pp. 327–328.

12 Ibid., p. 320.

13 Ibid., p. 328.

14 Arthur H. Beattie, introduction, in Michael de Montaigne, *In Defense of Raymond Sebond*, trans. by Arthur H. Beattie (New York: Frederick Ungar, 1976), p. ix.

15 Margaret Dauler Wilson, *Descartes* (London: Routledge and Kegan Paul, 1978), p. vii.

16 For this narration, see Adrien Baillet, *La vie de Monsieur Des-Cartes* (Paris: D. Horthemels, 1691), 2:160–166. This text is translated in Norman Kemp Smith, *New Studies in the Philosophy of Descartes* (London: Macmillan, 1952), (henceforth cited as *NS*) pp. 40–46. See also Descartes' letter to Villebressieu, AT 1:212–217. Appropriate selections from Pierre Borel's *Vitae Cartesii compendium* (1653) are given on pp. 217–218. In attempting to situate Descartes' thought within his narrative, one follows the maxim: "The philosophy of René Descartes cannot be rightly understood apart from his own person and life." Gilson and Langan, *Modern Philosophy*, p. 55.

17 Pierre Borel, *Vitae Cartesii compendium*, AT 1:217.

18 Baillet, *Vie de M. Des-Cartes*, 2:163. See *Regulae ad directionem ingenii*, 2, AT 10:362: "Atque ita per hanc propositionem rejicimus illas omnes probabiles tantum cognitiones, nec nisi perfecte cognitis, et de quibus dubitari non potest, statuimus esse credendum." (Henceforth cited as *Regulae*.)

19 Smith, *NS*, pp. 42–43.

20 Letter to Villebressieu, AT 1:213.

21 Webb, *Studies*, p. 296.

22 Smith, *NS*, p. 43. (Italics added.)

23 Webb, *Studies*, pp. 293–294. Unfortunately, the caution was in vain. The works of Descartes were placed on the *Index librorum prohibitorum* with the proviso *donec corrigantur* in 1663, thirteen years after his death. See Frederick Copleston, *Modern Philosophy: Descartes to Leibniz*, vol. 4 (Garden City, N.Y.: Image Books, Doubleday, 1963), p. 182.

24 Smith, *NS*, p. 45.

25 Collins, *History of Modern European Philosophy*, p. 139.

26 Etienne Gilson, *La liberté chez Descartes et la théologie* (Paris: Librairie Felix Alcan, 1913), pp. 161–163. A word about the subsequent history of the Sieur Chandoux: He was a physician given to explorations in chemistry. The latter interest led to his untimely end. Within a few years of the celebrated conference, Chandoux was convicted of counterfeiting and publicly hanged. See Smith, *NS*, p. 40.

27 E. M. Curley, *Descartes Against the Skeptics* (Cambridge, Mass.: Harvard University Press, 1978), pp. 37–38.
28 *Regulae*, 2, AT 10:362; 6, AT 10:384. This translation is a modification of the one found in H-R 1:17.
29 Curley, *Descartes Against the Skeptics*, pp. 38–41.
30 *Regulae*, 1, AT 10:360.
31 Ibid., p. 359: "Studiorum finis esse debet ingenii directio ad solida et vera, de iis omnibus quae occurunt, proferenda judicia."
32 AT 10:255 (italics added). Père Poisson cites these words from Descartes with this introductory note: "Ce sont à peu-prés les paroles de M. Desc. que j'ay leües dans un de ses fragmens manuscrits." See also *La Recherche de la verité par la lumière naturelle*: "les connoissances qui ne surpassent point la portée de l'esprit humain, sont toutes enchainées avec une liaison si merveilleuse, et se peuvent tirer les unes des autres par des consequences si necessaires, qu'il ne faut point avoir beaucoup d'addresse et de capacité pour les trouver, pourveu qu'ayant commencé par les plus simples, on sçache se conduire de degré en degré jusques auxplus revelées." AT 10:496–497. See p. 526.
33 *Cogitationes privatae*, AT 10:215.
34 *Regulae*, 2, AT 10:362.
35 Ibid. [M].
36 *Meditationes*, "Epistola sapientissimis clarissimisque viris sacrae facultatis theologiae parisiensis decano et doctoribus" (henceforth cited as "Epistola"), AT 7:1–2.
37 *Meditationes*, "Epistola," AT 7:2–3. See *Meditations*, Lafleur, p. 7.
38 Letter to P. Dinet, AT 7:581 [M].
39 Letter to P. Vatier, AT 1:564. See Jacques Maritain, *The Dream of Descartes*, trans. Mabelle J. Andison (New York: Philosophical Library, 1944), p. 205.
40 *Principles of Philosophy*, 10, H-R 1:222. See *The Search After Truth*, H-R 1:324: "There are certain things which we render more obscure by trying to define them, because, since they are very simple and clear, we cannot know and perceive them better than *by themselves*. Nay, we must place in the number of those chief errors that can be committed in the sciences, the mistakes committed by those who would try to define what ought only to be conceived, and who cannot distinguish the clear from the obscure, nor discriminate between what, in order to be known, requires and deserves to be defined, from what can be *best known by itself*" (italics added). Examples that Descartes gives of these self-evident notions are existence, thought, doubt, ignorance, volition, figure, extension, motion, unity, duration, and so on. See *Regulae*, 12, AT 10:419–420, 426.
41 AT 7:144.
42 AT 7:145.
43 AT 7:145 (italics added).
44 *Principles of Philosophy*, 204, H-R 1:300.
45 "Responsio ad secundas objectiones," AT 7:145.
46 *Regulae*, 2, H-R 1:4. See AT 10:364–365.
47 Cited in Gilson, *Unity of Philosophical Experience*, pp. 130–131.
48 *Regulae*, 2, AT 10:363–366.
49 *Regulae*, 4, AT 10:374–379. Why then did Descartes in his later works enumerate even mathematics among those things which could be brought under doubt? Gilson maintains that doubt can be brought to bear upon the *memory* of the reasoning behind a mathematical proposition, but not the *intuition* itself. L. J. Beck thinks that mathematics becomes doubtful when Descartes came to the

opinion that all judgments are forged by the will. Curley counters that this method of doubt can extend to mathematics because of the possibilities contained in a theology "of a God who can do everything," even deceive. This is the nagging possibility that Montaigne has left behind him, and although Descartes will call it "slight and metaphysical," there is no possibility of perfect certitude until he has put it to rest under the figure of the "malignant demon." See Curley, *Descartes Against the Skeptics*, pp. 41–43.

50 Giovanni Crapulli, *Mathesis universalis: Genesi di un' idea nel xvi secolo* (Rome: Edizioni dell' Ateneo Roma, 1959), p. 150. For the scholastic and the Greek heritage of such a conception, see L. J. Beck, *The Method of Descartes: A Study of the Regulae* (Oxford: Clarendon Press, 1952), p. 200.

51 Crapulli, *Mathesis universalis*, p. 113.

52 Crapulli, *Mathesis universalis*, p. 8 and passim.

53 Letter to Beeckman, March 26, 1619, AT 10:154–158; cited by Smith, *NS*, p. 14.

54 *Regulae*, 4, AT 10:378 (italics added). For the identification of the Cartesian method with the universal mathematics, see Roberto Perini, "Mathesis universalis e metaphysica nel metodo cartesiano," *Giornale di metafisica* (March–June, 1973) vol. 28, nos. 2–3: 161–173. Perini defends against J. P. Weber the thesis: "Anche la *mathesis universalis* è dunque considerata da Cartesio come un metodo, come la fonte del sapere anziché il sapere stesso. E fuor di dubbio, quindi, che l'applicazione del metodo matematico all' intera conoscenza della realtà constituisce il nucleo del concetto cartesiano di *mathesis universalis*." For Weber's contrary position, see *La constitution du texte des Regulae* (Paris: Société d'Edition d'Enseignement supérieur, 1964).

55 *Regulae*, 4, AT 10:378: "ac proinde generalem quamdam esse debere scientiam, quae id omne explicet, quod circa ordinem et mensuram nulli speciali materiae addictam quaeri potest, eamdemque, non ascititio vocabulo, sed jam inveterato atque usu recepto, Mathesim universalem nominari, quoniam in hac continetur illud omne, propter quod aliae scientiae Mathematicae partes appellantur."

56 *Discours de la methode*, 2, AT 6:19. A standard English translation is René Descartes, *Discourse on Method*, trans. Laurence J. Lafleur (Indianapolis: Bobbs-Merrill, 1979). When this translation is used, it will be cited as *Discourse*, Lafleur.

57 *Discours*, 2, AT 6:20. See *Discourse*, Lafleur, p. 13. The same doctrine is articulated in the *Regulae* together with an example of what is meant by proportion or relationship: "Thus I may easily deduce that there is the same proportion [*eandem esse proportionem*] between 3 and 6, as between 6 and 12, and likewise 12 and 24 so on, and hence that the numbers 3, 6, 12, 24, 48, etc. are in continued proportion [*esse continuè proportionales*]. But though these facts are all so clear as to seem almost childish, I am not able by attentive reflection to understand what is the form [*qua ratione*] involved by all questions that can be propounded about the proportions or relations of things [*proportiones sive habitudines rerum*] and what is the order [*quo ordine*] in which they should be investigated; and this one thing [*unum*] embraces the sum of the entire science of Pure Mathematics [*totius scientiae purae Mathematicae summam*]." AT 10:384–385. See H-R 1:17 (m).

58 *Meditationes*, 5, AT 7:65.

59 Beck, *Method*, p. 202.

60 *Regulae*, 6, AT 10:381–382.

61 *Regulae*, 5, AT 10:379 (italics and enumeration added). Descartes also styled

these two moments analytic and synthetic. See "Reply to Objections II," AT 7:155–157. For the history of "analytic" and "synthetic," see *Infra*, pp. 199–202.

62 These are termed "per se satis nota," *Principia philosophiae*, pt. 1, 10, AT 8:8. See *Regulae*, 6, AT 10:384.

63 Gilson, *Unity of Philosophical Experience*, pp. 155–158.

64 *Discours*, 2, AT 6:28: "Et en toutes les neuf années suivantes, ie ne fi autre chose que rouler çà et là dans le monde, taschant d'y estre spectateur plutost qu'acteur en toutes les Comedies qui s'y iouent."

65 *Recherche de la verité*, AT 10:515: "Hac enim universali ex dubitatione, veluti e *fixo immobilique puncto*, Dei, tui ipsiusmet, omniumque, quae in mundo dantur, rerum cognitionem *derivare* statui." This is to explain to Poliander, "qua ratione dubitatio istiusmodi possit principium esse, quod tam longe nos deducere queat" (italics added).

66 *Discours*, 2, AT 6:13–14. In his reply to the seventh series of objections Descartes uses the example of the basket of apples: "Supposing he had a basket of apples and, fearing that some of them were rotten, wanted to take those out lest they make the rest go wrong, how could he do that? Would he not first turn the whole of the apples out of the basket and look them over one by one, and then having selected those which he saw not to be rotten, place them again in the basket and leave out the others?" H-R 2:282.

67 *Discours*, 1, AT 6:10. For the reflexive, intuitive nature of the "Cogito ergo sum," compare "Responsio ad secundas objectiones," AT 7:140: "Neque etiam cum quis dicit, *ego cogito, ergo sum, sive existo*, existentiam ex cogitatione per syllogismum deducit, sed tamquam *rem per se notam simplici mentis intuitu* agnoscit" (italics added).

68 *Meditationes*, 2, AT 7:27.

69 *Principia philosophiae*, pt. 1, 9, AT 8:7: "Cogitationis nomine, intelligo illa omnia, quae nobis consciis in nobis fiunt, quatenus eorum in nobis conscientia est." See Anthony Kenny, *Descartes: A Study of His Philosophy* (New York: Random House, 1968), pp. 44ff.

70 *Meditationes*, 3, AT 7:45–46; *Meditations*, Lafleur, p. 44.

71 For Beck's disagreement with Serrus on this point, see Beck, *Method*, p. 287ff.

72 *Meditationes*, 2, AT 7:25: "Imo certe ego eram, si quid mihi persuasi. . . . Adeo ut, omnibus satis superque pensitatis, denique statuendum sit hoc pronuntiatum, *Ego sum, ego existo*, quoties a me profertur, vel mente concipitur, necessario esse verum." See also p. 27: "Hic invenio: cogitatio est: haec sola a me divelli nequit. Ego sum, ego existo; certum est. Quandiu autem? Nempe quandiu cogito; nam forte etiam fieri posset, si cessarem ab omni cogitatione, ut illico totus esse definerem."

73 *Principia philosophiae*, pt. 1, 11, AT 8:8–9; H-R 1:223 (m).

74 Maritain seems quite correct in his assessment of the second demonstrations: "The second Cartesian proof is merely an extension of the first. 'It matters little that my second proof, based on our own existence, be considered as different from the first, or simply as an explanation of the first.' To pass by way of causality from the idea of God to the existence of God, one can start from this idea itself, or from the thought which contemplates this idea." *Dream of Descartes*, p. 120. Maritain is citing Descartes' letter to Mersenne, May 2, 1644, AT 4:111. In the response to the first series of objections, Descartes wrote: "Ideoque ulterius inquisivi, *an ego possem existere, si Deus non existeret*, non

tam ut diversam a praecedenti rationem afferrem, quam ut eandum ipsam absolutius explicarem." AT 7:106. For the purpose of analysis, these proofs will be considered as three under the proviso that the second is really an extension of the first.

75 *Discours*, 5, AT 6:42.
76 "Reply to Objections I," H-R 2:14. See "Reply to Objections III," H-R 2:63–64: "since that which thinks is not nothing."
77 "Responsio ad quartas objectiones," AT 7:236: "Atque eodem modo, in omnibus aliis locis, ita contuli *causam formalem*, sive rationem ab essentia Dei petitam, propter quam ipse causa non indiget ut existat, neque ut conservetur, cum *causa efficiente*, sine qua res finitae esse non possunt, ut ubique illam a causa efficiente esse diversam ex ipsis meis verbis cognoscatur" (italics added). See also H-R 2:108.
78 "Reply to Objections IV," H-R 2:109.
79 "Responsio ad secundas objectiones," AT 7:135: "Quod enim *nihil fit* in effectu, quod non vel simili vel eminentiori aliquo modo praeextiterit in causa, prima notio est, qua nulla clarior habetur; haecque vulgaris, *a nihilo nihil fit*."
80 "Reply to Objections IV," H-R 2:110.
81 *Meditationes*, 3, AT 7:37.
82 *Meditationes*, 3, AT 7:40.
83 *Meditationes*, 3, AT 7:41; *Meditations*, Lafleur, p. 40.
84 "Reply to Objections I," H-R 2:11.
85 See Maritain, *Dream of Descartes*, p. 120; AT 4:111; AT 7:106.
86 *Meditationes*, 3, AT 7:50; *Meditations*, Lafleur, p. 47.
87 *Meditationes*, 3, AT 7:50.
88 "Reply to Objections I," H-R 2:13 (m).
89 "Reply to Objections I," H-R 2:13.
90 *Meditationes*, 4, AT 7:54; *Meditations*, Lafleur, p. 51.
91 "Reply to Objections I," H-R 2:19–20.
92 "Responsio ad secundas objectiones," AT 7:156: "Ego vero solam Analysim, quae vera et optima via est ad docendum, in Meditationibus meis sum sequutus."
93 *Discours*, 4, AT 6:36.
94 Descartes to Mersenne, November 25, 1630, AT 1:179: "la fable de mon Monde me plaist trop pour manquer à la parachever, si Dieu me laisse vivre assez long-temps pour cela."
95 *Meditationes*, "Epistola," AT 7:2.
96 *Meditationes*, 6, AT 7:71.
97 Maritain, *Dream of Descartes*, p. 27.
98 *Meditationes*, 5, AT 7:70; *Meditations*, Lafleur, p. 67.
99 Kenny, *Descartes*, pp. 188–197. In his consideration of the texts of Descartes which are liable to this charge, Kenny does not consider the one cited from the fifth meditation above.
100 *Meditationes*, 6, H-R 1:185.
101 *Meditationes*, 6, AT 7:71 [M]. "Certainty" is added in the first French edition. See *Meditations*, Lafleur, p. 68.
102 *Meditations*, 6, Lafleur, p. 71. See *Principles of Philosophy*, 2.1, H-R 1:254–255.
103 *Meditationes*, 6, AT 7:80 [M]. See *Meditations*, Lafleur, p. 76.
104 *Principles of Philosophy* 2.4, H-R 1:255–256.
105 *Principles of Philosophy* 2.8, H-R 1:258.

106 *Principles of Philosophy* 2.64, H-R 1:269.
107 *Les Principes de la philosophie*, preface, AT 9:14–15.
108 Gilson, *La liberté chez Descartes et la théologie*, pp. 94–95.
109 *Meditations*, 6, Lafleur, pp. 49–50.
110 *Discourse*, 5, Lafleur, p. 28.
111 *Discourse*, 5, Lafleur, p. 29.
112 Descartes to Mersenne, May 27, 1638, AT 2:138: "mais mesme que ces veritez qu'on nomme eternelles, comme que *totum est maius sua parte*, etc., ne seroient point veritez, si Dieu ne l'avoit ainsi estably, ce que ie croy vous avoir desia autresfois écrit." See answer to Arnauld, July 29, 1648, AT 5:223–224: "It is my opinion that one cannot say of anything that it cannot be done by God; as a matter of fact, the essence of the true and the good [*omnis ratio veri et boni*] depends upon his omnipotence, and I should not dare to say that God cannot make mountains exist without valleys or one plus two not be equal to three; but I say only that He gave me a mind of such nature that a mountain without a valley or a sum of one plus two not equal to three cannot be conceived by me." For translation, see Maritain, *Dream of Descartes*, p. 142.
113 Aram Vartanian, *Diderot and Descartes: A Study of Scientific Naturalism in the Enlightenment* (Princeton: Princeton University Press, 1953), pp. 13–14.
114 *The Search After Truth*, H-R 1:314.

Chapter 2: Section 2.

1 In general, the Latin edition of Newton's works which is used in this book is contained in *Isaaci Newtoni Opera quae exstant omnia*, commentariis illustrabat Samuel Horsley (London: Excudebat Joannes Nichols, 1779–1785), and cited as *Newtoni Opera Omnia*. The third and final edition (1726) of Newton's *Philosophiae Naturalis Principia Mathematica* has been assembled and edited by Alexandre Koyré and I. Bernard Cohen with the assistance of Anne Whitman (Cambridge, Mass: Harvard University Press, 1972) (henceforth cited as K-C). All the citations from the *Principia* have either been translated by the author from this edition or checked against it in his use of the English translation of Andrew Motte revised by Florian Cajori: *Sir Isaac Newton's Mathematical Principles of Natural Philosophy and His System of the World*, trans. Andrew Motte (1729), revised with historical and explanatory appendix by Florian Cajori (Berkeley and Los Angeles: The University of California Press, 1962) (henceforth cited as Cajori). Newton's correspondence is found in *The Correspondence of Isaac Newton*, vols. 1–3 ed. H. W. Turnball, vol. 4 ed. J. F. Scott, vols. 5–7 ed. A. R. Hall and L. Tilling. Published for the Royal Society (Cambridge: Cambridge University Press, 1959–1977) (henceforth cited as *Correspondence*). These seven volumes contain the correspondence up to the end of Newton's life. In M. Buckley, *Motion and Motion's God*, the text of the *Principia* and its theological argumentation is dealt with extensively.
2 *Principia*, "Auctoris Praefatio ad Lectorem," henceforth cited as the preface to the first edition, K-C 1:15; Cajori, p. xvii. The value of the preface in many mechanical and mathematical works rests with its discussion of the nature of the enterprise which lies before it or with the identification of the intellectual tradition which it claims. Such prefaces are often a few paragraphs of a metaphysical discourse on the organization of the sciences or of foundational studies on the subjects of mathematics or physics. It is profoundly misguided to dismiss

them as rhetorical exercises whose major purpose is *redere lectorem benevolem.*

3 Newton to Hooke, February 5, 1675[6], *Correspondence* 1:416. For a listing of the "giants" whom Newton honored many years after both Descartes and Hooke had been stricken from the catalogue, see Newton to Johann Burchard Menche, 1724, *Correspondence* 7:254–255. Tycho Brahe and Johannes Kepler head the index with Galileo coming between Otto Von Guricke and Torricelli. In his monumental biography of Newton, *Never at Rest*, Richard S. Westfall states that even the most original of Newton's discoveries evolved from processes of investigation which began with notes and commentaries on the writings of others. Richard S. Westfall, *Never at Rest* (Cambridge: Cambridge University Press, 1980).

4 *Principia* 1. 2, scholium following proposition 4, K-C 1:100–101; Cajori, pp. 46–47.

5 *Principia* 1. 1., scholium following corollary 6, K-C 1:66; Cajori, p. 22.

6 *Principia*, preface to the first edition, K-C 1:16; Cajori, p. xviii.

7 Halley to Newton, June 29, 1686, *Correspondence* 2:442.

8 René Dugas, *Mechanics in the Seventeenth Century*, trans. Freda Jacquot (New York: Central, 1958), p. 362. Halley summarized the conversation and its aftermath in this manner: "The August following when I did my self the honour to visit you, I then learnt the good news that you had brought this demonstration to perfection, and you were pleased, to promise me a copy thereof, which the November following I received with a great deal of satisfaction from Mr. Paget." Halley to Newton, June 29, 1686, *Correspondence* 2:442. I. Bernard Cohen writes in his magisterial *Introduction to Newton's Principia* (Cambridge, Mass: Harvard University Press, 1971), p. 47: "The history of the *Principia* begins with a definite event: a trip from London to Cambridge to see Newton, made by Edmond Halley. . . . The date is 1684, presumably August." See p. 49: "when Halley came to see Newton there was a general awareness that planetary orbits are elliptical, and there was good ground for suspecting that the force (if any) exerted by the Sun on the Earth must vary inversely as the square of the distance, but no one had yet shown—so far as Halley knew—a necessary (that is, a logico-mathematical or causal) relation between the two. There was only a surmise or a reasonable guess, of the kind that has no place in science save to serve as an inspiration for research. . . . But it was a feat of extraordinary consequence to have 'calculated' this result . . . because this feat implied that Newton was so perfect a master of mathematical celestial physics that he had been able to solve an outstanding scientific problem of the age: what makes the planets go?"

9 Dugas, *Mechanics*, pp. 363–366.

10 H. D. Anthony, *Sir Isaac Newton* (New York: Abelard-Schuman, 1960), p. 112.

11 *Principia*, preface to the first edition, K-C 1:16; Cajori, p. xviii.

12 Newton to Bentley, December 10, 1692, *Correspondence* 3:233.

13 For the critical importance of the much-neglected Tycho Brahe, see John Allyne Gade, *The Life and Times of Tycho Brahe* (Princeton: Princeton University Press, 1947.) Gade gives the following assessment of Tycho Brahe: "Properly weighed and valued, Tycho Brahe's achievements were, nevertheless, such that he ranks today as one of the two or three greatest scientists ever produced by the North-European countries. The treasure trove of his observations of the moon and planets exceeds even his determination of the positions of a thousand fixed stars. He was a link in the great chain: Copernicus, Brahe, Kepler, Galileo, Newton" (p. 189).

14 Dugas, *Mechanics*, p. 53.
15 *Principia*, scholium after the eight definitions, K-C 1:46; Cajori, p. 6.
16 *Principia*, preface to the first edition, K-C 1:15; Cajori, p. xvii.
17 Newton to Hawes, May 25, 1694, *Correspondence* 3:359–360.
18 *Principia*, preface to the first edition, K-C 1:15; Cajori, p. xvii.
19 Aristotle, *Eth. Nic.* 1. 3. 1094^{b}13–27.
20 Robert Boyle, *Some Considerations Touching the Usefulness of Experimental Natural Philosophy. Propos'd in a Familiar Discourse to a Friend by way of Invitation to the Study of it*, vol. 2 essay 1. 3, "Of the Usefulness of Mechanicall Disciplines to Natural Philosophy" (Oxford: by Henry Hall for Ric. Davis, 1671), p. 1.
21 *Principia*, preface to the first edition, K-C 1:15, Cajori, p. xvii.
22 Pappus of Alexandria, *Synagoge [Collection]*, 8, preface 1–3, in *Selections Illustrating the History of Greek Mathematics*, English translation by Ivor Thomas, Loeb Classical Library (Cambridge, Mass.: Harvard University Press, 1941), 2:614–620 [M]. Pappus makes quite clear that the understanding he is reporting is not one that is general among Greek theoreticians about mechanics by attributing it to the school of Heron of Alexandria. For Heron, it is the movement of the point which generates the line, the movement of the line which generates the surface, the movement of the surface which generates the solid. That science which studied or described movements thus would lie at the basis of geometry. See Heron of Alexandria, *Mensuration: Definitions*, 14.1–24, in *Selections Illustrating the History of Greek Mathematics*, 2:468–469. Newton held a similar position in his *Quadratura curvarum* (1687): "Quantitates Mathematicas, non ut ex partibus quam minimis constantes, sed ut motu continuo descriptas, hic considero. Lineae describuntur, ac describendo generantur, non per appositionem partium, sed per motum continuum punctorum; superficies per motum linearum; solida per motum superficierum; anguli per rotationem laterum; tempora per fluxum continuum; et sic in caeteris. Hae [*sic*] Geneses in rerum natura locum vere habent, et in motu corporum quotidie cernuntur." "Introductio ad Quadraturam Curvarum," *Newtoni Opera Omnia* 1:333.
23 *Selections Illustrating the History of Greek Mathematics*, 2:614.
24 *Principia*, scholium after the eight definitions, K-C 1:53; Cajori, pp. 6–8. The imperative under which the Newtonian inquiry into real motion labored was put laconically in a sentence: "Sic vice locorum et motuum absolutorum relativis utimur; nec incommode in rebus humanis: in philosophicis autem abstrahendum est a sensibus." K-C 1:49.
25 Galileo, Galilei, *Dialogues Concerning Two New Sciences*, third day, scholium following problem 9, proposition 23, trans. Henry Crew and Alfonso de Salvio (New York: Dover, 1914), p. 215. See also the fourth day, p. 244.
26 Galileo, *Two New Sciences*, third day, p. 154.
27 Galileo, *Two New Sciences*, third day, pp. 161–172.
28 Galileo, *Two New Sciences*, third day, theorem 2, proposition 2, p. 174 (italics added). Galileo's method in the science of dynamics is given at the beginning of his investigation of naturally accelerated motion: to construct a mathematical definition which exhibits the essential features of observed accelerated motion, to deduce the consequences of such a definition, and to test these consequences against experiential results for a confirmation of the original mathematical definition; see pp. 160–161. The reason that this is a "new" science for Galileo is not that observation has been added to mathematics, but that mathematics has been introduced into observation. See pp. 153–154.

29 Galileo, *Two New Sciences*, fourth day, p. 250 (italics added).

30 *Principia* 1, scholium after the sixth corollary of the three laws of motion, K-C 1:65; Cajori, p. 21.

31 *Principia* 3, General Scholium, K-C 2:764: "Et haec de deo; de quo utique ex phaenomenis disserre, ad philosophiam naturalem pertinet." See Cajori, p. 546.

32 John Wilkins, *Mathematicall Magick. Or, The wonders that may be performed by mechanicall geometry*, 2 vols. (London: by M. F. for S. Gellibrand, 1648), 1.2.12.

33 Boyle, *Some Considerations*, vol. 2, essay 1. 3, p. 1.

34 *Principia* 3, introduction, K-C 2:549; Cajori, p. 397.

35 *Principia*, preface to the first edition, K-C 1:16; Cajori, p. xvii (M). Among the authorities in rational mechanics, Pappus numbers Archimedes of Syracuse and Carpus of Antioch; see Pappus of Alexandria, *Synagoge [Collection]*, 7, preface, 1–3, pp. 618–620. See also T. L. Heath, Greek Mathematics (Oxford: Clarendon Press, 1921), 2:428–429.

36 Ernst Mach, *The Science of Mechanics*, trans. Thomas J. McCormack, 6th ed. (LaSalle, Ill.: Open Court, 1960), p. 301.

37 John Herivel, *The Background to Newton's Principia* (Oxford: Clarendon Press, 1965), pp. 93–117. For the Latin version of this tract and an English translation, see pp. 257ff.

38 A. Rupert Hall, *Philosophers at War: The Quarrel Between Newton and Leibniz* (Cambridge: Cambridge University Press, 1980), p. 146. Hall maintains that for Leibniz and Descartes, force "was only apparent, a kind of optical illusion; the reality lay in the movement of invisible, indetectable particles whose pressures on bodies cause the movements we attribute to forces." For the organization of the eight definitions and the comprehensive nature of "force" in Newton, see M. Buckley, *Motion and Motion's God*, pp. 171–177.

39 Mach, *Science of Mechanics*, p. 300: "The concept of mass is not made clearer by describing mass as the product of the volume into the density, as density itself denotes simply the mass of unit of volume. The true definition of mass can be deduced only from the dynamical relations of bodies." E. A. Burtt seems to grasp better the movement of Newton's method from the apparent to the real and remarks: "Having chosen to define it in terms then more familiar, rather than present it as an ultimate quality of bodies, [Newton] could hardly have done better." E. A. Burtt, *The Metaphysical Foundations of Modern Physical Science* (London: Routledge and Kegan Paul, 1949), p. 240, See also Stephen Toulmin, "Newton on Absolute Space," *Philosophical Review* 68 (1959): 19–20.

40 Dugas, *Mechanics*, p. 341.

41 For the eight definitions at the beginning of the *Principia*, see K-C 1:39–46; Cajori, pp. 1–6. That the definitional structure is so arranged as to reduce mass or body to force would be coordinate with the astonishing response which Clarke gives to Leibniz: "That some make the souls of men, and others even God himself to be a corporeal being; is also very true: but those who do so, are the great enemies of the mathematical principles of philosophy; which principles, and which alone, prove matter, or body, to be the smallest and most inconsiderable part of the universe." "Dr. Clarke's First Reply," *Leibniz-Clarke Correspondence*, ed. with introduction and notes by H. G. Alexander (Manchester: Manchester University Press, 1956) (henceforth cited as *L-C*), p. 12.

42 A. Rupert Hall records Leibniz's reaction to the attacks of the Newtonian David Gregory in his *Elements of Astronomy* (1702). To this attack upon the harmonic circulation throughout the solar system, "in a letter to Bernoulli, Leibniz could only feebly rejoin that if the existence of the deferent vortices in his system might be denied, still the need for the gravitational vortex remained; nor could any argument upset his own basic assumption that nothing could be moved save by the contact of another moving body 'and that solar attraction without the motion of matter around the sun, in which the planets swim, cannot be understood.'" Hall, *Philosophers at War*, pp. 160–161. For the various forms that the Cartesian vortices assumed among such neo-Cartesians as Huygens, Leibniz, Malebranche, Varignon, and Villemont, see pp. 148ff. What is consistent throughout is the priority of body over force as a principle of explanation.

43 Newton to Bentley, December 10, 1692, *Correspondence* 3:235. In all of these definitions, it is critically important that Newton's precisions be kept: "I here use the word *attraction* in general for any endeavor whatever, made by bodies to approach to each other, whether that endeavor arise from the action of the bodies themselves, as tending to each other or agitating each other by spirits emitted; or whether it arises from the action of the ether or of the air, or of any medium whatever, whether corporeal or incorporeal, in any manner impelling bodies placed therein towards each other. In the same general sense I use the word *impulse*, not defining in this treatise the species or physical qualities of forces, but investigating the quantities and mathematical proportions of them; as I observed before in the Definitions." *Principia* 1. 11, proposition 69, theorem 29, scholium, K-C 1:298; Cajori, p. 192. In gravitation, the "accelerative force" (Newton's term) includes what is now called G, the acceleration due to gravity, whereas the "motive force" (Newton's term) includes what is now called mG, the force due to gravity. Of course, in other examples, the accelerative force could correspond to other types of physical interactions, such as magnetism.

44 Richard S. Westfall, *Force in Newton's Physics: The Science of Dynamics in the Seventeenth Century* (New York: American Elsevier, 1971), p. 323.

45 *Principia*, definition 3, K-C 1:41; Cajori, p. 2.

46 *Principia*, scholium after the eight definitions, K-C 1:49; Cajori, p. 9.

47 *Principia*, scholium after the eight definitions, K-C 1:50. The Latin here is stronger than Cajori's translation: "Unde motus integri et absoluti non nisi per loca immota *definiri* possunt" (italics added).

48 Ibid.

49 Ibid., pp. 50–53; Cajori, pp. 10–12. "This argument is a mathematical one; showing, from real effects, that there may be real motion where there is none relative; and relative motion, where there is none real; and is not to be answered, by barely asserting the contrary. [14] The reality of space is not a supposition, but is proved by the foregoing arguments, to which no answer has been given." "Dr. Clarke's Fourth Reply," *L-C*, pp. 48–49.

50 This notion of absolute space as the condition for the possibility of motion finds early and very succinct expression in an early manuscript of Newton's. Though these precise lines are in the hand of Wilkins, the bulk of the work is in Newton's handwriting. The editor of the *Correspondence* hypothesizes that Wilkins may have been transcribing at Newton's direction: "There is an uniform extension, space, or expansion continued every way without bounds: in wch all bodyes are, each in severall parts of it: wch parts of space possessed and adequately filled by ym are their places. And their passing out of one place

or part of space into another, through all ye intermediate space is their motion."
Correspondence 3:60.

51 The story is related by Plutarch in his life of Marcellus, ch. 14. See also Heath,
Greek Mathematics, 2:18.

52 *Principia*, preface to the first edition, K-C 1:16; Cajori, p. xvii.

53 *Principia*, scholium after the eight definitions, K-C 1:53; Cajori, p. 12.

54 George Berkeley, *Principles of Human Knowledge*, #110; cited by Alexander
Koyré, *From the Closed World to the Infinite Universe* (New York: Harper,
1958), pp. 221–222.

55 Berkeley, *Principles of Human Knowledge*, #117. See Koyré, *From the Closed
World to the Infinite Universe*, p. 222.

56 See *The Thirteen Books of Euclid's Elements*, translated from the text of Heiberg
with introduction and commentary by Sir Thomas Heath, 2d ed. revised with
additions (New York: Dover, 1956), 1:137–140.

57 *Encyclopaedia Britannica*, 14th ed., s.v. "Harris, John," The *Encylopaedia
Britannica* salutes Harris' *Lexicon* as one of its ancestors and mentions that he
also delivered the seventh series of Boyle lectures in 1698 at Saint Paul's
Cathedral, titled *Atheistic Objections Against the Being of God and His Attributes Fairly Considered and Fully Refuted*. Harris was one of the early members
of the Royal Society and for a time acted as its vice-president. See H. D.
Anthony, *Sir Isaac Newton*, p. 188.

58 John Harris, *Lexicon Technicum: or, An Universal English Dictionary of the
Arts and Sciences: explaining not only the terms of art, but the arts themselves*
(London: D. Brown, 1704), s. v. "Analysis" and "Synthesis."

59 Isaac Newton, *Opticks, or a Treatise of the Reflections, Refractions, Inflections
and Colours of Light*, 3, query 31, based on the 4th ed. (London, 1730) (New
York: Dover, 1952), pp. 404–405. (Henceforth cited as *Opticks*.) For a history
of the various editions of the *Opticks* with the addition of Queries, see I.
Bernard Cohen's excellent preface to the Dover edition, pp. xxxiiiff. See also
Cohen, *Introduction to Newton's Principia*, p. 22. Since the purpose of this
study is not to trace the evolution of Newton's thought, but to determine its
finally formulated meaning and theological import, there has been no attempt in
this chapter to situate each statement of or about Newton as it emerged in his
personal evolution—unless this would make a critically important contribution
toward understanding, not Newton's development, but the final product which
influenced the world.

60 Newton to Cotes, March 28, 1713, *Correspondence* 5:397.

61 Newton to Oldenburg, July 6, 1672, *Correspondence* 1:210.

62 *Principia* 3, General Scholium, K-C 2:764; Cajori, p. 547. Newton had this
section included by Cotes in the second edition of the *Principia* through a letter
of March 28, 1713 (*Correspondence* 5:397). It is in this General Scholium that
Newton coined his famous: "*Hypotheses non fingo* [I do not frame/feign
hypotheses]." For an extended and nuanced treatment of this often repeated but
seldom grasped statement, see Alexander Koyré, "Concept and Experience in
Newton's Scientific Thought," in *Newtonian Studies* (Chicago: University of
Chicago Press, 1965), pp. 25–52. For the translation "feign," rather than
"frame," of *fingo*, see I. B. Cohen, "The First English Version of Newton's
Hypotheses non fingo," *Isis* 53 (1962): 379–388.

63 René Descartes, *Principia philosophiae*, 3, 44–47, AT 8:99–101. See also Koyré,
"Concept and Experience in Newton's Scientific Thought," p. 34.

64 *Principia*, preface to the first edition, K-C 1:16; Cajori, p. xvii.

65 Westfall, *Force in Newton's Physics*, pp. 323ff.

66 *Principia*, corollaries after the three laws of motion, corollary 2, K-C 1:59; Cajori, pp. 15–17.

67 *Principia*, corollaries after the three laws of motion, corollary 4, K-C 1:63 (M).

68 Edward Strong, "Newton and God," *Journal of the History of Ideas* 7, no. 2 (April 1952):167. Strong believes that Cotes's suggestions "might have prompted Newton to relax his caution as a scientist." See also p. 157.

69 See I. Bernard Cohen, *Introduction to Newton's Principia*, pp. 155–156. The reference which this review is making is to the first edition of the *Principia*, 3, proposition 8, corollary 5: "Collocavit igitur Deus Planetas in diversis distantiis a Sole, ut quilibet pro gradu densitatis calore Solis majore vel minore fruatur." This laconic statement, touching both upon the divine *dominatio* and the divine providence, was, under diverse incentives offered by many issues, expanded into the more complete thesis of the General Scholium. Cohen has pointed out that Newton, in the versions of the *Principia* elaborated before the first edition, "on at least two occasions turned to discussion of God." I. Bernard Cohen, "Isaac Newton's *Principia*, the Scripture, and the Divine Providence," in *Philosophy, Science and Method: Essays in Honor of Ernest Nagel*, ed. Sidney Morgenbesser, Patrick Suppes, and Morton White (New York: St. Martin's, 1969), pp. 431–522.

70 Newton to Bentley, December 10, 1692, *Correspondence* 3:233.

71 Edward Phillips, *The New World of Words: or, A Universal English Dictionary*, 5th ed. (London: R. Bentley and J. Phillips, 1696), s. v. "system."

72 "And the word Hypothesis is here used by me to signify only such a Proposition as is not a Phaenomenon nor deduced from any Phaenomena but assumed or supposed without any experimental proof." Newton to Cotes, March 28, 1713, *Correspondence* 5:397. See also Cohen, *Introduction*, pp. 156ff.

73 *Principia* 2.9, scholium after proposition 53, theorem 41, K-C 1:546: "Nam Planetae secundum hypothesin *Copernicaeam* circa Solem delati revolvuntur." For a discussion of the various uses of hypothesis in Newton, see I. Bernard Cohen, *Franklin and Newton* (Cambridge, Mass.: Harvard University Press, 1966), pp. 129–147.

74 Henry George Liddell and Robert Scott, *A Greek-English Lexicon*, 7th ed., s. v. σύστημα.

75 John Locke, *Essay Concerning Human Understanding*, 4.3.24. ed. Peter H. Nidditch (Oxford: Clarendon Press, 1975), p. 555.

76 John Harris, *Lexicon Technicum*, s. v. "system."

77 *Principia* 3, "Phaenomena," K-C 2:556–563. In the first edition of the *Principia*, these "phaenomena" were called "hypotheses," but they were not the kind of hypotheses he insistently repudiated, that is, ones "not deduced from phenomena" or elsewhere "a mere Hypothesis." See Newton to Cotes, March 28, 1713, *Correspondence* 5:397–398; Newton to Cotes, March 31, 1713, *Correspondence* 5:400. In the readjustments from the first to the third edition, the *Principia* seems to indicate the belief that astronomical observation has dealt a death blow to the Ptolemaic hypothesis, but it leaves open the question between Tycho Brahe and Copernicus. Brahe's geocentric system is ruled out because it fails to embody or account for the kinematic proportions which Kepler had established for the heliocentric universe.

78 *Principia* 3, propostion 7, theorem 7, K-C 2:576; Cajori, p. 414 (M).

79 *Principia* 3, proposition 13, theorem 13, K-C 2:588 (M).
80 *Principia* 3, "Regulae Philosophandi," n3, K-C 2:552–555; Cajori, pp. 398–400.
81 *Principia* 3, General Scholium, K-C 2:764 (M).
82 "Dr. Clarke's First Reply," *L-C*, p. 12.
83 "Dr. Clarke's Second Reply," *L-C*, p. 20.
84 Cited in Richard S. Westfall, *Science and Religion in Seventeenth-Century England* (New Haven: Yale University Press, 1958), p. 28.
85 Ibid., p. 34.
86 Ibid., p. 42.
87 "Mr. Leibniz's First Paper," *L-C*, p. 11.
88 Newton to Bentley, January 17, 1692/3, *Correspondence* 3:240.
89 *Principia*, corollaries after the three laws of motion, corollary 4, K-C 1:63 (M).
90 Strong, "Newton and God," p. 167. So Strong censures Clarke and Cheyne because "they did depart from his [Newton's] thought, however, in taking the religious addendum to be fundamental to his science, for therein they did violence to the autonomy of science in methods and results upon which Newton had clearly and vigorously insisted." It seems that Strong is reading his own sense of the "autonomy of science" into Newton.
91 *Opticks* 3, query 28, p. 369 (italics added).
92 Newton to Bentley, December 10, 1692, *Correspondence* 3:235.
93 *Principia* 3, General Scholium, K-C 2:760; Cajori, p. 544. Newton uses two words for system in Latin: *systema* and *compages*. The latter could equally well be translated as "structure."
94 Newton to Bentley, December 10, 1692, *Correspondence* 3:234. The value of these letters to Bentley lies in their amplifying the demonstration of the existence and attributes of God which Newton outlined in his published works. In so doing, they give an indication of what theological development would follow upon the influence of the *Principia* and the *Opticks*.
95 Newton to Bentley, December 10, 1692, *Correspondence* 3:235–236 (enumeration added).
96 Newton to Bentley, January 17, 1692/3, *Correspondence* 3:240: "I do not know any power in nature wch could cause this transverse motion without ye divine arm." Newton to Bentley, February 11, 1692/3, *Correspondence* 3:244: "And tho gravity might give the Planets a motion of descent towards the Sun either directly or with some little obliquity, yet the transverse motions by wch they revolve in their several orbs required the divine Arm to impress them according to ye tangents of their orbs."
97 Newton to Bentley, February 11, 1692/3, *Correspondence* 3:244.
98 Newton to Bentley, December 10, 1692, *Correspondence* 3:236.
99 *Principia* 3, General Scholium, K-C 2:760–761; Cajori, pp. 544–545 (italics added).
100 Berkeley, *Principles of Human Knowledge*, #117; Koyré, *From the Closed World to the Infinite Universe*, pp. 222–223. James Collins nicely summarizes Berkeley's view of the Newtonian theological enterprise with its many successors: "Berkeley greatly admired Newton's combination of reason and observation, in the development of a *natural philosophy*. But he opposed the pretentious claims being made by the Newtonians for this natural or experimental philosophy, whether the claims were made in the interest of religion or of irreligion." Collins cites Berkeley's letter to the American Samuel Johnson: "The true use and end of Natural Philosophy is to explain the phenomena of nature; which is

done by discovering the laws of nature, and reducing particular appearances to them. This is Sir Isaac Newton's method; and such method or design is not in the least inconsistent with the principles I lay down." Collins, *A History of Modern European Philosophy*, p. 397. Berkeley has significantly truncated Newton's method.

101 *Opticks* 3, query 28, p. 369. See also query 31, p. 405: "For so far as we can know by natural Philosophy what is the first Cause, what Power He has over us, and what Benefits we receive from him, so far our Duty towards him, as well as that towards one another, will appear to us by the light of Nature." Note that "Power" is again singled out as the primary and pivotal attribute.

102 *Principia* 3, General Scholium, K-C 2:762: "Deum summum necessario existere in confesso est: et eadem necessitate semper est et ubique." See Cajori, p. 545. That whatever necessarily exists, whatever cannot not-be, must be everywhere, will form a critical argument of Clarke's against the materialists.

103 *De gravitatione et a equipondio fluidorum*, ed. with an English translation in *Unpublished Scientific Papers of Isaac Newton*, ed. A. R. and Marie Boas Hall (Cambridge: Cambridge University Press, 1962) (henceforth cited as *De gravitatione*), p. 99: "[Extensio] habet quendam sibi proprium existendi modum qui neque substantiis neque accidentibus competit." See also Westfall, *Force in Newton's Physics*, pp. 339 ff. and 403n26.

104 *Principia* 3, General Scholium, K-C 2:762: "Totus est sui similis."

105 *De gravitatione*, p. 99.

106 *De gravitatione*, p. 136. See also Koyré, "Newton and Descartes," *Newtonian Studies*, pp. 85–86. For the historical context of this discussion of the nature of space, see Koyré, *From the Closed World to the Infinite Universe*, p. 227.

107 *Principia* 3, General Scholium, K-C 2:763; Cajori's version (p. 546) leaves out one of these sentences.

108 See Acts 17:28: "For in Him we live and move and are." Newton has shifted this statement to a statement about space and the lack of resistance. Thus Koyré can comment that this assertion is not to be taken "metaphorically or metaphysically as St. Paul meant it, but in the most proper and literal meaning of these words. We—that is, the world—are in God; in God's space, and in God's time." Koyré, *From the Closed World to the Infinite Universe*, p. 227.

109 *Principia* 3, General Scholium, K-C 2:764; Cajori, p. 546.

110 *Opticks* 3, query 31, p. 402. The Queries do *not* assert that God intervenes to reform this system, but only that the system will eventually need a reformation.

111 *Opticks* 3, query 31, p. 398.

112 "Dr. Clarke's First Reply," *L-C*, p. 14.

113 *Principia* 3, General Scholium, K-C 2:763; Cajori, p. 546. See Henry Guerlac and M. C. Jacob, "Bentley, Newton, and Providence," *Journal of the History of Ideas* 30, no. 3 (July–September 1969):317.

114 David Kubrin, "Newton and the Cyclical Cosmos: Providence and the Mechanical Philosophy," *Journal of the History of Ideas* 28, no. 3 (July–September 1967):325ff.

115 *Principia* 3, proposition 42, problem 22, K-C 2:757; Cajori, p. 541 (M).

116 *Principia* 3, General Scholium, K-C 2:760; Cajori, p. 544.

117 *Principia* 1. 14, proposition 96, theorem 50, scholium, K-C 1:344; Cajori, pp. 230–231.

118 *Opticks* 2, pt. 2, proposition 3, pp. 249–250.

119 *Opticks* 2, pt. 3, proposition 8, p. 267.

120 John Harris, *Lexicon Technicum*, s. v. "mechanical philosophy": "*Mechanical Philosophy* is the same with the *Corpuscular*, which endeavours to explicate the Phaenomena of Nature from Mechanical Principles; i.e. from the Motion, Rest, Figure, Position, Magnitude, etc. of the Minute Particles of Matter. And these Principles are frequently called *Mechanical Causes*: And also the *Mechanical Affections* of Matter."

121 *Opticks* 3, query 28, pp. 369–370.

122 *Opticks* 3, query 28, pp. 369–370 (italics added).

123 "Dr. Clarke's Second Reply," *L-C*, p. 21. Leibniz' attack was stated in his first paper: "Sir Isaac Newton says, that space is an organ, which God makes use of to perceive things by. But if God stands in need of any organ to perceive things by, it will follow, that they do not depend altogether upon him, nor were they produced by him." "Mr. Leibnitz' First Paper," *L-C*, p. 11.

124 *Opticks* 3, query 31, p. 397 (italics added).

125 Ibid., pp. 402–403. See p. 389: "I had rather infer from their Cohesion, that their Particles attract one another by some force, which in immediate contact is exceeding strong, at small distances performs the chymical Operations above-mention'd, and reaches not far from the Particles with any sensible Effect."

126 Ibid., p. 400.

127 Ibid., p. 402.

128 Isaac Newton, "A Short Scheme of the True Religion," quoted in Sir David Brewster, *Memoirs of the Life, Writings, and Discoveries of Sir Isaac Newton* (Edinburgh: Thomas Constable, 1855), 2:347–348: "Did blind chance know that there was light, and what was its refraction, and fit the eyes of all creatures, after the most curious manner, to make use of it? These, and such like consider-ations, always have, and ever will prevail with mankind, to believe that there is a Being who made all things, and has all things in his power, and who is therefore to be feared."

Chapter 3: Section 1.

1 Père Yves de l'Isle André, *La vie de R. P. Malebranche, Prêtre de l'Oratoire avec l'histoire de ses ouvrages* (Paris: Librairie Poussielgue Frères, 1886), pp. 11–12. One must not think that such philosophic moments of exuberance are confined to the West. The biographer of the Chinese philosopher, Wang Shou-jen (Wang Yang-ming) described the Master's abrupt entrance into en-lightenment one night in 1508, at the age of thirty-seven: "Suddenly, in the middle of the night, the meaning of 'the extension of knowledge through the investigation of things' dawned upon him. Without knowing what he was doing, he called out, got up, and danced about, so that the servants all became alarmed. Now for the first time he realized that for the Truth [*Tao*] of the stages, one's own nature is sufficient, and that it is wrong to seek for Principle [*li*] outside of it in nature and things." *Yang-ming Chi-yao* (Important Selections from Wang Shou-jen), trans. Frederick Goodrich Henke, *The Philosophy of Wang Yang-ming* (London and Chicago: Open Court, 1916), p. 13.

2 Henri Gouhier, *La vocation de Malebranche* (Paris: Librairie philosophique J. Vrin, 1926), pp. 13–35. Gouhier acknowledges that contemporary scholarship has been unable to determine the actual content of Malebranche's studies with exactitude.

3 Nicolas Malebranche, *Recherche de la vérité où l'on traite de la nature de l'esprit*

de l'homme et de l'usage qu'il en doit faire pout éviter l'erreur dans les sciences, ed. Geneviève Rodis-Lewis, in *Oeuvres complètes de Malebranche*, general editor A. Robinet (Paris: Librairie philosophique J. Vrin, 1962–). The *Recherche* occupies the first three volumes of this edition, henceforth cited as *OCM*. 1:9–11 (M). Idem, *The Search after Truth*, trans. Thomas M. Lennon and Paul J. Olscamp (Columbus, Ohio: Ohio State University, 1980) (hereafter cited as *Search*).

4 Descartes to Mesland, February 9, 1645, AT 4:167–169.

5 *Recherche*, preface, *OCM* 1:10; *Search*, p. xix.

6 *Recherche*, preface, *OCM* 1:10–11; *Search*, p. xx (M).

7 *Recherche*, 1.1.1, *OCM* 1:39; *Search*, p. 1 (M).

8 *Recherche*, 1.5.1ff., *OCM*, 1:69–77; *Search*, pp. 19ff.

9 *Recherche*, 1.13.4. *OCM* 1:46; *Search*, p. 62 (M) (italics added).

10 Nicolas Malebranche, *Dialogues on Metaphysics and on Religion*, 4.16–17, trans. Morris Ginsberg (London: Allen and Unwin, 1923) (henceforth cited as *Dialogues on Metaphysics*), pp. 134–135. For the French original, *Entretiens sur la métaphysique et sur la religion* (henceforth cited as *Entretiens sur la métaphysique*), *OCM* 12:100–102 (italics added).

11 René Descartes, *Principes* 1.71, AT 9, bk. 2, pp. 58–59. Desmond Connell remarks correctly that Malebranche "does not reject the explanation of Descartes but subordinates it to his own view that original sin is the ultimate source of our disordered dependence on sense." *The Vision of God: Malebranche's Scholastic Sources* (New York: Humanities Press, 1967), p. 12n 19. What Connell does not emphasize, however, is that this places all of Malebranche's philosophy within a theological context. Hence one of the radical differences between Descartes and Malebranche is that one of them is fundamentally a philosopher who occasionally dips into a theological issue; the other is one for whom theological assertions and theological evidence lie at the very basis of whatever philosophy he will do.

12 Francis Rouleau, S.J., "Maillard de Tournon, Papal Legate at the Court of Peking: The First Imperial Audience (31 December 1705)," *Archivum Historicum Societatis Iesu* 31 (1962):264–323. Ludwig von Pastor, *The History of the Popes from the Close of the Middle Ages*, trans. Ralph E. Kerr and E. F. Peeler (St. Louis: B. Herder, 1941), 33:393–490. William V. Bangert, S.J., *A History of the Society of Jesus* (St. Louis: Institute of Jesuit Sources, 1972), pp. 335–342.

13 Nicolas Malebranche, *Entretien d'un philosophe chrétien et d'un philosophe chinois sur l'existence et la nature de Dieu* (henceforth cited as *Entretien*), *OCM* 15:39. The English translation of this work is that of Dominick A. Iorio, *Nicolas Malebranche: Dialogue between a Christian Philosopher and a Chinese Philosopher on the Existence and Nature of God* (henceforth cited as *Dialogue*) (Washington, D.C.: University Press of America, 1980), p. 45. Iorios' introduction reveals a hopelessly faulty grasp of the issue of the Chinese Rites.

14 Wing-Tsit Chan, ed. and trans., *Reflections on Things at Hand, The Neo-Confucian Anthology compiled by Chu Hsi and Lu Tsu-Ch'ien* (New York: Columbia University Press, 1967) (henceforth cited as Chan, ed., *Reflections*), pp. xvii–xxi.

15 Fung Yu-Lan, *A History of Chinese Philosophy*, trans. Derk Budde (Princeton: Princeton University Press, 1953) (henceforth cited as *History*), 2:533.

16 Chan, ed., *Reflections*, pp. xxxviii–xxxix.

17 Chan, ed., *Reflections*, pp. 367–368. Even for the pioneer Jesuit missionaries, the terrible difficulties of translation took their toll. A letter of December 20, 1629, from the visitor to the missions, André Palmeiro, to the Jesuit General, Muzio

Vitelleschi, recorded the death of Nicolas Trigault, the great successor to Matteo Ricci, on November 14, 1628. Palmeiro writes in code to the General that Trigault's mind had collapsed and he had hanged himself, and that Lazaro Cattaneo had predicted that Trigault's intense concentration upon the enormous problem of the Chinese translations of Christian terminology would kill him. 'This is probably the clue to what happened. His mind gave way under excessive strain." George H. Dunne, S.J., *Generation of Giants. The Story of the Jesuits in China in the last Decades of the Ming Dynasty* (Notre Dame: University of Notre Dame Press, 1962), p. 213. See François Bontinck, C.I.C.M., *La Lutte autour de la liturgie chinoise aux XVIIe et XVIIIe siècles* (Louvain: Éditions Nauwelaerts, 1962).

18 Chu Hsi, *Chu-tzŭ Yü-lei (Classified Conversations of Chu-Hsi)* (hereafter cited as *Conversations*), 94.21, in Fung Yu-Lan, *History of Chinese Philosophy*, 2:535.

19 Chu Hsi, *Conversations* 4.6, *History* 2:535–536.

20 Chu Hsi, *Conversations* 94.11, *History* 2:537.

21 Plotinus, *Enneads*, 6.4.7: "Let us consider once more how it is possible for an identity to extend over a universe. This comes to the question how each variously placed entity in the multiplicity of the sense order can have its share in the one identical Principle. . . . Imagine a small luminous mass serving as center to a transparent sphere, so that the light from within shows upon the entire outer surface, otherwise unlit: we surely agree that the inner core of light, intact and immobile, reaches over the entire outer extension; the single light of that small centre illuminates the whole field. The diffused light is not due to any bodily magnitude of that central point which illuminates not as body but as body lit, that is by another kind of power than corporeal quality: let us then abstract the corporeal mass, retaining the light as power: we can no longer speak of the light in any particular spot; it is equally diffused within and throughout the entire sphere. We can no longer even name the spot it occupied so as to say whence it came or how it is present; we can but seek, and wonder as the search shows us the light simultaneously present at each and every point of the sphere. So with the sunlight: looking to the corporeal mass you are able to name the source of the light shining through all the air, but what you see is one identical light in integral omnipresence. Consider too the effect of bodies which intercept the sun's light (as in an eclipse): without letting the light pass through them to the side opposite to its source, they yet do not divide it. And supposing, as before, that the sun were simply an unembodied illuminant, the light would no longer be fixed to any one definite spot: having no starting point, no centre of origin, it would be an integral unity omnipresent." Plotinus, *The Enneads*, trans. Stephen MacKenna (London: Faber and Faber, 1930), pp. 524–525.

22 Chu Hsi, *Conversations* 94.41, *History* 2:541.

23 Chu Hsi, *Chu Wen-kung Wen-chi (Collected Writings of Chu-Hsi)* (henceforth cited as *Writings*), 58.5, in Fung Yu-Lan, *History* 2:542.

24 Chu Hsi, *Conversations* 1.1, *History* 2:544.

25 Chu Hsi, *Writings* 58.11, *History* 2:539. "There is Principle [*li*] before there can be the Ether [*ch'i*]. But it is only when there is the Ether, that Principle has a place in which to rest. This fact applies to the coming into existence of all [things], whether as large as Heaven and Earth, or as tiny as the cricket or ant. . . . If we are to pin down the word Principle, neither 'existence' [*yu*] nor 'non-existence' [*wu*] may be attributed to it. For before Heaven and Earth 'existed,' it already was as it is."

26 *Entretien*, p. 20; *Dialogue*, pp. 45–47.

27 *Dialogue*, pp. 45 and 47; *Entretien*, pp. 39 and 42.

28 For the history of the composition of the *Entretien*, see André, *La vie de Malebranche*, pp. 304–331. André expands the six errors which Malebranche listed into an index of nine dogmas of Confucius to which he adds this short introduction: "Les docteurs ou lettrés chinois, disciples de Confucius, qui est comme le Dieu des sciences en ce pays-là, tiennent pour dogmes fondamentaux de leur religion et de leur philosophie" (p. 309). For the contrasting stance of Leibniz, see his *Discours sur la theologie naturelle des Chinois*, trans. with introduction and notes by Daniel J. Cook and Henry Rosemont, Jr. (Honolulu: The University Press of Hawaii, 1977), monograph 4. Leibniz contrasts Spinoza's view with the Chinese understanding of *li*, see *Discours*, pp. 72, 87–88, 90. See also David Mungello, *Leibniz and Confucianism: The Search for Accord* (Honolulu: The University Press of Hawaii, 1977).

29 *Dialogue*, p. 65; *Entretien*, p. 4. In order to keep a consistency in spelling, Malebranche's *Ly* will be rendered *Li* in the English version. When it is used to denote a form of god, it will be capitalized.

30 *Dialogue*, p. 65; *Entretien*, p. 4.

31 *Entretien*, p. 3; *Dialogue*, p. 65.

32 *Dialogue*, p. 63; *Entretien*, pp. 55–56 (m).

33 *Dialogue*, p. 65; *Entretien*, p. 4.

34 *Dialogue*, p. 48; *Entretien*, p. 42.

35 *Entretien*, pp. 57–59. Unfortunately, this series of citations has been omitted from the English version, perhaps because of the notation which has been appended to them in the *OCM*, p. 57n 1: "Il est habile de faire appel aux Jésuites eux-mêmes pour combattre les critiques de Trévoux, qui atténuent l'Athéisme des Chinois. Mais ce passage aurait été ajouté à l'insu de Malebranche." The actual evaluation that Matteo Ricci made of the three received religious cults, especially of Confucius, can be found in his *Storia dell'introduzione del christianesimo in Cina*, ed. Pasquale M. D'Elia, S.J., in the series *Fonti Ricciane* (Rome: La Libreria della Stato, 1942), 1:115–132, especially pp. 115–117.

36 *Dialogue*, p. 84; *Entretien*, p. 20.

37 *Dialogue*, p. 66; *Entretien*, p. 4 (m).

38 *Entretien*, p. 7; *Dialogue*, p. 69.

39 *Dialogue*, pp. 67–68; *Entretien*, pp. 5–6.

40 *Entretien*, p. 3; *Dialogue*, p. 65 (M): "Le Dieu, que nous vous annonçons est celui-là même dont l'idée est gravée en vous, et dans tous les hommes."

41 Nicolas Malebranche, *Dialogue on Metaphysics*, 2.5, p. 90; *Entretiens sur la métaphysique*, p. 53.

42 *Dialogue on Metaphysics*, 2.5, p. 90; *Entretiens sur la métaphysique* p. 53.

43 *Entretiens sur la métaphysique* 2.3. p. 52; *Dialogues on Metaphysics*, p. 89.

44 *Recherche*, 1.3.2, *OCM* 1:64 (M), (*Search*), p. 15.

45 *Dialogue*, pp. 70–71; *Entretien*, pp. 7–10.

46 *Dialogue*, p. 73; *Entretien*, p. 10 (emphasis added).

47 *Dialogue*, p. 74; *Entretien*, p. 11. In the *Dialogues on Metaphysics*, the meditational nature of metaphysical reflection is even more evident. In order that inner truth will preside over the conversations, Theodore and Aristes leave the French countryside for the study where one can draw the curtains and leave the room in semidarkness. These dialogues begin with what must be one of the strangest introductions in the history of this philosophic form: "Be seated. Reject, Aristes,

all that has come into your mind by means of the senses. Silence your imagination. Let all things in you be in perfect silence. Forget also, if you can, that you have a body, and think only of what I am going to tell you." Theodore, or the devout Father Malebranche, is not inviting Aristes to a philosophical discussion, much less a mutual inquiry. He is giving him "points" for his future meditation. Descartes had used meditation as a method by which one could do his philosophy. Malebranche would go one step further. He would provide the matter for the meditations of someone else: "Meditate, Aristes, on what I have just told you, and to-morrow, I promise you, you will be ready for everything. Meditation will strengthen your mind and will give you enthusiasm and endow you with wings wherewith to soar beyond merely created things and ascend to the very presence of the Creator." *Dialogues on Metaphysics* 1.1, pp. 71, 1. 10, p. 85.

48 René Descartes, *Meditations*, 1, Lafleur, p. 17; *Discourse*, 2, Lafleur, p. 7.

49 *Dialogue*, p. 74; *Entretien*, p. 11. For the importance of this experience, see Joseph Moreau, "'Vision en Dieu' et 'Présence au monde,'" in *Malebranche: L'Homme et L'Oeuvre, 1638–1715* (Paris: Librairie philosophique J. Vrin, 1967), pp. 182ff.

50 *Dialogue*, p. 75; *Entretien*, p. 12.

51 *Dialogue*, p. 76; *Entretien*, pp. 11–12.

52 *Entretien*, p. 15; *Dialogue*, pp. 77–78.

53 *Dialogue*, p. 81; *Entretien*, p. 17.

54 *Dialogues on Metaphysics* 1.1, p. 72.

55 Ibid., 1. 2–3, pp. 73–74.

56 Ibid., 4. 11, p. 130.

57 Ibid., 7. 11, p. 191. The axiom with which Malebranche argues his case is: "The Creator alone can be the mover, only He who gives being to bodies can put them in the places which they occupy" (p. 190).

58 Collins, *God in Modern Philosophy*, p. 86: "In this respect, he [Malebranche] was forced to disagree with his own masters, St. Augustine and Descartes, who had distinguished between the causal power of finite things and its ultimate source in the creator of nature. But like other thinkers who failed to see in finite causality a manifestation of God's power and goodness, Malebranche was eventually obliged to make a covert restitution of some type of agency to finite things."

59 *Dialogue*, p. 83; *Entretien*, p. 19.

60 *Dialogue*, p. 88; *Entretien*, p. 23.

61 *Dialogue*, p. 87; *Entretien*, p. 22.

Chapter 3: Section 2.

1 Benjamin Hoadly, preface, *The Works of Samuel Clarke, D.D.* (London: John and Paul Knapton, 1738), p. i.

2 William Whiston, *Historical Memoirs of the Life of Dr. Samuel Clarke* (London, 1730), pp. 5–6.

3 Whiston is contrasting the situation of David Gregory's teaching of Newton at Edinburgh with the hold that Cartesianism continued to extend over Cambridge; *Memoirs of the Life and Writings of Mr. William Whiston* (London: Printed for the Author and Sold by Mr. Whiston and Mr. Bishop, 1749–50) 1:35–36: "After I had taken Holy Orders, I returned to the College, and went on with my own Studies there, particularly the Mathematicks, and the Cartesian Philosophy; which was alone in Vogue with us at that Time. But it was not long before I, with

immense Pains, but no Assistance, set myself with utmost Zeal to the Study of Sir Isaac Newton's wonderful Discoveries in his *Philosophiae Naturalis Principia Mathematica,* one or two of which Lectures I had heard him read in the publick Schools, though I understood them not at all at that Time. Being indeed greatly excited thereto by a Paper of Dr. Gregory's when he was Professor in Scotland; wherein he had given the most prodigious Commendations to that Work, as not only right in all things, but in a manner the Effect of a plainly Divine Genius, and had already caused several of his Scholars to keep Acts, as we call them, upon several Branches of the Newtonian Philosophy; while we at Cambridge, poor Wretches, were ignominiously studying the fictitious Hypotheses of the Cartesian, which Sir Isaac Newton had also himself done formerly, as I have heard him say."

4 Michael A. Hoskin, "Mining All Within," *Thomist* 24, nos. 2, 3, 4 (April, July, October 1961): 357–361. In the first edition of Clarke's translation and annotation of Rohault's work, as Hoskin points out, "there is no suggestion of a systematic refutation of the text and argument in favor of Newtonian philosophy, although historians who have confused the 1697 notes with those of later editions have often supposed Clarke to offer just this." Even in these modest beginnings, Clarke followed his exposition of the theories of Descartes, Hooke, and Barrow with this phrase which could stand for his whole life: "I hasten to the theory of the illustrious Newton (for I do not think that it is right to call it a hypothesis), by which the phenomena which we have detailed above and all others as well are given an explanation which is without peer," pp. 357–358 (M). Hoskin includes a very helpful list of the succeeding editions of Rohault's work. For a brief consideration of the history of Cartesian vs. Newtonian influences in England, see Florian Cajori's appendix to his translation of the *Principia,* pp. 629–632.

5 Hoadly, preface, *Samuel Clarke,* p. ii.

6 Hoskin, "Mining All Within," p. 361.

7 Whiston, *Memoirs of Samuel Clarke,* p. 4.

8 Joel M. Rodney, "Clarke, Samuel," *Dictionary of Scientific Biography,* ed. Charles Coulston Gillipsie (New York: Charles Scribner's Sons, 1971) 3:294.

9 Whiston, *Memoirs of Samuel Clarke,* p. 6.

10 Hoadly, preface, *Samuel Clarke,* p. ii.

11 James P. Ferguson, *An Eighteenth Century Heretic: Dr. Samuel Clarke* (Kineton: Roundwood, 1976), pp. 47ff.

12 Ferguson, *Heretic,* pp. 23–25. Rodney maintains that "at Norwich, Clarke gained a reputation as a preacher of clear, learned sermons; this led him to be chosen to present the Boyle lectures for 1704. He made such a favorable impression that he was asked to deliver an additional series the next year" ("Clarke, Samuel," p. 294).

13 Samuel Clarke, *A Demonstration of the Being and Attributes of God. More Particularly in Answer to Mr. Hobbs, Spinoza, and their Followers* (London: J. Knapton, 1705) (hereafter cited as *DBAG*) and *A Discourse concerning the Unchangeable Obligations of Natural Religion, and the Truth and Certainty of the Christian Revelation* (London: J. Knapton, 1706) (hereafter cited as *DNR*). Both works were published together as: *A Discourse concerning the Being and Attributes of God, the Obligations of Natural Religion, and the Truth and Certainty of the Christian Revelation* (London: J. Knapton, 1711). The edition cited throughout this study is the ninth (London: John and Paul Knapton, 1738).

14 Voltaire, "Platon," *Dictionnaire Philosophique, Oeuvres de Voltaire* (Paris: Chez Lefèvre, 1829), 31:445.

15 Voltaire, "Septième Lettre," *Lettres Philosophiques*, in *Oeuvres de Voltaire* (Paris: Chez Lefèvre, 1829), 37:144–147.

16 Voltaire, "Septième Lettre," pp. 144–147. The critical edition of Gustave Lanson amplified by André M. Rousseau is quite skeptical of the authenticity of this anecdote; see *Lettres philosophiques* (Paris: Marcel Didier, 1964), pp. 85–86.

17 Hoadly, preface, *Samuel Clarke*, p. xiv.

18 Voltaire, "Septième Lettre," pp. 144–147.

19 Voltaire to René-Joseph Tournemine, c. August, 1735. *The Selected Letters of Voltaire*, ed. and trans. Richard A. Books (New York: New York University Press, 1973), p. 51. For the French original, see *Voltaire's Correspondence*, ed. Theodore Besterman, (Genève: Institut et Musée Voltaire, Les Délices, 1954), 4:103–108.

20 *DBAG*, p. 1.

21 Newton, *Principia*, 3, General Scholium; Cajori, p. 546.

22 *DBAG*, pp. 2–3.

23 Ibid., preface.

24 Ibid., p. 8.

25 Ibid., preface.

26 Samuel Clarke, Latin translation and notes to Jacques Rohault, *Traité de physique* (1697); notes to pt 2, pp. 214–219. Any Latin citations from Clarke's translation of Rohault will be taken from or checked against *Jacobi Rohaulti Tractatus Physicus*, 2 vols., 2d edition (Cologne, 1713).

27 Roger Cotes, "Preface to the Second Edition," Cajori, p. xxxiii.

28 *DBAG*, preface.

29 Ibid., pp. 8–9.

30 Ibid., p. 9.

31 Ibid.

32 Ibid., pp. 11–13.

33 Ibid., p. 14.

34 Ibid., p. 15.

35 Elmer Sprague, "Clarke, Samuel," *The Encyclopedia of Philosophy*, ed. Paul Edwards (New York: Macmillian and The Free Press, 1967), 2:119. Sprague is also unhappy that in the defense of the second proposition, "Clarke made the slide from 'something' to 'being' without apology." Again, the "slide" does not seem to need apology. In proposition one, Clarke says that "something has existed from all Eternity"; and in proposition two, he refers to "Some One Unchangeable and Independent Being." Clarke is not using "being" to mean the act of being (*esse*), but something, or someone.

36 *DBAG*, p. 9.

37 Ibid., p. 16.

38 Ibid., p. 17 (italics added).

39 Ibid.

40 Ibid., p. 20.

41 Ibid., p. 21.

42 Ibid., pp. 17–18.

43 Ibid., p. 27.

44 Ibid., p. 23. See pp. 27ff. Clarke is at great pains to distinguish this issue from the issue of the eternality of the world. "The Question between us and the Atheists, is not whether the World can possibly have been eternal; but whether it can possibly be the Original, Independent, and Self-existing Being: Which is a very

different Question. For many, who have affirmed the One, have still utterly denied the Other" (p. 30). There is a second reason to insist upon the distinction of issues: "That the Material World is not Self-Existent or Necessarily-Existing, but the Product of some distinct superior Agent, may (as I have already shown) be strictly demonstrated by bare Reason against the most obstinate Atheist in the World. But the Time when the world was created; or whether its Creation was, properly speaking, in Time; is not so easy to demonstrate strictly by bare Reason, (as appears from the Opinions of many of the Ancient Philosophers concerning that Matter;) but the Proof of it can be taken only from Revelation" (pp. 36–37).

45 Ibid., p. 24.

46 Ibid., pp. 25–26.

47 Ibid., pp. 26–27. "For if a Being can without a Contradiction be absent from one Place, it may without a Contradiction be absent likewise from another Place, and from all Places: And whatever Necessity it may have of Existing, must arise from some External Cause, and not absolutely from itself: And consequently, the Being cannot be Self-Existent" (pp. 44–45).

48 Ibid., p. 39.

49 Newton, *Principia*, 3, General Scholium; Cajori, p. 545.

50 *DBAG*, p. 38. So, for example, Saint Thomas outlines his treatment of God in the very early parts of the *Summa theologiae*: "Circa essentiam vero divinam, primo considerandum est an Deus sit; secundo, quomodo sit, vel potius quomodo non sit; tertio considerandum erit de his quae ad operationem ipsius pertinent, scilicet de scientia et de voluntate et potentia" (1.2. Introductio). The reason for this correction of the second issue is given in the introduction to the third *Quaestio*: "Cognito de aliquo an sit, inquirendum restat quomodo sit, ut sciatur de eo quid sit. Sed quia de Deo scire non possumus quid sit, sed quid non sit, non possumus considerare de Deo quomodo sit, sed potius quomodo non sit" (1.3. Introductio). It is interesting to compare this order of the issues with that of the *Demonstration* of Samuel Clarke.

51 *DBAG*, p. 41.

52 Ibid., p. 44.

53 Ibid.

54 "Dr. Clarke's First Reply," *L-C*, p. 12.

55 *DBAG*, p. 45.

56 Ibid., p. 48.

57 Benedict de Spinoza, *Ethics*, 1, proposition 14, p. 51.

58 *DBAG*, p. 50.

59 Aquinas, *Summa theologiae* 1.14.1 (M).

60 *Principia* 3, General Scholium; Cajori, p. 545.

61 *DBAG*, p. 51.

62 Ibid., pp. 52–58.

63 Ibid., pp. 58–59.

64 Ibid., pp. 60–61.

65 In answer to the objection that colors and sounds and tastes are not qualities of an object, but result from figure, divisibility, mobility, and the other qualities of matter, Clarke remarks: "Colours, Sounds, Tastes, and the like, are by no means Effects arising from mere Figure and Motion; their being nothing in the Bodies themselves, the Objects of the Senses, that has any manner of Similitude to any of these Qualities; but they are plainly Thoughts or Modifications of the Mind itself, which is an Intelligent being; and are *not properly Caused, but only Occasioned,*

by the Impressions of Figure and Motion" (ibid., p. 54; italics added). The use of "occasion" in place of "cause" bears striking resemblance to Malebranche, though in the *Demonstration* it has a much more limited role.

66 Ibid., p. 56. "If they be really Compounds and Effects, then they are not different, but exactly the same that ever they were; as, when two Triangles put together make a Square; That Square is still nothing but two Triangles" (p. 57).

67 Spinoza, *Ethics*, 1, proposition 17, p. 57. This is cited in the Latin original by Clarke, *DBAG*, p. 64.

68 *DBAG*, p. 63.

69 Spinoza, *Ethics*, 1, proposition 29, p. 65.

70 *DBAG*, p. 66.

71 Ibid., p. 69.

72 Ibid., p. 70.

73 Ibid.

74 Ibid., p. 101.

75 Ibid., p. 108. It is only when freedom has been explored that Clarke can remark: "I shall, from what has been said on this Head, draw only this one Inference; that hereby we are enabled to answer that Ancient and great Question [πόθεν τὸ κακὸν] What is the Cause and Original of Evil. For Liberty implying a Natural Power of doing Evil, as well as Good" (p. 107).

76 Ibid., p. 109.

77 Ibid., p. 111.

78 Ibid., pp. 112–114.

79 Ibid., pp. 114–115.

80 Guillemi de Ockham, *Quaestiones in librum secundum sententiarum (Reportatio)*, ed. Rega Wood, Gedeon Gal, Romvald Green (St. Bonaventure, N.Y.: St. Bonaventure University Press, 1981), Q. 15, pp. 352ff. This allows the astounding propositions in the argument of the sixteenth question of the fourth book: "Deus potest praecipere quod voluntas creata odiat eum." *Quaestiones in librum quartum sententiarum (Reportatio)*, ed. Wood, Gal, Green (St. Bonaventure, N.Y.: St. Bonaventure University Press, 1984), Q. 16, p. 352.

81 *DBAG*, p. 114.

82 Ibid., p. 119. For the discussion about the freedom of creation, see p. 121.

83 Ibid., p. 126.

84 Ibid., p. 127.

Chapter 4

1 Diderot to Volland, October 18, 1760. Denis Diderot, *Lettres à Sophie Volland*, ed. André Babelon (Paris: Gallimard, 1930) (henceforth cited as *SV*) 1:243. Translation and citation from Arthur M. Wilson, *Diderot: The Testing Years, 1713–1759* (New York: Oxford University Press, 1957), p. 17.

2 Denis Diderot, *Oeuvres complètes*, ed. Jules Assézat (Paris: Garnier Frères, 1875) (henceforth cited as *OCD*) 6:182. Translation and citation from Wilson, *Diderot*, p. 18.

3 *OCD*, 6:182. Wilson, *Diderot*, pp. 20–22. Wilson cites a large portion of this paragraph, but translates "*un tempérament*" too narrowly as "sexual nature."

4 Wilson, *Diderot*, p. 22. For Diderot's final and complete rejection of the Jesuits, cf. "Jésuite," *Enc*, 8:512–516. Volume 8 of the *Encyclopédie* appeared in 1765, after the Jesuits had been expelled from France by the decree dated August 2,

1762. See Joseph Edmund Barker, *Diderot's Treatment of the Christian Religion in the Encyclopédie* (New York: King's Crown, 1941), p. 97.

5 Wilson, *Diderot*, pp. 49–53.

6 Denis Diderot, *Pensées philosophiques* (henceforth cited as *PP*), 61. The French text of this and other philosophic works of Diderot is taken from Diderot, *Oeuvres philosophiques*, ed. Paul Vennière (Paris: Garnier Frères, 1961) (henceforth cited as *OP*), pp. 48–49. The English translation, sometimes modified by checking against the French original, is taken from *Diderot's Early Philosophical Works*, trans. and ed. Margaret Jourdain (Chicago: Open Court, 1916) (henceforth cited as *DEPW*), pp. 66–67.

7 *PP*, *OP*, p. 9; see *DEPW*, p. 27; Wilson, *Diderot*, p. 64.

8 *PP* 1, *OP*, pp. 9–10; *DEPW*, p. 27.

9 *PP* 4, *OP*, p. 11; *DEPW*, p. 28.

10 *PP* 11, *OP*, pp. 13–14; *DEPW*, p. 31 (m). In *La promenade du sceptique ou les allées*, composed in 1747, shortly after the *Pensées philosophiques*, the internal contradictions in the designation of the god of religion were limned in the darkest irony: "L'empire dont je te parle est governé par un souverain sur le nom duquel ses sujets sont à peu près d'accord; mais il n'en est pas de même de son existence. Personne ne l'a vu, et ceux de ses favoris qui prétendent avoir eu des entretiens avec lui, en ont parlé d'une manière si obscure, lui ont attribué des contrariétés si étranges, que tandis qu'une partie de la nation s'est épuisée à former des systèmes pour expliquer l'énigme, ou à s'entre déchirer pour faire prévaloir ses opinions; l'autre a pris le partie de douter de tout ce qu'on en débitait, et quelques-uns celui de n'en rien croire." *OCD* 1:190. *La promenade du sceptique* is of considerable assistance in the determination of Diderot's early thought. Its seizure by the police soon after its composition effectively prevented its publication during Diderot's lifetime and isolated it from the evolving public discussions of the time. It was not published until 1830. See *OCD* 1:11.

11 *PP* 9 and 13, *OP*, pp. 13–15; *DEPW*, pp. 30–32.

12 Plutarch, περὶ Δεισιδαιμονίας (*De superstitione*), edited with an English translation by Frank Cole Babitt, Loeb Classical Library (New York: G.P. Putnam's Sons, 1928), 2:484–485. This passage is freely cited in *PP* 12, *OP*, p. 14, and *DEPW*, p. 31. Both Bayle and Shaftesbury indicate the influence of this section from Plutarch, Shaftesbury by citing it directly. See *OP*, p. 14n 1.

13 Plutarch, *De superstitione*, ch. 12, pp. 490–491.

14 René Descartes, *Meditations*, dedication, H-R 1:133.

15 *PP* 17, *OP*, p. 17; *DEPW*, p. 34.

16 Ambrose, *De Fide* 1.5.42. *PL* 16, 537A.

17 *PP*, 19, *OP*, p. 18; *DEPW*, p. 35.

18 *PP* 18, *OP*, p. 17–18; *DEPW*, pp. 34–35. The spelling of the names of each of these major figures, as that of so many names from the seventeenth and eighteenth centuries, varies in different transpositions into English.

19 *PP* 13, *OP*, pp. 14–15; *DEPW*, pp. 31–32.

20 *PP* 18, *OP*, pp. 17–18; *DEPW*, pp. 34–35.

21 Newton, *Principia*, preface to the first edition; Cajori; xviii.

22 Newton, *Principia* 3, General Scholium; Cajori, p. 546.

23 Gilson, *The Unity of Philosophical Experience*, pp. 149–150.

24 Hans Freudenthal, "Nieuwentijt, Bernard," *Dictionary of Scientific Biography*, ed. Charles Coulston Gillispie (New York: Charles Scribner's Sons, 1974), 10:120–121. Pierre Brunet comments: "C'est encore en 1715 que parut à

Amsterdam l'ouvrage de Nieuwentyt, dont les éléments avaint été, dès la fin du siècle précédent, réunis avec une patience scrupuleuse. Bien que l'auteur se propose avant tout de développer la preuve cosmologique de l'existence de Dieu, il ne se contente pas, à la grande surprise d'ailleurs et presque au scandale de Rousseau, de considérer l'ordre et harmonie du monde dans son ensemble; soucieux de retrouver l'action de Dieu jusque dans le moindre détail, il passe en revue la plupart des phénomènes, en y appliquant toutes les ressources de la méthode expérimentale. Constamment on retrouve dans cet ouvrage la défiance à l'égard des démonstrations fondées sur des raisonnements, auxquelles l'auteur oppose, en marquant sa préférence, les expériences évidentes et tout à fait exactes, auxquelles Newton a su se tenir." *Les physiciens hollandais et la méthode experimentale en France au XVIII siècle* (Paris: Librairie scientifique Albert Blanchard, 1926), pp. 46–47.

25 *PP* 18, *OP*, p. 17; *DEPW*, pp. 34–35.

26 See Brunet, *Les physiciens hollandais*, pp. 61ff. Noting the immediate influences upon him of 'sGravesande and Boerhaave, Brunet comments on the importance of Musschenbroek's inaugural address; "Musschenbroek allait donc marcher également sur les traces de Newton, dans la voie de la physique expérimentale" (p. 62). For the relationship between the laws which experimentation and observation established and "la volonté et la providence de celui qui les a établies," see Petrus van Musschenbroek's *Cours de physique experimentale et mathématique*, trans. Sigaud de la Fond, 1:8, cited and analyzed in Brunet, pp. 86ff.

27 Newton, *Principia*, Cajori, pp. 544–546.

28 René Descartes, *Meditations* 4, H-R 1:173. See "Concerning the Objections to the Fourth Meditation," H-R 2:223.

29 *PP* 21, *OP*, pp. 21–22; *DEPW*, pp. 38–40. See Herbert Westren Turnbull, *The Great Mathematicians* (New York: Simon and Schuster, 1962), pp. 89–90.

30 *PP* 19, *OP*, p. 18; *DEPW*, p. 35. Unfortunately, Jourdain translated *germes* as "germs." It should be translated "seeds," as in the above modification of Jourdain's translation. The actual sentence of Diderot reads: "La seule découverte des germes a dissipé une des plus puissantes objections de l'athéisme." Pensée 21 outlines this objection of the atheist.

31 Johannes Heniger, "Leeuwenhoek, Antoni van," *Dictionary of Scientific Biography*, ed. Charles Coulston Gillispie (New York: Charles Scribner's Sons, 1973), 8:126–129.

32 *PP* 19, *OP*, pp. 18–19; *DEPW*, p. 35.

33 *PP*, 19, *OP*, p. 18; *DEPW*, p. 35. For the importance of "organic finalism" in the *Pensées philosophiques*, see Aram Vartanian, "From Deist to Atheist: Diderot's Philosophical Orientation, 1746–1749," *Diderot Studies*, ed. O. E. Fellows and N. L. Torrey (Syracuse: Syracuse University Press, 1949), pp. 47–52.

34 *PP* 20, *OP*, p. 19–21; *DEPW*, p. 36–38 (m).

35 *PP* 22, *OP*, p. 23; *DEPW*, p. 40.

36 *PP* 24, *OP*, p. 24–25; *DEPW*, p. 41–42.

37 *PP* 25, 26, *OP*, p. 25–26; *DEPW*, p. 42–43.

38 *PP* 21, *OP*, p. 28; *DEPW*, p. 45.

39 *PP* 28, *OP*, p. 26; *DEPW*, p. 43.

40 *PP* 50, *OP*, p. 41; *DEPW*, p. 59.

41 *PP* 53, *OP*, p. 42–43; *DEPW*, p. 60–61. For the situation at Saint-Médard, see *OP*, p. 3n l, and Wilson, *Diderot*, p. 55.

42 Antoine Arnauld, *The Art of Thinking*, trans. James Dickoff and Patricia James (Indianapolis: Bobbs-Merrill, 1964), p. 293.

43 Cicero, *De divinatione* 2.11.27. Edited with an English translation by William Armistead Falconer, Loeb Classical Library (Cambridge, Mass.: Harvard University Press, 1953), p. 400. Cited, slightly altered, in *PP* 47, *OP*, pp. 38–39; *DEPW*, pp. 55–56.

44 *PP* 48, *OP*, p. 39; *DEPW*, p. 57.

45 *PP* 16, *OP*, p. 31; *DEPW*, pp. 48–49.

46 *PP* 46, *OP*, pp. 36–37; *DEPW*, p. 54.

47 *PP* 42, *OP*, pp. 31–32; *DEPW*, p. 49.

48 *PP* 50, *OP*, p. 41; *DEPW*, pp. 58–59. See also *PP* 52, *OP*, p. 42; *DEPW*, p. 60.

49 *DBAG*, p. 126.

50 *PP* 42, *OP*, pp. 31–32. *DEPW*, p. 49.

51 *PP* 56, *OP*, pp. 44–45; *DEPW*, pp. 62–63.

52 *PP* 58, *OP*, p. 46; *DEPW*, p. 64.

53 *PP* 59, *OP*, pp. 46–47; *DEPW*, pp. 64–65.

54 W. W. Rouse Gall, *A History of the Study of Mathematics at Cambridge* (Cambridge: Cambridge University Press, 1889), p. 84. Of these four sturdy figures, Saunderson seems to have possessed the easiest temperament. Isaac Barrow was reportedly so troublesome as a schoolboy that his father "was heard to pray that if it pleased God to take any of his children he could best spare Isaac" (Gall, p. 46). See also "Saunderson or Sanderson, Nicholas (1682–1739)," in *The Dictionary of National Biography* (London: Oxford University Press, 1937–38), 17:821–822.

55 Denis Diderot, *Lettre sur les aveugles à l'usage de ceux qui voient* (hereafter *LA*), in *OP*, p. 111. The English translation, *Letter on the Blind for The Use of Those Who See* (henceforth *LB*), is found in *DEPW* and is used here either fully or in modified form by checking it against the original. Henceforth just the title and the page in *OP* or *DEPW* will be cited; *LB*, p. 101; *LA*, p. 111.

56 *La promenade du sceptique*, pp. 220–221.

57 *LB*, p. 68–69; *LA* p. 81–82. Réaumur was one of the great universal geniuses who flourished during the first part of the eighteenth century. He contributed significantly to mathematics, natural history, biology, experimental physics, and technology, and is still celebrated for the thermometer which he invented and which bears his name. He became increasingly hostile to Diderot, finally charging him with plagiarism and the theft of drawings and engravings for use in the *Encyclopédie* in a letter to Jean-Henri-Samuel Formey, February 23, 1756. See Wilson, *Diderot*, pp. 242–243.

58 Nicholas Saunderson, *The Elements of Algebra* (Cambridge: Cambridge University Press, 1740–1741), 1:ix.

59 *LB*, "Note 2," pp. 219–220. For Cassiodorus, see Casiodori Senatoris, *Institutiones*, 1.5.2, ed. R. A. B. Mynors (Oxford: Clarendon Press, 1962), pp. 22–23. For the English translation, see Cassiodorus Senator, *An Introduction to Divine and Human Readings*, trans. Leslie Webber Jones (New York: Columbia University Press, 1946), pp. 84–85. For Trithemius on Nicaise de Voerde, see *De scriptoribus ecclesiasticis*, 876, in John Albert Fabaricius, *Bibliotheca Ecclesiastica* (Hamburg: Christianus Leibezeit et Theodorus Christoph. Felginer, 1713), pp. 208–209. Trithemius writes about Nicaise's achievements that because he had been without sight since his third year he presented to the fifteenth century the "miraculum" which Didymus of Alexandria had offered to his own.

60 John Locke, *An Essay Concerning Human Understanding*, bk. 2, ch. 9, sec. 8., collated and annotated by Alexander Cambell Fraser (New York: Dover, 1959), 1:186–187. Though Locke's *Essay* and *OP* spell Molyneux as Molineux, contemporary orthography has contentedly changed the *i* into *y*. This latter spelling is used throughout for consistency.

61 *LA*, p. 98; *LB*, p. 88 (M).

62 *LA*, p. 82; *LB*, p. 69.

63 *LA*, p. 141; *LB*, p. 134. The division of *LA* into two parts is confirmed by Diderot's own subsequent comments; see *Additions à la lettre sur les aveugles*, *OP*, p. 151; *DEPW*, p. 142.

64 *LA*, pp. 82–87; *LB*, pp. 70–75.

65 *LB*, p. 76; *LA*, p. 88(m). Gabriel Farrell, director of the Perkins Institution, is quoted by Arthur M. Wilson as saying: "Diderot seems to have been first to call the attention of the scientific world to the superior sensory capacities of the blind." Wilson, *Diderot*, p. 99.

66 *LB*, pp. 79–82; *LA*, pp. 91–94. Voltaire read Locke as introducing this possibility: "Mr. Locke after having destroy'd innate Ideas; after having fully renounc'd the Vanity of believing that we think always; after having laid down, from the most solid Principles, that ideas enter the Mind through the Senses . . . presum'd to advance, but very modestly, the following Words, 'We shall, perhaps, never be capable of knowing, whether a Being, purely material, thinks or not.' This sage Assertion was, by more Divines than one, look'd upon as a scandalous Declaration that the Soul is material and mortal." *Letters Concerning the English Nation*, intr. Charles Whibley (London: Peter Davies, 1926), pp. 77–78. For the French original, see *Lettres philosophiques ou Lettres anglaises*, p. 64.

67 *LB*, pp. 87–89; *LA*, pp. 97–99.

68 Diderot, *Réfutation de l'ouvrage d'Helvétius*, *OCD* 2:322. Consequently, in his *De l'Interprétation de la nature* (1753) (henceforth cited as *DIN*, with French text taken from *OP*), he contended that pure mathematics "ne conduisent à rien de précis sans l'expérience; que c'est une espèce de métaphysique générale, où les corps sont dépouillés de leurs qualités individuelles." Mathematics lives in its own intellectual world, "où ce que l'on prend pour des vérités rigoureuses perd absolument cet avantage, quand on l'apporte sur notre terre." *DIN*, 2:178–179. It was this persuasion that led Diderot to the astonishing prophecy that pure geometry could go no further and that in a hundred years there would not be three great geometers in Europe! The succeeding century, which saw such figures as Gauss, the Boylais, Lobatchewski, Riemann, Cayley, and Von Staudt might have thought that Diderot was somewhat premature in his obituary.

69 *LB*, p. 90; *LA*, pp. 100–101.

70 *LB*, pp. 90, 96; *LA*, pp. 100, 105.

71 *LB*, pp. 99–100; *LA*, p. 110.

72 *LB*, pp. 101–102; *LA*, p. 112.

73 *LB*, pp. 102–104; *LA*, pp. 112–113. See also the weary conclusion of the letter: "Thus we scarce know anything, yet what of numbers of books there are whose authors have all pretended to knowledge!" *LB*, p. 141; *LA*, p. 146.

74 *LB*, pp. 104–105; *LA*, pp. 114–115.

75 *LB*, pp. 108–109; *LA*, p. 118. At the beginning of the *LB*, Diderot defends the detail that he gives about the man of Puiseaux. Its purpose is "to convince you that the person I am speaking of is not imaginary" (*LB*, p. 69; *LA*, p. 82). By the third stage of his investigation, however, this interest has given way to imagina-

tion and drama, despite the assurance that one could verify the conversation in a work by Saunderson's pupil, William Inchlif's *Life and Character of Dr. Nicholas Saunderson, late Lucasian Professor of the Mathematicks in the University of Cambridge*, published in Dublin in 1747. Unfortunately, William Inchlif never existed, and his Dublin contribution to our understanding of Saunderson was never made. Diderot has simply recast for the title of this nonexistent work the ascription after the identification of Saunderson as the author of the *Elements of Algebra*; see Paul Vernière's note in *OP*, p. 125n 1; *LB*, p. 115. Periodically, Diderot can leave one with the unhappy impression that he was willing to do anything for the furtherance of the truth except stick to it.

76 *LB*, pp. 109–110; *LA*, 119–120.
77 *LA*, p. 121; *LB*, p. 111.
78 *LB*, p. 111; *LA*, p. 121.
79 See *LB*, p. 102; *LA*, p. 112 (M).
80 *LA*, p. 121, *LB*, p. 111.
81 *LB*, pp. 111–112; *LA*, pp. 121–122.
82 Titi Lucreti Cari, *De rerum natura* 5.837–838, 846–848, 855–856, in the critical edition and translation by Cyril Bailey (Oxford: Clarendon Press, 1947), 1:474–477.
83 Lucreti, *De rerum natura* 5.806 ff; Bailey, 1:474–475.
84 *LB*, p. 113; *LA*, p. 123.
85 Lucreti, *De rerum natura* 5. 830, 834–836; Bailey, 1:474–475. "Nature alters all things and constrains them to change . . . So then time changes the nature of the whole world, and one state after another overtakes the earth, so that it cannot bear what it did but can bear what it did not of old" (ibid.).
86 *LB*, pp. 113–114; *LA*, pp. 123. Lucretius emphatically denied that the origin of material combinations came about by design (*consilio*) or through a directing intelligence (*sagaci mente*). The motion of matter was caused by gravity and by concussion and the resulting chance combinations of every possible kind until "at last those come together, which, suddenly cast together, become often the beginnings of great things, of earth, sea, and sky, and the race of living things." *De rerum natura* 5.415–431; Bailey, 1:452–455. Diderot does not trace matter back to atomic principles moving in a void; he does have Saunderson attribute motion as an intrinsic property of matter and postulate that all present order is a result of combinations which have been able to perdure while other combinations perished.
87 *LB*, p. 110; *LA*, p. 120.
88 *LB*, p. 114; *LA*, p. 124.
89 John R. Baker, "Trembley, Abraham," *Dictionary of Scientific Biography*, 13:457–458.
90 Rachel Horwitz Westbrook, "Needham, John Turberville," *Dictionary of Scientific Biography*, 10:9–10. For the influences and intellectual atmosphere with which this shift of Diderot's took place, see Aram Vartanian, "From Deist to Atheist: Diderot's Philosophic Orientation, 1746–1749," pp. 57–59. Vartanian makes this comment on La Mettrie: "Man might still be a machine; but it was a curiously un-Newtonian machine whose parts continued to function after being dismembered. The doctrine of 'muscular irritability' in *L'homme machine* was but another example of the same tendency, which attributed a vital principle to organic matter in its primary states." Though Buffon's "système des molécules

organiques" was not yet published, Vartanian reasonably enough assumes that his ideas were already in circulation. On the other hand, there is little enough reason to suppose that Diderot took his evolutionary ideas and the survival of the fittest from Benoit de Maillet's *Telliamed* (1748) when they correspond so well to Lucretius' *De rerum natura*, a poem which Diderot knew well; see Wilson, *Diderot*, pp. 18, 124, and 195; Paul Vernière, *OP*, p. 121n 1 and p. 123n 1.

91 Vartanian, *Diderot and Descartes: A Study of Scientific Naturalism in the Enlightenment*, p. 259. Part of this atmosphere was the strange, sometimes even fantastic, work of Benoit de Maillet's *Telliamed, ou Entretien d'un Philosophe Indien avec un missionaire françois sur la Diminution de la Mer, la Formation de la Terre, l'Origine de l'Homme*, whether it had any direct influence upon *The Letter on the Blind* or not. His was a world based upon matter constantly renewing its forms through the motions characteristic of the Cartesian vortices, in which the earth was formed by the recession of the cosmic ocean and new forms of life developed through the transformation of primitive sea creatures. This occurred over billions of years. "After the usually ingenious but unconvincing attempt to affirm a harmony between the two accounts [*Genesis* and *Telliamed*], *Telliamed* was obliged to declare, in agreement with Cartesian precept, that the spheres of natural science and theology were mutually independent and deserved to be treated as such." Vartanian, pp. 109–110.

92 Diderot to Voltaire, June 11, 1749 (M). The critically edited text of this letter has been published in Arthur M. Wilson, *Revue d'Histoire littéraire de la France* 51, no. 3 (July–September, 1951): 258–260. Voltaire's horror at the narrative of Saunderson's atheism is countered by Diderot with the assurance that Saunderson does not represent his own opinon (p. 258) and the protest that the cry for mercy from the god of Clarke, Leibniz, and Newton is quite sincere and that it parallels the Jewish invocation of the god of Abraham, Isaac, and Jacob (p. 259). The reassurance and the protest are of autobiographical interest, and it is not impossible that they are honestly said. Whatever Diderot's private state of mind, his text leaves the only argument for the existence of god, that of biological design, pulverized.

93 Diderot to Voltaire, June 11, 1749, p. 259.

94 Denis Diderot, *Les Bijoux indiscrets*. Critical annotated edition presented by Jean Macary, Aram Vartanian, Jean-Louis Leutrat with the assistance of Jean Varloot (Paris: Hermann, 1978) (henceforth cited as *LBI*) vol. 2, ch. 5, p. 163. In other editions of this work, *LBI* is not divided into volumes and this section is given simply as chapter 38.

95 *LBI*, 2.5.164.

96 Ibid., p. 166.

97 Denis Diderot, *Discours de la poésie dramatique à M. Grimm*, (henceforth cited as *PD*), ch. 2, *OCD* 7:309: "Qu'il soit philosophe, qu'il ait descendu en lui-même, qu'il y ait vu la nature humaine, qu'il soit profondément instruit des états de la société, qu'il en connaisse bien les fonctions et les poids, les inconvénients et les avantages." The English translation, "On Dramatic Poetry," is found in *European Theories of the Drama*, ed. Barrett H. Clark, rev. ed. (New York: D. Appleton, 1929) (henceforth cited as *ODP*), p. 287.

98 *ODP*, ch. 2, p. 289; *PD*, p. 313.

99 *ODP*, ch. 4, p. 290; *PD*, p. 315. This persuasion of Diderot that drama and philosophy merge in the best theater lies behind what Edwin Duerr cites as his primary and startling contribution to the theory of drama: "First, he

advocated—a hundred and fifty years too soon—a thoroughly realistic, even naturalistic, theater." The second proposition which Duerr singles out as both new and critical reinforces the previous analysis made in this chapter about Diderot's essential philosophic method: "Second, he argued that actors should wake to the fact that they are the lively creators of the essential play, and that as such they could be artists of intelligence—and sometimes geniuses." The play is no longer just the world created by the playwright; it is continually recreated by every new perspective which each actor embodies. Edwin Duerr, *The Length and Depth of Acting* (New York: Holt, Rinehart and Winston, 1962), p. 256; Wilson, *Diderot*, pp. 268–274.

100 *ODP*, ch. 10, p. 296; *PD*, p. 328.
101 Denis Diderot, *Entretien entre d'Alembert et Diderot*, *OP*, p. 280. This work is the third part of a dramatic triptych which includes the much longer *Rêve de d'Alembert* and the brief *Suite de l'Entretien*. They will be cited as *EDD*, *Rêve*, and *Suite* respectively, with the page reference taken from *OP*. The English translation, occasionally modified by checking with the original, will be taken from *Diderot, Interpreter of Nature: Selected Writings*, trans. Jean Stewart and Jonathan Kemp and edited with an introduction by Jonathan Kemp (New York: International Publishers, 1963) (hereafter cited as Kemp). The individual works will be cited under the abbreviations *CDD* ("Conversation between d'Alembert and Diderot"), *Dream*, and *Conclusion*. Kemp's persistent footnoting of the text of Diderot with the canonical authorities in the Marxian tradition simply underscores the continuous Communist enthusiasm for Diderot, an enthusiasm that was kindled by a remark of Karl Marx that Diderot was his favorite prose writer. See Wilson, *Diderot*, p. 194. Diderot himself remarked that this set of dialogues which involved d'Alembert and his memoir on mathematics were the only works of his with which he was content. Kemp is probably accurate when he maintains that in these dialogues, along with *Rameau's Nephew*, is expressed in small compass "the quintessence of Diderot's genius" (Kemp, p. 20). Lester G. Crocker comments that "the tripartite *Rêve de d'Alembert*" is Diderot's "most important philosophical work. . . . This brilliant, imaginative dialogue, the most complete and far-ranging philosophy of materialism in the eighteenth century, contains the essence and ultimate reach of Diderot's radical thought." *Diderot's Selected Writings*, ed. Lester G. Crocker, trans. Derek Coltman (New York: Macmillian, 1966), pp. xiii–xiv.
102 *DIN* 15, *OP*, p. 189. On the *Interpretation of Nature*, Kemp, p. 45 (henceforth cited as *IN*). Truth and falsity are not in human notions or in a chain of reasoning; truth and falsity come into question when these notions or conclusions are related to nature, a relationship which can be established only through experimentation and observation. See *DIN* 7, *OP*, p. 184; *IN*, p. 43.
103 *ODP*, ch. 2, p. 288; *PD*, p. 312. Diderot was not sanguine about the possibility of the average author composing as well as he did: "All the objections made against this new type [Diderot's serious comedy, depicting virtue and the duties of human beings] prove but one thing, that it is difficult to write. It is not the sort of play that a child can write: It demands an art, a knowledge, a gravity and power or intellect, which are very rarely at the command of the dramatist." Happily, however, they were among the competencies of the author of *Le Fils naturel* and *Le Père de famille*. See *DPD*, p. 287; *PD*, p. 309.
104 *DPD*, ch. 2, p. 288; *PD*, p. 310 (m).
105 *DPD*, ch. 5, p. 291; *PD*, p. 317.

106 *DPD*, ch. 5, p. 291; *PD*, p. 318: "Ils agiront au lieu de se développer." There is a remarkable coincidence between this theory of drama and Diderot's insistence upon the development of species in the origin of life. In both cases, the intelligibility of nature is found in the observation of its development.
107 *DPD*, ch. 7, p. 291; *PD*, p. 320.
108 *DIN*, 20–21, pp. 191–192.
109 Denis Diderot, "Essai sur la peinture" (1796), *OCD* 10:512: "D'où l'on doit conclure que ce système de mesures d'ordres vitruviennes et rigoureuses semble n'avoir été intenté que pour conduire à la monotonie et étouffer le génie."
110 "Encyclopédie," in *L'Encyclopédie*, *OCD* 14:415. "En effet, le but d'une *Encyclopédie* est de rassembler les connaissances éparses sur la surface de la terre; d'en exposer le système général aux hommes avec que nous vivons, et de le transmettre aux hommes qui viendront après nous, afin que les travaux des siècles passés n'aient pas été des travaux inutiles pour les siècles qui succéderont."
111 "Encyclopédie," in *L'Encyclopédie*, *OCD* 14:458.
112 *DIN*, 1, pp. 177–178 (M). Ira O. Wade praises the suggestions which David Funt offers on the correlation between Diderot's aesthetic theories and his understanding of physical reality: Diderot's "vision is based upon a conception of matter, movement, and change, and ultimate interrelationships between these three elements. This activity is paralleled by the constant activity of consciousness. Sensations and perception follow a moving process, and this process which is essentially epistemological, is likewise ultimately esthetic." Wade, *The Structure and Form of the French Enlightenment* (Princeton: Princeton University Press, 1977) 1:308–309; Funt, *Diderot and the Aesthetics of the Enlightenment* (Geneva: Droz, 1968).
113 See Jacques Ehrmann, "Rameau's Nephew: An Existential Psychoanalysis of Diderot by himself," *Journal of Existential Psychiatry* 4, no. 13 (Summer 1963):60ff. For the various positions of the early and most unpublished manuscripts of Diderot, see Wade, *Structure*, 1:230ff.
114 Denis Diderot, *Rameau's Nephew and d'Alembert's Dream*, translated with introductions by Leonard Tancock (New York: Penguin, 1976), p. 137.
115 *CDD*, p. 49; *EDD*, pp. 257–258 (m).
116 Diderot to Duclos, September 10, 1765, *OP*, p. 258n 1 and pp. 261–262n 1(M). The article by Bordeu and Fouquet entitled "Sensibilité" is found in the fifteenth volume of the *Encyclopédie*.
117 René Descartes, *Principia Philosophiae*, 2.36, AT 8:61–62.
118 Gottfried Wilhelm Leibniz, *Specimen dynamicum*, pars prima (1695), *Leibnizens mathematische Schriften*, ed. C. I. Gerhardt, 2d ed., in *Leibnizens gesammelte Werke*, ed. George Heinrich Pertz. 3d ed.: Mathematik, sixth part (Halle: H. W. Schmidt, 1860), p. 238. For English translation, see René Dugas, *A History of Mechanics*, trans. J. R. Maddox (Neuchâtel, Switzerland: Griffon, 1955), p. 221.
119 *CDD*, p. 50; *EDD*, pp. 259–260.
120 Denis Diderot, *Philosophic Principles on Matter and Motion* (henceforth *PPMM*), Kemp, p. 128. For the French original, see *Principes philosophiques sur la matière et le mouvement* (henceforth *PPSMM*), *OCD* 2:66.
121 *PPMM*, p. 130; *PPSMM*, p. 68.
122 *PPMM*, p. 131; *PPSMM*, p. 68.
123 *EDD*, p. 264; *CDD*, p. 52.
124 *EDD*, pp. 264–268; *CDD*, pp. 52–54. For Lucretius' similar appeal to sponta-

neous generation as the contemporary analogy that illumines the first generation of all animal life, see *De rerum natura* 5.795–806; see also *De rerum natura* 2.865–903. One section from *De rerum natura* is remarkably parallel to Diderot's: "Inasmuch as we perceive the eggs of birds turn into living chickens, and worms swarm out when mud has seized on the earth owing to immoderate rains, we may know that sensations [*sensus*] can be begotten out of that which is not sensation [*ex non sensibu'*]." *De rerum natura* 2.926–930; Bailey, 1:284–285. Bailey points out the parallel theories in the Greek philosophers, perhaps most closely in Empedocles: "Trees were the first living things produced from the earth . . . and grew as they were raised up by the warmth in the earth, so that they were parts of the earth, like the embryo which is part of the womb in the stomach." *Aët.* 5.26.4. (Diels, *Fragmente*, A. 70). Empedocles analogizes the growth of vegetation from the earth to the growth of feathers and hair on birds and beasts after their birth. The theory that animal life, as well as plant, came from the earth was found in Anaximander, Anaxagoras, Empedocles, and Democritus. "It will be noticed that in these accounts the animals are said to have been produced by heat out of moisture, this Lucretius carefully reproduces." Bailey, 3:1452.

125 *CDD*, pp. 54–55; *EDD*, pp. 269–271 (M).
126 *CDD*, pp. 56–57; *EDD*, pp. 272–274.
127 *EDD*, pp. 277–278; *CDD*, p. 60. Diderot's continual argument from analogy, his reliance upon one level of reality as the microcosm of another, and the resemblance he drew between the movement of nature, the processes of thought, and the conversational method do not seem to have caught the attention of Michel Foucault in his attempt to characterize the philosophic discourse of the period extending from the seventeenth to the nineteenth century. This might have modified the requiem that he chanted for "resemblance" during the eighteenth century. *The Order of Things: An Archaeology of the Human Sciences* (New York: Random House, 1973).
128 *CDD*, pp. 57–59; *EDD*, pp. 274–276 (m) (italics added).
129 *EDD*, p. 276; *CDD*, p. 59.
130 *EDD*, p. 279; *CDD* p. 61.
131 *CDD*, p. 61; *EDD*, p. 279 (M).
132 *CDD*, p. 62; *EDD*, p. 280–281. This dismissal of the fantasies of the poet parallels an even sharper discrimination of the physicist and chemist from the geometer and metaphysician in the *PPMM*. The criterion for the distinction is the pivotal place occupied by nature in their reflections. "You can concern yourselves with geometry and metaphysics as much as you like; but I, who am a physicist and a chemist, I, who consider bodies as they are in nature and not as they are in my head, I see them existing, differing, having properties and actions, and moving in the universe as they do in the laboratory." Kemp, pp. 128–129; *OCD* 2:66. Remembering that d'Alembert is referred to in *EDD* as "un des plus grands géomètres de l'Europe," Diderot's placing him as the fundamental adversary of the universal sway of matter and skeptical defendant of the Newtonian god has already laid a prejudice on that position. *EDD*, p. 265.
133 *CDD*, p. 63; *EDD*, p. 283.
134 *CDD*, p. 60; *EDD*, pp. 277–278.
135 *DIN*, 58, p. 240 (M).
136 Jean Le Rond d'Alembert, *Preliminary Discourse to the Encyclopedia*, pt. 1, translated by Richard N. Schwab with the collaboration of Walter E. Rex

(Indianapolis: Bobbs-Merrill, 1976), p. 13. For the French original, see *Discourse préliminaire de L'Encyclopédie*, ed. F. Picavet (Paris: Armand Colin, 1919), p. 21.

137 *Dream*, p. 65; *Rêve*, p. 287.
138 Diderot to Sophie Volland, September 7, 1769, *OP*, p. 251; Kemp, p. 331.
139 Diderot to Sophie Volland, September 11, 1769, *OP*, p. 251; Kemp, p. 341 (m).
140 *Dream*, p. 76; *Rêve*, p. 305.
141 *Rêve*, p. 304; *Dream*, p. 75. The list is given by Bordeu.
142 *Dream*, p. 103; *Rêve*, p. 349.
143 *Rêve*, p. 306; *Dream*, p. 76.
144 *Rêve*, p. 288; *Dream*, p. 65. See *Rêve*, p. 306, for Mlle. de L'Espinasse's irritated assertion of the same certitude. When Bordeu asked her which issues in philosophy she found superfluous, she said: "Celle de mon unité, de mon moi, par exemple. Pardi, il me semble qu'il ne faut pas tant verbiager pour savoir que je suis moi, que j'ai toujours été moi, et que je ne serai jamais une autre." This leads Bordeau to adapt to the operational method the classic distinction between *le fait* and *la raison du fait*. See *Dream*, p. 76.
145 See Vartanian, *Diderot and Descartes*, pp. 270–274.
146 *Dream*, p. 68; *Rêve*, p. 293. Paul Vernière traces the *de facto* influence upon Diderot for this discrimination between the general life of the total living animal and the particular life of its organs back to Bordeu himself, but it was Diderot who extended this analogy to the issue of the origins of life. See *OP*, pp. 291–292 n 1.
147 *Dream*, p. 71; *Rêve*, p. 298 (m).
148 *Dream*, pp. 73–74; *Rêve*, pp. 301–302.
149 *Dream*, pp. 72–73; *Rêve*, pp. 299–300.
150 *Dream*, p. 74; *Rêve*, p. 302.
151 *Dream*, pp. 78–79; *Rêve*, pp. 310–311.
152 *Rêve*, p. 312; *Dream*, p. 79. It is at the completion of this discussion of formation that Bordeu makes the comment: "Voilà de la philosophie bien haute; systématique dans ce moment, je crois que plus les connaissances de l'homme feront de progrès, plus elle se vérifiera" (*Rêve*, p. 313). In Diderot, "systématique" has the force of a contemporary use of "speculative," highly theoretical and without an adequate experimental basis. Diderot was quite aware of the nature of his findings, and his use of the dream is indicative of this sensitivity.
153 *Dream*, pp. 80–81; *Rêve*, pp. 314–315.
154 *Dream*, pp. 82–83; *Rêve*, pp. 316–318.
155 *Dream*, pp. 84–87; *Rêve*, pp. 320–325.
156 *Dream*, p. 91; *Rêve*, p. 330.
157 *Dream*, pp. 91–92; *Rêve*, p. 331.
158 *Rêve*, pp. 337–339; *Dream*, pp. 95–96.
159 *Dream*, pp. 97–103; *Rêve*, pp. 341–349. There is no attempt in the pages above to do more than register the line of argument that Diderot evolves from d'Alembert's dream and the conversation it occasions, certainly no attempt to note each of the subissues he treats. It is critical to observe that the argument for a comprehensive material explanation deals with origins, internal structures, animal evolution, and the causes of life and death, and that it can subsume all of the topics ordinarily treated in tractates upon the human soul and the education of the human person.

160 *Dream*, pp. 111–113; *Rêve*, pp. 362–364.
161 *Dream*, pp. 114–117; *Rêve*, pp. 366–369.
162 *Conclusion*, p. 118; *Suite*, p. 372.
163 Horace, *Ars poetica*, 343.
164 *Conclusion*, p. 125; *Suite*, p. 383.
165 See Lawrence W. Lynch, *The Marquis de Sade* (Boston: Twayne, 1984), pp. 22–37. Lynch notes that it is curious that Sade did not know of Diderot's *Lettre sur les aveugles*, which, ironically enough, also landed its author in Vincennes. While Diderot is only occasionally mentioned by Sade, Baron d'Holbach was one from whom Sade particularly took his "direct ideological borrowings" (p. 25).
166 August Comte, *System of Positive Polity*, trans. J. H. Bridges and Frederic Harrison (London, 1876; reprint, New York: Burt Franklin, nd), 3:498. For Marx, see Franz Mehring, *Karl Marx: Geschichte seines Lebens* (Leipzig: Sociologische Verlagsanstalt, 1933), p. 551. For Diderot as Marx's favorite prose writer, see "Marx's Confession," in David McLellan, *Karl Marx: His Life and Thought* (New York: Macmillan, 1973), p. 456.

Chapter 5

1 R. Sasso, "Voltaire et le *systéme de la nature* de d'Holbach," *Revue Internationale de Philosophie* 32, no. 124–125 (1978): 280–281.
2 *Avertissement du clergé de France, assemblé à Paris par permission du Roi, au fidèles du royaume sur les dangers de l'incrédulité* (Paris: Desprez, 1770). See "Assemblies of the French Clergy," *New Catholic Encyclopedia* (New York: McGraw-Hill, 1967), 1:959–960; Jeroom Vercruysse, *Bicentenaire du Système de la Nature* (Paris: Lettres Modernes, 1970), pp. 23–24; Alan Charles Kors, *d'Holbach's Coterie: An Enlightenment in Paris* (Princeton: Princeton University Press, 1976), pp. 116, 238–242 (hereafter cited as Kors).
3 For a summary of the actions of the Assemblée général du Clergé de France regarding the growing dangers of disbelief, see the summary of the Procès-Verbaux of this Assembly formulated by P. Charbonnel in *L'Idéologie des Lumières, Colloque International*, directed by Charles Delvoye, edited by Jacques Sojcher (Brussels: Editions de l'Université, 1971) (henceforth cited as *IL*), pp. 267–269.
4 Kors, p. 240.
5 Kors, pp. 241–242; *IL*, pp. 267–268; Vercruysse, p. 24.
6 *IL*, p. 268. "La forme d'incrédulité la plus menaçante n'est plus le déisme à la Jean-Jacques Rousseau ou le théisme teinté de pyrrhonisme de Voltaire, mais cette forme toute différente d'incrédulité qu'expose avec une assurance dogmatigue, c'est vrai, l'auteur du *Système*."
7 R. R. Palmer, *Catholics and Unbelievers in Eighteenth Century France* (Princeton: Princeton University Press, 1939), p. 215. Palmer's work offers an extended and significant analysis of Bergier's engagements in the struggles between the Church and its critics.
8 Alfred J. Bingham, "The Abbé Bergier: An Eighteenth-Century Catholic Apologist," *Modern Language Review* 54, no. 3 (July 1959):349. For another review of Bergier's life and works, see E. Dublanchy, "Bergier, Nicolas-Sylvestre," *Dictionnaire de Théologie Catholique* (Paris: Bacant et Mangenot, 1910), vol. 2, cols. 742–745.

9 Nicolas-Sylvain Bergier, *Examen du matérialisme, ou Réfutation du Système de la nature* (Paris: Chez Humbolt, 1771), 1:154–55, 174–76; cited in Kors, p. 65n.

10 Louis-Mayeul Chaudon, *Anti-Dictionnaire philosophique* (Paris: Saillant & Nyon, 1775), 2:125–129; cited in Kors, p. 65n.

11 Ernest Campbell Mossner, *The Life of David Hume* (Oxford: Clarendon Press, 1970), pp. 485–488.

12 Edward Gibbon, *Autobiography: Memoir C.*, ed. John Murray (New York: Fred de Fau, 1907), p. 223.

13 Horace Walpole to Gray, November 19, 1765, *The Letters of Horace Walpole*, ed. Peter Cunningham (Edinburgh: John Grant, 1906), 4:436; and Horace Walpole to George Selwyn, December 2, 1765, *Letters*, 4:449.

14 *Memoirs of Dr. Joseph Priestly (written by himself) with a Journal of his Travels*, in the *Autobiography of Joseph Priestly*, ed. Jack Lindsay (Bath: Adams and Dart, 1970), p. 111.

15 Jean-Jacques Rousseau, *The Confessions*, trans. J. M. Cohen (Middlesex: Penguin, 1970), 11:523–524.

16 Denis Diderot to Sophie Volland, trans. and cited in Mossner, *Hume*, p. 483. Kors assumes the substantial truth of the anecdote, if not of d'Holbach's statement, because Diderot repeated it some sixteen years later to Samuel Romilly. Nevertheless, "in the absence of other corroborative documentaion, there is no reason why it is more valid to see d'Holbach's riposte as a factual account of things than, for example, to see it as a hyperbolic attempt to startle Hume or as a sarcasm directed to his friends at the table" (Kors, p. 41). See Denis Diderot, *Correspondance*, ed. George Roth (Paris: Editions de Minuit, 1959), 5:133–134.

17 Kors, p. 92, and pp. 9–10. Kors distinguishes between d'Holbach's Salon and the *coterie holbachique*, the latter being constituted by those in regular attendance, while the salon included all those guests who came to visit and enter into the conversations.

18 Kors, pp. 116–117.

19 Gay, *Enlightenment*, 1:399–400; see also Kors, p. 5.

20 Gay, *Enlightenment*, 1:18.

21 Daniel Roche, "Lumières et engagement politique: la coterie d'Holbach dévoilée," *Annales* 33, no. 4 (July–August, 1978):721. The entire article is a careful and positive evaluation of the work of Kors, *D'Holbach's Coterie*.

22 Kors, p. 49: "Naigeon himself, in his *Philosophie ancienne et moderne*, listed only six men as comprising the list of those of 'our modern atheists' whose names could be made public, four of whom had been members of the coterie: d'Holbach, Diderot, Roux and Helvétius."

23 Kors, pp. 56–58.

24 Kors, pp. 59–63. For the skepticism of Grimm about any attempt at scientific system, see his remarks dated July 1, 1764. The value of the study of nature does not lie with the system produced, but that one might "comprendre de bonne heure les bornes et la pauvreté de nos connaissances, à sentir combien il est difficile d'échapper a l'erreur, à apprendre le grand art de douter, de se défier de ses lumieres, d'être modeste et sage." Grimm, Diderot, Raynal, Meister, et al., *Correspondance littéraire, philosophique et critique*, ed. Maurice Tourneux (Paris: Garnier Frères, 1878), 6:23ff. The citation translated by Kors is taken from this text.

25 *DND*, 1.5.11–12(M). For the Ciceronian single method of *controversia*, see Michael Buckley, *Motion and Motion's God*, pp. 95–102.

26 *DND*, 1.6. 13 (M).

27 Etienne Bonnot de Condillac, *Essai sur l'origine des connoissances humaines*, in *Oeuvres philosophiques de Condillac*, vol. 1, ed. Georges Le Roy (Paris: Presses Universitaires de France, 1947), introduction, p. 3. All citations from Condillac's philosophic works in the original French are taken from this edition and cited as *OPC*. Idem, *An Essay on the Origin of Human Knowledge Being a Supplement to Mr. Locke's Essay on Human Understanding*, trans. Mr. Nugent (London: J. Nourse, 1756), reprinted with a new introduction by James H. Stein (New York: AMS Press, 1974), p. 1.

28 Condillac, *Essai*, introduction *OPC*, 1:4.

29 Ibid., p. 5.

30 Condillac, *Essay*, introduction pp. 6–7; *OPC*, 1:4 (m).

31 This is the burden of the *Essai*, reinforced by the further inquiries of the *Traité des Sensations*. See "Dessein de cet ouvrage," *OPC*, 1:222: "Le principe qui détermine le développement de ses facultés, est simple; les sensations mêmes le renferment. . . . Le jugement, la réflexion, les desirs, les passions, etc., ne sont que la sensation même qui se transforme différemment."

32 Condillac, *Extrait raisonné du Traité des sensations*, 1, *OPC*, 1: 325.

33 Condillac, *Traité des sensations*, 4.9, *OPC*, 1:314.

34 Ibid., 2.5.4–5, *OPC*, 1:256–57.

35 Condillac, *Essai*, 1.1.1, *OPC*, 1:6.

36 Condillac, *Essai*, 1.1.7, *OPC*, 1:7. For Condillac's natural theology, see his *Traité des animaux*, 2.6, *OPC*, 1:365–370.

37 Claude-Adrien Helvétius *De l'esprit*, ed. Guy Besse (Paris: Edition sociales, 1968), preface, pp. 67–68.

38 Helvétius, *De l'esprit*, Discours premier, 1, pp. 76–77.

39 Ibid., pp. 74–75.

40 Ibid., 1, pp. 79–80.

41 Claude-Adrien Helvétius, *A Treatise on Man; His Intellectual Faculties and His Education*, trans. W. Hooper (London: Albion, 1810), 1.2.7, pp. 124–126.

42 Julien Offray de la Mettrie, *Man a Machine*, French-English edition edited by Gertrude Carman Bussey (La Salle, Ill.: Open Court, 1943), p. 13 (French), p. 85 (English). (Henceforth, in citing this work, the page number from the French text will be given first and that of the English text second.)

43 La Mettrie, *Man a Machine*, pp. 14 and 86.

44 Ibid., pp. 72–73 and 142–143. "I believe that Descartes would be a man in every way worthy of respect, if, born in a century that he had not been obliged to enlighten, he had known the value of experiment and observation, and the danger of cutting loose from them. But it is none the less just for me to make an authentic reparation to this great man for all the insignificant philosophers—poor jesters, and poor imitators of Locke—who instead of laughing impudently at Descartes, might better realize that *without him the field of philosophy, like the field of science without Newton, might perhaps be still uncultivated*" (italics added). This linking of Descartes and Newton is significant in the twin influences it celebrates upon La Mettrie's own period and thought.

45 Ibid., p. 56 and 128. See "The excellence of reason does not depend on a big word devoid of meaning (immateriality), but on the force, extent, and perspicuity of reason itself." See also p. 15 and 87.

46 Ibid., pp. 69–71 and 140–141.

47 Ibid., p. 79 and 148.

48 Ibid., p. 50 and 122.

49 Ibid., pp. 51–53 and 123–125. Thus the conclusion from this repudiation of a natural theology which emerges from physics: "The weight of the universe therefore far from crushing a real atheist does not even shake him." See also p. 54 and p. 125.

50 Ibid., p. 55 and 126. The citation is from Vergil's *Eclogue* 3, line 108.

51 La Mettrie, *Man a Machine*, pp. 55–56 and 126–127.

52 La Mettrie, *Man a Machine*, pp. 79–81 and 148–149: "Let us then conclude boldly that man is a machine, and that in the whole universe there is but a single substance [matter] differently modified."

53 Voltaire to the Marquise de Florian, May 20, 1762, *Voltaire's Correspondence*, ed. Theodore Besterman. (Génève: Institut et Musée Voltaire, 1962), vol. 48, no. 9659, p. 259 (M). For a complete list of Voltaire's references to Meslier, see *Oeuvres complètes de Jean Meslier*, ed. Deprun Desné and Albert Soboul (Paris: Édition Antropos, 1970–1972) (hereafter cited as *OCJM*), 3:488–490.

54 Jean Meslier, *Mémoire des pensées et sentiments de Jean Meslier* (henceforth cited as *Mémoire*), "Septieme preuve," *OCJM* 2:471. *Abrégé de la vie de l'auteur*, *OCJM* 3:389: "Etant au seminaire où il vécut avec beaucoup de regularité, il s'attacha au système de Descartes."

55 *Abrégé*, *OCJM* 3:394 (M).

56 Ibid., p. 393 (M).

57 Roland Desné, "L'homme et son oeuvre," *OCJM* 1:lxiv–lxviii.

58 Ibid., p. lxi.

59 Ibid., p. lxix: "Il s'agit d'un acte de contrebande littéraire d'un plus haut eclat, un exploit en vérité, et le plus étonnant peut-être, dans l'histoire des lettres, par sa durée et par le nombre des lecteurs qui en furent les dupes: la réédition, sous le nom de Meslier, du *Bon Sens* de d'Holbach." Unfortunately, the edition most available in English is precisely one of those fraudulent works, published in the series *The Atheistic Viewpoint* under the general advisory editorship of Madalyn Murray-O'Hair: Jean Meslier, *Superstition in All Ages: Last Will and Testament*, commonly entitled *Common Sense*, trans. Anna Knoop (New York: Arno Press and the New York Times, 1972).

60 Gay, *Enlightenment*, 1:392n; Will and Ariel Durant, *The Age of Voltaire* (New York: Simon and Schuster, 1965), pp. 611–617. The Durants credit *Bon Sens* with being a summary of Meslier, done by Diderot and d'Holbach. Voltaire's failure to deal with the philosophical and social revolution in Meslier is noted by Jean Deprun, "Meslier philosophe," *OCJM* 1:lxxxii.

61 Jean Delumeau, *Catholicism Between Luther and Voltaire: A New View of the Counter-Reformation* (London: Burns and Oates, 1977), p. 141.

62 Voltaire to Jean Le Rond d'Alembert, February 10, 1762(c), *Voltaire's Correspondence*, vol. 68, no. 9527, p. 90(M). See also Voltaire to Jean Le Rond d'Alembert, Feb. 25, 1762, *Voltaire's Correspondence*, vol. 68, no. 9545, p. 111; Voltaire to François Achard Joumard Tison, Marquis d'Argence, March 2, 1763, *Voltaire's Correspondence*, vol. 51, no. 10245, p. 210; Voltaire to Jean Le Rond d'Alembert, July 16, 1764, *Voltaire's Correspondence*, vol. 55, no. 11149, p. 164. "Meslier" ends up "Mélier" in Voltaire's version of his name.

63 Meslier, *Mémoire*, "Septième preuve," *OCJM* 2:402. For a consideration of Meslier as a philosopher to which the above analysis is indebted, see Jean Deprun, "Meslier philosophe," *OCJM* 1:lxxxiff.

64 Meslier, *Mémoire*, "Septième preuve," *OCJM* 2:403.

65 Ibid., *OCJM* 2:245.

66 Nicolas Malebranche, *The Search After Truth*, English translation by Thomas M. Lennon and Paul J. Olscamp (Columbus: Ohio State University Press, 1980), 4.11.3, p. 323. See also 3.2.6, p. 232: "Finally, of the proofs of God's existence, the loftiest and most beautiful, the primary and most solid (or the one that assumes the least), is the idea we have of the infinite. For it is certain that (a) the mind perceives the infinite, though it does not comprehend it, and (b) it has a very distinct idea of God, which it can have only by means of its union with Him, since it is inconceivable that the idea of an infinitely perfect being (which is what we have of God) should be something created."

67 Meslier, *Mémoire*, "Septième preuve," *OCJM* 2:237–245. See also p. 245: "Donc il n'y a que la matiere qui puisse pousser la matiere, et que puisse faire effort et impression sur elle, et qui puisse la mouvoir, et par consequent ce qui n'est point matiere, ne peut mouvoir la matiere."

68 Voltaire, "Le pour et le contre" ("Epître à Uranie"), *Oeuvres Complètes de Voltaire*, ed. Louis Moland (Paris: Garnier Frères, 1877), 9:359.

69 Denis Diderot, "Les Eleutéromanes, ou les Furieux de la liberté," *Oeuvres Complétes de Denis Diderot*, ed. J.-A. Naigeon (Paris: Chez J. L. Brière, 1821), Romans et Contes 3:469. For the source of this remark in Meslier, see Meslier, *Mémoire*, "Avant-Propos," *OCJM* 1:23–24: "Il me souvient à ce sujet d'un souhait que faisoit autres fois un homme, qui n'avoit ni science ni étude mais qui, selon les apparences ne manquoit pas de bon sens pour juger sainement de tous ces détestables abus, et de toutes le détestables tyrannies que je blame ici. . . . Il souhaitoit que tous les grands de la terre, et que tous les nobles fussent pendus, et étranglés avec des boiaux de prêtres." Naigeon commented: "On écrira dix mille ans, si l'on veut, sur ce sujet, mais on ne produira jamais une pensée plus profonde, plus fortement conçue, et dont le tour et l'expression aient plus de vivacité, de précision et d'énergie." *Philosophie ancienne et moderne* 3, published in *l'Encyclopédie méthodique*, s. v. "Meslier"; see *OCJM* 3:509–510.

70 Paul Hazard, *European Thought in the Eighteenth Century: From Montesquieu to Lessing*, trans. J. Lewis May (London: Hollis and Carter, 1954), p. 125. For similar judgments of Cicero, see Michael J. Buckley, S.J., "Philosophic Method in Cicero," *Journal of the History of Philosophy* 8, no. 2 (April 1970):143–144.

71 Kors, p. 82.

72 Virgil W. Topazio, "Diderot's Supposed Contribution to d'Holbach's Works," *Publications of the Modern Language Association of America*, ed. William Riley Parker, vol. 69 (1954), pp. 187–188.

73 Roland Mortier, "Holbach et Diderot: Affinités et Divergences," *L'Ideologie des Lumières*, pp. 223 and 230.

74 Mortier, "Holbach et Diderot," pp. 236–237.

75 Kors, p. 82.

76 Vercruysse, *Bicentenaire*, pp. 12–13.

77 Henri Lion, "Essai sur les oeuvres politiques et morales du Baron d'Holbach," *Annales révolutionnaires* (1922), 14, p. 89; cited in Virgil W. Topazio, "D'Holbach, Apostle of Atheism," *Modern Language Quarterly* 17, no. 3 (September 1956):260. Vercruysse styles the work "cette véritable bible du matérialisme militant," maintaining that it surpassed anything which the eighteenth century produced. Vercruysse, *Bicentenaire*, p. 7.

78 René Descartes, *Le monde, ou Traité de la lumière* 7, AT 11:37.

79 Voltaire to Jean Le Rond d'Alembert, July 27, 1770, *Voltaire's Correspondence*, vol. 76, no. 15531, p. 65.

80 Sasso, "Voltaire," p. 280.

81 Baron Paul d'Holbach, *The System of Nature: or, Laws of the Moral and Physical World*, with notes by Diderot, trans. H. D. Robinson (New York: G. W. and T. Matsell, 1835) (hereafter cited as *System*), 1:11. The French edition of this work which is being used is that still attributed to M. Mirabaud, *Système de nature. ou Des loix du monde Physique et du monde moral*, new edition (London, 1771) (hereafter cited as *Système*), 1.1, p.1. The dubiousness of the Diderot attribution has been noted above.

82 *System*, 1.1, p. 12; *Système*, p. 5.

83 *System*, 1.1, p. 12; *Système*, p. 5 (m).

84 *System*, 1.1, p. 15; *Système*, p. 11 (m).

85 *System*, 1.2, p. 16; *Système*, p. 13 (m).

86 *System*, 1.2, p. 16; *Système*, p. 13: "Une Cause, est un être qui en met un autre en mouvement, ou qui produit quelque changement en lui. L'effet est le changement qu'un corps produit dans un autre à l'aide du mouvement."

87 Thomas Aquinas, *In XII libros Metaphysicorum Aristotelis Expositio* 5.1.751. See the edition of R. Cathala, revised by Spiazzi (Turin: Marietti Editori, 1935), p. 251. For a fuller development of causality considered in terms of being rather than in terms of motion, see *Quaestio disputata de potentia dei* 7.2.: "All the created causes communicate in one effect, which is being [*esse*], granted that each one of them has its proper effect, and this distinguishes it from the others. For instance, heat causes something to be hot, and the builder causes the house to be. Thus, these causes agree in this: they all cause being [*esse*], but they differ in that fire causes a fire and the builder causes a house" (M). See *Quaestiones Disputatae*, ed. Bazzi et al. (Taurini: Marietti, 1948), 2:191. For these texts and a commentary upon them, see Etienne Gilson, *Elements of Christian Philosophy* (Garden City, N.Y.: Doubleday, 1959), p. 189.

88 *System*, 1.2, p. 16; *Système*, p. 14 (m).

89 *System*, 1.2, p. 17; *Système*, p. 16 (m).

90 *System*, 1.2, p. 18; *Système*, p. 18 (m). For Toland's defense of motion as essential to matter, see John Toland, *Letters to Serena*, new facsimile of the 1704 London edition with an introduction by Günter Gawlick (Stuttgart-Bad Cannstatt: Friedrich Frommann Verlag, 1964), letter 5, pp. 163–239.

91 *System*, 1.2, p. 18; *Système*, pp. 18–19.

92 *System*, 1.2, p. 19; *Système*, pp. 20–22 (m): "Ainsi l'idée de la nature renferme nécessairement l'idée du mouvement." This has been classically true since Aristotle's insistence that a natural thing has within itself a principle of movement and rest (*Physics* 2.1.192b14). What Aristotle did not do, however, and what d'Holbach emphatically does, was to equate this principle with the matter of natural things and eliminate both internal form and all nonmaterial causality.

93 *System*, 1.2, p. 20; *Système*, p. 24.

94 *System*, 1.2, p. 20; *Système*, pp. 24–25n.

95 *System*, 1.2, p. 20; *Système*, p. 25 (m).

96 *System*, 1.2, p. 21; *Système*, p. 26 (m).

97 *System*, 1.2, p. 22; *Système*, p. 30 (m).

98 *System*, 1.2, p. 23; *Système*, pp. 31–32.

99 *System*, 1.2, p. 22n; *Système*, pp. 27–28n.

100 *System*, 1.2, p. 23; *Système*, pp. 33–34 (m).

101 *System*, 1.3, p. 24; *Système*, p. 35 (m).

102 Galileo Galilei, *Dialogues Concerning Two New Sciences*, English translation by Henry Crew and Alfonso de Salvio (New York: Dover, 1914), pp. 137–138.

103 Galileo Galilei, *Il Saggiatore*, #48. See also Edwin Arthur Burtt, *The Metaphysical Foundations of Modern Physical Science* (London: Routledge and Kegan Paul, 1949), p. 75 (m). This allows Galileo to distinguish "primi e reali accidenti" from any which described the reaction of the sensitive subject, "la quale affezione è tutta nostra." The precise vocabulary of primary and secondary qualities came from the *Origin of Forms and Qualities* of Robert Boyle, and found its classic formulation in the masterpiece of his friend John Locke, *An Essay Concerning Human Understanding*, 2.8.9ff; 1, pp. 170ff.

104 Descartes, *Meditationes* 2, AT 7:30–32; *Meditations*, Lafleur, pp. 29–30; *Principles of Philosophy* 4.198, 199, AT 8:210–212; H-R 1:295–296.

105 Isaac Newton, "Rules of Reasoning in Philosophy," rule 3, *Principia* 3, Cajori, p. 399.

106 Newton to Bentley, February 25, 1662/3, *Correspondence* 3:254.

107 *System*, 1.3, p. 24; *Système*, p. 35. Note that d'Holbach has significantly altered the understanding and the listing of the primary and secondary attributes of matter.

108 *System*, 1.3, p. 24; *Système*, p. 36.

109 *System*, 1.3, p. 26; *Système*, p. 42 (m).

110 *System*, 1.3, p. 27; *Système*, p. 43.

111 *System*, 1.4, p. 29; *Système*, p. 49 (m).

112 *System*, 1.4, p. 27; *Système*, p. 45 (m).

113 *System*, 1.4, p. 28; *Système*, pp. 46–47.

114 *System*, 1.4, p. 28; *Système*, p. 48 (m).

115 *System*, 1.4, pp. 29–30; *Système*, pp. 50–51.

116 *System*, 1.4, p. 30; *Système*, p. 53 (m).

117 *System*, 1.4, p. 31; *Système*, pp. 54–55.

118 *System*, 1.4, pp. 31–32; *Système*, pp. 56–57.

119 Voltaire to Marie de Vichy de Chamrond, August 8, 1770, *Voltaire's Correspondence*, vol. 76, no. 15548, p. 86.

120 *System*, 1.18, p. 163; *Système*, 2.1, p. 2.

121 *System*, 1.18, p. 163; *Système*, 2.1, p. 2.

122 *Système*, 2.1, p. 3; *System*, 1.18, p. 164 (M).

123 *Système*, 2.1, p. 3; *System*, 1.18, p. 164 (M).

124 *Système*, 2.1, p. 4; *System*, 1.18, p. 164.

125 *System*, 1.1, p. 12; *Système*, 1.1, p. 4.

126 *System*, 1.18, p. 165; *Système*, 2.1, p. 6.

127 *System*, 1.18, pp. 166–167; *Système*, 2.1, p. 8–11. See also ibid., p. 166: "It was in the lap of ignorance, in the season of alarm and calamity, that humankind ever formed his first notions of the Divinity." D'Holbach does not use the vocabulary of "magic," but it is to this that he analyzes religion.

128 *System*, 1.18, p. 170; *Système* 2.1, pp. 16–17 (m). See also *System*, 1.19, pp. 174–175; *Système*, 2.2, p. 28.

129 Sigmund Freud, *The Future of an Illusion*, ch. 7, trans. W. D. Robson-Scott (London: Hogarth, 1949), p. 64: "I have said nothing which other and better men have not said before me in a much more complete, forcible and impressive manner.... All I have done—and this is the only thing that is new in my exposition—is to add some psychological foundation to the criticisms of my great predecessors." For Freud's discussion of the transition from animism to theism, see *Totem and Taboo* trans. James Strachey (London: Routledge and Kegan Paul, 1950), pp. 75–78, 147–155, and *The Future of an Illusion*, pp. 39ff.

130 *System*, 1.18, p. 174; *Système*, 2.1, p. 27. This is to restore nature to the dignity that is rightfully hers for "it was upon the ruins of nature that the human person erected the imaginary colossus of the Divinity."

131 *System*, 1.19, p. 175; *Système*, 2.2, p. 29.

132 *System*, 1.19, pp. 176–177; *Système*, 2.2, pp. 31–33. The possibility of the hermaphroditic origin of the human species is an addition to the *Système* in a later edition. The two basic alternate hypotheses of d'Holbach are the eternal return and natural evolution.

133 *System*, 1.19, p. 177; *Système*, 2.2, p. 33.

134 *System*, 1.19, pp. 175–177; *Système*, 2.2, pp. 33–35.

135 *System*, 1.19, pp. 177–178; *Système*, 2.2, pp. 34–35.

136 *System*, 1.19, p. 180; *Système*, 2.2, p. 40 (m).

137 *System*, 1.19, p. 181; *Système*, 2.2, p. 43 (m). Both Montaigne and Xenophanes are enlisted to support this existentialist interpretation that the gods are human beings writ large, an opinion seconded by the axiom of Lamotte le Vayer: "Nous voyons que le Théantrophie sert de fondement à tout le Christianisme." *System*, 2.1, p. 191n; *Système*, 2.2, p. 43.

138 *System*, 2.1, p. 191; *Système*, 2.3, p. 61.

139 *System*, 2.1, p. 192; *Système*, 2.3, p. 62.

140 *System*, 2.1, p. 193; *Système*, 2.3, p. 66.

141 *System*, 2.1, pp. 195–196; *Système*, 2.3, p. 72 (m).

142 *System*, 1.1, p. 11; *Système*, 1.1, p. 2.

143 *System*, 2.1, p. 199; *Système*, 2.3, p. 80: "Ainsi de quelque façon que l'on envisage le systême Théologique, il se détruit lui-même."

144 *System*, 1.1, p. 12; *Système*, 1.1, p. 5.

145 Voltaire, "Septième Lettre," *Lettres philosophiques*, in *Oeuvres de Voltaire*, vol. 37.

146 *Système*, 2.4, pp. 108–109; *System*, 2.2, p. 211. See also *Système*, 2.4, p. 107: "D'âges en âges de nouveaux champions de la divinité, des philosophes profonds, des Théologiens subtils ont cherché de nouvelles preuves de l'existence de Dieu, parce qu'ils étoient, sans doute, peu contens de celles de leurs prédécesseurs." *System*, 2.2, p. 210. A printing error numbers this chapter as iv in Robinson's translation. Since the prior chapter is numbered i and the subsequent chapter numbered iii, this intervening chapter will be numbered ii in citations from Robinson's translation.

147 *System*, 2.2, pp. 211–213; *Système*, 2.4, pp. 110–114 (m). Because of this early priority that the *Système* gives to necessity, d'Holbach can claim that Clarke's third proposition merely repeats the first.

148 *System*, 2.2, p. 211n; *Système*, 2.4, pp. 108–110n. This extensive footnote in d'Holbach is the only ground for the above interpretation of his text. It is startling to see that d'Holbach does not consider Clarke's reasons for denying the very conclusion on which d'Holbach insists, namely that the necessary being finds its realization in the material universe itself.

149 *System*, 2.2, p. 213; *Système*, 2.4, pp. 114–115.

150 *System*, 2.2, pp. 213–214; *Système*, 2.4, pp. 115–118.

151 *System*, 2.2, pp. 214–215; "It is likewise in nature, that is formed intelligent, feeling, thinking beings; yet it cannot be rationally said, that nature feels, thinks, and is intelligent after the manner of these beings, who nevertheless spring out of her bosom." *Système*, 2.4, pp. 118–120.

152 *System*, 2.2, pp. 215–216; *Système*, 2.4, pp. 120–122 (M). The god of the theolo-

gians is no different from matter in the freedom projected upon him. He must also act according to the necessity of his nature: "Ask a theologian if God has power to reward crime, and punish virtue."

153 *System*, 2.2, p. 218; *Système*, 2.4, p. 128.

154 *System*, 2.2, p. 219; *Système*, 2.4, p. 129.

155 *System*, 2.2, p. 224; *Système*, 2.4, p. 143. D'Holbach traces these opinions of the theologians as well as the rites, the symbols, and the sacraments of Christian theology back to Plato. "It is this fantastical philosophy, which regulates all our opinions at present" (*System*, 2.2, pp. 219–220). What Clarke would have thought about his Newtonian orthodoxy being equated with Platonism is not hard to imagine. For a summary refutation of Clarke, see *System*, 2.2, pp. 224–225; *Système*, 2.4, pp. 145–147.

156 See M. Buckley, *Motion and Motion's God*, pp. 109, 116–117, 143–144.

157 *System*, 2.2, p. 205; *Système*, 2.4, p. 95 (m).

158 *Système*, 2.4, p. 95; *System*, 2.2, p. 205.

159 *System*, 2.2, p. 206; *Système*, 2.4, p. 98 (m).

160 *System*, 2.2, p. 207; *Système*, 2.4, p. 99 (m).

161 *System*, 2.2, p. 208; *Système*, 2.4, p. 102 (m).

162 *System*, 2.2, p. 218; *Système*, 2.4, p. 127 (m).

163 *DBAG*, p. 7.

164 *DBAG* p. 126.

165 *System*, 2.2, p. 218; *Système*, 2.4, p. 127. If pushed, the *Système* maintains, these special revelations indicate only another irreconcilable contradiction in the notion of god, here a god with universal love who favors only a small section of the globe.

166 *System*, 2.3, p. 225; *Système*, 2.5, p. 148.

167 *Meditations*, 3, Lafleur, p. 49. This text is cited directly from d'Holbach; see *Système*, 2.5, p. 149; *System*, 2.3, p. 226.

168 *System*, 2.3, pp. 225–226; *Système*, 2.5, pp. 148–150 (m).

169 Malebranche, *Dialogues on Metaphysics and on Religion*, p. 227.

170 See Thomas Aquinas, *Summa theologiae* 1.45.1: "Non solum oportet considerare emanationem alicuius entis particularis ab aliquo particulari agente, sed etiam emanationem totius entis a causa universali, quae est Deus: et hanc quidem emanationem designamus nomine *creationis*. . . . Ita creatio, quae est emanatio totius esse, est ex non ente quod est nihil."

171 *System*, 2.3, pp. 226–227; *Système*, 2.5, pp. 152–153 (m).

172 *System*, 2.3, pp. 277–279; *Système*, 2.5, pp. 153–158. On the influence of Newton through the corrections of Toland, d'Alembert, and Stahl, see Pierre Naville, *D'Holbach et la philosophie scientifique au xviiie siècle* (Paris: Gallimard, 1967), pp. 231, 239–240.

173 *System*, 2.3, p. 229; *Système*, 2.5, p. 157.

174 *System*, 2.3, p. 227; *Système*, 2.5, p. 154.

175 *System*, 2.3, p. 228; *Système*, 2.5, p. 155.

176 *System*, 2.3, pp. 228–229; *Système*, 2.3, pp. 156–157 (m) (italics added).

177 *System*, 2.3, p. 229; *Système*, 2.5, pp. 157–158.

178 *System*, 2.3, p. 229; *Système*, 2.5, pp. 158–159.

179 *System*, 2.3, pp. 229–230; *Système*, 2.5, pp. 159–161.

180 *System*, 2.5, p. 161; *Système*, 2.3, p. 230.

181 *System*, 2.3, pp. 230–231; *Système*, 2.5, pp. 162–163.

182 Newton, *Principia* 3, General Scholium; Cajori, p. 546 (M).

183 *System*, 1.1, p. 12; *Système*, 1.1, p. 5 (m).
184 *System*, 2.3, p. 229; *Système*, 2.5, p. 159 (m). Thus d'Holbach can write: "Les connoissances superficielles ou quelconques que nos sens nous fournissent sont les seules que nous puissions avoir."
185 *System*, 2.3, p. 231; *Système*, 2.5, p. 163 (italics added). See also Naville, *D'Holbach*, pp. 252–256.
186 *System*, 2.3, pp. 231–232; *Système*, 2.5, p. 166.
187 *System*, 2.3, p. 232; *Système*, 2.5, pp. 167–68 (M) (italics altered).
188 Aristotle, *Physics* 2.1. 192b8–20; 5. 197a10–35; 6. 197a36–198a12.
189 *System*, 2.3, p. 233; *Système*, 2.5, p. 170.
190 *System*, 2.3, pp. 233–234; *Système*, 2.5, pp. 170–172 (m).
191 *System*, 2.3, pp. 234–235; *Système*, 2.5, pp. 172–173 (m).
192 *System*, 2.4, p. 236; *Système*, 2.6, p. 179.
193 For the influences in the tradition which d'Holbach counted as his own, see Virgil W. Topazio, "D'Holbach, Apostle of Atheism," pp. 252–260. Topazio notes the presence in d'Holbach's library of almost all of the works of the important English deists and asserts that the ancient philosophers whom he admired the most were Epicurus, Democritus, and Leucippus, while the moderns were Hobbes, Spinoza, and Bayle.

Chapter 6

1 P. Damiron, *Mémoires pour servir à l'histoire de la philosophie au XVIIIᵉ siècle*, 2:417; cited in Kors, p. 279. For the collaboration of Naigeon and d'Holbach, see Kors, pp. 85–88, 141.
2 Hazard, *European Thought*, p. 126. Cornelio Fabro insists that "despite these philippics, Naigeon (if he is the author of the work in question [*Le militaire philosophe*]) is not the 'violently anti-religious' thinker he has been labelled by one scholar, even though he does show himself to be a drastic critic of positive (man-made—*factices*) religions." *God in Exile*, trans. and ed. Arthur Gibson (Westminster, Md.: Newman, 1968), p. 397. This opinion of so fine a scholar as Fabro may rely too heavily on this earlier work of Naigeon and fail to give appropriate attention to his *Philosophie ancienne et moderne*, his *Adresse à l'Assemblée nationale*, his edition of the *Oeuvres de Denis Diderot*, and his *Mémoires historiques et philosophiques sur la vie et les ouvrages de D. Diderot*. None of these works finds a place in Fabro's book, and they form the basis of the judgment given above.
3 Kors, p. 287.
4 Kors, p. 29.
5 Hazard, *European Thought*, p. 126. Maniac or not, Marechal's *Dictionnaire des athées* clearly included Naigeon among its heroes, to the scandal of Napoleonic France. Atheism had fallen from whatever public favor it had enjoyed; Marechal's celebration of Naigeon secured him additional time for his labors over Diderot, since it made it unthinkable that he would be advanced under the rule of Bonaparte. See Kors, p. 297. For the Marquis de Sade, see Lynch, *The Marquis de Sade*, pp. 124–127. Guillaume Apollinaire's judgment is given in his massive introduction to *L'Oeuvre du Marquis de Sade* (Paris: Bibliothèque des Curieux. Collection Les Maîtres d'Amour, 1909), p. 17.
6 Le Marquis de Laplace, *Exposition du système du monde*, 6th ed. (Paris: Bachelier, 1835), p. 466.

7 Laplace, *Exposition*, pp. 464–469.
8 Roger Hahn, "Laplace and the Vanishing Role of God in the Physical Universe," *The Analytic Spirit: Essays in the History of Science in Honor of Henry Guerlac*, ed. Harry Woolf (Ithaca: Cornell University Press, 1981), pp. 85–86: "At the turn of the eighteenth century, Laplace was considered the most accomplished physical scientist of his time, having written extensively on the system of the world, on the mathematics of probability, and contributing to physics and chemistry in smaller but no less respectable ways. He received the supreme accolade from his peers in 1827 when eulogists dubbed him the 'Newton of France,' one hundred years to the month after Sir Isaac's Westminster funeral."
9 Ernst Mach, *The Science of Mechanics*, p. 552 (italics added).
10 For a sympathetic and synoptic presentation of Kant's theological development, see James Collins, *God in Modern Philosophy*, pp. 162–200.
11 Immanuel Kant, *Critique of Pure Reason*, trans. Norman Kemp Smith (London: Macmillan, 1963), A602, B630, p. 507.
12 Immanuel Kant, *Critique of Practical Reason*, trans. and ed. Lewis White Beck (Chicago: University of Chicago Press, 1949), preface, pp. 121–122.
13 Ibid., p. 118.
14 Ibid., pp. 121–122.
15 Ibid., "The Dialectic of Pure Practical Reason," p. 226.
16 Ibid., p. 225.
17 Richard R. Niebuhr, introduction to Friedrich Schleiermacher, *The Christian Faith*, ed. H. R. Macintosh and J. S. Stewart (New York: Harper and Row, 1963), 1:ix.
18 Freidrich Schleiermacher, *On Religion: Speeches to Its Cultured Despisers*, trans. John Oman (New York: Harper and Brothers, 1958), pp. 11–12 (italics added).
19 Ibid., p. 13 (italics added).
20 Schleiermacher, *Christian Faith*, pp. 12–16. For the correct translation of this most vexed classic phrase of Schleiermacher's, and his situation within the development of Protestant thought, see Claude Welch, *Protestant Thought in the Nineteenth Century*, vol. 1, 1799–1870 (New Haven: Yale University Press, 1972), pp. 65–81. "Schleiermacher's proposal to develop theological statements as implications of the religious self-consciousness, and Coleridge's conception of a Reason (the "organ of the supersensuous") that at its highest is an act of will, a venturing forth and throwing oneself into the act of apprehension, also represented a new way of taking the believing self into the theological program. Consciousness of the truth was peculiarly one with self-consciousness. The religious subject—his point of view, his cognitive limitations, his 'interest,' his willing and choosing—had to be self-consciously and systematically recognized as ineradicably present in that with which Christian theological reflection begins. This theme is the *foundation* for a striking community of interest and effort in the whole course of Protestant theology in the nineteenth century" (p. 60; italics added).
21 Schleiermacher, *Christian Faith*, p. 17.
22 Ibid., pp. 17–18 (m).
23 Georg Wilhelm Friedrich Hegel, *Lectures on the History of Philosophy*, trans. E. S. Haldane and Frances H. Simson (Atlantic Highlands, N.J.: Humanities Press, 1983), 1:30, 37 (m).
24 Epistle to the Colossians 3:22; Epistle to the Ephesians 6:5.
25 Herodotus 1.1. See *Herodotus*, with an English translation by A. D. Godley,

Loeb Classical Library (London: William Heinemann, 1931), p. 2.

26 See Henry Cary, *A Lexicon to Herodotus* (Oxford: Printed for J. Vincent and Henry G. Bohn, London, 1843), s. v. ἱστορίη and ἀπόδεξις. Henry R. Immerwahr follows E. Erbse in translating the phrase "the setting forth of his research." See also *Form and Thought in Herodotus* (Cleveland: Western Reserve University Press, 1966), p. 17. John L. Myres writes of Herodotus: "In general, he agrees with Pindar that 'custom is king of all' (3.38); but what the customs are which govern events can only be ascertained by observation and comparison; this is ἱστορίη ("research"), to record and preserve events, and to discern their causes (1.1)." *Herodotus: Father of History* (Oxford: Clarendon Press, 1953), p. 46.

27 Hans-Georg Gadamer, *Hegel's Dialectic: Five Hermeneutical Studies*, trans. with an introduction by P. Christopher Smith (New Haven: Yale University Press, 1976), pp. 104–105.

28 J. N. Findlay, *The Philosophy of Hegel: An Introduction and Re-Examination* (New York: Collier, 1966), pp. 70–74.

29 Gadamer, *Truth and Method*, pp. 267–274, 305–341.

30 Nietzsche, *The Gay Science*, 3, fr. 125, p. 181.

31 Aristotle, *Rhetoric* 1.2.1356^{b}2ff.

32 Gadamer, *Hegel's Dialectic*, p. 19.

33 Gilson, *Elements of Christian Philosophy*, p. 43 (italics added).

34 Gilson, *Elements of Christian Philosophy*, p. 290.

35 Thomas Aquinas, *Summa theologiae*, 3, prologue (M).

36 Thomas Aquinas, *Summa theologiae*, 1. 2. 3.

37 Martin Heidegger, *Identity and Difference*, trans. with an introduction by Joan Stambaugh (New York: Harper and Row, 1957), p. 72. See also William J. Richardson, "Heidegger and the Problem of God," *Thought* (Spring 1965): 29.

38 Martin Heidegger, *Introduction to Metaphysics*, trans. Ralph Mannheim (Garden City, N.Y.: Doubleday, 1961), pp. 15–21.

39 Henri Bremond, *A Literary History of Religious Thought in France*, trans. K.L. Montgomery (London: SPCK, 1936), 3:191. Unfortunately, only the first three volumes of this monumental work have been translated into English.

40 Ibid., p. 192.

41 Nicolas Malebranche, *Dialogues on Metaphysics and on Religion* 7.10–11, pp. 189–191.

42 *DBAG*, p. 126.

43 "Dr. Clarke's First Reply," *L-C*, p. 12.

44 *DBAG*, p. 119.

45 *DNR*, p. 133.

46 Karl Marx, "The Leading Article of N. 179 of *die Kölnische Zeitung*," in Karl Marx and Friedrich Engels, *On Religion*, edited with an introduction by Reinhold Niebuhr (New York: Schocken, 1964), p. 38.

47 Francis Bacon, *The New Organon*, 1, aphorism 65 (Indianapolis: Bobbs-Merrill, 1960), p. 62.

48 Wolfhart Pannenberg, *Jesus–God and Man*, trans. Lewis L. Wilkins and Duane A. Priebe (Philadelphia: Westminster, 1968), p. 130.

49 Julius Guttmann, *Philosophies of Judaism: The History of Jewish Philosophy from Biblical Times to Franz Rosenzweig*, with an introduction by R. J. Zwi Werblowsky, translated by David W. Silverman (New York: Holt, Rinehart and Winston, 1964), pp. 5–6. See also the discussions in Michael Wyschogrod, *The Body of Faith: Judaism as Corporeal Election* (New York: Seabury, 1983), pp.

55ff. For the tension and irreducible conflict between Judaism and certain philosophies, see Gershom Scholem, "Das Ringen Zwischen dem Biblischen Gott und dem Gott Patons in der Alten Kabbala," *Eranos-Jahrbuch 1964* (Zurich: Rein-Verlag, 1965), pp. 9–50.

50 Blaise Pascal, *Pensées*, trans. with an introduction by A. J. Krailsheimer (London: Cox and Wyman, 1977), no. 449, pp. 169–170.

Name Index

Subject Index

Absolute, 17, 19, 110–118, 169, 181–182, 310–311; and relative, 82–83; Clarke on, 169, 181–182; Descartes on, 83, 87–88, 92; d'Holbach on, 280, 310–311; Diderot on, 233; Newton on, 107, 110–118. *See also* Force; God; Motion; Space; Time

Abstraction, 161, 246–247; and mathematics, 216–217; and sensation, 214–216; atheism as, 16, 337; Diderot on, 227, 233, 246–247; of philosophy from theology, 351

Act, 15, 24, 62, 159, 163, 188, 190; of being, 51, 54

Action, 41, 54, 85–88, 161, 176, 226; and reaction, 242, 278, 280; and religion, 41; Diderot on, 233–234; ethical, 263–264; of nature in drama, 226–227. *See also* Ethics; Force, motive; God; Moral life

Actional principle. *See* Principle, actional

Agnostic, 6, 10, 259, 372*n*34

Agnosticism, 10, 258–259, 268, 372*n*34

Analysis, 20, 24, 84, 94, 118–120, 124, 128, 131, 174, 180, 183, 186; d'Holbach on, 287–289; Euclid on, 118; Harris on, 119; Newton on, 120–128, 131. *See also* Method, logistic; Resolution; Synthesis

Antinomies, 69, 71, 86, 125, 154, 249, 275, 289, 327, 363. *See also* Dualism

Antitheism, 1, 2, 6, 251–252, 295

Apparent, 4, 111, 280, 300, 309; and atheism, 172–175; and rest, 223; and skepticism, 206–207; and theologians, 314–315; Clarke on, 172–175, 183, 300; Descartes on, 111; Diderot on, 240; Leibnitz on, 111; Newton on, 99, 104, 107, 111–118, 183, 233, 236, 240, 278, 300, 309–310, 390*n*39. *See also* Real

Appearance, 4, 6, 65, 302, 314, 354

Archetype, 90; in neo-Confucianism, 151, 158–159

Argument, 20, 22, 24, 31–32, 45–55, 71, 173, 187, 189, 200, 202, 208, 221, 252–253, 257; and drama, 226; d'Holbach and, 315–316; Diderot and, 218–219, 224, 228, 230–231, 236, 238, 244; from absurdity, 53–54; from existence, 53; from universal consent, 40, 48, 50, 53, 54, 193, 271, 304–306, 378*nn*45, 47; ontological, 51, 327, 348. *See also* Design

Art, 17, 49–50, 74, 214, 226–227, 267, 280–282, 317–318; divine, 53, 141. *See also* Theology, and beauty

Astronomy, 52, 54–57, 63, 101, 108, 127–130, 182, 189, 191, 325. *See also* Body, heavenly; Celestial mechanics; Planetary motion; Solar system

Athanasian Creed, 169, 354

Atheism, 3–6, 13, 16, 24–34, 38, 46–48, 60–61, 64, 95, 181, 185, 192, 203, 222, 259, 307, 314; and ambiguity, 9, 12–13, 337; and happiness, 267; apparent versus real and, 172–175; as literary event, 20; as theological issue, 37–41, 47, 65–67, 320; as transition, 16–17, 20, 24–25, 206, 222, 259, 332, 337–339, 360; Clarke on, 171–172; definition of, 9–11; dependency on theism, 14–17; d'Holbach on, 252, 275, 317; Diderot on, 199–200, 211, 222; history of, 14–15, 24–25, 27–32, 46–47, 223, 251–252, 253–256, 270, 273, 337–341; neo-Confucianism and, 150–157; paradox of, 1–36; self-denial of religion and, 37–41, 332, 359–360

Atheist, 4, 6, 12, 39, 56, 206; as term, 2–11, 258, 337–338, 372*n*31, 375*n*70

Atheists, 10–11, 27, 37, 46, 57–58, 69, 146, 171–172, 193, 255–258; Clarke on, 171, 182; Diderot on, 249; Lessius on, 46; lists of, 4–5, 46–47, 256, 258, 305, 323, 368*n*14; Maréchal on, 323, 424*n*5;